How to Catch
Salt-water Fish

How to Catch Salt-water Fish

BILL WISNER

DOUBLEDAY & COMPANY, INC.
GARDEN CITY, NEW YORK

All illustrations of fish, except the blueclaw crab, have been taken from *Fishes of the Gulf of Maine* by Henry B. Bigelow and William C. Schroeder, printed by the United States Government Printing Office, Washington, D.C., 1953

ISBN: 0-385-07217-1
Library of Congress Catalog Card Number 72–89130

To the memory of my dad, the late Bill Wisner, Sr., a lifelong fisherman who launched me in the sport, this book is dedicated affectionately.

"I couldn't let the book [Editor's note: an earlier, much shorter version] alone and I must say you have done it very well. I shall pore over it and keep it on board my boat the *Bugsy Seagull*. I know how difficult it is to write for the uninstructed. As far as I have read, your handling of that most important detail, feeding habits, is masterly. I guess the first thing to do always is to open the first specimen and to find out what they are eating. And sometimes they are eating very unusual things. . .

"Meanwhile, book in hand, I am going to try out your methods on my own."

JOHN STEINBECK

Contents

Contents

Introduction

Fishing's magnetism is compounded from many things. To begin with, it's a challenge. You match wits, often muscles too, with wild creatures in their native element. Much of the fun comes with meeting that challenge. And there's always suspense. You never really know for sure what you might catch. Fact is, in fishing, more than in any other sport, the unusual is usual.

Fishing is a common denominator, and this is another of its attractions. All anglers are on an equal footing. Your finned opponents couldn't care less who you are, what you are, or whether you're a millionaire or a pauper. And it's a sport in which everyone can participate, regardless of age. I know anglers—girls and boys and women and men—ranging from five and six years old up into the seventies and eighties. All of them have a ball. Still another attraction is that fishing can be as economical or as lavish as its participants wish. The guy perched on a bulkhead with a fifteen-dollar outfit derives just as much benefit from fishing as a fellow on a hundred-thousand-dollar cruiser.

Most important, fishing is extremely rewarding, physically and mentally: physically because it brings its followers out into the sun and air; mentally because it relaxes and gives the satisfaction of accomplishment. Few other pastimes pay such large bonuses in fun, health, and carefree relaxation. Salt air is a great tonic. In fishing you can't lose, even when you come home empty-handed.

As in any endeavor, though, the rewards are in direct proportion to the time, attention, and effort invested. Those last three details separate good fishermen from perpetual bumblers.

Every step in every procedure is based on simple logic. Once you know the reasons, the steps become easy. There's absolutely nothing difficult about successful fishing. If there's any "secret," it's only thorough familiarity with the reasoning behind procedures. What I've tried to accomplish in this book, therefore, is not only to show you what to do, but also *why* you do it. I'm a strong believer in the idea that we remember and do things better if we understand why we do them.

Yes, in case you're asking, there can be an element known as "luck." All fishermen, including experts, have their good and poor days. But much of the so-called luck is created by anglers themselves. The "lucky" ones are usually those who are well informed. Just remember that there's no magic or hocus-pocus involved. Some anglers are more talented than others, and for a solid reason. Not because of some special gift doled out among a select few, but because of knowledge and *experience,* augmented by little stunts and gimmicks picked up along the way. You can become just as talented by following the same route.

Many years ago an old-timer told me, "To be a good fisherman you gotta think like a fish." It was one of the best pieces of angling advice I've ever received. As I'll show you, it isn't as difficult as it might sound. It's just a matter of understanding the logic behind such details as selecting baits, fishing areas, and so on. And if this book starts you "thinking like a fish" it will have realized one of its objectives.

There's no substitute for actually fishing. Get yourself grounded in the basics, then go out and put them to work. Keep your eyes and ears open. Watch other fishermen, and never be afraid to ask questions of fellow anglers, tackle shop owners, and boat captains and mates. I should add that it's also worthwhile to join a fishing club, especially if you're a novice. And never hesitate to experiment. That's the way everything in fishing came about in the first place.

This book was written for *you.* I sincerely hope that it helps to make you a good angler . . . or, if you're already a good fisherman (or fisherwoman), a better one. I also like to think that it will go a long way toward contributing to the fun you'll derive from your chosen sport. With it go warm wishes for the best action always.

BILL WISNER

Brightwaters, New York
September 1973

Author's Note

Fishing is all the better for the fishermen you meet, new friends you make, and companions with whom you enjoy it. I'd like to give a nostalgic greeting to some among the many who have enriched my fishing life:

Capt. Dick Abrams, Superintendent, Captree and Robert Moses State Parks; Ray Adell of Radio Station WGSM, Huntington, N.Y., long-time fishing buddy with a great sense of humor (helpful in fishing); Hampton Bays, N.Y., tackle man Mickey Altenkirch and his sister Miriam, both crackerjack anglers; Bill Beckmann of Beckmann's Fishing Tackle, Lynbrook, N.Y.; freelance fishing writer Frank Bruce; retired magazine publisher Russ Crandall (*Sportsmen's Life*), another fishing companion with a great sense of humor; Gus Dinger of The Shoals, Great Kills, Staten Island; Capt. Marty Fisher of Freeport (N.Y.) Boatmen's Association; Capts. Jim Gillen (boat *Capt. Gillen*), John Gutman (*Angler*), and Remy Haynes (*Capt. Haynes*) of Captree Boatmen's Association; retired skipper Bill Golder of the *Lucky Girl*, Greenport, N.Y.; Joe Huether, Pop's Fishing Station, Seaford Harbor, N.Y.; John Kronuch, Johnny's Tackle Shop, Montauk, ace surf fisherman; "Lefty" Kreh, Director, Metropolitan Miami Fishing Tournament; Dick Lewis, Wilmington, N.C., lifelong friend with whom I shared the Peconics and their delights; Ed Lemp of Lemp's Rod and Gun Shop, Glen Cove, N.Y.; Herb and Bill Lieblein, Port of Egypt Fishing Station, Southold, N.Y.; Bill Leitz, Orange, N.J., another lifelong friend with whom I've wet lines on many occasions; retired skipper Carm Marinaccio of the *Duchess II*, Freeport, N.Y., one of the best bluefish and tuna skipper-guides who ever lived; shark fishing skipper-guide Frank Mundus of the *Cricket II*, Montauk; Mike Mafai, Mike's Tackle Shop, Sheepshead Bay; Capt. Sol Newman, *Ventura II*, Bronx; Dr. Ross F. Nigrelli, Director, New York Aquarium and its Osborn Marine Laboratory, a very special friend of long standing; marine biologists Dr. Alfred Perlmutter, John Clark, Irwin Alperin, and John Poole; Harry and Milt Powles, Veteran's Fishing Station, Cold Spring Harbor, N.Y.; Virgil Price, with whom I've fished in Mexico and Australia; Bill Perry, Maryland's Department of Chesapeake Bay Affairs; Gerry Ruschmeyer of Ruschmeyer's Hotel and Motel, Montauk, whose friendship and hospitality I've enjoyed for lo, these many years; Walt Squires of Walter's Rowboats, Hampton Bays; oceanographer-ichthyologist-author Dr. F. G. Walton Smith, Dean, Rosenstiel School of Marine and Atmospheric Science, University of Miami, a long-time friend; Capt. John Suydam, National Party Boat Owners Alliance; fishing columnist Charley Vaughan of the Philadelphia *Inquirer,* a great friend, fishing buddy, and companion on many jaunts throughout these United States; Edmund von Bonde and his wife, Jo, with whom I fished in South Africa; Capt. Al Veltman of the Hampton Bays boat *CMB;* Art White, A. P. White Bait Shop, Greenport; Capt. Art White of the *Angler,* Point Lookout, N.Y.; Capts. John and Walter Wiegand of the *Flamingo II,* Sheepshead Bay; and Roger Whitehouse, Freeport, N.Y., with whom I fished Zachs Bay at High Hill Beach, N.Y., in the long ago.

Last but far from least, some of my fellow fishing writers in the Rod and Gun Editors Association of Metropolitan New York, all esteemed angling companions on trips to all points of the compass, near and far: Bill Backus, dean of East Coast fishing columnists; Herb Blackwell; Nick Karas; Frank Keating; Jerry Kenney; Dave Knickerbocker; Frank Moss; Guin Polevoy; Milt Rosko; Jim Salvato, codean with Bill Backus of Atlantic Coast angling columnists; Hank Schaefer; Mark Sosin; Hugo Uhland; and Fred Walczyk.

And in memoriam:

Charles ("Chuck") Altenkirch, fisherman
Cecil Clovelly, fisherman-photographer
Richard Cornish, fishing columnist
Charles Curtis, fisherman
Capt. Walter Drobecker, skipper-guide
Carter Henderson, bayman-fisherman
Richard Alden Knight, fisherman-writer

Lawrence J. Kresek, fisherman
Victor Librizzi, fishing station operator
Hans Poser, fishing station operator
Capt. Frank Rhodes, bayman-fisherman
Capt. Thomas Raynor, bayman-fisherman, my grandfather
John Steinbeck, author and fishing companion
Capt. Sonny Smith, skipper-guide

How to Catch
Salt-water Fish

CHAPTER 1

Choose Your Weapons

When I was a kid, a family physician was a GP, a general practitioner. He delivered babies, treated diphtheria, set cracked bones, removed warts, and performed minor surgery.

The passage of years has wrought many changes in medicine. Nowadays, except in rural areas, general practitioners are only slightly more numerous than Masons at a Knights of Columbus picnic. Such has been the profession's expansion that specialization has become compulsory. A wit once quipped that someday we'll have specialists treating only the left nostril, middle finger of the right hand, and so on.

That's exaggerated, of course. I don't believe they'll slice it that thin. But it points up an analogy in fishing tackle.

Returning to when I was a youngster, fishing tackle was like a GP's practice. One outfit was many things to many anglers. Sure, there was some specialization in equipment. The more precise fishermen—today we call them purists—divided tackle into weight classes to better adapt it to various assignments; but in the main, your average angler clomped around with one rod-reel-line ensemble for whatever might swim his way.

Those were years before synthetic fishing lines. Linen was the thing. Linen lines were fabricated from individual threads, usually in multiples of three, with a wet test strength of three pounds per thread. Thus a nine-thread linen line was rated at twenty-seven-pound test, a twelve-thread at thirty-six, etc.; and you had them up to fifty-one threads or so. This led to a system of matching rods, reels, and lines in graduated combinations known as balanced tackle. It was a good idea. The only trouble was, no one but purists paid much heed to it. The average guy still clomped around with his one all-purpose outfit.

A VAST FOREST OF TACKLE The years have spawned many alterations in that situation. In a way, fishing tackle has moved into an era of specialization. Or maybe I should call it finer division.

Today's equipment can be more precisely adapted to various angling assignments, from ultralight salt-water fly casting to muscle-bulging arguments with finned opponents going a thousand pounds and up. Back in simpler fishing days of yore manufacturers outshopped many models of reels and rods, but there was only one basic type of gear, the so-called conventional kind. Now there are two: conventional and spinning, or three, if you count marine fly tackle. Today's fishermen can select from a horde of rods and reels to find those best suited to his purposes.

And there are lures. By the thousands! If you started counting right this minute you'd be like a Chinese census taker. You couldn't keep up with them because more are coming out all the time.

And there are lines. Good grief, are there lines! None of that simple business with just linen anymore. Fact is, a host of synthetic lines of nylon, Dacron, and other test-tube-created materials have pushed linen into limbo. Some of these are braided. Others, called monofilament, are a single strand. All are marketed in various strengths under dozens of trade names.

A single chapter couldn't possibly embrace a complete discussion of tackle. It would only confuse you anyway. Entire books have been devoted to the subject, and even they can't cover everything. What I'll do, therefore, is wade through the thickening jungle of available paraphernalia, cull out items I think are useful to you, and then boil the whole thing down to a reasonably simplified guide to choice of tackle.

PRELIMINARIES In general simplification, modern fishing tackle is catalogued in five major sizes or "calibers." Progressing upward, according to increasing size and weight, they are: ultralight; light; medium; heavy; and extra-heavy.

These are flexible gradations. You'll encounter variations in definitions of where each begins and ends, according to whomever is doing the cataloguing; and if you were to put all the opinions together in a consensus you'd find some overlapping. Don't let it bother you. By and large, such differences aren't great enough to be important.

You should keep in mind that selection of all angling gear, even to hooks, eventually comes right down to the user's personal opinions. Those opinions, in turn, are molded by experience and preferences. Too, grading of tackle often is made according to techniques and sizes of fishes involved. Equipment considered light for their kind of fishing by one group might be heavy for another set of conditions, and so it goes. Like a doctor friend of mine once remarked, an itch to one man is an ache to another. Everything is relative.

Right here, before we get into specifics, is a good place to tell you that I won't dwell on ultralight tackle—such as that employed in salt-water fly casting—in this book. That equipment is for highly experienced fishermen (no reflections on you, you understand). Besides, it's a specialty, a subject unto itself. You can pursue it later.

In your selection of tackle you can be guided by three cardinal details. Follow them and you won't go wrong.

1. Match your weapons, generally, to the sizes of fishes you intend to catch. If most of them will be small, bay species, such as flounders, porgies, and the like, you can go light. If they'll be more in the size class of striped bass and large bluefish, you can look more to medium-caliber tackle. At the extreme, if your efforts will be targeted at larger, stronger combatants—finned game weighing a hundred pounds or more—choose appropriately heavy equipment.

What I'm saying is, don't expect the same outfit to satisfactorily handle a wide range of assignments under an assortment of conditions. Similarly, don't go to weird extremes, like using a heavy rod on small species, or trying very light equipment on big game (until you're ready for it).

Matching tackle to the kinds of fishing done isn't a matter of hair-splitting precision. There's leeway. If you select tackle, within reasonable limits, for the kind of angling you expect to do, it will handle most of the fishes you contact.

2. Make an honest appraisal of your ability and experience. This applies especially if you plan to be adventuresome and put light equipment to the larger opponents.

Tarpon, big striped bass, even white marlin, are taken on fly tackle, and sharks up to two hundred pounds-plus have been whipped with spinning rods, but only by very skillful anglers. There's an old maxim that declares: The lighter the tackle, the greater the sport. It's true. But it's also a fact that you must exercise judgment and not go to extremes in light weapons until you're ready. For now, a wise procedure is to gain experience and "graduate" to progressively lighter tackle as ability and desires dictate.

3. Choose equipment that is comfortable for you to handle. This is purely personal, governed by such intangibles as likes and dislikes and by such variables as individual height, build, arm length, stamina, and conditions. It's a detail in which a book can help you only so far. You'll have to take it from there.

Rods have two main sections, butt (or handle) and tip, the longer portion beyond the butt. Pay particular attention to butt length. Comfort or discomfort in wielding a rod lies there. Butt length also is important because it determines the amount of available leverage, a detail of increasing value with larger fishes. The tip section is extremely important, because with it you'll hook, play, and eventually conquer your fish. Most rods of a given caliber have tip sections that are more or less standardized for length. Differences in how they will perform lie in their taper from where they join the butts on out to their tiptop guides. A tip can make a rod too "bendy" or too stiff for the kind of angling at hand. Variations in over-all rod lengths within the various weight categories are usually due to differences in butt sections.

For a given kind of fishing, whatever it may be, the ideal rod is one whose butt is long enough to furnish sufficient leverage, but not so long as to be awkward to use; and one whose tip section has backbone for when it's needed to provide resistance, yet also possesses plenty of flexibility for maximum sport. There are rods, incidentally, whose tips taper in such a way as to provide spine when needed, yet are sensitive enough to cast small lures and baits.

Combined weight of rod and reel can be important to your comfort too. But here I don't think you'll run into any problem unless you go into big-game tackle or heavy-duty conventional surf gear. The former takes a bit of getting used to, but you'll be in a fighting chair. If it turns out that you just can't adjust to heavy conventional surf tackle, you'll just have to go to a lighter outfit or to spinning equipment.

A smart prelude to buying tackle, particularly for beginners, is to try friends' outfits. Actually fish with them. See how they feel to you. When you find a combination that seems to suit you, note its size and manufacturer.

ACCENT ON TACKLE SHOPS Tackle stores provide assistance in choice of equipment. Establishments dealing exclusively in fishermen's gear are specialists. Frequently their staffs are anglers themselves. What's very important too, from the ringing of their cash registers, they know what lures, rigs, etc., are producing best locally. They're also gathering places for experienced rod-and-reelers. Still further, many are service and repair centers for the brands of equipment they carry.

If you're green as grass, don't be afraid to admit it. If you can't take a seasoned angler friend along with you, lay your cards on the table for a member of the store's staff. He'll listen to your story and make personalized recommendations. Pick up a few rods, "heft" them, see how they feel to you. Ask the store's man to mount an appropriate reel on it, and test it again for feel. How is it for your height and arm length? Can you handle the outfit comfortably?

Be sure to tell the guy the type of fishing you intend to do —trolling, surf casting, or whatever—and the species of fishes you'll be hunting. Above all, don't hesitate to ask questions. Answering them is part of his job. The better he satisfies you, the more likely he is to gain you as a steady customer.

BEWARE OF "BARGAINS"! Like everything else, including people, fishing tackle comes in a wide range of quality. In the cellar is the junk. Among that junk are inferior rods and reels made by obscure manufacturers here and abroad. A "bargain" there is rarer than a three-legged duck. At the other extreme is custom-quality tackle, with reels to five hundred dollars and more, and rods to two hundred dollars and up. This is superb equipment. If you can afford it, bless you. Just remember that the most expensive gear in the world won't, in itself, catch any more fish for you than less costly tackle. But it will perform beautifully, backed solidly by its builders, and give you pride of ownership.

Assuming you're like me, slogging through life without a Rolls-Royce, you'll find excellent tackle within the broad zone labeled Medium-Priced. Within that cost spread are outfits that will serve you well; fit your budget; and reward you with long, dependable use. Dependability is a key word in fishing tackle. Unreliable equipment isn't worth the powder to blow it to glory.

START OUT RIGHT   Get yourself good stuff right at the beginning. There's excellent tackle in the medium-price range. There's no excuse for buying cheap equipment today.

Buy name brands, tackle turned out by such esteemed manufacturers as Heddon, Garcia, Penn, and the like. You benefit from their decades of experience, research, and field testing. They guard their reputation for quality and dependability, and back their products accordingly. Further, their advanced manufacturing techniques enable them to provide high-quality tackle at economical prices. And, very important, they maintain a network of far-flung service centers with good parts inventories.

CONVENTIONAL AND SPINNING TACKLE, A COMPARISON

You'll select your gear from either or both of two types: the older conventional or "standard" kind, and the relatively newer spinning equipment. Some comparisons will help. First, though, I'll ask you to keep this in mind from here on in: Although it's brought into play in just about all angling methods, spinning tackle was designed primarily for casting; and it's there that it stars. I'll elaborate on that as we go along.

REELS   For openers, there are striking differences in the reels. Whereas a conventional "mill" has a revolving spool, that of a spinning reel is stationary. In another radical contrast, the axis of the former's spool is at right angles to the rod, but that of a spinning reel's spool is aligned with the rod's long axis. As if those details were not enough to separate the two, a spinning reel is mounted on the underside of its rod instead of on top; and its crank is on the left (for right-hand users) instead of on the right.

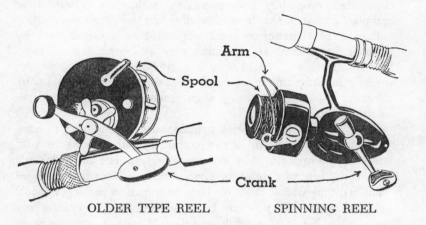

OLDER TYPE REEL   SPINNING REEL

Incidentally, there are spinning reels with cranks on the right for southpaws. Also available are models that can be flipped, quickly, for operation by either hand.

A simple demonstration will show how a spinning reel's fixed spool pays out line. Hold a spool of sewing thread, one end pointing toward you. Pull the free end of the thread away from you in the same direction as the spool's long axis. Note how it leaves the spool in little coils that straighten out as tension is maintained. Line leaves a spinning reel's spool in the same fashion. And it's because of this that spining reels became a marvelous innovation in casting.

A conventional reel's spool turns as line leaves it. So far so good. It's when line zips off too rapidly to be controlled, as can happen in casting or when a fast-running fish catches an angler off guard, that problems develop. What occurs is this: The spool immediately gains momentum, turning faster than it can release line. It overruns the line and winds it back on the spool. The result is a backlash, which is a euphemism for the most gosh-awful tangle or "bird's nest" you ever saw. If there's a fish on, the line will come to an abrupt stop and break. For years back-lashes were the bane of casters' existence. Not only are they annoying, their untangling costs precious fishing time and lost fish.

Although there are devices to lessen backlashes, they can't be eliminated completely on conventional reels. Too, casters often complain that such refinements cut down on their distance.

Because of its stationary spool, a spinning reel minimizes snarls. A spool that doesn't revolve can't very well overrun line going out. Elimination of backlashes is a tremendous advantage, especially in night fishing. A tangle is bad enough in daylight. In darkness it's enough to make a guy take up something easier—like sleeping.

When first wielding spinning tackle after being used to conventional gear, mounting of the reel underneath the rod, with its crank on the opposite side, looks peculiar and is a bit awkward. It takes some getting used to. There are reasons for this arrangement. To understand them we have to return to the reel's spool.

If you're a novice you may be wondering how a spinning reel can retrieve line if its spool doesn't turn. "I can see how line peels off," you say, "but how does it get back on?"

The answer is in a pickup device. We can liken it to a curved arm. When you turn the crank, this appendage pulls line through the rod's guides, gathers it in, and deposits it on the spool. It's because of this arrangement that a spinning reel functions better on its rod's underside instead of on top. And the crank is on the side opposite to that of a conventional reel to leave the more skillful other hand free to tend brake, pickup mechanism, and line.

Another anatomical difference between a conventional and spinning reel lies in location of the brake's (drag's) control. On the former, the drag control is most frequently a star-shaped wheel (hence the name star drag) mounted on the same side as the crank. On some conventional reels the drag control is a clutchlike lever, also on the crank's side. On spinning reels the drag usually is tightened or loosened by means of a knob at the end of the spool. Or there's a lever arrangement. If there's an advantage, it lies with a spinning reel whose drag control is more accessible to the free hand.

RODS Spinning rods, understandably, also have to be different in some respects. And these too are based upon the reels' methods of paying out and retrieving line.

A major difference is in the sizes and numbers of guides. A spinning rod has more of them than its conventional counterpart, they're larger, and they're on the rod's underside. Those guides

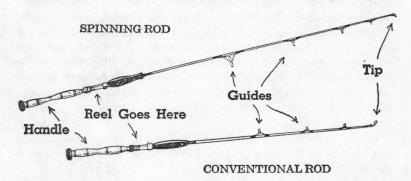

SPINNING ROD

Tip

Guides

Reel Goes Here

Handle

CONVENTIONAL ROD

progressively closer to the reel are especially large. They have to be, because line leaves the reel in coils. Too, large guides are more suited to the pickup arm's method of functioning.

Some spinning rods, you'll also notice, are longer and more willowy than conventional counterparts in approximately the same caliber. This goes back to the fact that they were originally designed for casting.

WHICH IS FOR YOU? A question frequently asked by less-experienced anglers in the market for tackle is, Should I buy spinning tackle or a conventional outfit?

Because personal tastes, kinds of fishing contemplated, and locations are involved, the answer can become complex. I'll give you generalizations that will aid in making decisions.

First off, recall what I said earlier about spinning tackle being primarily for casting? In that it does an excellent job, especially for novices. Beginners can learn to cast easier, achieve casting distance sooner, and handle the equipment with greater facility once they get used to the equipment's anatomical peculiarities. Often less-experienced anglers become the most enthusiastic spin-

ning tackle buffs. The only trouble is, too many fishermen—
including seasoned hands—become so enthusiastic about its performance and easy casting that they try to employ it in all angling
assignments. That's a mistake.

True, there's husky spinfishing equipment for heavy-duty surf
use and even for the larger offshore gamesters. But the lighter
gear is not for trolling or bottom fishing when heavy terminal
tackle—rigs, artificials, baits, or sinkers—is involved. Many spinfishing outfits are designed to accommodate light lines and cast
light lures, some weighing only a fraction of an ounce. Such
equipment would be out of its depth in, say, trolling a twelve-to-
sixteen-ounce natural squid, or in deep-water bottom fishing,
where strong currents necessitate sinkers weighing eight ounces
or more, or in shark angling, where baits can weigh a pound
or more.

In that sense spinning tackle is limited. Mind you, I said
limited, not restricted. There's a difference. So long as it can handle the rigs, baits or artificial lures, lines and/or sinkers involved, it can be employed in many techniques. The fact is,
spinning gear often provides more sport than conventional tackle
of comparable size.

Nevertheless, a key to spinfishing success is to recognize its
tackle's limitations. Don't try to make it be all things to all kinds
of fishing. Sooner or later a drawback will show itself when attempts are made to extend spinning tackle beyond its capabili-
ties. The results are clear-cut: popped lines, goodbye to rigs and
lures, lost fish. One, two, three.

If you're going to do much of your fishing on party boats I
should apprise you of another detail. With a really flexible spinning rod you won't be able to exert as much control on a fast,
wildly running fish as you could with a stiffer conventional
"stick." Your fish could be all over the place, getting your line
fouled up with others. On a crowded party boat that's calculated
to make other fishermen eye your throat speculatively.

If you plan to do any casting at all, you should consider spinning tackle. And keep in mind that casting of natural baits and
artificial attractors such as plugs, spoons, etc., is done from boats
as well as from beaches, jetties, piers, channel banks, and the
like. Casting from a boat is great sport, and it comes in mighty

handy when striped bass, bluefish, and other targets are beyond shoreside casting range.

It's difficult to precisely prescribe tackle for *you* as an individual, because I haven't any notion of what kind of fishing you'll be doing. It's almost like trying to recommend a well-fitting suit when you haven't even seen the guy who will be wearing it. But I'll offer a suggestion: If casting figures in your plans at all, it might pay you to own two basic outfits, one spinning, the other conventional. It will give you added scope, particularly if the two outfits are of different weights; and the cost isn't prohibitive. What's more, the spinning combination could serve as a lighter-tackle spare.

CHAPTER 2

Tackle Specifics

I mentioned that classifying tackle by weight—ultralight to extra-heavy—is a general, somewhat flexible yardstick, subject to a certain amount of variation and overlapping. It's convenient for designating outfits of various calibers, and it aids in closer suiting of tackle to jobs at hand. The only thing I don't like about it is that it might give an impression of semirigid restriction of tackle usage to those classifications. That isn't so. Conceivably, it also could complicate matters for less-experienced fishermen. It doesn't have to.

In fact, for this book's purposes I'm going to simplify the whole business and set up my own classification of tackle. It will apply to both types, conventional and spinning.

I'll boil the five weight classifications down to three: light, medium, and heavy. I'll concentrate on those because they'll handle just about all the finned game you're likely to encounter. In the interest of completeness I'll mention ultralight and extra-heavy gear in passing, just so you'll know what is involved.

ULTRALIGHT TACKLE

Salt- and fresh-water fly fishing equipment comes under this heading. Rods go from about 8 to 9½ feet long or so, very skinny and extremely flexible. They have to be because of the lures and very nature of fly casting. Fly reels are in a family by themselves too. They come in various sizes to accommodate the desired lengths of fly lines, sometimes backed by 100 yards or more of regular line in varying strengths for larger marine game fishes such as tarpon.

Fly lines also are something else. Here you get into such intricacies as lines of uniform diameter, those with a double taper (thickest in the middle, thinner at the ends), and those of the weight-forward variety, where the greatest diameter is more toward the lure end.

Fly fishing is an art unto itself. Whole books have been devoted to it. Salt-water fly fishing is even more of a specialty. For that reason, and because it's for those with enough mastery of other kinds to tackle to search for superthrills, I'm going to dispense with it in this volume. But don't lose sight of it. It's supreme sport. Later, when you feel you're ready to graduate to ultralight gear, get yourself a book on the subject.

Ultralight spinning tackle would include the very lightest freshwater outfits, sometimes used in salt-water fishing for greater action. This tackle generally is more delicate than its salt-water counterpart because it handles very small fishes. Don't go out and buy a fresh-water outfit to put some added oomph in your marine angling. If you already possess one, okay, but remember that salt air and water can do a corrosion job on fresh-water tackle, so be prepared to clean it thoroughly afterward.

A better bet would be to use the lightest possible salt-water spinning tackle, and consider that as ultralight. Try it on somewhat larger fishes than you usually catch. That will give you an ultralight tackle effect.

LIGHT TACKLE

CONVENTIONAL Rods that can be included in this category are the smaller so-called boat rods. Five or 5½ to 6 feet long overall, they're light and whippy, yet have some backbone too. They're good all-purpose rods in the lightweight division, just right for fishing on bays, creeks, and other moderately shallow bodies of water where strong currents aren't a factor. They're also fine for fishing from docks, channel banks, and locations in sheltered areas of inlets.

Light conventional rods will handle all the standard bottom rigs used for such smaller species as flounders, fluke, porgies, mackerel, kingfish, sea bass, croakers, weakfish, and bluefish to a couple of pounds. In bottom fishing they'll handle sinkers to 5 or 6 ounces. Where currents and depths demand heavier sinkers, these sticks become a bit too light. They'll catch any of the smaller fishes, even some of the heavier bluefish; and if bay fishing is your cup of tea, they should do the trick.

A reel to complement a rod of this caliber is a size 1/0, whose spool will take 100 to 200 or 250 yards of line in strengths to 20-pound test or so.

SPINNING   A balanced light outfit would include a 6-to-7-foot rod and a spinning reel accommodating 150 to 250 or 300 yards of lines to about 10-pound test. The rod will fish lures up to about 1½ ounces and, in bottom fishing, sinkers to 3 ounces.

Like its conventional cousin, a light spinning combination can be used for fishing the bottom, intermediate levels, or top, aboard boat or from shore. It's fine for flounders, mackerel, sea bass, porgies, small- to medium-size bluefish, and others. I don't recommend it for trolling. It's too light, although it probably would be all right at slower trolling speeds for small fishes. You can use it in light-tackle casting, as from a boat, jetty, or pier; or even in the surf, so long as distance isn't a requirement, heavy lures or baits aren't rigged, and you're not tangling with opponents apt to make long runs when hooked.

SURF GEAR   Because of surf angling's common demands—casting distance and fairly heavy rigs—its tackle is scaled accordingly.

A light surf spinning combo suggests a rod 7 to 9 or 9½ feet long overall. A good tip section is one that tapers from enough thickness to give it backbone for fighting stubborn opponents, to a slender section with a lot of flexibility to cast the smaller 1-to-2-ounce surf artificials. Butt lengths vary somewhat, but the criterion is one that's long enough to let you swing it with both hands for leverage—comfortably. In bottom fishing the surf this rod will handle sinkers to about 3 ounces. It will take somewhat heavier ones when currents and backwashes necessitate it, but they're harder to handle.

Complementing this stick is one of the small surf spinning reels holding 200 to 300 yards of line up to 20-pound test. Lines usually employed with this outfit are 10-pound test or thereabouts. Such a reel also can be mounted on other spinning rods.

Light surf tackle will give you lively activity with weakfish, northern whiting, small- to medium-size bluefish, school-size striped bass, kingfish, and other surf-running species. But don't expect it to be all-purpose. Remember that it's light and has certain limitations.

CONVENTIONAL TACKLE A light conventional surf stick goes about 8 to 9 or 9½ feet long, tiptop guide to end of butt. Handle lengths vary but will be long enough—20 inches or better—for two-handed use. A conventional rod in this class combines sufficient resiliency to cast artificial lures up to 2½ or 3 ounces with enough spine to handle sinkers to about 4 ounces when angling is on the surf floor, as it sometimes is for striped bass, among other gamesters.

Matching this stick is one of the small surf reels with a capacity of 150 yards of 20-to-30-pound line. Thirty-pound test is close to maximum for this outfit. Later I'll tell you what to look for in surf reels.

With such an outfit you can argue with surf-foraging battlers of fair size, including striped bass, bluefish, channel bass, and others up to 20 or 25 pounds, maybe even 30 pounds or so.

MEDIUM TACKLE

Conventional and spinning equipment in this class is often recommended as good for all-around purposes. In other words, one of those happy mediums people go around striking.

One reason is that the rods have enough whip to cast artificials and sufficient "muscle" to manage rigs and medium-weight sinkers in bottom fishing.

CONVENTIONAL TACKLE Medium conventional gear is among the most popular of all salt-water tackle. Versatility is the reason.

It's one of the most widely used aboard boats, in a variety of methods, bottom fishing to trolling. It can take lines up to 30- and 40-pound test (provided the rods are rated for it, a system of grading I'll explain later). It can be brought into play when heavier baits are rigged and/or in fairly deep water where currents necessitate sinkers as heavy as 8 and 10 ounces.

A medium conventional outfit is good all-around boat fishing equipment (unless you're a real light-tackle nut). With it you can take bottom, intermediate-level, and top species ranging from, say, 4 or 5 pounds up to 25, 30, or even 40 pounds. That gives you a lot of latitude, since it encompasses most of the fishes you'll encounter. It's not the best tackle for gamesters beyond the extremes of that size range I mentioned. You'll lose appreciable action with opponents smaller than 4 or 5 pounds (and even with those) because the gear is too heavy for them. Conversely, it's too light, for the average angler, for such larger offshore species as big school tuna, swordfish, and the like. I should add, though, that with experience you'll be able to whip some of those bigger fighters, including white marlin, sailfish, tarpon, and some of the sharks, with this gear.

Although employed frequently for bottom angling, this outfit also will give you service in trolling for albacore, bonitos, dolphin, large bluefish, and the heftier striped bass. And you can use it on piers, jetties, and bridges. Although not as good as equipment designed for surf fishing, it can double in that service, provided casting distance and extremes in lure sizes aren't involved.

Medium boat rods range from about 5 or 5½ feet to 6 or even 7 feet overall. Being sturdier, they naturally have more backbone than light tackle. But they also are resilient for lively action.

A reel to go with such a rod accepts 150 to 200 or 250 yards of lines to 40-pound test. How much you'll require will depend upon water depths in the areas where you'll be doing most of your fishing, and also, to a certain extent, whether or not you'll be tangling with scrappers that make long runs. By and large, 150 yards will suffice for most conditions. For shallow water angling you could get away with 100 yards and a 1/0 reel. But a 2/0 reel, with its greater line capacity and more rugged insides, will give you greater scope.

SPINNING COMBOS Medium spinning rods measure 7 to 9 or 10 feet long, of which 14 or 16 to 20 or 22 inches are butt. They'll handle lures to 2½ or 3 ounces, and sinkers to 4 ounces or so. Twelve- to 20- or 30-pound lines are more or less standard.

"Medium" becomes a very flexible term when applied to spinning reels in this category. Their capacities range from 150 yards up to 300 or even 400 yards, according to line strengths. And they have a versatility of their own because they also can be mounted on medium surf spinning sticks.

Like its conventional-type running mate, a medium spinning combination is a good all-around instrument. With it you can fish aboard boat at various levels, bottom upward, including trolling, so long as the artificials, baits, rigs, and sinkers aren't too heavy. You also can take it along for jetty, pier, and bridge service. And you can adapt it to surf fishing if you keep in mind its limitations in weights of terminal rigs it can handle.

With its greater length, a spinning rod in this class is more willowy than a conventional equivalent. This spells greater sport, ounce for ounce of fish; but it also could mean some difficulty if you tie into a fairly large opponent. In the main, this outfit will take care of the widest single range of sport fishes in the spinning tackle department.

SURF EQUIPMENT, REGULAR AND SPINNING Here again I'm going to ask you to look in your wallet. If you're going to be doing appreciable amounts of both boat fishing and surfcasting, I suggest you get yourself two outfits. On the other hand, if surf fishing is going to be your bowl of chili, equip yourself accordingly.

Another "if": If you lean more toward conventional tackle than spinning gear, a medium outfit of the former type would be the one to buy. It's versatile, handling a wide assortment of lines, natural baits, artificials, rigs, and sinkers. That isn't to state that it will serve equally well in every conceivable situation, but it will do fine under most conditions, catching the greater majority of battlers you're likely to encounter in the surf. That includes channel bass, stripers, and the biggest, roughest 'n' toughest bluefish. (With smaller fishes, though, you'll sacrifice some action, because of its caliber.) Further, it will handle lines in the 30-to-40-pound bracket, which enhances its value on rocky coasts, where abrasion of line is a calculated risk.

Medium conventional surf rods go 8½, 9½, and 10 feet long, with butts of suitable length for leverage. All-around rods in this class have enough stiffness to let you rig sinkers to 5 and 6 ounces and fair-size baits, yet also are flexible enough to cast the lighter artificials, 1½ ounces or so, and provide fun with smaller but active species.

A reel to match this rod of yours can be found among many excellent models marketed by the better-known manufacturers. A 200-yard spool capacity is about right. You can get away with less yardage, but be influenced by the heavier lines involved. In other words, since lines to 30-pound test are fished with this tackle, choose a reel whose spool will accommodate at least 200 yards of such lines.

If you have a medium-caliber all-purpose spinning outfit you also own a combo that can double in surf fishing. But I repeat that the equipment best suited to this phase of angling is that designed specifically for it.

Medium surf spinning sticks, overall, go 8 to 10 feet long, of which anywhere from 18 to 24 inches are handle section. Those butt lengths will give you good leverage for casting and playing a fish, and among them you'll find one suited to your general build and arm length.

If you recall, I said that the smaller surf spinning reels also can be mounted on medium rods. For service on a rod in this category (and to double in brass on a lighter stick) I suggest a surf spinning reel with a capacity of 250 to 300 yards. And since lines of 12-to-20-pound test commonly are fished on medium spinning rods, you can be governed by the 20-pound mark when considering spool capacity.

A medium combo is a fine all-purpose spinning weapon. It casts lures as light as an ounce, as well as heavier artificials to 3 ounces, which covers a flock of the fish-getters rigged in surf spinning. And the rod is stiff enough to handle baits and sinkers to 4 ounces when fishing the surf bottom.

HEAVY TACKLE

As its name hints, this gear is intended for the bigger, tougher, more rambunctious game fishes. In this category are tackle's "big guns."

For the greater majority of fishes, methods and angling conditions covered by this book you won't need heavy gear. But there are situations where you could require it. Here's a sampling:

1. In deep-water bottom fishing or deep trolling for some of the larger species.
2. Surf fishing in strong currents and undertows and/or with the heaviest rigs, artificials, and natural baits.
3. In big game angling for brutes such as swordfish, blue marlin, giant bluefin tuna, large sharks, and the like. Here you won't have to buy appropriately heavy gear unless you're equipping your own boat. You can hire a charter boat. With it will come the necessary tackle.

I suggest you give some thought to how much time you'll be spending in the foregoing situations before investing in heavy equipment. It can be expensive.

CONVENTIONAL TYPE Heavy conventional tackle is brought into action in fishing the sea floor and deep water around reefs for hefty battlers such as groupers and deep-swimming sharks. It also can be used in drift fishing at various levels (a sharking technique we'll come to later). And you can wield it in trolling for the largest school tuna, as well as swordfish and marlin.

Rods in this class are about 6 or 6½ feet long, of which 16 to 18 inches are butt. They usually have a metal cap on the butt that fits into a fighting chair's gimbal or socket. Suitably stout and strong, they're made to handle lines up to at least 80-pound test, along with the heaviest terminal rigs.

Most heavy-caliber rods come outfitted with roller guides instead of the ring type. (Even the lighter rods in offshore fishing today have roller guides—if not throughout, at least the tiptop guide is a roller.) Many also have a double-locking reel seat as a safety precaution.

Reels mounted on these rods range from a 3/0 or 4/0, on the lighter side for the category's lighter sticks, to 6/0, even 9/0, with capacities climbing from 300 to 500 and 600 yards of line. Reel sizes are governed by rods, lines, kinds of fishing, sizes of the game sought, and skill of the anglers involved. Personal preference is a factor too. Sizes 4/0 to 6/0 would constitute an average.

HEAVY SPINNING GEAR   You'll find "big guns" here too. Although the rods do not match some of the conventional sticks for stoutness of tip sections, they exceed them in length, going to 9 and 10 feet-plus. Among them are spinning rods developed for offshore big game angling. The stronger spinning lines are used. The maximum safe strength for a particular rod is usually indicated on it. Lacking that label, it should be learned from the tackle dealer or manufacturer. It's vital to the life of *any* rod.

There are big, heavy-duty spinning reels to balance these rods. They're the spinning reel family's largest, characterized by extra-strong parts and roomy spools that accept up to 500, 600, or more yards of line to 40-pound test.

SURF TACKLE, CONVENTIONAL AND SPINNING VARIETIES   You've heard the saying, "Never send a boy to do a man's job." Designers must have had something like that in mind when they created heavy-duty surf equipment. Everything about it is scaled to rugged proportions. It is, in fact, a specialized weapon, developed for surf combat under the roughest conditions imaginable. That means the biggest, toughest surf-run battlers, a heavy, beach-slamming surf, stiff breezes, strong currents, and big rigs that have to be flung across appreciable yardage.

Heavy surf rods measure up to 12 feet long, with appropriately long butts and muscular tip sections. They're made to cast big baits, such as whole eels, handle heavy sinkers up to about 8 ounces, and toss artificials going 5 ounces or thereabouts. The reels are correspondingly buxom, with strong innards, and spool capacities ranging to 250 yards of 40- and 50-pound line.

Conceivably you could encounter most or all those aforementioned rugged conditions in one place simultaneously. But unless you'll be doing considerable surf fishing where such conditions prevail, you can write off heavy surf tackle for now. The word "heavy" refers to more than its caliber. It's heavy to handle, and becomes progressively more so when you cast with it for any length of time. It can be fatiguing to wield. It's time enough to consider this equipment when you find yourself ambling up and down a coast where truly rugged conditions prevail.

Heavy-caliber surf spinning rods measure about the same as conventional equivalents, which is to say up to 12 feet. Their handles also are long, up to 24, 26, and 28 inches for the required leverage. Similarly, their tips are proportionately sturdy to wrestle with the huskiest surf-prowling gamesters. They'll cast artificials up to 4 and 5 ounces, including big plugs and metal squids, as well as rigged eels within that weight range. In surf bottom fishing they'll enable you to rig large baits and sinkers to 6 ounces.

Lines employed with these king-size spinning sticks usually go 20-, 30-, and 40-pound test, suited to the larger fishes and rocky areas where lighter lines might be chafed through. Accommodating sufficient yardage of line in such strengths naturally calls for a reel with a roomy spool. The large surf spinning models can hold up to 400 yards. Also usable with heavy surf sticks are those big offshore spinning reels I mentioned earlier.

EXTRA-HEAVY WEAPONS

These are the battleship 14-inchers of sport fishing, the big, BIG guns. And you'll find them in the conventional category. I include them here because you should know about them. There's no need to even flirt with the idea of buying an extra-heavy outfit unless you especially want to own one and are prepared to spend anywhere from about $350 to $1,000 or more to satisfy the whim. The chances are that any extra-heavy tackle fishing you'll do will be aboard either a charter boat or a suitably equipped private vessel.

Rods in this class are like those in the heavy division, only more so. They're characterized by a very strong butt, with a metal end to seat itself in a fighting chair's gimbal, an exceptionally stout tip section, able to fish lines up to 130-pound test, double-locking reel seat, and big roller guides throughout. They can cost up to a couple of hundred bucks apiece, and that's without two pairs of pants.

On them are clamped the biggest of all reels, literally young winches with extremely strong gears and drags. On the "smaller" side is the 10/0. From there, sizes range up through 12/0 to a monstrous 16/0. (A 12/0, maybe 14/0 at the outside, is about the largest in popular use.) To give you an idea of the bulk of a 16/0, its spool will hold about 1,100 yards of 150-pound line, and proportionately more of the 130-pound stuff. Incidentally, for official world record purposes, the strongest line recognized by the International Game Fish Association, arbiter and final authority in such matters, is 130-pound test. This is the strength usually fished with extra-heavy tackle.

GENERAL POINTERS

There you have a catalogue of the various calibers of conventional and spinning tackle. It covers all the equipment you could possibly use anywhere. From it, with an accent on light to heavy gear, you'll make your selections. Now I want to add some suggestions.

1. Don't go crazy buying tackle right off the bat. You'll acquire enough as time goes by. For a starter, decide what kind of fishing you'll be doing most of the time, then outfit yourself accordingly. If you're a real newcomer, you can't go far wrong in choosing either light all-purpose tackle if your angling is going to be exclusively for the smallest species in bays and other sheltered waters, or medium all-purpose gear for larger fishes, inside and out.

2.—and important: You won't find it on all rods, but many carry a label indicating the heaviest line they can handle safely, without damage to the rod. For example, let's say a rod is labeled "30 pounds." The heaviest line you can fish with it is 30-pound test. You can go under that, but not over. If a rod you select carries no such designation, ask the tackle dealer or manufacturer. Then stay within the recommended maximum; otherwise you could be shopping for a replacement.

3. Don't try to become a light-tackle user overnight. If you're at all in doubt about your experience and skill, lean more toward sturdier equipment than in the opposite direction. You'll sacrifice

some action, but you'll also save on lines, lures, rigs, and maybe rods. You can always progress to the lighter equipment.

RODS, CONVENTIONAL AND SPINNING   Most rods today, lightest to huskiest, are made from fiberglass. You can't beat 'em for toughness, serviceability, and long life—all at modest cost. And, unlike wooden rods, they demand relatively little maintenance.

In case you're asking, yes, you can buy wooden rods, such as split bamboo models and the like, but they don't match fiberglass for over-all ruggedness. They're more likely than glass to "take a set" (develop a permanent bend in their tip section) after long, repeated use or if stored improperly, and they require revarnishing periodically. Moreover, good wooden rods can be expensive.

There are one-piece rods, but most of those used in salt-water fishing are two-piece, with a ferrule uniting butt and tip section. Some anglers favor one-piece sticks, believing that a ferrule joint discounts some of the tip section's action. That's a quarrel with metal ferrules, but not a serious one except for purists. And for them there are rods with fiberglass ferrules that bend with the tip.

Take-apart rods are the most popular because they're easier to carry and store, especially the long surf models. All you have to do is keep both parts of the ferrule joint clean and, if metal, free of corrosion. A touch of light machine oil, sparingly applied, will help a ferrule to function smoothly.

Focus a sharp eye on the reel seat and ferrule(s) of any rod you buy. Salt-water rods turned out by reputable manufacturers have heavily plated hardware, strongly resistant to corrosion and rust. Be sure the reel seat aligns the reel accurately with the guides to avoid unnecessary line wear.

Check the rod's guides. If they're the ring type, the most common, they should be of Carboloy or other tough material to resist line wear. Cheap guides become grooved in time, exerting unnecessary friction on lines and shortening their life. Weakened lines will cost you fish. If you're getting a rod with roller guides, insist on good ones. When you examine a rod's guides, look at their wrappings. Guides on a good rod are wrapped strongly and securely.

Roller guides have frames of various materials. Some are of corrosion-resistant, anodized aluminum. Others are nylon, favored by some fishermen because they tend, more than metal, to "give" with the rod's bending and therefore are less likely to interfere with its resiliency. Whatever the frames' material, the rollers should be of metal—many are stainless steel—and freely turning.

REELS—ALL KINDS Its drag is a very important part of your reel. It provides resistance when a fish takes line, helping you to better control him and eventually wear him down. The drag must be absolutely dependable and function smoothly, without jerkiness or binding. These are qualities incorporated in reels produced by reputable builders.

I've already mentioned that the drag control on most conventional reels is a star-shaped wheel, while that on spinning reels commonly is a knob, which can be mounted on the spool's outer end or at the opposite end of the reel. I also mentioned a lever-like control, called a quadrant brake, found on some conventional reels. Often there's a multicolored band right alongside the lever to indicate varying degrees of drag tightness. I don't want to dwell on this except to comment that I prefer the lever arrangement to a star wheel, which has no calibrations to show just how tight or loose a brake is—you go by touch. I prefer the quadrant brake because it's easier to return, with some precision, to a desired setting. The only trouble is, this type is found on more expensive reels.

Now I want to tell you about some of the various line-retrieving devices found on spinning reels. Since their spools do not revolve, there has to be some way to get line back on them.

The simplest of these mechanisms is the manual type. To retrieve, the angler simply hooks his line with his forefinger and deposits it on a roller that guides it onto the spool as the reel's crank is turned. Another system is in the arm or finger pickup. Here a curved arm or finger on the reel automatically sweeps into position and gathers in the line for spooling when the crank is rotated. Third is what they call a bail or full-bail pickup. The bail is a curving metal appendage extending from one side of the reel to the other (in contrast to the arm or finger type, which is shorter and open on one end). The instant a retrieve is begun, this bail gathers incoming line and guides it back on the spool.

There are pros and cons for the various types of pickups, based chiefly on personal preference.

The manual kind, being simplest, is least likely to develop "bugs," and so is fancied by many anglers. Another advantage claimed for it is that it's better for casting heavy lures. They've been known to interfere with operation of the spring mechanism of automatic pickups. It requires practice to learn to use, but that's no problem. More of a drawback is the time lapse between picking up the line with the forefinger and the start of a retrieve. It's a very short gap, but it assumes importance when fast reeling is necessary.

An automatic arm pickup does its job, but for casters it poses a drawback. When casting on windy days the line may get snagged on the arm. Another source of trouble arises if the pickup arm becomes bent enough to impair its function. But that headache is more likely to occur on inferior reels than on good ones.

The bail type has probably been the most popular of the trio. It's automatic, easy to use, and gathers in line immediately when a retrieve is begun. That last virtue may not seem to be major, but often it's necessary to start a retrieve as quickly as possible. This necessity arises when slack develops in the line as a fish alters the direction of his run. Bluefish are one species famous for that tactic. If slack develops, you want to take it up quickly so as not to give your opponent a chance to throw the hook. Another circumstance in which instant retrieve is desirable occurs when casting lures whose action should begin the instant they hit the water. A possible drawback to the bail pickup is that it's a bit more complex mechanically, and therefore (theoretically, at least) more subject to little operating difficulties than simpler types. But here again most such bugs have been eliminated in well-built reels.

If you're newcomer or a fisherman with little experience, I'd suggest a bail-type pickup.

Depending upon model and make of reel, its spool may be made from metal or plastic. Both serve their purpose. Many fishermen who do a lot of casting, from shore or boat, like plastic spools. Since they're lighter, they do not gain as much momentum as fairly heavy metal spools during casts. Therefore they're less likely to overrun the line and cause backlashes. I should quickly add, though, that there are lightweight metal spools that also lessen overrunning. Some plastic spools do have a flaw in that they've been known to crack under heavy strain when a particularly belligerent fish is being played. Similarly, weak plastic spools have cracked under the pressure that builds when monofilament is packed tightly on them during a battle.

For all-around service I recommend a metal spool.

Spools on conventional reels come in varying widths, the widest being those on surf models. If I were you, I wouldn't trouble myself with the detail of spool widths at this stage of the game. Later, if you become technically minded as regards your tackle, you can recall these details: (1) The wider a spool, the more chance for line to pile up unevenly during a retrieve. Uneven accumulations of line increase chances of line tangles on the spool and backlashes in casting. (2) In casting, a wide spool is less apt than a narrow one to gain excessive momentum leading to "birds' nests." That's why many surf fishermen favor reels with wide spools. (3) Although line is less likely to "bunch up" unevenly on a narrow spool than on a wide one, the former's mechanical advantage can change as line pays out or is cranked back in. Such changes may necessitate drag adjustments at various stages of combat.

Tip: Mark this well. With any reel, regardless of type or model, drag effect increases as more and more line goes out. In other words, *the less line left on your spool, the greater the braking effect.* With smaller fishes and those not inclined to make long runs, this doesn't mean beans. But with larger opponents and considerable line out it could mean that you'll have to slack off your drag somewhat or risk a popped line.

Standard on conventional reels are a free-spool clutch and a clicker. The former is a kind of neutral gear, allowing the spool to turn freely, independently of the crank. It's useful when paying out line (but not when a fish is on!). A lever throws the reel into free spool, and the line's outflow can be controlled by thumb pressure on the spool. When sufficient line is out, the lever is thrown to re-engage the spool's gears.

The clicker is an internal ratchet, activated by a sliding button on the reel's side plate. One of its functions is to serve as an audible alarm, warning that a fish is fooling around with the bait. That comes into its own when a rod is left unattended in a holder. The clicker also is useful when it's advantageous to leave the reel in free spool. Then the clicker supplies just enough drag to prevent line from being pulled off the reel by currents or the boat's motion. You'll get to know the difference between the lackadaisical, quieter sound of a clicker in false alarms and the steady, loud, angry "Zzzzzzzz!" when it means business.

An antireverse lock is a useful feature on spinning reels. This is a mechanism that permits the crank to turn only during retrieves. With the antireverse on, any line pull meets resistance from the drag; and the clicker, if on, sounds a warning.

This device "pays for its keep" in several ways. In trolling, for instance, you can keep the lock off until enough line is paid out (a kind of free spool arrangement), then throw it into "On." That will hold your lure at the desired distance astern. Or you can use it in jigging and bottom fishing to maintain your rig at the desired level. And when carrying your outfit it will prevent line from peeling off the spool or collecting on it in loose coils.

On spinning reels, the roller over which line passes may be fixed or revolving. Many anglers like the fixed type because a little sand or dirt can be enough to make a movable roller bind, imposing unnecessary friction—and wear—on both line and roller. In any event, the roller should be of hard, durable material. A soft roller will groove in time, shortening lines' life through extra wear.

There are two more features incorporated in some conventional reels that merit mention.

One is an antibacklash device. There are different types: magnetic, hydraulic, and one that's a kind of air brake. All are designed to prevent a reel spool from gaining excessive momentum during casts and overrunning the line. They do just that, at a price. By the same token they also reduce casting distance. For that reason die-hard casters dispense with their services and rely on an educated thumb, applied to the reel spool, to do the trick. Incidentally, there are antibacklash devices adjustable to weights of lures used. There are also some that can be turned off, giving a double advantage of full freedom in long casts and a backlash minimizer in short and medium casts.

The other extra found on certain conventional reels is a level wind mechanism. It's geared to the crank, and when you reel in, it shuttles back and forth, neatly and evenly laying the line on the spool. A level wind is handy but not necessary. You can guide line back on a spool fairly evenly with a finger. The device's advantage is that it performs this chore automatically. Disadvantages are that it cuts down on casting distance (which isn't a worry when casting isn't involved) and that it must be kept clean (otherwise sand or grit will impair its function).

Many reels, conventional and spinning, offer an easy-take-apart feature. Very handy for do-it-yourself cleaning and lubrication—especially surf reels, when sand gets into their insides. Along the same lines, many models also have an interchangeable spool feature. You can carry one or more extra spools, each with a line of different strength, to suit a variety of conditions.

Finally, there's the detail of exteriors. Any salt-water reel's exposed metal surfaces must be protected—by chrome plating, anodizing, or enamel—against the ravages of corrosion and rust. Those two saboteurs will make short work of an insufficiently protected reel. And there you have still another strong reason for buying the product of a reputable manufacturer. His competitive research has come up with the best possible protection.

CHAPTER 3

Lines and Lures

Once upon a time, believe it or not, fishermen used lines fabricated from *horsehair*. There also was an era in which hooks were dangled on ordinary cotton sewing thread. Then came linen. For decades that was *the* material for fishing lines, and those made from Irish flax were among the most desirable.

But in time linen was doomed. Research chemistry did it by finding synthetic substitutes for the plant fibers used in line manufacture. Today's synthetics are superior to yesterday's linen in many ways.

Prime among synthetic lines' bonuses is their imperviousness to water. Since they do not absorb water like linen lines, all the drawbacks—rot, mildew, and swelling—noted for linen are eliminated, or at least minimized. Another advantage of synthetic lines, and a very important one, is that they incorporate greater strength in smaller diameters than their linen predecessors. This means more line on a reel spool, decreased visibility in water, and less water drag. (The less water drag the better. Appreciable drag in bottom fishing can lift a rig off bottom, necessitating heavier sinkers. In trolling, if great enough, it can break a line.) Last but not least, since they do not absorb water they do not require the maintenance demanded for longer life among linen lines.

Yes, the synthetics have a lot going for them. But they're not completely devoid of drawbacks. One that has been mentioned frequently over the years is stretch.

A certain amount of stretch in a line is all right, and in most angling will do no harm so long as it isn't excessive. In fact, sometimes a certain amount of "give" is an advantage after a fish is hooked. Here you have a kind of rubber band effect that maintains tension on the line and helps to minimize slack. Too much stretch, on the other hand, is a built-in handicap, notably in trolling and deep-water bottom fishing with heavy rigs and large baits. When a line stretches excessively it absorbs some of the jolt of a strike, interfering with the force that helps hook the fish. Similarly, excessive give makes it harder to set a hook by lifting the rod tip. Much of that lift's oomph is lost in the line's stretch.

Excessive stretch may also mask the bait-nibbling actions of smaller or lightly biting fishes to the extent that an angler doesn't realize he has a customer. It also can complicate the playing of a hard-running fish that peels off a lot of line, especially if he changes direction often. Then stretch costs the fisherman a certain amount of control. It also provides the fish with more opportunities to develop slack in the line and possibly throw the hook.

Other criticisms that have been leveled at some synthetic lines over the years are that they're a bit stiff and/or tend to coil when they leave the reel and that there's no tension on them. Certain synthetics also have been accused of being more susceptible to abrasion when they rub against rocks and other underwater objects. Since abrasion can weaken lines, it becomes something of a calculated risk when angling in rocky areas. For this reason fishermen often employ somewhat heavier lines in such places than they would ordinarily.

Improved manufacturing methods have done much to remove objectionable stretch and excessive stiffness, as well as that aforementioned tendency to coil when leaving a reel, from synthetic lines. And although some of those negative properties may still be present, in varying degrees, among certain lines, they're outweighed by synthetics' virtues.

TYPES OF SYNTHETIC LINES   Forerunners of all synthetic lines were those made from nylon. The early nylons had all the plus features of synthetic lines, but they stretched like the dickens, so much so that many anglers wouldn't use them. It was almost like fishing with a long rubber band, if you imagine such a thing. Modern nylon lines still have inherent give—more so, maybe, than other synthetics; but their stretch has been lessened appreciably.

The synthetic lines that have earned great popularity in recent years are those fashioned from Dacron, a material introduced to the sport fishing fraternity-sorority back in the 1940s.

Dacron lines offer all the virtues of synthetics, and then some. To start with, they have relatively little elasticity, a characteristic that makes them fine for trolling and bottom fishing. Another bonus lies in the fact that they incorporate even greater strength in even finer diameters than other kinds of lines. They wear well, too; and, characteristic of synthetics, are less likely than linen to deteriorate with age.

I've shown you why greater strength in a finer diameter is an important line quality, accenting that business of water drag. Now let me cite a couple of examples.

Let's take trolling. You'd be surprised at the amount of water drag on a line when a boat is in motion. It's considerable. In trolling you can pay out line—without a lure or anything else on it—to the point where water drag becomes great enough to snap it. When water drag is lessened by a finer diameter, chances of a line popping because of it are decreased.

As I've said, drag also is a factor in bottom fishing in deep water and/or strong currents. Here the thrust against a line can be sufficient to lift your rig off the sea floor, away from where it will do its work. Sometimes fairly heavy sinkers are required to offset this thrust. That's where finer-diameter lines come into their own. With their decreased drag you can rig lighter sinkers —say, 5 ounces instead of 8, or even 10. Furthermore, a lighter sinker, coupled with less drag on the line, means just that much less strain to detract from your opponent's fight. A sinker is dead weight against which a fish must battle in addition to you at the line's other end. Throw in water drag, and the fish will tire that much more quickly, giving you correspondingly less sport.

Tip: I'll probably have occasion to repeat this from time to time when we get to some of the fishes you're going to catch. Never use any more weight in a sinker than you need to keep your baited rig on the bottom where it's supposed to be. Excess sinker weight serves no purpose. It only robs you of some action with your fish.

Synthetic lines can be divided into two broad categories. One consists of braided or multistrand types—designations that are self-explanatory. The other general category embraces lines known as monofilament. And in that name you'll find a clue to their construction. "Mono-" means "one-" or "single-"; "filament" means "strand." Hence a monofilament line is a single strand, as opposed to, say, a line of several strands braided or twisted upon each other. Synthetic lines are marketed under many brand names created by their manufacturers, but they all belong to either of those basic families, braided or monofilament. Both kinds see service with conventional and spinning equipment.

BRAIDED TYPES   Nylon and Dacron are common materials among braided lines in strengths up to 130 pounds or so. As usual, a choice between the two is a matter of personal preference, influenced by kinds of fishing done.

Braided nylon lines have found popularity among casters, particularly surf fishermen using conventional gear. They're the ones you'll hear surfcasters refer to as "squidding lines" because of their use with metal squids. They come in varying degrees of suppleness, according to their manufacturers' processing. Some are quite soft and pliant, and are favored because they cast better than stiffer lines. Other anglers like somewhat stiffer lines, even though they might not cast quite as well, because they're less susceptible to injury from abrasion in rocky or boulder-strewn areas. Braided nylon lines in general are susceptible to abrasion. If they're fished in rocky places they should be checked frequently for signs of weakening wear.

Braided Dacron lines are used in casting too, but are less in favor than nylon for that purpose among some fishermen because of their finish, which is harder on the thumb when casting any distance. Braided Dacron lines' real popularity is in boat fishing, for trolling, jigging, and bottom angling. In those techniques they're favored over nylon because they possess less stretch and incorporate greater strength in a smaller diameter.

THE MONOFILAMENTS   Another offspring of the wedding of chemistry and modern fishing line manufacturing processes is monofilament line, commonly called mono for short. Monofilament lines are made from nylon and other synthetic materials by a process called extrusion—like a spaghetti machine, you might say.

Available in a wide range of strengths from very light to heavy, monofilament lines can be used with both spinning and conventional tackle. Originally there were problems in their use with conventional reels because the lighter mono lines' finer diameters caused them to work their way inside spools' flanges, causing real foulups. But subsequent improvements of the lines and modifications of reels have eliminated that difficulty to a great degree. So their use has broadened, bringing them into service in all kinds of boat fishing and in casting.

The monos have a number of good features. They're synthetic, which means they resist rot and deterioration. They wear better than braided and twisted types. They're also more resistant to abrasion damage, which leads to their use in rocky places. Further, they offer finer diameters than other lines of comparable strengths, and you know what that means. Many anglers fishing with other kinds of lines capitalize on mono's lower visibility in water by tying in a length of it between their terminal rig and regular line. Too, mono lines retain their rated strength for a long time. Finally, because of all their qualities, they're economical to use.

Excessive stiffness was an objectionable trait of early monofilaments. They refused to lie snug on a reel spool, and in general were awkward. Some mono lines, notably those in the greater strengths, still possess a certain amount of stiffness; but much of that problem has been licked by improved manufacturing techniques and by creation of lines that are oval, instead of round, in cross-section. Because of their cross-sectional shape and greater suppleness, oval mono lines lie snugger on a reel spool than the round types and are less likely to billow outward in casts. It's the generally increased suppleness of mono lines, incidentally, that has aided their adaptability to conventional reels.

Nylon, as a pioneering synthetic, was the granddaddy of materials for fabrication of mono lines. With it came nylon's chief drawback, excessive stretch. But here again manufacturers heard the squawks of fishermen and devised improved processing to cut down on an objectionable trait. Nylon monofilament lines still have appreciable elasticity, but this can pose a problem only when fishing deep water with heavy rigs or while playing a fast, hard-running fish with considerable line out.

WIRE LINES   Their name tells the story. Made from metal, they are, in essence, pliant, flexible wires.

Why use wire for line? Well, wire lines were created especially for deep trolling. In that sense they're specialists. Their function is to carry lures deeper than they would go with linen or synthetic lines. Wire lines, naturally, are heavier than those other kinds. In that respect they have a kind of built-in sinker, you might say. With them you reach fishes wandering along the deeper levels between surface and bottom. Sometimes that's the only way you'll contact the larger individuals of certain species —bluefish and striped bass, to name two. At such times with lines other than wire you usually have to add a trolling sinker or other gadget to your terminal rig to bring it down to where the beasties are. With wire, its weight alone is often enough to do the trick.

During their development over the years, wire lines have been manufactured from a variety of metals, including copper and stainless steel. There also have been developed various types, such as twisted, braided, and a solid, single-strand wire, a kind of monofilament in metal. The three kinds have their individual advantages and drawbacks. The twisted and braided types, for example, are somewhat more supple and therefore a bit easier to handle than the solid variety. And they're less apt to kink. On the other hand, they have greater diameter per pounds-test rating. Consequently, there's greater water thrust against them, and they do not ride as deep as solid wires. Subsequent years brought a trend toward wire lines of the solid, single-strand type, with a nickel alloy known commercially as Monel finding favor.

Wire lines are sold in a wide range of strengths to handle the various species for which deep trolling is the technique. A common procedure is to have the wire line backed by regular line of whatever kind the angler is accustomed to using. That is, at least half the reel's spool, we'll say, receives the regular line, after which the desired amount of wire line is secured to it to fill all or part of the remainder of the spool. The wire is in about the same strength as its backing line. Unless enough wire is used so that there's always some on the reel, there's really no point in using a greater strength than the backing line. After all, the combination's maximum strength is that of its weakest component.

Wire lines have a lot in their favor (which isn't to say they should be substituted for other kinds). Being metal, they naturally are impervious to water, and can't rot or swell; and those made from Monel or stainless steel can't rust. They're strong and wear well. The solid types can't fray, and they're not sensitive to abrasion like braided synthetics. Monel solid wire line has some other features on its bragging list. It has high tensile strength for its diameter; its surface resistance to water is fairly low, hence there's decreased drag; and it sinks deeper, at the same trolling speeds, than some other kinds of lines because of its greater density and lower water drag.

Wire lines have two shortcomings: They're not as easy to handle as other varieties; and they kink. Both of those shortcomings are due to the fact that the lines are metal.

Although modern wire lines are quite flexible and pliant, there's no escaping a certain amount of metallic stiffness. As a result, they're not as easy to reel as other lines. Nor do they lie as flat and snug on the reel spool. In fact, an annoyance with wire line is that its stiffness causes it to develop loose coils on the spool when there's no tension on it. You have to watch that. If a spool should overrun with wire line—that is, revolve too fast as line pays out—the resulting snarls could make you wish you'd taken up another activity. *Here's a tip:* When you let wire line pay out, keep your reel's clicker on to maintain some resistance against overrunning.

Kinking is the really serious drawback in wire lines. Even a small one can spell headaches. A kink can cause a snarl when it's in among coils on the reel spool. It can snag in the rod's guides as it passes through. Worst of all, a kink weakens wire; and sometimes attempting to straighten it out only intensifies the weakening.

Care should be exercised in handling wire lines to minimize kinking. Check them periodically for signs of it. You'll have to use your own judgment as to how bad a kink is before you attempt to straighten it. If you try, avoid excessive bending that will weaken the wire. If a kink is really bad, or you're at all in doubt about it, play it safe and remove that section of wire. You'll lose enough finned opponents to kinks as it is. They've been known to develop while playing a fish.

If you plan to use wire line to any extent, your rod's tiptop guide should be a roller rather than a ring type. Extensive use of wire is apt to groove a ring guide.

THE SUBJECT OF LURES

Considering the different models, along with the assorted weights and color patterns in which they come, there are thousands of artificial baits or lures on the market. They range from small, fractional-ounce attractors, for spinning, on up to big bunker spoons. To merely *list* only part of those hordes of artificials would make this book read like a tackle manufacturer's catalogue, and it's unnecessary.

Don't let that huge army of lures scare you. For your purposes you'll have no use for the vast majority of them, but they'll be there should you ever want to try them. As you gain experience you'll be surprised at how easy it will be to thread your way through the assortments, selecting those best suited to your purposes. And always you can be guided by the advice of local tackle dealers. From the jingling of their cash registers they can tell which models are the most effective at given times.

Often several different kinds of lures can be rigged for a single species. Or, conversely, a single artificial can be fished for several species. To include all those possibilities here would only lead to confusion and monotonous repetition. Suffice it now to cite some general types you'll employ for fishes covered by this book. Specific lures will be spotlighted in chapters dealing with those species.

FEATHERS   Among the widely employed artificials within the scope of your book are the feather lures—feathers for short.

The term "feather" has come to include the entire lure, but actually it applies to only part of it, a kind of skirt surrounding the hook. The feathers in this type of salt-water artificial are mounted in a fairly heavy, bullet-shaped head of metal so that they trail out behind it. The head is given added attraction by bright plating, and many models carry large red eyes to further the illusion of some kind of living creature scooting through the sea. The wire leader on which a feather lure is rigged is fed through a lengthwise hole in its head. The hook, secured to the leader, rides hidden among the feathers.

The idea, of course, is that a fish—a tuna or whatever—sees this thing moving along, decides it would make a tasty snack, and gets himself a mouthful of hook. No one has ever explained satisfactorily why anything with feathers would look natural to a fish, but it works. The fact is that feather lures are used in many parts of the world for a variety of gamesters. I've fished them as far away as the Indian Ocean off Cape Town, South Africa, for yellowfin tuna.

Natural feathers are used. Sometimes you'll hear these lures referred to as "Jap feathers," a term supposedly stemming from the fact that they're taken from the necks of Japanese chickens noted for the quality of their feathers. Whatever their source, the lures' feathers come in various colors and color combinations: all white; red and white; green and yellow; a shade called tangerine; blue and white; black and white, etc. Designed for trolling, they're killers for tuna, albacore, bonito, and dolphin, among others. If you plan to do any offshore fishing, a few feather lures in different color combos (keep red and white in mind) are a must.

Not all the so-called feather lures have natural feathers. Also grouped in the family today are artificials with skirts of strands of nylon and other synthetic materials. These too come in various colors—red, yellow, etc.—and color combinations. And they can be effective on species for which natural feathers are trolled. You should include a couple of these in your kit too.

SPOONS Here's a large family. Widely rigged in both salt and fresh-water angling, they're on the scene in a multitude of shapes and sizes.

Commonly they're oval or teardrop in shape, or like the bowl of a teaspoon. Some are elongated or shaped like a little fish; some are flat; certain models are bent or otherwise curved to give them a wobbling or other eye-catching action. They're also marketed in different finishes, which include chrome, silver, nickel, and stainless steel. Many models are enameled in gaudy combinations of white, red, yellow, etc. Sometimes bright-colored

beads are incorporated for additional attraction. Spoons' effectiveness is based on a combination of flash, or brightness, and
action.

Those most widely used are models ranging up to about three
inches long, and they can be armed with single, double, or treble
(gang) hooks. Then there are the larger spoons going up to six
inches and more in length. Largest of all are those bunker spoons
I mentioned earlier. Shaped something like a canoe paddle's
blade, and up to about a foot long and four inches wide, they're
made to simulate the mossbunker or menhaden, a popular food
fish among striped bass, bluefish, and other species. There's an
old joke about these monster spoons. It says that if you can't
hook a fish with one, you can club him to death with it.

The smaller spoons, those to three inches long or so, naturally
are rigged for smaller fishes and lighter tackle. They can be lethal
in trolling and casting for many different kinds of sport fishes.
The larger models, up through the huge bunker spoons, are
trolled on somewhat heavier tackle and will take the bigger
striped bass, bluefish, and other marine battlers.

SPINNERS These are kissin' cousins of spoons. They too are oval,
roundish, or teardrop in shape, and come in different finishes. As
in the case of spoons, popular spinner finishes for salt-water fishing include chrome, silver, nickel, and stainless steel. As their
name implies, they're intended to spin or turn in the water; and
they depend upon flash, glitter, and motion to lure customers to
their waiting hooks.

Spinners are primarily trolling lures, but they also can be
added to other rigs to furnish additional eye-catching attraction.
Fluke fishermen, for example, will attach one or two small spinner
blades to their terminal rig to provide flash and movement as it
drifts along the bottom. They also can be effective when allowed
to drift out from a pier or other shoreside structure, or from a
boat, then retrieved slowly. Sometimes a rig consists of a single
spinner blade and a hook. Or two or more can be rigged, according to personal preference and theory. Some spinner assemblies
include beads (red is a common color) for added attractiveness.

Spinner rigs often are most effective when their hooks are
baited. Popular baits include sandworm, piece of pork rind, strip

of squid, and some small bait fish such as killy or spearing. Such outfits can be trolled, drifted, or cast and retrieved slowly. They're particularly good for fluke and striped bass.

PLUGS One of the largest lure families of all is that gathered under the heading Plugs. An endless parade of them troops through sport fishing, carrying colorful names such as Goo Goo Eye, Big Daddy, and the like. They come in a host of designs, a rainbow of colors, and assorted finishes, all with various types of hook arrangements. Whatever their anatomical details, plugs find their world in casting and trolling.

Within the plug tribe are several subgroups. For example, take the darters, so named for their darting, zigzag motion. You'll hear about poppers. They're made with a concavity in front to generate popping sounds when in motion. And there are divers and swimmers. Many plugs have a single-piece body. Others are jointed in one or more places to impart undulating movement. The list of antics performed by plugs includes wiggling, splashing, fluttering, and all kinds of erratic actions. Some models have built-in sonic effects as extra attention-getters.

For many years plugs have been fashioned from wood. Today you see more and more molded in plastic. Wooden plugs have painted or enameled finishes. The plastic jobs usually are color-impregnated.

Some models are designed to do their work at the surface, creating splashing disturbances that draw top-feeding species. Others are made to travel at intermediate levels to contact fishes traveling along those planes. Still others ride deep. Their color patterns include every conceivable hue of the rainbow—and then some, singly or in combinations. There are smooth finishes and those that mimic fishes' scaly skins. Some carry tiny propellers to lend extra attraction. Certain models are outfitted with a metal lip in front, which can be bent to make them dive to desired levels. And so it goes, *ad infinitum*.

As you'd expect, there's a multitude of sizes too. Smallest are the fractional-ounce fellows, created for spinfishing. From there, sizes range upward to six inches and more.

Whatever their individual design, size, color pattern, action, etc., all plugs have one thing in common: They're designed to imitate, in one or more ways, various small fishes, eels, or other creatures on which game fishes prey. Often their appearance is a major key to their success. More frequently, it's a combination of their appearance and the way their owners work them in the water.

Hook arrangements on plugs vary considerably. Some carry only one hook in the rear, or a trailing, swinging treble hook. Another model will be armed with two treble hooks, one aft and the other at about its midsection. Among seasoned fishermen the hook armament often is rearranged according to individual ideas, with hooks added or removed. You'll probably experiment too.

Plugs are versatile artificials, racking up a variety of marine gamesters in trolling and casting, from shore and boats. Bluefish and striped bass are among the species that respond.

BUCKTAILS AND JIGS   In the section about feather lures I mentioned models that are included in that group but have skirts of nylon or other synthetic material instead of natural feathers. These nylon feathers, as they're sometimes called, can be included in this section too because of their artificial skirts.

Incidentally, many experienced fishermen favor those synthetic skirts over natural feathers, because the former stand up better under repeated attacks from the harder-hitting sport fishes—bluefish, for example.

Bucktail lures function along the same lines as natural feathers and their synthetic counterparts. Differences are anatomical, chiefly in shape and size. Bucktails are smaller, kind of stubby, and relatively heavy for their size. Another difference is the one that gave the attractor its name. A bucktail also has a skirt around its hook, except that it's short and made from coarse animal hairs, originally those from the tail of a buck deer. A bucktail further differs from the other two in that its hook is rigidly fixed, whereas on a natural or nylon feather the hook is free to swing. Too, a bucktail and its hook comprise a unit, with attachment of the leader made directly to its body.

You'll encounter numerous variations in designs among bucktails, but mostly they follow a basic blueprint calling for a characteristically heavy body and short skirt. Colors vary among different models, going to bright yellow, all white, red and white, etc. Many a striped bass has found them fatal.

Bucktails can be classified with a large tribe of artificials lumped under the broad heading Jigs. Their weight range extends from types as light as one-eighth ounce for spinning up to about four ounces. Similarly, their hooks cover a good spread in sizes.

According to their designs, jigs can be cast, trolled, or jigged (kept in motion by jerking the rod tip or by continuously lowering the lure to a desired depth and reeling it upward). They see a lot of service on oceanfronts, inlet shores, channel banks, bays, deep sea grounds, piers, and bridges. And they can be rigged for a whole host of salt-water gamesters. The members of the jig clan are legion, so for now I'll mention only a few of those—standards, you might say—you'll use for fishes covered by this book.

The diamond jig is one. Originally so called because of its elongated diamond shape, this artificial bait has a narrow body tapering at each end. It may carry a single hook, imbedded in its metal body, or a swinging treble hook at the tail end. Diamond jigs are fairly heavy and come in graduated sizes. For effectiveness they rely on a combination of shape, motion, and glitter, giving an illusion of a small bait fish. Some diamond jigs have bodies of lead, which is okay, except that repeated salt-water immersion dulls their finish, necessitating periodic light scraping or sandpapering to restore their shininess. Many diamond jigs are chrome plated to eliminate that nuisance.

Mackerel, sea bass, bluefish, and striped bass are but four species that can be caught on diamond jigs.

Another popular member of this family, especially among surf anglers, is the metal squid. Many models are available, with or without chrome plating, in a range of designs and weights. I've always maintained that the term "squid" is misleading when applied to these lures, because they do not closely resemble that cousin of the octopus. Besides, natural squid are used as bait. But apparently fishes couldn't care less, and metal squids spell their undoing time and time again. Their popularity in surfcasting, notably for striped bass and bluefish, added the word "squidding" to fishermen's lingo.

Depending upon angling technique and species sought, jigs may be fished with or without bait. In fishing for Boston mackerel, for instance, a plain diamond jig without any garnishing of its hook will take fish like crazy. On other occasions anglers bait a jig's hook with a piece of pork rind, sold in bottles for that purpose. Or they may add a sandworm or other goodie as an added come-on.

Some fishermen add a second or tail hook to a jig, attaching it by its eye to the bend of the hook already on the lure. The tandem hooks then can be baited with a single strip bait, such as a piece of natural squid, or a strip cut from the white underside of a mackerel or other fish. Some of the strip bait is left free to dangle and flutter in the water. Tail hooks are particularly useful in the case of what we call short-strikers. These are the exasperating rascals that come up behind a bait, chop it off just short of the hook, and escape. A tail hook provides a surprise party for these thieves.

Like other artificials, jigs come in a variety of finishes. Some are natural metal or chrome plated. Many are painted bright colors to enhance their appeal (to fishermen as well as fish, I sometimes suspect). Some are decorated with small, bright-colored feathers or skirts of nylon or animal hairs. In cross-section they range from oval to flattish to a diamond shape. Certain models carry a little keel along their underside as a kind of stabilizer.

AND STILL OTHERS One of the oldest lures is the cedar jig. If the truth were known, the cedar jig is probably the forerunner of many of today's jigs, plugs, and many other artificials. It's still with us, still a killer for tuna and bluefish, among other finned game, including such billfishes as marlins.

It's a simple gadget. In profile it resembles a torpedo. At the front is a bullet-shaped metal head, often lead, with a simple eye for securing to a leader. The body is wooden—cedar, commonly. At the lure's narrowly tapered stern end, firmly lodged in its body, is its one hook. Cedar jigs are sold in a wide assortment of lengths and weights, armed with hooks of appropriate sizes. For ocean fishing it won't do you any harm to carry at least a couple in the three- to six- or seven-inch range.

In recent years, thanks to developments in plastics, a whole new family of artificials has swarmed into the picture. These are lures fashioned into clever imitations of different food items on which game fishes dine. There are plastic eels that look and wiggle like the real thing. There are all kinds of small bait fishes, such as mullet, herring, and *balao* ("ballyhoo"), that last a food fish that marlins find attractive. Plastic-lure makers also have created realistic bloodworms and sandworms; and there's a plastic squid, complete with fluttering tentacles. Many of these phoney creatures are amazingly like their real-life counterparts. Some even have a fish-attracting scent built right in.

You also can select from a large assortment of artificials that include such unusual types as the Knucklehead, a gaudy, plug-like lure originating in Hawaii and proven effective on swordfish and marlins. The fertile minds of lure designers are constantly dreaming up new types, including weird-looking hybrids combining the better features of other types.

TO SUM UP All artificial lures are created to appeal to fishes' appetites and/or feeding habits. The route to hooking any fish lies via his stomach's naggings. Every bait, man-made or natural, is used with that route in mind.

Don't figure you have to own representatives of every conceivable type of salt-water artificial. You won't need to. Besides, you could go broke trying to keep up with that parade. And in the third place, an unnecessarily vast collection could become so much excess stuff to lug around and maintain. But don't go to the other extreme either and skimp. Acquire a good, versatile assortment, well suited to your kinds of fishing.

In the chapters dealing with the various sport fishes I'll indicate recommended artificials. These can form a nucleus for your collection. You can build around it as you go along.

THE HOOK DEPARTMENT

Fishhooks are practically as old as man, yet down through ages their *basic shape* hasn't changed. Excavated hooks used by beetle-browed fishermen far back in time prove it. But then, just how much can you do with a basic hook shape?

Of course, there have been countless refinements. In materials, for instance. The guy who looked like a monkey but walked like a human had hooks fashioned from wood or V-shaped twigs. Later arrivals, including our American Indians, went ancient cave dwellers one or two better, adding graceful curves and carving their hooks from bone. Then somebody got the idea of using metal, and so were born the ancestors of our present fishhooks.

There have been many other improvements too, not only in the materials used but also in their anatomical details. And right here, for the benefit of newcomers to fishing, is a good place to explain the anatomical terminology of a hook.

All hooks have five basic parts: *shank*—the straight or (usually) longest portion; *bend*—the curved section; *point; barb*—a short, needle-sharp, backward extension of the point, the part that keeps the hook in a fish's mouth once it has been planted; and the *eye*—its place of attachment to a line (commonly in either of two forms, a hole in the shank, like the eye in a needle—and called needle-eye type, or a ringlike eye, called ring eye, formed by bending the end of the shank in a loop).

Refinements in fishhooks down through the decades have involved one or more of the aforementioned portions, leading to an enormous assortment of variations. Here's just a sampling: extra-long shanks; bends that are widely rounded and those that are U-shaped; long, conical points; shanks that are flattened on the sides, instead of round; hooks with curved shanks, instead of straight; ring eyes that are bent at an angle to the shank; tiny barbs on the shank to better hold a bait and prevent it from "bunching up" on the bend; and so on, for dozens of others.

The upshot of all these many variations is that we have many patterns or designs among hooks, each with its own set of characteristics. And each pattern carries a name. You'll run across many such pattern names: O'Shaughnessy, Sobey, Chestertown, Sproat, Carlisle, and so on. There are also types that bear the name of their manufacturer or a brand name created by the maker. Prominent among these are the Mustads and Eagle Claws (Wright & McGill).

Hooks are made from a variety of metals, including steel and nickel, and come in different finishes, even gold plate. Many come in double and triple strengths per given size. Sometimes it's advantageous to have that extra strength without increasing your hook size.

GRADING FOR SIZES   There are hook sizes for every known kind of sport fish, fresh and salt water, from little panfishes weighing a matter of ounces up to black marlin and sharks going a thousand pounds and more. Naturally there has to be some system of indicating these graduated sizes.

The system is numerical and has two parts, one for the smaller hooks, the other for their larger brethren. Those in the smaller half of the range are designated by "No.," followed by a figure. Starting with No. 1, they progress through No. 10 onward. On this side of the size scale, *the larger the number, the smaller the hook.* Thus a No. 5 is smaller than a No. 1, a No. 10 is smaller than a No. 5, and so on. In the upper half of the scale, sizes are designated by a number, followed by a slash and zero: 1/0, 2/0, 3/0, etc. On this side, *the larger the number preceding the slash, the larger the hook.* A 1/0 is the next largest after a No. 1, after which the series indicates progressively larger hooks up to 12/0, 14/0, etc.

The system has been used for years, and it serves its purpose. Its only flaw lies in the fact that hook sizes aren't standardized among the patterns and/or manufacturers. So a 1/0 of one style, we'll say, will be a bit larger or smaller than a 1/0 of another pattern. But don't let that fret you. In most instances the discrepancies aren't great enough to cause problems.

Tip: If you're ever in doubt as to what pattern and size to get when buying hooks, tell your tackle dealer what you want them for. He'll fix you up.

Except when fishing artificial lures, which can carry single, double (two hooks in one unit), or treble hooks, you'll be rigging your hooks individually. Most hooks, except those in rigs sold already made up, are marketed separately for that purpose. They're just plain hooks, nothing added. However, you also can buy hooks that come outfitted with short lengths of gut, nylon, wire, tarred line, etc.—called snells—for attachment to your line. You'll encounter snelled hooks in various kinds of fishing (for flounders and cod, to name two). But presence or omission of snells is a matter of preference, and maybe convenience. You'll make your choice.

In due course I'll suggest patterns and sizes you can rig for the different species.

CHAPTER 4

Accessories

The fishing fraternity has its gadget collectors, and some of them go overboard. I've known guys who couldn't pass a tackle shop without going in and buying something, whether they needed it or not. Don't get me wrong. I'm not against amassing equipment. Certain items are essential to full enjoyment and success in fishing. I just think it's foolish to go to the expense of acquiring a lot of things you may never use.

What I'll do first, therefore, is steer you to items you must have. Later we'll get to accessories that are helpful but not absolute musts.

ESSENTIALS

TACKLE BOXES You can select from among hundreds of models. You'll be governed by your tastes and wallet, of course, but let your needs be a criterion too. It will help if you know beforehand how much gear—reels, extra spools of line, lures, and small accessories—you'll be lugging around with you. Remember, you probably won't be toting all your equipment at a given time.

All tackle boxes consist primarily of a main compartment for reels and equally large items and one or more compartmented trays for lures of various sizes and miscellaneous small items such as sinkers, swivels, etc. Their range is from small, simple carriers, with a main section and only one tray, up to large boxes with roomy bottoms and as many as four compartmented trays. Among the more elaborate boxes with two or more trays, the trays are cantilevered to swing upward and outward to better present their contents and provide access to the main section underneath. There are even models with battery-operated lights for night fishing. Other refinements include recessed handles, special safety locks, and no-tip balance.

There are tackle boxes made from steel and aluminum, anodized or enameled or otherwise protected against corrosion and rust. There are handsome carriers made from wood, with brass hardware and fancy price tags. But extremely popular are the boxes made from strong, impact-resistant plastics. Some are guaranteed unbreakable. The better of these plastic carriers are resistant to oil, gasoline, soft plastic lures, insect sprays, and scratching. They're also impervious to salt water and can't rust or corrode. At least that's true of their plastic portions. The metal hardware might be something else again. That brings up *a tip:* When you buy a tackle box, whatever its construction, get one whose metal parts are resistant to the ravages of salt water and weather.

Manufacturers offer excellent selections within price frameworks everyone can afford. Buy one from a reputable maker. A good tackle box doesn't cost that much more, and it will reward you with years of service.

CUTTING INSTRUMENTS   You should have a good knife. A knife has a multitude of uses: cutting bait; cleaning fish; severing line and leader material (except wire), etc. Here again you choose from among many good, reasonably priced models, domestic and imported. Most popular are those of the hunting knife style, carried in a sheath on the belt. Its length is optional, but ideally the blade should be able to retain an edge. You might investigate one of those knives whose blade has a cutting edge on one side, a fish scaler on the other. I don't suggest a pocket knife. You're not going to want to reach for it with your hands full of gook.

Another valuable addition to your kit is a pair of fisherman's pliers. They're very useful for cutting and bending wire leaders, opening the ring eyes of hooks, and other chores in which pliers come in handy. They too come in a sheath to be worn on your belt.

For your knife and—more importantly—for your hooks you should carry a small sharpening stone. Frequently hook points and barbs rust or otherwise become dull, interfering with their penetration. A small hone is great for correcting that condition.

SURF AND JETTY FISHING ITEMS In the interest of saving you a broken leg or worse, I'm putting this item first: safety footwear. If you're going to be scrambling around on jetties, you should have some kind of nonslip footwear. There are the so-called creepers that strap on. Some "jetty jockies" use heavy-tread golf shoe soles, cementing or otherwise attaching them to their footwear. The main thing is to have something to give you secure footing on wet rocks. Slippery stones are very treacherous, doubly so if they have any vegetation on them—ask the jetty fishermen in traction.

In summer you can fish a surf in swim trunks (better wear a top too if you're a female). But for spring and autumn you should consider hipboots or waders. Many times, depending upon the shelving of a beach and the mood of its surf, boots will allow you to walk out far enough. But when the surf is surly, or conditions demand that you wade out farther, perhaps to reach a slough along a sandbar, waders are the ticket. Being a combination of boots and overalls in waterproof material, they'll keep more of you dry than boots. They'll also provide more warmth.

For both surf and jetty angling you'll need a gaff. This device, simply a fishhooklike head affixed to an aluminum or wooden handle, will help you land your catches. Sometimes a gaff is a must, especially in jetty work. The only difference between surf gaffs and jetty gaffs is in the lengths of their handles. The former are short and can be attached to the belt. Those wielded on jetties, where often it's impossible to get close to a fish, have correspondingly longer handles. There are telescoping aluminum gaffs that give you the advantage of two or three different lengths.

A sand spike is a good accessory in beach fishing. It's a rod holder that can be plunged into the sand. It will hold your outfit while you're busy with something else, keeping your reel out of the sand.

NEAR-MUSTS AND AIDS

Let's draw up a checklist. Make mental notes of the items you might want for your kind(s) of fishing.

1. *Lights.* A flashlight is practically indispensable in any kind
of night fishing. On beaches and jetties it's a must. A good gadget
is a headlight, similar to that a miner wears, made especially
for fishermen. Leaves your hands completely free.

2. *Landing net.* A small hand net is useful for lifting small fishes
out of the water, rather than dangling them on a line. It cinches
capture of ambitious rascals that are likely to flip themselves off
the hook or tear free as they're being extracted from the water.
Fluke, for example, are notorious for their stunt of slapping
against the sides of boats and right off the hooks. Weakfish are
another species you have to watch. Their delicate mouth parts
can cause a hook to rip out if their weight is suspended too long
from a line as they're being cranked in.

There are collapsible landing nets that fold up into a tidy little
package for easy carrying.

3. *Gadget bag.* This is primarily for surf and jetty fishermen
and other shoreside anglers who want to move around without
being encumbered by a full tackle box. The better gadget bags
are made from canvas or duck, and have a couple of compart-
ments and a flap or cover to keep the contents from spilling.
They sling over the shoulder. There's room in them for an extra
reel, a plastic box containing sinkers, swivels, etc., some lures, a
few gadgets, and sandwiches.

4. *Service kit.* Most anglers have one, although they might not
recognize it by that name I coined for it. All it consists of is a
few items for service and emergency repairs of tackle in the field.
Each guy makes up his own, but here are some of the things such
a kit might contain: oil for reels; electrician's tape for emergency
repair of loose rod guides; reel wrench and screwdriver for take-
apart of reels; red nail polish to mark line to indicate when desired yardage is out; clear nail lacquer to repair broken guide
winding; and a piece of clean, preferably lint-free, cloth for wiping reels, plus an old towel for cleaning hands. Carrying a few of
the more important spare parts, such as reel drag washers, isn't a
bad idea either.

5. *Fish carriers.* There are various arrangements for toting fish.
On boats, of course, there's no problem; and at dockside in most
sport-fishing centers they sell large plastic bags for catches.

It's shoreside fishermen, especially those wandering some distance from their cars, who have to improvise. Simplest for surf, jetty, and channel bank anglers is a stringer, similar to that used by their fresh-water brethren, fashioned from strong twine or a short length of clothesline. Or they can take along a couple of those plastic bags I mentioned a moment ago. If there isn't too much shifting of position so that it doesn't have to be toted appreciable distances, a portable ice chest will help. In summer it can be filled with ice and beverages on the way out. Homeward-bound, the ice will refrigerate the catch. The only trouble is, carrying one of these can be a two-man job, and its capacity is limited. It can't be used for fish of any size unless they're dressed or filleted.

Really hot weather is when a problem can arise—preventing spoilage, particularly when there's an appreciable interval between catching and icing or refrigerating the catch. The problem is acute with oily or soft-flesh species such as bluefish and mackerel. They can spoil quickly. On a boat there's no sweat, because you can carry ice. On lonely beaches is where the headache arises. Here you might *have* to take ice in a chest. Failing that, your best bet is to gut the fish as soon as possible after catching and protect them from the sun, even to burying them in *cool,* damp sand.

Incidentally, if you're aboard a small boat that has neither fish box nor ice, contrive to keep your catch out of the sun. Place the fish under forward decking, if available. If the boat doesn't have that either (rowboats do not), cover the fish with something—a piece of cloth, kept wet, or a tarpaulin, or in a pinch, even a jacket or wetted newspapers.

The important detail in warm weather is to ice your catch for the trip home. Ideally, the fish should be at least gutted beforehand, perhaps on the way back to the dock or on the dock. Then get yourself two of those large, strong plastic bags. Put one inside the other. Your fish, of course, go in the inside bag, after which you can fill the space between the two bags with chopped ice. You also can use a single bag, putting both fish and ice in that. It's easier, 50 percent cheaper, and it serves the purpose; but it's inferior to the two-bag method because that one keeps fish and water from the melting ice separated. Either way, on a long ride home the ice can be replenished if necessary.

It's preferable not to carry your catch in your car trunk in hot weather, for obvious reasons. Put it on the back seat floor where it will be cooler and the ice won't melt as rapidly.

6. *Sunglasses.* Don't think these are solely for sun worshipers out for a coat of tan to show back at the office. They're an important fishing accessory, afloat or ashore—if they're the right kind. Don't buy a junky pair. Get good ones. You want eye protection.

I recommend those with Polaroid lenses. They screen out water surface glare and harmful rays. Having glare bounce into your eyes all day long is annoying, fatiguing, detrimental to good vision, and possibly harmful. Aboard boat, killing glare and reflection will better enable you to spot surface and subsurface finned game such as tuna, swordfish, sharks, and marlin. Polaroid lenses also are protective and helpful in surf and jetty fishing. As you know, the reflected rays of a bright sun bouncing off a white beach are hard on the eyes. Effective sunglasses eliminate that annoyance. By cutting water surface glare Polaroid lenses will aid in spotting sand bars and sloughs—places in which surf species may be feeding—just off the beach.

7. *Hook disgorger.* This is a short, simple, metal device (one type consists of a straight shaft with a rounded, grooved end) to help dislodge hooks when fish are landed. Commonly a fish will take a hook 'way down in his throat somewhere, and extracting it can be a minor project. That's where a disgorger helps. It can be particularly helpful when your catch has a mouthful of needle-sharp teeth, like a bluefish.

8. *Binoculars.* In surfcasting these come in handy for studying the beach and water at a distance when searching for sand bars, sloughs, and other likely-looking places. They're useful for spotting sea birds that might indicate a school of striped bass, bluefish, or other gamesters down the beach. They're also good for spying on other anglers to see how they're doing, without them knowing you're watching. (If burying fish in the sand to hide them from other surfcasters is fair, so's this.) Binoculars could save you a lot of walking.

In boat fishing they're an obvious aid to navigation in detecting buoys, channel markers, etc. Similarly, they assist in relocating fishing grounds by picking up landmarks, etc. for "fixes." Binoculars can be invaluable for sighting sea birds that indicate the presence of surface-feeding fish, for determining whether or not a distant surface disturbance is merely a wind riffle or an actual group of fish, and for spotting top-cruising game such as swordfish, marlins, and sharks.

A 6 x 35 binocular will do nicely, but the additional magnification afforded by a 7 x 35 is even better. And if you're going to be doing any night navigation, a 7 x 50 is better yet.

ABOUT SEASICKNESS I'm not plagued by *mal de mer* or other forms of motion sickness, but many people are. I suspect that seasickness keeps a lot of folks from enjoying fishing more fully, and to them I offer some suggestions, for whatever they may be worth:

1. On the eve of a boat trip, especially one offshore, get a good night's sleep. If you drink, hold it to a low level. You can have cocktails or highballs when you get back to the dock.

2. On the morning of sailing avoid heavy, greasy, and/or fried foods. Stick to something bland. (Some people favor dry cereals.) Don't fill your stomach with a lot of coffee. You can make up for a light breakfast later.

3. Carry one of the popular motion sickness preventives sold under such names as Bonamine, Dramamine, Marezine, etc. Take according to directions.

4. Aboard boat, avoid places in the cockpit where you might inhale gasoline or diesel fumes—especially the latter.

5. If someone near you becomes ill, get away from him if you can, or at least avoid looking at him.

6. Should you start to feel queasy, in spite of all precautions, stay out on deck in fresh air. As much of a temptation as it might be to go below and stretch out in a berth, resist it. Often it's the worst thing you can do. Out on deck it may help if you fix your vision on something steady—the horizon.

And if all else fails, you can try the old mariners' facetious suggestion: a couple of hours' rest under a shady oak tree.

There now, I think you're pretty well set as regards the basics of tackle, accessories, and miscellaneous gear. If you can't amass all the desired equipment at the outset, don't worry. Few of us do. And sometimes it works out better that way, because as you go along you acquire items better suited to *your* individual needs.

CHAPTER 5

Albacore and *Bonito:*
Streamlined Wallopers

Alphabetically, albacore and bonito take the lead in the parade of sport fishes swimming their way through this book of yours. As fighters they deserve a leading position too. Pound for pound, they rate among your more worthwhile finned opponents in the angling arena.

If we're going to consider our fishes in terms of family relationships, the albacores and bonitos belong right next door to the tunas and mackerels, because in a sense they're all related, like the Kellys, Flannagans, and O'Gradys. So it comes about that some authorities catalogue albacores and bonitos as members of the tuna tribe, a family that embraces such species as the bluefin, big-eye, Allison or yellowfin, blackfin, and so on, while other ichthyologists are inclined to lump them with the mackerels. That's why, in the old days, giant bluefin tuna were nicknamed "horse mackerel."

The tunas, bonitos, mackerels, and albacores comprise a large, far-flung family, with representatives in seas all over the world. Its members with which we'll come in greatest contact in these pages are: Boston mackerel; bluefin tuna; albacore; and two species of bonito, common and oceanic. In addition to the tunas I mentioned earlier, other members of the clan include the Oriental bonito, Pacific mackerel, dog-tooth tuna, Mexican bonito, and several more.

You've probably noticed (if you haven't, you're not paying attention in class) that when I just mentioned albacore and bonito I cited not two kinds of fishes, but three: one albacore and two bonitos, common and oceanic. Let's invite them into our parlor one at a time and meet them.

ALBACORE

This is the name applied most commonly to this particular finned dynamo in areas he visits. You may also hear him referred to as "false albacore," an alias he acquired to set him apart from other fishes of the same name. And in various locales he has been given such regional nicknames as "little tuna" and "mackerel tuna," both of which I suggest you promptly forget, since they're confusing. "Skipjack" is another regional nickname.

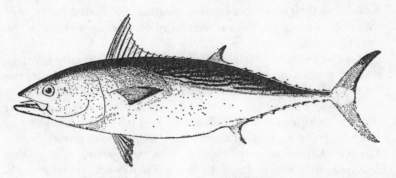

FALSE ALBACORE (*Euthynnus alletteratus*)

This species of albacore we're looking at right now could become a case of a name being misleading. Some of the modern schools of ichthyological thought classify him as a bonito, not an albacore. In fact, my friend Edward C. Migdalski, Yale University's noted ichthyologist, has given him the name Atlantic spotted bonito. If Ed catalogues him with the bonitos, that's good enough for me. For now, though, until it comes into popular usage, you'll just have to go on calling him albacore or false albacore to avoid misunderstanding. I'll do the same.

WHAT HE LOOKS LIKE, WHERE HE LIVES   This Atlantic spotted bonito (whoops, I mean albacore) has a form typical of tunas and other fishes in that big family I mentioned earlier. The anatomical characteristic they all share is a superbly streamlined body. Another physical trait common to many members of the tribe is a noticeably crescent-shaped caudal fin or tail. Still another is the finlets. These are small, rigid, more or less triangular processes that appear in two rows, one above the other, along the midlines of the back and underside near the tail. No one knows what function the finlets perform, if any. My guess is that they're vestigial remains of fins carried by their ancestors in the remote past.

The false albacore is a good-looking fish, as fishes go. Along the back he's a dark blue, overlaid conspicuously with darker, wavy markings, which start at about the middle of the first dorsal fin and extend aft to the base of the tail. Below each pectoral fin is a group of small, dark dots whose number, size, and shape vary among individuals.

He's one of the smaller members of the tribe of scombroid fishes, as tunas, mackerels, and their kin are called by scientists. An approximate weight span for most of those you'll encounter goes up to ten or twelve pounds. There are occasional heftier specimens in the fifteen-to-twenty-five-pound bracket.

Overall, the species' distribution is along the Atlantic seaboards of North and South America from about southern Massachusetts to Brazil, including both coasts of Florida, the Gulf of Mexico, Caribbean Sea, and waters surrounding Bermuda and the seven-hundred-island Bahamas archipelago. Additional distribution is listed for the Atlantic Ocean's eastern side in the Mediterranean region.

This albacore is essentially a warm-water resident, as evidenced by centers of abundance around Bermuda and the Bahamas. Accordingly, numbers of the fish taper off progressively in the more northern parts of their range. Also pointing to their warm-seas habits is the fact that they're encountered in the northern coastal regions of their range during the warmer seasons; and the farther north you go, the later they start to appear for a season. Off Florida, for example, they can begin to show in April. Off New Jersey and New York they usually start turning up offshore in July and August, depending upon seasonable weather. In some warm-water regions—Bermuda is one—the species is encountered just about all year long.

HABITS OF IMPORTANCE TO YOU   As you now can see, this scombroid is a migrator. He also is pelagic, which is a high-falutin'
way of saying he frequents open seas.

False albacore travel in schools, some of them large; and it's
not uncommon to find relatives, such as oceanic bonito, journeying along with them, or at least in the immediate area. It's probable, I've always figured, that albacore schools travel to
Maryland, New Jersey, New York, and southern Massachusetts
with the Gulf Stream, capitalizing on its northward transportation, warmer water, and supply of food.

These albacore scout for food offshore and inshore, which
means you'll find them in both of those oceanic zones. They're
fast, active feeders. Among items listed for their menu are squids
and assorted smaller fishes.

From Maryland northward the sport fishing season for them is
from about June or July through the remainder of the summer,
deep into September. Once autumn's frosty weather begins
chilling the water, they depart for warmer climes.

Fast, hard fighting is characteristic of tunas and their relatives.
False albacore and school-size bluefin tuna are among the gamest
sport fishes. Pound for pound, they're tough to beat.

COMMON BONITO

Two kinds of bonito figure in the Atlantic Coast recreational
angling theater. One is the so-called common bonito. The other
is the oceanic bonito. We'll take them in turn.

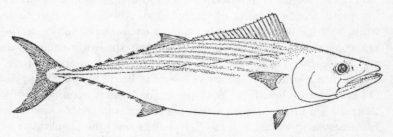

COMMON BONITO (*Sarda sarda*)

The common bonito, perhaps more accurately called Atlantic bonito (but not to be confused with the character we just met, the Atlantic *spotted* bonito), is another fish that has accumulated a fair number of nicknames during his career as an angling target. Among those I've run across are "skipjack," "little tunny," "green bonito," "frigate mackerel," "California bonito," "bonejack," and "African bonito." I mention those only as a matter of transitory interest. Don't take them seriously. They're apt to contribute to confusion.

IDENTIFICATION AND DISTRIBUTION The common bonito is among the smaller representatives of the tuna-bonito-albacore-mackerel combine. Only the common or Boston mackerel comes in littler packages. Lengths to 2½ and 3 feet, with weights up to 10 or 12 pounds, are recorded for the species; but those you'll hook into are more likely to go to 5 or 6 pounds, tops.

Size is one detail enabling you to separate this fish from his relatives. Others are his color pattern and certain physical traits.

In profile he's unmistakably a scombroid: superb streamlining; two dorsal fins, the first (front), as usual, higher than the second; and a tail that's concave in outline. His body has scales throughout and is somewhat more slender (shallower) than the forms of his relatives. His mouth, proportionately, is larger.

His body's upper half is darkish blue, sometimes with a greenish tinge. Aiding in identification is a series of darker stripes that run horizontally but more or less obliquely from the tail section forward to his gill covers. From his body's midline downward the color disappears, yielding to a silver. On some individuals there are iridescent gold or yellow tints in the silver on the sides.

A complete picture of this fellow's over-all distribution is yet to be drawn. Authorities aren't sure of its extent, especially in the western and eastern South Atlantic Ocean. But for your purposes that's purely academic. More important to you is a general range that extends from about New England southward to at least Florida. Some of them wander northward beyond New England, as far up as Nova Scotia, but those nomads are considered stragglers.

In the interest of completeness I'll point out some other regions for which common bonito have been reported. These include the Gulf of Mexico, waters off Brazil, the Mediterranean, and the eastern Atlantic from Scandinavia to North Africa, and even as far down as South Africa.

On one point most ichthyologists agree: These bonito are warm-water fish and migrate.

In northern segments of their U. S. East Coast range, say from New Jersey on up, some action with common bonito can come any time from late June or early July onward, depending upon how soon summer temperatures warm ocean waters thereabouts. Often the fishing is better in August, and it lasts on into September.

A FEW HABITS OF NOTE   Common bonito usually travel in schools of varying sizes. As in the cases of false albacore and other relatives, it also is possible to run across them singly or in pods (small groups). Small schooling fishes, along with squids when available, comprise their chief bill of fare; and in search of food they'll prowl offshore or in closer to a beach. They frequently feed at the surface, where their prey can be found; but, like all fishes, they go where the chow is, and if need be they'll extend their foraging to deeper levels.

Common bonito are active feeders and fast swimmers—aggressive, you can call them. They're attracted to moving prey, which is precisely why they get themselves hooked on trolled lures.

Count on them to give you a run for your money. They fight like the dickens, with a resistance that's magnified in proportion to the lightness of your tackle. On really light gear they're wild sport.

OCEANIC BONITO

At one time or another you may hear this gamester referred to variously as "Arctic bonito," "skipjack," "striped tuna," and/or "watermelon." Set that last one aside for a second and cross the other three off your mental list. The only one of the trio for which there's an excuse is "skipjack," because the fish has a habit of

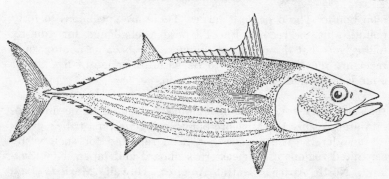

OCEANIC BONITO (*Euthynnus—*or *Katsuwonus—pelamis*)

"skipping" clear of the sea when in a surface feeding frenzy. But that's a nickname shared by several species, so toss it out.

If you must have an alias for him, stick to "watermelon." At least that will help you remember a couple of identification details, one of which is his shape; the other is a series of dusky or blackish stripes extending horizontally along his lower sides and belly. Their location, I should point out in passing, is in contrast to that of the common bonito's bands, which are on the upper sides and back. The rest of the oceanic bonito's color scheme consists of a deep blue on his upper surface and a silver farther down to the belly. On some specimens I've noted iridescent pink and gold tints on the sides.

The shape is typical of scombroid fishes, except that this bonito is a bit deeper-bodied, giving him a kind of fullness that also contributed to the "watermelon" nickname. Other characteristics aiding in identification: a comparatively high first dorsal fin whose height falls away abruptly after the first few spines; a well-developed tail, like a quarter moon in profile, attached to the body by a very slender caudal peduncle (as the base of a fish's tail is called); and a body that's free of scales except along a lateral line on either side and in the region of the pectoral fins. As a scombroid, the oceanic bonito has the characteristic finlets along the upper and lower midlines in his body's posterior segment.

Size is another detail separating him from his cousin, the common bonito. The oceanic is larger. There are specimens to forty pounds-plus on record. But I'll pose a challenge for you by telling you that those are real biggies. The oceanic bonito you'll meet are much more likely to be within a range of five or six pounds to ten and twelve, maybe fifteen.

THEY'RE GREAT ROVERS Some findings indicate that oceanic bonito are possibly the albacore-bonito-mackerel-tuna tribe's greatest wanderers. The species has been reported for such vastly separated regions as our eastern seaboard and Japan, New Zealand, North Africa, Central America, Hawaii, Mexico's Baja (Lower) California, the Bahamas, the Indian Ocean, and far-flung reaches of the central Pacific Ocean.

Off the U. S. Atlantic Coast oceanic bonito are encountered in varying numbers from the Bahamas and Florida (spring and summer in both regions) on up to New York state and, to a lesser extent, even farther north. Ed Migdalski notes that these fish commonly show in large numbers in the Pacific, where they're seen in enormous schools strung out over impressive distances. He adds that nowhere on our East Coast can they be described as really abundant.

My experience with them on our Atlantic Coast has been that they're erratic in both "timetable" and numbers. I can recall seasons when we boated only a few or practically none at all. On the other hand, I also remember a summer when my friend Capt. Carm Marinaccio, then skippering his charter boat *Duchess II* out of Freeport, N.Y., docked with tremendous catches of oceanic bonito. One season can be radically different from the next. Nor does there seem to be any way of predicting when they'll arrive within sport fishing range. Perhaps they're most erratic in the northerly part of their Atlantic coastal range.

HABITS TO NOTE Oceanic bonito travel in schools, for the most part. This gregariousness leads to enormous groups, probably containing thousands of individuals. If it's ever your good fortune to contact a big school, and they're hungry, you're guaranteed the liveliest kind of action for as long as they're interested in your lures. At the other, more frequent, extreme, you'll pick up a scattered few during a day's offshore trolling.

I knew and fished with famed author John Steinbeck, who had a summer home in Sag Harbor, Long Island. And one of our off-shore trips was aboard a boat called *Salty,* owned by attorney-sportsman Arthur Klorfein and piloted at the time by one of the best skipper-guides on the entire East Coast, the late Capt. Walter Drobecker of Montauk.

Well sir, John had done a lot of angling on our Pacific Coast off his native California, but the Atlantic was still rather new to him. He hadn't had a personal introduction to our East Coast oceanic bonito. With Walt at the helm he met them that day off Montauk. We were trolling "blind" for bluefin tuna, there being no schools in sight on the surface at the time, and a couple of husky oceanic bonito smacked John's feather lure. I can tell you he was impressed.

Most of the oceanic bonito with which I've had better than a nodding acquaintance were contacted well offshore—say, twenty miles or more. But there's no law that says they can't come appreciably closer inshore on occasions. There's no way of predicting where you'll find them, although I think your chances are better at distances of ten miles or more from the beach.

Since they're warm-seas fish, they usually do not venture into northern segments of their range until summer. An unseasonably hot June could lure scatterings by late in the month, especially off such southernmost reaches of New Jersey as Cape May. But under standard conditions even July is a bit early. It takes a long time for a summer sun to warm the Atlantic to the north. By and large, August is the best month from New Jersey northward; and you can figure on any that have appeared to linger as long as summery weather lasts in September.

HOW TO CATCH FALSE ALBACORE, COMMON BONITO, AND OCEANIC BONITO

Like school-size bluefin tuna (you'll meet 'em later), these three battlers are caught chiefly by trolling. Occasionally some will wander into a chum line set out for bluefish—and surprise some guy no end by yanking his rod out of his hands, but in the main they're trollers' targets. The same basic tackle can be used for all three, as well as for school tuna, which makes it nice all around. I should add, though, that any of the sturdier outfits wielded on the larger school tuna are too heavy for common bonito.

I won't even suggest fly tackle for these fishes. That ultralight equipment is for experts. I also consider spinning tackle impractical here, except in the hands of well-seasoned users. Unless you fit in either of those categories, stick with conventional gear.

A medium-weight boat or all-purpose outfit (it can be on the lighter side in this category if you wish)—fiberglass rod and matching reel—will cover all assignments, with possible exception of the heavier school tuna going fifty, seventy-five, or a hundred pounds or better. It will handle lines to thirty- and forty-pound test. They, in turn, will hold all the albacore, common and oceanic bonito, and the majority of schooling bluefin (and yellowfin) tuna you're likely to encounter. It will have enough suppleness to provide plenty of action, simultaneously possessing enough backbone to lend authority to your argument.

In selecting line you'll have to exercise judgment, taking into consideration your own ability and approximate sizes of the albacore and bonitos currently in residence. While you're at it, inquire about the general weights of any school tuna that might be in the neighborhood at the time. What I'm saying is, while twenty-pound test—even ten—can handle false albacore and both bonitos, it would be wise to go to at least thirty-pound line when school bluefins are about. Don't use unnecessarily heavy line, but be prepared for possibilities. Remember that you'll be doing a lot of blind trolling, so you have no way of knowing what might seize your lure.

Dacron is good, and for this offshore trolling you should spool at least 150 yards of it on your reel. Two hundred would be even better, in case some larger, long-running sportster should accept your offering. The chances are that you won't need as much as 200 yards; but you already will have some line out, just in presenting your artificial. Some extra yardage always provides for a comfortable margin.

I suggest either a 3/0 or 4/0 reel. It has to be large enough to accommodate the size and yardage of your line. Using light line, you can get away with a 2/0, but those two larger sizes have the generally heavier construction desirable in offshore fishing. By the same token, you can go to a lighter conventional outfit entirely, but keep in mind what I said about an honest appraisal of your own experience. It's all right to milk maximum action from a fight, but not at the cost of broken rods or lost fish.

Here's a maxim you can tuck away for future reference in your mental file of angling lore: *The lighter the tackle, the greater the sport with any fish. But—and this applies especially to the harder-fighting and larger opponents, the lighter the tackle the greater the angling skill involved and the longer the time required to land the fish.*

LURES, HOOKS, AND RIGGING In all fishing, marine and fresh water, attractors fall into one of three basic classes: (1) natural baits— items of food on which the species dine; (2) artificial baits—lures or man-made creations designed to simulate, in appearance and action, articles of natural food that fishes find attractive; and (3) combinations of artificials and naturals, such as a spoon garnished with a worm.

For false albacore and the two bonitos you'll use artificials— specifically, feather lures.

Except when already made up as complete rigs for specific species, feather lures are sold without hooks. The reason is that it allows buyers to choose the hook patterns and sizes they want.

For albacore and the two bonitos you can select hooks from among many good patterns—a Mustad, Martu, Pfleuger, Pfleuger-Sobey, O'Shaughnessy, etc. Eventually you'll form your preferences. Meanwhile, you can't go wrong with any of those just mentioned. You have latitude in sizes. By and large, all members of the albacore-bonito-mackerel-tuna tribe have generous mouths, so a hook size one way or another isn't a matter of precision. What is important is hook strength. Some anglers go to double (designated as XX) or even triple (XXX) strength for the larger scrappers. Figure on a range of 5/o to 8/o, with a 6/o or 7/o, as a happy medium for false albacore, common bonito, and oceanic bonito. For that second species you can go smaller than a 5/o, but then it might become a calculated risk when contacting the other two and tuna.

Reminder: There's no predicting what feather color combina-

tion these fish will fancy on a given day. Carry at least a few
different ones, and be sure to make one of them red and white.

In the same vein, *this tip:* When trolling feathers, whatever
the species sought, try putting out two or more *different* color
combinations at varying distances—say, 50 to 150 feet—astern.
Note which one takes the first fish, and how far out it was. Then
replace the other feathers with the same color combo and vary
their distances astern accordingly. This experimentation often is
productive when trolling other kinds of artificials too.

You'll rig your feathers on wire leaders, choosing between
stainless and the so-called piano wire. It's purely a matter of
personal preference. Whichever type you select, use about a No.
7. That will give you a pounds-test strength in the neighborhood
of 69 to 76, which is more than enough. Actually you can go
lighter if you find the finer wire easier to handle. I suggest a No. 7
as a safe size. Figure on about 8 feet of it. You can rig a 10-to-
12-foot leader if you wish, although I can't see a proportionately
greater advantage. Besides, the longer a wire is, the harder it is
to handle.

Rigging a feather lure is simple:

1. Attach your ring-eye hook by its eye to the leader. Fashion
a small loop in the wire through the hook's eye. Twist its free
end around the main wire with your fisherman's pliers, making
six or eight tight turns right alongside each other. Break off (don't
cut) any excess close to the leader by bending it back and forth.
If you cut it, there will be a small but sharp burr that can tear
the hands.

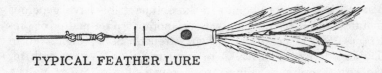

TYPICAL FEATHER LURE

2. Your hook attached, feed the leader's free end through the
lengthwise hole in the lure's metal head. That head, of course,
should be aimed away from the hook, in the direction the lure
will be traveling. Slide the artificial down on the wire as far as
it will go so that the hook will be in among its feathers.

3. In the same way you made a loop for the hook, fashion another at the leader's free end for attachment to your line. It has to be only large enough to accept the snap end of a snap swivel (which will be on your line). That completes your rig. Unless you're going to use it right away, coil it neatly. Wrapping its free end loosely around the coils a couple of times will hold them. If you've used a wire that's rustable, store the rig in a dry place. Some anglers even give such wire a thin coating of light machine oil.

Tip: Whatever the leader material, wire or other, and whatever the kind of fishing involved, you'll find it to be of great practical advantage to rig your leaders with a small loop on their free end for connection with a snap swivel *on the line.* (A snap swivel is like the connector on the end of a dog's leash for attachment to his collar.) The advantage in this arrangement, as opposed to a more permanent type of connection, as with a regular swivel, is that it allows fast, easy changing of terminal rigs. It comes in very handy when you want to switch lures or baits for one reason or another, or when a leader is damaged. Such quick changes become important when action is hot.

SEASON AND ARENA False albacore, common bonito, and oceanic bonito are summer visitors in the northern segments of their distribution along the U. S. Atlantic Coast, which is to say from about Cape May, N.J., up to southern New England. (Some may go beyond that, but I'm citing regions of greater summer abundance.) Weather having been seasonably warm—or, better yet, hotter than normal—long enough, they can start to appear offshore almost any time in June in those segments. Understandably, the southerly parts of their range receive them first, after which they extend their migrations northward as waters warm to their liking.

Ordinarily their showings develop with real summery weather, gaining substance in July and August. Barring a premature autumn chilling spell or severe storm, they can be caught on into September. Weather is a key throughout. Available food supply is a major factor too. Squid and smaller fishes such as menhaden, silversides, sand launce ("sand eels"), and the like are on their menu. Naturally they stick around longest where the larder is best stocked. Conversely, they'll move on to seek a better "supermarket" when food supplies are short.

Like school tuna (the four species often are linked in habits and showings), false albacore and the two bonitos can't be forecasted with any accuracy—not with such variables as water temperatures and food playing such big roles. It's been my experience in the New Jersey–southern New England region that common bonito are more dependable—if that's the word—than the other two, with albacore second and oceanic bonito last. Perhaps because they're high seas rovers, oceanic bonito often are a hit-or-miss proposition. I should qualify that by adding that in seasons when they're sparse in the sport fishing theater it could be that there are large schools offshore, but beyond the reach of boats.

In any case, the ocean is your arena. Generally speaking, false albacore and the two bonitos can be contacted both offshore and inshore, in a coastwise belt extending from a couple of miles off the beach out to thirty miles or more. Again, water temperatures and available food are key factors. I think you'll find that albacore and oceanic bonito are more likely to be encountered well offshore. *Tip:* Water depths can play a part too. Watch local newspapers' fishing columns in season. Often they mention compass courses to the action, along with distances and water depths currently frequented by the fishes.

SIGNS OF LIFE There are no signposts out there on the broad briny, pointing to particular places and saying FISH HERE. There are few expanses, short of the Sahara Desert, that can appear as open and vacant as an ocean. But they may not be as devoid of finned game as they seem. They may not be teeming with targets, but usually there's some kind of fish to be had. It's up to the angler to find them.

Sometimes there are signs that help; sea birds such as gulls, terns, gannets, and Mother Carey's chickens, for example. *Always maintain an alert watch for sea bird activities.* If the birds are merely winging along in the sky, ignoring the sea's surface, they're only going from hither to yon. But if they circle low over the surface, occasionally swooping or diving, keep an eye on them. They may be feeding on small fishes chased upward by larger game, or on scraps resulting from a predators' dining orgy. "Birds working," as this activity is called, can indicate the presence of surface feeders such as albacore, bonitos, tuna, bluefish, and other species.

Another sign you can watch for is a surface ruckus caused by the game fishes themselves. You may see a large patch of water being agitated quite violently. Get close enough without scaring them into sounding, and you'll probably see the agitators. They may leap out of water in their feeding frenzy. Or you may glimpse small fish jumping clear of the sea in a frantic effort to escape their pursuers.

There will be days when there are neither birds nor surface indications to give you a clue. You have no choice then but to troll blind, covering as much territory as you can, all the while watching for signs. Keeping a sharp eye on the sea is also a way to locate swordfish, marlin, blue sharks, and other game loafing along on the top or close to it.

Tip: The more eyes watching for finned game, the better. If the boat has a flying bridge, at least one spotter should be up there to take advantage of the better visibility afforded by greater height. For the same reason it's even better if the boat has a tuna tower.

PREPARATIONS FOR BATTLE Die-hard surfcasters and other hardnoses may criticize trolling for one reason or another, but the fact remains that it covers a lot of water and increases chances of contacts proportionately. Moreover, it effects contacts that wouldn't be possible from shore or an anchored boat.

Ideally, a boat trolling offshore should have four rigs out. Two can go directly from rods ("flatlining"), the remaining two from outriggers. It's even possible to utilize six rigs by having two more rods in holders in the cockpit. The more rigs out, the greater the opportunity to test lures or baits and trolling distances astern. The only trouble with having as many as six rigs out is that if you were to meet a school of tuna, there's a distinct possibility that all the lures could be hit. Let me tell you, that creates pandemonium.

Let's say you're going to try four rigs. As a start you might try a quartet of feathers in different color combinations (make a red-

and-white combo a must); or maybe natural feathers on three of the lines and a nylon "feather" in red or yellow on the fourth. Vary their distances astern. False albacore and the two bonitos aren't particularly boat-shy under these circumstances. The fact is that they may be intrigued by the white water churned by a boat's propeller, as are school tuna. But by and large they're not as brassy as tuna, and usually won't venture as close to a boat's transom, although I've hooked common bonito only about twenty to twenty-five feet astern. Try one rig that close if you want. It might pick up a young bluefin. But usually distances of, say, forty or fifty feet to seventy-five or eighty, even a hundred feet astern are better for albacore and the bonitos. Those are approximate figures, you understand, and quite flexible. There's nothing in the book to stop you from experimenting.

You can try varying your trolling speeds too. All three species are fast swimmers and hunt moving prey. I suggest keeping under seven or eight miles an hour, at least as a starter.

You also can experiment with trolling depths. Start with them all near the surface, since they normally travel there when trolled. If that draws a blank after a reasonable interval, try small pinch-on sinkers on one or two leaders to make them ride a bit deeper.

Set your reel's drag moderately. Not too tight, or a hard strike will pop the line; not too loose, because you want to have enough resistance to set the hook and also to prevent your fish from peeling off line like crazy. Choose a setting somewhere in the medium range. If anything, favor a lighter side of that range over a heavier. At the beginning some anglers like to keep their drag at what is called a strike setting, which may be on the stiffer side of medium, until they plant the hook, then ease off as required during playing. Setting a drag is an intangible thing, a detail best learned through experience. If you're at all in doubt about how to go about it, ask your skipper or an experienced fisherman. Remember this general principle; it's especially true when using lighter gear for heavier fish: At the start don't set your drag too tight. A hard hit could cause something to give. And don't go the other extreme, setting it too loose. A fast, vicious strike could peel line off too fast, causing a backlash tangle that leads to trouble.

Leave the reel's clicker on. This, along with the drag, provides some resistance to prevent line going out while trolling. It also is an audible signal to warn you of a fish at the bait.

Beforehand you should decide whether you're going to battle your fish standing up or in a fighting chair. With smaller game, of course, you'll stand. But with larger opponents, including the bigger albacore, oceanic bonito, and school tuna, you can choose between the two. If you're inexperienced, I suggest using a chair until you get the feel of things. With really large opponents the decision will be made for you. You'll fight them from a chair.

Unquestionably, standing up is the most exciting way to fight a fish. It teaches you more about their combat tactics and how to cope with them. It also gives you mobility with fishes that tend to run in wide arcs. When you're standing you're better able to cope with such maneuvers, especially if a fish suddenly streaks under the boat or swims swiftly and unpredictably from one side to another. With an angler in the fighting chair, the boat often has to be maneuvered to compensate for such antics, and it may not be possible to do it fast enough.

But you'll have to exercise judgment as to the maximum sizes you can handle while standing. These will vary with species. For example: You probably would have no difficulty arguing with a sixteen-pound fluke. But a sixteen-pound tuna or other swift, hard fighter might be something else again—if you're inexperienced, that is.

Just one thing: Whenever you fight a fish of appreciable size, speed, and/or toughness, *wear a gimbal belt.* This is a simple contraption, just a belt with a socket or a swiveling gimbal to take the butt end of the rod. If you have your own boat and plan on offshore fishing, at least a couple of gimbal belts should be part of her standard equipment. You might be able to get away without a gimbal belt up to a point, but beyond that is to court injury.

THE STRIKE AND THE FIGHT   Albacore, bonito, and tuna all attack a lure in the same fashion: enthusiastically. *Wham!* Suddenly the fish is there, often hooking himself with the force of his strike, and the reel's clicker is buzzing angrily as line zips out. The boat slows and the fight is on.

False albacore and the two bonitos are real sluggers. They'll fight you toe to toe, so to speak, in a slambang series of runs, adding spice by dashing off in different directions.

More often than not, the sheer force of the hit will set the hook. If not, a short, smart, upward lift of your rod tip will do it. Now you can turn off the reel's clicker and make any drag adjustments that may be necessary. You'll have to do the latter by feel. If he's taking line much too easily, tighten the brake a bit. Conversely, if you sense a strain on your line and rod tip because of a stiff drag, slack off a little. Either way, adjust by degrees.

When they demand line they'll get it, and neither you nor the reel's drag is going to prevent it. You let them go, pitting the resistance of the rod and the reel's drag against them and controlling them whenever and however you can. Don't ever try to stop, or even slow, the first power surges of a fast, hard-running fish. All it's liable to get you is a broken line or rod.

Tip: Always fight your fish—any fish—primarily with your rod. Your reel is basically a repository for line, with its drag providing supplemental resistance.

A battle with a truly scrappy fish is a tug-o'-war. Your opponent is going to draw on all the muscle at his command in an effort to get away. You, in turn, endeavor to regain line at every opportunity. You'll sense those chances when you feel the fish slow down or pause between rushes. You capitalize on those little recesses by pulling upward and backward on your rod to pull the fish toward you, then bending forward quickly, cranking as you go to put line back on the spool.

In most instances with all fishes, the first one or two, maybe three or four, power surges are the greatest and longest. After that the tendency is for the fight to resolve itself into shorter runs and a bulldog type of resistance. Some of the really big rascals will go deep, then sort of lie there, using sheer bulk to defy capture. Other fishes have been known to deliberately turn broadside to the angler to put up more resistance. They have all kinds of tricks.

There will be times when you think you're gaining ground. Line is coming back on the reel—slowly, maybe, but surely. Then, abruptly, your opponent summons reserve strength and streaks away, taking all the line you regained, plus additional yardage as a penalty for your being overconfident. That's the way it will go, until finally the battle enters its closing phase. This is when the fish tires and the superior strength of you and your tackle prevails.

Tip: Sooner or later you're going to have a fish torpedo under the boat. It's a common maneuver. It's also a smart one, whether or not the fish realizes it, because it puts the angler at a disadvantage. Line drawn under a boat is difficult to slow or retrieve. What's worse, it can be frayed through by barnacles on her bottom or keel, or become fouled in the propeller or rudder and snap. If you happen to be in a fighting chair with a back harness clamped to your reel, and the fish is big, you have yourself a dilemma. Only quick maneuvering of the boat may prevent a lost fish. If you're standing, or can get out of the fighting chair and still handle the tackle, you'll have to execute a lively maneuver yourself. The thing to do is hurry to the side of the boat where the line is and lower your rod, tip downward, as far as you can (hold onto it!)—in water up to the reel if necessary—in an effort to keep your line clear of the boat's underwater obstructions. Then you walk around the transom—watch out for your line on rudder and prop!—to the side where the fish now is, and resume the debate.

LANDING YOUR FISH When your wire leader breaks water alongside the boat there should be someone there to grasp it. On charter and party boats a mate handles that chore. On a private boat there has to be a volunteer. If given a chance, the angler can place his rod in a holder and seize the leader himself, but it's better to have someone standing by for the job. And whoever it is had better be wearing some kind of work gloves—cheap cotton ones will do. Wire line can cut, painfully.

The leader handler should have a straight gaff instantly ready for use. Gaffing even the smaller common bonito can save some time. It also can save some fish. They've been known to throw a hook right at the boat. With a gaff in them they can't get away. The gaffer has to be reasonably careful when he swings that weapon. Ideally, he should try to plant the gaff's hook on the first shot. I'll always remember losing a beautiful school tuna in the forty-pound class because a well-meaning but inept aide swung his gaff poorly and actually knocked the fish off my hook.

False albacore, oceanic bonito, and common bonito are first-rate fighters, usually rated in that order for combat qualities. Some fishermen rate the albacore superior to school tuna, pound for pound. I'll argue with that, but let it pass. When you come down to it, it's a matter of personal opinion. I suggest you reserve decision until you've tangled with the two of them.

Tip: When you sight a school of fish feeding at the surface, and you're trolling, have your lures out and move in. Do it cautiously. You don't want to scare the fish into diving. Your strategy is to approach close enough to troll your lures along the school's edges. If you can get the artificials farther in among the fish, so much the better. Don't barge right into the middle of the school with the boat. The chances are you'll scare them and they'll go down.

All the foregoing—setting the hook, adjustment of drag, fighting, and bringing to gaff, is your general blueprint for combat with any toughie, regardless of species.

CHAPTER 6

Blackfish:
Seagoing Bulldogs

Here's a fish that has acquired almost as many regional names as he has scales. Up New England way fishermen call him "tautog," stemming from an Indian word. In New York and New Jersey they know him as blackfish, or just plain "black." In other places and other times he's been tagged with such nicknames as "oysterfish" (presumably because of his habit of dining on mollusks), "moll" (!), "black porgy" (a bad one because it leads to confusion with another species), "salt-water chub," and "white-chin."

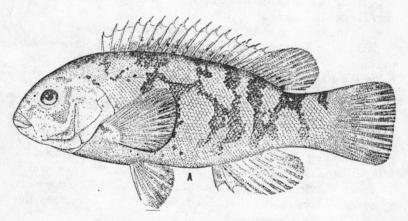

BLACKFISH (*Tautoga onitis*)

You can take your pick of those odd monikers if you're of a mind to, but if I were you I'd stick with either "blackfish" or "tautog"; otherwise no one may know what you're chattering about. You go around mumbling about molls and white-chins and somebody is apt to think you've lost your marbles.

The blackfish is catalogued with the wrasse family, a large tribe of fishes credited with between four hundred and five hundred different members throughout the world. All things considered, he's quaint. He must have been hiding someplace when they gave out streamlining. His body is deep, tending toward stubby stoutness. In profile his head curves downward precipitously, giving it a blunt appearance; that, coupled with his thick-lipped, determined mouth, is hardly calculated to make lady fishes swoon or ask for his autograph. Except, maybe, lady blackfish. His tail is broad and ends abruptly, looking as though the quitting-time whistle blew before it could be finished. His dorsal fin begins as a series of spines and ends as a rayed, rounded lobe.*

His drab body color is subject to variations from place to place and includes shades of grayish brown, dark gray, greenish gray, dusky brown, and brownish black. It's mottled and blotchy, and sometimes there are vague, irregular bars. Usually the mottlings, blotches, and bars are a darker tone of the body color. The belly is generally a lighter color, and there's an off-white patch in the chin (hence that nickname white-chin).

As in the cases of many species, this body color tends to vary in darkness or lightness according to the kind of bottom on which the fish are residing. The darker the bottom, the darker body color. It's a form of camouflage to help protect them against predators.

Of special interest to anglers is the blackfish's mouth. Its thick lips are very tough, often making it difficult to set a hook. The mouth is equipped with two sets of teeth. Right up front is a set resembling Bugs Bunny's. These are his nippers, used to bite off barnacles, mussels, and other shelled creatures on which he feeds. Farther back in his mouth is another set. These are his grinders, equivalent to our molars. With them he crushes the shells of barnacles, clams, mussels, and crabs he eats.

When I call the blackfish "quaint" I have some of his habits,

---

* Spines are more or less rigid structures, firm to the touch. Among some species they have sharp, exposed points that can inflict painful punctures if handled carelessly. Rays look something like spines, but are softer and flexible.

more than his looks, in mind. Consider, for instance, the way he takes his leisure by lying on his side on the bottom or in some convenient cubicle. Or he might enjoy a fish's siesta by remaining motionless, head downward, in a rock crevice. His table manners are odd too. Often he eats while practically standing on his head, feeding in a series of rapid, triphammer blows, like a woodpecker after grubs in a tree trunk.

Of importance to fishermen, he's a very independent fellow with surprising strength for size. That, coupled with his habits, makes him a cagey, stubborn opponent on the end of a line.

The species' over-all range on North America's eastern seaboard is from New Brunswick and Nova Scotia on down to the Carolinas. But the centers of greatest abundance are in southern New England, around Long Island—both shores, and along the New Jersey coast. Throughout their range blackfish are littoral in nature, which is to say they stick quite close to shore. Ten to twelve miles, perhaps a little more—depending upon water depths—seem to be about as far as they'll wander off a coast. Although they frequent deeper waters in some locales, they seem to favor depths no greater than about ten to twelve fathoms (sixty to seventy-two feet). They're not extensive migrators. Any mass movements on their part consist merely of shifts to deeper (warmer) water, offshore if necessary, for the cold season, then back to shoaler areas in springtime.

PLACES, SEASONS, AND SIZES You'll find blackfish in the Atlantic, in the surf in rocky areas, around oceanfront jetties, in inlets, and in sounds, bays, and harbors. In all those places you're most likely to find them around wrecks, shellfish beds, rocks and boulders, bridge abutments, trestles, and other submerged objects that have collected growths of barnacles and mussels. Artificial reefs,†

† Finally man is putting something into the sea (besides pollution), instead of only taking from it. Artificial reefs are created by dropping quantities of such items as old car bodies, large chunks of masonry, etc., to the sea floor in a planned pattern. Recently it was discovered that discarded automobile tires filled with concrete make superlative reefs (while also providing a neat, nonpolluting way to dispose of those tires). Whatever their composition, artificial reefs are a substantial contribution to angling because they provide a haven for little fishes and other creatures that attract larger game. Often fishing clubs join federal, state, and local government conservation

of which there are growing numbers on U.S. coasts, are good blackfishing sites for this reason.

In normal seasons blackfish are ubiquitous—everywhere. It's one of the things making them a popular sport fish. Also under normal conditions, they can be depended upon to show in their customary areas year after year, usually in large numbers. What's more, they sportingly provide anglers with two excellent opportunities by running in the spring and again in the fall. Both runs generally are good. Sometimes their spring performance is superior for sheer numbers, but the autumn run compensates by offering larger fish, since the tautogs have had all summer to feed and grow.

Sizes. On the lowest rungs of the size ladder are little guys going to a pound, maybe a pound and a half. Moving up the ladder, weights increase to 6 and 8 pounds; then, with lesser frequency, to 10 and 12. The potential climbs, but uncommonly, to 14 and 16. Blackfish of 10 pounds and heavier are real hefties for this species. Ichthyologists Henry B. Bigelow and William C. Schroeder have said that the maximum size is about 3 feet. But that, you can be sure, is the very outermost limit, and chances of hooking one that length are remote indeed. However, rare giants, caught commercially, are on record. Among them is a 36½-inch, 22½-pounder, taken off New York many years ago.

Generally speaking, blackfish hooked in bays and other sheltered waters range from 1 or 2 pounds up to 6, occasionally laced with biggies to 8 pounds, while the larger fish are caught on ocean grounds and around oceanfront jetties, where the size potential goes up to 10 and 12 pounds, occasionally heavier. You can figure on an average span of 2 to 8 pounds.

Wherever found—mark this—tautogs are ground fish (bottom dwellers). Often they favor somewhat deeper places in a given area, since water temperatures at those levels are more to their liking, cooler in summer heat and warmer in chillier weather. (The layers of water above act as an insulator against heat and cold, you see.) In spring you *might* be treated to the unusual spectacle of a tightly knit group of blackfish frolicking at the

---

or research agencies in cooperative construction of these reefs, with private companies donating certain essential services.

surface. This is a kind of courtship party in spawning. The gallivanting bunch is probably a squadron of romantic, eager males pursuing some of the girls. You know how it is with love in springtime. Far and away the greater part of the time, though, blackfish remain fairly close to the bottom. That's a detail of cardinal importance to rod-'n'-reelers, since it governs the way they'll rig their hooks.

Another detail of importance to fishermen is one I mentioned earlier, about blackfish frequenting places where there are rocks and other submerged objects that have accumulated barnacles and other forms of shelled life on which *Tautoga onitis* dines. These are blackfish restaurants. The larger an underwater object is, and the longer it has been submerged, the more of a magnet it is for tautogs.

SPECIAL NOTE ON PLACES Blackfish are encountered in many places in numbers, but don't think for a minute that you'll find them just anywhere. The fact is that in few other kinds of angling is it so important to pinpoint a spot and place your terminal rig in precisely the right location. Here's why:

For some reason, close-togetherness is a big thing among blackfish when they feed. Thus a comparatively small area may be literally crawling with them, packed shoulder to shoulder almost, while the surrounding area, maybe only twenty-five to fifty feet away, will be completely barren of them. Your line, therefore, could be only twenty feet or so out of place and you wouldn't get so much as a nibble, whereas if you were on target you'd get plenty of action. It's that trait that prompts professional sport fishing captains to use depth sounders to anchor their boats precisely over a wreck or other location where blackfish may be concentrated, employing two anchors if necessary to hold position.

Tip: If you're fishing with a party boat skipper you won't have to worry about locating a payoff spot, but if you're ocean fishing aboard your own craft you'd better learn how to locate grounds by using a compass, charts, and a depth sounder. All these come in handy in all kinds of deep-sea fishing. When you're working a bay or other sheltered waters for blackfish it will pay you to inquire locally about the best spots at a fishing station or bait depot.

And you can use landmarks—water towers, shoreside buildings, etc.—to help guide you to those locations again.

GETTING BACK TO SEASONS   During winter, tautogs kill time in a kind of "hibernation." It's not true hibernation, but more a period of lethargic inactivity. In deeper water to protect against the cold they laze away the weeks in among rocky crannies, eel grass, or large stones, keeping their activities at a minimum. During milder winters scatterings of blackfish may be caught from November on through February. One skipper I know, Capt. Ernie Schiller of the *Mijoy* out of Niantic, Conn., fishes regularly for tautogs during the winter in deeper areas beyond Montauk Point. But for most blackfish hunters winter is an off-season.

Comes spring, blackfish begin to stir, prompted by their appetites. Given unseasonably mild weather, the first of them may be caught before April is out; but the real spring run comes in May, after waters have had a chance to warm. An old fishermen's saying has it that a spring blackfish run is under way when dogwood trees are in bloom. It often works out that way, when temperatures are right for both. But tautogs never did hear that old fishermen's saw; and even if they had, they couldn't care less. Water temperatures are the key. The air might be warm enough to inspire dogwoods to bloom, yet the water could still be too cool for the fish to stir.

Once a spring run is established in May, it quickly gains substance to build to its peak. You can figure on it lasting at least through June, even later if weather doesn't turn too hot.

Although blackfish can be caught all through the summer, it isn't the best season. Tautogs dislike temperature extremes. When shallower regions—bays, close-inshore ocean zones, and the like —become too warm for them they seek deeper, cooler places. If you have the patience to seek such areas you'll find some blackfish.

Tip: In summer, in addition to looking for deeper places, confine your blackfishing to the cooler hours of early morning and late afternoon or evening. Your chances will be better.

The spring run is good. So is its autumn successor. That latter phase commences with an onset of somewhat cooler weather in September and follows the spring blueprint of gaining momentum rapidly. With seasonable temperatures it lasts through October, then begins a gradual tapering-off as it enters November. Just as they dislike heat, so do blackfish avoid very cold water. And small wonder. It can kill them. They've been destroyed by the thousands when trapped in shallow bays by a sudden, severe cold snap.

Their autumn performance's duration depends upon how quickly local waters absorb the deepening chill that is the tautogs' signal to move on. Unseasonably mild weather can hold them, although in fewer numbers than earlier, right on through November; but by that time their fall run is shot. Most of them have gone on to insulated deeper, warmer locations.

THERE'S NO BLACK MAGIC TO FISHING Successful angling doesn't require some mysterious abracadabra. A little luck at times, maybe, but no magic. Every step has a sound, logical basis. If you keep that in mind and search for the logic, the technical aspects of fishing will be vastly simplified, and you'll be a better fisherman for it.

Every sport-fishing method, fresh-water and salt-water, no matter what species is involved, has its foundation in fishes' feeding habits. In other words, if you can appeal to their stomachs you're well on your way toward catching them. There's more to fishing, of course, but that's the keystone. The best anglers are those who have learned the whys, wheres, whens, and hows of capitalizing on the feeding habits of their intended opponents.

Just as with any other finned game, you must offer an appeal to a tautog's belly or you won't hook him. And the surest way of teasing a fish's appetite is to tempt him with some item of natural food (or an artificial designed to simulate some such item). The first thing to do, therefore, is to look to the species' normal diet.‡

‡ Occasions may arise, as in an unfamiliar region, where you'll have no way of knowing what this is, and there's no opportunity to inquire. Never be afraid to experiment, either with a natural bait or an artificial one. By the same token, just because certain baits and lures are specified doesn't mean that the fishes involved will reject everything else. Other attractors may not have been tried. That's why I'll always tout the value of experimentation. How do you suppose the effectiveness of known baits and lures was discovered?

BAITS AND BAITING   Blackfish eat several things in addition to
barnacles and mussels. They also have a passion for crustaceans
of various kinds, including (accent these first two) fiddler crabs,
green crabs, hermit crabs, blueclaw crabs, shrimp and small lobsters. They'll also devour marine worms and small clams. The
list expands to include spearing, small sand eels (true name, sand
launce, not an eel), meat from skimmer or ocean clams, and peri-
winkles (the larger ones cut into pieces of suitable size). Often
blackfish scout for food over oyster beds and in creeks and channels where mussels congregate along the banks, and they frequent
locations where small crabs abound. All those are potential natural attractors. Let's look at the best prospects from the bait angle
to see which are most practical.

Practicality is important and is judged on the basis of a couple
of details. The first is availability. A bait's excellence is one
thing, but if it's difficult to obtain or the supply is very erratic,
it isn't practical. Second, how well does it go on a hook? Does it
tear badly or otherwise come apart? If so, forget it. Third, how
durable is it on a hook? Some baits are tough (strips of squid,
for instance) and remain intact for a long time. Others, being
more delicate, disintegrate faster and must be replaced more
frequently.

For blackfish bait we can eliminate barnacles. Tautogs like
them, but they're small and would be difficult to impale on a
hook. (Besides, you'd have to get your own.) Scratch off infant
lobsters too. You can't get 'em. They're illegal to catch. All the
others you can keep on your list. For the most part they fulfill
the requirements of good blackfish baits. I say "for the most part"
because sometimes certain items fall into short supply. Bloodworms and sandworms do the job, but they tend to soften and
become washed-out-looking, less attractive. Too, prolonged exposure on a hook leaches out much of their attractive scent. Those
aren't serious drawbacks, however. They simply mean that you'll
have to freshen your bait at intervals.

Among the most popular blackfish baits are fiddler crabs,
green crabs, and sandworms, plus, for ocean angling, the meat
from skimmer clams. In case you're asking, blueclaw crabs in
both the hard shell and shedder states also can be used, cut into
pieces.

Despite their diversity of tastes, blackfish may show a prefer- ence for one kind of bait over all others. It may be a day-to-day sort of thing, or longer; and it can vary from place to place. Be- cause of these periodic displays of finickiness it's always wise to stop at a local bait depot or fishing station to learn what baits the fish in that area favor at the time. It's also a good reason for carrying along a couple of different kinds of baits, just in case.

Tip: Sometimes during the early part of a spring run, bay blackfish may exhibit a marked preference for one of the soft baits, such as sandworm or a piece of clam, over harder baits, even the favored fiddler and green crabs. No one knows why. Maybe it's one of those displays of cussedness that all fishes exhibit peri- odically. Or perhaps, as a fishing station once theorized, they're "teething" at that time and their mouths are sore. Only the fishes' dentist could reply to that, but the fact remains that sometimes they do favor softer baits in the spring.

Bay and harbor blackfish will bite on pieces of sandworm or clam (hard, soft, skimmer), but they may show a preference for worms. It depends upon locale. During the summer these fish also will accept shrimp; and a combination bait consisting of shrimp and a piece of clam to conceal the hook's point has been known to succeed where other enticers fail.

A popular bait for ocean tautogs is the skimmer or sea clam, removed from its shell and cut into pieces. The shells can be dropped overboard alongside the boat as chum. Also usable in deep-sea blackfishing are pieces of squid, blueclaw crab, and worms, as well as spearing. The same baits, along with others I've mentioned, can be tried in jetty fishing and the surf.

Fiddlers and green crabs are high on the list of come-ons for bay blackfish. They're impaled on the hook to hide its point and barb. In the case of fiddlers it's done in a special way. The fiddler crab gets his name from the fact that one claw is larger than its mate's, and movements of these appendages appear as though he's "playing" that oversized claw like a violin. Anglers remove the big claw and insert their hook in the hole it leaves.

As already noted, blueclaw crabs can be rigged for blackfish bait in either the hard-shell or shedder state (a phase we'll ex- amine in the chapter on the blueclaw crab). A procedure is to lift off the back of the shell and break off the claws and appendages, leaving the joints closest to the body. The crab then is cut into pieces, each portion having a leg joint. To bait, run your hook's point in through the piece's body section, then out into the leg joint, leaving the point and barb concealed in the joint.

Clams and worms are cut into pieces. Squid is impaled on the hook as pieces or small strips. Small spearing and sand eels can be used whole if very small, or cut into pieces.

Tip: Unhappily for anglers, blackfish often are accompanied by relatives known as bergalls or cunners, which are pestiferous bait stealers and less desirable. When bergalls are especially numerous, blackfish won't get a decent crack at your bait because their larcenous cousins will steal it nearly every time. Very frustrating. But there's a way you can thwart the cunners' larceny. A fishing station operator showed me the trick long years ago. What you do is this: Bait with small, whole, soft-shell clams, leaving the shells on. Crack each shell carefully, only enough to allow body juices to escape to attract blackfish, then impale the clam on your hook, burying its point and barb in the meat. Now, a tautog will seize a bait that has a shell because he feeds on such items anyway and can crush the hard outer covering with his grinders to get at the morsel inside. A bergall won't bother with such baits because he isn't equipped to mash the shells. In conjunction with this stunt it helps to do a little chumming with cracked clams or mussels first, dropping a liberal quantity of them overboard alongside the boat.

METHODS AND TACKLE You can catch tautogs by fishing at anchor, by casting or dropping your baited rig alongside a jetty, sea wall, bridge abutment, trestle, pier, bulkhead, in among rocks, or by surfcasting from a beach, placing your bait in a rocky area, deep hole, or near a jetty. On oceanfront beaches those structures known as groins—either bulkheads or piles of stone, extending to seaward to minimize erosion—also are places with blackfishing potential. And don't overlook creeks and channels where there are likely to be collections of bank mussels.

However you fish for them, tackle must be reasonably sturdy. Sporting flexibility is desirable in all rods, but those used for blackfish must also have some backbone, for several reasons:

Blackfish often must be struck hard to set a hook in their leathery mouths. With a light rod that's too flexible, much of the hook-setting force is absorbed by the rod's bending. Too, you may be fishing for them in places where tidal currents are strong, necessitating fairly heavy sinkers. The rod will have to reckon with this weight in addition to the fish's. Further, blackfish are surprisingly strong for their sizes, and persistently stubborn. Still further, one of their favorite gambits when they feel the restraint of hook and line is. to go into a power dive for the nearest rock cranny or opening in a wreck. When they execute that maneuver they must be kept away, as much as possible, from rocks and other barnacle-encrusted obstructions, by sheer force if necessary. Otherwise there's a chance that they'll bring your line in contact with something that can sever, fray, or snag it.

That's why I don't recommend extra-light tackle, conventional or spinning, for blackfish. An exception is when out after the small bay fish, and then only in shallow water where currents are weak and there aren't obstructions.

Depending upon whether you seek small-to-medium-size bay blackfish or their larger oceanic brethren, your rod can be a light-to-medium stick of the so-called boat or all-purpose type. Conventional tackle is suggested. If you use spinning gear, fish a rod with a reasonable amount of spine. A spinning rod that's too willowy makes it difficult to control the larger tautogs. Try it if you want, but be prepared to lose rigs and fish.

On your rod you can mount a 1/0 or 2/0 revolving spool reel (or spinning equivalent if you insist on using that type of tackle).

Line strength isn't a matter of precision. You can gauge it close enough according to the sizes of the fish currently running. Ten-pound test, even a pound or two lighter, will handle most of the blacks you'll encounter. If heavyweights are anticipated, you can go to twenty. You also can go to a heavier line if you're fishing rocky areas. The greater diameter of somewhat heavier line will provide a measure of protection against chafing and cutting. You won't need a lot of line. Fifty to a hundred yards should be ample, even for deeper blackfish water.

All the foregoing details apply in surf fishing for tautogs too, except that you'll probably be wielding surf tackle, conventional or spinning, instead of a boat rod. Light equipment will suffice, and I recommend the conventional type. Because of the species'

habits, much of the angling will be done around stone jetties or
in rocky or boulder-strewn areas. Conventional tackle has more
backbone to handle the somewhat heavier lines used to minimize
chafing on rocks and to argue with the stubborn "bulldogs" when
they take refuge in nooks and crevices. Arguing a husky tautog
out from among rocks with a spinning rod can be tough.

Casting distance won't be requisite. Most of the time in shore
blackfishing you'll be working your rig fairly close to where you're
standing on a beach, bank, sea wall, or jetty. For this reason you
can often get away with a boat or all-purpose outfit instead of
a surf combination.

RIGGING   Blackfish are bottom residents; therefore you'll rig your
terminal tackle—hook and sinker—for the bay or sea floor.

Hook design is a matter of personal choice. There's a style
called a Virginia often suggested for tautogs. There's also one
designated as a standard blackfish hook, with or without a snell
of gut, tarred line, or synthetic material. By and large, one pattern is as good as another, so long as the hooks aren't oversized.
Tautogs' mouths aren't particularly large. Hooks for them range
in size from a No. 8 to slightly larger No. 7 for small bay fish up
to a No. 2 or No. 1, even 1/0, for large oceangoing toughies. A
No. 8 or No. 7 will hold blackfish to two or three pounds. A No. 6
will handle specimens to five and six pounds, even up to eight,
but care must be exercised when arguing a blackfish that size out
of a tight place or when lifting him from the water. Under real
strain certain types of hooks in that size could straighten out at
the bend. Actually a No. 3, which is stronger than a No. 6, is safer
for blackfish in the six-to-eight-pound bracket. If heavier fish are
expected, a No. 2 or No. 1 is better yet.

Tip: Any hooks rigged for blackfish must have good points for
penetrating the critters' tough mouths. Always make certain beforehand that your hooks have clean, rust-free, needle-sharp,
unbent points. Their barbs must be sharp too. These hook requirements apply in all kinds of fishing, but they're especially
important in blackfishing.

Another tip: For all your fishing maintain a running inventory
of your hooks. Make sure you have enough. Always carry spares,
including some for your artificials. You never know when you'll

need replacements. Check your hooks periodically *before* you go fishing. Examine them for dullness, rust, and bent points. Even a slightly bent point will have its penetrating ability impaired or lost. Rusty hooks are weakened. Very slightly rusted ones can be cleaned with fine emery cloth or sandpaper. Discard and replace badly rusted hooks.

When fishing around submerged objects, as for blacks, you can expect snagged rigs. A certain amount of "hanging up" on some underwater obstruction is unavoidable. Hooks and sinkers get caught on all sorts of things down there, and you'll have to anticipate rig losses.

In some instances you'll be able to pull your rig free. Other times, the more you try to work it loose, the more firmly it becomes lodged. Up to a point you can endeavor to get your rig clear, but it isn't worth risking a broken rod to persist. If efforts to free it fail, the only thing to do is kiss that rig goodbye, cut the line with minimum loss, and rig up again. Right there is the best reason for carrying spare hooks, sinkers, and swivels. On some party boats you can buy replacements from the skipper or mate, but I wouldn't count on it, and tackle shops are mightily scarce out on the water.

A hook-saving device: Here's a stunt that will cut down on hook losses in all kinds of fishing around obstructions. It's an old gimmick and very simple. When you attach your sinker, don't tie it in directly. Instead, attach it by means of a very short length of ordinary string. The string should be strong enough to keep the sinker in place, yet sufficiently weak to break if the sinker becomes entangled in an obstruction. In that way you stand to lose only a sinker, not hook, sinker, and some line. A variation of the same trick, designed for use when chances of snagging are great, is to substitute a little bag of sand for the metal sinker, attaching to the line with a short piece of break-away string as before. This can save sinkers as well as hooks, but necessitates fashioning the little sand sacks beforehand. They're easily made from squares of discarded cloth and filled with beach or ordinary sand. Ideally, the amount of sand should be measured out in ounces to provide equivalents of lead sinkers and avoid excess weight. Then, if you want to be really practical, you can tie the bags shut with string of different colors to indicate their weights.

Although crafty in their own way, blackfish aren't especially shy. Leaders, therefore, aren't required. (One purpose of a leader is to get the bait or lure away from anything, such as a sinker, swivel, or line, that might make a fish suspicious or shy.) Hooks for blackfish can be attached directly by their snells or on a short length of monofilament, about the same strength as the line. Attachment can be made with or without a standard two-loop barrel swivel. Some anglers prefer to omit the swivel, feeling that it's just so much unnecessary hardware. But a swivel minimizes tangling of hook and line, and I think it's desirable.

One or two hooks can be rigged. Some eager beavers use three. You can do as you please, but I suggest holding it to two, maximum. Theoretically, multiple hooks boost chances of contacting fish; but in blackfishing, much of which is done around underwater obstructions, they also increase possibilities of getting snagged. In fact, where chances of becoming "hung up" on something are great, it might be best in the long run to stick to one hook.

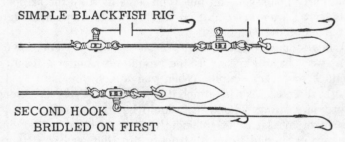

SIMPLE BLACKFISH RIG

SECOND HOOK
BRIDLED ON FIRST

Okay, rig up, using swivels or not as you see fit. Your sinker goes on the end of your line. If only one hook is employed, it should be tied into the line about an inch or two above the sinker. Should you want to try a second hook, you can use either of these arrangements: (1) Tie it to the line a few inches above the first, only high enough to prevent the two from tangling; or (2) bridle the second hook to the first by tying it (no swivel) midway on the snell of the latter, giving you a Y-shaped rig. If a third hook is used, it's attached a few inches above the second (or the bridle arrangement), just far enough to keep it from tangling with the others.

In *any* bottom fishing you can use the so-called bank-type sinker, the most popular for this type of angling, or a round type. Some fishermen favor the latter for areas where there are obstructions, but I don't think there's that much difference. I do recommend, though, that you carry sinkers in assorted weights, from one or two ounces up to at least five ounces. For ocean fishing you may need eight ounces or more.

Remember: Use only enough weight to keep your rig on bottom. It may be necessary to experiment a little, trying various weights until you find the one that keeps your rig where it belongs. You can determine when your rig is on bottom by bouncing your sinker—raising your rod tip a few inches and letting it drop back. If your sinker is holding bottom you'll feel a dull thud when it hits.

HE'S TRICKY Another feeding characteristic of importance to fishermen is the tautog's habit of eating in a series of fast, darting nips, like a bird pecking seeds. This trait, along with his leathery lips and surprising agility, makes the blackfish a cunning imp. He can steal bait with the best of them. And his rat-a-tat-tat feeding procedure has fostered a little debate among fishermen for years as to the best way to hook him. I'll present both sides so that you can try them.

One school of thought calls for the hook to be set the instant a blackfish nibbles. The plot here is to plant its point in some part of his mouth before he gets a chance to swipe the bait and move off.

The other plan, a direct opposite, says *not* to set the hook at the first sign of nibbling, but to wait until the fish has ticked the bait a couple of times. Proponents of this technique point out that blackfish seldom gulp a bait. When biting off food such as barnacles they first cut them free with their front teeth, then pass them back to the masticators to be crushed. You don't gain anything by impetuously trying to set the hook right off the bat, say the delayed-action fellows. Their reasoning is that if the fish becomes suspicious about something in his food—such as a hook buried in bait—he'll reject the offering anyway and leave. The way to set the hook, they advise, is to wait until pecklike attacks on the bait give way to a more or less strong yank that unmistakably indicates the fish has taken the hook, then set it. These anglers point out further that attempting to set the hook on an initial nibble is likely to jerk the bait away and cause a blackfish to lose interest. What's more, they add, often the larger blacks are the slowest to really accept a bait, and therefore must be handled with patience. That's true of some of the big tautogs, incidentally.

There's something to be said for both those schools of thought. Personally, I think the technique to be used varies from fish to fish. I suggest you try both for your own satisfaction. Blackfish usually are plentiful enough so that you can afford experimentation. To help you form your own opinion, try the instant-strike method on the small-to-medium blacks, and the delayed-strike procedure on the bigger fish. Another combination is to set the hook fast when using soft baits such as worm or clam to prevent the crafty visitor from cleaning your hook. When fishing with hard baits, such as crabs, give your quarry a chance to get the offering past his front teeth. He won't be able to denude your hook as readily as in the case of a soft bait. Besides, it's a fact that you risk losing your fish by attempting to set your hook at the very first ticking of a hard bait.

When a blackfish seizes your hook and starts for other places there won't be any doubt that you have a tough customer. The forward and downward power surges of even a two-pounder are surprisingly strong. He's clever too. It's second nature for him to race for haven in among rocks or the shadowy recesses of a wreck, and he seems to instinctively know how to bring a line against something that can part it. He'll make you earn him. He hasn't been nicknamed "bulldog" for nothing. You'll find that his drive, stubbornness, and little tricks all go to make blackfishing an interesting game. You'll enjoy it. And for extra spice there's always that possibility of tying into a toughie going ten or twelve pounds, or even heavier.

Finally, to top the whole thing off, blackfish are good eating. They can be prepared in any way that you'd cook other fishes. If they're large enough they can be filleted; or, if you don't mind bones, they can be cooked whole after gutting and removal of head and fins. I should add that a blackfish has a rather tough skin. If it's to be removed before cooking (some people like to leave a fish's skin on), a method that has been suggested to facilitate skinning is to literally freeze the fish first, or at least give it a chance to chill through in a refrigerator. But if you do that, cook the fish right after thawing. Don't refreeze the meat.

Now I ask you, what more could you want than good sport topped off by good eating?

CHAPTER 7

Bluefish: The Assassins

For utter savagery, for uninhibited killer instinct, this muscular, trim-bodied battler ranks among the oceans' most bloodthirsty marauders. He has few equals in the sea when it comes to destroying other fishes, whether for eating or for sheer pleasure of butchery. His carnage would give a hungry shark an inferiority complex. With a mouthful of needle-sharp teeth, a seeming love of slaughter, and the way he goes stark, raving mad when he tastes the blood of prey, the bluefish is a reasonable facsimile of South America's dreaded piranha.

Unlike the terrible piranha, though, the bluefish confines his murderous attacks to other, usually smaller, finned residents of the undersea world—so far as we know, that is. Anglers are bitten by blues, but this generally happens only in careless handling.

BLUEPRINT FOR MAYHEM   In the vast kingdom beneath the waves bluefish rate with the boldest, most vicious assassins, roving seas in various parts of the world in vast schools. In all seas they frequent, including the Indian Ocean off South Africa and the Pacific off Australia, they constantly stage murderous attacks on smaller neighbors. Their destruction staggers belief.

It seems to be their desire to kill, mangle, eat, or otherwise destroy every smaller fish in their path. They travel in gigantic schools, some of which are strung out for miles, pursuing schools of menhaden, herring, mackerel, or other grouping species. They literally "ride herd" on their prey, much as cowboys round up cattle, driving their victims into a closely packed, panic-stricken mass. Then the butchery begins. When a slaughter takes place in a surf the smaller fish sometimes become so wildly panicked that they're driven right out onto the sand. So savage and persistent is the onslaught of the blue killers that they almost follow their prey up onto the beach.

Having driven their victims into an hysterical mass, the blues go to work with their teeth, biting and slashing like so many hedge clippers gone berserk. Quickly they reduce the unfortunates to shreds, or chop them to ribbons, or bite chunks from them, littering the sea with entrails and body fragments and streaking it crimson with blood. You may come across the aftermath of such an encounter. You'll see the evidence, a long trail of mangled remains of fish in ominous red clouds.

The strange part of their wholesale butchery is that much of it seems pointless. In other words, they don't kill for food alone, but massacre other fishes for the love of it. If bluefish had a whale-size need for food you could understand their murderous harvests, but they couldn't possibly eat all the fishes they destroy. The fact is that they eat until their stomachs bulge, then vomit the contents and start the gluttonous orgy all over again. They might repeat this idiotic performance several times. When it bores them they keep right on killing out of pure deviltry.

The numbers of smaller fishes destroyed by bluefish is beyond calculation. One scientific observer has estimated that each blue destroys at least twice his own weight daily. Let's say, just to use round figures, that there's a school of ten-pound blues numbering one thousand individuals. Their daily tally would be in the magnitude of twenty thousand pounds. Other authorities have calculated a full-grown blue's daily score at one thousand fishes—and more.

But let me hastily jump to the bluefish's defense. Dame Nature doesn't create creatures purely for the purpose of slaughtering others senselessly. There's invariably a good reason. Pointless murder would ruin the balance of life in the sea. An educated guess as to the reason for the blue's attacks on other fishes is that it's part of maintaining that balance. It should be noted that blues prey chiefly upon fishes that breed in astronomical numbers. Menhaden or mossbunkers are one. Mackerel and various kinds of herring are others. A logical speculation is that bluefish prey upon those prolific species as part of a natural scheme to keep their numbers down. In other words, were it not for bluefish we might be up to our behinds in mossbunkers.

One thing is for sure: Dame Nature didn't figure on man's greediness. In his way he's good competition for bluefish in the wholesale destruction department. And he doesn't limit himself to mass-produced species.

DISTRIBUTION AND SEASONS 'Way back in 1758 a Swedish botanist-biologist named Linnaeus tagged the bluefish with the Latin handle *Pomatomus saltatrix,* which always sounds to me like a guy trying to talk with a mouthful of dry crackers. The species' family name subsequently came to be Pomatomidae.

His descriptive name, bluefish, the most commonly used in the United States, probably was bestowed by some unidentified angler(s) in the distant past. In waterfront jargon it's often shortened to "blue." Nowadays you'll also hear him called "chopper" because of those habits mentioned earlier.

"Tailor" is another moniker given to bluefish. It's used in Australia, but here in the States it's regional in nature and you'll seldom if ever hear it on our Atlantic seaboard. In regions throughout the world where he's known, the blue-and-silver speedster has acquired quite a collection of nicknames over the years. Here's a sampling: "blue runner"; "blue snapper"; "greenfish"; "fatback"; "skip mackerel" and "snapping mackerel" (both bad, even as nicknames, since the bluefish isn't even related to mackerels); and "skipjack." One of the oddest I've run across is "tassergal," origin unknown. Another odd one, considering the species' disposition, is "ballerina" (!), possibly for effeminate blues.

When I was fishing in South Africa I encountered two more. In the Cape Town region a bluefish is called an "elf." Up in Durban, on the Indian Ocean, they speak of bluefish as "shad" (also a bad misnomer, since blues have no kinship with shad).

All those aliases are of historical interest, but they might best be forgotten so as not to contribute to confusion. There's enough of that with fishes' names as it is.

The bluefish is the only known member of the Pomatomidae family, and is considered by many ichthyologists as having no very close relatives. Ed Migdalski notes, however, that some scientists like to classify blues as being allied with the jackfish tribe (Carangidae), while others see a relationship with sea basses, primarily because of certain similarities in skeletal structure. And my friend Dr. Ross F. Nigrelli, director of New York

Aquarium and Osborn Marine Laboratory, believes there might just be some distant tie between bluefish and piranhas, citing similarities in jaw structure and habits as possible evidence.

Bluefish are erratic ocean wanderers, widely but irregularly distributed throughout temperate and warmer seas. Along the Atlantic seaboard of North and South America they're encountered from Massachusetts—and occasionally northward as far as Nova Scotia as strays—down to Florida, the Gulf of Mexico, Brazil and, to a lesser extent, as far south as Argentina (hence another nickname, *salmon Argentino*).

The toothy terrors also are found in the Mediterranean Sea, on Africa's northwestern coast, on both the Atlantic Ocean and Indian Ocean sides of South Africa, around Madagascar, in waters of the Malay Peninsula, and "down under" in Australia and New Zealand.

In late spring, northbound migrations up our Atlantic seacoast bring schools sometimes estimated to extend as much as twenty miles. We know relatively little about their travels, other than that they migrate. We also know that warmer weather heralds a northward trek up our East Coast by schools. There's evidence that some of the huge main bodies of fish remain offshore, while smaller groups—splinter schools, we might call them—break away from the main packs and head inshore.

You'll meet blues both offshore and inshore, sometimes just beyond where breakers are thundering on a beach. They enter inlets too, to invade bays and harbors. Larger, semi-enclosed bodies of water, such as Long Island Sound, also are host to bluefish schools. In search of food they'll race into creeks and channels.

Commonly they're seen at the surface, raising hob with schools of smaller fishes. Evidence indicates that their vertical scope extends from there, down through intermediate levels, to depths of several fathoms. Sport-fishing evidence—you'll learn this for yourself—is that the larger blues tend to seek deeper planes than their younger brethren. And there are times when blues are caught quite close to the bottom. In fact, they've been caught by bottom fishermen out after other species.

Water temperature is a major factor in determining whether or not areas within their distribution will harbor bluefish. Ed Migdalski suggests 58° to 60° F as about the lowest temperature they'll tolerate in any numbers. Waters cooler than that, he says, seldom contain blues. It's been my theory that when unsatisfactorily cold water is encountered by northward-migrating bluefish it can be as effective as a brick wall in halting their travels. For instance, schools might be advancing up the coast off Maryland and Delaware at a good clip (blues move fast when they're on the march), covering many miles practically overnight. Then, abruptly, somewhere off New Jersey, they slow down, even stop, and several days may elapse before they cover the relatively short distance between there and New York. Conversely, with favorable water temperatures ahead, they can be in New Jersey waters one day and off Long Island the next.

Similarly, water temperatures can determine how long blues will remain in a given area. Dropping of the thermometer, as in a hurrying autumn, can dispel them, perhaps only temporarily or maybe for the rest of that season. It's also possible that water temperatures are a factor in their disappearances, sometimes for years, from regions they ordinarily frequent.

Factors other than water temperatures also could contribute to such antics. Salinity, or saltiness, of local waters might play a part. Different fishes have varying salinity requirements. Some, such as striped bass, can even adapt to fresh water. Salinity is a variable. Bluefish could be very sensitive to changes. Food, of course, is a cardinal factor. It is with most fishes, and especially with blues. Where a food supply is adequate, and other environmental conditions are favorable, bluefish linger. When the supply is poor, they go elsewhere. It's as simple as that.

Bluefish are warmer-weather species; and because they participate in coastwise migrations their seasons naturally vary accordingly in progressively northern parts of the Atlantic seaboard. Starting with Florida, for example, where waters are warm much of the time, they seem to be most numerous in dead of winter. In the Carolinas schools "appear" offshore along about March or April, moving along to show in the offing of Delaware later on in April, then in the southern part of New Jersey during the latter part of that month or in May. By May, all things being favorable, they start to turn up in more northerly New Jersey waters and in the ocean off Long Island. Toward the end of

May or perhaps in early June, they're swimming in Massachusetts waters.

That's a rough timetable for their offshore appearances. Anywhere from a couple of weeks to a month can elapse, after those dates, before sizable schools part company with the main bodies of fish and work their way inshore more within reach of anglers.

By June hordes of choppers are swarming offshore and inshore, and even in bays and sounds, throughout much of their northerly distribution, building to a season's peak by or before July. With food and water temperatures at appropriate levels, they linger throughout the summer and into October. How deep into that month they remain depends upon those two cardinal factors just mentioned. Autumn storms can play a role too, depending upon their severity. Sometimes a fall blow only drives them into deeper water. A really severe storm can chase them away completely for that season.

Whatever their region, when their run is over they vanish. We don't know for certain where. The chances are, it's to offshore regions; but we have yet to pinpoint specific ocean areas. Nor do we know whether they congregate out there or simply roam willy-nilly. In any case, when they go that's it until their next seasonal showing.

Although bluefish are numerous in the over-all picture, their visitations in various regions can be erratic and subject to radical fluctuations between the extremes of great abundance and complete absence over a period of years. Commercial and recreational fishing's history of their presence in North American waters is a long series of such fluctuations. Anglers refer to those radical variations as "bluefish cycles."

You can bet that their cycles are a mystery only to man, not to the blues. There have to be substantial, logical reasons for them. Among the possibilities are radical variations in spawning and/or in combinations of food availability, water temperatures, and salinity—or any one of those three by itself. Perhaps there are cyclic diseases that claim huge tolls of breeding females and/or bluefish of certain ages. Or there may be years in which an overabundance of certain kinds of predators destroy extraordinary quantities of bluefish eggs and infants. There are several possibilities, alone or in combination. And there may be still other factors of which we're not yet aware.

Causes of the erratic comings and goings of *Pomatomus saltatrix* are still within the realm of speculation. Not until much more data have been amassed by research studies will we be able to accurately explain bluefish cycles. Meanwhile, let's be thankful for when the choppers do show.

BLUEFISH CLOSE-UP   Once having seen a bluefish in life, or even in an illustration, you'll be able to identify this famous sport fish thereafter.

His body shape is one clue. It's classified as fusiform, which means it's like a spindle—deepest in the middle, tapering toward its ends. Bluefish are streamlined, but some of it is lost as they grow older. Like many humans, they have a trim figure when young, but expand around the middle with advancing age.

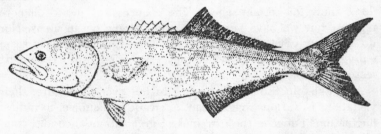

BLUEFISH (*Pomatomus saltatrix*)

Prominent among physical traits distinguishing the bluefish is his mouth. It's of generous size, extending downward at a slight angle. Above it his forehead curves to form a rather blunt snout. His jaws are well-defined and strong. Characteristically, the lower jaw projects a bit beyond the upper. His mouth is armed with many sharp teeth. Those in a large specimen can be a quarter of an inch long. This oral cavity, with its powerful jaws and dental armament, is ideally suited to the kind of killing for which its owner is (in)famous.

Our toothy friend is a swift, strong swimmer, thanks to a muscular body and fine propulsion equipment. Notable in the latter department is his caudal fin or tail, well-developed and deeply forked. There are two dorsal fins, the first being comparatively small, rounded in profile, and spined. The second, larger dorsal is higher, shaped like a sail, and rayed. Helping identify the bluefish is the fact that his single anal fin is very similar to the second dorsal and positioned almost directly under it, giving a kind of profile symmetry.

A prime characteristic, of course, is the color giving the species its name. Basically it's a shade of blue, subject to some variations, which include a darkish tone and a greenish hue. This color is most pronounced on his back and upper sides. Lower down it fades to a lighter shade, finally giving way to silver-white on the belly.

In North American waters the growth potential of *Pomatomus saltatrix* goes to a length of approximately 3 feet and a weight of 20 to 25 pounds. Larger bluefish have been captured. It's reported, but apparently wasn't authenticated, that blues weighing *30 to 50 pounds* (!) were caught commercially in the 1800s.

Africa has some real huskies. In its waters, it's been said, 20-pounders aren't uncommon, and brutes up to 30, 40, and 45 pounds have been reported. When I was in South Africa not long ago I was told that blues to 35 pounds are commercially caught at Saldanha Bay, northwest of Cape Town on the Atlantic Ocean side.

Once upon a time blues in the 20-to-25-pound bracket constituted world records. But the mark has crept upward. Now a record hopeful has to fix his sights at the 30-pound-plus level.

Bluefish caught by recreational fishermen span a range of sizes. In the main that range extends upward to 12, 13, and 14 pounds. There are also jumbos going up to 16, 18, even 20 pounds. Most sport-caught blues, however, are smaller than those last "maximums." Eight to 10 or 12 pounds is about tops, with a majority weighing up to about 6 pounds. It's interesting to note that some areas seldom see bluefish larger than approximately 4 pounds, while other places will have concentrations of tacklebusters topping 10 pounds. Similarly, there are seasons when the smaller fish predominate, and other years that bring numbers of the big fellows.

For bluefish there's a general nomenclature/size yardstick that goes like this: Bluefish to a pound or so are dubbed "snappers" (because they deserve it, they're given a chapter by themselves in this book). Those individuals heavier than snappers and going up to about 2 or 2½ pounds are often referred to as "snapper-blues," indicating an intermediate stage between snapperhood and maturity—the older kids, in other words. Specimens weighing more than 2 or 2½ pounds and going to about 4 pounds sometimes are called "harbor blues," from their habit of coming very close inshore and infiltrating inlets and bays. Finally, individuals above 4 pounds are full-fledged bluefish. Snappers and snapper-blues usually are bay visitors. Harbor blues can be encountered in open ocean, sounds, surf, bays, and harbors. Adult blues are met just about everywhere in their range, but the heavier fish generally frequent the open sea and large sounds.

There's also a length/weight yardstick. Like the foregoing classification, it's approximate and flexible. You'll come across variations in both from region to region.

The length/weight yardstick is close enough to give you a clue to the weights of your catches when a scale isn't available. It's provided by ichthyologists Henry B. Bigelow and William C. Schroeder, and goes like this: 13 or 14 inches, 1 pound; 17 inches, 2 pounds; 20 to 21 inches, 3 pounds; 24 inches, 4 pounds; 28 to 29 inches, 8 pounds; and 30 inches, 10 to 12 pounds.

Blues are superb game fish. Pound for pound they rate among the best battlers. They have all the qualities of what might be called a perfect game fish. There's their inherent savagery. The viciousness making them unholy terrors to their small neighbors is an excellent contribution to their high desirability as rod-and-reel opponents. In addition, they have the muscle and dogged resistance for even more authority. They're extremely active and aggressive in their hunting habits, details that make them slam-bang contestants on the end of a line. And bluefish are fast swimmers. Unofficial estimates have pegged their speed at close to 40 miles an hour when in "full flight." Then there's the detail of quantity—very important. Fortunately for anglers, bluefish are prolific and gregarious, traveling in large to astronomically huge schools. That, of course, spells good catches.

A FIGHTING TRICKSTER Any bluefish, even a youngster, is a rip-snorter. When blues are in an eat-'em-alive mood, which is a good part of the time, they'll snap those fangs at practically anything, especially if it's moving. They've been known to snap at bubbles on a line, sometimes with disastrous results to that line. When a blue grabs your offering and feels the hook's bite, hold onto your hat!

A blue demon hits your rig like this, *whammo!* You'll know all about it. There's no daintiness, no pussyfooting around the bait. He doesn't tiptoe in. He zooms in and wallops it. Hooked, he's instantly mad at you. He'll demand line and take it, and you'd better be prepared to yield yardage. His gears will mesh in high at once, and he'll be away at full throttle.

A bluefish's initial maneuvers after the strike are unpredictable, another detail making combat with him so interesting. In his first power drive he might plunge downward into the dark green shadows . . . or he might streak away like an arrow, just under the surface . . . or he might hurtle skyward, exploding through the surface like a water-to-air missile, flashing blue and silver in a geyser of foam and shaking his head in an effort to rid himself of your hook. He may change direction suddenly, even doubling back on his former course. Again and again he'll demand line, forcing you to give it to him or risk a popped line.

Here's a cardinal law in playing bluefish: *Never allow him as much as an inch of slack line!* He's an expert at dislodging a hook. Let him have even a little slack, even for an instant, and he might toss your hook and be gone.

A fighting bluefish has a bag of tricks. One of his battle tactics is to race away from the boat on a straight run, then suddenly alter course, swinging in a wide arc or even rushing *toward* the boat. In that latter gambit he can create a lot of slack line fast. You'll be fighting him when suddenly your line "goes dead," giving you an impression you've lost your fish. What the blue is doing is easing the pressure on himself. If you don't reel in slack immediately you could give him a chance to get rid of the hated hook. You must tighten your line by cranking furiously—even walking away from him as you do, if necessary.

Bluefish can create line slack in other ways too. Suddenly slowing his forward rush is one, or a combination of that and abruptly changing course. Leaping out of water is another. Blues can be quite acrobatic in their maneuvers to get off a hook. Always be alert to the split-second possibility of your opponent pulling some stunt that will cause line slack.

Yes indeed, a bluefish is full of cute tricks. Often he's at his slyest in the fight's final phase. Frequently he keeps one special tactic in reserve, an ace in the hole, as we say in stud poker. He plays that ace like this: You're retrieving line—not fast, maybe, but it's coming back on your reel steadily. Your opponent is beginning to yield. You can tell he's tiring. The fight is about over.

That's what *you* think.

Suddenly he puts on the brakes, practically within sight of the boat. Then—*whoosh!*—away he goes on another run as though freshly hooked. Which is all right if he dashes *away* from the boat. If he turns and arrows under the boat, you have problems. Now the danger is that your line will be cut or rubbed through by something on the boat's bottom or keel, or become fouled in her prop or rudder.

You can anticipate this maneuver to a certain extent by feeling for his movements, especially a reversal of course. Should it seem as though he's going to run under the boat, try to control him to prevent it, exerting a safe amount of pressure with your rod tip. If that fails, and odds are it will, aim your rod tip toward the stern as much as possible in an effort to guide your line around it. If he dives directly under the boat, guard against slack and follow the plan of retaliation I described in the chapter on albacores and bonitos.

TECHNIQUES AND TACKLE

Bluefish are caught by several techniques. All are effective, but some may be more productive than others in certain areas. For example, chumming is the preferred method in that great oceanic triangle formed by the coasts of northern New Jersey and southern Long Island, with New York City at its apex. (Trolling also is done in that region, but chumming is favored because it's a better producer there.) Out at Montauk Point at the eastern end of Long Island, trolling is *the* technique, rather than chumming. Just to the north of Montauk, in waters off Long Island's other easternmost tip, Orient Point, jigging is often the preferred method. Up and down the coast, Florida to New Jersey, you'll find various techniques in use. That's why it's advisable to check locally as to the method *currently* realizing the best results when you're in an unfamiliar area.

Tips on bluefishing hours—for all methods: Broadly speaking, optimum times for bluefishing are during early morning, in very late afternoon or evening around sunset, and at night. A commonly accepted reason is that choppers do not like the warmer water encountered in uppermost levels on hot days, so they go deep or move offshore to cooler locales. I believe too that blues are more active feeders during the day's cooler periods and at night. Not that you won't catch any blues at all during a summer day's midsection, you understand. It's just that your chances will be upped considerably at those other times.

TROLLING, SURFACE AND NEAR-SURFACE   This is one of the most popular methods. It has an advantage in that it covers more territory than other techniques, increasing the chances of encountering roving bands of blues. It can be employed anywhere. Most important, it produces.

When trolling it pays to constantly watch for signs of blues in the area. Here are signals you can look for:

(1) Surface disturbances generated by the fish as they feed. Blues feed in a frenzy, making the water look as though it's boiling. You may see fleeting flashes of silver as their frightened prey desperately try to escape by leaping into the air, with pursuing bluefish right behind them. (2) Seagulls, terns, or other sea birds swooping and diving toward the water's surface, squawking and squabbling among themselves. They're feeding on small fish driven upward by attacking bluefish, or on scraps of the blues' victims. (3) A profusion of dead and dying fish, along with fragments of same. They could be the remains of a bluefish raid. Tinges of blood in the water indicate that the carnage was quite recent, and the marauders might still be in that general area.

Absence of such signs doesn't necessarily mean there are no blues around. The fish could be deep. Conversely, the presence of such clues doesn't guarantee bluefish. Signal No. 1, for instance, could be caused by another species feeding or just frisking at the surface. Too, the combination of wind and tidal currents creates surface agitation, which at distance could be mistaken for a commotion of feeding fish. The only thing to do is check it out. Signal No. 2, birds working, isn't absolute proof that bluefish are underneath them. The sea birds could be dining on schools of little food fish. Signal No. 3 can be accepted as reasonably conclusive evidence that a school of blues passed through. But it doesn't hint that they're still around. By then they could be miles away. Bluefish travel fast. But you'll keep your eyes open anyway.

A crowd of come-ons, natural and artificial, has been brought into play successfully in bluefishing.

Artificials for blues preferably should be bright, flashy, or colorful, easily seen, designed to attract by brightness and action as they're trolled. Several different kinds are effective at one time or another. The parade includes: feathers, such as those rigged for school tuna and their relatives, in various color combinations; spoons; metal squids, chrome-plated for maximum flash; bright spinners; plugs of assorted types; bucktails; cedar jigs; the so-called chicken bone lures; and eelskin rigs. *Tip:* Check locally as to which is currently getting results.

Natural baits can be employed in bluefish trolling too. Among the more effective are strip baits. These are rather thin pieces, about a half to three-quarters of an inch wide and a few inches long, cut from herring, mullet, mackerel, squid, and other bluefish prey. Ideally they should be cut from a fish's lighter-colored underside so they can be better seen by blues. Strip baits stand up fairly well in trolling. Some, such as those cut from a squid's mantle, are tough and outlast others. Sooner or later, however, you'll have to replace a strip bait because it has become tattered or too washed-out. Blues can mangle a bait and render it useless, and escape in the process.

Whole natural baits such as small mullet and butterfish also are rigged for bluefish trolling. Whole eels are used too, as well as a hybrid gimmick known as an eelskin rig, part natural bait and part artificial (we'll get to eel rigs in the chapter on striped bass).

Whatever the natural baits foisted on bluefish, they should be as fresh as possible. The old maxim, *the fresher the bait, the greater its effectiveness,* holds for all kinds of angling.

Rigging artificials for bluefish—whether they're spoons, sub-surface plugs, or whatever—is essentially the same as rigging Jap feathers, as outlined in the chapter on albacore and bonitos. I do, however, want to accent two details. First, *always use a wire leader for bluefish, whatever the method.* Their teeth make short work of lines. Leader length varies according to individual preference, and can range from about three to six feet. Actually you need only enough wire to protect against their teeth; and it doesn't have to be heavy. The other point I want to stress is that you make your attachment of leader to line through a snap swivel, on the line, to permit fast, easy changing of rigs.

Strip baits are easily rigged. Terminal tackle consists of a hook of appropriate size and a wire leader. Attachment of leader to line is made in the same fashion as just noted. The strip is impaled on the hook securely, preferably near one end so that the remainder is free to flutter in the water as it moves. Whole natural baits such as butterfish, small mullet, etc., can be hooked through the head or jaws to make them travel in a fairly lifelike manner.

Hook sizes with artificials and natural baits go from about a 3/o to 6/o, even to 8/o, depending upon sizes of the blues currently running. Bluefish mouths are of sufficient size that gauging hooks to them doesn't have to be precise. You match them reasonably closely, but a hook that's a *little* too large or undersized needn't be a cause for concern. Only with extremes—hooks really unnecessarily big for small blues or those too small (and too weak) for hefty choppers—could you have problems.

There are refinements and special rigs employed in bluefish trolling. One is a trolling keel. This is a small, flat piece of metal incorporated in the terminal tackle between line and leader. Serving as a kind of stabilizer, it lessens spinning of a lure or bait and consequent twisting of the leader. It isn't a must, but it's helpful with attractors that tend to spin like crazy when towed.

There are special rigs calling for more than one hook. Multiple-hook arrangements often are used with artificial lures and strip baits. Sometimes an artificial will be armed with two sets of treble (gang) hooks, one riding right behind the other. Or they may be outfitted with two single hooks in similar fashion. Still another setup is to take an eyed hook, open its eye, then close it on the bend of the first hook, so that one dangles from the other. Another arrangement consists of rigging two single hooks in tandem, the second trailing the first on a couple of inches of wire.

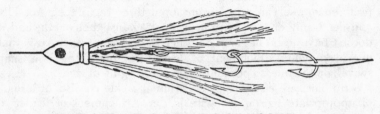

EYE-AND-BEND LINKING OF HOOKS

The purpose of multiple-hook rigs, of course, is to heighten the chances of nailing a fish should he miss one hook or set of hooks. That tandem hook deal just mentioned can be especially effective with strip baits. Among bluefish and other species—fluke are one—there are "short strikers." A short striker is a fish with larceny in his soul. He comes up behind a bait, strikes it, and chops it off just short of the hook, escaping with the tidbit. Now you have to put on a new bait. The trailing hook in a tandem rig is intended to minimize short strikes. If a fish smacks the trailing end of a strip bait so armed he gets himself a mouthful of hook.

Still another arrangement combines artificial and natural baits. Here a plug, jig, or whatever has its hook garnished with a piece of bait. It could be squid, or a small strip cut from a fish belly, or a piece of the pork rind sold in jars expressly for that purpose. It serves as an added attraction.

It's impossible to state which attractors, natural or artificial, may be best for bluefish. Too many variables are involved: the area fished; technique; and the fish themselves. Blues may favor certain come-ons over others from time to time. The thing to do, therefore, is first to inquire in the area you intend to fish. Find out which method is preferred and what attractors are most effective that season. In any case, it does no harm to have an assortment of artificials and/or natural baits aboard, in case bluefish tastes change unpredictably. Nor can you lose by experimenting with different come-ons and hook arrangements.

Also among terminal tackle for bluefish is the so-called Scotch rig. There are several versions. The one I'll describe here comes from Freeport, N.Y. charter skipper Carm Marinaccio.

Basically a Scotch rig consists of a series of lures, often of small-to-medium size, armed with hooks in sizes proportionate to the blues being sought. The choice and number of artificials are up to the user—wide open in accordance with his own ideas. "Surgical tubes" (about which more in the striped bass chapter), spoons of various types, etc., are among the selections, and it's a multilure rig. The artificials can be rigged in series, spaced just far enough apart to minimize tangling.

Carm has fished his version both with and without wire leaders. The latter instance is one of the very rare exceptions to the rule that wire always should be used for bluefish, because of their teeth. (Another occurs when long-shank hooks are rigged for snappers and small blues. Here the hooks' long shanks serve the same purpose as a wire leader.)

In the wireless version the lures are rigged on monofilament leaders a few inches long. The only advantages with this wireless rig might be that it's a bit easier to handle and the mono offers somewhat less visibility than wire in the water. But it's definitely a calculated risk, and I'm not sure it's worth any advantages it might have. A school of hungry blues can bite at its monofilament leaders, severing them.

Much better, I think, is Carm's version in which about six inches of light wire leader is incorporated between each lure and its monofilament. That won't eliminate damage entirely, but it will cut down on it.

A Scotch rig can be drifted as well as trolled. Trolling should be done very slowly. When drifted, a Scotch rig should be jigged or jerked spasmodically at intervals to give added motion to its lures. Scotch rigs have been proven bluefish killers in Long Island Sound, on both the Connecticut and New York sides, and the reason, I'm convinced, is because these multilure ensembles look like small schools of bait fish to the predators.

DEEP TROLLING   Sometimes bluefish travel at levels well below the surface. They may be searching for food or just traveling. Or they may have been driven there by a storm. Whatever the reason for their "submarining," it becomes necessary to deliver the lures to them. Deep trolling accomplishes it.

The lure rigged in deep trolling for bluefish may be one of several types (another memo to check locally before going out). Among them are spoons and metal squids of assorted designs, including models known as the Huntington Drone spoon, Belmar squid, and squid-spoon. Of more recent inception are the so-called surgical tubes, and this is as good a place as any to describe them.

Surgical tube lures get their name from the fact that they resemble the tubing used in transfusions and intravenous feeding. They are, in fact, tubing, like very coarse spaghetti. Made from plastics, this tubing comes in various diameters, colors, and wall thicknesses. There's no need to go into specific measurement figures, since the surgical tubes used in sport fishing are within a more or less standard range of diameters and wall thicknesses. Roughly, the diameter range of many in use is from just under a quarter inch to just under a half inch. You ask for surgical tubes for a specific kind of fishing and you'll get the right diameter. Surgical tubing colors include red, black, amber, brownish, and an off-white. Those commonly used in sport fishing are the first two, with an accent on red. In lure use their lengths vary, but usually are a matter of inches, perhaps three to five or six. A hook of suitable size is "buried" in the tubing.

Surgical tube lures also are killers for striped bass.

As always for blues, you gauge your hooks approximately to the predominant sizes of fish currently running, the scale going up to a 7/0 or 8/0 if really hefty choppers are anticipated.

Except in the case of surgical tubes, which are relatively light, and plugs designed to ride at or near the surface, the weight of artificials such as spoons and squids helps to carry them down a way. Many times, though, it isn't deep enough to contact blues; or currents and/or the boat's forward motion thrust the artificials too high. Then additional weight is needed.

Wire line, substituted for regular line, supplies some of this additional weight, and can be enough to take a lure down to where blues are. Twenty-to-thirty- or forty-pound test is a broad range. Many anglers favor a dull- or darker-finish wire to a shiny kind, feeling that the latter tends to "spook" the fish. Lengths of wire vary and can go, say, fifty yards or more (the more wire out, the greater the weight and the deeper a lure will travel). Often the wire line is backed by regular line to fill the reel spool.

At times blues travel very deep; or currents may be so strong that the combined weight of wire line and lure won't take a rig far enough down. Still more weight must be added. This is accomplished by incorporating a drail between leader and line. This is a trolling sinker. Made from lead, drails take various forms, come in graduated weights up to a pound and more, and have swivels fore and aft for attachment. The most common type of drail is simply a rather slender, elongated, spindle-shaped affair, included between leader and line by attachments to swivels at either end.

How much drail weight you need will be dictated by how deep you want your rig to go, strength of the current, and trolling speed. You may have to try a few different weights before hitting the right one.

RIG FOR DEEP TROLLING

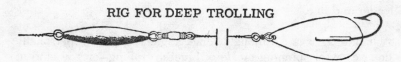

Another device for taking a rig deep is a trolling planer. It vaguely resembles an airplane, with its short wings and tapered, weighted "fuselage." Installed in the terminal tackle between line and leader, it can be adjusted to "fly" at different depths. Like drails, trolling planers can be used with lines other than wire.

Except for addition of a drail or trolling planer, the deep trolling rig for lines other than wire is substantially the same as that fished in surface and near-surface trolling. The lure is on six to eight feet of No. 6 or No. 7 wire leader. If a trolling sinker or planing device is added, it's tied in between leader and line.

Among rigs employed with *wire* line there are variations. Here are two you might try:

1. Secure your lure to a six-to-eight-inch length of No. 6 or No. 7 wire leader. Omit a swivel here. Blues would only snap at it. Connect leader and line through a swivel. An ordinary two-loop barrel swivel can be used instead of a snap swivel if preferred, unless you're figuring on experimenting with different rigs or lures. Incidentally, a wire leader is used even when the line is wire because the latter tends to kink, whereas wire leader material, being stiffer, remains straighter. Kinked wire close to a lure contributes to a rig's visibility and lends an unnatural appearance. A drail or trolling planer can be tied into the outfit between line and leader as before; and since those gadgets usually carry their own swiveling attachments, other swivels may not be needed.

2. The lure is secured to a short wire leader, without swivel, as before. Then a length of monofilament leader (for decreased visibility), about three feet and in about the same strength as the line, is attached to the wire leader through a barrel swivel. Finally, the mono leader is connected to the line. Joining can be made via another barrel swivel; or, if changing rigs is contemplated, use a snap swivel on the line and a loop in the leader. Again, if a trolling sinker or planer is used it's tied in between leader and line.

TROLLING TACKLE   Although some anglers use it, I personally don't care for spinning tackle in bluefish trolling—or any kind of trolling, for that matter. Appreciable weight—rigs and lines—is involved. I think spinning rods are too willowy.

For surface and upper-level operations you can wield a medium, all-purpose, conventional boat rod. You can go lighter, but the main thing is that the rod is rated to handle the pounds-test strength of the line involved. On this stick you can mount a 2/0 or 3/0 conventional reel.

Line material is your choice. Dacron is good. Some fishermen use braided types. Others go with monofilament if their conventional reels can take it. One hundred to one hundred fifty yards should suffice. Line strength is also a matter of personal ideas. Twenty-to-thirty-pound stuff is a safe range, capable of handling even the larger choppers. You can go below 20-pound line for medium and smaller blues, down to 10-pound test or so. Unless you can be reasonably sure that only small-to-medium blues are involved, don't go much below 10-pound test.

In deep trolling you'll go to wire line sooner or later. Here strengths can be about the same as for synthetics. Lengths can be approximately the same too. Depending upon how deep you want your rig to go (and water depths), you can use less wire, backing it with regular line to fill your spool.

For wire lines you may have to revise your tackle somewhat. The rod may have to be somewhat sturdier than the one you ordinarily wield, since it will be handling heavier lines, possibly heavier lures, and maybe the added weight of a drail or trolling planer. Too, in deep trolling there's always a possibility of contacting jumbo-size bluefish, to say nothing of fairly husky striped bass. Further, an added strain will be imposed on your rod by the amount of line out.

Tip: In any trolling, but more at shallower planes than deep, there are chances of contacting tuna and albacore. Your tackle should be able to handle them.

For better handling of wire line your rod should have at least one roller guide, its tiptop. Even better is a full set of roller guides. Wire line can groove some ring guides. However, I don't think you have to consider roller guides unless you'll be doing an appreciable amount of wire line fishing, but you can keep in mind that roller guides are fine for other kinds of lines too.

Your reel in deep trolling for bluefish will go to a 3/0, or a 4/0 if other, larger battlers are anticipated. In the latter case it should have a spool able to accommodate enough yardage of line in strengths up to about 40-pound test.

GENERAL NOTES ON TROLLING You'll hear differing views as to proper bluefish trolling speeds. The truth is that they vary and depend to some extent upon the moods of the fish. Particularly aggressive bluefish might respond to lures trolled at higher speeds—perhaps as fast as fifteen or twenty miles per hour in some instances, while blues in another group might hit on a slower troll, maybe four or five miles per hour. There's no predicting what the right speed will be, so experiment. Bluefish can be as erratic as all get-out. You might start at a slower speed, and try that for a while. Then, if it draws a blank, gradually increase your speed, giving each level a reasonable chance to produce. What can save you experimentation sometimes is to seek out flotilla trolling boats that are nailing bluefish and pace your speed with theirs.

Every bluefishing skipper has his own ideas about trolling speeds. Some professional skipper-guides like a five-to-six-knot range. That's a bit faster than speeds used by others. Speeds also are lower than that, as a general rule, when trolling for bluefish and striped bass together. In still other instances the trolling speed for blues may go to eight knots or higher.

Current velocity is a factor affecting trolling speed. So is wind. You'll have to judge the extent of their force on your boat as best you can. Sometimes you'll be going with those factors; on other occasions you'll buck them; at still other times you'll be riding with one but bucking the other. You'll have to go by trial and error, adjusting your throttle accordingly.

The slower you troll, the deeper your lure rides. Remember that in areas where obstructions thrust their way upward to appreciable heights from the bottom. They can cost you rigs. Also at slower speeds, your rig may travel too deep for bluefish schools in that sector, in which case you can bring your rig higher by shortening the line. The faster you troll, the greater the tendency for your lure to be thrust upward. Then you may have to either add weight or lengthen your line if you want it to scurry along at a greater depth.

In surface and near-surface bluefish trolling you also should experiment in the amount of line you pay out. Frequently it isn't necessary to let out a lot. Blues, like school tuna, have been known to come right up in a boat's bubbly wake, maybe only fifty feet or less astern, sometimes. Often you'll be able to nail them less than a hundred feet astern. What you might do at the onset is put out two or more lines, each at progressively greater distances between fifty and a hundred feet. When you get a hit, note which line did the trick, then adjust the others accordingly.

Oddly enough, although bluefish are bold enough to come right up into a boat's wake, the bulk of a craft's hull barging into a surfaced school can cause the otherwise aggressive gamesters to sound. If you cut into or across a school, your chances of hooking surfaced blues are decreased. The odds are that they'll dive the minute a boat enters their midst, if not sooner. If they're real hungry you might hook a few before they get too deep, but you can write off the rest. The school might reappear nearby; but, what is likely, it will be some distance away.

When you sight a school at the surface a strategy is to approach the fish cautiously and skirt the school, maintaining a discreet distance so as not to drive them down, simultaneously maneuvering the boat to swing the lures into the school's outer perimeter. In other words, get as close as you can without spooking the school, then work your lures in among the fish as much as possible.

Use the same principle when trolling tide rips and other places where blues are seen or thought to be. The odds are apt to be more in your favor if you work the edges of such areas, rather than cutting back and forth across them.

There will be occasions when, having contacted a bluefish school, either at the surface or while trolling blind, you'll extract some fish, then the action will cease as the school sounds or moves on. It's frustrating, and efforts to find the school again can be futile . . . but you can try.

Try to guess the distance between the boat and where the school *was*, and the direction it was heading at last contact. This is purely a gamble, since chances are you'll be off on both guesses. Besides, the blues may be moving swiftly. But it might help, especially when trolling blind, to toss over a buoy of some sort (it can be retrieved later), or even a floating beer can or piece of paper, to mark the place where the fish hit. With or without such a marker, you can attempt to relocate the school by swinging the boat and her lures through an ever-widening circle, like a giant pinwheel course. The chances aren't rosy, especially if the blues were at full gallop, but you might get lucky.

Another procedure can be tried when a surface school vanishes before you have a chance to work it. You estimate the direction the school was headed when last seen, then try to sail a course parallel to that of the fish, at the same time working your lures along the route you think they might be traveling. Sure, it's difficult when you can't see your target, and you might be 'way off. But what do you have to lose? If that fails to relocate the school after a reasonable try, go into the pinwheel search pattern.

If all that fails, don't waste any more time. Go looking for another school.

CHUMMING   For the benefit of newcomers in our crowd I'll take a minute to explain what chumming is. It's a very important phase of angling, employed for a number of different species.

Chumming is a sport-fishing procedure in which some item of fishes' natural food—clams, shrimp, small fishes, etc., or other tidbits (dyed rice, cat food, etc.—we'll get to those later on) is distributed overboard continuously to lure finned game to a boat's vicinity and hold them once they've arrived. This largesse is called chum.

Depending upon species sought, chum varies. For example, grass shrimp can be used for weakfish, clams for striped bass, mussels for flounders, and so on. Sometimes one kind of chum —ground-up menhaden or mossbunkers, for example—can be used for several different kinds of battlers (sharks, bluefish, mackerel, etc.). Similarly, their form as used in chumming varies. Small butterfish may be used whole or cut into halves. Moss-bunkers and other fishes are ground into a mushy pulp to be ladled overboard. Mussels and clams can be used whole, with their shells cracked to let attractive body juices escape, or cut into pieces, or ground up. Small shrimp are used whole and dropped overboard alongside the boat in little clusters at intervals. And so on.

In other words, chumming is a handout, a kind of line of communication with fishes out some distance away from the boat. A continuous procession of such goodies is known variously as a chum line, chum slick, or chum streak. When established and maintained properly—which is to say unbroken—it forms a continuous teaser, which attracts sport-fishing targets to where baited hooks are waiting. Chumming is important because, first, it's a magnet that draws fishes that otherwise might not come anywhere near the hooks, and second, it heightens chances of better catches by keeping fish in the boat's vicinity. In that latter capacity it can be especially helpful with fast-moving species such as bluefish.

Chumming can be employed for many kinds of sportfishes, fresh and salt water, since its underlying principle remains constant: It appeals to a fish's appetite. And that, after all, is the underlying principle of baiting too.

It's standard procedure, wherever possible, to use some favored food of the species sought as chum. In the case of bluefish, therefore, mossbunkers are a natural. 'Bunkers are high on the blues' menu. As a matter of economy and to effect maximum distribution, mossbunkers are run through a meat grinder to yield a mushy, oily, blood-laced pulp. On hot days this mush sometimes hammers on human nostrils with fists of scent, but to bluefish it's ambrosia.

Some bluefishermen buy 'bunkers whole, fresh or frozen, and grind them to pulp themselves by running them through a home meat grinder. They grind a supply beforehand, or take a grinder along, clamp it aboard boat, and crank out the mush as needed. Use of home meat grinders isn't calculated to endear fishermen to their wives. Besides, unless you find the process intriguing, or sexy, or something, it hardly seems worthwhile to go to the trouble and mess, because you can buy 'bunkers already ground and packed in cans, ready for use.

In poor commercial fishing seasons menhaden will be in short supply. You may have to substitute some other kind of fish. Mackerel can be used; so can herring. These too are ground up and must be kept under refrigeration. In a pinch, get hold of a commercial fisherman and ask him to save his trash fishes for you. See if you can't have the use of a big grinder somewhere. Preparing chum on a little home meat grinder is a laborious, time-consuming chore.

CHUMMING PROCEDURES Judging the amount of chum required, beforehand, whatever its kind and application, is often a by-guess-and-by-golly calculation, since there's no way of telling accurately in advance how much is going to be required. Two of the biggest factors involved are current speeds and fishes' response, both variables. A faster current naturally carries chum away from the boat more rapidly, thereby necessitating more of it. So far as fishes' response is concerned, a chum line may be effective in a matter of minutes or require an hour or more to get results.

From experience—especially when you're laying out money—you'll derive pretty good estimates of how much you'll need. There will be times when you underestimate and run short, a deplorable state of affairs, especially when you're holding a school of blues and they're biting like crazy. At the other extreme will be trips when you overestimated and bought too much chum; and that, of course, is better than running out of it. But don't let such miscalculations disturb you. They're made by the best of us.

Tip: Buy your 'bunker chum—or any ground-fish chum—the night before a trip and leave it out of refrigeration to thaw. Fish pulp chum kept under refrigeration for any length of time develops ice crystals, which make the stuff buoyant. Unthawed chum, therefore, tends to float. Not only does that curtail its distribution and consequent effectiveness, it also provides a buffet, attracting seagulls from miles around . . . and maybe they'll be all you'll attract until the stuff thaws. If you purchase the pulp on the morning of sailing, leave it uncovered in the sun to thaw on the way out; or, if the boat's engine housing is roomy enough, place it in there. Packaged frozen baits—butterfish, spearing, etc. —also should be given a chance to thaw so that they're not stiff and unnatural on a hook.

The technique is basically the same in all chumming, whatever the material. Small quantities of chum are ladled (pulp) or dropped (pieces) overboard at regular intervals to form an unbroken line. Accent that word *unbroken.* It's of utmost importance. Unless a chum line is continuous and uninterrupted you might as well forget it. Well, here, let's see what happens in the case of a broken chum line.

You have a line established. Then whoever is doing the chumming decides on a sandwich or a beer. He leaves his post to find same. Now, supposing the chum was starting to get results out yonder. Fish have picked it up and are following it toward its source and waiting hooks. Abruptly they come to the end of the handout, the interruption caused when the chummer went for that sandwich or can of beer. Finding no more yummies, they lose interest and swim away. Unless the resumed line just happens to catch their attention, or it attracts other customers, all the earlier effort was a waste.

Another tip: Whenever possible, chum in an area where there's little or no chance of boats cutting across the line and possibly interrupting it. Outside in ocean waters or on large, open bays you won't have any trouble—except, maybe, from an occasional yahoo who doesn't know any better. But in more or less confined waterways with heavy weekend boating traffic you may have a problem, particularly if you're drifting while chumming. Under such circumstances it's better to do your chumming on weekdays, when fewer boats are in operation, if you can. The only alternative on a busy weekend is to seek out areas with minimum traffic.

Although frequency of chum distribution in any kind of angling is governed by current velocity or by the boat's speed if she's drifting, or both, there's a general rule of thumb you can follow: Ladle or drop your chum overboard in a small quantity right alongside the boat, wait until it almost disappears from view, then repeat, and so on, continuously. You'll be able to adjust your rhythm, chumming faster or slower as required.

More tips: (1) When you're about to start a chum line with the boat at anchor, let her settle down first to see which way she's going to ride in the current and breeze. Then chum on one side or in the stern, as the case may be. (2) When the boat is drifting, chum on the side *away from* the direction in which she's moving. The idea behind this is that the boat won't glide over the chum right after it's dropped, possibly scattering it prematurely. Ideally it also should be a side away from the wind, but this isn't always possible, notably in instances when it's wind, not current, causing the drift. But don't worry about any breeze that may be blowing on your chumming side. If you drop your chum overboard with reasonable care the wind won't strew it in midair.

Ground mossbunkers are a standard chum for bluefish. The pulp also attracts several other species, including mackerel, bluefin tuna, albacore, bonito, and sharks.

Since it comes in cans, the pulp is tightly packed. Using it in this concentrated form is neither necessary nor economical. Besides, you only want to tease your intended opponents' appetite, not fill their bellies so they'll ignore your bait. This chum should be diluted. Simply add small amounts of sea water, stirring it in and breaking up any large chunks until you create a mixture with the consistency of stew. If the can is too full at the start, take some out for the time being. You don't have to dilute the can's entire contents right off the bat. Mix the sea water as you go along, just enough to give you a ready supply of stew. Any container big enough to hold about a teacupful of this witch's brew will do as a ladle. Many skippers nail a can on the end of a stick eighteen inches long or so. It serves nicely—it's cheap and easily replaced too.

Ladle this 'bunker stew overboard, letting it drop into the water alongside the boat. *Don't sling it.* Slinging it as though you were sowing grass seed gives any breeze a chance to scatter it, probably half of it on the boat or on you. It's wasteful and messy. As each ladleful plops into the water it will begin to spread outward and downward, carried away as a cloud of meat tidbits, body juices, blood, and oil globules, all an *aperitif* to fishes. Just before that little cloud begins to move out of sight, drop another ladleful, and so on.

Whatever the chum involved, always give a line a reasonable chance to produce—I'd say at least an hour—before abandoning it for another locale.

In bluefishing you'll find that chumming works in two ways. It can draw fish from some distance, or it can halt a school that happens to be passing at the time. When it stops a passing school, especially a sizable one, its frequency often has to be stepped up. Blues on the run move swiftly. If you manage to detain such a galloping group momentarily, you'll have to feed the stuff to them at an accelerated rate to hold them; otherwise they'll take off like jets. I've seen everyone aboard get into the chumming act when a school of blues was stopped, fishing with one hand and plopping chum overboard with the other, busier than the proverbial one-armed paperhanger with hives. Such instances, by the way, are another good reason for having an ample supply of chum. I suspect that when an appreciable number of boats chum an area regularly, day after day, it helps considerably to keep schools in that place.

TACKLE AND RIGGING FOR BLUEFISH CHUMMING   Bluefish chumming usually operates with the boat at anchor. (But let me add quickly that there's no law that says it can't be tried while drifting.) Because it's a method that can attract the largest blues, tackle must be sturdy enough to absorb the punishment those bruisers mete out. Any bluefish, even little guys, are tough customers. The heftier choppers are real slammers.

That's why I do not recommend spinning tackle for bluefishing by less-experienced anglers when any of the heftier fish are around. Sure, there's spinning gear to handle even the heaviest blues; and light-caliber weapons in the hands of a seasoned wielder will cope with the toughest of 'em. And it's great sport. But I still won't suggest it for fishermen with little experience, and definitely not for green beginners. Even in capable hands spinning tackle is likely to require more time than conventional tackle in which to land a bluefish, if for no other reason than that a chopper may be hard to control. Among the results can be tangled lines and all sorts of foulups. From these comes a vexation all around, more calculated to make enemies than friends.

Also to be considered in this bluefishing technique is the possibility of chum attracting school tuna, albacore, and even sharks of considerable size. I've known big mako sharks—up to 400 pounds-plus—wander into a chum line out for mackerel. Now, you can't be expected to fish for blues with equipment husky enough to cope with beasts that size, but if your bluefishing gear is sturdy enough—and you know how to wield it—it can handle albacore and some of the smaller bluefin tuna.

I'd suggest medium-caliber boat or all-purpose conventional tackle: Say, a rod rated for 20- or 30-pound lines, or even to 40-pound test if you don't mind sacrificing some sport with blues to a possibility of tangling with appreciably heavier fishes. On your rod you can mount a 2/0 or 3/0 reel on which you've spooled 100 or so yards, maybe 150, of line.

If you persist in the idea of wielding spinning tackle, in spite of what I've said, the selection of weapons is yours. You can swing one of those medium-weight fiberglass sticks, 7½ feet long or so, and matching reel. Just be sure your rod can handle the maximum-strength line you might use. You can go to lighter gear if you want added thrills, accompanied by increased chances of losing fish. Or, conversely, you can fish one of the heavier combinations. That will still give you action while shaving the odds in favor of lost blues. Your line will be monofilament, and its strength will be your choice up into the 20- or 30-pound class: or, if you want to play it close to the vest, 40-pound test.

If you should use spinning tackle for blues, and a 40-to-50-pound school tuna grabs your bait, don't say I didn't warn you . . . and don't come around sniveling and tugging at my sleeve.

The terminal outfit employed in bluefish chumming couldn't be much more basic. There are two fundamental rigs. I'll label them "A" and "B." You can vary them as you see fit.

"A" consists merely of a hook attached to about 6 feet of wire leader. That leader, in turn, can be connected to your line through a two-loop barrel swivel or—better yet, as I've pointed out—via a snap swivel. In bluefishing the latter has a double advantage. Not only does it let you change rigs in a hurry when action is fast and furious and your bait has been mangled or stolen, it's also helpful when you don't want to take time to unhook a blue you've just caught.

CHUMMING RIG

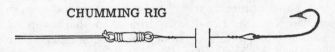

Chumming rig "B" is just a variation of "A," but is favored by some bluefishermen for daylight angling in clear water because of its lesser visibility. Here a 3-foot length of monofilament, about the same strength as the line and up to, say, 40-pound test, is substituted for the wire leader, tying it into the line as outlined for "A." And since we still must have protection against our toothy friends' sharp fangs, we use extra-long-shanked hooks. They're the type used for imbedding in metal squids, and can be bought separately.

A variation of "B" for a spinning outfit suggests 6 to 8 inches of wire between monofilament line and hook, the short leader being preferred because of its easier handling. Should a leader be desired (although I can't see why it's necessary if you're using monofilament anyway), you can follow the example of some anglers who vary the setup further by interposing 6, 8, or 10 feet of mono, in somewhat greater strength than the line, as a low-visibility leader between wire and line.

Bluefish chumming hooks run a gamut of sizes, gauged approximately to the general weight range of the opponents expected. Thus a 2/0 to 4/0 can be rigged for smaller-to-medium blues, and a 6/0 to 8/0 for heavier rascals. The main thing is that they're strong enough. If big blues are around, better have some hooks up to at least a 6/0 along.

CHUMMING BAITS When they're hungry, bluefish will accept a wide variety of baits. In chumming, a piece of mossbunker is good because it matches the chum, so to speak. Not as effective is a piece of one of the other species you might be using as ground chum. A cut piece of butterfish is another good bait. Blues like those little fish too, and they're sold in packages for baiting. Really small butterfish can be impaled on a hook whole. Those that run more than about 2 inches long can be cut into halves or generous pieces. If you have plenty of butterfish aboard, cut some into small pieces to fortify your chum line at intervals.

BOTTOM FISHING Mention of this time-honored procedure in connection with bluefish may lift some eyebrows, even among regulars. But there are occasions when neither chumming nor trolling is particularly effective. Sometimes blues go very deep, maybe to feed down near the sea floor. Ordinary deep trolling doesn't reach them; chumming can't raise them. Sometimes it will take place unpredictably during a run's early phases. Or it can happen toward the end of a run, especially if there has been a fairly severe storm. When blues go that deep there's a procedure that has a chance of reaching them. It's good old-fashioned sinker-bouncing, done at anchor.

The idea is the same as in fishing for any bottom species: Get those baited hooks down to where the fish are. I can suggest two rigs.

The first arrangement is superior in strong current, and with Dacron line its drag is lessened. On the end of your line tie a drail as its sinker. Its required weight will be dictated by current strength on the grounds fished. The important thing is that it be heavy enough to keep your rig on bottom. Drails come with swivels at either end for attachment. To the remaining swivel on your drail attach 2½ to 3½ feet of monofilament of about the same strength as your line. This will serve as a low-visibility leader. The mono is followed by 6 inches of No. 6 wire as a bite-proof leader. At the end of that goes a 6/o or 7/o hook, baited with a piece of butterfish or mossbunker.

The second rig resembles one used for fluke. At the end of your line is tied a standard bank type sinker of sufficient weight to hold bottom in the area fished. About 4 to 6 feet above the sinker on the line, tie in this "subassembly": 3 feet of monofilament (approximately the same strength as your line) as a leader, 6 inches of No. 6 wire, and a 5/o to 7/o hook. Attachment of the mono leader can be made directly to the line or through a three-loop swivel. Use of a swivel offers an advantage because it lessens fouling of leader and line. This rig also can be baited with a piece of butterfish or 'bunker.

Your tackle for bottom bluefishing can be in the medium range, as long as the rod has enough backbone to handle fairly heavy rigs and large bluefish. Again I'd rule out a spinning rod because of its willowyness. Favor a conventional stick, such as a boat rod able to take lines to 30-pound test or so, and a 3/o reel. Twenty-to-30-pound line, 100 to 150 yards, should suffice.

DEEP CHUMMING I've set this apart from the other bluefish chumming because it's a specialized technique and allied, in a way, with bottom angling.

Deep chumming can be brought into play when it's suspected that blues may be lurking near the ocean floor. It's done with the boat at anchor and is an alternate to deep trolling when the latter isn't possible. It also can be tried for other bottom-roving species.

In essence it's the creation of a vertical chum line, used in conjunction with a regular chum slick. Its sole advantage over the latter is that it goes deeper.

This vertical chumming consists of filling a meshed bag—such as those that oranges and onions come in, except with a finer mesh—with ground mossbunkers (or, if that pulp isn't available, try some other kind of ground-up fishes such as mackerel, whiting, etc.), weighting it with sinkers, and attaching it to a length of stout twine. This chumpot is lowered to the sea floor, where it's bounced to release some of its chum through the mesh. Then it's gradually raised toward the surface, and jerked like a Yo-Yo on the way up to release more of the chum. This procedure sometimes helps to lure blues up from deep water to baited rigs waiting in a regular chum line.

Old-timers will tell you about a variation in which a few strong paper bags are filled with chum, plus a weighty stone in each as a sinker. Each is tied to a length of twine or old fishing line. The first bag is lowered all the way to the bottom. En route it becomes weakened by water soaking, and when it reaches the bottom a tug on its line causes it to rupture and discharge its contents. A second bag is lowered to an arbitrary level so many feet above the first, and its contents released. The procedure is repeated with other bags at increasingly shallower planes until a vertical chum line has been set up between sea floor and surface. This too can be a magnet drawing blues up from the "cellar."

A third stunt works along the same lines. For this you mix some beach sand in with a quantity of your stew made from 'bunker pulp and sea water. The mixture is ladled overboard just as when establishing a regular chum line. You are, in fact, doing that too, but with this difference: Your chum goes out as usual, but the beach sand, being heavier, sinks to the bottom. And since it has sopped up some of the oil and scent from the 'bunker pulp it becomes a kind of chum too. The result is two chum lines, one traveling outward with the current as usual, the other sinking vertically alongside the boat. This also helps a bit to stretch a supply of fish pulp chum.

Tackle and rigs for deep chumming can be the same as for bottom bluefishing.

SURF FISHING Every angler entertains an idea of the sportiest fishing method. But one declaration that will meet no argument is to say that surfcasting for blues is in a class by itself. Tying into a big, rough, tough, bluefish in a white water surf is real, basic, toe-to-toe combat with a finned opponent. Many fishermen would rather catch blues (and striped bass) that way than by any other method. Be advised, though, that it places demands on skill, which is why some tournaments pay more points for surf-caught fish than for those landed on boats.

At times bluefish move in close to a beach. Even curling breakers hold no terror for them when they're determined to fill their stomachs. It will pay you to "read the surf" for signs of bluefish activity. Here again you look for gulls and other sea birds concentrating on a patch of water beyond the breakers. Birds swooping and squabbling can indicate the presence of a marauding band of blues below them. I should add, though, that unless the fish are a safe distance beneath the surface the birds may not be diving. Even they seem to have instinctive respect for choppers' teeth. Active birds, incidentally, also can herald the surface or subsurface presence of striped bass, also pursuing prey. Not uncommonly the two species are encountered in the same area.

Lacking such winged signals, you can study the surf for other clues. Here's where a pair of Polaroid sunglasses comes in handy to cut surface glare. If you can get up on a high dune nearby, so much the better. One sign to watch for is a top-water ruckus caused by the fish themselves as they plunder a school of smaller fish. Another is a surface disturbance caused by tide rips. These often are marked by white water, eddies, and swirls. Most of the time you'll spot them quite readily. Tide rips can be generated by several different combinations of conditions, such as a collision of opposing tidal currents, as at an inlet's mouth or at a point of land; a strong tide bucking the wind; and a strong current meeting opposition from a point of land, shoreside structure, or a sand bar. Bluefish often lurk in such places, waiting for confused little neighbors to be swirled their way.

"White water" is a busy sea, not necessarily heaving with large waves but active enough to create some whitecaps and foam. Winds and currents are its creators. White water areas can produce blues because here again small fishes are tumbled around in the turbulence, often helpless and confused. Bluefish know this and prowl the perimeter, looking for victims forced their way. Blues aren't exactly ninnies, you see.

Look for white water turbulence around sand bars lying just off and parallel to an oceanfront beach, around points of land—even jetties and groins—jutting out into the ocean or into channels and bays where there's a free-wheeling tide, and around inlets—at their outside and inside mouths, as well as in the waterways proper. And mark this: Striped bass also are fond of food shopping in white water places, so be prepared for those too. There's never a guarantee that you'll nail fish in such areas, but they demand a try.

Tip: Study beforehand any stretch of beach you plan to fish, whatever the species sought. Note its configuration. Consider the beach's slope—note whether it's gradual or steep. Look for sand bars (water over them is lighter) and points of land where there may be current rips at certain tides or in wind. Watch too for current-eroded sloughs, those deeper troughs—detected by their somewhat darker water—that may extend seaward from a beach or lie along either side of a sand bar, parallel to shore. Such sloughs can harbor smaller fishes that draw blues and striped bass. In general, note the deeper and shoaler areas along the beach. Varying degrees of darkening of the water's color are clues to its depths. Whenever possible, climb the highest sand dune in the vicinity to scan the beach. Its added height will give you superior visibility. Last but not least, study your beach at different tides and under varying conditions of weather and wind.

A *word to the wise:* The best surf fishermen are those who know their beaches like the palms of their hands. Moreover, it becomes especially helpful to familiarize yourself with a stretch of beach beforehand when you go night surf fishing.

PLACES AND FRUSTRATIONS Sooner or later you'll face the frustrating circumstance of seeing unmistakable evidence of bluefish activity, or maybe a strong potential, out beyond casting distance. Don't work yourself into a snit. That won't bring 'em in. If the looked-for sign is a tide rip, forget it—you can't reach it— and move on. If the signal is birds working or a commotion caused by fish, keep your eye on it, following it along the beach if necessary. The fish could move within casting distance at any time as they pursue prey. If it becomes obvious they won't, look elsewhere.

Around inlets—along oceanfronts too—bluefish activity frequently is a hit-and-run deal, with the choppers on a fast march. This is especially true in inlets, where blues tend to move in and out in a hurry when searching for food or chasing it. You may get only a few minutes' action as a school whips by. That's why, more often than not, surf angling for blues at inlets is an instance of being in the right place at the right time. It can be a sometime proposition, with much left to luck.

But you can bolster your chances by fishing an inlet frequently, testing various locations and noting correlations between tides and showings of the fish. It's possible to have two cracks at inlet bluefish, once when they come in and again when they leave. Inlets are most likely to be productive when they have a fairly deep channel and there are brisk tidal flows in and out. The greater the volume of water sluicing through an inlet, the more food fishes it can transport to lure blues (and striped bass).

Naturally you're going to try different spots along an inlet, both sides. But if one side has a deeper channel or cut, while its counterpart has shallower water, a common condition in inlets, favor the former. Fish different stations along the gateway's shores at various phases of tides. *Tip:* Try a place near the inside mouth as the tide builds toward its peak. When the tide turns and begins to ebb, take a position at the outside mouth.

Here's an interesting fragment of bluefishing lore, for whatever it's worth to you: It's been said that bluefish are "left-eyed" or "left-handed feeders." In other words, they tend to be more attracted to prey they see with their left eye or are on their left side. The theory's proponents suggest presenting a bait or lure to bluefish on their left side whenever possible. In practice that could influence your choice of which side of an inlet to fish. Conceivably it might also have something to say about how you'd approach a bluefish school when trolling.

Although optimum bluefishing times generally are during early-morning hours, in late afternoon, in the evening, and at night, this doesn't necessarily mean that you won't contact blues along a beach during a day's warmer hours, but, rather, that your chances might be better at those other times.

Tides are a factor you'll reckon with in surf bluefishing. Because they're extremely active feeders, blues usually respond best during some phase of a free-wheeling tide, rather than at slack water. It can be a falling tide or a rising phase, so long as it's moving. The brisker it flows, the better. Although there are always exceptions, the more productive periods along surf fronts and inlets generally occur during the last hour or two of a rising tide and the ensuing hour or two as the tide ebbs.

SURF TACKLE   Your choice of weapons will be influenced by certain factors, but selection isn't as involved as it might sound. Between you and me, *any* surf fishing gear—and a lot of boat tackle too, conventional and spinning—will take bluefish. It's just that a few recommendations better suit the tools to the job.

As I was saying, a few factors can have a say in the surf tackle you employ for blues—or any species, for that matter. Prominent among them is the artificial or bait you're using. Obviously, tackle has to be reasonably sturdy to fling the heavier plugs and big come-ons such as eels and eelskin rigs. And that would rule out much of the lighter spinning and conventional equipment.

You also should give thought to the size range of blues currently running, bearing in mind that even if the majority of fish being landed are in a range up to only six pounds there's always a chance of tying into rod-benders going ten pounds or more. Too, there's the possibility that striped bass weighing up into the teens, twenties, even thirty or forty pounds or more, will find your offering interesting. Your tackle has to be able to cope with those muscular gents.

Frequently emphasis (too much, if you ask me) is placed on casting distance as a prerequisite of surf tackle. True, there are places and times when considerable casting distance is a must to reach fish, or when breezes pose a problem. By and large, however, most of the surf catches you take home to brag about will be nailed within a hundred feet or so from where you're standing. Too, your reach will be extended if you can wade into the surf or get out on a jetty. So don't figure you have to be Olympics casting material to achieve success in surf fishing.

In average use you can wield medium-caliber conventional or spinning surf equipment. When heavier lures and/or appreciable casting distance are involved, you'll probably have to go to heavier gear. Conversely, for small lures and relatively short casts you can go to lighter tackle, including rod-reel combinations you'd fish aboard boat. In that latter instance, though, keep in mind the potential weights of the fishes being sought. Arguing a husky striped bass or bluefish in through breakers can be tougher than from a boat.

You can go to 20-, 30-, even 40-pound lines (so long as your rod is rated to handle them). The larger sizes often are preferred to minimize abrasion problems when fishing rocky places. For such areas some anglers favor monofilament over braided lines for the same reason. Mono is less likely than braided line to rub through on contact with rocks. An alternative to going to a heavier line is to interpose 10 yards or so of mono, in about the same strength as the line or somewhat heavier, between lure or leader and line, if your line is a braided type. If your line is monofilament, that interposed length of mono can be somewhat heavier, say 10 pounds or thereabouts. Figure on 150 to 200 yards of main line. You want a comfortable amount on the reel spool in case your opponent takes it into his head to tear off on long runs. With a comfortable surplus you won't have as much of that automatic drag-tightening effect that comes with less and less line on the spool.

SURF RIGS FOR BLUES   Among basic surf rigs are two commonly employed. One is for fishing bottom with bait. The other is brought into service with artificials. They can be used for any surf-run species calling for those techniques.

An old faithful for bait surfing is a simple one used by such

KRONUCH SURF RIG

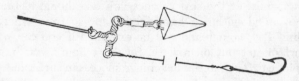

experts as Johnny Kronuch, veteran beach fisherman and head man in Johnny's Tackle Shop, Montauk.

A distinguishing component of this and other surf bottom fishing rigs is a pyramid sinker, so designed to dig in and hold bottom against surges of waves, undertows, and currents. The swivel is a "three-way" or three-loop style. The connector attaching swivel to sinker has a sliding collar that allows it to be opened and closed easily for quick change of sinker weights, a handy feature when you discover you need more to keep your rig on bottom. (Carry pyramid sinkers in a graduated selection of weights.

You may require up to five ounces or more.) Completing this terminal outfit is a wire leader, about fourteen inches long (say, twelve to fifteen), securing hook to swivel. The swivel's remaining loop is reserved for your line.

A variation of the foregoing setup is the so-called fish-finder rig. It will give you a lot of service in surf bottom angling and can be used for practically any species thus encountered. For its details I refer you to the chapter on striped bass, with this important memo: A wire leader is a must for blues with this rig too.

Surf-run bluefish will respond to several different baits. The list includes: piece of mossbunker, mullet, or herring; strip of squid; whole small butterfish or half a large one; small bait fishes such as sand eels and silversides or spearing; a chunk of blueclaw crab in the shedder or soft shell state; and a strip cut from the lighter underside of some schooling species such as mackerel. With some baits, notably those with soft or mushy flesh, it may be necessary to secure them to the hook with a few turns of strong thread to lessen their disintegration during use.

Live baits such as killies and small crabs will take blues too, and in fact are favored by some anglers because of their lifelike action in the water. Eels and eelskin rigs, long-time attractors for striped bass, also are rigged in surf bluefishing and are especially effective on choppers in evening and night angling. Eels are nocturnal feeders, a habit that hasn't escaped the notice of bluefish and stripers. Whole eels and eelskin rigs are weighty and demand tackle sturdy enough to cast and work them. They're discussed in the chapter on striped bass.

When surf bluefishing along an open beach, or at an inlet or on a jetty, whether using natural baits or artificials, you want to place your come-on where it will do the most good. If you can lob it near a school of feeding blues, great; otherwise you'll have to seek out such tide rips and sloughs as I mentioned earlier. In bait fishing, the current will impart some action to your offering. You can enhance it by occasionally lifting your rod tip and by alternately reeling in a few feet of line and letting it drift out again.

The other of the two basic surf bluefishing rigs is that for artificial lures. It too is simple. Components of a common form of this outfit are a wire leader about eight to ten inches long (that somewhat shorter length is easier to handle with artificials), a hook of suitable size, and a snap swivel between leader and line. Here again a snap swivel is superior to a standard two-loop barrel swivel (which can be used) because it facilitates changing of lures, a process sometimes necessary to determine which will elicit the best response. Therein is a cue to carry at least a small assortment of artificials, including some for stripers when they're in the same area. The snap swivel goes on the end of your line. Connection is made by means of a small loop in your wire leader.

Rigging for surf spinning is essentially the same as in fishing of artificials with conventional gear. But here's something you might try: Between your wire leader and line tie in twenty feet or so of somewhat heavier line than that on your reel. Why? Because it will lessen chances of your main line popping during the first part of a vigorous cast and during the final phase of combat when a rambunctious blue is being coaxed to the beach.

There's a little army of man-designed lures that will take surf blues. Among them you'll find: metal squids of various types, such as one molded to simulate the undulating form of a sand eel, in graduated weights, and often chrome-plated for greater eye-catching talent; bucktails and jigs of assorted kinds; and plugs, including surface and subsurface types, divers and deep runners, darters, poppers, etc. Some have jointed bodies to increase their wiggle. Others are designed to mimic an injured fish's movements. And so on. They come in a rainbow of colors and color combinations, with various finishes. The heavier models are for conventional tackle. There are light, scaled-down versions for spinning equipment.

Since surf lures are variables that change from place to place and time to time, it's wise to check at *local* tackle shops when making your selections. Often you'll be able to choose artificials that are also effective on stripers and other surf-running gamesters. Generally speaking, metal squids are good. You should have an assortment of those anyway, in different designs and weights. A tackle dealer's plug recommendations are particularly valuable because frequently specific models bring better results than others.

TECHNIQUE POINTERS   Bluefish are aggressive hunters and delight in moving prey (it arouses their competitive instinct). Therefore, you should always keep your artificial in motion, *whatever kind it may be.* In this respect surf angling for blues is like trolling, except that here you'll have an advantage in that you'll be better able to control your lure's action and speed.

Any movement of a surf lure, including its own peculiar antics, is up to you and will be effected on a retrieve. You cast your lure to where you want it, then reel it in to impart action. That's why a retrieve should be started the instant an artificial hits the water. Seasoned surf fishermen sometimes begin their retrieve during the final seconds of a cast, while the lure is still airborne. This requires precise timing, throwing the reel from free spool into gear just seconds before the artificial plops into the water. But it's tough on reel gears, and really isn't necessary. It will suffice if you start your retrieve the instant of "touchdown." By day you'll be able to see that instant. At night you'll have to rely upon hearing it, or by guessing as best you can.

The fastest, surest way you can begin your retrieve when your lure hits the water is to immediately step back a pace or two, simultaneously lifting your rod tip a few inches. As you do, you engage the reel's clutch (the reel was in free spool when you cast), and with your hand on the crank you're ready to retrieve at once. A bluefish strike can come at the precise instant your lure starts moving back toward the beach.

For the most part, bluefish artificials are retrieved at a moderately brisk pace. But retrieve rates vary and are influenced by certain factors. The type of lure is one, together with the depth at which you want it to travel. For instance, a metal squid is heavy and consequently tends to sink. Therefore, a somewhat faster cranking will be required if you want to fish that lure in upper levels. Similarly, along a gradually shelving beach you'll have to retrieve a sinking-type artificial rather rapidly to keep it up where you want it. Conversely, on a beach that drops off abruptly into deeper water you may find a slower retrieve effective. The nature of a surf running at the time and its undertow (a dragging effect away from the beach) are also factors, along with currents, since waves can push a lure toward the

beach. Currents move it this way and that, and an undertow
tends to pull it to seaward.

You can be guided by any instructions that accompany an
artificial. Often manufacturers advise how best to work their
lures. A tackle dealer will give you helpful suggestions too. But
they can't possibly account for every combination of conditions.
Surf moods change. That's why it will pay you to experiment
with retrieve speeds. Start arbitrarily with a moderate rate. If
that doesn't produce after a fair trial, have a go at faster and
slower speeds. Sometimes a combination of all three will give a
lure an erratic action that tickles a bluefish's fancy.

Whatever your artificial, the most important things are these:
(1) Keep it constantly in motion. (2) Retrieve it at a rate that
best capitalizes on its built-in action. (3) Never allow any slack
line when retrieving. Should a bluefish smack your lure during
slack, he could throw the hook or get off it before you could
tighten your line.

SURF HOOKS   Sizes are about the same for both a natural bait and
an artificial. Patterns differ according to personal preferences.
Another major variation is that a standard bait rig calls for a
single hook, whereas artificials may carry more than one. Too,
hooks employed in bait and lure fishing with the lighter spinning gear are scaled-down versions of those used with conventional tackle. In general, surf bluefish hooks range from about a
2/o or 3/o on the smaller side upward to a 6/o, a scope that
will handle just about any blues you nail beyond the breakers.
When equipment or preference dictates, an angler can inject an
added measure of safety with the smaller hooks by using those of
double, even triple, strength.

PLAYING THE BLUES   When a bluefish grabs your bait or artificial
in the surf, the blueprint for battle is essentially the same as when
boat fishing. Control him as best you can, don't try to force him
in when he's on his power surges, retrieve line whenever possible,
and never allow any slack. In combat here you'll have a little
more latitude than on a boat because you can follow your fish
along the beach when necessary.

The final phase can be tricky. Now you have to be doubly

careful about slack line developing. The bluefish may cause it by suddenly running toward the boat, perhaps to ease the hook's pressure. Or, if he's fighting at the surface, waves may thrust him beachward. Let him take yardage when he insists upon it. Keep your line taut at other times. When you've argued him in close enough in the breakers' wash you can clinch victory by gaffing him. Lacking a gaff, at least let him get out of the breakers' clutch before you try to unhook him. Be extremely wary about trying to complete the capture by grasping a blue with your bare hand. More than one surfcaster has been bitten that way.

GENERAL SURF FISHING TIPS 1. Some artificials are most effective by day, others get better response at night. Some types produce at both times. Certain models elicit more response early in a run, while others come into their own later on. Those are more reasons for your making inquiries in areas you want to fish.

2. An old rule of thumb has it that working a lure in daylight and/or clear, calm water should be faster than at night and/or in rough or murky water. The theory is that an artificial must be retrieved faster in conditions of better visibility to prevent the fish from getting close enough to the attractor to discover it's a fake. In conditions of poor visibility the slower retrieve is intended to give a fish a better chance to spot the come-on.

3. If I've given an impression that there's no one all-purpose artificial for surf bluefishing, and no single, fixed method for working same, it was deliberate. I want you to start building a collection of lures. Don't go hog wild. You can start with a modest assortment of versatile models. It will be a worthwhile expenditure because it will better equip you for your sport, thereby adding to enjoyment and success.

BAY BLUEFISHING By and large, blues of the open sea are the family's larger, more muscular members, while those fish invading inlets, bays, and harbors are the younger, smaller individuals. (Maybe, being younger, they're more reckless.) There are exceptions, of course. Not uncommonly blues in an oceangoing school will be in the 3-to-6-pound class. Conversely, big slammers come into inlets and sheltered waters on occasion.

Never underrate smaller blues because they fall short of their big brothers in avoirdupois. They're just as scrappy and tricky. The over-all size range of bay and inlet blues is from 1½ or 2 pounds to 4 and 5, occasionally 6. And, as I just pointed out, there are chances of heavier choppers.

Bay bluefishing's principal techniques are trolling and chumming, the latter either at anchor or while drifting. Jigging can be done too. We'll get to that later.

Bay chumming for blues is done in the same fashion as in ocean angling. Ground mossbunkers make good chum here too. You also can use killies and/or spearing, chopped fine. A chum line is established precisely as outlined earlier. The only thing is, in enclosed waterways such as bays, channels, and inlets you may have a problem finding a location where other boats won't cut across your chum line.

Bay blues dine on killies, spearing, small herring, and other available little fishes. So they can be used for bait. Live killies are especially good because of their action and hardiness. To keep them alive, however, requires careful hooking; you'll find details in the chapter on fluke. Spearing, a common bait, are almost impossible to keep alive on a hook. You'll have to compensate by using the freshest possible spearing. Buy them alive if possible. Use packaged, frozen spearing as a second-best alternate. Also used, notably during periodic killy shortages, are pieces of mossbunker, shedder crab, and butterfish. Strips cut from the undersides of snappers and larger bluefish have drawn results too.

Trolling for bay blues is the same procedure as when "scratching" the ocean for larger choppers. The major difference is that you can wield lighter equipment, conventional or spinning. Everything is scaled down, you see. Even the lures are smaller. These artificials include small plugs, feathers, and spoons. The lure is rigged on a short, fine wire leader connected to the line via a snap swivel or two-loop barrel swivel.

For bay bluefishing you have plenty of leeway in tackle. A light, all-purpose boat rod, conventional kind, with a 1/0 reel will handle most bay blues. So will light-to-medium spinning gear. Your line can be light. Ten-pound-test monofilament or braided line will serve nicely. The general range of hook sizes is from a 1/0 for smaller fish to a 3/0 or 4/0. You can go up to a 5/0 or 6/0 for the very largest blues, the real tackle-wallopers.

OTHER BLUEFISHING METHODS

BOAT CASTING   Great sport, this can be done anywhere—in bays, channels, inlets, around tide rips, in sounds, and in the ocean beyond the breakers. It's done with the craft anchored so that an artificial or bait can be cast into a school or likely place. That means that you need good ground tackle—anchor and line—to hold your boat in position.

Boat casting beyond the surf has an obvious advantage in being able to contact fish that can't be reached from shore; and it often accounts for heavyweights. It also has drawbacks. The boat's anchor system must be able to hold her securely. Most important, your boat must have a dependable engine, just in case. I don't think I have to draw a picture of what could happen in the event of engine failure just off a surf. Because this kind of fishing entails a risk, doubly so in rocky areas, I suggest that you either be an experienced boatman or go with someone who is.

Plugs and spoons are popular boat casting attractors, and they run a gamut of types and sizes. You also can try any of the standard natural baits for bluefish. The idea is to place your offering close to—or, better yet, in among—a school, or to flip it into a place where you think they might be skulking. Be alert for schools surfacing nearby. In fishing a surf a procedure is to maneuver safely beyond the breakers' grasp and cast in toward them. Always, of course, an artificial has to be worked, and some action should be imparted to a natural bait.

Bait casting tackle is good. Spinning gear gives lots of action. All-purpose boat tackle is okay. Gauge your line to the sizes of the blues. Rig simply with a short wire leader.

FISHING FROM A SHORESIDE STRUCTURE   Possibilities are offered by docks, piers, bulkheads, channel banks, and seawalls, where there are enough food and current activity to draw the hungry rascals. Mostly these are two-to-four-pound scrappers, occasionally laced with heavier specimens. On a seawall you might be lucky enough to get into arguments with blues up to ten or twelve pounds and better.

Tackle is the same as for bay bluefishing, and you have a choice of two basic techniques. In both you rig as you would for chumming: a short wire leader between line and lure or bait. If line other than monofilament is used, try a couple of feet of low-visibility mono between leader and line. In any case, connection at the line can be made directly or through a small standard swivel. Hook sizes go from a 1/o or 2/o to 3/o or 4/o, up to 5/o and 6/o when bluefish weights merit it. Good in bait fishing is a hook with a spiked shank to better hold the offering.

Both techniques can be employed on a boat or on an inlet shore where there's a tidal flow.

In one method your bait or artificial is allowed to ride out into the current's mainstream. Leave it there for a few minutes, then reel it in a little way, pause again, retrieve some more line, and so on. The current's thrust gives the attractor constant movement, and retrieving contributes to an illusion of an edible creature struggling in the flow. A very brisk current will tend to shove the lure or bait upward toward the surface, maybe higher than you want it. Correct for this by adding a small, fractional-ounce, pinch-on sinker or two on your line to carry the rig deeper. Don't position the weight too close to the hook or it will interfere with the attractor's action.

In this technique a live killy is often effective. And, as in other kinds of live-bait fishing, many anglers favor a finer-diameter hook to lessen chances of killing or injuring the bait. In any case, caution must be exercised when impaling any live fish on your hook. A worthwhile addition to this rig is a small cork affixed a couple of feet ahead of the bait to offset the wire leader's weight and drag on the killy.

In the other method you cast across the tidal flow, either at a right angle or obliquely. Here the effect is rather like that in trolling, with the current giving motion to the lure or bait; but the difference is that you retrieve. It's a good idea to try different retrieve speeds while working the lure or bait with your rod tip.

JIGGING This procedure takes two forms. One occurs during trolling—I call it jig trolling—and supplements that technique. The other is a method in itself.

Jigging while trolling can be a helpful assist when out after bluefish, striped bass, and other species. All it consists of is alternately lifting the rod tip a short distance and letting the lure drop back, in a more or less continuous process. Its advantage is that it gives some extra motion to the attractor. I can tell you, though, that if you do it constantly, hour after hour, it becomes fatiguing. Do it for a while, then take a breather before going back to it.

The other kind of jigging, a technique in itself, is a method usable for mackerel, sea bass, porgies (scup), and other kinds of sport fishes, in addition to blues. It can be done at anchor or while drifting, and its sole purpose is to impart attractive action to a lure or natural bait. It isn't a prime bluefishing technique, but it's effective at times.

"Standard" jigging calls for an artificial known as a diamond jig. It's an old, popular lure deriving its name from its vague resemblance to a diamond—elongated. Diamond jigs are slender for their length, many of them being thickest in the middle and tapering toward their ends, and quite heavy, going up to eight ounces and more. Most commonly their bodies are of lead. Many models have a bright chrome plating to enhance their eye-catching ability. Frequently anglers try out their own ideas by dressing up a jig with a bright-colored feather, or even a little piece of red cloth, to add even more attraction. Jigs' hook armament varies. One model has a single, fixed hook imbedded in its body. Another carries a treble or gang hook—three hooks in one, like a sand anchor or grappling iron—swinging at its free end. All diamond jigs have a loop or swiveling arrangement for attachment to a line.

Whatever its size and hook armament, a diamond jig's function is to look like a little food fish to its prospective victims. That's why it's important that it maintains a shiny surface to draw attention. Jigs with lead bodies, no plating, become dull in time, and therefore should be scraped or lightly sanded at intervals to bring out their glitter again. Jigs that are made from bright metal or are chrome-plated retain their luster. It's also important that a diamond jig be kept in motion to further add to the illusion of a small, live creature. That's where jigging comes in.

There are various jigging procedures, all substantially the same. One basic jigging technique consists merely of letting the jig go to the bottom by throwing the reel into free spool. When the lure hits bottom, the reel's clutch is engaged. Jigging is accomplished by repeatedly lifting the rod tip and letting the lure drop back to thud on the bottom. When it's desirable to cover levels higher off the bottom, the jig can be cranked upward a few feet, then allowed to return by throwing the reel into free spool. When the lure hits bottom, the reel is thrown into gear and the cycle is repeated.

In another basic jigging technique, just a variation of the one just described, the jig may be cranked all the way to the surface before being allowed to fall back to the bottom. But this too is a continuous process.

Both methods have their applications.

Several layers of water, from bottom to top, can be covered by reeling the jig upward a few feet, pausing to make it dance with the rod tip, cranking the lure higher, pausing to jig it again, and so on until near the surface. Then the jig is lowered to the bottom and the whole process repeated.

Use of the reel—rather than just lifting of the rod's tip—often becomes necessary in deep-water jigging in places where a fairly strong current is running. In that circumstance, you see, you have so much line out that merely lifting the rod tip would serve only to take a little of the "bellying" or curve out of the line, and no movement would be given to the lure.

In bluefish jigging keep your lure constantly in motion, up and down like a nonstop elevator. If a blue is going to hit he's likely to do it while the jig is going through that elevator routine. Try jigging through various levels, from the very bottom on upward. By such experimenting you'll cover a number of different planes, including those at which deep blues (often the larger ones) may be traveling.

At first, raise the jig only a couple of feet off bottom before letting it drop back. Then try reeling it a bit higher, and so on. If necessary, you can keep rough track of the heights to which you're raising your lure by counting the turns of your reel crank.

One thing you'll have to watch: When the jig is falling back to the bottom, your reel will be in free spool. You'll have to be alert for a strike, ready to throw your reel into gear instantly. Otherwise that fish will strip off line in a flash and create one awful bird's nest backlash on your spool. If your line tangles and stops abruptly while he's taking it out, it could break.

Tip: Jigging while drifting covers more territory than at anchor. Either way, there's nothing to prevent you from combining some chumming with the jigging.

For bluefish jigging your tackle should be reasonably sturdy. Often it's done in fairly deep water where strong currents prevail. Such a combination calls for a moderately heavy jig; and that, along with the amount of line paid out and chances of connecting with a bluefish weighing 10 pounds or more, necessitates tackle with some backbone. Spinning equipment is used, but conventional gear is recommended.

For deep-water bluefish jigging you may want to go to a reel with a somewhat faster than average retrieve ratio—say, 3½ to 1 (3½ turns of the spool to 1 revolution of the reel crank). The higher that gear ratio, the better able you'll be to take up any bellying in your line to impart motion to the jig. A reel with a lower retrieve ratio isn't ruled out, you understand, but with it you'll have to be more alert to avoid slack in your line. Ideally, a reel for this kind of angling is one that has a fast retrieve for jigging, then shifts to a lower ratio for playing a fish. A fast retrieve reel sometimes can make it a bit more difficult when battling a deep-fighting bluefish, but its ability to give action to the lure and keep slack out of the line compensate for any extra effort.

Bluefish jigging lines go as low as 10- or 12-pound test, and from 20-pound test through 30 to 40. That last is rather heavy for the assignment, but some like it as a measure of safety in event of tangling with jumbo blues, known to come in wild packages up to 16 or 17 pounds, or even heavier. Braided lines are used; so is mono. A hundred to 150 yards should suffice.

Here's where finer-diameter, minimum-stretch lines come into their own. Less diameter, of course, means less water drag, with decreased bellying in the line. Minimum stretch is important because it lessens the "give" between rod and lure. Excessive line stretch in deep-water fishing costs lure action and makes it more difficult to set the hook. There's another interesting angle: A line with excessive stretch is almost like a rubber band under stress. Should the hook happen to fall free when your bluefish breaks the surface, the jig could come hurtling in your direction like a bullet. Chances of it happening are unlikely, but being smacked by half a pound of metal—carrying a sharp hook, yet—whistling through the air could give you pause for thought.

As always when fighting blues, you must guard against any line slack. Jigged blues often are still full of fight when you get them close to the boat. Landing those dynamos is lively business. Don't try to boat a jigged bluefish with your rod alone. You're very likely to lose him. If you're careful you can boat him by hand. Reel him as close alongside as you can, keeping a taut line. With your rod in one hand, grab the line as near to the jig as you can—safely, but don't get too close to that fish's mouth. With luck you may be able to swing him into the boat. You can gaff him if you're adept at hitting a moving target. Or you can maneuver a landing net under him, preferably while he's still in the water. With gaff or net you'll have to be extremely careful not to knock him off the hook.

FINALLY, SOME ODDS AND ENDS   Before we leave the choppers to go on to other finned game I'll throw in some miscellaneous tidbits culled from bluefishing lore. No guarantee accompanies them, but you might find them helpful.

1. In spring or at a season's start the first-arriving blues may be in small, scattered groups, rather than in large, concentrated schools. Chumming is an aid in attracting strays, but it isn't as much a quantity producer as it is later, when hordes arrive.

2. When fishing a surf early in the season try working your artificial deep. Or fish the bottom with natural bait.

3. In summer and early autumn some good bluefishing opportunities come when a flood tide's last phase is at dusk or shortly afterward.

4. At times bluefish seem to move to seaward on a falling tide and return inshore with a rising tide.

5. An old bluefishermen's saying has it that some of the best action is around the time of a full moon.

6. When beach fishing, keep your bluefish in the water as long as you can, particularly when you get him into shallow water, and most especially if you have him on a plug. Many bluefish have been lost during those final moments as they were brought in close.

7. If you've had a hit and missed your fish, let the lure rest a second and start reeling again. He might return for another go at it.

8. During a normal run, there's invariably good-to-excellent bluefishing during the period from around sundown on into the night. It equals and often surpasses daytime action. By day in hot weather the superior action is likely to be early, say, from just before sunup until the sun's heat is beginning to be felt by midmorning. Similarly, some of the better daytime action can occur in late afternoon. During the hours in between, in my opinion, the upper levels of the water become too warm for blues. You might try deeper or near-bottom fishing at those times if working of upper levels proves unproductive.

In any event, keep an eye glued to fishing columns in local newspapers for word of when current bluefishing is most productive, by day or at night. Remember that bluefishing ports usually have party boats that make regular night trips.

CABOOSE There's still another part to the bluefish story. It concerns the youngsters of the breed, the lively little characters familiarly nicknamed "snappers." They possess all their elders' characteristics, right to the aggressiveness, scrappiness, and needle-sharp teeth. In fact, they're so much fun to catch and such a delight to eat that they rate their own chapter.

CHAPTER 8

Cod: The Gluttons

Ever hear of a man named James Buchanan Brady? Or maybe he'd sound more familiar if I called him by his nickname, Diamond Jim. James Buchanan Brady lived during a glittering era that straddled the beginning of the twentieth century, and he became a legend. Diamond Jim was a financial genius. He made a whale of a lot of money. He also spent a lot of money, much of it on diamonds, which was how he acquired his nickname. And he was extremely generous to people he liked and those less fortunate than himself. One way he shared his wealth was to endow the James Buchanan Brady Urological Institute at Johns Hopkins University in 1912.

He was a big man all around. Two things matched his generosity: his appetite and his waistline. He made enormous contributions to both. It once was reported that he ate three dozen oysters *before* breakfast. A man eschewing alcoholic beverages, he engulfed orange juice by the gallon. One time, a story has it, he gave a dinner party for several guests, and when they didn't appear he ate all the food himself.

Well sir, I didn't know Diamond Jim Brady personally, but I know his counterpart among fishes. It's the cod, *Gadus callarias*.

The fact is that the cod goes Diamond Jim a few better, pound for pound. Here's a fish that eats practically anything and everything. If there ever was a character with a cast-iron stomach, this kid is it.

Among the natural items he devours on a lavish scale are marine worms, starfish, squid, rock eels, shrimp, clams, mussels, crabs, small lobsters, and forms of bottom life such as sea cucumbers. He also devours smaller fishes—including flounders, herring, his own relatives, and any other food "on the hoof" you might have kicking around the place—in wholesale lots, as well as their eggs and young. Even the hard shells of lobsters up to six and eight inches long can't discourage his gluttony, and he's especially fond of those crustaceans when they're only two to four inches in length. Next to man, the codfish is probably lobsters' greatest enemy.

Even sea birds have fallen victim to the cod's omnivorous demand for food. Whether or not the birds are alive at the time they disappear down a cod's cavernous maw is open to debate, but it's recorded that in olden times in New England the flesh of a sea bird called the shearwater was used as codfish bait.

A cod can devour clams and mussels much in the same fashion as you'd eat peanuts, except that he doesn't bother to shell them first, but gulps them as is. Inside his rugged gut the meat is digested out, after which the empty shells are stacked, like nesting ashtrays, to be eliminated. It's said that many years ago conchologists—shell collectors—capitalized on this situation by letting cod do some gathering for them. It came in handy for obtaining specimens that were far out of their reach on the ocean floor.

Nor does the cod limit his diet to natural food. He'll take a whack at anything that looks interesting to him, and practically everything does when his appetite nags. Like people, I suppose, he always has an eye open for new or exotic menu entries. Only he chooses the craziest things. Found inside his digestive tract have been such bizarre morsels as electric light bulbs, tobacco tins, pieces of wood and cloth, rope, and hunks of metal such as nuts, bolts, and bottle caps. One big cod was reported as having swallowed a whiskey bottle (empty, much to the fisherman's disappointment). Another was found to have the jagged bottom of a beer bottle in his belly. Why it didn't cut him internally I'll never understand. Then there was an instance some years ago when an angler called me to announce he'd found a lady's necklace (probably lost at sea) inside a cod he caught. Last I heard, he was going to have it appraised.

AN INDIVIDUAL AND A FAMILY In its broad sense the term "cod" applies not only to a distinct species, but also to an entire family of fishes, at least in some ichthyologists' cataloguing. Thus, enrolled under the codfish banner we also find the American pollack, haddock, northern whiting, tomcod, and cousins known as cusks and hakes.

Within this tribe the species we call cod moves with a dignity and authority befitting his size, for he's the largest of the lot. Only two relatives come anywhere near him for size, and they're no competition in that department. One is the pollack, which can attain weights up to 30 or 35 pounds in exceptional instances. Well astern is the haddock, which has been known to weigh as much as 25 pounds, but averages far less.

The king of the clan, in dramatic contrast, comes in packages ranging from 5 or 6 pounds among the youngsters up into the 40s. Fifty-to-6o-pound specimens are boated by anglers at intervals, and there have been some up into the 70-, even 80-pound class. A sport fishing record 98-pounder was caught off Massachusetts. I have no doubt that cod of 100 pounds, perhaps more, prowl deep-sea grounds and far-offshore wrecks.

Cod up to 50, 60, and 70 pounds are big, make no mistake, but they're dwarfed by monsters reported for Georges Bank and New England commercial fisheries back in the 1800s. Georges Bank yielded a bruiser weighing 138 pounds *dressed*—probably about 180 in life. Others in the 100-to-160-pound range have been recorded for New England. And the all-time granddaddy was a brute captured by commercial fishermen off Massachusetts in May of 1895. That monster was 6 feet long and tipped the scale at a whopping 211¼ pounds!

All those king-size beasts are exceptional, of course. In the sport fishery a weight span is more like 5 or 6 to 10 or 12 pounds, and up through the 20s into the 30s, 40s, even 50s. As I noted earlier, even heftier fish are caught on occasion, but they don't belong among average catches.

NOTES ON IDENTIFICATION His profile is one clue to recognition of the cod. As you can see, he's a fairly plump, deep-bodied fish. His head is rather large, proportionately, and is characterized by a gradually sloping forehead. Note too that he has a large mouth, in keeping with his huge appetite. The chin often carries a barbel, which is a small, fleshy process hanging down like a Van Dyke beard.

Although there are reddish and greenish variations, the general color scheme of cod calls for a brown or grayish-brown back and upper sides, peppered with reddish-brown dots. The

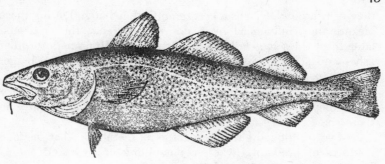

COD (*Gadus callarias*)

underside is a cream color or off-white. Typical and noticeable is a pale lateral line, a single, very narrow stripe that runs from just behind the gill cover to the base of his tail on either side.

Also an aid to identification of a cod are his three dorsal fins (one or two more than many other species possess), two anal fins (one more than the usual quota), a pair of rather small pectoral fins below and behind the gill covers, and a nearly straight-edged tail.

Since they all share a kind of family resemblance, cod, pollack, tomcod, and haddock sometimes are confused for each other by inexperienced sport fishermen. Greater size, of course, is a detail distinguishing cod. Aiding identification are their color scheme, pale lateral line, and forked tail. The tomcod is set aside by his size. He's much smaller than all the others, and he's the only one in the group possessing dark, irregular mottlings or markings on his back and fins. Haddock are rather exclusive in that they are the sole owners of a conspicuous *black* lateral line and a darkish spot on either side near the pectoral fins.

SPAWNING AND GROWTH   I mention breeding to show that cod do everything on a gargantuan scale. Our mass production is nothing when compared with the prolificness of lady cod. Commonly an average-size female will lay three million to four million eggs a year, while the larger ladies have been found to contain as many as nine million to ten million during the spawning period.

The eggs are buoyant and very small. Once they've been released by Mrs. Cod and fertilized in the water by her husband, they drift around, free as a breeze, until they hatch. During those meanderings, influenced by winds and currents, the eggs—and later the babies too—fall prey in astronomical numbers to other fishes and adverse environmental conditions. One of the bigger culprits in the destruction is the cod's own cousin, the pollack. Sharks take a toll too. Considering what cod do to their neighbors when they grow up, maybe there's a kind of poetic justice in there somewhere.

As I've mentioned elsewhere, there's a method in that seeming madness of predators' wholesale gobbling of eggs and young. It's part of a system of population control.

Many cod eggs and infants survive the continuing raids of predatory neighbors. The survivors reach a length of approximately 7½ to 8 inches their first year, and 15 or 16 inches by their second birthday. My friend Ed Migdalski of Yale provides this approximate length-weight relationship of growing cod in his excellent book, *Angler's Guide to the Salt Water Game Fishes, Atlantic and Pacific* (New York, The Ronald Press Company):

Length in Inches	Weight in Pounds
20	3
25	6
30	9
35	17
40	23
45	32
50	45
55	55

Cod are at the not-so-tender mercies of all sorts of foes while in the egg stage, as babies, and while growing up. Very early in life environmental conditions such as adverse water temperatures can take their toll. From the egg phase onward there are many assassins lurking about. Life can cease abruptly. Once cod reach a fair size, however, the story takes a reverse twist. With cod now the hunter instead of the hunted, it becomes relentless and awesome. Few smaller fishes are immune from attack —except, maybe, blowfish that can inflate themselves to become too large to seize, and other critters that are too prickly or spiny to swallow. Cod roam the ocean like pirates, bringing terror to those that once made life a nightmare for them when they were kids. It's vengeance with 1,000 percent interest.

HABITS AND SEASONS   Some cod populations seem to stay more or less put in a given region, provided water temperatures and food supplies are to their satisfaction. An outstanding example of populations that hang around in one region occurs in deeper-water areas off Montauk and Block Island. More about that later.

It appears that greater numbers of cod migrate than stay put. Some of their migrations are fairly extensive on our Atlantic Coast, a detail that accounts for their being seasonal game in most areas. It has been said that some individuals even stray across the North Atlantic to Europe.

In the broad sense cod are classified as ground fish or bottom dwellers. But it isn't a strictly accurate term when applied to the family, because some of its members—the pollack is one—have been encountered at various ocean planes, from the sea floor right up through intermediate levels to the top, where they've been seen and caught at times. Young cod also have been observed near the surface. By and large, though, cod are bottom-living, deep-water residents, traveling right over or a few feet above the ocean floor. And they've been found at depths as great as nine hundred feet. You won't fish for them that far down, but it's important to remember that they're essentially ground fish, because that governs rigging and angling procedures.

Cod favor cold water. So you're not apt to find them in the more southerly segments of their Middle Atlantic–North Atlantic coastal range during the summer. But a couple of areas are noteworthy exceptions. One includes grounds between Montauk and Rhode Island's Block Island, some fifteen miles east of Long Island's most seaward tip. Another is Cox's Ledge, a deep-water place southeast of Block Island and reached by Montauk party boats. In those places cod can be caught all year, and it's something of a phenomenon that their summer runs, featuring fish up to forty pounds-plus, are often better than the usual winter runs in many other locations.

I should add that in recent years some of the larger party boats sailing from ports on Long Island's South Shore have been traveling to remote offshore wrecks to find warmer-weather cod angling. Here too are some heavy fish up into the forty-to-fifty-pound bracket. Montauk boats have made special trips to the remains of the ill-starred liner *Andrea Doria* and have reported huge cod prowling the area. But it's a long haul to those far grounds, one that only real codfishing *aficionados* and a few skippers are likely to make. Small craft and/or amateur boatmen shouldn't even think about attempting it.

Elsewhere, New Jersey northward, cod are chiefly autumn-winter-early spring targets.

In the oceanic expanse beyond Long Island's southern coast the season's first cod usually are in evidence as autumn progresses and October's brisk air removes the last traces of Indian summer. During this initial phase, which lasts until mid-November or so, the fish frequently dally quite close inshore, foraging over shell-fish beds in water about fifty to sixty feet deep. Sometimes the majority of these cod are the smaller fish.

Then comes a second stage, the real run, which commences sometime during November's last half and endures through the winter into early spring. In this phase the fish shift offshore to deeper water, probably to escape extremes in cold (the water above them acts as an insulator), where they're hooked in depths to 100 or 120 feet.

When spring begins to warm ocean waters, cod start their migrations to cooler regions to the east and north. By April the normal winter run in southern parts of their range has just about had it.

And that's their pattern, in general, throughout the segment of Atlantic seaboard they inhabit.

RANGE AND DISTRIBUTION Although cod like cold water, there are limits to what they will tolerate. They want to feel comfortable, not freeze to death. Drs. Bigelow and Schroeder peg the lowest temperature at which cod feel at home at approximately 32° F, which is pretty frosty, when you stop to think about it. Water frigid enough to form anchor ice—ice on the bottom, that is—can be lethal.

There are limits for them on the upper side of the temperature range too, of course. These are about 50° to 55° F. Bigelow and Schroeder note that smaller cod are somewhat less sensitive to

higher temperatures than their elders, which would account for
visitations by numbers of them in relatively warm, shallower
areas. Larger cod, it seems, tend to shy away from water warmer
than about 50° F. There are, however, the inevitable exceptions.
Some, cited by Bigelow and Schroeder, have occurred on Nantucket Shoals, Massachusetts, where appreciable numbers of
larger cod have appeared when waters were as warm as 58°
or 59° F. The two authorities, incidentally, also cite Nantucket
Shoals as an all-year cod ground.

So water temperatures, along with available food supplies, are
a key factor in determining the species' range and movements.

Cod are encountered on both sides of the North Atlantic Ocean.
On the western side their range is described as extending from
western Greenland, Davis Strait, Resolution Island, and Hudson
Strait on the north on down almost to Cape Hatteras, N.C. The
Continental Slope is about their offshore limit on the North
American seaboard. Centers of abundance are scattered from
Labrador to New Jersey. On the European side of the Big Pond
their range is from Norway and the Baltic on down to the Bay
of Biscay between France and Spain.

Cod are a popular marine sport fish in the British Isles, notably
Scotland and England. And those anglers are real buffs. There
was an account in a British sport-fishing periodical of three fans
out after cod in Scotland in weather so cold their worm baits
froze stiff and became as brittle as dried twigs.

COD HABITS OF PARTICULAR INTEREST TO FISHERMEN   (1) Although
cod, like other species, probably can discern food, including baits,
when reasonably close to it, and are attracted to moving prey
when they can see it, evidence suggests that they depend heavily
upon scent in foraging. To support this, Bigelow and Schroeder
point out that cod bite as readily at night as during the day.
Further, they greedily seize "nude" baits, such as the meat of a
skimmer, which they don't encounter in that condition in nature.
(2) Cod frequently seek food over beds of sea clams (skimmers),
mussels, and the like. Other gathering places include wrecks,
rocky areas, sandy and pebble-strewn bottoms, and the deeper
slopes of coastal ledges, where they prowl among gardens of
marine vegetation.

(3) Broadly speaking, the larger the cod, the more they keep to the bottom or just over it. But occasionally they, like their smaller brothers, will prowl for prey or pursue it upward into levels closer to the surface. That wildfowl, such as ducks and sea birds, are found in the bellies of big cod from time to time indicates that the heavyweights can be drawn even to the surface on occasion. (4) Cod spawn during the colder weather, from about December or January to March, possibly as late as early April, depending upon areas. During spawning it isn't uncommon for them to fast. That could account for sporadic lulls in action that occur during a season.

TACKLE   If you've gathered by now that codfishing gear must be reasonably sturdy, you've gathered correctly. This tackle has to be able to handle not only bulky fish, but also the moderately heavy terminal rigs employed in the sport. The main thing is that your rod have sufficient spine, but with flexibility too. You don't want to fish with a stick that has the "give" of an oar handle. On the other hand, you don't want to wrestle cod with anything as "whippy" as light spinning gear. Forget spinning tackle for this assignment. Go with conventional equipment.

If you own a couple of outfits, say, a medium and a light, you can switch according to sizes of cod currently running. A medium, all-purpose boat rod handling lines to about 30-pound test will do fine. You may sacrifice some action with smaller cod, but you'll be outfitted for the heftier ones. On this you can mount a 2/0 reel. You probably could get away with a smaller 1/0, but the stronger innards of a 2/0 are more suited to deep-water angling for husky cod.

Here's where Dacron line with its lower water drag comes into its own, letting you use sinkers somewhat lighter than with some other lines. Line strength is up to you. Twenty-pound-test stuff will handle the majority of cod you encounter. Thirty-pound line will give you a margin of safety when big cod are about or when fishing in rocky areas. Some anglers, I suspect, go to 40-pound line for those two reasons. You won't require a lot. A hundred to 120 feet are about the maximum depths at which you'll fish for cod, and they're not long-running fighters. A hundred yards of line should suffice; any over that would be more than enough.

Cod have big mouths and will accept good-size baits, so a hook of appropriate size is indicated. There are so-called standard codfish hooks, some of which come on short lengths of tarred line for attachment. But you can rig any pattern, and sizes aren't a matter of splitting hairs. The over-all range goes from a 4/0 for the smaller fish up to a 7/0, even an 8/0 or 9/0, for the lunkers. A 6/0 is a good medium.

You'll rig the common bank type of sinker. It need be only heavy enough to keep your rig on bottom against the thrust of currents. Its weight, therefore, will vary according to current strengths in areas fished.

RIGGING   You have a choice of two basic, time-tested methods. You can use one, two, or even three hooks, as preference dictates. The only purpose in rigging more than one hook is to cover levels above the sea floor. In wreck fishing you might find multiple hooks more of a nuisance than an advantage, since they increase chances of getting fouled on underwater obstructions. No leaders are needed. Cod are anything but shy. Connections can be made directly by the hooks' gut or tarred line snells, or even by short lengths of line of suitable strength. Or they can be tied in via three-loop swivels. These aren't essential, but they do help minimize fouling of hooks and line.

If you elect to use a single hook, tie it into your line just above the sinker. Some fishermen make the attachment immediately

A BASIC COD RIGGING (RIGS I and II)

above the weight, but you can go to twelve to eighteen inches above it. If a second hook is rigged, tie it two or three feet above the first. If a third hook is used, connect it eighteen to twenty-four inches above the second.

A variation of the foregoing is basically the same, except that the first hook is tied in directly above the sinker, and other hooks, if used, are attached to the line just far enough to prevent all three from tangling with each other.

You may wonder why I mention two basic cod rigs instead of one, especially when they're quite similar. I do that because both are in use. If an angler favors one over the other it's because that particular variation has produced best for *him*. I suggest you try both and so arrive at an arrangement that's best for *you*. Feel free to vary the distances between hooks.

Tip: Codfishing skippers usually have recommendations for rigging in specific areas. Ask the boat's captain or mate before you rig.

A SPECIAL THREE-HOOK OUTFIT   In the Montauk-Block Island region there has been developed a special three-hook outfit that can be brought into service when cod, pollack, and large flounders (nicknamed "snowshoes" at Montauk, about which more in the chapter on flounder) are encountered on the same grounds. It's a form of high-low rig (that is, high hook and low hook), with an intermediate hook thrown in for added versatility. You might also try it, with appropriate baits, when bottom fishing for species other than those mentioned here.

Pay attention, because this gets a little involved in places.

The arrangement starts with a bank sinker of suitable weight, then incorporates the following (all hooks in sizes for species involved):

1. A cod hook on a snood or snell of tarred line twelve to sixteen inches long, attached immediately above the sinker by a three-way swivel. The sinker ties to one of the swivel's three eyes.

2. Here's a tricky detail. *Midway* on that codfish hook's snell you tie a flounder hook on a clear gut snell twelve to sixteen inches long. No swivel is used there. Attachment is made directly, and the connection secured with water-resistant tape to keep the two snells separated.

3. About five feet up from the sinker you attach a three-loop swivel. Your line will use two of those three eyes. On its free loop is tied a hook for pollack on a four-foot leader of clear gut or other low-visibility material. For this hook the length of line between its swivel and the sinker should be longer than the pollack hook's leader. Got it?

That comprises the multiple-hook rig for cod, pollack, and snowshoe flounders. We'll talk about its baiting later.

COD BAITS   Since cod are omnivorous, aggressive feeders, they'll accept a wide variety of baits. Among those used successfully are strips of squid (purchased whole in packages); hard and soft clams; pieces of herring; calico crabs, especially in the shedder state; and even strips cut from other fishes, such as bergalls.

One of the best cod baits of all is that ocean clam known as a skimmer. Mollusks such as this form a large part of the species' diet. Except, maybe, in seasons of poor harvests, these big clams are readily available as cod bait. They're also an effective chum for cod. The clams can be cracked with a sharp blow, enough to let body juices escape, and dropped overboard, singly or a few at a time, at intervals. You can even use the empty shells as chum after the meat has been removed for bait.

Use a generous piece of the meat, but don't overdo it. It once was believed that the bigger the bait for codfish, the better; but an oversized bait has been proved unnecessary. Although the old maxim of big baits for big fish and small baits for small fish holds true, there are limits. Use a chunk of fair size, not a big blob. And don't go to the other extreme and skimp.

In the case of the multiple-hook rig fished for cod, pollack, and snowshoe flounders, you divide a skimmer clam into three portions and bait thusly: A sliced-off end of the skimmer's body goes on the cod hook; a "center cut" of same goes on the pollack hook; and the "lip" or tough outer edge of the mollusk's body is folded on itself and impaled on the snowshoe hook.

BATTLEGROUNDS   You have plenty of latitude. You'll encounter cod in ocean areas of varying depths, ranging from shoals and inshore zones with 40 to 60 feet out to depths of 100 to more than 120 feet. Remember what I told you earlier about places with codfishing potential—wrecks, rocky bottom, etc. Wrecks can be among the more fertile areas, since they harbor lesser creatures that attract cod. Some of the larger, more muscular gents are met in the vicinity of such submerged structures. Numerous are deep sea skippers' and skindivers' stories about huge cod finning their way through the shadows around wrecks. U. S. Coast and Geodetic Survey Charts, intended primarily for navigation, can be helpful in codfishing. In addition to indicating depths they show the nature of the bottom in various areas and pinpoint wrecks and other submerged objects of appreciable size.

If you fish on a party or charter boat you won't have to worry about locating a good place to drop your rig. That will be the captain's responsibility. A professional sport-fishing skipper will find fish, if any are to be had. He'd better, or he'll be collecting unemployment insurance.

When fishing around such undersea obstructions as wrecks and boulders you have to be prepared to lose sinkers and hooks, just as in blackfishing. That's why I commented before that multiple hooks in such places can be more of a nuisance than an advantage. Of course, if you don't mind occasional hangups and rig replacements, that's something else. Often you can buy hooks and sinkers aboard a party boat (on a charter boat *all* the tackle is furnished as part of the deal), but if you're wise you'll carry extras, just in case. And remember that hook-salvaging gimmick detailed in the chapter on blackfish.

Except, maybe, when they've gorged themselves on small schooling fishes, or during a spawning fast, cod are ready to dine almost any time. When one strikes your hook there won't be any doubt that you have a fish on. When it comes to feeding their faces, cod won't fool around. They hit with sincerity and enthusiasm—*KALUNK!* Then you'll experience an exhibition of dogged resistance . . . not spectacularly lively, perhaps, but muscular and determined. Set your hook with a short, firm, upward lift of your rod tip, if the fish hasn't already planted the barb for you. Often a cod will smack your bait with such ferocity that the hook is set right off the bat. There also will be times when one hits with such enthusiasm that the impact tears your hook loose before it has had a chance to really dig in. You'll feel a jolt, then nothing. Obviously the fish is off the hook. Be patient. Leave your rig where it is, or give it just a little motion. He might come back. A cod can't resist a handout even if it costs him a torn mouth. If several minutes pass without further response, better check your bait. He may have swiped it.

Tip: You can add a bit to your fighting time with any deeper-water fish if you bring him up slowly, pausing long enough at

various levels to allow him time to adjust to decreasing water
pressures. The fact is that when catching bottom fishes, such as
whiting, for live bait, you should reel them in slowly in fairly
deep water to let them adjust; otherwise you'll have badly injured or dead bait.

BONUSES   During normal runs cod yield good-to-excellent catches.
Another bonus is an ever-present possibility of tying into huskies
weighing thirty pounds and upward. A third bonus is their
food value. With a deep-freeze unit you can double that last one.

If, as I did, you had to gulp mouthfuls of awful cod liver oil
as a kid, you may have a thing against these fish. Do as I did and
forget it. Cod are excellent eating, tasting not at all like that
stomach-churning medicinal oil from their livers. You'll be shortchanging yourself in the seafood dining department if you don't
devour your catches. Cod can be prepared in a number of ways:
baked; as steaks or fillets; fried; broiled; salted; in a New England boiled dinner; as finnan haddie; in fishcakes and chowder;
with fancy sauces, and so on. They're tasty in all of them.

HISTORICAL NOTE   You may not be aware of it, but cod were
tied in with the early growth and economy of the United States.
From colonial days, 'way back, they've been an important food
fish, and at one time harvesting them commercially was a major
industry in New England. The fact is that it created prosperity
for many citizens of another era. All of which led to coining of
the term "codfish aristocracy" for folks who suddenly became
rich, and maybe didn't wear their wealth too gracefully.

You won't join the codfish aristocracy, but you'll have angling
sport and plenty of good eating.

CHAPTER 9

Bluecraw Crab:
A Trickster in Armor

Beneath the breeze-rippled surface of a bay is a strange, wonderful, incredible world teeming with a fantastic assortment of creatures that swim, crawl, burrow, drift lazily with the tide, or scoot along the bottom as though in a race with time or each other. From our side of the surface this underwater cosmos appears calm and peaceful. We see only the small, dancing triangles of waves and fluid shadows below. We hear not a sound. But if we could see and tune in on the "audio" of what goes on all the time in this submarine kingdom we might very well shudder and be glad we don't live in such a nightmarish place.

Despite the face of serenity it presents to outsiders, the underwater world is a scene of constant violence and, I hate to say it, sudden death. Assassins come in a multitude of shapes and sizes. They hide behind rocks, or streak down from above, or dart out from innocent-looking arbors of seaweed gardens, or lie in wait, buried in sand or mud. Day and night, undersea residents are kept busy in an unceasing struggle for survival. There's something doing all the time. Never a dull moment.

Right through the thick of this merciless competition for the privilege of living marches a crusty little character who doesn't give a hoot for anybody or anything, regardless of size, including humans. This toughie is the blueclaw crab, also known as the "blue crab."

He's a very confident, self-assured fellow. He's also belligerent, ready for combat at a moment's notice. Much of this attitude is due to his being better equipped than many of his neighbors to deal with assaults by bullies, and even dish out a little mayhem of his own. He's one of nature's forerunners of all the armor ever devised by man, including modern tanks. Completely encased

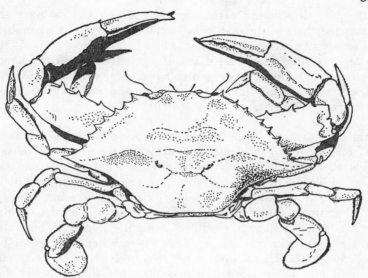

BLUECLAW CRAB (*Callinectes sapidus*)

in a hard, extremely tough outer covering, the crab is a combination of knight in armor, submarine, and highly maneuverable light tank.

He has his own "artillery," a pair of strong, sharp-pointed nipping claws that can puncture or tear, thereby lessening the enthusiasm of just about any foe who comes along, including human types. To make things even more interesting, he can walk, scramble like a football quarterback, swim, dart, and burrow. He can move up and down like an elevator, or backward, or sideways; and he's able to bury himself in sand or mud with a speed that puts burrowing land animals to shame. In short, the blueclaw crab can get from here to there in a twinkling by any of several different maneuvers.

Unhappily for this spunky crustacean, though, we and some of his finned neighbors find him good to eat. Worse yet, his human enemies are a lot smarter, and those finned foes are often faster and more powerful. Complicating matters and making him a bad insurance risk, he likes to eat and can be tempted by many kinds of morsels. Freshness of food is no criterion. He finds long-dead fish quite delectable. In this respect the blueclaw, along with other members of the crab tribe, could be considered a member of nature's Department of Sanitation.

Many anglers hunt blue crabs. If you haven't tried crabbing, you should. You'll enjoy matching agility with the rascals. They're a challenge, make no mistake. And not only are they fun to catch, they're a gastronomic delight.

THE CRAB "STORE" Distribution of blueclaw crabs on the U.S. Atlantic Coast is considerable, extending all the way from Massachusetts down to Florida's eastern seaboard, thence over into the Gulf of Mexico to Texas, and even as far south as northern South America. Throughout that range they favor warm, comparatively shallow water, and dwell in bays, coves, harbors, creeks, canals, and estuaries. Although classified as marine animals, blue crabs also are found in brackish locations where water is a mixture of salt and fresh. They'll even move into fresh water on occasion. They'll also loiter along sandy and muddy shores beside the ocean, where beaches shelve away gradually to deeper water; but it's not their custom to set up housekeeping any great distance at sea. They're essentially littoral or coastal residents.

Despite their extensive distribution, blueclaw crabs are considered nonmigratory. Their travels are confined chiefly to wandering into backwaters and to shuttling back and forth between shoals and deeper areas where, as winter touches their environment with icy fingers, they dig into mud to escape hibernal cold.

From a conservation standpoint it's vitally important to keep in mind that blueclaws are nonmigratory and consequently do relatively little traveling. What this means in practical terms is that each area has its own crab populations, which do not receive periodic reinforcements from other places. If local populations are cleaned out by imprudent fishing, therefore, it's conceivable that the carelessness could spell the end of crabbing in that locality. Pollution could bring the same dismal results.

SEASONS Because they fancy warmish water, in the more northerly segments of their range blueclaw crabs wait until spring is about over and summer has a start before moving about to see what's doing in the neighborhood. In those more northerly regions, some of the more enterprising and hungry individuals will show before June is out. Usually, however, summer heat is needed to call them forth in respectable numbers.

As summer turns on its fire they move into arms of bays, canals, and small creeks, their numbers increasing steadily. And as they feed, they grow. In August and September they're at their peak in sizes for that season. Crabbing can last into October if weather doesn't turn too frosty, because it takes a while for bays to chill after absorbing a summer sun's warmth for weeks. Often crabs are at their fattest and sassiest during the last act of their performance in late summer and early fall.

LOVE LIFE OF A CRAB   No one would call crabs romantic—except, maybe, another crab. But neither do they take their reproductive duties lightly. During the spawning season, which generally lasts from June through August in temperate regions, each female can extrude anywhere from about seven hundred thousand to more than two million yellowish eggs, each something like one one-hundredth of an inch in diameter. These are fertilized by a male.

After releasing her ova, the mother totes them around with her in a roundish mass, nicknamed a "sponge," on her abdomen until they hatch.* Water with low salinity (saltiness) is one of the adverse factors that can be detrimental to successful hatching, so the mamas carry their precious cargoes into water with a higher salt content or to where conditions are more favorable. As they do, embryos develop within the eggs. Hatching requires nine to fourteen days, depending upon water temperatures and other environmental conditions. It goes without saying that not all of those countless numbers of eggs survive to hatch.

Those that do enter the world as tiny larval crabs, only about a hundredth of an inch wide, are called *zoea* by the scientific boys. At that stage they look more like insects than the offspring of respectable crustaceans. As such they mingle on or near the surface with plankton, minute forms of marine animal and plant life, on which they feed. (Plankton comprise the start of the sea's

---

* Females bearing egg masses are called "sponge crabs," and should not be kept by fishermen. The conservation reason should be obvious. Do your part to preserve the blueclaw crab fishery. Return sponge crabs safely to the water.

food chain, nourishing tiny creatures on which larger ones dine, and so on up the size scale.) There the larval blueclaws are borne about, willy-nilly, by tides and winds. Astronomical numbers of them vanish into the maws of predators. Other unfortunates succumb to a hostile environment, such as water that's too cold.

There, incidentally, is another reason for man giving attention to every detail of conserving the blueclaw fishery. Nowadays the crabs need all the help they can get. What with such natural factors as poor breeding seasons and those mentioned in the preceding paragraph, theirs is uphill going as it is. Now increasing fishing pressures and water pollution make it even more so.

A "CLOTHING" PROBLEM   From infancy to maturity the crab's life is punctuated by a series of moltings or shell sheddings. Probably a nuisance to him, they're a vital part of his growth.

A crab's skeleton isn't like ours. He wears his on the outside in the form of a hard exterior shell that has no stretch. Naturally, the fleshy internal parts of his body require more room as he grows; but that hard, tough exoskeleton, being of unstretchable material, doesn't yield to the expansion going on inside. As you can imagine, a crab would be in an awful pickle if something weren't done. Alterations in his "suit" must be made; otherwise he'd find himself in a bad bind, to put it mildly.

Tailor shops are few and far between in the underwater world. There's no place where a crab can drop in and say, "Lengthen the sleeves a bit," or "I wish you'd let the pants out at the waist." So nature comes to his aid, solving the alterations problem. It's accomplished by a series of discardings of old shells and growths of new ones. He simply sheds his shells as they're outgrown and develops roomier "clothing."

From the larval stage blueclaws graduate to a kind of miniature crab status. Measuring only about an eighth of an inch wide, they no longer mingle with the plankton set, but settle to the bottom, where they get down to the serious business of looking and acting like crabs. During development young blueclaws are like so many girls and boys continuously outgrowing their clothes. They must molt or discard their old shells, now too small, and patiently await development of successively larger ones that keep pace with their internal expansion. During early stages growth is so rapid that molting occurs about every six days. Gradually the intervals between molts lengthen, still keeping pace with growth inside, until about twenty-five days elapse between sheddings. A female repeats molting some fifteen to twenty times before she can wear the same ensemble month in and month out. A male usually requires three additional sheddings before he can wander around in the same suit for the rest of his life.

With each shell change, blueclaws increase approximately one-third in size until maximum growth is attained and alterations are no longer necessary. Maturity, according to one authority, occurs during the second summer of life, when the crabs are twelve to fourteen months old.

Mating occurs during a female's final molt, and she mates but once. Certain storage facilities she possesses enable her to fertilize all eggs in future spawnings after only one mating. Convenient, but not very romantic.

Female blueclaws first spawn during their third summer, when two years old. They may spawn twice that season. It's believed that some females live through the following winter to spawn again during the fourth summer at the age of three. The majority of them die during their third winter, however, and it's thought that the males' life span is about the same.

Many people (not in the know as you are) hear the terms "shedder crab" and "soft crab" and think they represent distinct kinds, different from blueclaws. They're not. "Shedder" and "soft" are merely names for stages a crab goes through while molting. The shedder phase is the time when an individual discards an outgrown shell to make way for the new, more spacious one forming underneath. Once the old shell has split to let its dissatisfied owner crawl out of it, the blueclaw becomes a soft crab or "softy."

At this stage of the game the new shell is soft and pliable, rather like heavy parchment. It soon reaches normal hardness, but during the waiting period its owner is practically defenseless against attacks by enemies and in the frequent squabbles that occur among these pugnacious crustaceans. Crabs are a quarrelsome lot among themselves, often biting off each other's claws during arguments. The vulnerability of soft crabs is well known to commercial breeders who produce blueclaw crabs on a wholesale scale for market. Since missing claws detract from their value, softies are carefully segregated from their hard-shelled kin.

A softy's only defenses are to maneuver quickly out of harm's way and a talent for making himself as scarce as possible, preferably hidden somewhere. It's been said that sometimes a softy will form a temporary alliance with a hard-shelled friend, moving about on the latter's back. I can't vouch for that, but I can tell you that softies try to keep themselves concealed and out of the paths of trouble, including any threatened by humans, as best they can. That's why soft-shelled crabs bring fancy prices. They're hard to get in nature.

Among blueclaws' worst foes during the soft-shelled stage are people. Fried soft crabs are a dining delight, much favored by seafood gourmets. But soft crabs are very good at making themselves scarce. You'll earn any you catch.

GOIN' CRABBIN'   In addition to the benefits of being a lot of fun and providing mouth-watering morsels for the table (hard-shell blueclaws are good eating too), crabbing has other things going for it. Except when traps are involved, there's a certain amount of skill. Nice catches can be made during normal runs. Equipment is simple and inexpensive. Folks of all ages can enjoy it. What's more, a boat isn't an absolute necessity. A boat is a definite advantage, no two ways about it, because of greater mobility. With a boat you'll cover more territory, reach otherwise inaccessible places, and find areas where there won't be competition from other crabbers. But you can catch blueclaws without one.

Those are all reasons why crabbing is one of the most popular kinds of fishing in many areas.

TECHNIQUES   Three crabbing methods are in common use. Take your pick. Better yet, try all three.

The simplest procedure demands the least expenditure of effort. It also is the least fun, in my opinion. This is the technique that employs a trap designed specifically for the assignment. Inexpensive, this trap is a boxlike contraption fashioned from strong wire with a large mesh. Its top and bottom are fixed, secured to each other by corner posts. But its four sides are hinged on their lower edges and collapsible so that they can be raised and lowered. To the top—in the middle—of each of those four

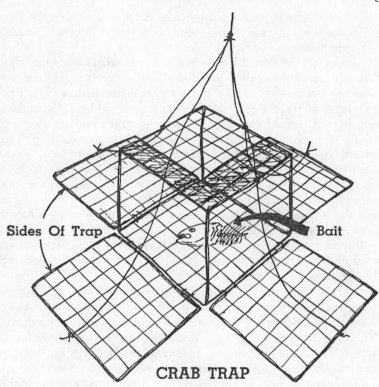

Sides Of Trap   Bait

CRAB TRAP

sides is tied a length of suitably strong cord. All four lengths should be the same—just enough to let the sides drop down all the way when the trap is in use. These four lines are tied to a main line, another length of stout cord, of suitable length for the depths of water fished. The main line serves a dual purpose. It lowers the entire trap to the bottom, and raises it for emptying. It also lowers and raises the four sides.

When the trap is lowered to the bottom or brought up for checking or emptying, tension exerted by the main handline on the four lines to its hinged sides keeps those sides up in position, forming a square cage. When the trap is in position on the bottom, slack in the main line permits the four sides to drop down and serve as ramps up which crabs walk to get at bait inside.

When the trap is raised periodically, tension on the main line pulls the sides up and closed, imprisoning any blueclaws inside. It's a simple device and quite effective.

Almost any kind of fish, or a part of same, can be used as trap bait. Earlier, you recall, I mentioned that a crab's appetite is his undoing because he can be lured to his doom with a variety of things. A piece of fish is good; even a head will do. Crabs like any part of a dead fish, even if it smells strong enough to move by itself. A couple of fair-size chunks will do for one trap. You can try fresh or frozen mossbunkers, for example, cut into pieces. Crab traps also can be baited with small, whole dead fish, such as killies, spearing, and butterfish. A hunk of salt pork and a piece of beef heart have been known to work too. You also can use the entrails, heads, and other discard fragments of fish you may have hooked that day.

But no matter what kind of bait is employed, it must be tied securely to the inside bottom of the trap; otherwise wily, thieving blueclaws will boldly carry it off.

A crab trap was designed for lazy fishermen or for anglers occupied with more desirable targets at the time. Baited, it's lowered to the bottom, where its sides are allowed to drop down. Then the user secures its main line so it won't slip overboard, and waits. He can do other fishing meanwhile as he waits for the trap bait to attract customers. After a reasonable length of time he pulls on the main line, closing the sides abruptly, and hauls the contraption to the surface. He empties it of any prisoners, checks the bait to see if there's still enough, then returns the trap to the bottom. The device's advantages are that it can be used from a dock, creek bank, boat, or pier, and it works for his owner while he's enjoying rod-and-reel angling.

Personally, I don't care for this kind of crabbing as a method. No sport.

A crab-catching device that's simpler than a trap is a little gismo called a killy ring. It will test your reflexes.

A killy ring is merely a small circle of wire, maybe three to five or six inches in diameter. Any kind of wire will do so long as it's stiff and heavy enough to maintain a ring shape, yet soft enough to be bendable in the first place. This ring must be fashioned with a simple catch so it will stay closed to prevent its bait from

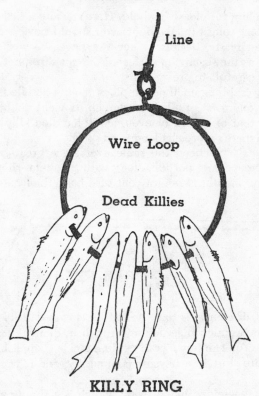

Line

Wire Loop

Dead Killies

KILLY RING

sliding off. Bending a crude catch, one end hooking into the other, after the ring has been baited will do.

You can bait the ring with dead killies or spearing, running the wire through their bodies to make a kind of necklace of bait. An alternate is pieces of fish, similarly strung and with some ends dangling.

Tied to the baited ring is length of twine or old fishing line, enough to let the ring reach bottom. Lower the gismo to the bay floor, keeping the handline just taut enough so you can detect any crab attacks on the bait. When you have a customer, little tugs will inform you that a crab is working on the bait, tearing or pinching off tiny pieces to thrust into his mouth. Raise the ring *slowly and very carefully* so as not to alarm your visitor and cause him to release his hold. Here's where a little craftiness on your part comes in. By rights you should have a crab net or landing net ready, because blueclaws have the vexing habit of letting go as they near the surface. You can slip a net under him —if you're careful—to prevent this.

A third crabbing method employs a long-handled net alone. I like this one most of all, even though its yield might not measure up to that of a trap, or even a well-handled killy ring. I like it because there's more challenge and sport.

Crab nets have been the same ever since great-granddaddy. The implement's net portion, along with the metal ring holding it open at the mouth, is reminiscent of a basketball hoop. The big

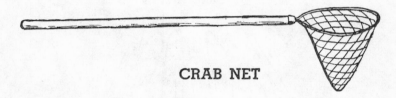

CRAB NET

difference, of course, is that the former is closed at its bottom. Its handle is a wooden pole, about an inch in diameter and six feet or so long. You can buy a crab net in a tackle shop, fishing station, or hardware store in a bayside community, and it won't cost you much.

The net is wielded like a scoop, which is a simple enough procedure. But catching crabs with it is something else again.

Blueclaws sometimes cling to the pilings of docks and bulkheads, where they can be seen if you look carefully. The protective green color of their shell calls for a sharp eye. Keeping your net ready as you walk along, you can slip it under them. Don't be fooled. It isn't as easy as it sounds. Crabs are agile and quick. It requires a little practice to outmaneuver them.

Occasionally, in certain places at certain tides, you'll see blueclaws riding along with the current just below the surface. If you're adept enough you can net a nice mess of them. Don't bank on this situation, though; it doesn't happen too often.

The way I like most to hand-net blueclaws is to slowly pole my way along a shallow creek in a rowboat, keeping the net handy for when I spot one on the bottom. It requires a bit of looking, but they can be seen even if they're standing still. It's better, actually, to have someone pole the boat while you stand in the bow, net poised. It's a lot of fun, moving silently up a lonely little creek among the reeds and cattails, trying to detect blueclaws. Often small creeks, even tiny ones, wriggling their way into salt marshes or those islets called hassocks are productive.

Refraction makes catching crabs with a net rather tricky. Water bends light rays, and the resulting refraction makes blueclaws look like they are where they ain't. That refractory illusion, coupled with their agility in sidestepping capture, adds to the sport. Makes the crabs taste better too.

There's a fourth crabbing technique called jacking. It's done at night with the aid of a fairly bright lantern, and again a net is involved. When jacking for blueclaws a fisherman places his lantern as far up in the boat's bow as it will go so it casts a circle of light down into the water. The boat drifts or is poled along slowly, and any blueclaws seen on the bottom or swimming in the circle of light are scooped up with the net. Some fishermen favor jacking because its being done at night lends an unusual note (there's less competition too) and because, like daytime netting, it permits selection in advance of the size blueclaws taken. That can't be done with a trap or killy ring.

Speaking of sizes reminds me of a favor I want to ask of you. When you go crabbing, practice conservation. Return all small blueclaws and sponge crabs safely to the water. Give little fellows a chance to grow for better catches. There isn't enough meat in undersized crabs to merit cooking them.

Whatever technique you use, maybe you'll be lucky enough to get yourself a few softies for frying now and again.

HANDLE WITH CARE! Our truculent friend the blueclaw crab is outfitted with five pairs of appendages. One pair, located at the rear of his carapace or shell, has flat, roundish blades on the ends. These are what we call swimmerettes. With their broad blades they're like little canoe paddles and are his propulsion machinery. The next three pairs, progressing more toward the front of his body, are more like legs. These are adapted for strolling on the bottom. Then, right in front, where they can do the most good (or harm, in the case of a foe) are the two largest appendages of all. These are muscular and armed with pincers. They serve as their owner's knife and fork in dining and as effective weapons of offense and defense. They're strong enough to sever a crab opponent's claw and can deliver a startling nip to a human finger. You'll be wise to respect them.

The blueclaw has a disposition to match his weapons. He's a chronic grouch (hence the term "crab" for grouchy humans). Practically everything except food can annoy him to belligerency, and he'll carry the argument right into the enemy camp if need be. With two strong, puncturing, tearing pincers, a discourteous manner, and considerable agility, this crab is a formidable opponent for his size. His spunk has to be admired.

To pick one up, first place your foot (having it in a shoe is recommended) over his shell—don't squash him!—in such a way that the pinching claws are pinned down. With thumb and forefinger grasp him firmly at the back of his shell between the swimmerettes. When you remove your foot and lift him he'll try to get at you with those pliers of his, but if you're holding him correctly he'll fail. If you're not grasping him properly you'll learn your first (painful) lesson in the handling of blueclaws.

Lots of times, especially within the confines of a small boat, a blue crab will scamper to a corner somewhere and face outward, pincers waving menacingly, eyes alert for trouble. A safe way to handle him then—or any time, for that matter—is to dangle a piece of cloth in front of him, let him seize it, and lift him quickly into a pail or box.

Memo: If you catch any softies (you can distinguish them by the abnormal softness of their shells), keep them separate from the others; otherwise they can be damaged or killed by their hard-shelled companions.

Crabs will live for quite a while out of water if kept cool and moist. You can meet that requirement by placing them on a layer of wet seaweed and covering them with another layer: or by alternating layers of seaweed and crabs, finally covering the container with newspapers or a burlap bag and placing it in a cool, shady spot. Above all, protect them from the sun's direct rays. Keep them in the shade if possible. If there's no shade, at least cover the container with a newspaper, wetted cloth, or burlap bag. If they're not covered by damp seaweed, toss a little water on them now and again. If you find any dead crabs when you get home, *play it safe and discard them.*

DON'T OVERLOOK AUTUMN Blueclaw crabs are most abundant in summertime, notably during the "dog days" of July and August. But what many crabbing novices do not realize is that the season for the ornery crustaceans doesn't end with the closing days of summer. *Au contraire,* as the French say (that's a little culture I'm tossing in), there can be good crabbing through September and even on into October, if the weather doesn't turn too cold. In the fall blueclaws usually are at that season's peak for size. They're also apt to be at their season greediest for food, since they're storing up nutriments to sustain them through their winter stay in the bottom. Some of the biggest, meatiest crabs are caught in autumn. Give them a whirl. If you're going flounder fishing, take along a net, trap, or killy ring.

ON THE TABLE Hard-shell blueclaws are cooked whole and alive in boiling water. Some people with kind-hearted intentions kill them immediately beforehand by thrusting a knife point deep into the crab in his vulnerable place between the eyes. Frankly, I'm not so sure it's merciful, since scalding hot water does the job quickly. The knife bit just adds an extra step.

Some home chefs add varying quantities of beer to the water, claiming it adds to the flavor. Personally, I can't taste any difference. I never could see how beer penetrates that hard covering to get into the meat. So far as I'm concerned, all the beer might do is make the crab's final fraction of a second a bit gayer. Removed from the pot, they're allowed to cool, after which the meat is extracted with the aid of a nutcracker and pick. Hard crab eaters generally concentrate on the succulent meat in the big claws.

There are several ways of enjoying hard crabs in addition to eating them like walnuts. One of the most delicious—a procedure that originally came from the great blueclaw state of Maryland, I believe—is to devil the meat and serve it in the upper portion of the shell. Or the meat can be removed, shredded, and served in a seafood cocktail. Shredded, it also can be mixed with chopped onions and whatever and served as a salad on a bed of lettuce or in a sandwich.

Soft crabs are fried in deep, very hot fat and presented with French fries, plus tartar sauce as a garnish. You eat every scrap of them, claws and all. Delicious!

Sorry, but I'll have to stop talking about crab dishes. That business about the fried softies did it. It's got me drooling here, and all the typewriter keys are starting to sticktogetherlikethis.

CHAPTER 10

The Eel: "This unloved, elongated thing..."

I can think of no better way to launch this chapter than with a certain little poem. It was penned by an author identified only by the *nom de plume* The Sunrise Trailer in my copy. Walter Squires, a long-time friend and operator of Walter's Rowboats, a fishing station in Hampton Bays, N.Y., sent it to me many years ago. I don't know if Walt wrote it, but I thank him for it. If he was not its creator, my apology to The Sunrise Trailer for not being able to identify him (or her) further. The poem goes like this:

ODE TO THE EEL

Let poets heap their praises on
The soaring gull, the graceful swan,
The fleeting goose or blue-winged teal,
While I extol the lowly eel.

Fresh from his beauty pack of mud,
With summer coursing through his blood,
Supremely happy, blithe and gay,
He's frolicking about the bay.

Without a voice his joy to sing,
This unloved, elongated thing,
'Neath placid calm or billows rough,
In sweet contentment does his stuff.

No wolf in sheep's attire, he;
Rather, a fairy of the sea,
Who's neither horrid nor benign,
Despite his serpentine design.

The bard whose gaze is on the sky
Is bound to think of things that fly,
Not seek or ever try to feel
The friendship of the lowly eel.

Now, maybe that isn't deathless poesy, a Byron or Keats masterpiece, but it sure summarizes the eel's case among us humans. Here's a little guy, a regular sort, just trying to eke out a living; and because he looks something like a black snake— through no fault of his own, mind you—people give him the cold shoulder. Call that brotherhood, fair play, and justice?

Unquestionably, the eel's snakelike appearance is the biggest thing against him in human eyes. Most of us aren't particularly fond of snakes. To some folks, I suspect, an eel is a snake or reasonable facsimile. That, of course, is ridiculous. An eel isn't any more a snake than one of those long, skinny Polish bolognas. He's every bit as much of a fish as a cod, flounder, striped bass, or marlin. He breathes with gills and has fins. His form happens to be nature's way of adapting him to his particular way of life. He could shudder when looking at *us*, you know. So don't hold his looks against him. For our purposes he's a versatile chap.

A MYSTERY AND A MARVEL   One of the first things you should know about eels is that they're catadromous. That's a one-word way of saying they spawn in salt water but spend at least part of their lives in fresh water. "Catadromous" is the opposite of "anadromous," a term applied to fishes that spawn in fresh water but spend at least a portion of their existence in salt water. Striped bass and certain species of salmon are classic examples of anadromous fishes.

Eels have been known to man since time immemorial, but it was only comparatively recently that he learned where the interesting critters came from. Some of the early theories, dating back to the 1600s and earlier, about the origins of these fish were fantastic. Even more fantastic, they were believed.

One theory, for instance, seriously propounded that eels sprang from inanimate matter, such as dirt. Even the immortal Izaak Walton wasn't exactly a bright light when it came to theorizing about their origin. Having seen them in rivers, old Izaak declared they must have come from dew along the banks. For centuries thereafter even the best ichthyologists and naturalists weren't much more knowledgeable than Ike. As late as 1862 an obscure observer named Cairncross solemnly declared that the "progenitor of the Silver Eel is a small beetle." Other theories had it that they originated from hairs that fell into the water from horses' manes, or sprang from the gills of other fishes, or developed from fragments of skin or body scraped off on rocks by other eels.

The fact is that going into the twentieth century, scientists still didn't know the origin of eels.

It remained for Dr. Johannes Schmidt, a Danish biologist, to unravel the mystery. His persistent, meticulous detective work in the 1920s discovered some eggs, identified as those of eels, in a deep-water region far offshore of the southern United States. Subsequent investigation by Dr. Schmidt revealed that eels have a major spawning ground in the deeps between Bermuda and the Leeward Islands. Still more research indicated that two closely allied and very similar species, the American and European, share a common breeding ground.

Eel eggs have been recovered from the Atlantic at a depth of five hundred feet in the spring, siring a belief that they're released by the females for fertilization at depths ranging from there on down to a thousand feet, perhaps more, rising slowly toward the surface thereafter and incubating into larval fish as they go.

During early developmental stages larval eels are as unlike the adults as they could be. They're leaflike in shape, not tubular, quite transparent, without pigmentation, and very delicate. They're so unlike their elders at that stage that even erudite scientists were fooled when they first saw them. Thinking the larvae were some kind of previously undiscovered fish, they gave them the name *leptocephalus,* which freely translates as "thin head."

In the leptocephalic phase the infants are only about a quarter of an inch long. From then until they approach their destinations along distant coasts months later, the infants are mere bits of transparent ribbon, so to speak, transparent enough for the individual sections of their backbone to be counted. This counting of vertebrae led to discovery of a subtle difference between American and European eels: The latter have a few more.

Now we come to one of the most fascinating of all marvels in the fish world.

That eel spawning ground in the deeps between Bermuda and the Leeward Islands is only a jumping-off place. From there the babies travel to remote shores. They have no parents, or even hired tour guides, to steer them on the incredibly long journey, and they set out over routes over which they've never traveled before and about which they know nothing. Yet they find their way unerringly. Without instruments and charts, guided by some mysterious instinct alone, they do a navigation job that would make even Magellan green with envy.

Here's something even more remarkable.

American and European eels are born in the same general oceanic region, and the two species look enough alike to be indistinguishable except to a trained ichthyologist. Yet when the time comes for the two groups of infants to seek their respective fortunes, there's no confusion. They embark on their journeys with fixed purpose. Baby European eels head unerringly for Europe, and American eels always head for American shores. No one gets on the wrong bus. Possibly both species start out together, then separate at some point along the route. However the sorting is accomplished, it's accurate. Members of neither group get sidetracked to the wrong destinations. As development progresses, the infants grow to a stage at which they're called elvers. For three years the European elvers keep going until they get across the Atlantic to the places that will become their home. Their American cousins need about a year to reach our shores.

How do such mites, hardly brainy children, know the right course to cruise? What draws them across an enormous expanse of open ocean swarming with perils? Why not stay where they were born and live happily ever after? How do the European youngsters know enough to go to Europe and not stay with American small fry headed for our shores? By the same token, how come the American kids don't become confused? How do they know when they've arrived? And how do they know who is who? They must all look alike to each other, and they're much too young to count vertebrae.

Obviously, instinct and great drive are involved, guiding them and pushing them on the long voyage because it's part of their life pattern. These are built-in forces. Nature takes care of those. But what about those questions we asked above?

Famed British zoologist John Roxborough Norman offered a plausible explanation that provides some answers. He based it on a difference in the development times of the American and European babies. The former grow more rapidly than the latter, he said. From egg to elver stage the Americans require about a year. The same metamorphosis takes three years for the Europeans. In each case the development span is suited to the time needed for their long journey. If the European babies were to steer westward toward the North American coast, they would arrive before attaining the elver stage. Conversely, if the American larvae were to head toward Europe, they would become elvers far at sea. Apparently nature sees that they don't make those mistakes because their chances of survival might be lessened considerably.*

GROWTH AND LIFE CYCLE By the time American elvers near the coasts, estuaries, and rivers that will become their home for a good part, if not most, of their lives, they have attained a length of about three inches, but still retain that weird, uneellike appearance of the larval stage. This soon changes, however. They begin to assume the familiar elongated, tubular form of the adults, although their bodies still have a glassy, transparent look, without pigmentation. In time this too is altered, and the kids take on another new look. As they move into bays, sounds, and mouths of rivers their bodies become pigmented to darken like those of their elders.

Elvers enter the brackish water of estuaries in astronomical numbers. Here a separation by sex takes place. The young females, slightly larger than their boy companions, swim upstream,

* The "biological clock" probably is a strong factor in the migration. This is a marvelous built-in timing device possessed by all living creatures, including man. It tells fishes when to spawn, birds when to migrate, bears when to hibernate, etc. It also influences human physiology. In the case of the baby eels it probably tells them when to start out on the long trip, keeps them on it the proper amount of time, and tells them when they've arrived at their destinations.

sometimes for incredible distances. En route they can overcome tremendous obstacles, in the manner of spawning-bound salmon, to reach headwaters far inland. Occasionally they become land-locked in fresh-water ponds or lakes and live there for many years. The young males, meanwhile, tend to confine themselves to tidal waters along the seaboard, growing during the warmer weather and wintering in the mud.

Male American eels grow to a length of about two feet, while females can reach three or four feet. (The presence of some specimens larger than two feet in coastal waters has led to a speculation that not all females journey inland.) Some eels are believed to mature at age seven or eight, others not until twelve or older.

With maturity comes another mysterious summons, a silent invitation to a spawning migration. Down from rivers and streams to the sea come the ladies, to be joined by the gents residing in bays and tidal tributaries. On signal, in a huge squadron, the adult fish say goodbye forever to their American homes and un-erringly find their way back to their birthplace in the deeps between Bermuda and the Leeward Islands, a journey that this time consumes one or two months. There they spawn a new generation and die. Their amazing life cycle has come full turn. It's interesting to note that as many as twenty years may elapse before an eel undertakes the return voyage to the breeding region.

Spawning appears to occur in midwinter. European eels are among the most prolific of fishes. An average female can discharge five million to ten million eggs to be fertilized by male sperm in the water. A larger lady has a production potential estimated up to fifteen million to twenty million. Presumably the American females are just as prolific.

RANGE The American eel (*Anguilla rostrata*), sometimes called silver eel and fresh-water eel, has wide distribution in the western Atlantic. Overall, the species' range is described as extending from western Greenland, eastern Newfoundland, and the Gulf of St. Lawrence's northern side on down to Bermuda, the Gulf of Mexico, the West Indies, and Panama, and even as far south, although rarely, as the northern shores of South America.

As long as there's food, eels thrive no matter where they are.

As you've seen, they adapt readily to brackish and fresh water. Commonly in salt water they're found over a mud bottom in more or less calm places such as coves, canals, and creeks winding through salt marshes. But they'll also inhabit rocky locales, and often are found over sandy bottom in freely flowing trout streams. In contrast to the deeps of their birth, they spend most of their lives in comparatively shallow water. Eels can tolerate a wide range of temperatures. But they seem to favor reasonably warm water, and generally escape winter cold by "hibernating" in mud bottom.

IDENTIFICATION, HABITS, AND SEASONS We hardly need to dwell on identification of this fellow, but I do want to point out a few characteristics, including some that set him apart from the American conger eel, commonly caught by bottom fishermen.

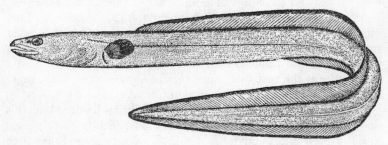

AMERICAN CONGER EEL (*Conger oceanica*)

The serpentine shape, of course, is the most obvious characteristic (of both species). The color pattern varies considerably, according to the bottom over which they live. Thus, eels residing over mud are darker than their kin living on sand. The color pattern is a shade of muddy or greenish brown on the back and upper sides, often tinged with a dirty yellow on the sides. This brown becomes lighter lower down on the sides and may be more yellowish. The belly is a dirty white or yellowish white.

Distinguishing the American eel is a long, continuous dorsal fin of more or less uniform height that originates well aft of the pectoral fins, then continues around the body's pointed end to become, so to speak, a long, continuous anal fin of uniform height.

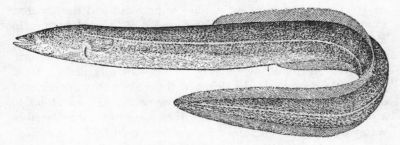

AMERICAN EEL (*Anguilla rostrata*)

In the dorsal fin is a difference between this eel and the conger. The conger's dorsal arises just behind his pectorals. Like the conger, the American eel has a pointed snout and a fairly large mouth, but there's a difference in their jaws. The conger's upper jaw projects beyond the lower. The opposite is true on the other eel.

American eels will eat just about anything. They are, in fact, quite greedy. They devour small fishes of many kinds—whatever species happen to be available, along with shrimp, small crabs, and lobsters and other crustaceans. Of prime importance to you as an eeler is the fact that, since they're omnivorous eaters, practically any kind of bait can be used to catch them.

They're chiefly nocturnal in their feeding habits, but this doesn't rule out catching them by day. They'll bite readily then too. But their night activity is a habit known to game fishes such as striped bass, sharks, and others. Anglers are aware of it too, and capitalize on it by using eels as bait for such game fishes during hours of darkness.

Although the better catches of eels often are made during the warmer months, a change of fishing methods can make them an all-year target.

HOW TO BE AN EELER You can catch eels by any of several techniques that are adaptable to places and seasons.

During the winter, when the fish are ensconced in mud for their hibernal siesta, spearing is the method. There's an implement just for this. An eel spear is a long-handled weapon bearing a passing resemblance to a giant seafood cocktail fork. Its closely spaced tines have barbs to keep the slithering fish from sliding

EEL SPEAR

or wriggling free once the spear has nailed them. You probe the bottom with this weapon in a continuous succession of jabs, jabbing away to find a spot where the fish are "bunched up," almost like a ball, in the mud. Such a nest of lethargic eels can yield a good catch.

An eelpot will account for good takes too. This is a trap, a cage with a rounded roof, made from nylon or wire mesh. It has a

 EELPOT

wide mouth that leads into a funnel-shaped throat, so designed to let eels get at the bait inside but prevent their return to freedom. An eelpot can be baited with clam or mussel meat, killies, spearing or other dead fish, crushed crab, or other natural food attractor. Preferably a bait should give off oil, bits of body flesh, or at least a scent to lure the victims. Even bread has been used. This draws little fishes which, in turn, lure eels to their point of no return. Eelpots are most effective when set out at night, with a small buoy at the surface to show their location, to take advantage of eels' nocturnal feeding habits. They can be raised and emptied and rebaited the next day.

Jacking is also an eel-hunting method. The procedure is very similar to that employed in jacking for blueclaw crabs, except that a spear is substituted for a net. Jacking also takes advantage of eels' night feeding activities. You get yourself a small boat, such as a rowboat, one that can be handled easily in poling or drifting, and place a bright lantern 'way up in her bow to shed light down into the water. As you glide along you peer down into that circle of light and stand ready to spear any eels that

swim into it. Sometimes the light attracts little fishes that draw
eels.

ON ROD AND REEL   Here you can have yourself some fun. A lively,
wriggling eel on light tackle—the lighter the better—puts up surprising resistance. What's more, rod and reel can account for
nice catches through the summer into fall.

Eels have been reported to reach weights of 10 pounds and
more. Bigelow and Schroeder mention weights up to 16½. But
these must be uncommon, king-sized specimens, for the average
weights in sport-fishing catches are well under 10 pounds, or even
8. A broad average is from just under a pound to 2, perhaps 3.

So your tackle should be light, even ultralight. A suitable
conventional-tip rod with a 1/0 reel, or equivalent spinning gear,
will do. Line should be light too. Any kind will suffice. You won't
need much because you'll be eeling in shallow water. Twenty-
five to 50 yards is plenty.

Hooks should be in proportion to eel mouths. The range is
from about a No. 6 to a 1/0 at the outside, depending upon sizes
of the fish currently running. If you're in doubt about hook sizes,
favor the smaller ones. Better those than oversized hooks.

SIMPLE EEL RIG

Hook baits for eels include pieces of bloodworm, sandworm,
shrimp, beef heart, shedder crab, or clam—hard, soft, or skimmer.
The larger eels also will accept a small dead killy or spearing.
Lacking any of the foregoing, you probably could try a piece of
squid or a small strip cut from the underside of some fish.

Eeling with rod and reel is simple bottom fishing. Use a bank
type sinker, only heavy enough to hold bottom. Your hooks, without leaders, are tied into the line, with or without swivels, as
close as possible to the sinker. There's little advantage in rigging
more than two hooks. More than that only enhances the annoyance of their tangling with each other, and you can't tie them too
far apart or too high up because eels are less likely to take a bait
higher than 3 or 4 inches over the bottom.

Another eeling technique, also involving rod and reel, is called bobbing. For this you can choose between two bobs or rigs.

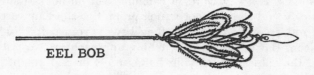

EEL BOB

One type of eel bob calls for a length of coarse yarn, rough and strong enough to catch and hold an eel's tiny teeth. On this length of yarn, with a needle of suitable length, you thread some whole bloodworms or sandworms, after which the yarn's free ends are wrapped around the bait a few times, just enough to minimize its being torn off but not enough to conceal it. This lovely necklace of worms then can be fashioned into short loops or a ball-like mass to make the bob.

With a sinker attached just under it, the bob is secured to your fishing line and lowered to the bottom. Your bob must be right on the floor. The idea behind this gismo is that eels attack the worms and get their little dentures caught in the yarn, whereupon the action is transmitted to your end. Hauling them in becomes a little tricky, with much depending upon how well the bob has caught their teeth. They can wriggle free. You can heighten your chances of capture by reeling the bob up at a steady pace, keeping your line taut, and having a landing net handy for when the bob nears the surface.

Another type of eel bob, less work and no prettier, can be fashioned by taking a lady's fine-mesh hairnet (first making sure the lady is out of it) and filling it with bloodworms or sandworms, or 'arf 'n' 'arf if you so desire. This grotesque-looking thing is weighted with a sinker and attached to your line in the same manner as the other bob. What happens is that hungry eels try to get at the worm handout and get their teeth fouled in the hairnet's mesh. Again you'll have to reel in carefully, even more so than before because there's a greater chance of an eel dropping off.

A simple handline can be substituted for rod and reel with

both kinds of bobs. In the case of the hairnet stunt it may be necessary to use a handline or a stiff stick for a light rod because of the bob's weight.

Promptness is a key word in catching eels on hooks too. Eels bite quickly and slyly. If not struck promptly—short upward lift of your rod tip, not a wild jerk—they'll swipe your bait, skin your hook clean. If you've had a twitching approach or two without hooking the culprit, check your bait. An eel or crab might have been indulging in a little larceny.

Eels are hardy. Just as they adapt readily to brackfish and fresh water, and can switch back to salt again, they can stay alive for a respectable time out of their native element. I suggest, though, that you put them in a bucket of sea water after catching, and protect them from the sun's direct rays. Changing the water once in a while doesn't do any harm either. You want to keep them alive as long as possible so they'll be really fresh for cooking.

HANDLING EELS   You'll make things easier for yourself if you wear a pair of cheap cotton work gloves, or use a piece of burlap or cloth, when handling eels. The expression "slippery as an eel" isn't without foundation. With a naturally slippery skin, and going into all kinds of contortions to escape, a live eel is a real handful. He can be dislodged from a bob by vigorous shaking over a receptacle. In unhooking an eel you can anticipate his wrapping himself around your hand and fist. But don't let it disturb you. You'd do the same thing if you were in his fix.

Preparing eels for cooking isn't a particular jolly chore, but it's not so bad once you get used to it. One way to do the job is to grasp the eel firmly near the head with gloves or a piece of cloth, then make a deep cut across the throat (his, not yours). Slit the body open on the underside (you may have to pin down his tail end with your foot) from the throat incision to the vent, and gut him. Continue that throat cut right on around, through the skin. Using his head as a handle, strip the skin from the body. A pair of pliers will give you a good grip for this operation. (If you're a striped bass fisherman, get the skin off in one piece and use it for an eelskin rig.) With dead eels—be sure they're fresh! —the process is the same, but not as lively.

After eels are gutted, skinned, and beheaded, they can be rinsed *lightly* in cold, salted tap water and drained on absorbent paper. Or you can remove excess moisture with a damp cloth. Then they're cut into sections two or three inches long, rolled in flour or cracker meal mixture, and fried like other pan fish. They're good eating (better than rattlesnake, I can tell you). The meat has a delicate flavor, rather like flounder. There are bones to contend with, but they're easily removed with a fork.

Incidentally, if you're pan frying very fresh eels don't be dismayed if the sections quiver or twitch a little. The fish are quite dead. Those movements are just involuntary muscular reactions to heat.

Eels also can be pickled, like lambs' tongues and pigs' feet. They're delicious when smoked. There are portable fish- and meat-smoking devices on the market. Quite inexpensive and easy to use, they come in handy for smoking many kinds of fishes. An alternate arrangement is to see if you can locate a professional smokehouse in your area.

EELING PLACES The elongated fish are caught in many locations throughout bays, harbors, coves, channels, and creeks. They can be found over mud and sand bottoms, but often prefer the former. The deeper spots of shoal areas can be productive. Look for holes. Eels also are encountered along sod banks of canals and creeks where the water isn't very deep at high tide. Such locations are good on dark, moonless nights when the tide is at flood stage. When a tide begins to ebb you can find them in drains crossing flats that are above water at low tide.

In spearing them during the winter, through ice or in open water, you'll have to use the by-guess-and-by-golly methods, probing various places. But it will help if you know beforehand where the mud bottoms are. Be extremely careful about venturing out on ice in any kind of fishing, *doubly so on salt-water ice*. Salt-water ice not only can fool you as regards its thickness, it's apt to be porous in places and treacherous. It takes a real spell of truly cold weather to form salt-water surface ice of safe thickness. If you're not sure of the ice, stay off it. No fishing in the world is worth a winter dunking—or worse.

A VERSATILE GUY   In addition to their contribution to tasty seafood platters, eels serve anglers well as bait for larger, more desirable game fishes; striped bass, for instance. Whole live eels
are rigged as come-ons for stripers. Dead eels, intact or in sections, come into play for striped bass and other gamesters. Cut
into pieces with the skin left on, eels are an effective bait when
pestiferous crabs are around, since the tough hide resists the sly
attacks of such thieves.

Whole eels also are rigged for some of the billfishes, such as
white marlin and swordfish. Sharks will accept them too. Then
there are those eelskin rigs for stripers, which you'll learn about
in the chapter on those fish. Eels in one form or another, by themselves or in combination with artificials, also have accounted for
bluefish, weakfish, cobia, and other marine battlers.

There now, don't you have more affection for our "unloved,
elongated thing," the eel? I think his many services earn him a
little respect around here, even if given grudgingly. In my opinion he's a pretty good guy to have with us.

BELIEVE IT OR NOT   I can't leave this chapter without telling
you an amazing eel story. It's incredible, but it happened. The
source of the story was no less an authority than Dr. Edward
Gudger, then Curator Emeritus of Fishes at New York's Museum
of Natural History.

It happened in The Bronx, New York. In some apartment
houses the supply of water to tenants was suddenly cut off or
seriously impaired. The cause was a mystery. When the trouble
was scouted it was discovered—are you ready for this?—that
there were eels in the plumbing. You read correctly. Eels in the
plumbing.

Dr. Gudger was called in on the weird case and solved the
mystery of how those crazy eels got themselves trapped in, of all
places, Bronx plumbing. Here's the way Dr. Gudger recon-
structed the situation.

Originally the pipe-trapped eels were part of a migration moving up the Hudson River. Along the way they passed the mouth
of the Croton River, which branches off the Hudson, so they
turned in there and headed up that route. After a while they
encountered a dam right smack in their way. You'd think that

would have ended the wanderers' excursion. Not at all, said Dr. Gudger. On a damp or rainy night they could slither through wet grass, aided by the natural mucous lubricant on their skin, and go right up the grassy slopes on either side of the dam. At the summit there was only a road to cross. When wet that would pose no more of a problem than the slopes. Once on the other side, it was all downhill into the Croton River again.†

From there they made their way into a reservoir. En route they encountered another barrier. This one consisted of a double set of screens, one at either end of a conduit entering the reservoir. That problem was solved by the eels patiently waiting until the screens were raised for their periodic cleaning. Once in the reservoir, the eels continued their journey via pipes and eventually wound up as unwilling occupants of Bronx apartment houses' plumbing.

As I said, the eel is quite a character.

† Eels can live for quite a while out of water. There have been many stories about their ability to move across land when determined to find a body of water. There are accounts of the fish slithering across meadows on damp or rainy nights in the British Isles and elsewhere in transfers from one body of water to another.

CHAPTER 11

Flounders: The World's Most Popular (?) Marine Sport Fish

No one ever took a census, but it would be my guess that more people wet a line for flounders than for any other salt-water species. I base that on the hundreds of rowboat stations and party boats and their tens of thousands of customers in Rhode Island, Connecticut, New York, and New Jersey, prime home of the popular flatfish. I doubt, though, that the little honeybunches appreciate the distinction, since it means their winding up in skillets. That's their "reward" for being so much fun to catch, so numerous, and for tasting so good.

The species of flounder we're spotlighting is one caught along middle and northerly segments of the U.S. Atlantic seaboard, a member of a very large, far-flung family collectively grouped under the name flatfishes. It's estimated that more than five hundred kinds of fishes belong to this enormous tribe. Among them we find such names as: starry flounder; hog choker; lemon sole; diamond flounder; Dover sole (England's famous flatfish); northern fluke or summer flounder; a small, semitranslucent fellow called a window pane; and the mighty halibuts.

All of these flatfishes share a family resemblance: a broad body, flattened in the horizontal plane, with both eyes on the same side of the head. That last detail makes them unique among all fishes in both salt and fresh waters. There are certain color similarities among many of them too; and a typical flatfish, whatever his breed, has his pigmentation on the upper surface of his body, while his underside is a shade of white.

But they differ considerably in size. The flounder we're talking about here is one of the family's smaller members, along with the little window pane. Far and away the largest, king of the entire clan, is the Atlantic halibut. This fellow is a fish of great size in any league, and you can throw in marlins, sharks, and tuna. Here's a brute with a body as broad as a tabletop and as thick through as a man at his beltline. In old-time commercial fishing records are notations about Atlantic halibut weighing as much as five hundred, six hundred, and even seven hundred pounds.

A "TWISTED CHILDHOOD" A detail that makes flatfishes especially unusual, even in a kingdom abounding in strange citizens, is a weird developmental stage that takes place when they're young.

Our friend the flounder—like all his relatives—starts out in life just like any other fish. His body is more or less oval in cross section and symmetrical, and his eyes are positioned in standard fish fashion, one on either side of his head. But then, when he's three months or so old, something very odd occurs. Very odd indeed. As if in response to a cue, his entire frame begins to alter. The head bones gradually twist to one side. His body commences to flatten out from side to side horizontally, like a phonograph record, instead of gaining depth. And his internal organs rearrange themselves accordingly.

Also remarkable, one eye—his left—gradually "migrates" until it comes to its permanent position alongside its mate. The entire body continues its broadening until it attains the characteristic flatfish form. Its upper side becomes pigmented to give the fish his color, while its "blind" side underneath remains ghastly white.

For the remainder of his life the flounder blithely swims around like an undulating plate moving through the water. His colored side is always uppermost. Both eyes are now atop his head, and he can't see beneath him very well. This is why his belly is called a blind side.

The flounder's color pattern provides camouflage protection above. The grayish brown, and variations, of his topside resemble the bottom on which he dwells. It enables him to blend in with his surroundings and so escape detection from enemies—larger fishes—by being inconspicuous. It can be quite difficult to spot a flounder at rest on the bottom. If his coloration doesn't enable him to elude foes he should get his money back, because that's the idea behind it, and it's a drab decoration. His white underside serves camouflage purposes too. From underneath he's less noticeable in light filtering down through the waves.

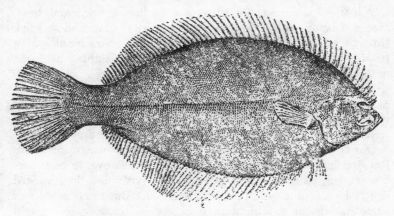

FLOUNDER (*Pseudopleuronectes americanus*)

Another unusual detail of the flounder and his flatfish kin is the size, shape, and positioning of the dorsal and anal fins. Most fishes wear their dorsal fin on the back and their anal fin underneath, near the tail; and the customary arrangement is for the former to be appreciably larger than the latter. Not so with the flatfishes. They wear theirs around the edges of their disclike bodies. Moreover, their dorsal and anal fins are quite similar in size and shape. They get around beautifully by an undulating motion of these fins, coupled with the fanning motion of a well-developed tail.

DISTRIBUTION AND HABITS   This flounder with the long Latin scientific name, *Pseudopleuronectes americanus*, is classified by some authorities as one of the most common shallow-water flatfishes on North America's eastern coast. The approximate extremes of the species' range are from as far north as Nova Scotia and Labrador on down to Georgia. Some of its greatest centers of abundance are in bays of New Jersey, New York, and Connecticut, and throughout the generous reaches of Long Island Sound. Throughout their range these flounders can be encountered from very shallow bays and coastal inshore zones on out to less deep ocean grounds. At least those are depths in which the greatest numbers are caught. The sport fishery, for the most part, is confined to waters well under 100 feet deep—even under 50 feet in many instances.

But these flatfish have been caught commercially at levels farther down. On the famed Georges Bank grounds off eastern Canada, for example, they've been taken at depths of 150 to 270 feet. Drs. Bigelow and Schroeder say that 70 fathoms (420 feet) is about the deepest they've ever heard for *Pseudopleuronectes americanus*.

These flounders aren't migratory. On the contrary, they're among the most stay-put fishes along the eastern North American seaboard. They're not inclined to wander about extensively or go on long coastwise cruises. Tagging experiments have underscored flounders' lack of interest in travel. Tagged specimens were recaptured only relatively short distances from where they were marked.

No, flounders are more the homebody type. Each region along the coast is believed to house its own populations. They there are born, grow up, and die of old age—unless humans get to them with hooks and cooking fat, without even visiting cousins Nancy and Elmer in another county. It's a dull, unimaginative existence by our standards, but the flatties like it.

Natural foods of the species include marine worms, tiny crabs, and other little crustaceans, and assorted lesser creatures such as minute shellfish and amphipods, a group that includes our so-called sand fleas.

ACCENT THIS HABIT As a fisherman, the most important thing for you to remember about these flounders is that they're exclusively ground fish or bottom dwellers. They spend their entire lives right on a bay or ocean floor, seldom venturing more than a few inches above it. That's one of the big differences between them and their cousins the fluke or summer flounders. Fluke are more aggressive and active. They'll pursue food—or baits and artificials—right to the surface if the spirit moves them. Not flounders. They're more independent. Or maybe they're lazier. Often they lie, buried in sand or mud with only their eyes showing, waiting for prey to come their way. They also actively shop for food, but always it's close to the bottom.

You must remember this because it governs the way you rig

for them. If you endeavor to hook flounders anywhere but on the bottom or very close to it—even a foot or so can make a difference—you'll fish till kingdom come without so much as a nibble. A common mistake made by novice flounder fishermen is to rig their hooks too far off the bay floor. They invariably come home empty-handed. As I said, flounders are very independent.

Commonly you'll find the flatties over mud or sandy bottom, or a floor that is a kind of muddy sand. If it's broken by patches of eelgrass, so much the better. A hard bottom, such as clay, also surrenders flounders in some areas, as do bottoms of gravel and pebble-peppered sand.

Flounders like the waters in which they reside to be cool, but not too cold. Unacceptably frigid water can kill them. This mortality sometimes occurs when a sudden cold snap overtakes them in very shallow water (which chills quickly). Similarly, they can't tolerate fast, high rises in water temperatures. Such extremes, low and high, have been known to slaughter flounders by the thousands when they're trapped, so to speak, in very shallow water.

SEASONS   Water temperatures are most suitable to flounders in spring and autumn. Consequently, they're most abundant and active in their usual haunts during those seasons. Because conditions are optimum in spring and autumn, those are the best times of year to go for flounders. They follow a yearly timetable with regularity. They're very faithful.

We can break into their cycle anywhere to trace it, but let's arbitrarily start with autumn. Summer over, and the first signs of cooler weather making themselves felt, flounders start moving back into bays, coves, harbors, channels, and the less deep parts of sounds after having summered in deep water, perhaps outside in the Atlantic, to escape the heat. (Real shallows, you see, become more unbearably hot or cold than deeper places.) They're not only numerous at this time, they're also at that season's best for size, having had several months in which to stuff their little stomachs and grow. It's also the time of year in which they're apt to be very lively feeders, storing up nourishment against the relatively inactive winter ahead.

Their autumn performance's duration is regulated chiefly by

the thermometer and how quickly it lowers water temperatures. September's latter half and the entire month of October are generally flounder harvesting weeks throughout much of their range. The farther south you go in their range, the longer their fall run endures. Even in November, at least in temperate portions of their habitat, local waters may not be cold enough yet to drive them away completely. Water temperatures usually lag behind air temperatures. But in November there usually comes a marked decrease in numbers.

As late fall moves in and really asserts itself, poking chilly fingers into shallower areas under clouds threatening snow, the waning numbers of flatfish seek haven from the increasing cold. By or before the end of November their autumn run is over.

As winter approaches they bury themselves in mud, or at least move into deeper, warmer places. There they wait out the winter, pondering whatever it is flounders think about. Not infrequently during mild winters some flatties continue to swim around in search of food. At such times it's often possible to hook at least a few. But scarcity of fish, unavailability of boats, ice on the water, and polar winds add up to a less-than-ideal flounder fishing season.

By December most of the flatties are holed up somewhere in mud or deeper water until the approach of spring. Their reappearance on the spring fishing grounds also is governed by the thermometer, aided to a certain extent by the intensity of their hunger at the time. On Long Island, N.Y., it's an old fishermen's saying that spring flounder angling begins around St. Patrick's Day. But there and in New Jersey bays to the south they can and often do jump the starting gun by beginning to show in February—not in any great numbers, however. Frequently the first flounders of a new year still carry smears of mud on their backs, indicating that they emerged from their winter bungalows only recently.

From March on, encouraged by gradually warming waters and prodded by a nagging appetite, flounders pop out of the mud and move into their usual bay haunts from the ocean and deeper areas where they wintered. Spring, like fall, is an excellent flounder fishing season, although at that time you'll usually find a larger percentage of small and undersized fish, the products of recent spawning.

Provided local waters do not become overheated, they can maintain a good level of abundance well into May, even June. As water temperatures climb, the majority of flatties shift elsewhere from the bays to find cooler levels. Their spring run tapers off. But often you can make catches, some of them good, right on into summer if you seek out deeper, cooler sections of bays, channels, inlets, and sounds.

Finally summer falls astern, as summers do with regularity, and fishermen begin thinking about the flat-bodied targets again. We move toward autumn, flounders start to "reappear," and another year-long cycle is complete.

Fall and spring, then, are major flounder fishing seasons. And since water temperatures are a big factor, the lengths of their autumnal and vernal runs vary somewhat, but overlap, from one large segment of coast to another. Broadly speaking, the farther south in their range they live, the sooner they show in prespring weeks and the longer they linger into fall.

MASS PRODUCTION Again depending upon water temperatures, flounders spawn any time from about January to as late as May. They're considered winter and early spring breeders.

An average female releases approximately five hundred thousand eggs annually. Some of the larger producers can turn out a million or more. These ova aren't buoyant, so they sink to the bottom, where they cling together in clusters, like grapes. Typical of fishes, these extremely small eggs are fertilized by sperm discharged into the water by males.

Take half a million to a million or more eggs laid by a single female and multiply them by thousands of lady flounders, and you have a mess of eggs indeed. But by now you know what happens to many, if not the vast majority, of them.

Ova lucky enough to be fertilized in the first place, then survive the forays of hungry neighbors and hostile environmental conditions, soon hatch into larval fish. (Infant fishes probably are called larval at this stage because so many of them look more like some kind of insect larvae than fish.)

Subsequent growth is fairly rapid as the infants forage for the

minute tidbits on which they feed. Their childhood is far from
happy and carefree. Getting sufficient food is only one worry.
Looming even larger is the distinct possibility of becoming an
item on the menu of many foes. Baby fishes never know from
one instant to the next whether they'll eat or be eaten. Fortunately they're not given to worrying about it, otherwise they'd
all be little nervous wrecks. But I'll tell you, lucky indeed are
the little flounders that survive their hectic childhood and ado-
lescence to grow up.

Naturally, countless thousands of them do survive, otherwise
the species would be as extinct as the dodo. Those on which Lady
Luck continues to smile attain a length of about 4½ inches by
the end of their first year. That increases to 7½ or so by their
second birthday. At age 3 they're some 9 to 10 inches long. By
the time they celebrate their 6th anniversary they're fairly big
boys as their breed goes, having reached 13 or 14 inches.

The average weight range of the majority of bay-caught flounders is ½ pound to 1½ or 2 pounds. But there are larger fellows,
often dubbed "sea flounders," that can hit over 3 pounds. Spring
and fall, with an accent on the former season for the very little
guys, you'll find a range that goes from a few ounces for "postage
stamps" to 1, 1½ and 2 pounds.

There are even larger specimens; but the bigger they become,
the fewer of them that are hooked. Among these are the flatties
which, because of their size and shape, have come to be nicknamed "snowshoes" on eastern Long Island. Thereabouts snowshoes seemed to be confined for the most part to waters off
Montauk Point and Block Island. Late spring, along about May or
June, is the best time to hook them, although some are boated
throughout the better part of summer. A special rig that can be
used for these flatties, cod, and pollack simultaneously is detailed
in the chapter on cod.

These are the largest known representatives of the species.
They may inhabit areas as yet undiscovered. The only grounds
on which I've heard of them being taken are the aforementioned
Montauk-Block Island sector and Georges Bank off eastern Canada. On Georges Bank 5- and 6-pounders are commercially
caught. Such sizes are seen among sport catches of snowshoes,
but not in numbers. The ceiling is more like 3 or 3½ pounds

there. The biggest snowshoe I've ever seen weighed 8 pounds, 6 ounces and was boated off Montauk Point many years ago.

TACKLE TALK   All you need by way of gear for flounder fishing is a light rod, 5 to 6 feet overall, conventional type or spinning. Accent lightness and flexibility. Flounders are small fish, and you want to get as much action from them as you can. Besides, you won't be fishing in very deep water or using the heavier sinkers. Too, flounders can bite rather delicately. If you sit there with a rod built like a small tent pole you might not even feel the fish nibbling. In that case your hook will become a free lunch counter, and if flounders had sleeves they'd be laughing up them.

Your reel can be a simple 1/0 of conventional type, or one of the small spinning "mills."

Because of its flexibility, a light spinning rod is fine for flounder angling, since heavy rigs aren't involved. Any one of the small spinning reels will match it nicely. You can even wield fresh water spinning tackle here, but if it has metal parts that aren't corrosion-resistant you may have to clean them after each use to guard against damage by salt air and water.

Line should be correspondingly light. Its material is immaterial, mono or braided. Fifty yards at the outside should be more than sufficient. Six-pound test is strong enough.

A hook pattern that does a good job on flounders is the long-shank Chestertown. This style is practically standard in sinker-bouncing for the flatties. The Chestertown's bend is well suited to flounders' small mouths. The term "long shank" means that the hooks' straight portion is extra long. This is good. Flounders have a habit of taking a hook deep inside their gullet. A long shank makes it easier to unhook them. Chestertown hooks generally come with snells of gut or other material attached. These are for attachment to your rig. Long-shank Chestertowns, sizes No. 9 to No. 6 (*not* 9/0 to 6/0!) are suggested for flounders. If you can't remember the name and sizes when you buy them, just ask for flounder hooks.

Important: Since flounders have little mouths, your hooks must be small too. If you're in doubt about what size to rig, favor the smaller size, rather than risking one that might be too large. Flounders won't accept hooks that are too big for their mouths.

A fish can't very well swallow something he can't wrap his mouth around, now can he?

You want to get right down to the bottom and stay there, so you'll need sinkers. You can tie any type of sinker onto your rig. Actually an old bolt or other small piece of metal of sufficient weight would serve to hold your rig on bottom. But we usually employ a sinker of the bank type.

Always carry sinkers of assorted sizes so you can vary the weights as conditions dictate. For flounders you'll be fishing mostly in fairly shallow water and/or places where currents aren't too stiff. Two or three to five ounces should do, but if currents gain strength on certain phases of the tide you may have to go a bit heavier. Just don't overdo it. Use only enough to hold bottom, no more. Small opponents such as flounders are outclassed by the combination of your tackle and superior strength as it is. Don't add an extra-heavy sinker for them to battle too. With practice, bouncing your sinker on bottom will notify you when you have enough lead.

RIGGING This is a detail separating greenhorns from successful sinker-bouncers. Flounder fishing is simple, but with improper rigging all you'll get is a little exercise.

TYPE I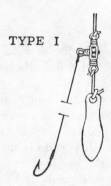

There are two basic kinds of flounder rigs. I'll designate them as Type I and Type II.

Type I is quite serviceable, but seldom is used anymore, the reason being Type II, which we'll get to in a minute. Type I calls for one or two hooks. If you rig a single hook, tie it into the line immediately above the sinker by its snell. A two-loop barrel swivel isn't a necessity in making the attachment, but it minimizes the snell twisting on itself or tangling with the line. If a second hook is incorporated, connect it to the line, with or without a swivel (again the latter is preferred), just above the first. Bear in mind that both hooks must be as close to the bottom as possible. This Type I rig's big drawback is that when two hooks are used they tend to tangle with each other, a nuisance.

Type II is the most popular flounder rig. The fact that it has been fished almost universally for decades is eloquent testimony to its efficiency.

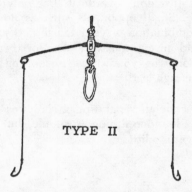

TYPE II

This terminal setup calls for a simple device known as a spreader. It's only a piece of stiff, fairly heavy wire, slightly bent like a bow, with a loop at each outer end. On top, middle, is a swivel arrangement for attachment to the line and to give the spreader freedom of movement to minimize line twisting. Underneath that, in the middle, is a place to tie a sinker.

To ready this gadget, all you do is tie it to your line, attach a sinker of suitable weight (tie it close to keep the rig right on bottom), and connect a flounder hook by its snell to each of the eyes at the spreader's outer ends. Bait up, and you're in business.

A spreader has big advantages. It enables you to use two hooks, keeping them apart so they won't tangle with each other. Two hooks, in turn, give you a chance to try two different baits simultaneously, and will get you two fish at a time when flounders are running well.

There's a third setup that is more or less a variation of Type I. It's sometimes employed in drifting for flounders, especially in rocky places where it may not be quite as likely as Type II to get fouled in obstructions. In this Type III you tie in your first hook as you did in Type I, right above the sinker. A second hook then is attached by its snell to the snell of the first hook, at about the midpoint.

I suggest you stick to Type II. If flounders are available, it'll get 'em. But keep Types I and III in mind. You might want to experiment.

Note: All the foregoing tackle and rigging have been targeted at fishing for flounders of "standard" size. Snowshoes weren't included. If you fish the special three-species rig detailed in our chapter on cod—the one for cod, pollack, and snowshoe flounders simultaneously—you'll be wielding heavier tackle because of larger fishes, a heavier rig, bigger baits, and a heavier sinker to hold against fairly strong currents. If you fish for snowshoes alone you may have to go to somewhat heavier equipment than for the smaller flatties, because here again you'll probably be in deeper water and require a heavier sinker.

BAITS To catch fish you naturally have to offer a come-on. Not even the densest dumdum of a fish is going to be attracted by just a nude hook.

Flounders' natural foods include marine worms and small clams and mussels. So what we try to do in the bait department is match those items as closely as possible, or at least offer something equally appealing. In bloodworms, sandworms, clams, and mussels we have the answers.

Bloodworms and sandworms are among the attractors most widely offered, and they rate among the most successful. You'll find, though, that flounders' tastes in baits can vary. Thus in some areas at certain times they may exhibit a preference for sandworms over bloodworms, or vice versa. Or they may respond more readily to a piece of clam than to worm. You're usually safe with bloodworms, but if you want to play it smart, take along a couple of different kinds of baits. Combination baits, such as a piece of worm and a bit of clam or mussel on the same hook, can be productive too. If you have some mussels, they also can be used as flounder chum.

Tip: If you have, say, two kinds of baits, try one of each on your spreader at the start of fishing. Note which gets the quickest response, then change the other bait accordingly. This also can be helpful when fishing is slow.

Regardless of what bait is used for flounders, it must be in small pieces. That's important. As you now know, flounders have little mouths. Your bait, therefore, like your hook, must be small so the fish can wrap his hungry little mouth around it. Beginning anglers often make the mistake of thinking that the bigger a bait is, the better their chances. In flounder fishing it works the opposite way. An oversized bait is an unnecessary waste, to begin with; and all that's likely to happen is that it will be nibbled away by thieves of one kind or another. Cut your worm, clam, or whatever (if you don't have a whatever, use mussel) into pieces a half inch or so long. Impale that bait on your hook in such a way that its point and barb are hidden. That's enough.

After a spell in the water, with no takers, baits are apt to be rather washed-out and blah, their scent and flavor leached away. That's especially true of bloodworm. Come-ons in that condition have lost much, if not most, of their appeal. (How would you like gray, tasteless roast beef?) I believe in checking flounder baits at intervals when they're not getting results. First, I want to make sure they're still present. Second, I want to see if they look faded, unattractive. Generally I put on fresh bait at intervals anyway. To my way of thinking it's false economy to sit there with a bait that might be only half effective.

Periodically there come seasons when bloodworms and/or sandworms are in short supply, even impossible to get, for one reason or another. The supply is entirely dependent upon professional diggers and their success. If crops are skimpy, you're going to have a tough time getting worms. You'll have to turn to substitutes.

A good one is the dyed clam stunt. It's simple, it's effective, and it has saved many a day when worms were scarcer than fur-covered pool tables.

What you do is this: Get yourself some clams. Skimmers will

do fine. You can use other hard-shell clams too, such as the kind served on the half shell, but they're more expensive. You won't need many. You also buy some vegetable dye, the kind bakers and housewives use to tint pastries and cake icing. It's sold in food stores. In this gimmick either red or yellow dye can be used. Red is favored by many sinker-bouncers, but it won't do any harm to try both.

Put your dye in a jar according to instructions accompanying it. Having extracted the clams from their shells, you can immerse them whole or cut into pieces. Put them into the dye. Since there's no predicting what intensity of color flounders will fancy on a given day, you might dye the clams to different shades, pale to bright. Increasing their immersion time, of course, heightens the color.

I don't think clams, dyed or otherwise, are ever quite as good as bloodworm or sandworm for flounders, although there are occasions when the little guys show a marked preference for clams (much depends upon the locale, I suppose, and what kind of natural food prevails there). But I'll tell you this: Dyed clams will catch flounders, and they fill the bill neatly when worms are scarce. They're also handy when you have only a few worms and want to stretch your bait supply. With a spreader you can bait one hook with a piece of worm and the other with a little hunk of gaudy clam.

Here's another stunt: Sometimes a piece of shiny tinfoil wrapped around a hook's shank just above the bait acts as an extra attraction.

CHUMMING Chumming has been an integral part of sport fishing for many years, employed successfully for gamesters such as bluefin tuna, sharks, striped bass, and others. It has come into increasing use for flounders too. Here it can be advantageous because sometimes the fish are feeding at varying distances from the boat and otherwise couldn't be drawn to her vicinity.

The simplest way to chum for flounders is to crack the shells of mussels—just enough to release body juices and minute bits of meat, don't stomp 'em to death—and drop them overboard right alongside the boat, a few at a time. Fishing stations and rowboat liveries peddle mussels just for that purpose.

CHUM POT

A superior way to chum for flounders is to fashion a chumpot. A small sack with a coarse mesh, such as one of those bags oranges and onions come in, will do. Or fashion a bag from a square of netting, tied at the neck. Into this sack you place some mussels, their shells cracked as before. With the bag's neck closed, tie a length of stout twine to it so it can be lowered to the bottom and raised. Make the twine long enough so that you can tie it to an oarlock or bitt so you won't lose the chumpot.

Lower this sackful of cracked mussels to the bottom. Every so often bounce it vigorously on the bay floor, the idea being that juices and tiny fragments of meat from the mussels will seep out into the water and lure flounders to your vicinity. At the start of fishing there may be no flatties in your immediate area, but when they get a "whiff" of those succulent mussels it's like an appetizer, or so you hope. They become interested, zero in on that trail of mussel juice and tiny tidbits, and follow it to its source. And there, lo and behold, is the main course, your bait. The appetizer is free, but the main course means a trip to a frying pan, yet flounders never seem to catch on.

Chumming is a must when flounder angling is slow. Many sinker-bouncers use it in any case.

Mussels are good flounder chum, but there are other items you can employ when those aren't available. Ground skimmer clams are one. Another is canned fish food for cats. Rice, colored yellow with vegetable dye, also has served. So have dried bread crumbs—in a pinch. If a chumpot's mesh weren't too coarse, I suppose ground mossbunkers would work too. Canned kernel corn also has been used, but now we talk against it. Flounders can't digest corn, and we believe it can kill those not caught.

Another method of chumming, especially suited to a mud

bottom, involves an oar, boathook, or simple pole. It has to be long enough to reach bottom. With it you stir up the bottom occasionally. This dislodges tiny shellfish, worms, and other tidbits, which attract flounders to the spot. Party boats carry long poles just for this purpose. Lacking something long enough to reach bottom, you can agitate the bay floor by bouncing your boat's anchor at intervals. When you're out in the bay, see if there's a clamdigger or dredge at work, and anchor nearby. They'll do the stirring up of the bottom for you. There's often good flounder activity around such agitation.

So . . . now you have your tackle and bait, you're rigged, you have some ideas on chumming, and you're ready to go. Let's find a place that should yield fish.

AREAS WITH POTENTIAL   Another reason flounders are such popular finned game is that they're found in so many places. During a normal run they're all over inside waters, in bays, coves, harbors, canals, channels, and inlets.

Because of this ubiquitousness there's no hard-and-fast rule about *good* flounder spots. Areas differ from one another in conducive conditions they offer to flounders. Too, the fish move around in search of food. Thus a place can be productive as all get-out one day and be practically barren the next. And when I say "place" I mean one small area, not an entire bay or harbor.

There are, however, some general suggestions I think you'll find helpful:

1. One spot with potential is over soft, black mud in water about six to twelve feet deep or so at high tide. Check the nature of the mud by dropping your anchor and pulling it up to examine blobs of mud clinging to it. Ideally, the mud should be coal-black with a velvety touch, and no strongly offensive smell. If it's flecked with tiny white specks, so much the better. These are minute shellfish on which flounders feed. If the mud has an unhealthy-looking grayish hue, feels slimy or greasy to the touch, and smells awful, move on to another place, because that stuff will lessen your chances. The odds are that such a bottom is barren of vegetation that attracts the lesser creatures on which flounders dine.

2. It will help to remember that at high tide flounders tend to scatter over submerged mud flats and sand bars, but in channels are apt to loiter around the edges. When a tide drops, they have a habit of seeking out deeper spots or holes in channels and canals. A sharp bend in a channel, where tidal currents have eroded a slough or deep cut, can be productive.

3. Look for holes in the bay bottom. They don't have to be huge or very deep to yield flatties. The same goes for channels and creeks. Try along creek or channel banks where there are fairly deep holes or hollows. You'll be able to detect all these deeper places when your sinker takes more line to find bottom.

4. When you're fishing channels or canals, try their deeper water first. Start at the center of the waterway first (if you have a boat) at low tide, move to a position between the center and a bank at the middle of the tide, then along the bank at high water.

5. Channel approaches to inlets often are productive places, not only for flounders but also for other species (bluefish, fluke, and striped bass, to cite three). The closer you get to the inlet, generally speaking, the better the fishing. The reason is that fishes move in and out of those gateways when food shopping.

Caution!: You may be doing much of your fishing, for flounders or whatever, in channels. I can't impress upon you too strongly the danger of anchoring in the middle of busy waterways. Not only is it a violation of boating safety and a breach of common sense, it invites serious trouble, especially if you happen to be in a rowboat or small outboard. With all due respect to the boating fraternity, most of whom are sane, capable pilots, you never know what idiot might come down the water road. In an argument between a cruiser and rowboat, the latter invariably loses.

Also in the interests of safety—yours—and proper conduct, avoid tying up to piles directly alongside low bridges. Boats coming from the opposite direction may not see you until too late. And don't tie up to buoys and other channel markers. It's illegal, to begin with, and by so doing you obscure those markers for other boat handlers. It's almost like standing in front of a stop sign at a busy intersection.

Here's another *tip on locations:* Flounders do not always leave inside waters completely with the increasingly warmer weather of late spring and summer. Deeper places, notably those around inlets, still have potential. The same goes for the colder weather of late autumn.

BE PATIENT, OLD BUDDY   When you reach a place where you'll test your luck, take a minute to study the bottom, as I suggested earlier. Remember that flounders move over sand as well as mud. If you feel the spot has promise, anchor your boat with just enough line to hold her steady. Stir up the bottom a little for openers. Get your chum over, if you're using any. Then bait up and go to work. Raise and lower your rod tip a few inches occasionally to bounce your sinker and make sure you're right on bottom. A sandy floor will produce a dull thud when the sinker hits. Mud can cause a kind of sucking, grabbing effect, but you'll know when you're on the floor. If you don't get a muted feeling of your sinker when it's allowed to drop back, it hasn't been on bottom. Current is thrusting it upward and away. You'll probably notice more line going out. You'll have to use a heavier sinker.

Check your bait periodically—not every five minutes, but at least once in a while. Crabs, blowfish, bergalls, and other sly robbers are adept at swiping bait. If your offering looks pale and bedraggled, replace it with fresh stuff.

Above all, don't be impatient. A prime virtue in successful angling is patience. If, after a reasonable interval, you've had no nibbles, and even chumming doesn't seem to provoke responses, pull up anchor and shift to another spot. Sometimes only a couple of hundred yards will make a difference. Flounders might be feeding not far from your initial location. But if that shift fails to produce, try another place altogether.

I've told you that flounders are independent cusses. Even though they're all over a bay, you may have to hunt them. On certain days you'll find good action at your very first location. You may even be able to fish it for hours. On other trips you may have to shift two, three, or more times before making contact. Then there are those frustrating days—not numerous, fortunately —when they don't seem to want to bite at all, no matter where you go. These are the times when chumming, agitating the bottom, and even dragging your anchor like a plow for a short distance can help. Trying various baits is an aid too.

During a normal flounder run, if you've done everything you can and done it properly, it's very doubtful that you'll be "skunked" (come home with excuses instead of fish).

Incidentally, somewhere along the line, in one kind of angling or another, there will be days when you're skunked. Don't let it bother you. The best of us get blanked at times. I don't like coming home with poor catches or no fish any more than the next guy, but in a way I approve of such trips. After all, what kind of challenge would angling be if you could be assured of good catches every time out?

HITS AND MISSES   Flounders bite lightly. They don't smack a bait viciously. Nor do they keep toying with an offering, without actually mouthing it, as some other species do. They tend to nip at a bait and release it. So they should be struck at once. The instant you feel a substantial nibble or tug, try to sink your hook. Here you have to exercise a little care. A short, smart, upward lift of your rod tip usually will plant the hook. Don't jerk the rod upward as though you had a tuna or marlin. An upward jerk that's too long or violent will yank the bait away before the flatty has had a chance to get it, and your hook, into his mouth.

Not infrequently flounders nibble at a bait so daintily as to barely be felt. When this occurs you'll have to coax your flounder. Give him a few inches of line. Depressing your rod tip a little may be enough. Wait a second or two, then tighten your line carefully. If he really has taken the hook you'll feel his weight, whereupon a short, steady pull, rather than an abrupt, vigorous yank, will nail him. Raising your rod tip a few inches will usually do the trick. You'll know when he's on.

An old stunt: If you hook one flounder on a spreader, first make sure he's securely hooked, then leave your rig on bottom for a minute or so. Sometimes a hooked fish attracts another to the same fate. If, after a short wait, there's no additional pull to tell you a second victim has taken a hook, reel in your catch.

By the way, doubleheaders are common in flounder fishing. Two flatties will accept your hooks practically simultaneously.

Don't ever look down your nose at flounders because of their size. They may not be big, but they put up lively resistance, especially on very light tackle. The tug-o'-war can be fun. When a flounder run is on you'll have one peppy little battle after another.

CONSERVATION NOTES—ALL SPECIES Contrary to popular opinion, the sea and its tributaries are not one vast, inexhaustible cornucopia of fishes. Research studies seem to indicate that the sea is a kind of vast watery desert, with scattered populations of fishes as oases. Makes sense. Considering that sea covers most of our globe's surface, if every acre of it were inhabited by fishes and other creatures, they couldn't survive. There wouldn't be enough food to go around.

We must exercise conservation common sense with all fishes, salt-water and fresh-water, whatever their species. There is NOT an endless supply, and the need for sensible use of our fishery resources becomes more and more urgent as recreational and commercial fishing pressures mount. We must be especially conservation-minded in the cases of localized, nonmigratory species such as flounders.

Once populations of nonmigratory species are cleaned out in an area, whether through overfishing—sport or commercial—or because they're destroyed by pollution, loss of breeding grounds, or some other negative by-product of today's living, we've had it so far as those fishes are concerned in that area. When fish are nonmigratory there's little hope of populations being revitalized by "transfusions" from another region.

In the interest of wise use of our priceless fishery resources I ask you to keep no more flounders (*or other fishes*) than you can use. That means however many you need at home, plus some others for relatives, friends, and neighbors. Every season I hear about one-, two-, three-, and four-angler flounder catches in the hundred- to three-hundred-fish range. Now I ask you, what on earth could they do with that many fish? Can you imagine how long a local population of flounders would last if every fisherman were to catch them at that clip?

When I hear about such gluttony I'm willing to bet that a sizable percentage of the fish are undersized. That compounds the felony. Undersized flounders are a waste of time, both to catch and to cook. They're not sport, even on ultralight tackle. They're too small to fillet, and if cooked whole are mostly bones.

So I ask you another favor: Please don't keep those "postage stamps," the tiny flounders that aren't even pan frying size. *Don't keep undersized fish of any kind.* They're of no use to you, believe me. Give them a chance to grow up. They'll be more fun to catch and much better for dining purposes. Most important of all, they'll have a chance to breed and so perpetuate the fishery.

HOW TO RETURN FISH TO THE WATER   Releasing a hooked fish of any species for return to his native element unharmed calls for reasonably gentle treatment.

First off, remove the hook carefully. Sometimes a fish will take a hook in such a way that it's impossible to remove without fatal results, but that's a different case. Do the best you can, endeavoring to take it out without tearing the poor critter to pieces internally.

Handle a fish as little as possible. The mucous coating on fishes' skin is there for a reason. It helps prevent penetration by bacteria and other harmful organisms. Minimum handling keeps that protective coating intact.

Once the hook is out, return fish to the water quickly. Don't throw them hard or scale them through the air like a discus. That can injure or kill. Get them back by holding them gently and placing them just below the surface so they can swim away. When you can't reach the water, you'll have to drop them in. Do it carefully.

Releasing fishes too large to handle naturally calls for different tactics. Here the usual procedure is to simply cut the leader. The hook remains in the fish, but eventually rusts out without harm. With these larger fish you have to spare the gaff, bringing them alongside close enough with rod and reel to cut the leader. At times you'll have to exercise judgment as to whether or not to cut the fish free. He may be nearly dead from exhaustion after a long fight, or he may have taken the hook 'way down in his gut and be seriously or fatally injured. In such cases it might be more merciful to bring the fish in, rather than to leave him to die slowly or become the prey of sharks.

If you handle fishes properly it's possible to get a picture or two and still release them satisfactorily. Minimum handling is the key. Again the gaff must be spared. The fish is brought into the boat by line and hand, someone helping to support the weight. A camera is ready beforehand, and a picture snapped quickly, after which the fish is released. If the hook can be removed easily, fine; otherwise simply cut the leader. Smaller specimens of billfishes, such as white marlin, can be brought into a boat for photographing by grasping them by their long snout or bill (use gloves!).

In passing I should mention that more and more angling contests are stressing releases of catches by awarding more points for a fish that's turned loose than for one brought to the dock.

A released fish won't thank you, but he or she will show their appreciation in one fashion or another in the future.

P.S. I don't think I have to tell you that flounders are good eating. If they're large enough and thick enough they can be filleted. Smaller ones have to be cooked whole. There are lots of bones in these, but they can be lifted out with a fork, and the meat's sweetness far outweighs that minor inconvenience.

If the fish are to be cooked whole, or the skin is to be left on fillets (some people think it adds flavor), flounders will have to be scaled. That's no great chore. If they're to be cooked whole it's necessary to dress them. Using a sharp knife, cut the head off just behind the gills. All the viscera should come out with the head. Then you can clean out the body cavity. Light rinsing will do it. The fins can be sheared off close to the body and the tail severed with a knife.

If they're to be filleted there's no need to remove the head, entrails, and fins. But you'll need a very sharp knife; preferably it should be one designed just for fish filleting. Laying the flounder white side down and grasping him by the tail, you begin your incision just beyond the base of the tail. Working as close to the bones as you can—your knife in a horizontal plane, naturally—you carefully cut toward the head and slice that broad slab of meat free. If you want to remove the skin, cut it free. Let me advise you that this should be done with care; otherwise you'll waste a lot of meat. Afterward the fillets can be rinsed lightly in salted tap water.

Flounders can be pan fried, deep fried, broiled, or baked, according to taste. Frying is the most popular cooking method. But no matter how it's cooked, fresh flounder is a gustatory delight. And it tastes twice as good if you caught the fish yourself.

BLOWFISH

A KIND WORD FOR A PEST   In late spring, during a period that straddles the late phase of the flounder run and the seasonal appearance of fluke, there occurs in bays from Delaware to New York what might be called a plague of finned locusts. It's the annual visitation by puffers or blowfish. They invade bays in astronomical numbers, where they make life miserable for bottom fishermen by relentlessly stealing bait intended for more desirable species.

For years fishermen vented their hatred of the little thieves by killing them and tossing them overboard as trash. It was a losing battle, like trying to bail out a river with a Dixie cup.

Then, somewhere along the line, word spread that blowfish are a dining delicacy, and that tempered anglers' dislike of them. Now many a rod-'n'-reeler is glad to take home a mess of blowfish for the table, especially when he found fishing slow in other departments. The fact is that under such high-falutin' names as "sea squab" and "chicken of the sea" blowfish appear on restaurant menus and command fancy prices.

Blowfish are very good eating. The only trouble is, it's a bit of a chore to prepare them for cooking. Actually it's not so bad when you learn how to do it and gain some practice. What you can do, before you attempt it yourself, is arrange a practical briefing. Have a party boat's mate, or fishing station operator, or fellow angler show you how it's done.

Here's an outline of the steps in the surgery:

First, get yourself a pair of work gloves. You can do the job barehanded, but the blowfish's sandpaperlike skin is tough on the hands. You'll also require a knife. It doesn't have to be large, but it must be sharp. Any wide piece of wood will do as an operating table. Or you can use several layers of newspapers. The latter serve a double purpose by providing something in which to wrap discarded parts.

1. Grasp the fish firmly with your free hand, belly down, its head to your right if you're right-handed, to the left if you're a southpaw.

2. Make an incision, behind the head, at right angles to the blowfish's long axis, as though you were going to cut the head off. Cut down through the backbone. You don't have to go through the body entirely. Halfway or so will do.

3. With the backbone severed, hold the fish securely with one hand and grasp his head with the other. Now, by tugging on the head, you literally turn the fish inside out, pulling it away from the body. With it should come skin and insides. Further pulling will tear those disposable parts away from the desired piece of meat inside.

4. Proper cleaning leaves a slab of firm, white meat. In shape it bears a vague resemblance to a chicken drumstick.

5. Attached to the chunk of meat will be the tail and some "roots" of fins. Lop off the tail and remove those bony fin portions with your knife.

Everything except that slab of meat is discarded. Certain internal organs are poisonous.

Caution! Don't ever give any of a blowfish's entrails to a pet. It could be a lethal "treat." The liver and internal reproductive organs can be especially poisonous.

That's all there is to it. After practice you'll become proficient enough to dress a blowfish in less time than it tells how to do it. You can, if you wish, *lightly* rinse the meat by dunking it in salted water before storing or cooking, letting it dry on absorbent paper. But it hardly seems necessary if it hasn't come in contact with dirt or other foreign matter.

Ideally, as in the case of any fish, blowfish should be dressed as soon as possible after catching, then eaten at the first opportunity after that, for maximum freshness and flavor. Also like any other species, the fish or meat should be iced on trips home and the meat placed under refrigeration as soon as possible.

The meat, often called "blowfish tails," can be broiled, fried in butter, or rolled in cracker meal and deep fried. And I'm sure that when you savor that sweet, delicious meat you'll be inclined to forgive puffers their bait stealing—for the moment, anyway.

CHAPTER 12

Fluke: Flounders' Bigger, Bolder, Aggressive Cousins

In the chapter about flounders I mentioned that they belong to a large family of flatfishes. Well sir, step up and meet another member of the clan, the fluke. He's a highly respected relative of the flounder, extremely well liked in his own right.

This fellow is a flounder too, really. How he came to be dubbed "fluke" I can't say. I never did hear an origin for that term.* But a more accurate name is summer flounder. This is a handle he goes by in ichthyological literature, along with his scientific name, *Paralichthys dentatus,* and was given to him because he's most commonly found inshore and in bays during the warmer months. Northern fluke is another name tacked on him by some authorities to distinguish him from a close relative, the southern fluke, found in more southerly U.S. waters. Most anglers know him simply as "fluke." We'll stay with that.

Distribution of fluke along the U.S. Atlantic seaboard is from Maine to the Carolinas. Some authorities extend the lower limit to northern Florida. But reports of these fish that far down could be in error, since southern fluke resemble their northern cousins rather closely. Specimens of *Paralichthys dentatus* hooked below North Carolina could be strays. In the northern segment of their range fluke are encountered as far up the coast as Maine, but in progressively and markedly decreasing numbers north of Massachusetts, even beyond Cape Cod.

During normal runs, centers of abundance include bays on the South Shore of Long Island and in New Jersey, along with inlets in those regions. For sport fishermen, that is. Fluke also are hooked, but to a lesser extent, in inshore ocean zones of New

* The Oxford Universal Dictionary suggests a possibility of "fluke" stemming from an old German word, *flach,* meaning "flat."

Jersey and New York. Commercially they're netted inshore and offshore.

DISTINGUISHING FLUKE FROM FLOUNDERS   Being in the same family as flounders, fluke naturally resemble their smaller relatives in certain ways, so much so that some folks experience a little difficulty in telling one from the other when sizes are about the same. This is understandable, at least for beginning fishermen, because both species possess a broad, flat body—colored on top and white underneath—both eyes on one side of the head, and similarly shaped and positioned fins. Like all flatfishes, both species go

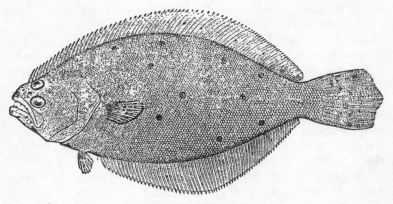

FLUKE (*Paralichthys dentatus*)

through that unique body-twisting process I described for flounders. But once you know how, it's easy to separate fluke from flounders.

The most obvious difference is one of size. Except when young, fluke are appreciably larger. Whereas 6 to 8 pounds constitute a rare giant among flounders, and then only in "snowshoes," such weights are common among fluke. The larger flatfish commonly attain weights of 10, 12, or 13 pounds. Even heavier fluke have been recorded for sport-fishing catches, and those of record caliber go to over 20 pounds. Somewhere in the sea, I suppose, are aging giants weighing as much as 25 pounds. Specimens in the

8-, 9-, and 10-pound or heavier bracket are nicknamed "doormats" because of their size and shape.

There are times, notably in late spring or early summer, when fluke and flounders mingle on the same grounds and approximate each other in size. Young fluke can weigh 1½ to 2 pounds, thereby matching the sizes of the larger flounders. It's then that new anglers may have difficulty differentiating between them.

A time-honored way of separating the two cousins involves "right-handedness" and "left-handedness." If you hold a flounder with his head pointing away from you, his flat body in the vertical plane, and his mouth underneath, his pigmented upper surface and eyes will be at your right hand. That's where the right-handed business comes in. Hold a fluke in exactly the same manner, and his colored surface and eyes will face your left hand. So he's "left-handed."

The only trouble with this identification method is that it isn't 100 percent sure-fire. Although it's practically infallible, sometimes Old Ma Nature indulges in a little whimsy and turns out left-handed flounders and right-handed fluke. Then, once in a blue moon, there turns up a rare freak that is either albino—no pigmentation at all—or colored on both sides.

A good way to distinguish between the two species is to examine their mouths. The flounder's is small. His jaw structures aren't too well defined, and his teeth are tiny and not too numerous. In contrast, a fluke has a fairly large mouth, well-developed jaws, and a fine set of dental equipment.

There are some other differences. Body shape, for example. The flounder's is broader, proportionately, whereas the fluke's tends to be more elongated. Then there's the detail of color, and in the fluke's case this is an interesting characteristic. Like a flounder, a fluke can alter his pigmentation to more closely resemble the color of the bottom where he resides, except that he's even more adept at camouflage. The way a fluke can change the color pattern of his body's upper surface is amazing.

In general, the coloration of a fluke's upper surface is a mottled brown or greenish brown, punctuated by circular whitish and darker markings. But this pigmentation is subject to considerable variation. He can and will alter not only the color, but also its lighter and darker shadings to better blend in with his environment.

For instance, if a fluke happens to be on a sandy bottom at the time, the color and pattern of his pigmented topside "automatically" lightens to simulate the details of the surrounding bay or ocean floor with incredible fidelity. Similarly, it will darken and become more uniform over a dark mud bottom; or assume a lighter, pebbled effect over a pebbly floor; or take on a mottled, kind of medium shade on a mottled, medium-colored bottom. In aquarium experiments they have been placed on a tank bottom consisting of a piece of checkered tablecloth, and they assumed a startling checkerboard pattern, complete with regularly formed, alternate light and dark squares! It's nature's camouflage talent at its best.

FLUKE HABITS   It's believed that fluke spawn sometime during the period of late autumn into winter or even early spring, most likely at sea. In springtime, following a spawning, young fluke find their way from deeper places offshore into shallower coastal zones where, like adult fish, they live on the bottom or fairly close to it. While inshore in littoral (coastal) belts, fluke favor sandy or muddy floors. And in addition to their camouflage talent they're able to bury themselves in a bottom with amazing swiftness, leaving only their eyes exposed like stubby little periscopes to watch for passing prey.

Fluke are classified as ground fish or bottom dwellers, but they do not restrict themselves to that lowermost level as much as flounders. When a search or pursuit of food demands, they'll shoot upward through intermediate levels to the very top. They've also been known to approach the surface at night and during early morning hours when feeding. For the most part, though, fluke are bottom fish, and that should be remembered when angling for them. Another detail that should be kept in mind is that even when down at that lowermost level, fluke do not hug bottom as closely as flounders. Whereas the latter stay right on the floor or no more than six inches or so above it, fluke can prowl anywhere from a foot to three feet over a bottom, perhaps even a bit more.

Fluke are voracious, only a cut or two below bluefish and cod in that respect. They seem to have an ever-present, omnivorous appetite, and it goads them into being savage in their own way, relentless hunters, especially attracted to moving prey (another detail I want you to remember). Their stomach capacity is commensurate, and its demands drive them to forage for food at frequent intervals. Concealed in sand or other bottom, or prowling over an ocean or bay floor, they devour other smaller fishes, including young flounders, along with shrimp, squid, marine worms, assorted small crabs, and shellfishes—just about anything, in fact, that can be accommodated by their toothy jaws. Which brings up another detail you should keep in mind: Fluke possess a roomy mouth, which means that they can take fair-size baits and hooks.

A little incident illustrates our friend's traits:

One day a fellow was fishing for flounders from shore when he felt a nibble, unmistakably that of a flounder. He hooked his fish, a small one, and began reeling in. Suddenly there was a smashing strike. This newcomer was no flounder! Perplexed, the angler had a lively tussle with his muscular second opponent on his light flounder tackle, but finally brought him to the beach. There was a flounder on his hook all right; and securely attached to the flounder, his teeth anchored in the smaller fish's flesh, was a whopper of a fluke—an eighteen-pound doormat, as it turned out. The big prowler had spotted the flounder moving through the water as the small fish was being reeled in, and struck. In attempting to swallow this morsel he too was reeled to his doom. Maybe there's a moral in there somewhere, if you like probing for morals.

Fluke can be remarkably fast. Their appearance is deceptive. Broad and flat, like a platter for a roast, they have none of the fusiform streamlining that characterizes sharks, bluefish, tunas, and other racers of the deep. But don't underestimate them. They might not be any match for such speed merchants as bonefish, bluefish, and others in long stretches, but they're capable of lightning-swift darts, fast enough to capture killies and other lively prey, and that isn't exactly dragging their fins.

OTHER HABITS, SEASONS   Compared with flounders, fluke are reasonably active migrants—not long-distance travelers, maybe, but they get around more than their smaller relatives. In winter they live offshore in the ocean, some distance from land, probably seeking depths of eight to ten fathoms (forty-eight to sixty feet) or more to escape the cold. Comes spring, with gradual warming of waters in shallower areas, they start their move inshore. As milder weather gives indication of being here to stay, they infiltrate coastal zones. Some remain there throughout the summer if they find things to their liking. Many others fin their way through inlets into bays for the warm months. In their respective seasonal neighborhoods they spend the summer, eating ravenously and growing larger. Hence the name summer flounders.

In late summer, along about September, those that have been in bays gather—"school up," as we call it—and begin to move seaward out through inlets. In coastal ocean waters they join those that have summered in littoral zones, and the whole kit and kaboodle shifts to the open ocean beyond to spend the winter.

If spring comes early, bringing unseasonably warm weather, fluke will start to trickle into inlets and bays before flounders have moved out entirely. Depending upon temperatures and other conditions, this can occur late in May, and even earlier in southerly parts of their range. Then, as waters warm inshore and in bays, their numbers increase. If that year's run is to have substance, it will begin to show signs in June, hitting its customary stride from then on into July.

Once their run is established, fluke can be caught on inshore ocean grounds, in and around inlets and their feeder channels, in other channels, and in bays and harbors. Occasionally they're hooked in the surf. Surfcasting for fluke, however, is more likely to be productive along the shores of an inlet, especially where there's a deep cut, than along an oceanfront beach.

sizes Fluke sizes inch upward as a run progresses. During a showing's early phases, fluke are boated that weigh about two or three pounds. Mixed in are some a little smaller and larger. As the season advances, their weight range is revised upward gradually. First you see more four-to-six-pounders on docks, followed after a while by a better percentage of flatties to eight, even ten, pounds. When a run reaches its season's zenith, here come doormats ripping scales at twelve, thirteen, fourteen pounds and more. There are unpredictable exceptions. Sometimes doormats up to thirteen pounds and heavier—I've known a few to hit sixteen and seventeen—appear during a run's early stages.

TACKLE TALK Fluke fishing gear is a matter of personal preference. You can wield either conventional equipment or a spinning outfit, and it can be light. A light conventional boat-fishing or all-purpose rod and 1/o reel will serve nicely. So will that outfit's spinning equivalent. Flounder tackle will do the job.

Don't go to either extreme in weapons for these flatties. Fluke are muscular in proportion to their size and good fighters, but you don't need heavy-duty gear to bring them in. On the other hand, if you go to real light stuff you can expect a real tussle with doormats.

If you choose spinning tackle or very light "standard" gear, keep in mind that fluke run appreciably heavier than flounders, that you'll be fishing in somewhat deeper water—especially in channels and outside in the ocean or in a large sound—and that currents in inlets, channels, and other locales with freely moving water may necessitate heavier sinkers than in shallow-water bay angling. Further, you might want to try trolling for fluke. If your spinning outfit can meet the foregoing conditions, okay; otherwise, I suggest you go to a somewhat heavier combination or switch to conventional gear. I doubt that any conventional outfit you use for flounders would be too light for fluke, but with real big doormats you might have your hands full.

Incidentally, I suspect that some fluke may pull the same stunt as certain other species when being reeled in—that is, they turn their bodies broadside to the direction of the pull to increase resistance. If so, that increase could be appreciable, with a body as broad as this flatfish's.

Line also can be light. Although there's always a chance that you'll tie into a doormat going up to 14 or 15 pounds or even heavier, it's more likely that your fluke will range up to 8 or 10, possibly 12 or 13 pounds at the outside, with the average well below that. Ten- or 12-pound test line, therefore, is strong enough. It will handle all the fluke you encounter, including the very largest doormats—provided you don't try to lift them clear of

the water with it. A hundred yards should be more than sufficient.

You needn't be overly concerned about hook sizes. I mean,
you don't have to be precise. Fluke have large mouths. Hook
sizes are more or less gauged to the weights of fluke currently
running. An over-all range goes from a 1/o to 5/o or 6/o. A
1/o will nail small fish—say, 1½ to 3 or 4 pounds. A 2/o
will take medium-size flatties, up to 6 pounds or thereabouts. A
3/o to 5/o or 6/o will secure the larger fellows, including hefty
doormats. You could employ the smaller hooks for the larger fish,
but it's a calculated risk, because they could be straightened out
by really muscular fluke.

As for hook patterns, you can use any of them. The Carlisle is
one that has found favor among fluke fishing regulars. The Sproat
is a good design. There are others, including the Eagle Claw
and O'Shaughnessy. Still another is the long-shank Kirby bass
design, liked by its riggers because its long shank facilitates hook
removal. Like flounders, fluke can take a hook deep.

RIGGING   There are a few ways to catch fluke: drifting; fishing at
anchor, with or without chum; trolling; and—least used—surfcasting. For now I give them a mention only in passing because
it's germane to a consideration of rigs. I'll detail them later.

The simplest fluke rig of all, one with minor variations, goes
thusly: *First,* to the end of your line tie a three-loop swivel. *Second,* to another eye of the swivel attach a sinker of suitable weight.

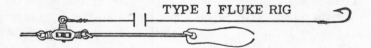

TYPE I FLUKE RIG

It can be tied close to the swivel's eye or on three to six inches of
line. The arrangement varies according to anglers' preferences.
Personally, I don't think it makes much difference, although I'm
inclined to tie the sinker close. The main thing is—you guessed
it—that the sinker is heavy enough to hold bottom. *Third,* to the
swivel's remaining loop tie your hook on two or three feet of
leader. This can be monofilament, gut, nylon, or whatever, in
about the same strength as your line.

We'll call that Type I. You can use it in drifting or for fishing
at anchor.

Tip: For either method you can rig a bank-type sinker. Better,
though, is a round or egg-shaped sinker with a built-in swivel.
It rolls with the current or drift, gives more freedom and action
to the rig, and is less apt to foul in bottom obstructions.

Type II rig is essentially the same as Type I, except that spinners—small, shiny, metal blades about the shape of a teaspoon's
bowl—are affixed to the leader for added attraction. They're a

TYPE II

good addition to a fluke rig. Because fluke are aggressive hunters,
alert to movement of prey, the spinners' glitter and turning contribute to a rig's eye-catching appeal. Spinner blades can be
bought separately, or you can purchase fluke rigs already made
up with spinners incorporated. If you buy them separately you
can attach one or two. Some fishermen even use three. Their
location on the leader is arbitrary, but attachment usually is made
just ahead of the hook.

Here's Type III:

First assemble these components: A June Bug pattern spinner,
about Size 2 or 4, with two-loop barrel swivel; five or six inches
of No. 7 steel wire (stainless is preferred here; piano wire rusts);
and a double hook. For beginners I should explain that a double
hook is just as its name implies. It consists of two complete hooks,
their shanks parallel—back to back, so to speak—and their bends

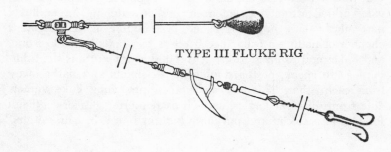

TYPE III FLUKE RIG

curving upward in opposite directions. Usually they're separated
except at the top, where they're joined by a loop for attachment.
Their size can be a 3/0 to 6/0. The heavier the fluke running,
the larger the hooks.

Here's how you put the rig together: (1) Make a small loop
or eye at each end of the wire by twisting it on itself in tight
turns. When completed, the section of wire and its loops
shouldn't be much more than about two inches long, overall.
(2) Attach your spinner. One end of it has a loop kept closed
by a sliding collar. Slide the collar away, open the loop, attach
it to one eye in your short piece of wire, and slide the collar back.
(3) Feed your double hook through the wire's other loop. (4)
Tie the two-loop barrel swivel to the spinner's free end. That's
all there is to it.

With this outfit you can use a leader about three feet long,
monofilament or whatever, in about the same strength as your
line. Tie it to the barrel's remaining loop.

Connection of this terminal tackle to your line will be made
via a standard three-loop swivel. One of the swivel's loops, of
course, is for the line. Another gets a sinker. You can use a bank
type, but the outfit functions best with a round or egg-shaped
weight, preferably with a built-in swivel arrangement to allow
it maximum movement. You can tie the sinker close to the swivel
or on two or three inches of line, but I can't see any advantage
to the latter.

Now the three-loop swivel on your line has one eye left. This,
of course, receives the rig's leader. You can make the attachment
directly if you wish; for purposes of quick, easy changing of
rigs, however, it's preferable to tie a small snap swivel to your
leader and snap that on the line's swivel.

Several advantages are claimed for Type III. Its spinner provides added attraction, which can aid in catching larger fluke,
particularly late in the season. The double hook heightens
chances of nailing a fish, since it offers two baits instead of one,
and fluke tend to be gluttons. Also cited as a feature is the "aim-
ing," so to speak, of the double hook's points and barbs away
from each other. This can make an approaching fluke vulnerable from different angles, as well as rendering it more difficult
for him to sneak in and purloin a bait, or bite it in half, without

lethal results. Fluke are notorious for their cute tricks with bait. The Type III rig is nicely suited to either drifting or fishing at anchor.

As this book was being prepared I ran across another type of fluke rig suggested by Claude Rogers of Virginia Beach, Va., a well-known Old Dominion fisherman and tournament director. I understand it has proved effective down there. At the time I first heard about it the rig hadn't been used extensively for northern fluke, but I can't see why it shouldn't be productive.

A variation of Claude's rig goes like this:

You'll need a piece of monofilament or leader material about a foot or so long, approximately the same strength as your line; two small synthetic "feather" lures (skirts of nylon or other synthetic material), in white or bright yellow, each armed with a hook of appropriate size and each tied on three to four inches of the same material as the "leader." Claude uses Mylar for all three. The so-called leader is attached to the line. Tie it directly or use a two-loop barrel swivel. Even better is a snap swivel for easy changing of rigs. This is tied to the line and connects to a loop in the leader. A sinker goes on the leader's free end. Here again a round or egg-shaped sinker is preferable to a bank type.

About three inches above the sinker is tied the first lure on its short leader—directly, no swivel. The second lure goes three inches or so above that in the same fashion. The hooks are baited with any of the standard fluke attractors (strip of squid, etc.). Hook sizes are the same as for other fluke rigs. Try a 3/0 or a 4/0. And the outfit is suited to drifting or fishing at anchor.

The simplest kind of trolling rig will do if you're going to "scratch" for fluke—that is to say, a short leader, three or four feet, of mono or other material that carries a suitable lure and is attached to the line directly or via a barrel swivel or snap swivel. Only thing is, you'll have to incorporate some kind of weighting device, such as a small drail or trolling sinker, or pinch-on sinkers, to get your rig down. Weight of the lure alone may not be enough. A small drail can be included in the rig between line and leader. Pinch-on sinkers can be attached to the line just ahead of the leader. Depending upon your boat's speed —it will be quite low here—pinch-on sinkers may not be enough.

In very slow trolling you also can use any of the rigs I described earlier for fluke bottom fishing and drifting. A possible difficulty here, however, is the increased chances of getting "hung up" on some bottom obstruction, especially in rocky areas where angling for these flatties is done. All I can say is, be prepared to lose rigs and have replacements.

Casting from shore will land fluke too, but it is less popular than boat fishing. For now suffice it to say that any of the bottom rigs will do. For the surf you might want to try the fish-finder rig, detailed elsewhere in this book.

BAITS, BAITING, AND ARTIFICIALS Such are a fluke's appetite and mouth size that you can lure him with several different kinds of

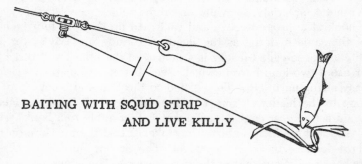

BAITING WITH SQUID STRIP
AND LIVE KILLY

baits, singly or in combinations. At one time or another the flatties will respond to a strip of squid, live killy, whole spearing, piece of clam, worm or shedder crab, and strips cut from porgy, mossbunker, herring, sea robin (a pest fish by which you'll be bothered from time to time), snapper (young bluefish), or even fluke. Keep those fish strip baits in mind for when you run out of more desirable come-ons. Always cut them from the lightest part of the fish's underside.

Superior fluke baits are a strip of squid, live killy, and a spearing. The chances are that you won't go wrong with either of the first two. Best of all, in my opinion, is a combination of a squid strip and live killy on the same hook. Its effectiveness is due to the eye-catching whiteness and fluttering of the squid strip combined with the live killy's movements. There's an attractive scent to those baits too.

Squid are sold frozen in packages. Let them thaw so they'll be limber. Cut your strips from the creature's mantle (skirtlike portion), three or four inches long and half an inch or so wide. If the outer skin happens to be colored a bit, peel or cut it away to expose the bright whiteness underneath. Slit one end of each strip up the middle for about an inch to create two little tails that will flutter in the water for even more eye appeal. Feed this strip on your hook, just enough so that about an inch and a half dangle free, and imbed the point and barb.

Squid strips and live killies can be used separately or in combination with each other. Similarly, a squid strip can be rigged with a spearing or other bait, and a live killy can be used in conjunction with some other fish strip bait.

In any case, the little fish must be put on the hook very carefully so as not to injure or kill. You can accomplish this by gently passing the hook's point upward from underneath through the lower and upper jaws, just behind the lips. The point should emerge through the forward, upper part of the snout. Slender-bodied hooks are preferred for live-bait fishing by many anglers because of minimal damage, but unless they're strong there's a chance of their straightening when playing a fish.

There are other methods, but I prefer the above because it presents a killy in lifelike fashion. I should tell you, though, that it increases the chances of a fluke biting off the bait and escaping the hook.

A less satisfactory technique is to hook the killy through the base of his tail or the flesh of his back. Special care must be exercised in the second location to avoid injuring or killing the fish. After all, the idea is to keep the bait alive as long as possible. Hooking a killy in either of these ways is unsatisfactory because it presents the bait in an unnatural way. Impaling him through the tail has him moving through the water backward, which looks peculiar, even to a fluke. Besides, it's apt to kill the bait by "drowning." Hooking him through the back gives him an odd appearance too, since he'll tend to spin, moving through the water in strange ways and twisting the leader in the bargain.

Killies are very hardy. They'll stay alive on a hook for a long time if placed there in the right way. This is a big advantage when dealing with gamesters that favor moving prey.

Spearing, another popular small-bait fish, are something else again. They're practically impossible to keep alive on a hook. They die quickly out of water, especially with handling, so you invariably wind up with a dead one on your hook. For live bait for fluke, stick to killies. Spearing can be used, don't misunderstand. It's just that live killies are preferable for fluke. But you may have to settle for spearing when there are killy shortages.

Spearing are sold, live, at bait depots and fishing stations. They also come frozen in packages. Get them alive whenever you can, because they're fresh. Spearing in combination with a squid strip is a good fluke bait, superior to the fish alone. Hook one just as you would a live killy. Less desirable, I think, is to pass the hook in through the little fish's mouth and out under a gill cover.

Live killies also are purchased at fishing stations, rowboat liveries, and bait depots. They're kept alive and active very easily in a bait car, which is left in the water alongside the boat. You can have a few closer to you for convenience in a pail of salt water.

A bait car is a simple, inexpensive contraption. It will be worth your while to own one if you do an appreciable amount of fishing. Essentially it's a small cage, made from wood so it will float. Its top has one or two lids, hinged or removable, for access to its passengers. A short length of stout twine prevents it from drifting away.

Like squid, whole fish baits such as menhaden are sold, frozen, in packages and should be thawed for easier handling. Whenever you can get fresh-caught baits, even if they're dead, give them preference over frozen stuff. The fresher a bait—any bait—for any kind of fish, the better. There are a few exceptions, such as the attractors for blueclaw crabs, but in the main a fresh bait is invariably tops. With some battlers you must use a fresh bait for best results.

When you set up a combination bait consisting of a strip of squid or fish belly and another item, feed the strip on your hook as before, but leave its point and barb free for impaling the live killy, spearing, piece of clam, or whatever. Bury point and barb in that. For fluke I don't think you can beat a bright-white strip of squid, tails fluttering, and a plump, bottle-green live killy about three inches long.

Artificial baits—lures—are employed in trolling for fluke, although you can try them in drifting too. Small, shiny spoons get results; so do spinner lures with flash and glitter; and so do small feather lures, natural or artificial. Sometimes a strip of squid is added to a lure's hook for extra attraction. You might also try a small artificial sometime if you're casting from an inlet shore.

METHODS Before we get rolling on this piece of business let's take a very brief refresher course on two cardinal points: Fluke feed chiefly along or near the bottom; and they're attracted to moving prey. Whatever your angling technique, it should take those details into consideration.

Drifting is an excellent fluke fishing procedure. It can be done from any size craft, rowboat to cruiser. It's very effective because it keeps the bait in motion, creating an illusion of live food. It has a great advantage over fishing from shore or from an anchored boat because it covers more territory. Fluke may be traveling along "lanes" in search of food, or congregating in places where chow is abundant. Drifting betters your chances of making contact in those situations. For it you can use any of the fluke baits, bottom rigs, and tackle mentioned earlier.

The boat is allowed to glide along, propelled by wind or tide, whichever is stronger. Your baited rig rides just over the bottom. Ideally, drifts should be across a channel or inlet area, straight or diagonally, in a kind of zigzag pattern.

Conditions aren't always favorable for drifting. Wind or tide may be too strong, or moving in the wrong direction for a particular locale. Or boat traffic might be too heavy. You really need plenty of room for drifting. That's its only drawback. In any case, be careful. Watch out for other boats under way, and for sand bars and rocks if those hazards are present. Be ready to move under power at a moment's notice.

When conditions aren't conducive to drifting, try an alternate procedure.

One is fishing at anchor with a chumpot. The method is substantially the same as chumming for flounders, except that ground mossbunkers replace cracked mussels (they can be used too).

You pack your chum in a meshed bag and bounce it on bottom alongside the boat at intervals. Another chumming method is to drop cracked mussels, a few at a time, right alongside every so often, just as in flounder fishing. We've also chummed with the canned fish food they sell for cats.

There probably will arise an occasion when conditions are adverse for drifting, but you have no chum. In that situation do this: Anchor in what you think is a likely spot—a channel, maybe, or a broad inlet mouth—being careful not to violate any of the rules of sane boating. Use a bottom rig, and cast away from the boat. As soon as your sinker hits bottom, steadily retrieve line at a slow-to-moderate rate. Repeat this casting and retrieving. If you're anchored in a waterway where the current is moving at a fair clip, let it carry your rig away from the boat (use a round or oval sinker) instead of casting, then reel in as before and repeat.

The casting act can be performed while chumming at anchor too, but here you want to keep your rig within the chum's sphere of influence. In casting you won't cover as much ground as in drifting, but at least you can impart motion to the bait.

Trolling for fluke promises interesting possibilities. Prime among them is the sport angle. A fluke hooked while trolling is lively sport because he has pursued the lure and is determined it won't escape. Trolling also provides a suspense angle, because you never can be quite sure what you might hook. It might be a striped bass or a bluefish—and one of the heftier ones at that— or a weakfish. (Conversely, deep trolling for blues sometimes produces fluke.)

Trolling can account for big fluke. Whether this is because those larger flatties are more excited by a trolled lure than their kid brothers, or because they're more aggressive and more inclined to push an attack, I don't know. But it does seem that trolling increases chances of getting doormats. One of the largest fluke I've ever boated, a 14-pounder, was taken while trolling a small feather—red and white, I think it was. I should add, though, that I've never found trolling to account for as many fluke as drifting. It's a quality, rather than quantity, technique, you might say.

Fluke trolling speed is a matter of opinion and experimentation. I suggest keeping the boat's engine well down on low throttle, enough to gain headway of about 1½ or 2 miles an hour. Here's where outboard motors designed for fishing come in handy. They throttle down nicely for varied low speeds.

The technique is to go deep. Use a small drail or trolling sinker if necessary. As the boat moves ahead slowly, let your rig sink to the bottom. When you feel it hit or touch, lift it a foot or two. This is the plane at which it will travel. The distance above bottom at which the lure is trolled is a variable. Experiment, varying its level a few inches either way, but keep it reasonably close to the bottom. Spasmodically raising and lowering your rig tip in a jigging motion at intervals will impart added action and attraction to the rig.

Feather lures, natural and those of the nylon skirt type (all white, red and white, yellow, and other color combinations), along with small spinners, bucktails, and spoons, are among the artificials trolled for fluke. Try 'em all. There's room for lots of experimentation. For example, you can dress the lure's hook with a trailing strip of squid, and so on. Rigging is the same as for an artificial in bluefish trolling.

For tackle here I suggest conventional equipment rather than spinning gear. The latter is too "bendy."

Still another method combines trolling, drifting, and bottom fishing. For this too I suggest conventional tackle over spinning equipment. A single-hook bottom rig on a two- or three-foot leader of monofilament, gut, or other material, weighted with a sinker of suitable size, is the terminal outfit. You start out by letting your rig find bottom, whereupon the boat eases ahead slowly to troll it. Try that a short distance, then let the rig settle and drift for a while. And that's the procedure, alternately trolling and drifting.

Fishing from shore—a dock or bank on a channel or inlet—or from a beach along such waterways or an oceanfront beach or jetty, has caught some big fluke, but it usually isn't a quantity technique. Casting is the procedure, and you can try both a bottom rig and an artificial. In either case the idea is to keep your rig in motion by retrieving it. Let it travel on or close to the bottom (no more than two or three feet above it, at most, for an artificial). Try both steady and varied speeds of retrieve, jigging the bait or lure at times.

You don't necessarily need a surfcasting outfit for this. Casting distance probably won't be a requisite. A light or medium conventional rod with 1/o or 2/o reel, or a spinning combination of similar caliber, will do (so long as that spinning combo can handle the terminal tackle). Line (give yourself a hundred yards or so), hooks, and sinkers are as in other fluke fishing methods. Rigging, of course, will go according to whether you use a bottom rig with natural bait or an artificial.

A surfcasting outfit, conventional or spinning, isn't ruled out, you understand. In certain areas it may be necessary to fling your rig out to where it will do some good. Too, there may be other, larger species in the area, such as bluefish and striped bass, at the time. For fluke alone you could stay with lighter equipment, but with chances of blues and stripers you might want to go to somewhat heavier gear. It will cost you some sport with fluke, but at least you'll be ready for any heavier scrappers.

The odds are that if you're fishing an oceanfront on bottom (as is done for stripers at certain seasons), you'll be using a fishfinder rig, and any fluke you catch will be incidental. I mean, not too many surfcasters work an ocean beach especially for fluke.

There's a fluking method I'll mention in passing, and only to ask you to shun it like a plague. It's jacking. I won't even go into detail. Suffice it to say that it consists of going out with a lantern at night, looking for fluke at rest on the bottom in shallow water, and spearing them. From every angle—sport, conservation, and otherwise—this is bad. Talk about shooting fish in a barrel! If you're a sportsman you not only avoid fluke jacking yourself, but also endeavor to discourage it in others.

Assuming you're not a "meat fisherman," one of those characters for whom no trip is a success unless he groans under the weight of his catch, you'll hook satisfactory takes of fluke during normal runs. You won't hook them in such quantity as flounders, for example, or Boston mackerel, even during the best runs. But there's compensation in fluke sizes. You don't need many of them for a good catch.

Equipment note: This is important. Always carry and use a landing net when fluke fishing. Fluke have a cute habit of wiggling violently as they're being hoisted from the water. If not hooked solidly they can flip themselves free. Be especially cautious when reeling them in close alongside a boat, particularly a boat whose cockpit is well out of water. Fluke can slap themselves against a hull with sufficient force to knock themselves off hooks. Whenever possible, slip your landing net under a fluke just before lifting him clear of the water. Do it carefully so *you* don't knock him free. A landing net, incidentally, comes in handy for boating other species too. If you get one with a telescoping handle, or handle extension, you'll find use for it on docks and jetties as well.

NOTES ON HOOKING AND PLACES   Fluke aren't as noise-shy as some other species—weakfish, for one, fresh-water bass for another; but in shallower areas they're inclined to be boat-scared at times. In shoal locations, therefore, the rig should be kept well away from the boat. Depending upon depths, 50, 75, or 100 feet of line paid out usually will be enough. In very shallow places you may have to let out as much as 150 to 200 feet. Be sure your reel is filled accordingly.

Often fluke take bait in a fast, ravenous gulp, then be off to the races when they feel the hook. Their strikes can be quite savage. They might even set the hook themselves. If not, a short, brisk, upward lift of the rod tip usually does it.

Not infrequently you'll encounter a sly rascal who wants to toy with your bait. You'll feel his cuteness as a series of rapid, firm twitches. This indicates that the fish has either taken a chomp or two at the bait or has seized it and is trying to back away with it, probably wondering what's holding the tidbit. Give him a *little* line, then retrieve *slowly,* feeling for his weight. If the teasing continues down there, retrieve a few more inches. If he still hasn't really taken the bait, feed him a little line again and repeat the slow retrieve. If nothing at all is felt after some of this jockeying, better reel in and check your bait. Don't be surprised if the hook is clean, or has only half a killy or a fraction of its squid strip.

This business of lopping off a portion of a bait and escaping is called short striking, and fluke are adept at it. A simple arrangement will take care of many (but not all) short strikers. You add a ring-eye hook of about the same size or slightly smaller than the one already on your rig. Open the second hook's eye enough to go on the bend of your original hook, and close it. This second hook dangles from the bend of the first. Feed a strip bait on the original hook as before, then bury the dangling hook's point in the strip's trailing portion. You can impale a live killy or a spearing on the first hook as before. Just be sure to cut your strip bait long enough to accommodate the second hook. But don't make it too long; otherwise a fluke will have a chance to lop *that* off without being nailed by the trailing hook.

Fluke range widely over open sandy and muddy bottoms, in inside waters and outside. They're also encountered over pebble or gravel floors and in rocky places. They seek out all sorts of places where they can find chow.

A freely moving, fairly deep channel with a clean, sandy bottom is often good fluke-hunting territory. Deep creeks with steep banks also are productive. Other areas with potential are: the junction of a channel and creek; where an inlet and channel meet; at the tapered ends of sand bars or in current-made sloughs flanking such bars; and at the tips of points of land, where currents swirl food to lurking fluke.

Inlets between bays and ocean, or sounds, frequently pay off. Some of the larger flatties, wise in their seniority, frequent these gateways because they've learned that tidal action will tote morsels their way. Fish, like people, believe doing things the easy way whenever possible.

Generally speaking, fluke are more apt to bite during a running tide than at slack water in bays and channels, again probably because they instinctively know that currents will transport food their way.

Personally, I prefer a boat for fluke angling because it can cover more ground. That's a big advantage, especially during a poor run. But I must caution you not to overlook piers and jetties on inlets or deep, freely moving channels. They have a lot of potential. So do shores along such waterways, provided boat traffic isn't heavy and you can get your rig into fairly deep water.

SPECIAL RIG   Years ago I learned about another fluke rig that I'd like to pass on to you for trial sometime.

This outfit starts out like a basic rig I detailed earlier, but adds another hook. The first hook is tied to a three-loop swivel via

a two-to-three-foot length of leader material. The second hook—
with a snell only, six inches or so long, no leader—is tied into
that leader just a little below its midpoint.

Two kinds of bait can be tried simultaneously with this setup.
One hook, for instance, can be baited with a squid strip alone,
while the other carries a live killy (or spearing) or squid-killy/
spearing combo. Or you can try the combination attractor on
one hook while you garnish the other with some kind of bait
you want to test. Whichever hook takes the first fluke will govern
how both are baited that day.

SO GO, ALREADY! I've given you all the fundamentals that come
to mind. Now it's up to you to get out there and use them.

Only one detail remains, and that is to comment on fluke
edibility. I'll sum it up in one word: excellent.

Fluke are dressed in the same manner as flounders, then prepared as fillets or whole (or cut into sections, depending upon
sizes of fish and methods of cooking). They lend themselves
better to filleting than flounders because they're larger and
thicker. Again, depending upon whether they're prepared as fillets or whole, they can be cooked by any of the popular methods
employed for fish.

Fluke meat is white, firm, and sweet, with a delicate flavor.
Personally, I think it's a bit better than flounders', but that's a
matter of taste. As fillets they present solid slabs of delicious
meat. Cooked whole, there are bones to contend with, but usually the entire skeleton can be lifted out intact after cooking,
leaving only a few stray bones. As in the case of flounders, this
is only a minor inconvenience, a very small price to pay for
such delightful dining.

CHAPTER 13

Kingfish: Little Guys,
but Lively

I don't know about you, but I was an "Amos 'n' Andy" fan for years. From the time I was knee-high to a superheterodyne I followed the hilarious (mis)adventures of the two lovable title heroes, Madame Queen, Henry Van Porter, Miz' Blue, Algonquin J. Calhoun, and all the other delightful characters created by Charles Correll and Freeman Gosden. First on radio, then on television.

Maybe that's why nearly every time I hear the name kingfish it conjures up a recollection of the predatory, conniving, slightly larcenous, yet likable fellow of the same name in "Amos 'n' Andy." George Stevens was his name in the show, you'll recall if you were one of its buffs, and Kingfish was his title as head of the Mystic Knights of the Sea, an organization to which Amos and Andy belonged. As Kingfish he used his exalted position frequently to bilk Andy out of any coin of the realm the latter might have at the moment.

The character we're going to spotlight here isn't the colorful Kingfish of radio and television history, but a smaller, considerably more honest individual that also has recruited quite a following. I mean the marine kingfish, northern version.

And right off the bat I might just as well attempt to clear up a confusing tangle in nomenclature. Another name for this particular kingfish is northern whiting. It's rarely if ever used among anglers fishing for them. I mention it here because you may see the species listed under both names. (For some reason, even ichthyologists can't always get together on names for certain fishes.) In this instance that second name is doubly confusing because there's a common species called whiting that inhabits the same general region, and is no relation. Commenting on that, a wag once said, "There are three Whiting brothers: North-ern, King, and Southern."

As if two more or less official names were not enough, anglers and others get into the act by contributing regional names. Have a sampling: "northern kingfish," "king whiting," "sea mullet," "shore whiting," "sea mink"(!), "surf whiting," "ground mullet," and "round-head."

Most of those names are rarely, if ever, used. I daresay you've never heard of some of them before. Unfortunately, though, they pop up occasionally, adding to confusion. The fact that there are distinct species of mullet doesn't help matters. Nor does the applying of the name kingfish to other species in various parts of the country—the king mackerel of southern climes, for example, often called "kingfish" or "king," just like the species we're dis-cussing here.

Along about now you may be asking, "If this kingfish also is called northern whiting, then what is that other fish called whit-ing that frequents the same general region?"

Good question. That *whiting* (his popular name, by the way) is a silver hake (*Merluccius bilinearis*), a member of a group called hakes, related to cod, pollack, and haddock. You'll meet him in another chapter.

Let's forget all that and call this kingfish a kingfish, shall we? Then we'll all know what we're discussing.

IDENTIFICATION This kingfish, scientifically labeled *Menticirrhus saxatilis,* is most easily recognized by his size, coloring, and first dorsal fin.

He'd rank as a small fish anywhere. Weights up to a pound and a half or two pounds are par for his course. Except during exceptionally good runs, a more average range is from a half pound to a pound and a half, with approximate lengths of ten to fifteen inches. In a good run of kings their maximum size is in the neighborhood of eighteen inches and three pounds, but that's a nice-size kingfish. It's reliably reported that they can grow to weights of five and six pounds, but I've never seen one that large. It takes some fishing to find one as heavy as three pounds.

The kingfish's color scheme is a thousand miles from being

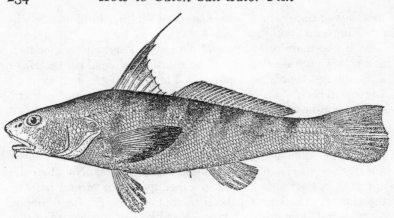

KINGFISH (*Menticirrhus saxatilis*)

glamorous. His back and upper sides are a nondescript gray or brownish gray, sometimes greenish gray. On some specimens this color is quite dark. Often there are iridescent silvery tints. Farther down on the sides and on his belly the color becomes whitish, yellow-white, or silver. Noticeable are wide, irregular, dusky, barlike markings on his upper surface. These are darker than the body color. Most of them run diagonally downward and forward on the body's upper half. On some the first bar, just aft of the gill cover, extends downward in the opposite direction and meets with the second bar to form a "V" in the vicinity of the pectoral fin.

His profile provides other identification clues. He has two dorsal fins, and an aid to recognition is the first dorsal fin. Appreciably higher than its mate, it's shaped like the mains'l on a Marconi-rigged sloop. This first dorsal has spines (as opposed to rays, which are softer and more flexible), and usually one of the leading two or three is extended to add to the fin's height. The second dorsal fin is appreciably lower, roughly rectangular in outline, of fairly uniform height. Another identifying profile detail is the S-shaped trailing edge of his dorsal fin or tail. Still other clues are his comparatively small mouth and a chin ornamented by a fish's equivalent of a Van Dyck beard, a small, fleshy, dangling process called a barbel.

Another anatomical detail, interesting but not detectable unless you dissect him, is his lack of a swim bladder, a kind of stabilizer. This kingfish, some of his immediate relatives (which include the black drum), and the Atlantic or Boston mackerel (no kin) are among species sharing this seeming oversight by Ma Nature. Although obviously not a fatal omission, lack of an air bladder prevents the kingfish from coming to rest in the water —hanging suspended in his native element—without at least fluttering his fins. Therefore, he has to keep in motion more or less continuously or sink toward the bottom. This is a trait that can influence his attack on a bait.

There's another interesting shortcoming in connection with the omission. Many fishes use their swim bladder as a kind of resonance chamber in connection with production of sounds—grunts, croaks, and the like. But the poor kingfish, having no such aid to sonic talent, goes around silent as a clam. The omission becomes all the more odd when you consider that some of his relatives not only have a swim bladder, but also are quite vociferous in production of sounds.

Among other relatives of this kingfish are a southern version, a Gulf of Mexico cousin, and the California corbina. Many authorities group our kingfish friend under the mass heading croakers, drums, and weakfishes, placing them all in a large family called Sciaenidae. I'll mention in passing that this kingfish often is found in company with the northern weakfish on common grounds.

THE KING'S COURT Kingfish are bottom dwellers, their preference running to areas with a floor of clean sand. You'll encounter the game little guys in the surf, in moderately deep water around sand bars, and on clean, sandy bottoms of bays, channels, and inlets.

They're rather widely distributed on the U.S. Atlantic seaboard, their overall range going from about Massachusetts on down to Florida. They're known to stray farther north occasionally, and presumably they may straggle below Florida when a mood prompts them. Among their greatest centers of abundance are areas within that stretch between Long Island and New Jersey to Chesapeake Bay.

In the more northerly segments of their Atlantic Coast range they're warm weather visitors. They begin appearing as spring advances, along about May or so. Once in seasonal residence, they stay right on through the summer. A climatically average September has kings still around. How much longer they stay after that depends upon water temperatures. When autumn's cooler weather bears down, the last of them take off, presumably moving offshore to the ocean's deeper, warmer layers.

These kingfish are a schooling species, a gregariousness that accounts for bountiful catches during a good run. When they appear for a stay in a region they confine themselves to inside waters and to close-inshore zones. This is a restriction that bay and surf anglers keep in mind.

Available supplies of kingfish are subject to considerable fluctuation between rich and scanty, at least in some areas. During certain seasons you'll hear of relatively few being caught. In other years they'll be all over the place and surrendering good catches.

Such variations could well be caused by radical differences in spawning success, occasional high mortality among eggs and fingerlings, and/or other cyclic factors. On the other hand, in seasons of apparent scarcity, maybe poor catches are due to small numbers of anglers fishing for them, rather than to an actual dearth of fish. There's a big competition angle. I have to say that these kings aren't among the most sought-after gamesters; and if bluefish or some other equally popular battlers are around in force it's quite possible that kingfish would be given a mass cold shoulder. A choice between blues up to ten pounds and better—in quantity—and kingfish to a pound and a half or two pounds wouldn't require a coin toss in most instances.

NATURAL FOODS, FEEDING HABITS, AND BAITS   Not particularly fussy when it comes to food, kingfish delight in any local menu that proffers shrimp, marine worms, small crabs and lobsters, clams and other mollusks, assorted little fishes, and the so-called sand bugs that reside in colonies along oceanfronts.

From a fishermen's point of view, the kings' varied appetite is a gesture of cooperation, since it allows a selection of several different baits. On the list of attractors that will lure kingfish to hooks are small shrimp (such as the grass shrimp used for weak-fish); the table variety of shrimp cut into small pieces; sandworm and bloodworm (the former often is preferred by anglers because kings like sandworm, and marauding crabs are more likely to swipe bloodworm bits); a piece of squid (good for weakfish too); a bit of hard or soft clam; a sand bug; and a piece of shedder crab. Since kingfish have a little mouth, any bait must be proportionately small.

AND OVER HERE, THE TACKLE With weights going only to 2, 2½, or 3 pounds at the outside, kingfish are no muscle-bound behemoths, but they wage a nice scrap on light tackle. And there, in light tackle, you have the key to maximum action with these little fellows.

In bay kingfishing you can go to very light equipment if you wish, since the fish are small, waters will be comparatively shallow, and rigs are light. The choice between spinning tackle and conventional gear is yours. Your flounder outfit is just right; or you can wield the lightest spinning tackle. Here's where spinning equipment is good. With small fishes in inside waters, the more flexible the rod, the better. The reel, of course, matches the rod—1/0 in the case of a revolving spool type; small model in the case of a spinning "mill." Use light line, certainly no heavier than ten-to-twelve-pound test (if that) at the very outside. Fifty yards are more than enough.

In short: Any light, all-purpose weapons you use for bay angling will do fine.

Favor light tackle when surf kingfishing too. Again, it can be spinning or conventional, but here you may have to strike a compromise. Use tackle sufficiently light to give you action with kings, yet capable of handling a bottom fishing rig in casting. You also have to be prepared for any larger species that might be around—striped bass, for example, or bluefish, or weakfish. If it's known that larger battlers are in the surf it might be wise for you to use proportionately heavier equipment and sacrifice some of the sport with kingfish—that is, if you feel you might not be able to handle the bigger gamesters on really light weapons.

Casting distance may or may not be a factor, depending upon how sharply the beach shelves away, where the fish are feeding at the moment, and the strength and direction of any breeze. You'll have to gauge your tackle accordingly.

A spinning outfit can fill the bill nicely when surfing for kings. With it even beginners can get fairly good casts when a certain amount of distance is involved. It can handle the smaller rigs, has plenty of flexibility for lively sport, and—used properly— can take on surf-run fishes of fair size.

There's one condition that will arise with light tackle in the surf, however. If currents are fast and strong they'll tend to lift your rig off the bottom and/or wash it toward the beach, so that fish do not have a chance to get at it. You can offset this problem by trying to locate a hole, deeper area, or a slough in the lee of a sand bar where currents' and waves' forcefulness is cur- tailed.

Like baits used for kingfish, hooks should be small. As in the cases of flounders and other small-mouthed species, it's better that a hook be a mite undersized than too big. For kings the range is from about a No. 6 or No. 5 to a No. 1 at the largest. Between those extremes you'll find a satisfactory medium. You can make a selection from among several patterns. The Chester- town, the same hook that is so popular for flounders, will do a job. So will O'Shaughnessys, Sproats, Carlisles, Eagle Claws, and others. Don't worry about patterns. Matching a hook's size to your bait and to the fish's mouth is more important.

Now step over here to the sinker section so we can get you outfitted with weights.

The usual bottom-fishing sinker rule is your guide: Use only enough weight to keep your rig on bottom, no more.

For bay kings, ideally, your sinker should have sufficient weight to keep the rig on bottom, yet not be so heavy as to prevent it from being carried a short distance by the current when you lift your rod tip slightly. A good bay kingfishing technique is to raise the sinker a little way—just a few inches—off bottom at intervals to allow the current to move the rig along until it has traveled maybe a hundred to two hundred feet from the boat or channel bank. A standard bank-type sinker can be rigged, but a round or egg-shaped weight is superior because it's better able to roll along the bottom.

For bottom fishing the surf, whatever the species sought, a

pyramid sinker is the type usually employed, because with its corners and shape it holds better against currents, undertows, and waves.

RIGGING   To rig for bay kingfishing, start by tying a three-loop swivel to your line. To its bottom eye attach your sinker, close

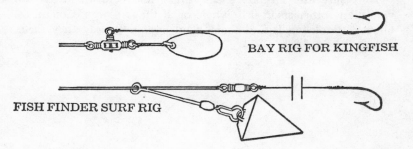

BAY RIG FOR KINGFISH

FISH FINDER SURF RIG

to the swivel. To the remaining loop tie your hook on a piece of monofilament, gut, or other leader material about twelve inches long.

For surfcasting—and this applies in bottom fishing for stripers and others, as well as kings—you can use the Kronuch surf rig detailed back in the chapter on bluefish, or the popular fish-finder setup and its variations, also described elsewhere in this volume.

OF SEASONS AND OTHER THINGS   As I said earlier, kingfish like warm weather. In the more northerly sectors of their range they start showing in springtime in the surf and, at about the same time or shortly thereafter, in inlets, bays, and channels. The run builds as the weather warms. Whatever its quality that season, it peaks in July and August, then begins to taper off in September.

During average or better runs catches are good, usually better in inside waters than along surf fronts. When runs aren't up to par they're scattered in bays and channels, and you'll work for any you hook. The same goes for the surf, where they're landed, along with a sprinkling of weakfish, by persistent regulars.

Kings bite with enthusiasm and resist with vigor. They'll provide lively little action sequences on light tackle. In their resistance kingfish won't disappoint you if you don't look for too much, like the bulldog pull of a husky pollack or the head-tossing antics of an annoyed bluefish. Know what I mean? After all, you wouldn't expect David to have Goliath's muscles, now would you?

"Are they edible?" you ask.

They sure are, I reply. Clean, dress, and cook them as you would any other small fish, whole or, if they're large enough, as fillets. I think you'll find them good eating. I'd say they taste rather like weakfish.

CHAPTER 14

Ling and *Whiting:*
They've Moved into a
Respectable Neighborhood

(Sounds cryptic? It will be explained.)

It used to be that when I heard these two fishes mentioned together, as they often are, I'd think of other name couplets, like
Horn & Hardart, Hans and Fritz, franks and beans. They also
suggest a vaudeville act to me. If you were around when we
still had vaudeville you'll recall the signs that were put up at
either side of the stage to identify each act. This pair could have
had one that read

LING & WHITING

Comic Juggling

or maybe

LING & WHITING

Songs, Dances, and Snappy Patter

You've probably guessed it anyway, but I'll tell you that ling
and whiting never were in show business. They've never even
seen a movie. But the two species often are mentioned in the
same breath, the reason being that they can be caught on the
same grounds. That's why I've maintained the partnership here.*

---

* Speaking of fishes being in show business, I have to tell you a joke. (It
fits here, and I may not have an opportunity later.) A drunk staggered into
a tavern carrying a live lobster. Pretty soon he decided the bartender was
his best friend, so he offered him the lobster. The barkeep politely refused
the gift, but the more he refused, the more persistent the lush became.
Finally wearying of this nonsense, the bartender decided that the line of
least resistance would be to accept the lobster. "Okay," he said to the drunk,
"I'll take him home to dinner." The drunk was horrified. "Don't do that!" he
hiccuped. "He's already had dinner. Take him to the movies."

Messrs. Ling and Whiting didn't always reside in a respectable neighborhood. What I mean is, there was a time when many fishermen looked down their noses at this pair. The fact is that ling bordered on being trash fish in the eyes of some anglers. In those days whiting weren't as low as ling in sport fishermen's opinion; but still, if you said you were going whiting fishing you risked being looked upon as a mild eccentric. Even whiting were considered as a kind of something's-better-than-nothing alternate when other species were slow. At that time ling and whiting lived in a poor, rundown neighborhood on the wrong side of the tracks, you might say.

Ling and whiting always have suffered by comparison with bigger, gaudier, and/or more athletic sea neighbors down through the years. Neither is a particularly good-looking fish. Some might even call ling ugly. His looks haven't helped his cause in angling circles. And the actions of both species are pedestrian and unspectacular by sport-fishing standards. They've even been called nuisances at times.

All that is unfair, not only to the fishes but also to anglers. I'll endeavor to show you why.

First off, ling and whiting have moved to a more respectable neighborhood in the view of many rod-and-reelers. You won't find as many anglers giving them a Harvard stare anymore, especially whiting. Times and conditions have brought a big change of heart. This is partly because fishermen have learned that they can enjoy light-tackle fun with the two, and partly because ling and whiting have spelled the difference between catches and skunkings when more desirable species were absent. A hungry man might crave a steak, but he won't sneer at a liverwurst sandwich. (That's a little philosophy I threw in to add class. Feel free to quote it at parties.)

FACE TO FACE, LING

By way of getting to know the two species better we'll peek into their private lives, starting with Louie the Ling.

I hate to launch the introduction with a problem, but we have one in connection with the popular name of this fish—"ling," that is, not "Louie." Here's what we're up against:

For reasons that elude me, sport fishermen everywhere fancy the name "ling." They've slapped it on, oh, I don't know how many different kinds of marine and fresh-water fishes, mostly as a nickname, here and abroad. For instance, it's an "alias" for the burbot or lawyer, a North American fresh-water relative of the cod family. It's also a nickname for the Pacific cultus, a codlike sport fish encountered on the California coast. "Ling" is one of several names applied to the cobia, a warm-water game fish. And there are European fishes carrying "ling" as a handle.

I can't understand why fish namers, amateurs and pros, are so enamored of that word "ling." I'll be doggoned if it doesn't sound almost obscene, something to be whispered behind the back of one's hand (as in someone saying, "Don't look now, but your ling is showing.").

Well, no matter. "Ling" is this species' popular name, so we'll ride with it. If you're a stickler for more correct names you have a choice. Drs. Henry Bigelow and William Schroeder call this ling a squirrel hake, giving red hake as another name. Dr. Alfred Perlmutter favors red hake. All three agree that "ling" is a popular nickname and that the scientific handle is *Urophycis chuss*. In regions the species frequent I suggest you use "ling"; otherwise few listeners will know what you're talking about.

FAMILY GET-TOGETHER   Our ling here is but one of several hakes. Others grouped around him in the family portrait are the white (also nicknamed ling), blue, spotted, and long-finned hakes, as well as a cousin known as hakeling. Those authorities with whom I've consulted believe in a family relationship between the hakes and the cod family. Like cod, the ling and some other hakes have a small barbel on their chin, and their heads bear a passing resemblance to those of cod, pollack, and haddock, although more slender. But there the resemblance ends, as you'll note if you compare profiles.

WHERE THEY'RE AT AND WHAT THEY DO   These ling inhabit both American and European sides of the Atlantic. Because of their abundance on those seaboards they've carved fair-size niches for themselves in commercial fishing at one time or another. Takes from U.S. waters alone have run into millions of pounds annually. You may have eaten ling, either as your own or someone else's catches, or perhaps as fresh or frozen fish sticks or fillets from markets. Or maybe in that dish called finnan haddie.

Distribution of ling along North America's front yard on the Atlantic Ocean ranges from Newfoundland's frigid waters southward to Virginia. In season, ling can be especially abundant in the New York-New Jersey region, at which times deep-sea party boats land all they want of them, whether they want them or not.

Spawning is thought to occur in spring and summer, during a period from about April into July. That doesn't jolt anyone, but what makes it interesting is the species' prolificness. Like cod, female ling are great believers in mass production. An average lady can release as many as two million eggs at a single spawning. They're fertilized by males in the water, after which, being buoyant, they float around until hatching takes place or a neighbor gulps them as caviar. Newly hatched babies remain close to the sea's surface, nourishing themselves on plankton and other minute forms of marine life. When they attain a length of about two to three or four inches they head for the bottom, where they reside happily ever after, more or less, satisfying their appetite with calico and sand crabs, mollusks of various kinds, and other soft-bodied creatures.

Typical of the eat-and-be-eaten pattern in the sea, astronomical numbers of ling eggs and babies fall prey to hostile environments or disappear down the gullets of hungry predators. Yet sizable numbers of them survive. Since these survivors undoubtedly represent only a fraction of the original lot, production of eggs and infants must be fantastic.

Ling are primarily ocean citizens, residing inshore and offshore. Some invade harbors, even estuaries, on occasion, but for your purposes they're ocean game. Although they will pursue food upward into near-surface levels, they're bottom dwellers. That's another detail of importance to you. Generally they favor soft bottoms such as mud or muddy sand.

As far as has been determined, ling are not truly migratory. At least they do not travel long distances. They confine themselves mainly to inshore-offshore movements in tune with seasons. The shore-to-seaward scope of their distribution extends from close-inshore waters as shallow as a couple of fathoms on out to depths well beyond fifty fathoms. Ling can tolerate a water temperature spread from as low as 33° F up to 70° F, and even higher in some parts of their range when chasing prey near the surface.

The young have a curious habit worth mentioning. At times they take refuge inside the shells of live giant scallops. They do not eat the scallops, but merely use their shells as hideouts. It's a good deal for the hakes. The giant scallops' reactions aren't recorded.

IDENTIFICATION AND SIZES Typical of his group, the ling is a slender-bodied fish, gracefully streamlined. Characteristic are a

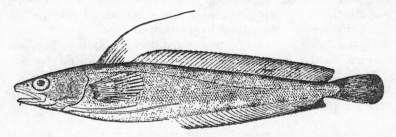

LING (*Urophycis chuss*)

long second dorsal fin of fairly uniform height and a "matching" anal fin that isn't quite as long or high. Other identification aids: (1) a relatively short first dorsal fin, sail-shaped, higher than the second dorsal, with a filamentlike extension of one of its first rays; (2) long, skinny, unusual pectoral fins, originating just behind the gill covers; (3) a tail that is longer than it is deep, with convex outer edge; and (4) large eyes placed high in the head.

Then there's his color. This is a kind of nondescript brown, reddish, greenish, or muddy, often quite dark. Sometimes this is a solid color; on other specimens it's mottled with darker blotches. That's on the back and upper sides. Farther down it often is a kind of dirty, yellowish brown, occasionally peppered with dark dots. The belly is white, off-white, gray, or a sort of yellowish white.

Maximum attainable length is in the vicinity of thirty inches, but that's exceptional. So are maximum weights in the magnitude of six, seven, or eight pounds. Such specimens would be large ling indeed, the products of commercial operations. For recreational fishermen the weight range is more like one to three pounds.

WILLY THE WHITING

Here's another fellow whose name contributes to confusion in discussions of sport fishes. When you consider that some ichthyologists place another group of fishes under the name whiting (like the kingfish and his cousins in another chapter), and that "whiting" is a localized nickname applied to species that aren't whiting at all, the whole thing becomes very involved. So involved, in fact, that it would do nothing here except confuse.

I will tell you, though, that authorities Perlmutter, Bigelow, and Schroeder give "silver hake" as another name for this species, along with the scientific label *Merluccius bilinearis*. "Whiting" is the popular name in areas of sport-fishing abundance, so we'll go with that.

YOU CAN TELL A WHITING FROM HIS RELATIVES WITHOUT A PROGRAM
This whiting belongs in a family with the fancy Latin name of Merlucciidae. His clan is so closely allied with the codfish tribe (Gadidae) that some authorities have considered the two families as one. Other ichthyologists prefer to keep the two separate, but say that they're very closely related.

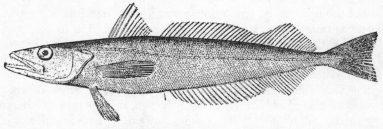

WHITING (*Merluccius bilinearis*)

In any case, the whiting can be readily differentiated from those relatives by several characteristics. Size, for instance. Like the tomcod, this whiting is one of the families' smaller members. The species can attain maximum sizes of 2 to 2½ feet and weights up to 7 or 8 pounds. Most of those you'll tie into, however, will go 14 or 16 inches, maybe even 18 or 20 here and there, and weigh 1½ to 2½ or 3 pounds. Hook a 4-pound whiting and you can brag† about one of the better ones.

Other anatomical traits setting this whiting apart from cousins in the codfish family include his body profile. He's more slender-bodied than cod, pollack, and haddock. Further, his head is flatter in profile. Like them, though, his mouth is large, and it's well outfitted with sharp teeth. Absent is the chin barbel frequently seen among certain members of the cod clan.

Still another distinguishing characteristic is the whiting's possession of two dorsal fins, whereas cod, pollack, and haddock carry three. In addition, his second dorsal closely resembles, in shape and size, the large anal fin positioned directly under it.

If you want, take a minute to compare profiles. I'll wait.

This whiting's coloring is silvery, overall, hence the name silver hake. But his back and upper sides exhibit a dark gray, brownish, or brown-gray cast. Farther down on his sides this turns to silver, sometimes with golden or purple reflections. His belly is silvery.

WHITING WHEREABOUTS Distribution of these fish spans a long, wide belt on the North American seaboard, Newfoundland down to the Carolinas. Dr. Alfred Perlmutter notes that they also travel into deeper areas to the Bahamas. Throughout their Atlantic coastal range whiting are encountered from shoal inshore waters on out to depths of 250 and 300 fathoms. They've been reported for levels as far down as 400 fathoms beyond the Continental Shelf off southern New England. You'll be fishing for them in considerably shallower water, however. I should mention in passing that while whiting are an oceanic breed they also make themselves available to anglers in Long Island Sound,

† I forgot to tell you: Boasting is an accepted practice in angling, especially during off-seasons, when no one can disprove anything.

notably in its eastern expanse, between Connecticut and Rhode Island on one side and Long Island on the other.

Silver hake—or whiting—are represented in the Gulf of Mexico by a species thought to be closely allied, and on the far side of the Atlantic Ocean by the European hake, a close relative.

Like ling, with which they're sometimes caught on common grounds, whiting are bottom feeders. They tend to favor the deeper places of areas in which they happen to be at the time. They also like sandy or pebbly bottoms. In the southernmost parts of their range they're generally found chiefly in deeper waters.

FOOD, DINING PROCEDURES, AND OTHER MANNERISMS   Whiting are voracious feeders and fast swimmers. Their ability to move swiftly makes them superior to ling as rod-and-reel targets. The fact is that ling are rather weak, sluggish swimmers.

Hunting actively, whiting prey upon smaller finned neighbors —young mackerel and menhaden are among their victims, crabs of various kinds, squid and shrimp.

In scouting food, as in their community life in general, whiting travel in large schools. These big, marauding bands can wreak havoc on schools of smaller fishes. Their hunting strategy seems to be to herd their prey into panic-stricken masses, then go to work . . . which is smart, since it makes getting a belly-filling meal easier.

If there's a single habit for which whiting are best known, it's their demoniacal persistence when raiding a school of prey. They just won't give up. Theirs is a wild determination. They'll pursue prey recklessly into shallow water, even into a surf's breakers.

Whiting have two unusual nicknames, neither of which you're likely to hear anymore. One is "winter weakfish." It stems from a fancied resemblance to northern weakfish, no kin, and the fact that they can be caught during the colder months. The other alias is "frost fish." It too was acquired because whiting are encountered during colder weather.

In fall and winter, especially at night, it isn't uncommon for hungry whiting to chase smaller fishes right into a surf. There in the breakers their recklessness can catch up with them as they're seized by waves and flung up on the sand. When large schools of whiting are occupied with such suicidal missions, numbers of them are stranded on the shore.

Coastal residents long ago learned about such strandings and turned them to their advantage. Thus was born an activity called frost fishing. Carrying lanterns and, later, flashlights, with baskets, frost fishermen walked beaches on cold nights, capturing marooned, flopping whiting with hand nets, homemade spears, and even by hand, thus harvesting a very nice mess of fish. Beach fires provided warmth when the going was slow and a polar wind became biting. Frost fishing came in for a good play in the old days. Today, as in the case of taffy pulls and horse-drawn buckboards, you don't hear much about it. Somewhere, maybe, a few old-timers are keeping it alive.

There's a modern version of "frost fishing," this one done with rod and reel. We'll get to it later.

NOW, LING AND WHITING TOGETHER

For most intents and purposes, there are two principal sport-fishing seasons for ling and whiting. One falls in the spring, roughly from April on into June. The other springs up in the fall, along about late September or October, and can last well into November.

I say there are "two principal seasons" for these fishes because they can be hooked at other times too. Ling are landed by ocean party boats through the summer. And whiting, in a sense, are an all-year species, since they too can be caught in summer and also are hooked in winter.

METHODS AND TACKLE   For both species you'll fish the sea floor. They can be caught by either of two common techniques: regular bottom fishing or jigging a small mackerel jig. Both are simple procedures, the major difference being that jigging employs an artificial and requires a little more effort. You can wield the same equipment in both.

Suit yourself as regards tackle, conventional or spinning. You have wide latitude. But you'll have to exercise judgment in your selection. For ling and whiting alone you can lean toward lighter outfits because those fishes are small. At the same time, though, you have to realize that you'll be fishing in places where fairly heavy sinkers may be required to keep your rig on bottom. Too, cod may be encountered on the same grounds in spring and autumn. Your rod must possess a certain amount of spine to meet those possibilities. If cod and/or pollack are known to be present, you might be wise to use conventional tackle instead of spinning gear, especially if lunker-size fish have been boated. An all-purpose boat outfit in the medium range will handle cod and pollack, but if it's on the heavier side of medium it will cost you some action with whiting and ling.

For those two species your line needn't be stronger than 10- or 12-pound test. Fifty or 75 to 100 yards should be ample. I doubt that you'll be fishing in much more than 100 feet of water, maybe 120 at the outside. You can spool this line on a 1/0 or 2/0 reel (or spinning equivalent, if that's what you're using). Here great line length isn't a factor, since ling and whiting aren't long-running scrappers, so you can get away with one of the smaller "mills."

If you go to somewhat heavier gear to accommodate cod in the area, particularly if they've been running upward of 20 pounds or so; you'll use proportionately heavier line, say, 20-pound test or thereabouts. To handle it, a 2/0 reel would be better. Or you can mount a 3/0 on your rod, if that's what you have. I suggest going with conventional tackle when there's a distinct chance of cod.

Ling and whiting have fairly roomy mouths, so hook sizes aren't a critical detail. A 1/0 or 2/0 will fill the bill. You can even go a size or two larger if cod are around. O'Shaughnessy, Sproat, and Virginia are among time-honored patterns. So are Mustads in various designs.

If you jig for these fishes, get yourself a couple of small mackerel jigs, about two ounces, armed with a 1/0 to 3/0 hook. This type of artificial bait consists of a streamlined metal body, of lead or with a chrome finish, in which the hook is imbedded. Some have a built-in swivel for attachment to the line, and the lure's weight serves as a sinker. These jigs should be kept shiny. Their glitter aids their attraction. With a chrome finish, wiping them off does the trick. If they're lead they'll become dull in time, due to corrosion, but rubbing with fine sandpaper or emery, or light scraping with a knife restores their luster.

Bottom angling for whiting and ling consists merely of lowering your baited rig to the sea floor and waiting for a customer. You'll find, though, that imparting some motion to your bait by lifting your rod tip a few inches and letting the rig drop back to the bottom will enhance your chances of getting whiting. They're active feeders and chase moving prey, remember. Ling, on the other hand, aren't as ambitious.

Jigging becomes a matter of lowering the artificial to the bottom, reeling it upward a couple of feet, then letting it drop down again. This cycle is repeated continuously. Jigging the bottom also can account for sea bass, notably around wrecks, I might add. And keep jigging for whiting in mind for when mackerel fishing is slow.

RIGS AND BAITS   Here are two bottom rigs you can consider. Both are simple. Both call for two hooks.

For rig No. 1 you tie a three-loop swivel to your line. To one of its two remaining eyes you attach your first hook by its snell. No leader is used for either hook in this arrangement. One loop of the swivel is left. To that you tie about eighteen inches of your fishing line. On the free end of that goes another three-loop swivel. To one of its remaining eyes tie your second hook, by its snell as before. To the last loop, on three to five or six inches of line (don't fuss; its length isn't a matter of life or death), affix your sinker. Some anglers ring in a third hook, tied into the line by its snell, with or without a swivel, about five feet above the sinker to be ready for any higher-cruising whiting.

Rig No. 2 is a kind of hybrid. I don't know if it has any advantage over No. 1, or that it's any less effective either. I mention it here as a matter of interest.

I call it a Y-rig. The first step is to tie a leader of monofilament or other material, about eighteen inches long, directly to the line close to the sinker. Both hooks are attached by their snells to the end of this leader. The result is a Y-shaped arrangement. If desired, attachment of leader and sinker can be made via a three-loop swivel on the end of the line (tie your sinker close to the swivel). With these two bottom rigs you can use a bank-type

SIMPLE RIG FOR LING AND WHITING

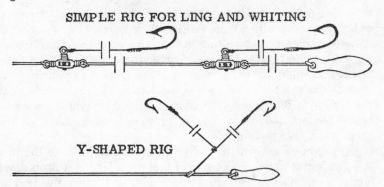

Y-SHAPED RIG

sinker of appropriate weight to keep your rig on the bottom.

There's a third rig, one you can employ when jigging for whiting, mackerel, sea bass, and other species. Here, as I indicated earlier, you'll fish a small mackerel jig, two ounces or so. All you do is tie it to the end of your line, with or without a two-loop barrel swivel according to preference (a swivel will lessen line twist). The jig itself serves as a sinker. If you're wondering why it shouldn't be heavier, it's because it doesn't have to hold bottom.

Whiting will respond to sand eels, spearing, shrimp, and pieces of bloodworm, blueclaw crab, mackerel, herring, squid, and smelt. And I should mention in passing that they frequently pursue sand eels. Ling will respond to the same baits. A good bait for both species is a piece of clam, and your best bet is skimmer.

In jigging, the artificial generally is left unbaited. Adding a bit of clam, however, does no harm. Similarly, you'll run across jiggers trying various added garnishes, such as a piece of red feather or maybe a strip of pork rind, to heighten the lure's attraction.

"FROST FISHING," MODERN STYLE   Today's frost fishing for whiting might better be called frosty fishing, for it's done in late fall and even during the winter, often at night. In its way it separates the true believers from the half-hearted. Even more than a diehard striped bass hunter who gets out of a warm bed to fish a lonely beach in the predawn hours of an autumn day, your true frost fisherman has to be fond of his sport. Being out there at night in the dead of winter, with a polar wind whistling in out of the north, it's an activity calculated to separate the men from the boys. Or maybe the nuts from the sane people, depending upon how you look at it. Be advised, though, that you won't freeze to death (it will only seem that way at times) if you dress for it.

This kind of hibernal fishing doesn't exactly attract overwhelming numbers of followers. I mean, I doubt that you'll encounter competition for a place to stand. Nevertheless, it does draw surprising numbers of men, women, and youngsters at times in places where facilities are available. If winter boat fishing offshore isn't your cup of tea, you might try the shoreside versions of frost fishing for an interseasonal fill-in.

Action is predicated upon schools of whiting prowling for, or chasing, bait fishes close to shore. Needless to add, what activity there is is concentrated in more northerly segments of the species' range. It usually begins in November and lasts on through the winter. Surf fishermen get a crack at whiting while casting such artificials as squids and plugs for striped bass in late autumn. If they're interested, they can catch whiting by switching to small bucktails.

More commonly the fishing is done from oceanfront piers and party boats. In recent years a few party boats in the New York-New Jersey region have specialized in night trips for whiting, while a couple of the few oceanfront piers available in that region have played host to beachbound groups. The boats generally are well lighted and have heated cabins to which passengers can retire to thaw out. Piers catering to winter whiting fishermen usually are well illuminated too. Lots of light aids fishing by attracting lesser creatures, which in turn draw whiting. Some piers augment the magnetism by feeding a steady stream of ground fish chum overboard.

Tackle for either boat or pier frost fishing can be on the light side, conventional or spinning. These whiting go only about a pound or so. Use that bottom rig No. 1 detailed earlier, arranging two or three hooks, No. 1 size, according to your preference.

Tip: On a pier or boat, jig your bait a little. You don't have to reel it off the bottom each time; just lift your rod tip a few inches, letting the rig drop back down. Bait motion is attractive to whiting.

Ideal winter whiting fishing nights are those that are clear and with little wind. Even with little or no breeze it can be cold; that's why I accent dressing for warmth. Thermal underwear is helpful. Another aid to warmth is an outer garment that keeps the wind out. In the wind is a chilling factor that makes cold colder, if you know what I mean. Take along a Thermos or two of hot liquid—soup, bouillon, coffee, or tea. Soup is especially good because it not only provides internal warmth, but also is food when salt air hones appetites. Not to be indelicate, but if you take coffee or tea on a pier fishing excursion you'd better check beforehand to learn if there are rest rooms. Nothing spoils fishing more than being chilled to the bone, unless it's having to go to the bathroom, and no toilet handy.

ON THE TABLE   Neither ling nor whiting rate among prime sport fishes, but they can be fun on light tackle. They're also the makings of a good meal.

Ling are meaty, have relatively few bones in comparison with some other food fishes, and when cooked as fillets are as tasty as cod. Their meat also can be used as a prime ingredient of fish chowder; or cooked and shredded for fishcakes; or cooked, cut into small pieces, and chilled for seafood cocktails.

There's no sweat to filleting ling. They're scaled first (this is easy when they're fresh-caught) if the skin is to be left on the fillets; otherwise they're filleted like any other fish and the skin carefully cut away.

Whiting can be cooked just about any way at all, including baking, broiling, and frying. They can be prepared as fillets or whole (dressed, of course). The meat has excellent flavor. Whiting also can be smoked, and as such they're delicious.

One more note about whiting, then we'll go on to the next chapter: Whiting, alive or dead, but preferably the former, are excellent bait for sharks, giant bluefin tuna, and other marine gamesters. I mention that as a tip to take along a whiting outfit on offshore trips for the larger battlers.

CHAPTER 15

Mackerel: A Case of
Feast or Famine

You've heard the phrase "feast or famine," I'm sure. It's applied
to anything that's alternately very abundant and scarcer than
giraffes in Times Square or triangular pool tables. I haven't the
foggiest notion who coined it, but I could believe it if I were told
the originator had Atlantic mackerel in mind. "Feast or famine"
describes the blue-and-silver beauties to a T. You'll learn why.

Atlantic mackerel, also called Boston mackerel (often shortened to "Bostons," naturally) and common mackerel, are members of a huge tribe that embraces such other mackerels as the
cero, king, Spanish, chub, sierra, and Pacific. That group, in turn,
generally is considered as being affiliated with tunas, bonitos,
albacores, and the fish whose name sounds like a shout of glee,
the wahoo.

If you compare this mackerel with some of his distant kin, such
as the common bonito and bluefin tuna, you'll see certain family
resemblances. All are handsome fishes, with crisp, clean-cut lines
and superb streamlining. Their tails are somewhat alike in profile
too, you'll observe. And widespread among them all are little
finlets. These are small processes, suggestive of triangles, along
the body's midline between dorsal fin and tail topside and between anal fin and tail on the underside.

CLOSE-UP The Atlantic mackerel, scientifically catalogued as
Scomber scombrus, isn't a difficult fish to identify. Size is a major
clue. These mackerel attain lengths just under 2 feet, although
specimens 20 to 22 inches long aren't run-of-the-mill. An average
range is more like 14 to 18 inches, with weights for those sizes
going approximately 1 to 2 or 2½ pounds. Larger individuals up
to 20 and 22 inches long can tip the scale at 3 to 4 pounds.

MACKEREL (*Scomber scombrus*)

Other aids to identification are shape and colors. This mackerel's body is an example of Ma Nature's streamlining at its best. His body is fusiform—spindle-shaped, tapered at its ends. Its surface is as smooth as glass. The whole idea, of course, is to keep water resistance at an absolute minimum. As a result, the Atlantic "mack" is a fast swimmer. I've never heard of him being clocked, but it wouldn't raise my eyebrows if I learned he could hit 40 miles per hour.

His color pattern, while not the underwater world's most distinctive or vivid, is attractive. His back is a dark, steely blue or greenish blue. This becomes a blue-black on the head. Characteristically, dark, wavy, irregular bands run transversely down the upper sides to near his body's midline. Sometimes the sides have brassy tints. The belly is silvery. Often this mackerel's body has a metallic sheen throughout.

He possesses a good quota of fins, the most notable of which are a well-developed, deep-V tail and a second dorsal and anal fin very similar in shape and size and positioned symmetrically.

His head is fairly long, proportionately, and his mouth is generous in size. In the dental department he's outfitted with numerous small, sharp teeth.

In one respect the Atlantic mackerel is freakish among fishes. He lacks a swim bladder, the hydrostatic organ that would give him poise, shall we say, when he chooses to pause. Because he lacks that little gas-filled sac, he must keep more or less constantly in motion. Otherwise he might drift toward the bottom. You'll witness that necessity when fishing for mackerel near the surface. You'll observe how, even though they're interested in your bait, Bostons can't tarry to investigate it leisurely. They'll either seize it or, if only looking it over, keep moving, either way.

DISTRIBUTION   Atlantic mackerel, *Scomber scombrus,* are colder-water fish. In its broadest scope their distribution on our North American seaboard is from the Gulf of St. Lawrence down to North Carolina. When the fish are available, great centers of abundance are the ocean waters off southern New England, New York, and New Jersey. Long Island's South Shore and New Jersey play host to incredibly large schools of these fish.

Scomber scombrus also is represented on the European side of the North Atlantic, where the range is described as extending from Norway to Spain.

Incidentally, in your waterfront travels you'll hear the words "spikes" and "tinkers" mentioned in connection with these mackerel. Don't be confused. Fishermen use them to denote certain size stages, as "snappers" and "snapper-blues" are applied to bluefish. When so used, "spikes" indicate mackerel up to about seven or eight inches long. In the ten- or eleven-inch class they're commonly referred to as "tinkers." Beyond those lengths they're often called "Bostons" to indicate the larger, more desirable macks.

OF MIGRATIONS AND THINGS   These mackerel are wanderers of the open sea. They travel in schools that can number astronomical numbers of individuals. During seasons of abundance you'll hear about mackerel schools strung out over miles of ocean. Interestingly, like young bluefin tuna, all the fish in a given school are much the same size. In fact, sameness of size is apt to be more precise in the case of mackerel. By actual measurement, those in a particular group won't vary more than an inch in length, indicating that they're all of the same age.

They're quite migratory, moving from hither to yon and back to hither again in food searches. They do not travel such great distances as, for example, some of the tunas and albacores. Evidence indicates that most of their wanderings are up and down the Atlantic seaboard, including offshore-inshore round trips, within their range. It's also believed that they do not travel much farther offshore than the limits of the Continental Shelf.

Studies have indicated that Atlantic mackerel winter offshore in waters fifty fathoms to as much as one hundred fathoms deep along the edge of the Continental Slope, a submarine shelf flanking the U.S. eastern coast. Although they like cool water, they won't tolerate temperatures lower than a certain level. Ed Migdalski points out that commercial harvests seldom, if ever, are found in waters colder than about 45° F. Although scatterings of them are encountered in early winter on cod grounds, those waters, with their temperatures of 35° to 39° or 40° F, are generally too cold for them, so they seek deeper water along the Continental Shelf where it's a bit warmer. There, it's thought, they spend the coldest months in areas thirty to one hundred miles from the nearest coast. There they also could be trawlers' targets.

In spring they move shoreward into littoral belts. During seasons of abundance they may appear simultaneously along many miles of coastline. These "sudden" appearances aren't surprising to mackerelwise anglers. The chances are that those sage rod-'n'-reelers have been keeping posted on the macks' progress through commercial fishing reports.

It's been suggested that one pattern of this springtime inshore movement goes like this:

When a signal is received, presumably triggered by rising water temperatures, a tremendous body of mackerel—uncountable thousands of fish—streams toward the coast. At a certain point the gargantuan parade divides to form two lengthy processions, each strung out several miles. One swings southward to arrive in coastal waters off Chesapeake and Delaware Bays in March or April. The other parade, meanwhile, fins its way shoreward on a more northerly course, threading into coastal zones above those bays in April or May.

According to this theory, both parades then move, at an estimated six miles per day, on a northeasterly heading up the coast in a spawning trek. Ordinarily they're in Massachusetts waters by or before late May, if they're to show. About a month later, schools of them have circumnavigated the elbow of Cape Cod and are journeying northward toward the Gulf of Maine. From those two coastwise processions, again according to the speculation, come populations (northern procession) that summer in the Gulf of St. Lawrence and other groups (southern parade) that spend the warmer months in the Gulf of Maine.

It would seem that this inshore migration *en masse* is connected in some way with spawning, and that the process occurs en route. The multiplication takes place in spring or summer. The spawning arena is vast, extending from about offing of Chesapeake Bay up to the Gulf of St. Lawrence, but breeding occurs at progressively later dates northward as waters warm.

They're prolific rascals. A medium-size female can release about five hundred thousand eggs. Multiplying that by countless thousands of lady mackerel would make for a crowded neighborhood, except that they're released in batches of forty thousand to fifty thousand at a time during the spawning season. Even so, they all add up to a mind-boggling number of eggs.

After fertilization by the males, these eggs drift about the sea in lackadaisical fashion while they incubate. Meanwhile, of course, there are the inevitable mass mortalities due to predators and adverse environments. Those ova that survive to hatch produce larval mackerel that reach a length of only about a third of an inch after their first forty days of life. After sixty days they attain lengths of about two inches, and growth is rapid.

Fantastic numbers of Bostons survive egghood and infancy, just by virtue of super mass production, I suppose. I've seen proof of it in early summer in the Atlantic when millions of youngsters, only two to four inches long, swarmed all over the sea. Even more dramatic proof is their presence in unending hordes in good years.

When they're about ten or eleven inches long, mackerel are in the early part of their second year. Later, when fully two years old, many are mature enough to spawn their wholesale contributions to perpetuation of the species. In their third summer they're approximately fourteen inches long, big enough to matriculate as full-fledged Bostons. By their sixth summer they've attained lengths of sixteen inches. A seventeen-incher is roughly eight years old. As for corresponding weights, an old fishermen's gauge says "a pound a foot."

A GLUT OR A SCARCITY Few other marine species (bluefish are one) exhibit such erratic, extreme, unpredictable fluctuations in abundance as *Scomber scombrus*. One season, or maybe two, three, or more in a row, they'll be around by the millions. Another year you might not see hide nor hair of them. They're so unpredictably erratic that commercial fishing for them is labeled an uncertain way to make a living. Either they're so scarce that decent catches are an impossibility, or so numerous as to drive market prices into the cellar.

Wholesale destruction of eggs and babies is one factor that can cause a severe scarcity. Such a calamity occurred in 1932 when there was a fantastic destruction of baby macks, with various causes as the culprits. It was estimated that only 4 fish out of each 1,000,000 eggs spawned managed to survive the first 2 months of life. The effect wasn't felt immediately; but a couple of years later, when many of those other 999,996 fish could have been swimming around, but weren't, catches were miserable.

Another cause of scarcity is the species' erratic migratory movements and behavior in general. The schools' travel plans tend to be so eccentric as to be difficult, if not virtually impossible, to predict. Some seasons they won't put in an appearance at all, or in widely scattered numbers, in their usual haunts. Here the famine is due simply to absence, not an actual scarcity.

Water temperatures, availability of food, and searches for satisfactory spawning grounds are thought to be among the variables influencing migratory patterns and so causing the vagaries of these fish. In the summer of 1937, for instance, the New England coast sweltered in unusually warm weather, resulting in extraordinarily high surface temperatures in adjacent waters. Even though there was substantial evidence of a large supply of mackerel in the Atlantic, fishermen just couldn't locate the schools, and the commercial catch was one of the lowest in years.

So it comes about that variable factors, working independently or together, can precipitate a radical scarcity of these fish.

Fortunately, all the ledger's ink isn't red. There's a credit side too. And what a credit side it can be!

If spawning is good and a high percentage of larval mackerel survive the nursery stage, if food supplies and other environmental conditions are favorable, and if the schools don't scatter to the four winds—a lot of "ifs," but they must be mentioned

—you can look forward to a feast phase. And I mean it will be a bonanza.

The fish then appear offshore and inshore in astronomical numbers, hordes of them, seemingly without end. Schools half a mile wide and strung out over twenty miles of ocean have been sighted. When mackerel are in their feast phase you can catch them until you stand chin-deep in them, if you fancy being up to your Adam's apple in dead fish. (I hope you're not that kind of "meat fisherman" or fish hog.) Add to such abundance the fact that these macks are scrappy for their size, and you have action-packed angling.

Frankly, I don't enthuse over mackerel storms myself. Party boat skippers like them, naturally, because they spell business. It's fun to catch a nice mess of fish, sure, but when they're so easy to take in such numbers a lot of the sport evaporates. The fact is that it can reach the edge of monotony.

SEASONS AND GUIDEPOSTS What with their movements inshore in spring and offshore in autumn, and their coastwise migrations, Bostons can give fishermen two excellent opportunities. Two mackerel fishing seasons, in other words. But I say "can" because there are years when such opportunities aren't forthcoming. They might show en masse in the spring, and not at all or in considerably fewer numbers that fall. Not infrequently their spring performance far outshines its autumn followup. Then there are years when they won't show during either season.

When they come inshore in the spring, and during their stay in coastal regions, they tend to wander at middle and upper levels, depending upon which depths are most productive of food.

A trick in mackerel angling is to watch for "sea signs" indicating the presence of fish. These signs are similar in nature to those sought when hunting bluefish and school-size bluefin tuna. One is a surface disturbance betraying fish feeding at the top. Another is the presence of sea birds, circling an area, swooping, and picking up items in the water as they feed on lesser fish chased to the surface by predators underneath.

One such bird to look for is the gannet, a fairly large fellow, included in the order of pelicans, and characterized by a spindle-shaped body; long, pointed wings; and a fair-size head armed with a large, sharp bill. Gannets will feed on smaller fishes being pursued by mackerel, and even on the mackerel themselves. Often these birds fish by diving from a height, and they can even swim underwater in pursuit of prey.

Capt. Russ Redfield of Freeport, New York, one of the U.S. East Coast's better skipper-guides before he retired from the field, used to place a lot of faith in gannets as mackerel indicators. When he spotted a gannet placidly floating on the ocean's surface he headed his *Capt. Russ* right for the bird. If the gannet showed a reluctance to leave, Russ interpreted it to mean that the bird had found pretty good dining in that spot—mackerel, perhaps. And if, on becoming airborne, a gannet jettisoned his stomach contents to better gain altitude, Russ would pause to look at the regurgitated material to see if it contained identifiable pieces of mackerel, a sign that Bostons were somewhere in the area.

A very noticeable sea sign occurs when hungry mackerel attack schools of small menhaden, herring, mullet, or other food fishes at the surface. Such a ruckus—the prey breaking water, jumping, skittering along the top in frantic efforts to escape, with mackerel right behind them—is almost like a giant finger pointing to the place.

Many times there are no such guideposts. That's when chumming does the trick.

GEAR AND RIGGING   To extract the most from mackerel fishing you should use light tackle. Rod flexibility is a criterion for lively sport. A light boat or all-purpose outfit, conventional or spinning, such as you'd wield for any kind of bay or ocean fishes of comparable size will do fine. Your line, whether Dacron, monofilament, or whatever, need be no heavier than ten- or twelve-pound test, and you can go lighter. Incidentally, I think a green-tinted line is better than white for mackerel. It's less conspicuous and "spooky" in the water.

Mist-colored leader, a couple of feet of it, is a good component for your terminal tackle. We'll get to its attachment in a moment. A small, chrome-plated mackerel jig carrying a No. 1 or 1/0 hook completes your rig.

Rigging procedure: (1) Tie about three feet of mist-colored

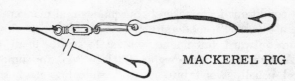

MACKEREL RIG

leader material or monofilament in about the same strength as your line (if you're not using mono line, that is) into your line. (2) Attach your mackerel jig to the leader's free end. This connection is made in any of three ways. You can tie the jig directly to the leader or through a two-loop barrel swivel. Some anglers omit this swivel, considering it just so much unnecessary hardware. Personally, I don't think it makes that much difference, one way or another. A third procedure is via a *small* snap swivel on the leader, which accepts the jig. The advantage here is simple removal of the artificial, and at a certain stage of the game you may want to take it off. (3) Generally the jig is left unbaited initially.

This is your basic starting rig. If you wish (you can do it now or later) add a snelled flounder hook, such as a Chestertown, to your rig. If it's incorporated at the start of fishing, it's tied into the leader just ahead of the jig by its snell in such a way that it stands practically straight out. In due time this will be baited. If you decide to wait before adding the flounder hook (and it may turn out that you won't need it that day) it can be substituted for the jig by connecting the loop in its snell with the snap swivel on your leader.

GETTING DOWN TO BUSINESS Having spotted promising sea signs, or having selected an area you think might hold promise (keep an eye out for other mackerel boats), and dropped anchor, your first step is to get a chum line going.

Chumming material and procedure are the same as for bluefish (which see, if you haven't already). Results are same too. The chum's globules of oil, laced with blood for spice, and bits of meat ride out with the current and diffuse. In time (or so you hope) this buffet is smelled and sampled by roving bands of mackerel and they start strolling up the chum corridor to waiting hooks.

Ideal conditions for mackerel chumming—and mackerel fishing in general—include a moderate current, moving enough to carry the chum outward, but not so swift as to scatter it all over the ocean. A slight chop in the water is helpful too. For some reason, mackerel usually won't bite as well on calm, glassy-sea days as they will when the water's surface is ruffled a bit.

Tip: Take along some white beach sand on chumming expeditions for mackerel and other species. If the tide is just a mite too strong for a good chum line, mix some of the sand with your 'bunker pulp. It not only will help to prevent the chum from straying too far, but also absorb some of its oil and strong flavor, thereby augmenting the pulp. You can stretch your chum supply this way too.

Angling for mackerel necessitates a certain amount of preliminary experimentation to determine the depth at which they're traveling at the time. At the start of fishing there's no way of knowing how deep they are. They might be twenty feet down, or forty, or up fairly near the surface. Unless you can actually see them, which happens, you'll have to do a little probing.

As a starter I select some arbitrary intermediate level in the depth of water being fished—say, twenty to thirty feet down. If there's no action there after jigging the lure for a reasonable length of time, I try a lower or higher plane. At this stage it's a definite advantage to have a number of people fishing, each with a jig dangling at a different depth, maybe fifteen feet to thirty or forty feet. When the first mackerel is hooked, the angler should note at what depth he had the strike and notify the others so they can make the necessary adjustments. What you can do is mark your line in some way (here's a use for that red nail polish) so that you can return to the right level after reeling in a fish.

REACTIONS When mackerel are available in good supply their answer to your chumming call is usually a concerted response. And when several boats are chumming the same area, ladling ground mossbunker pulp overboard in quantity, the reaction can take on the aspects of a mass assault.

Mackerel often will bite wildly on unbaited jigs for the first hour or two of fishing. Then, after a while, for no apparent reason, they may lose interest in those shiny attractors, and catches will taper off sharply. This is a signal to commence fishing with bait. This is also when that flounder hook I mentioned earlier comes into service. If it's already part of your rig, you're all set. Remove the mackerel jig or leave it on as a sinker. Some anglers favor its removal so their bait will sink in a more natural fashion. If mackerel are biting like mad that isn't a critical detail. If the current is brisk and you've taken your jig off, you can add a half-ounce split shot or two, or a small sinker, to the leader to carry your rig down. If you didn't include a flounder hook earlier, do it now as described.

This hook is baited with a small strip of squid or mackerel belly, sliced from the fish's silvery underside. Considered very good mackerel bait is a mossbunker heart. Only trouble is, you'll have to paw the chum bucket to find one, and there aren't many.

Once again you may have to determine where the Bostons are hanging out. They might still be at the level where you caught them earlier . . . or deeper . . . or shallower. They might even be up within three to six feet of the surface, in which case you'll see them. I've seen them so close to the top that I could watch each fish approach the bait and grab it. Again you'll have to adjust your rig so that it dangles at the proper level. That's determined by sight of the fish or by the first strike.

When mackerel are in abundance they can be hooked practically without limit. (Unfortunately, a lot of fishermen take advantage of this and keep many more than they can use.) The scene created by a boatload of fishermen excitedly hoisting mackerel inboard as fast as they can, then getting their rigs overboard again, becomes wild at times. It also can be like a sequence in an old Mack Sennett comedy film. Many a guy has had his favorite fishing hat knocked off or been slapped in the face by a wiggling mackerel coming inboard. Fish and scales fly all over the place. It doesn't take much more than looking at Bostons to make their scales come off. Fish slither around the deck, and from bow to stern there's a kind of organized pandemonium . . . but fun.

BIG COMPETITION   If there's anything that can put a crimp in mackerel action it's a shark. Sharks—notably makos—dine on mackerel; and chum naturally attracts *them* too. Periodically a big-bellied pirate will be drawn to your chum line by the combination of ground menhaden and the mackerel. Sometimes sharks will come right up to your boat with the macks.

If mackerel action is lively, then stops abruptly like water turned off at a faucet, the odds are that a shark has glided into the scene. There isn't much you can do about the intruder unless you have appropriately strong tackle aboard. The cue then is to hastily rig a hook of suitable size, bait it with a whole mackerel, and try to remove the shark from circulation.

Or you can try this stunt: Tie a strong hook, say, a 9/0 to 12/0, to a few feet of stout cord or old fishing line. To the other end attach an empty beer can. Bait the hook with a whole mackerel and toss the works overboard, can and all, preferably close to the shark with the bait where he can see it. Or if you can tease him into taking the bait by dangling it in front of him, so much the better.

What's supposed to happen is this: When the shark gulps the bait he feels the hook and starts to move off. As he does, his forward motion brings the beer can against his side, nudging him. This prompts him to move faster. The faster he goes, the more that can thumps him. If the length of line is right, the can will smack him just about where he would sit down, if sharks sat down. Users swear it can make a shark nudge himself into the next county. I can't vouch for that.

Down on the Gulf of Mexico in Louisiana, marlin fishing members of the New Orleans Big Game Fishing Club have a variation of that gimmick they use to eliminate two sharks at once. With two hooks and some line they fashion a Y-shaped rig. On the single, free end of the "Y" they attach one of those plastic bottles household bleach comes in. Its hooks baited with whole fish, the rig is tossed to the interlopers. If it works, two sharks grab the hooks and tug against each other and the plastic bottle, thereby becoming too busy to bother more desirable game.

SPECIAL   If you want to enjoy some real sport with Bostons, go boat casting for them with light spinning or conventional tackle —especially the former. Chumming is part of this, the boat at anchor or sometimes drifting. Maybe a school has been sighted at the surface, in which case you attempt to hold it around the boat with chum. Or maybe your chum line attracts a wandering school to your vicinity.

In any case, when the fish are within range you cast to them. Hungry mackerel will accept a variety of small, bright, eye-catching artificials, including spinners, bucktails, etc. A two- or three-pound Boston on light spinning gear will give you lively action.

Here's another stunt: Inevitably there will be occasions when chum pulls macks to your boat, yet they don't seem to want to accept *any* lure. It's worth a try to rig a small hook, a No. 2 or so, on a couple of feet of mist-colored leader or monofilament, bait with a small piece of mackerel or herring belly, or squid if those aren't available, and let the rig drift in among the chum.

FOR THE TABLE Bostons are too oily for my taste, unless cooked a certain way. Many seafood eaters share that sentiment, which is why mackerel are difficult to give away. But they're good food fish, my taste notwithstanding. The fact is that the oiliness that some people find objectionable is that extra that others like about the fish. The same goes for their somewhat stronger flavor.

If you're one of those folks who can do without the oil, there are ways to drain a mackerel's crankcase. One is to cut out any darker streaks of meat while dressing the fish for cooking. (I happen to dislike dark meat in any kind of fish, but here again there are differences in diners' tastes.) The other procedure is this. After scaling, gutting, removing head and fins, etc., rinse the fish gently in a pan of cold, salted tap water. Drain on absorbent paper or remove excess moisture with a damp cloth. Cut two to four lengthwise slits through the skin on the belly. Broil the fish, belly down, on a rack, with a pan directly underneath to catch the oil rendered out. Cooked properly, mackerel meat is sweet and firm, darned good eating. With most of the oil gone, and no strong taste, I like it.

LAST WORD When mackerel fishing is slow, skippers mutter, "We got a pick on 'em." When action is lively, captains chortle, "We got 'em leapin'!" Here's hoping you'll have 'em leapin' when you go mackerel fishing.

CHAPTER 16

Pollack: Scrappy Cousins of the Cod

Early one spring, when juice was beginning to run hot again in fishermen's veins after a long winter, I listened in at a friendly but supercharged debate between a fresh-water angling faithful and a longtime crony of his, a Long Islander who was just as enthusiastic about salt-water fishing. They had locked horns in a generations-old argument as to which offers the most sport, fresh-water angling or its marine counterpart. As usual, as in debates about religion and politics, they were arguing to a Mexican standoff.

On this occasion the famed fishing port of Montauk, N.Y., crept into the conversation, dragging with it the subject of pollack, a springtime target out there. The lake-and-stream angler had heard of pollack, but never had wet a line for them. No pollack, he was sure, could match a husky largemouth bass. That was his irreversible verdict. He had spoken. Period.

But his salt-water buddy wasn't finished with him. No one was going to slam the door on pollack—or, for that matter, any other marine battler—while he was around. He hung on like a barnacle. "Charley," he growled, "you've got a mind about this broad." He held up his thumb and forefinger to measure off about an eighth of an inch.

The argument blossomed all over again, the Izaak Walton becoming smugly complacent while his friend's blood pressure soared like a kite in a wild March sky. Neither side got anywhere.

Finally the salt-water buff—call him George—frustrated and exasperated to the brink of a stroke, seized a telephone. Instead of braining Charley with it, as I half expected he would, he dialed a Montauk captain he knew and booked a boat for a date in May to go trolling for pollack off Long Island's easternmost tip.

"I'll show you!" he snorted, banging the telephone down in its cradle. "We'll see what you do at Montauk, wise guy!"

Charley accepted the challenge. His grin as much as said he knew this was going to be a no-contest affair. But he'd humor his buddy, give pollack a whirl. Maybe he could shut George up for once and for all.

You may have guessed the outcome. I'm sure you have if you've ever trolled for pollack in the rough-and-tumble tide rips beyond Montauk Lighthouse in the spring. After wrestling with those fish Charley returned to his lakes-and-streams bailiwick with a healthier respect for pollack and a completely renovated opinion of salt-water fishing in general.

Of course, trying to equate fresh- and salt-water fishing is foolish business anyway. But that's another story.

The fact is that Charley, like many a salt-water brother, had his eyes opened by tangling with muscular pollack. That's why pollack hunting, both at anchor and trolling, is amassing its own corps of followers.

PERSONAL GLIMPSES Pollack have acquired the usual quota of regional nicknames. In various places they've been called "green cod" (because of their greenish tinge) and "Boston bluefish" (you've got me there!). They've also been given such unexplainable handles as "Quoddy salmon," "coalfish," "saithe," and "sea salmon." Those aliases are interesting, but they only confuse the issue. Stick with "pollack." The species' scientific tag is *Pollachius virens.*

Pollack are in the codfish tribe. If you take a moment to compare our profiles of cod and pollack you'll note a family resemblance. Go ahead, take a look. I'll wait.

I want to point up certain details in particular that they share. One is that they're both fairly deep-bodied, although cod sometimes have an edge in that department. Other shared traits are three dorsal fins and two anal fins, a common arrangement in the cod clan. Then there's the characteristic pale-colored line extending laterally along each side from the gill cover region to the tail's base. Representatives of both species also sport a barbel, a small, pointed, fleshy process hanging from the chin.

A greenish tinge usually is quite noticeable among pollack. As

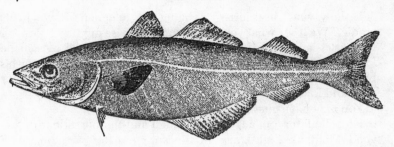

POLLACK (*Pollachius virens*)

in the cases of many other marine fishes, though, their color
scheme is subject to variations. The back and uppermost sides
can be green-gray, or greenish brown, or olive, or brownish. Farther down on the sides this has a paler hue; or it may be gray
or yellowish, or a blend of those two colors. Their belly is a gray-
silver mixture.

Cod and pollack are the two members of the codfish family
with which you'll come in contact most frequently. Although
they share a very noticeable family resemblance, they're not difficult to separate. One aid is their respective color patterns, with
an accent on the pollack's greenish tinge. Another clue is our
friend pollack's more deeply forked tail.

Size differences are another field mark. Cod attain considerable
length and weight. Pollack are smaller. Over-all, their range is
from a couple of pounds for youngsters up to twenty-five and
thirty pounds. Specimens heavier than thirty pounds are unusual,
and a rare one over thirty-five pounds would be world record
material. Among sport-fishing catches the average scale is from
about three, four, and five pounds up into the twenties. Pollack
weighing in the teens or early twenties are fairly common.

Here's an approximate length-weight yardstick: twenty-four
inches long, four or five pounds; thirty inches, eight to nine
pounds; thirty-five inches, fourteen to twenty-one pounds; and
forty inches long, twenty-five to thirty-five pounds. Weights in
relation to lengths among pollack are variable, notably among
larger specimens, and depend to an extent upon their physical
condition at the time.

SPAWNING AND OTHER HOUSEHOLD HABITS   The love life of pollack is by no means an open book, but indications are that they breed during late autumn and winter. The mating takes place offshore in water 150 to 250 or 300 feet deep.

Depending upon the size of the lady involved, a female can produce anywhere from a couple of hundred thousand to more than 2,000,000 eggs. One conscientious breeder, weighing 23½ pounds, was found to contain in excess of 4,000,000.

Pollack eggs measure about $\frac{1}{20}$ inch in diameter and are buoyant. They're fertilized in the water by males' sperm. Being buoyant, they drift around in the sea in rudderless fashion until they either hatch or are gulped by hungry neighbors. Incubation time is governed by water temperatures. The warmer the water, the sooner hatching occurs.

Larval pollack are roughly ⅕ inch long. That's tiny anywhere; and in the sea's merciless milieu it's precarious indeed. These infants have to take their chances, drifting aimlessly at or near the surface for several weeks, then seek the ocean's lower levels to better find the sort of food they need at that stage.

Pollack eggs hatching in midwinter produce babies to 2 inches long by that spring. In summer they reach 3 to 5 inches. By their second spring, when a year old, they're 5 to 7 inches long. After that, the age-length relationships go about like this: age 2, 12 or 13 inches; age 3, 17 to 18 inches; age 4, 21 to 22 inches; by 5½, to 25 inches; at 6½, 27; at 7½, 28; at 8½, 29; and between 9 and 10 years, 30 inches. Ed Migdalski says that pollack are known to live as long as 19 years. Presumably some of the senior citizens top 20.

Voraciousness runs in the codfish family. Pollack exhibit it too. I think cod top them, since I haven't heard of pollack wolfing bottles, electric light bulbs, and other junk. Pollack seem to draw the line at such unpalatable items of hardware. But their appetite doesn't have to take a back seat to the cod's. Pollack are ravenous predators, glutting themselves on crustaceans and small fishes of assorted kinds. Family sentiment has no place in their makeup. They devour the young of their cod cousins as readily as those of any other species. Pollack are notorious for eating great quantities of young cod, herring, hake, and haddock. A classic example of pollack voraciousness is a nine-inch specimen that had engulfed seventy-seven herring, the largest nearly three inches long.

This enormous, varied appetite gives fishermen latitude in selection of baits. Also noteworthy is the species' lively hunting of food. They're very active in this respect, with *sight* playing an important part in capture of prey. Their aggressiveness and hunting by sight form the basis for choosing trolling as a pollack fishing technique. Since the fish like their prey on the move, a moving lure is a logical way to tempt them. Furthermore, their liveliness and their respectable amount of muscle combine to make them worthy rod-and-reel opponents.

DISTRIBUTION AND DEPTHS   Pollack inhabit both sides of the North Atlantic. On our North American seaboard their range extends from about the cold Gulf of St. Lawrence and northern Nova Scotia on down to New Jersey. Fringe regions include southern portions of Newfoundland and Labrador on the north, and Chesapeake Bay and North Carolina to the south. European pollack have been reported for Iceland, Norway, the North Sea, the English Channel, and on down to the Brittany Coast of the Bay of Biscay.

On our side of the big puddle they appear in good numbers in Nova Scotian waters and the Gulf of Maine. I can attest to the former region's pollack (and cod) fertility. I've fished for them out of Wedgeport. The waters beyond Montauk Lighthouse, eastward to Block Island and the offshore grounds of Cox's Ledge, also harbor good numbers of pollack. Among them are some of the larger specimens, weights at least into the twenties.

As you can see from its distribution, this is a cold-water species. And throughout their range pollack are ocean dwellers.

They travel at varying depths, water temperatures and food being major influencing factors. They're encountered near or at the surface when the sea's upper levels aren't too warm for them. Ed Migdalski has said that the larger fish are rarely, if ever, found near the surface when the temperature is higher than 52° F. Yet they can be quite numerous down a few fathoms where it's cooler. These are details you should keep in mind when trolling for them. They determine whether you tow a lure near the top or deeper.

Pollack also are found at intermediate levels and down near the sea floor, where they're often caught by codfishermen.

SEASONS Depending upon areas, and satisfactory coolness of waters therein, pollack can be hooked during just about any of the four seasons. Understandably, quantities vary from place to place and season to season. Some grounds and/or times of year naturally are better producers than others. Too, catches depend upon how many anglers fish for them and how well they concentrate on them.

I come back to Montauk as a case in point. I cite this eastern Long Island peninsula because there's probably as much, if not more, pollack fishing there than just about anywhere else. Much of the time pollack are caught incidental, more or less, to cod in that region. And since Montauk codfishing is an all-year deal, sinker-bouncers find several months' action with pollack too.

For my money, though, it's in the spring that Montauk pollack action really comes into its own. This is when we troll for them there, and it's fishing in a class by itself.

Water off Montauk Point becomes quite turbulent with the right combination of tides and winds, for it's here that gigantic masses of water rolling in from the Atlantic encounter shallower depths. There's nowhere for this water to go but upward; and with tide and wind battling each other, it goes upward in big lumps. Small fishes are knocked about by this turbulence, a situation of which pollack are well aware. So they come into the tide rips to feed. That's the time to troll for them.

Pollack trolling in Montauk's tide rips can start any time after mid-April. It usually reaches its zenith in May, and can extend into June. Pollack probably could be trolled there—deep—well into summer, but by then Montauk anglers' attention is drawn to other gamesters, not the least of which are swordfish, white marlin, and assorted sharks.

As I said earlier, pollack are commonly caught by bottom fishermen out after cod, and they're boated on many ocean grounds from Nova Scotia to New Jersey. Because not too many anglers sail expressly for pollack, there are probably many regions—some as yet undiscovered in that respect—with good-to-excellent supplies of the fish.

TROLLING COVERS TERRITORY   A surface disturbance generated by a school of food-mad pollack is an obvious signpost. You could hardly miss an acre or so of boiling sea. Another indicator, not as dramatic, is a squadron of seagulls hovering over a particular spot, giving it their raucous attention.

When pollack are evident at the surface, you can troll the school's edges. Don't plow through the fish. Maneuver your boat —long, curving swings are one strategy—so that the lures flash through the thick of activity.

When the only promise of action is sea birds working, and pollack aren't actually seen, you'll have to "scratch" that area and experiment with trolling depths to make contact. If the gulls seem reluctant to leave that spot, you have a pretty fair sign that some kind of fish is underneath. Here, as always, it's an advantage to have three or four rigs out, each set to ride at a different level, from within a few feet of the top down to intermediate planes. When one nails a pollack, others are adjusted accordingly.

More often than not, pollack and marine birds won't be so obliging as to hand out such strong hints. Pollack are most likely to keep their whereabouts and depths to themselves. That's good, more of a challenge.

They might be near you or some distance away, or absent entirely. They might be finning along only a few feet below the surface, or a few fathoms down, or low over the ocean floor. Right at the start you have a hide-'n'-seek game on your hands, with the problem of guessing the level at which to begin. You have to "feel the fish out."

When there's no clue as to where pollack might be, I usually begin the feeling-out process by trolling deep, somewhere near the bottom. I also believe this is a good starting plane when near-surface waters are likely to be warming. The rig is carried deep by a drail or trolling sinker of suitable weight or by a gismo such as an adjustable trolling planer. Wire line also helps to place a rig deep. At the same time it's helpful to have another rig, or even two or three, riding at shallower levels above the deep rig. Also at this stage, a worthwhile maneuver is to swing the boat in a wide arc or a long U-turn every so often. This tends to bring lures up nearer the surface, towing them through different levels along which pollack might be swimming. In these maneuvers you'll have to be especially alert to note the approximate depth at which a fish is caught so that all rigs can be adjusted accordingly. Trolling in long arcs and U-turns, you see, covers ground in both horizontal and vertical planes.

When you come right down to it, almost every aspect of pollack trolling calls for experimentation each time you go after them. Lures are another instance.

When pollack are hungry they're apt to be in the market for just about anything that moves. They've been known to respond to such artificials as metal squids, bucktails, streamers, spinners baited with a strip of squid or pork rind, small plugs, and feather lures, both natural and synthetic. A natural feather lure, the same as that trolled for bluefish and tuna, often is effective for pollack. Jigs with metal bodies and long, colorful nylon skirts also will take them on occasion. But there's no predicting what color or combination of colors in a lure's skirt, natural or synthetic, will elicit the best response on a given day. It's usually necessary to try one, then another, or, better yet, different colors simultaneously, before making contact. An added attraction can be given to any lure by garnishing its hook with a squid strip or piece of pork rind.

You also will have to experiment with trolling speeds and the distances astern at which your lures travel. Wind and current strength, and whether you're moving with them or against them, will be factors to reckon with. There's no rule of thumb for pollack trolling speeds. Vary them, but don't go to extremes, especially on the faster side. As for your lures' distances astern, you might hook pollack only twenty to thirty feet off the transom, possibly even closer, or it might be fifty to sixty feet or more. Here again having two or more rigs out is an advantage. They can be trolled at varying distances.

RIGGING FOR POLLACK TROLLING There are various rigging arrangements for pollack trolling *near the surface*. Anglers fiddle around with rigs to suit circumstances and their own ideas. You should too. I'll get you launched with some basics.

A feather lure or other skirted artificial can be rigged in the same fashion as for bluefish and young tuna—that is, the hook is attached to a wire leader, then the artificial is slipped on the

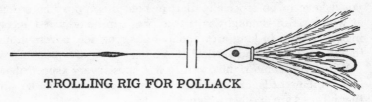

TROLLING RIG FOR POLLACK

leader's free end and shoved down to the hook. About six feet of No. 6 or No. 7 wire are satisfactory. The best attachment of leader to line, when lure experimentation is involved, is through a loop in the wire and a snap swivel on the line. Other artificials, whatever they may be, are rigged in a similar manner. About the only major variations in such rigs are the selections of lures. A minor variation is in leader lengths.

For trolling deep and at intermediate levels you'll have to adopt another procedure. A hundred feet or so, maybe fifty yards, of wire line on top of your regular line—that is, between your regular line and rig—will carry your lure deeper than ordinarily. Here you may elect to omit a wire leader, attaching lure to wire line through a snap swivel. If wire line doesn't take your come-on deep enough, you'll have to incorporate a drail or trolling sinker in the system. This can be inserted between line and wire leader.

Whenever there's a situation that calls for experimentation with lures, make attachments through snap swivels to facilitate changes.

In pollack trolling you can rig one or two hooks. If a single hook is used, attach it to the leader in the customary manner. If you decide on a second hook you'll need one with a ring eye. Connect it to the first by the eye-and-bend method. Open the second hook's eye, slip it over the first hook's bend, then squeeze the eye closed. Don't use this tandem arrangement if you're trying for an IGFA record, though. The rules bar it.

Pollack have roomy mouths. Hook sizes go from about a 6/0 for the smaller fish to a 9/0 for the heftier ones. A 7/0 or 8/0 is a serviceable medium. Any of the well-known designs—O'Shaughnessy, Sproat, Eagle Claw, Mustads, etc.—will do a job.

SINKER-BOUNCIN' Time of year, location, and conditions may not be conducive to trolling for pollack. So who's worried? We'll go bottom fishing.

Sinker-bouncing for pollack is essentially the same as bottom fishing for cod. The only difference is that pollack may be wandering around at a higher level than their cousins, especially in rocky places and around wrecks. You rig accordingly. A high-low rig takes care of that difference in traveling levels, and with it you'll make mixed catches of the two species.

Basically this outfit consists of a low hook attached to the line just above the sinker and a high hook connected to the line a few feet above that. When cod and pollack are on the same grounds, the low hook is for the former. This cod hook is attached to the line via a three-loop swivel, the sinker tied to one of its eyes and close to the swivel. The high or pollack hook goes about five feet above that, also connected to the line through a three-eye swivel. The cod hook can be tied in by its snell. Your pollack hook is on a leader—gut, monofilament, or what have you—two to four feet long.

This fundamental high-low rig is open to all sorts of variations. For instance, the low hook, on a short leader, also can be for pollack. Or you can vary the height of the high hook above the sinker, trying it at three or four feet, six feet, etc. You also can experiment with its leader length. Still another possibility is a high high hook, if you follow me. Low and regular high hooks are rigged for cod and pollack as before, with the high high pollack hook, on a leader a couple of feet long, tied in two to five feet above your second hook. That will give you two hooks for pollack at different levels, plus one right on the bottom for cod. That lowermost hook also could nail a "low-flying" pollack, just as either or both of its mates might catch a cod traveling above the sea floor. If you want all three hooks expressly for pollack, with cod as a distinct possibility too, try rigging the low one a foot or two above the sinker, then space the others at arbitrary distances of a few feet above that. All three pollack hooks should be on leaders. Two to four feet apiece is enough.

And don't forget that rig designed for cod, pollack, and big flounders. It's detailed in the chapter on cod.

TACKLE SUGGESTIONS Since pollack reach fairly good sizes, with muscle to match, tackle should be sturdy for both bottom fishing and trolling. Conventional equipment is indicated. In bottom angling you may be working in fairly deep water, with a heavy

sinker to hold against strong currents. Your terminal tackle, carrying two or three baited hooks in addition to a sinker, will be
heavy too. On top of that, there are chances of latching onto cod
going 20 pounds or considerably more. In trolling you have
considerable drag on line and lure; and that, coupled with the
possible necessity of having to use a trolling sinker or drail,
rules out spinning tackle so far as I'm concerned.

An all-purpose boat rod handling lines to about 30-pound test
will serve for both pollack and cod. Ideally it should combine
flexibility with backbone. On the rod will go a 2/0 (suggested
minimum) or 3/0 reel. The recommended line is Dacron. Even
with some of the heavier cod around it needn't be stronger than
20- or 30-pound test. A hundred to 150 yards should meet both
trolling and bottom fishing requirements.

SPORTING QUALITIES   It's been said that of all the members of the
cod tribe only the pollack is a true gamefish. That's all right, but
it's a mite harsh on cod. I'd revise it to read: Of all the members
of the cod family, the pollack is the best fighter.

It isn't easy to describe a pollack's strike. It isn't the savage
wallop of a large bluefish. Nor is it the grab-lunch-on-the-run hit
of a surface-feeding weakfish. Nor is it a dainty, toying, or teasing
type of response. A pollack's smack is somewhere in between
the extremes, but closer to strong than weak, if anything. One
way to describe it—and this is perhaps truer when trolling than
when bottom angling—is to say that it feels like suddenly tying
into an unyielding object that stands still for a moment, then begins to move away in low gear. In bottom fishing there's also this
strong, bulldog kind of obstinacy, and the fish may throw in an
extra by swimming in a wide circle.

No matter where you hook him, a pollack shows muscle in
proportion to his size. He might make one powerful, bull-like run
at the outset, but that's often it . . . no fireworks as exhibited by
flashier gamesters. After that initial exhibition of rebellion the
argument resolves itself into a steady tug-o'-war. With a good-
size pollack there will be minutes when it feels as though he
brought along friends as anchormen. You might even think you're
tied into some submerged object. There will be phases when you
won't be able to budge him—at least not without some rough
horsing. He'll pause, and neither side will gain an inch. There's

life down there, though, never doubt it. He'll prolong his show of stubborn resistance as long as he can, usually deep. Sooner or later he'll tire, and you'll reel him toward the boat.

Once you've slugged it out with husky pollack I think you'll come back for more.

TO MAKE YOUR MOUTH WATER   A couple of years ago I fished out of Wedgeport, Nova Scotia, aboard a Cape Islander, one of those boats peculiar to the region. They're rugged, very seaworthy craft, well suited to lobstering, setlining for cod, and sport fishing for giant bluefin tuna in the famous Soldiers Rip off Wedgeport. Our skipper was a grizzled veteran, the iron-gray stubble from a couple of shaveless days standing out against a face the color of mahogany.

Two giant tuna in the eight-hundred-pound class had been caught out there a few days earlier, but we were finding the going slow. By late morning we hadn't enjoyed so much as a strike, and a fog bank was moving toward us. Without a word the skipper stepped to a gunnel and dropped a bottom fishing rig over the side. In a matter of minutes he was cranking in a pollack, six pounds or so, maybe. Working quickly, he gutted and filleted the fish right at the coaming, then disappeared below.

It seemed as though only minutes had passed before the most delicious aroma imaginable came wafting out of the cabin. We zeroed in on it and traced it to a small, beat-up, propane-fired stove, where the skipper was stirring some concoction in an equally beat-up pot. When he was satisfied that his creation was ready, out came the darnedest assortment of containers you ever saw: metal mugs, thick bowls, even old tin cans with their labels long gone. Anything that would hold liquid was pressed into service. In those vessels was a pollack chowder that was sheer ambrosia.

I have a recipe that I'll pass on to you. I got it from Ed Migdalski. He extracted it from one of the Nova Scotia skippers. Traditionally it calls for either cod or haddock, but pollack also is used. For that matter, you can use just about any kind of fish. Here's the way it goes:

1. Gut your fish, removing head and fins, and skin it.
2. Slice some onions—the quantity to your taste—and put them

into a large pot in which a generous hunk of butter is sizzling.

3. Brown the onion slices. That done, add enough water for the required number of servings and bring it to a boil.

4. While you're waiting for the water to boil, peel a few spuds and cut them into small pieces. When the water boils, add them to the pot.

5. When the potatoes are just about cooked, add the fish. Put it in whole if it will fit; otherwise cut it into halves. Now sit back and let your nostrils be entertained by the aroma.

6. Finally, check the chowder at intervals. It's done when the fish meat comes off the bones easily (testing with a fork will show this). Remove as many bones as you can, breaking the meat into bite-size pieces. Add pepper and salt to taste, and stir a few times. Dish it out piping hot. For added touches, serve with a pat of butter floating in each bowl and good old-fashioned pilot crackers.

Chowder isn't the only form in which you can serve pollack, of course. They can be baked (even stuffed), broiled, steaked and barbecued, fried as fillets, boiled New England style for a boiled dinner, cooked in one way or another and served with fancy sauces, creamed like cod and served on toast, or made into fish cakes.

Good fishing. Good eating.

CHAPTER 17

Porgy: Sometimes Fickle, Often Cooperative

Do you suppose the immortal George Gershwin had this character in mind when he penned his delightful classic *Porgy and Bess?* Probably not. So I guess no one would object if I were to write a marine musical comedy someday and title it *Porgy and Bass.*

Nothing like a little levity to start things off. Now let's get down to the business at hand.

Like so many fishes, the porgy has been saddled with a collection of names over the decades. Up New England way, for instance, you'll hear him called "scup"* or "northern scup." This is probably a shortening of the Indian-sounding "scuppaug" and "scuppang," two names hung on him long ago. Around New York and New Jersey (two of the species' major fishing regions) and to a certain extent in neighboring Connecticut, the preference is "porgy," sometimes changing to "pogey" in waterfront vernacular. Farther south, in regions including Chesapeake Bay, he has been dubbed "fair maid" (!) and "maiden" (now, *there* are two fine monikers for a manly little fellow!) and "ironsides" (that's better). "Paugy" and "common scup" are two more regional names he has acquired over the years.

Technically minded readers might like to know that he's listed in the scientific catalogue as *Stenotomus chrysops,* a label tacked onto him by Swedish naturalist Linnaeus 'way back.

DISTRIBUTION, FAMILY ALBUM Overall, this species' range is from Maine on down to South Carolina. However, porgies are more numerous south of Cape Cod, Mass., than north of there.

---

* "Scup" is favored by some ichthyologists as the correct name for the species. Others use "northern porgy," popularly shortened to "porgy."

As far up as Maine they'd be classified as stragglers. Some of their greatest centers of abundance are on our Atlantic Coast from New York and New Jersey to Chesapeake Bay, inclusive. Throughout that range they're encountered offshore in water as deep as fifty to ninety fathoms (by commercial fishermen) as well as in inshore ocean waters, sounds, bays, and harbors.

This particular species is but one in a family of porgies. Among other family members, distributed chiefly in warmer regions from North Carolina southward to the Gulf of Mexico and the West Indies, are the jolthead, southern, saucer-eye, and grass porgies. Another relative of the northern porgy is the sheepshead. Once abundant around New York and New Jersey (a leading New York sport fishing port, Sheepshead Bay, carries their name), the species has taken its business elsewhere and gone south. Also in the porgy's family album is the Bermuda bream, a silvery beauty distributed in warm seas from Bermuda to Argentina and rated as lively sport on light tackle.

IDENTIFICATION   His profile provides the best clues. Note, first of all, that his body is deep in the vertical plane. This deepness,

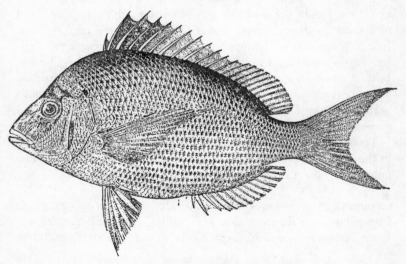

PORGY (*Stenotomus chrysops*)

coupled with body shape, has spawned the nickname "dinner plates" for larger specimens. You'll see too that the porgy's forehead is steep and tends to be slightly concave. His eyes are of fair size, high in the head. A detail of major importance to you as an angler is his small mouth. That means your hooks and baits will have to be of proportionate size.

For the most part, a porgy's body is silvery, darker on the back and upper sides, pearlescent silver on the lower sides and belly. Sometimes his dorsal surface has brownish gray or blue tinges, and there may be darker shadings of same. Younger specimens often carry dark, indistinct, horizontal bars. Darker blotches mark the heads of some individuals. The porgy's well-developed, deeply concave tail is dusky and flecked with blue, as are the dorsal and anal fins. His pectorals are pale, almost filmy. The ventral fins may be whitish or dusky.

His body has scales that are comparatively large and thick, and tough to remove. The porgy is one of the toughest fishes to scale. That may be one of the reasons why mumps are easier to give away than fresh-caught porgies.

ROMANCE AMONG PORGIES, AND THEIR SIZES Porgies winter offshore in deep water. It's there that commercial trawlers harvest large catches of them from about January until April. When this ocean harvesting is overdone, as it once was by foreign trawlers off our shores from New England southward, it can have serious repercussions in the sport fishery.

After wintering offshore, the fathoms of water above them serving as a shield against bitter cold, porgies turn their little snoots shoreward and head for the coast in a more or less northwesterly direction. They arrive in the inshore ocean belt off Chesapeake Bay along about April, and in coastal waters and bays of New York, New Jersey, and southern New England in May or June. From the time of their inshore arrival on into August they spawn, the breeding peak occurring in June. Females release eggs in great numbers to be fertilized in the water by amorous males. Their ova are spherical, very small and transparent (no privacy for the occupants).

Spawning regions double as nursery areas for the babies, and the wee ones ravenously fill their bellies with minute forms of marine life. Growth is fairly rapid. By their first autumn of life they reach an average length of 4 inches. These youngsters, along with many somewhat larger brethren, are the so-called sand porgies that swarm into bays and harbors of New Jersey, New York, and Connecticut in countless thousands during the summer.

Growth is not as rapid after the 4-inch mark. At the end of the first year it has increased less than an inch. Thereafter, this is an approximate age-size scale: age 2, 6½ inches; age 3, 7 to 7⅛ inches; age 4, 9 inches; and by age 5, 9¾ to 10 inches. By then they weigh roughly ¾ pound.

Except for the little sand porgies you'll hook in sheltered waters, the average range in sport catches is from ½ pound or ¾ pound to 1, 1¼, and 1½ pounds. Larger ones, dubbed sea porgies, grow to 3 pounds and better. Occasional 4- to 5-pounders are reported, but I wouldn't count on any if I were you.

SEASONS AND HABITS   Porgies favor warmer water, a trait of appreciable interest to anglers, since it not only governs the species' seasons, but also the numbers of fish in a given area from time to time. Those, I might add, can be quite variable.

Porgies are quite sensitive to cold water and drops in water temperatures. I believe this is the chief cause of their seemingly erratic behavior at times. One day an area will house a good supply of them. The very next day that place may be all but barren. Such radical changes are common in the sport fishery. My belief is that they can be caused by only a couple of degrees' difference in water temperatures.

Their fondness for reasonably warm water is what drives porgies offshore in winter to take advantage of the sea's protective insulation. It also prompts large numbers of them to winter off Virginia and North Carolina. It's said that in winter they favor temperatures of at least 45° F, which is pretty warm for a winter sea. Bays and harbors, being shallower, naturally chill faster and more thoroughly in autumn, and porgies get the message quickly. Fleeing a falling thermometer is a matter of survival. So sensitive are they to drops in water temperatures that they can be killed en masse when trapped in shoal areas by a sudden cold snap.

The angling season throughout their range is dependent upon how soon inshore zones and bays warm in the spring. Similarly, how long they remain after summer is governed by how rapidly local waters chill. In its broadest scope the sport-fishing season begins as early as April in more southerly regions below New Jersey, then gets under way in May and June progressively farther up the seaboard. By midsummer their run for that year reaches its zenith, and with real hot weather little sand porgies make their multitudinous presence known in bays and harbors.

In normal seasons the best ocean action with porgies is during the summer. It's also at this time that they join sea bass to contribute to good mixed catches on deep-sea party boats. But, as I pointed out earlier, porgies sometimes make themselves scarce for days at a time, then "come back" on the same grounds in force.

Bay fishing is apt to be more consistent than ocean angling, by and large, probably because the shallower waters are more consistent in maintaining temperatures to porgies' liking.

With occasional exceptions, bay porgies are smaller than those swung inboard on ocean boats. Weights to three pounds aren't uncommon among the latter. In bays a pound, maybe a pound and a half, is about maximum.

If local waters remain warm enough for them, porgies will linger on into September—even into October in an unseasonably mild fall. By then, though, the run's peak has long since passed, and catches taper off. Understandably, their season ends somewhat earlier in northerly parts of their range and lasts a bit longer in southerly sectors.

Porgies normally travel in schools, some of them very large. They're primarily bottom feeders, and they like a sea or bay floor of smooth, clean, hard-packed sand, favoring it to rocky areas and "broken ground." In that bottom-feeding habit is a clue to rigging procedure. I'm sure you caught it.

On the menu of natural foods gulped by porgies are tiny mollusks and crabs, marine worms, very small fishes, and occasional samplings of sea plants. In their way they're hearty eaters. This is good for them. It's also good for you, because it means they bite greedily.

BAITS   Porgies will accept a lot of things, within reason. At one time or another they can be enticed to hooks with pieces of skimmer clam, bloodworm or sandworm, hard or soft clam, squid, shedder crab, and shrimp. Note that those baits follow rather faithfully the items on their natural menu.

Some fishermen swear by hard clam as the best porgy bait. It's good, but nowadays hard-shell clams are expensive, unless you can tread your own. Skimmer or ocean clam also is effective porgy bait. Bloodworms and sandworms usually rank second and third, respectively, after clams. Skimmers are a popular bait for ocean porgies.

I remind you that the porgy mouth is a comparatively small one. Pieces of bait should be cut accordingly. You don't have to be microscopic about it. Don't go to the other extreme either, figuring that the larger the bait the better your chances. Impale a fair-size piece on your hook for sea porgies. Scale it down for the smaller bay fish. For the littlest fellows of all, sand porgies, use tiny baits.

Sand porgies offer a splendid route to getting youngsters interested in fishing. Quantity is the key. The little fish are usually around in numbers. Sand porgies might not be fun to you, but on extra-light tackle they'll give kids a whale of a time. And children won't be bothered by the sizes. To them a fish is a fish.

Kids want action. They're impatient. Too, their span of attention can be very short if things are slow. A sure way to discourage them right off the bat in an introduction to fishing is to take them on trips where there are long pauses between catches. They won't have those pauses with sand porgies, or with some other species such as flounders and young bluefish (snappers).

When quantity is involved it's also an excellent opportunity to indoctrinate kids into conservation, explaining the meaning and consequences of overfishing and showing how to return undersized fishes to the water. Youngsters should learn conservation as an integral part of their sport right at the very start.

TACKLE RECOMMENDATIONS   Don't underestimate porgies because of their size. Like many small fishes, they'll surprise you with their resistance, especially on really light tackle. Much of porgies' popularity among rod-'n'-reelers stems from their liveliness when hooked. The lighter the tackle, of course, the more that resistance comes through.

A light spinning rod and small matching reel are fine for bay porgies—excluding sand porgies for the moment. So are a light conventional-type glass or split-bamboo boat rod and 1/o revolving spool reel. You won't need much line, since you'll be fishing in shallow water. Fifty yards are more than enough. It can be very light, well under ten-pound test and as low as, say, two or three. The same gear will take the little sand porgies. You can't go too light for these. Ultralight tackle is best if you're to get any action at all from them.

Light, all-purpose conventional or spinning equipment can be brought into play for ocean porgies too, with a couple of modifications. Your line will be somewhat stronger than for the small bay fish, but under ten-pound test still will do. Fifty to seventy-five yards will be enough. Just remember, though, that you'll be fishing in deeper water, with a heavier sinker to hold bottom, and that ocean porgies run larger than their bay brethren. Your rod, therefore, has to have sufficient backbone—and accent that in the case of a spinning rod. Just don't carry that backbone detail too far. If you fish with a rod that has the flexibility of a rake handle you're not going to have much fun. A small spinning reel will do; so will a 1/o—2/o at the outside—reel of the conventional kind.

Give attention to the sizes of the hooks you rig for porgies. For sand porgies you'll have to go very small—I'd say no larger than about a No. 10, preferably a bit smaller. Even the hooks rigged for the larger bay fish should be small—suggested is a No. 10 or No. 9 Chestertown, or a No. 7 Sproat or Carlisle. For sea porgies you can rig a No. 1 O'Shaughnessy or Sproat, or something like a No. 6 in the Virginia pattern. Any hook design will do, so long as you avoid sizes that are too large.

Bank sinkers are rigged for inside and outside porgies. The only requirement is that they're heavy enough to find bottom and hold it.

RIGGING From 1 to 3 hooks are employed in porgy angling, depending upon where the fishing is being done. For bay sport, you can choose between 2 or 3. No leaders are required. Each hook is tied into the line by its snell, with or without a swivel according to preference. Personally, I think it's better to use

swivels. They give more freedom to the rigs and minimize twisting. Hook No. 1 is attached to your line right above the sinker.
No. 2 is connected above No. 1 at a distance about equal to the
length of its snell, or only far enough apart to prevent the 2 hooks
from tangling. If a third hook is put to work, tie it into the line
a snell's length above No. 2. Try a 3-hook outfit for the little

SIMPLE PORGY RIG

sand porgies if you wish, but I think 2 hooks are sufficient for
those fish in the ¾-to-1-, 1½-pound class. Two of those on your
line simultaneously will give you something to do with your
hands.

Another bay porgy rig that has proved to be effective is a 2-
hook arrangement assembled like this: One hook is tied into the
line via a 3-eye swivel, the sinker being tied close to the swivel's
lowermost loop. A second hook is tied onto the snell of the first,
at about where the snell of the first hook meets its shank. A small

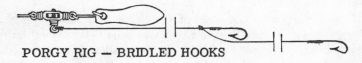

PORGY RIG — BRIDLED HOOKS

pinch-on shot can be added to the snell of each hook to keep it
closer to the bottom. It will get you your share of doubleheaders
when a porgy run is in high gear.

Also effective is a high-low rig that is brought into service when
porgies and weakfish are on the same grounds. I'll save that one
for the chapter on weakfish.

The terminal tackle in ocean fishing for porgies is a simple
bottom rig, basically the same as that for bay angling. Your
choice is between a single hook or twins. In either case, one
hook is attached to the line by its snell—no leader, with or without a swivel—right above the sinker. The second hook can be
tied into the line in similar fashion, about the length of its snell
above the first.

When there's a mixture of porgies and sea bass around in the summer—a common occurrence on ocean grounds and in some bay areas—you might want to go to a form of high-low rig de-

SEA BASS AND PORGY RIG

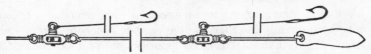

signed to nail both species. You'll find an illustration of it here, and the details in the chapter on sea bass.

PORGIES GET TO THE POINT (IN MORE WAYS THAN ONE)   Every fish has his own particular approach to a bait, both as a species and as an individual. Why should the porgy be an exception?

This kid usually doesn't fool around. No cat-and-mouse game. No prolonged toying and teasing. The hit can be fairly light or a healthy smack, but it's clean-cut. A porgy's customary procedure is to take the bait at once. Therefore, you should set your hook immediately. A short upward lift of your rod tip will do it.

Most times porgies are very sociable toward fishermen, which is pretty generous of them, considering that it's fatal. They're so cooperative that, during a good run, if you don't find fish in one spot within a reasonable length of time, you can be sure that there are none in that area. Try another location. Sooner or later you're bound to hit fish.

At one time or another you'll be annoyed by sea robins. These strange-looking fish can be the bane of a bay porgy hunter's existence. Persistent bait pirates, these notorious pests will denude a hook of its offering repeatedly before porgies can get so much as a smell of it. You can't eliminate sea robins, but there's a little stunt that will minimize their raids and even get rid of them for the time being.

All you need is some skimmer clams and patience. When the sea robins appear, crack the skimmers' shells and drop them overboard, a few at a time. At first the sea robins' assaults on your bait will continue. But after a while the skimmer chum will attract some porgies. Along about then you'll start to pick up a porgy or two among the sea robins. Gradually the percentage of sea robins will decrease, and the number of porgies will increase. In time you'll be hooking only porgies. What happens is that the clam chum brings porgies around in such numbers that they elbow the pesky sea robins out of the picture.

WHEN GENEROSITY GETS YOU NOWHERE   Unless you have acceptance beforehand, don't try to give porgies away—to anyone who knows them, that is. It isn't that porgies aren't good eating. It's because they have a reputation for being tough to dress. Actually this is difficult only if you scale them.

Long ago I heard that the best way to scale porgies is to dip them briefly in boiling water first. This is supposed to loosen the scales and thus facilitate their removal. Frankly, I can't be bothered. I always figured it was easier in the long run to skin the little beasts.

I'll give you some tips on that surgery, but first this reminder: There's a gadget that makes dressing any kind of small fish easier. It's a board, with a nonskid surface, at one end of which is a strong clamp. All you do is lay the fish on the board and put its tail in the clamp's jaws. This holds the fish securely and leaves both hands free.

Incidentally, there are electric fish scalers on the market. They probably would do a fast job on porgies, but unless you have some passion for eating their skin I think it's just as well to get rid of it—and the scales—beforehand.

If your porgies are large enough you can fillet them. You'll need a sharp knife.

If the fish have already been gutted, okay; otherwise, don't bother. Lay the fish flat. With the tail anchored, either in that clamp board I mentioned or grasped by your hand. A piece of cloth will give you a better grip, start slicing carefully near the base of the tail, proceeding toward the head. Take your time. Work as close to the backbone as you can to minimize waste. Slice the fillet right up to just behind the gill covers and cut free. Turn the fish over and repeat the operation on the other side.

Skin (with its scales) can be removed from fillets by getting it started with a knife, then peeling it free with pliers. Peel it away carefully, using firm, steady pressure, so as not to take chunks of meat with it. Use your knife in an assist if necessary. Should you have any trouble removing any fins with the skin, cut them off close to the body with scissors.

Some "surgeons" behead and gut the fish and remove the fins with shears before filleting. I can see the gutting as a precaution against spoilage, especially in hot weather, if there's to be an appreciable time lapse before the fish can be adequately refrigerated (in any case they should be iced down for the trip home). But the rest seems to me to be wasted effort if the porgies are to be filleted eventually.

If you're going to cook the fish whole—as you'll have to do when they're too small for filleting—the procedure is standard. Leaving the tail on for the time being as a handle, cut off the head and remove the entrails. Skin or scale as desired. Side fins can be snipped off close to the body or removed with the skin. Dorsal and anal fins can be removed by either of two methods— which can be employed for other species too, by the way. The easier of the two procedures is to amputate them by shearing close to the body. The other technique is to "run" them with a knife. Just make two parallel cuts, one on either side of the fin at its base and quite close to it. With pulling and a couple of extra slices, the fin will lift out. The entire backbone of a fish can be removed in similar fashion, although you have to cut away some lesser bones to do it.

On a party boat you can pass the chore of dressing your catch on to the mate. Tell him how you want the fish prepared, as fillets or whole. He'll do the job one-two-three, and it's worth the tip. A similar service is performed by charter boat mates, and usually is part of the service for which you're going to tip him anyway. If you're on a private boat and want to duck the chore, you'll have to try to stick someone else. Plead ignorance, while praising the other guy's ability as a fish cleaner. Or tell him you have arthritic fingers, holding up a twisted hand. Just be sure the patsy doesn't find you out.

Porgies are a fine table fish. Anyone who can't be bothered fixing them for cooking doesn't deserve the eating pleasure. Amen.

CHAPTER 18

Sea Bass: Summer Staple

Whenever I hear the quainter nicknames applied to fishes I wonder who coined them, and when, and whatever prompted those particular names. Most of them, I suppose, were conceived by fishermen in the long ago, generations before our time. Old-time mariners had a hand in the coinage too. Others have come down to us from the American Indians, either as reasonable facsimiles of the originals or as phonetic corruptions of same.* Whatever their sources, they've persisted down through the years, even though little used anymore, outliving their originators and coming to us all salt-encrusted, sometimes smelling faintly of tar and bilges, and all comprising another colorful part of the lore of fishing and the sea.

Now you take our friend here, the sea bass, *Centropristes striatus*. He has quite a collection of aliases. Some of them, I should point out right away, conflict with the popular names of other species. "Blackfish," for instance. This sea bass has been called that in southerly segments of the Atlantic seaboard, probably because of his darkish hue. It's a bad nickname because it conflicts with the common name for the tautog. Another misnomer for this sea bass is "bluefish," also because of his color, which can be indigo blue.

In the Chesapeake Bay region he's been referred to as "Black Will." "Black Harry" is another obscure nickname. Two of his more unusual aliases (sources and vintages unknown) are "talywag" and "hannabill." Still another misnomer applied to this species is "black perch," bad because it leads to labeling him as a perch, instead of a bass, and to confusion with a California species of the same name. The list of nicknames also includes "rock fish" and "rock bass." Although the "rock" part suits

* Witness such Indian heritages as *squeteague* for weakfish, *tautog* for blackfish, *scuppaug* for porgy, *mummichog* for killy, etc.

the sea bass so far as certain habits are concerned, both of those names are confusing because they conflict with regional nicknames (around Chesapeake Bay, to name one place) for striped bass.

Depending upon which authority you read, this species will be listed variously as common sea bass, black sea bass, or just sea bass. That last will do nicely for our purposes.

LARGE FAMILY, LARGE RANGE   The marine basses, among which our buddy here belongs, are a large, worldwide group that comes under the technical family heading Serranidae. Serranidae are related to the fresh water basses whose group name is Centrarchidae. The two big families, marine and fresh-water versions, resemble each other in such respects as body shapes, arrangements of fins, and certain other anatomical details. One of the more unusual fresh-water relatives of our sea bass is the Nile perch, a bruiser going to two hundred and three hundred pounds and found in tropical Africa.

The family Serranidae also embraces many species of groupers, among them the king-size models called giant sea basses, specimens of which have been known to attain weights of five hundred to six hundred pounds and reportedly reach as much as seven hundred and eight hundred pounds.

Close relatives of our sea bass here—I'm talking about good old *Centropristes striatus* now—are the striped bass, white perch (a bass that looks quite a bit like a striper without the stripes), and wreck fish or wreck bass. You'll meet that first guy later on in this book. The less-famous white perch—another misnomer, so far as I'm concerned—is a small marine bass inhabiting salt, brackish, and occasionally fresh waters along our Atlantic Coast. The wreck bass is widely distributed on both sides of the Atlantic, but seldom is encountered, as far as I can determine, by sport fishermen along our East Coast.

The sea bass we're spotlighting in this chapter are an Atlantic coastal species whose distribution is strung out from Maine (but they're strays this far north) to Florida. Their greatest populations are encountered from southern Massachusetts to North Carolina. Throughout their range, in season, they're hooked on offshore grounds, in inshore ocean waters, and in sounds and bays. They're found in waters of varying depths, shallow to quite deep.

SEASONS   Sea bass winter offshore, eluding bitter cold by seeking deep water. Some of their main winter resorts are believed to lie off New Jersey, Delaware, and North Carolina. Comes spring, they cruise inshore on a somewhat northerly heading. There, in coastal waters, they're thought to spawn during May and June.

Throughout the major portion of their range—which is to say from Cape Cod and Long Island Sound down to about Cape Hatteras—sport fishing activities open up at varying times in May and June, depending upon weather conditions, food, etc. During normal summer runs they comprise a mainstay of the party boat fishery in many areas from Connecticut and Long Island to New Jersey.

You'll find sea bass on bay, sound, and ocean grounds through the summer, building to that season's peak along about July. As the season advances in September their numbers start to decline, usually in proportion to the coolness of autumn's approach. Fair numbers may linger into fall, even as late as November in some sectors, if local waters do not turn too frigid for them. But autumn rings down the curtain on angling for them. The fish assemble in ragged parade formation as they turn to the open sea, reversing their spring itinerary and moving offshore on a somewhat southerly heading.

That's about the extent of the species' migrations.

HOW TO TELL A SEA BASS WITHOUT A PROGRAM   Size and color pattern are among the details helping to identify this fish and separate him from his relatives, the striped bass and white perch.

His fins are important identification clues too. Check our illustration as I point them out. Look at the dorsal fins. Technically there are two: the first dorsal with spines, and the second dorsal with rays (it's softer) and a rounded edge. These two fins are confluent and so appear as one. On the striper and white perch the two dorsals are more distinctly individual. Note the sea bass's tail. Its trailing edge has a vague S shape. Among larger specimens there's usually an extension of one of this fin's rays beyond its outer edge. Note too the rounded edges of the pelvic

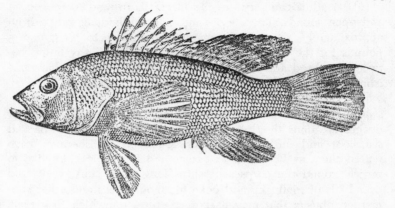

SEA BASS (*Centropristes striatus*)

and anal fins. Finally, a good clue: rather large pectoral fins, with rounded edges, that arise just behind the gill covers and reach almost to the beginning of the anal fin.

This fellow's body shape is typical of basses, with a fairly large head, proportionately, and mouth of generous size.

As a bottom species, sea bass exhibit color variations. You'll catch specimens that are dark brown or brownish gray. You'll hook some whose color is a deep, rich indigo blue. Still others will be practically black. Whatever their basic color may be, it extends almost entirely throughout the body, more or less uniformly, although it may be a bit darker along the back and upper sides. At the last minute this body color gives way to a paler shade or off-white on the belly. Often the body is overlaid with vague bars or blotches in a darker shade of the basic color. A rather unusual effect is achieved by the bases of his scales being lighter then their edges, giving an appearance of rows of dots.

Sea bass come in assorted sizes, each representing a stage in development. The smallest fish hooked by sinker-bouncers are youngsters living in bays and coves. They weigh anywhere from a few ounces to ½ pound or ¾ pound. You'll hear these little guys nicknamed "pin bass." They're the individuals that turn up in inside waters in summertime. Also during that season, conditions being conducive, inside waters play host to larger fish weighing up to 1 or 1½ pounds.

In the adult category are the larger fish found in the ocean and open sounds. These more muscular individuals range from approximately 1½ pounds among the juniors to 3, 4, and 5 pounds for the seniors. Older *males* develop a fleshy hump between the head and leading edge of the dorsal fin, a characteristic that has given rise to another nickname, "humpback."

HABITS   Sea bass are bottom dwellers. In the ocean and other deeper locations they have a fondness for a clean, hard-packed sea floor and fairly deep water. Commercial fishermen have netted them as far down as 120 to 180 feet. They also like to prowl around the corpses of ships long since sunk, seek food over beds of mollusks, and poke in among rocks and other submerged objects that may harbor creatures on which they feed. There you have reasons why man-made fishing reefs can be productive of sea bass . . . and blackfish and other gamesters.

In bays and other sheltered waters their preference for some depth prompts them to seek out water that's at least 10 to 15 feet deep at low tide. They're even happier with 20 to 40 or 50 feet of water between them and the surface. These bay residents are like their oceangoing brothers in that they like to explore rocky places, sunken boats, and other submerged objects, as well as prowl around pilings, bridge abutments, and shellfish beds. That's all part of their search for food.

They also go shopping in briskly moving, deep-running channels. Sometimes they wander into creeks and canals bordered by sod banks that drop abruptly into water that is about 15 or 20 feet deep at low tide. In these locations they search for tidbits deep beneath the banks' shadows.

SPAWNING—AND AN ODD NOTE   Sea bass breeding takes place in the prescribed fashion among fishes. The females release multitudes of ova into the water, and the males faithfully discharge sperm to fertilize them. The eggs are buoyant, and they drift about willy-nilly as incubation progresses. Eggs and babies are subjected to usual environmental and predatory hazards, and the toll is high at times.

So far all is as usual, but there's a weird side to their sex life that sea bass keep hidden from all except scientific investigators.

Evidence indicates that hermaphroditism, the condition in which an individual carries reproductive organs of both sexes, exists among sea bass. In fact, it appears—and I wish you wouldn't spread this around—that they change their sex.

The larger sea bass hooked by anglers are invariably humpbacks; and, as I told you earlier, these are males. On the other hand, females predominate among the younger individuals, research indicates. As those younger fish grow older, however, the proportion of females decreases. This diminishing goes on until about the tenth year, after which females seem to "disappear." Males, in contrast, carry on for at least another decade. Further, an investigator named Nathan Lavenda found regressive (atrophying or shrinking) ovarian tissue, associated with their sperm ducts, in males.

All these findings strongly suggest hermaphroditism in sea bass, and that the fish undergo a sex change. The alteration is believed to occur sometime after the fifth year, on which occasion females become males. All of which prompts me to suggest that maybe sea bass have more fun than anybody.

Instances of hermaphroditism and/or changes of sex are known to exist among underwater creatures. There's a species of shrimp, for example, that spends part of its life as a male and part as a female. Hermaphroditism is thought to exist among some other members of the sea bass's tribe, as well as among some of the porgies.

Who would think of it to look at them?

NATURAL FOODS = LOGICAL BAITS Small fishes of assorted species are on the menu for sea bass. So are crustaceans of various kinds, such as shrimp and little crabs, as well as small mollusks. Marine worms are acceptable for lunch too, and squid also are consumed when available.

From that menu we can draw a pretty good list of potential attractors.

Bay bass will bite on sandworm, bloodworm, shrimp, or a piece of squid, skimmer clam, or shedder crab. Generally they're not too hard to please. One of the few times when they might be at all finicky can occur during a bay run's early phase, at which time they might exhibit a marked preference for a worm bait, notably sandworm. But that fussy phase ceases, after which they readily take such baits as squid, clam, shedder crab, etc.

Later in the summer the larger bay dwellers may be slow to respond to any of the more common baits, in which case you should try a small, live killy, hooked carefully through the lips. Periodically sea bass show a preference for live baits such as killies. Usually they draw the line at artificials, but jigging a small metal jig will get them, and occasionally they can be teased into grabbing a small spoon trolled just off the bottom.

Baits employed to attract the larger ocean-swimming sea bass to hooks include skimmer clam, squid, hard clam, and shedder crab. The first named is one of the most popular. Skimmers are easier to obtain than some of the other baits, they can be used for various species, and they're effective.

About the only artificial used to any extent for the ocean bass is a diamond jig. We'll get to that soon.

As his profile reveals, this fish possesses a fairly large mouth. He's like his cousin the striper in that respect. So baits of reasonably generous size can be impaled on your hooks. All you need do is gauge the sizes of the pieces, approximately, to the sizes of the sea bass being hunted: smallest for the little "pin bass"; medium for those fish going 1 to 1½ pounds; and largest for fish to 3 pounds and more. But don't stew about that matching. It isn't a matter of micrometer precision.

HOOKS AND RIGGING Hook sizes are graduated upward in proportion to the fish currently running. Here again, though, as in the case of bait sizes, it isn't a critical matter of precision. The overall scale is from about a No. 6 for small pin bass, through a 1/0 for the larger bay fish, up to a 2/0 for ocean humpbacks. Even larger sizes, up to a 4/0, have been used for the bigger ocean-run sea bass, but I don't think those greater sizes are necessary. True, humpbacks have roomy mouths, and somewhat larger than ordinary bait might be a little more attractive, but the fish aren't that heavy.

Hook patterns are your choice. You can't go wrong with types such as Mustad, Sproat, O'Shaughnessy, Virginia, Aberdeen, etc. I've known fishermen who favored the Aberdeen because its slenderness makes it a little less visible in water and is an advantage when hooking live baits such as killies.

Substantially the same rig, with only minor variations according to individuals' ideas, is used to catch sea bass of all sizes. About the only differences among these variations are the number of hooks involved, their sizes, and weights of sinkers required. Whatever their minor differences, they all share one cardinal detail: Since sea bass are bottom feeders, hooks are arranged accordingly.

I'll give you the basics. You can experiment with variations as your experience dictates.

For pin bass. These little guys are usually eager feeders, not at all shy. You needn't bother with leaders. You can fish with one hook or two. Some sinker bouncers go to three. Hook No. 1 is tied into the line by its snell. Use a swivel if you want, but it isn't a must. This hook must be close to the sinker, preferably no more than about two inches above it. Attach hook No. 2 in similar

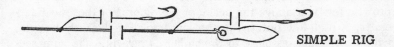

SIMPLE RIG

fashion, just far enough above No. 1 to keep the two from tangling. If you put hook No. 3 to work, attach it in the same manner as the other two, only far enough above No. 2 to prevent the two from snarling with each other.

Tip: In the foregoing rig, if no swivels are used, it will help to keep your hooks separated if you attach their snells in such a way that they're at approximately right angles to the line.

For the larger bay bass. These fellows may exhibit coyness when summer is well along, perhaps because they're not as ravenous as they were earlier. When they play harder to get it often helps to use leaders. Tie a piece of monofilament, gut, or leader

RIG WITH LEADERS

material (in about the same strength as your line) 2½ or 3 feet
long to the hook and connect this to your line, directly or via a
3-loop swivel, according to preference, 4 to 6 inches above the
sinker. If a second hook is rigged, give it a 2-foot leader and attach it to the line in the same fashion as its predecessor and
about 16 to 18 inches above it.

For ocean-run sea bass. Rigging for these approximates the first
bay version, with a choice of one or two hooks. Tie your hooks
into the line by their snells—swivels are optional—as close to the
sinker as possible and only far enough apart to keep them from
interfering with each other.

Tip: I don't recommend three hooks in the rigs for the larger
bay bass and their ocean-run brethren. You may be fishing around
wrecks, rocks, or other underwater obstructions, such as artificial reefs; and the more hooks you use, the greater your chances
of getting hung up down there and losing rigs.

RIG VARIATIONS   Although sea bass are normally bottom feeders,
there are times, notably in the vicinity of wrecks, when they
prowl a few feet above the ocean or bay floor. For those wanderers try a high-low outfit. Rig the low hook for the very bottom,
without a leader, as close to the sinker as possible. Tie your second hook in by its snell, no leader, a couple of feet above No. 1.

Still another variation of the ocean rig comes in handy when
there's a mixture of sea bass and porgies on the same grounds.
Two hooks are rigged, each on a snell ten inches or so long. The
bottom hook is for sea bass. Tie this one into your line, with or
without a swivel, anywhere from immediately above the sinker
to the length of its snell above it. Hook No. 2 is for porgies, and
of suitable size for same. This one is affixed to the line, with or
without a swivel, the length of its snell above the sea bass hook.
No leader is used on either hook. Baits for the porgy hook include
a piece of skimmer clam (a bait you may already be using for
sea bass) or squid.

In all rigs, whether for bay or outside angling, a bank-type
sinker is used. Required sinker weights will graduate upward
when you fish in deeper water and/or stronger currents.

RIG A JIG   The terminal tackle for sea bass jigging couldn't be
simpler. Get yourself a three- or four-ounce standard diamond jig,

one with a bright, shiny finish and armed with a 2/o to 4/o hook. Tie this artificial directly to the end of your line. No bait is

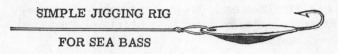

SIMPLE JIGGING RIG

FOR SEA BASS

needed, although some anglers feel that it's an added attraction if the hook is garnished with a small piece of skimmer or squid, maybe just enough to cover point and barb. The jig's weight is a built-in sinker.

The procedure consists of lowering this flashy lure to the bottom, reeling it upward several feet, letting it drop to the bottom again, and so on in a continuous process. The jig's shininess is an eye-catcher, and so is its motion. Further, alternately raising and lowering it through several feet covers different planes along which sea bass may be swimming. Jigging can be particularly effective around wrecks.

TACKLE CHATTER Light gear, spinning or conventional, will do nicely for bay-visiting sea bass. And if you take those little pin bass into consideration you'll need the lightest kind of gear. Conventional equipment such as you wield for flounders and other small species is all right. Light spinning tackle is a natural here.

Tackle for the ocean bass should be somewhat sturdier, since the fish are larger, the rigs go a bit heavier, and depths and currents are factors. Suitable is a standard all-purpose outfit that includes a 1/o or 2/o reel, whichever size better complements the rod. An equivalent spinning outfit also fills the bill, but the rod is going to need some spine in case you have to argue a 4- or 5-pound humpback up from depths that can go to 100 or 120 feet. The spinning reel, of course, should match that rod.

Your line needn't be heavier than about 10-pound test for ocean sea bass; and it can go lighter for bay fishing. I'd suggest at least 50 to 75 yards for ocean angling; 50 yards are ample for bay service.

Memo: In any kind of angling around wrecks and other underwater obstructions, and over shellfish beds and other rough floors, you can expect your rig to get snagged periodically. Sometimes you'll be lucky enough to pull it free. At other times you can

302   *How to Catch Salt-water Fish*

figure on cutting your line and losing that terminal outfit. *Carry spare hooks and sinkers.* Allow some extra line too when fishing such areas. You'll lose varying amounts of yardage when you cut rigs free. *Tip:* Back in the chapter on blackfish I detailed a gimmick that will cut down on the mortality rate of sinkers and hooks lost in hangups.

GO AHEAD AND PLAY For sea bass you'll fish at anchor, whether bottom fishing or jigging. Use of government-issued navigation charts will help you to locate expanses of clean, sandy bottom; wrecks; and other areas where the fish linger. On open bottom there's nothing especially tricky about anchoring, just as long as the "hook" digs in properly and holds. Let the boat settle on her anchor line in the breeze or current. Anchoring around wrecks, man-made reefs, and the like is something else again. Here the idea is to anchor securely so that the boat will swing into a position that enables you to fish close to the wreck or whatever, yet keep hangups at a minimum. This is a trial-and-error procedure in which a depth sounder is helpful.

Bay bass, although not reluctant to take hooks, sometimes will test your patience by nibbling at a bait before mouthing it. Until they do mouth it you're not likely to hook them. They might even seize an edge of your bait and move away with it a few feet, still ticking away at the morsel. Play the game their way. Carefully feed them a little line. There won't be any real pull on the line when they toy with a bait in this manner; and you won't be able to set your hook until they finally decide to mouth the offering. Be patient. Keep your line as taut as you can without pulling the bait away. Maintain contact with your fish all the time. When they finally take a bait—really grab it—you'll feel a more determined, steady tug. A short, smart, upward lift of your rod tip will drive the hook home.

When bay bass are biting well they'll take baits without any preliminary dickering and start to run off. Simply tightening your line usually sets the hook. Sea bass can be surprisingly energetic, particularly when the bait is a live killy. They'll hit quickly, with enthusiasm, often setting the hook themselves as they apply tension to the line.

There are also times, especially with a live killy, when they fool with a bait before gulping it. In the case of a killy they frequently go for the tail end, grasping it but not going anywhere in particular. (Maybe they're "casing" the setup.) This comes through to your end of the line as a series of nibbles or gentle twitches. It'll test your self-control, because your first impulse will be to set the hook—a mistake. You'll have to resist that reaction, because if a sea bass is struck then, either the killy will tear off the hook or your opponent will release his hold, or maybe bite off the killy's stern end and leave. In any case, you'll lose him.

To avoid that loss, keep your line as tight as possible, but not overly so. If he starts to move slowly, pay out line, just inches at a time, constantly feeling for the nature of his assault on the bait. Your bass may take away slowly for several feet; or he might make a short, gentle dart or two. But unless he has felt the hook there won't be any show of force. After he has moved off a few feet he'll probably pause to mouth the bait. Now you'll feel a series of spasmodic, sharper tugs on your line. Get ready. When he really takes the bait into his mouth he'll feel the hook and move off in a strong rush. Then he can be struck. If he hasn't already planted the hook himself, a slight upward lift of your rod tip will do it.

The larger oceangoing sea bass generally do not believe in monkeying with a bait. They usually hit with genuine enthusiasm, then exhibit a strong desire to go elsewhere. They put up a sporting argument.

HANDLE WITH CARE Watch your hands when handling sea bass, alive or dead. They're not vicious fish, but the forward section of their dorsal fins is armed with stiff, needle-sharp spines that can inflict punctures that hurt. When the fish is dead this spiny portion of the dorsal lies down against the back, but still can jab in careless handling. When the fish is alive he's apt to erect those spines, and anyone not according them respect is in for a painful surprise.

GOOD EATIN' You'll never hear complaints about sea bass as scrappers. Nor will you hear adverse criticisms of their meat, which is white, sweet, and delicious. Some people grouse about the number of bones in sea bass; but that's a minor squawk, really, when you consider that the fish provide both lively angling and a good seafood dinner. After yanking the poor fish out of their happy home and eating them, it isn't very polite to begrudge them a skeleton. After all, they don't complain about *yours*.

Sea bass can be prepared whole or, in the case of those of suitable size, as fillets or even small steaks. Dressed whole, they're gutted, beheaded, and definned by any of the standard methods. If the skin is to be left on (some seafood fanciers feel that the skin adds flavor), the fish must be scaled thoroughly. Or they can be skinned, which eliminates scaling. The same choice goes for fillets and steaks. If the fish is to be steaked—a *modus operandi* for which the largest fish are best suited—you first gut, behead, and defin the fish as before. If the skin is to remain during cooking, you'll have to scale the bass, and this should be done before steaking. If the skin is to come off, you can cut it free before or after steaking, without scaling. To steak any fish, simply cut it into sections of desired thickness for broiling or barbecuing.

Personally, I think skinned fillets are best, but that's only *my* choice. There's a minor annoyance with bones when sea bass are cooked whole, but they can be easily separated from the meat with a fork when eating.

I believe sea bass are among my favorite eating fish. To my taste their delicate flavor is delightful. I like them with boiled potato, salt and pepper on both. If there's piping-hot corn on the cob to go with it, dripping butter, or maybe some sliced beefsteak tomatoes, so much the better.

If you see any spots on this page, they're my saliva.

CHAPTER 19

Sharks: The Mako and Others

Considering the millennia during which sharks have been around this old globe of ours, and the fact that people all over the world have been aware of them for countless generations, we were a l-o-n-g time recognizing their sport-fishing value. The fact is that angling for sharks, as a sport unto itself, is relatively new. It really didn't come into its own until after World War II.

Before we get into that, let me give you a little shark background.

Sharks comprise one of the older forms of animal life still around on our planet. Estimates vary (no one knows for sure), but most researchers seem to agree that they've been in existence for at least three hundred million years, give or take some millions. Carbon analyses of fossilized shark teeth have dated them back one hundred million years and more.

Therein lies a detail that is unfortunate, yet points up an important anatomical characteristic of sharks.

Bony fishes—flounders, sea bass, trout, and others—lend themselves to fossilization, leaving lifelike imprints of themselves in rock. Beside me as I write this are two such imprints. Both came from an Eocene Period lake bed in Wyoming. Clearly discernible are the outlines of little fishes, together with their spinal columns and bones. Both swam that prehistoric lake fifty million years ago.

In contrast to bony fishes are the sharks. Their internal framework is cartilage.* Consequently, they do not lend themselves

---

* There is no true bone in sharks. Certain portions of the "skeleton" in some species, notably the skull, contain calcium and are partially ossified; but in the main, their internal framework, including the jaws, is cartilage. For this reason sharks are considered to be among the more primitive fishes.

readily to fossilization. Instead of "turning to stone," so to speak, like bony fishes, sharks tend to disintegrate and vanish. As a result, about all we have left to tell of their presence is their teeth.

The enormous length of time they've prowled the seas of our globe is only one of many fascinating things about sharks. Another is that they've changed relatively little throughout that expanse of millions of years. In this sense they're "living fossils." (So too, you might be interested to learn, is that familiar seaside figure, the horseshoe crab. He probably has changed even less than sharks over millions of years.)

THE FAMILY TODAY Even in our time, with all the how-to talent, equipment, and modern research procedures at our command, we know comparatively little about sharks. In fact, we know absolutely nothing about many species, other than that they exist.

One of many things we don't know about sharks, at least not with any precision, is how many different kinds inhabit the world. Accordingly, estimates vary widely. Figures range upward to 200 to 250, and occasionally to 300, depending upon who's doing the estimating. Those figures are for *recognized* species. Not taken into consideration are kinds not yet detected. As recently as 1945 another species of hammerhead, *Sphyraena bigelowi,* was "discovered." Who can say how many others have eluded nets and hooks, or remain secluded in the great offshore deeps, still unknown to man?

Of one thing we're certain: Sharks comprise a large, universal tribe that has fanned out to inhabit even the most far-flung waters. Their habitats extend from polar seas to the tropics. They're represented in frigid waters by the sluggish Greenland or gurry shark. Temperate zones harbor many species. So do tropical regions. Sharks are even represented in fresh water by the dangerous Lake Nicaragua shark of Central America.

The largest known member of the tribe today is the whale shark, *Rhincodon typus,* believed to attain lengths of sixty feet and more, with weights of several tons. Next comes the basking shark, *Cetorhinus maximus,* credited with reaching lengths up to forty and fifty feet, also with a bulk measured in tons. Oddly enough, both of these giants are harmless to man. They're easy-going brutes, possessing unbelievably tiny teeth, that feed principally on small fishes and other little critters.

Third in size is the white shark or maneater, *Carcharodon carcharias*, known to grow up to twenty-five and thirty feet, even thirty-six, and thought to reach forty feet and possibly more. His

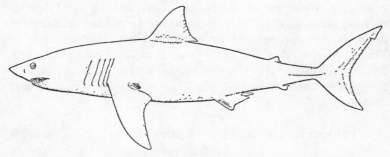

WHITE SHARK or MANEATER (*Carcharodon carcharias*)

weight also is reckoned in tons. A seventeen-to-eighteen-foot specimen harpooned by Montauk charter skipper Frank Mundus off Amagansett, L.I., weighed an estimated forty-five hundred pounds. Also on record is a twenty-one-footer weighing seventy-one hundred pounds. (Weights vary greatly among white sharks, hence the startling difference between Frank Mundus's fish and that twenty-one-footer.)

As their other name, "maneater," hints strongly, white sharks are extremely dangerous to humans. Large, powerful, and armed with a mouthful of vicious-looking teeth, white sharks are proven man-killers. Moreover, they're among the more aggressive of sharks, and there are recorded instances in which they attacked small boats.

THE ANGLING ANGLE   There has been a commercial shark fishery of sorts (liver oil, food, hides, fertilizer from the dried flesh, etc.). But not until fairly recent years did angling for sharks become a recognized, well-defined sport. Prior to that it was a kind of neglected stepchild. Sure, there have always been some rod-and-reelers who sought combat with the beasts, but by and large, action with sharks was more or less incidental to other kinds of sport fishing.

Sport fishing for sharks no longer is a neglected stepchild. This action has been developed as an integral part of marine angling. Moreover, it has achieved status by having several species recognized by the International Game Fish Association as being worthy of world record contention. Shark angling has taken its rightful place in the rod-and-reel scene. Increasing numbers of fishermen are appreciating its suspense, action, and excitement. Very important, they're realizing that here is a kind of big game fishing within the reach of everyone, with chances of success far greater than in hunting such monarchs as swordfish and marlins.

"AND IN THIS CORNER, WEARING THE BLUE TRUNKS . . ." Theoretically, all the known kinds of sharks are sport-fishing targets. In practice, however, many of them are undesirable as rod-and-reel game for one reason or another. Size—one extreme or the other—is one reason. The sharks may be either too small (like the dogfishes, erroneously called "sand sharks") or too large (like the whale and basking sharks and the larger whites). Some simply do not take a hook often enough, like the sand tiger, a common species on our Atlantic Coast. Others aren't numerous enough in certain regions, like tiger sharks in the more northerly segments of the U.S. East Coast. Some are not hunted, I suspect, because disposal of their carcasses, particularly in the case of the bigger

BLUE SHARK (*Prionace glauca*)

specimens, would pose a problem, or at least an inconvenience. And so on.

So far, because recreational "sharking" is so relatively new, only a handful of species are involved in the sport fishery. Among them are these: makos, blues, duskies, tigers, porbeagles, browns, threshers, hammerheads, whites, and black-tipped sharks. There are others in various parts of the United States and abroad, but it isn't necessary to list them here. Suffice it to say that almost every species of shark, wherever it may be encountered, offers sport-fishing potential. Because of their fighting qualities, sizes, and/or numbers or availability, principal sport-fishing species include makos, blues, porbeagles, browns, tigers, duskies, hammerheads, and, to a lesser extent because of their great size and fewer numbers, white sharks. Of all those, the mako is the most highly desirable. We'll concentrate on that species. The reasons for the makos' popularity will turn up as we go along.

IMPORTANT PREFACE   Before we get into such topics as tackle, rigging, baiting, and techniques, I want to give you this tip: Although there are certain specializations and adaptations in fishing for sharks, basically the same equipment, procedures, rigs, and types of baits can be employed for any and all species. That's a rule of thumb. Understandably, however, your tackle, baits, and, in some instances, methods of landing sharks must be suited to the sizes of the critters involved.

And there's always room for experimentation, testing of ideas. That goes double in a sport as "new" as shark angling.

SHARK TACKLE, GENERAL   As shark angling developed in the 1950s it became obvious that there was a need for a grading of tackle specifically for that sport. It's easy to see why when you consider that sharks caught in the sport-fishing theater go up to one thousand pounds and more. Obviously, tackle generally graded as light for other kinds of angling would be too weak for sharks. Similarly, gear rated as heavy for some types of fishing would be considered light in combat with large sharks. For the new sport the entire calibration of tackle had to be revised upward to better suit the assignments.

Using the system of grading tackle according to the maximum-strength lines that rods can handle, a table of tackle classifications for shark fishing has been devised. You'll note differences between these gradings and those employed for other sport fishes in this book. You'll see, for example, that even "ultralight" shark tackle is heavy by some other standards. Here's the cataloguing:

Ultralight	to and including 20-pound lines
Light	over 20 to 45-pound test
Medium	over 45 to 60-pound lines
Heavy	over 60-pound test to 80-pound
Extra-heavy	over 80- to 130-pound test and up

See what I mean by shark tackle being generally heavier than gear used for other gamefishes? Keep that grading in mind as we go along, because that's what I'll be referring to when I speak of tackle in this chapter.

SHARK SIZES, ONE CLUE TO TACKLE   Sharks come in a wide assortment of sizes, according to species. Too, there are often considerable variations among individuals within a given species.

I offer a quick-reference table to give you an idea of weights. It's general, approximate, and for the sport-fishing arena only.

Species	Potential Weight Range in Pounds	Potential Maximum in Pounds
Mako*	Under 100 to 200, 300	400, more
Blue	Under 100 to 150, 200	Over 200
Dusky	To 400	To 600
Porbeagle	Under 100 to over 200	To 300, 350
Thresher	To 100, 200	Over 300 (It's believed the very largest threshers can go to 800, even 1,000 pounds.)
Brown	Under 75 to 125, 150	About 200
Tiger	Over-all, extremely variable, from under 500 up to 700, 800	To 1,000, 1,200

* Pacific makos grow larger than their Atlantic kin. The potential maximum among the former is over 1,000 pounds.

Great hammerhead	Well over 100 to 500 and more	Probably to at least 1,000
Common hammerhead	Under 100 to 200 or so	Not established in the sport-fishing theater, but possibly to 500 and more
Large black-tipped	Not established in the sport fishery, but probably from under 100 to 200, 250	Open to speculation, possibly to 400
White or Maneater	From 500 to 1,000 on up to at least 2,000	3,000, 4,000, more

Now you see why we had to upgrade tackle classifications to better suit the assignments at hand.

SHARK TACKLE: SOME SPECIFICS   Selection of weapons is up to you. But let me spell out the situation.

First off, you must keep sharks' sizes in mind. Even the largest striped bass, white marlin, and Atlantic sailfish are "killies" alongside some sharks. Even swordfish, with weight potentials up to five hundred pounds (to eight hundred and one thousand pounds in the Pacific off South America) and black marlin, with a potential to over two thousand pounds in Australia) are dwarfed by the heftier white sharks. You also must remember that, while you might not be purposely fishing for such monsters as the bigger whites, duskies, and tigers, there nevertheless is a chance that one might wander your way. He won't ask you beforehand if you're ready. If you're a true shark fishing buff you'll always be ready for such possibilities.

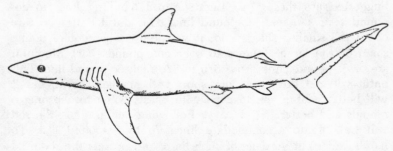

DUSKY SHARK (*Carcharhinus obscurus*)

Another factor to guide you in selection of shark tackle is your experience and ability. If you're a newcomer to shark angling, or are inexperienced with larger game fishes, lean toward heavier gear. You won't have quite as many thrills as the wielders of light tackle, but you'll have a better chance of landing your fish. Later, if you wish, you can graduate to lighter equipment.

Factor No. 3 in choice of tackle is equally important, but trickier because it involves an unpredictable variable. Pay attention, class. We won't have a quiz here. Your "exam" will come out there on the briny somewhere, and you won't have time to consult your notes.

No. 3 enters the picture when you can't see the shark that's about to smack your rig. Sometimes you'll catch a glimpse of your intended opponent before contact, perhaps loafing along at the surface or moving in along your chum line, and have an opportunity to match your tackle accordingly. On other occasions—these are common—you won't see your target beforehand. It frequently happens when deep rigs are involved. This is a calculated risk. If you happen to be fishing lighter tackle, you hope it's strong enough. If you're fishing heavier gear, it will cost you some action if the shark is one of the smaller specimens. I should add that, generally speaking, it's the larger sharks that hit the deeper rigs, down out of sight. There isn't very much you can do about this blind situation except to be prepared beforehand. If you're in doubt, go to heavier tackle. If you persist in using lighter equipment, be ready to lose fish.

Ideally, to be fully equipped for shark fishing you'll carry or have access to conventional outfits in three different calibers. Suggested are these: (1) Light: A rod handling lines to 40-pound test; 4/o reel; 40-pound line. This outfit will take care of all the smaller sharks and, if you know what you're doing, some of the larger fellows to over 200 pounds. (2) Medium: 50- or 60-pound (line) rod; 6/o to 8/o reel; 60-pound line. This outfit will cut down on your sport with smaller sharks, but it will better enable you to cope with beasts going to 200 or 250 pounds and better. (3) Heavy: Following our grading, the rod will be able to accommodate lines up to 80-pound test. To handle sufficient yardage of such lines, and possess the required ruggedness, the matching reel should be at least a 9/o, and can go to a 10/0. Such equipment, worked properly, will defeat sharks of 300 pounds and upward to 500 and even heavier. (4) Extra-heavy: If real biggies, such as whites, tigers, or the huskier duskies are in the area, or if lack of experience dictates, you might want to go to correspondingly stronger equipment. Here your rod should be able to fish lines up to 130-pound test. Your reel will be a 10/0, if not a 12/0, and your line strength will be rated at 130 pounds. This tackle will handle just about all the big sharks you're likely to encounter, with the possible exception of real behemoths.

You see, there's no one all-around rod-reel-line combination for shark angling, any more than there can be one that will handle flounders to swordfish with equal facility. You say, "Well, that's all very nice, having two or three outfits in different calibers, but suppose I'm not prepared right now to go out and invest that much in tackle. What then?" The answer, of course, is to do your shark fishing on charter boats. They carry gear in a wide range of sizes.

If you're going to collect your own tackle, there's one outfit you can assemble as a starter, a kind of happy medium for those who are inexperienced, yet don't want to go to the heaviest outfits. My suggestion is a rod able to handle fifty-pound line and a 6/0 reel spooled with fifty-pound line. This combo will cost you some action with small sharks, but it will enable you to battle many, if not most, of those with which you're likely to come in contact. What I'm saying is that most of the sharks you're going to fight probably won't go over three hundred pounds. When you gain experience with this outfit you'll be able to handle sharks weighing more than three hundred pounds—maybe. Later you can add lighter and heavier tackle.

ADDITIONAL NOTES ON GEAR (1) Braided Dacron line is recommended because of the virtues noted for it in an earlier chapter. Monofilament lines also are used. If the synthetic you have has some stretch, don't worry about it. A certain amount of stretch can work to your advantage in shark fishing by maintaining tension on the fish, like an elongated spring. And it isn't likely to interfere with your setting of the hook, as in the case of some smaller finned game. (2) Rods preferably should have at least one roller guide, the tiptop. It's even better if they have roller guides throughout. They function better than ring guides in big game angling. (3) Reels must have a dependable, *smoothly operating* drag. In this game there's no room for a drag that has even a threat of stickiness. A little of that nonsense and—*bang!*— there goes your line. (4) Don't skimp on lines. Figure on at least 250 or 300 yards. Hard-running sharks can peel off 100 yards or more at a clip. By rights, a reel's spool should be filled with line for maximum advantage. The more line peeling off a spool, remember, the greater the braking effect. Keep yardage and line strength requirements in mind when selecting a reel. It's better to have more than enough line than too little. Few things are more frustrating than to stand by helplessly while a long-running fish makes line evaporate from the reel.

TO SPIN OR NOT TO SPIN   In all the foregoing chatter about tackle you must have noticed the absence of the word "spinning." The omission was deliberate.

Not that spinning tackle can't be used in shark fishing, you understand. It can be, and it is. The fact is that spinning tackle has accounted for sharks up into the two-hundred-to-three-hundred-pound class, and the heavier equipment probably could take even bulkier fish. The point behind my not mentioning spinning tackle is that I don't recommend it for sharks. It provides all kinds of action, no doubt about it, but it also demands more skill and costs more fish. Furthermore, it extends fish-playing time; and since your companions should have their lines out of the water while you're arguing with your opponent, you're cutting down on their opportunities for action, something that won't endear you to them if you do enough of it.

In this game, spinning tackle is light gear. By all means try it, if you wish, but if you do I suggest that you equip yourself with one of those heavy-duty rod-reel combinations designed for larger battlers. Here, as in the case of spinning tackle, your spinning rod must be able to fish lines of suitable strength. In keeping, the reel has to be large enough to hold sufficient yardage of those lines, as well as possess a smooth, dependable drag mechanism and sturdy guts to stand the stresses and strains of combat with boys who play rough.

Unless you've had appreciable big game angling experience, or until you gain it, stick with conventional tackle for sharks.

HOOKS Even anglers are amazed sometimes by the sizes of the hooks rigged in sport fishing for sharks. I mean, they're surprised at their smallness. They expect to see huge hooks, about like those suspending beef carcasses in meat packing houses.

They *are* small, when you consider the sizes of the fishes involved. A 14/0 or 16/0, for example, will take even a hefty maneater. The reason for this comparative smallness of shark hooks is that *they're matched to the baits, not to the fishes themselves.* That, in turn, has a reason. Although sharks aren't the brightest critters in the world, they're not total dummies either. Like most fishes, they tend to be sensitive to foreign objects in baits. (If you bit down on something hard in scrambled eggs you'd be suspicious too, wouldn't you?) In the first place, a great big hook protruding from a bait might just give a shark pause for thought. Or if he felt a huge hook when he mouthed the bait he might very well think that something peculiar was going on here and reject your offering. The chances are that you won't get a chance to convince him otherwise.

Shark sport-fishing hooks range from about a 6/0 up to a 14/0 or 16/0. Sizes 8/0 to 10/0 or 12/0 will take any shark caught on medium tackle. With heavier or lighter gear you can go larger or smaller in proportion.

Although hooks are matched primarily to baits, shark sizes do influence hook calibers in a way, but indirectly, since baits can be progressively larger for bigger opponents. You don't have to be exact in hook sizes. Sharks have large mouths. A size or two one way or another isn't going to make a critical difference, as long as the hooks are strong enough. Hook strength is very important. Hooks that are too weak—even those of adequate size —can straighten out during the power surges of a muscular shark. I recommend, therefore, that you always rig triple-strength hooks for sharks.

Hook patterns aren't of cardinal importance. Any of the popular designs will do the job. In time you'll develop your own preference. For a starter I suggest the Martu pattern. Because of the design of its point and barb, a Martu has good penetrating and holding ability.

Tip: Rust your shark hooks. That's what I said, make them *rusty.* It sounds crazy, but it has a purpose. It makes them less conspicuous in a bait. The rusting is only superficial, however, not enough to affect the hooks' strength. In time, should rusting become extensive enough to affect a hook's soundness, discard that hook. Shark hooks can be readied by simply leaving them in a can of water until a thin patina of rust has eliminated their shiny glitter. To speed up the process, leave them in some Clorox, or a mixture of Clorox and water.

Rusted or no, shark hooks must have sharp points and barbs. You'll have to pay special attention to this detail if you camouflage them by rusting. Keep them keen with a small hone made just for sharpening hooks—you should have one of these little stones anyway. But be careful when honing the barb. Confine your sharpening to its *point.* Sharpen any more than that and you'll risk having the hook cut its way free after it has been set.

WIRE LEADERS: A MUST Mark this well: *For sharks you must always incorporate a wire leader in your terminal setup.* No ifs, ands, or buts. Sharks' teeth can sever fishing line faster than a knife. Further, their skin is strongly abrasive. When rubbed toward the fish's head, shark hide becomes coarse sandpaper. A line merely has to brush against it to be rubbed through. Wire affords some protection if your shark rolls up in the leader, a common occurrence with certain species. Wire won't completely prevent severing of the line by abrasion because some sharks with a large girth will roll themselves in a leader until the line can't help but come in contact with their hide. This is a calculated risk.

Two types of wire are commonly employed as shark leaders. One is made from stainless steel. The other is popularly called piano wire. Each has advantages and disadvantages, as shown in the following comparison:

Stainless steel wire. Not as strong per diameter as piano wire, but it doesn't rust. It will kink, however, and a kink is a weak spot, a place where the wire can part under strain. Stainless steel wire can be used over and over again until it catches its first shark. Then, by rights, it should be discarded because of the danger of kinks.

Piano wire. Stronger per diameter than stainless steel, piano wire doesn't pose as great a kinking problem as the stainless stuff, but it rusts quickly and is weakened thereby. A piano wire leader should be used the same day it's made up, then discarded, whether it has caught a fish or not. If you want to prepare piano wire leaders in advance, keep them immersed in oil until used.

Strengths of wire leaders are in proportion to diameters, and those diameters are indicated by numbers: No. 5, No. 6, etc. The larger the number, the greater the diameter and the more strength. In shark fishing the range is from about a No. 9 to a No. 12. A No. 12 in stainless steel wire is rated at 174 pounds test. Its piano wire counterpart has a pounds-test strength of 198.

No. 9 wire, stainless steel or piano, is strong enough for many of the sharks you'll tie into. Go to the next largest size if you want to, but actually it doesn't contribute to the over-all strength of your line-leader combination. The maximum strength of that combo is only as great as the line. If your line is eighty-pound test, we'll say, it doesn't make any difference how strong your leader is. The combined strength of line and leader is still eighty-pound test. The only conceivable advantages in a somewhat heavier wire would lie in its being perhaps a bit tougher to bite through if the shark happened to seize it, and in its added strength when the leader is grabbed to bring the fish to gaff. Back on the debit side again, the heavier a wire leader, the harder it is to handle.

"How long should this leader be?" you ask. Well, you can figure on fifteen to eighteen feet. Those lengths are sufficient in the majority of cases. I say "in the majority of cases" because some sharks, notably blues and porbeagles, tend to roll up in a leader. When that happens you'd better hope they don't use up enough wire so that their skin comes in contact with your line.

You say, "If that can happen, why not use longer wire?" My answer goes back to something I said earlier: The longer a wire leader is, the more difficult it is to handle—and, theoretically, at least, the greater the danger from kinks, because there's more of it. Even fifteen to eighteen feet can seem like a half mile to the guy handling it when a particularly lively rascal is brought alongside the boat.

Stick to fifteen to eighteen feet, using the longer of the two for species that tend to roll up in the leader.

If you become record-minded in shark fishing you'll have to observe International Game Fish Association laws governing leader lengths. These rules, applying to all IGFA entries, specify that wire leaders, whatever their composition and strength, can be no longer than fifteen feet for lines up to and including fifty-pound test. For lines stronger than that they can't exceed thirty feet. Violations automatically disqualify contenders.

You'll hear talk about cable leaders in shark fishing. The accent is usually on their strength, which often is greater than need be. A cable leader will do the job, and when it's one of those plastic-coated types it's a bit easier to handle than wire. But it has a drawback in sharking.

Being cable, it's made from several fine strands of wire twisted or braided together. Along the sides of his jaws a shark's teeth mesh closely, like well-ground gears, creating a formidable cutting apparatus. If he gets a cable between those meshing teeth, as can occur if he's hooked in the side of his mouth, a combination of their shearing power and motions of his head will sever those strands one by one. If he manages to cut enough of them, the cable weakens sufficiently to let go. After a long battle that could happen before you have a chance to gaff your fish.

That's why wire leaders are preferred to cable in sharking. Let me hastily add that wire leaders aren't totally immune to severing by sharks' dentures. Sooner or later you'll have one get your wire between his teeth just right, and pop goes the weasel. But this too is a calculated risk.

Important: When you measure off your fifteen or eighteen feet of wire, be sure to allow some extra for making attachments to swivel and hook. Eighteen inches or so should do it.

RIGGING   Your basic shark rig calls for one hook. There are three ways of attaching it. One is what we call a fixed hook; next is a loose or swinging hook; third is a live bait setup. The swinging hook and live bait setups are substantially the same, with a varia-

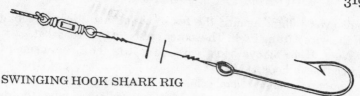

SWINGING HOOK SHARK RIG

tion. Familiarize yourself with all three. You'll use them, depending upon whether you fish with live or dead bait.

Fixed hook—for dead baits only. This favors a needle-eye hook over the ring-eye type. As its name implies, the former has its eye right in the shank, like a needle. A ring-eye style of hook has an eye that has been formed by bending the end of its shank around to form a small loop. This kind of hook also can be used in a fixed-hook setup, and it's just as effective. The only quarrel with it is that it makes a bulkier-looking connection than a needle-eye hook. If you don't have needle eyes with you, rig ring eyes.

In the fixed arrangement your hook is attached to its leader in a stiff or rigid fashion. Therein lies the principal difference between it and a swinging hook.

Run the free end of your wire through the hook's eye. Give yourself several inches to work with. Make two tight turns around the shank, below the eye but close to it. These are what make it a fixed hook. Be sure there's enough wire left over after those turns—you're going to need it. Now feed the end back through the eye again.

To finish the connection, make what is called a bailing wire twist. With the leader's free end, fashion eight to ten loose twists with the wire proper. It's important that the wire cross itself like an "X" in these twists (rather than the free end just wrapping around the leader) so they'll retain a looseness. Finish up with six or eight tight turns around the wire, leaving a couple of inches of free end sticking outward, aimed in a direction away from the hook's point. This short, protruding piece of wire will help to secure the bait to your hook and prevent its sliding up the leader. You'll see how it functions when we come to baiting.

Maybe you're wondering why we put those bailing wire twists in there instead of using all tight turns to finish the connection. Well, if you were to make only tight turns, under strain they'd pull even tighter against the hook, posing a distinct possibility of the wire cutting itself. The looser twists first prevent that.

Note: If a ring-eye hook is used, rig it in the same manner as a needle-eye hook.

Loose or swinging hook. This also is for dead baits. In addition to using a ring-eye hook instead of a needle-eye type, the difference between the swinging and fixed setups is that in the former you *omit the two turns around the shank* when first threading your wire through the eye. Otherwise it's rigged in the same fashion as a fixed hook, with eight or ten bailing wire twists, then six or eight tight twists to finish it. Here too you leave a couple of inches of free end sticking out to pin the bait. About the only advantage I can see for this particular rig over a fixed-hook arrangement is that it lets a bait have a little more freedom of movement.

Live-bait hook. This is intended primarily for live baits, but it also can be employed with dead ones. Here again you use a ring-eye hook. Feed the wire through its eye, again allowing a few inches to work with. *Don't make any twists around the shank;* otherwise you'll wind up with a fixed hook. Bend the wire to make a small loop—not too small—through the hook's eye, then proceed as before with eight or ten bailing wire twists and six or eight tight turns. Don't leave any wire protruding, because you won't pin a live bait. Apart from injuring or killing the fish, it would hamper its action, which defeats the purpose of a swinging hook. Break, rather than cut, off any excess wire, close to the leader, so as not to leave a hand-tearing burr. Bending the wire back and forth will cause it to part.

Connection of leader to line. This should be made by means of a snap swivel, tied to the *line,* which accepts a small loop in the end of the wire. This arrangement, as you now know, facilitates changing of rigs, a very handy feature in sharking.

All swivels come in various sizes. The larger they are, naturally, the stronger they are. Those selected for shark rigs must be suitably strong. Generally speaking, they'll meet that requirement if you follow this tip: Use a snap swivel that's too large to even enter your rod's tiptop guide, much less pass through it. It's important that the snap swivel not be able to go into that guide at all. If it can enter it, it could become wedged there. Should your shark decide on a last-minute display of muscle at that precise time, you could wind up with a fractured rod or broken leader.

Making the loop on your leader. Follow a procedure very similar to that for attaching a hook. (1) Bend a small loop in the wire's free end. It needn't be any larger than about a half inch in diameter. (2) Holding the loop with one hand, or with pliers or in a vise, make six bailing wire twists. Remember that these should be like an "X." (3) Take six tight turns around the leader proper, each lying snugly next to its neighbor. (4) Finish by breaking—not snipping—off any excess close to the leader. Here too the purpose of the bailing wire twists is to prevent the loop from pulling tight like a hangman's noose under tension. Not only would that pose a risk of the wire cutting itself, it also would make it difficult to remove your leader from the snap swivel. That would defeat the arrangement's purpose.

Tip: Make up at least five or six terminal tackle assemblies, complete, ready to go. Vary leader strengths and hook sizes according to the general sizes of the sharks you're most likely to encounter. The hooks on these most likely rigs can be fixed or swinging, governed by whether you're most apt to use a dead or a live bait. It would be smart to have some of both. If you want to rust your hooks, as suggested earlier, do it beforehand, checking the sharpness of their points and barbs when you rig them. If you use piano wire, keep it in a light oil until used.

Baits. Whenever you can, use the freshest baits possible for sharks. 'Way up at the top in order of preference is live bait. Then comes a *fresh* dead bait. Third, and inferior to the other two, is a frozen bait. Avoid frozen baits for sharks if you can. Hold those as a last resort.

NATURAL FOODS = BAIT CHOICES By and large, sharks are omnivorous feeders, dining on a variety of creatures. Their menu lists smaller fishes of many kinds, squids, and an assortment of crustaceans. Commonly they favor species that travel in sizable schools, such as menhaden, mackerel, herring, mullet, bonitos, young tuna, and so on. And why not? Charging into such groups makes feeding easier. For the same reason sharks are always on the lookout for strays, among marine mammals as well as among fishes. An animal or fish that lags behind the others because of age, weakness, or fatigue is a prime target for sharks. Not only does this provide lunch for predators, it's also part of nature's selective breeding, an elimination of the unfit. The same thing happens in the world of land animals.

Similarly, sharks are attracted to hooked fishes that are being played or reeled in. The sounds of such fishes' struggles can draw sharks in out of nowhere, as many an angler has discovered when he reeled in only the head of his opponent. If hunger nags them enough, sharks will attack larger, more solitary fishes. Makos, for example, have a taste for swordfish, even as you and I—except that they like theirs on the hoof, instead of broiled, with French fries. The carcasses of dead animals, sea or land, also will draw sharks. Find a dead whale, and chances are there are sharks chomping on the corpse.

Theoretically, therefore, any fish—or piece of fish—of suitable size for impaling on a hook is potential shark bait. Species that have been used, alive and/or dead, include northern whiting, eels, mackerel, sea bass, menhaden, porgies, bonito, herring, mullet, and dozens of other regional kinds. Sharks are cannibalistic, so you can even use their own kind to lure them to hooks, if you find specimens small enough. (Unless you crave risking bites, you rig them dead.) I've baited with whole dead blue sharks, twenty, twenty-four or so inches long, and hooked their big brothers.

In addition to whole smaller fishes the list of shark come-ons embraces strips, fillets, or chunks cut from larger species. Fillets or strips cut from white marlin, swordfish, and other billfishes have been effective. Here, however, you're likely to meet stiff objections from fellow anglers if you go to whittle baits from such catches. It's much easier to capitalize on sharks' cannibalisms and slice the goodies from a specimen already caught. Blue shark fillets, for example, are effective.

You ask about animal flesh as shark bait. The reply is yes, it has some magnetism, depending upon its nature and freshness. At least meat cut from marine animals such as whales, porpoises, and seals has some attraction. But why offer sharks animal flesh when they're primarily fish eaters? Fish baits are much easier to

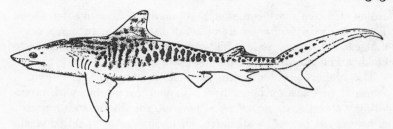

TIGER SHARK (*Galeocerdo cuvier*) (young specimen; markings may fade with growth)

obtain. Besides, if you have in mind to try for an IGFA record, forget animal flesh of any kind. The rules forbid it.

POINTERS 1. Sharks have lusty appetites, but they're not insatiable gluttons. Like animals, they exhibit a disinterest in food —including your bait—when their bellies are full.

2. Although they're omnivorous feeders, sharks can and do become persnickety at times. They'll favor certain baits over others at intervals. On occasion even highly favored items elicit no response. That's your cue to have a variety of baits whenever possible.

3. Forget the popular notion that sharks will eat anything, anywhere, anytime. 'Tain't so. Don't think for a minute you can just toss over a baited hook and have a shark zero in, practically sobbing with gratitude. You'll learn that shark baiting is a little art in itself.

4. Wherever you may be sharking, try to learn what kinds of baits the marauders favor in that area. Failing that, inquire as to what schooling smaller fishes visit local ocean waters at that particular time of year. Any of these, some more than others, are potential shark baits.

SPECIFICS Live baits are favored; but the only way you're going to get 'em is to catch 'em yourself. I believe their superiority justifies the extra effort.

An excellent shark bait is live northern whiting, the same fish we looked at in an earlier chapter. You can carry a suitable bottom fishing outfit and bait for these. Live Boston mackerel also are an effective shark come-on, and you know how to catch them. There are many other kinds of small fishes—eels, to name one— that can be rigged as live baits. Ask for recommendations as to tackle and techniques for catching these fishes.

The biggest problem with live baits is keeping them alive. If the boat in question has a live bait well, preferably with circulating water, there's no sweat. Otherwise you'll have to improvise. A watertight box or small barrel, or one of those so-called washtubs, will suffice. But unless you have provision for aerating its water, you'll probably have to freshen it at intervals. You also should shield it against direct rays of the sun, so its water doesn't overheat. Certain kinds of bait fishes can't be kept alive even under optimum conditions. Others require constantly circulating water, and even then may not remain alive for long. On the credit side are those rugged species that can be held in a large bucket, as long as it's kept out of the hot sun and its water is freshened at intervals.

With many bait fishes you'll have to determine yourself which kinds will survive and under what conditions. In any case, if you can't keep them alive you'll have the next best thing, a fresh dead bait.

Catch an adequate supply before you start shark fishing. Figure on at least one or two for each rig you intend to put out, plus a couple of extras. But don't put too many in the same container. Crowding can kill them. If your supply runs short, you'll have to catch more.

Don't try fishing for live bait if sharks are cruising around under the boat. You won't stand the proverbial Chinaman's chance of getting a bait fish up past them, and you won't nail a thief on that light gear—without a wire leader, yet. Put aside your bait-hooking gear for the time being and go to a dead bait.

Squid are shark bait and are fine for swordfish and marlin too. Live or dead eels also are shark bait. You can catch them and keep them alive in a pail or tub without difficulty. Small dead fish—mossbunkers, mackerel, bluefish, and others—are used whole. Larger ones can be cut into halves. And then there are those fillets or strips cut from sharks or other large fishes. You might try tuna here too.

PREPARATION OF BAITS A dead bait, fresh or frozen, will have more action in the water if its backbone is removed. That gives it flexibility. For the same reason, hard-frozen baits should be thawed before use.

A bait fish's backbone can be removed by either of two methods. In one the fish is slit open along the back and the spinal column cut free, after which the incision is sewed shut with a few stitches of twine or strong thread. The other method calls for a deboner. A deboner is simply a metal tube, brass or aluminum, with a cutting edge on one end and a handle on the other. The tube is forced into the fish and around the backbone, which it cuts free as it is worked. Out comes the backbone inside the tube.

You can fashion a deboner yourself, but why go to that trouble when they can be bought? A deboner a half inch in diameter will handle most of the baits you'll rig for sharks and other offshore gamesters. Later you can add a somewhat larger one for really big baits. With a deboner carry a dowel or similar gadget to shove the backbone out of the tube so the instrument will be ready for use another time.

Preparation of fillet baits. Cut a fillet of suitable size from the side of the fish. You want to wind up with rectangular pieces, roughly 8 to 10 inches long, 2 or 3 inches wide, and 1½ inches or so in thickness. If the fillet has a silvery skin, you can leave it on. Otherwise remove it so that the flesh is exposed. This is particularly important when the flesh is whitish. Whiteness is an attractor. Cut the fillet into rectangular pieces of the sizes I just gave you. Cut each rectangle diagonally, corner to corner, giving you two triangles. These are your baits. For added attraction, split each one at its pointed end for a couple of inches to create two taillike appendages that will flutter in the water.

Strip baits. I prefer fillets to strips for sharks, but that doesn't rule out use of the latter. Strip baits of various lengths and widths can be rigged. Generally they're cut from the silvery or whitish side or belly of a fish, thick enough to give them some substance on a hook, but not so thick as to impair their action in the water. Silver or whitish skin is an attractor, and leaving it on gives the strip some toughness.

You'll save fishing time by preparing dead-bait rigs on the way out. Thaw frozen baits beforehand. Baits can be deboned and secured to hooks, and their wire leaders neatly coiled, to be ready for use when you reach the arena.

BAITING TECHNIQUES   *Live fish.* Using a swinging hook, run its point through the flesh of the back just behind the dorsal fin. Be careful! The idea is to hook the bait securely without injuring or killing it.

Whole dead fish. Use a fixed hook. Thrust its point upward through the fish's jaws from underneath, just far enough back to leave room for that protruding piece of wire on the leader. The hook in place, force that short, free piece of wire (left sticking out when you completed your fixed-hook rig) up through the roof of the bait's mouth and out the top. Bend it over and take a couple of turns around the leader proper. If you see you're going to have some excess, it might be a good idea to break (not cut) it off before making the turns. Bend the end as close as you can to the leader.

Fillets. Simply run your hook through the triangular piece of bait near its wider forward end. Some anglers leave the point exposed. Others bury it in the meat. The main thing is that it's securely hooked and that its narrow free end is free to flutter.

Chunks or halves of fishes. Imbed the hook securely in the bait, leaving its point hidden.

Strip baits. The procedure here is essentially the same as for fillets. The hook's point goes through the strip near one end, after which that end is moved up on the bend a bit, and the point thrust through the bait again. It depends upon the strip's thickness, but you probably will have to leave the hook's point and barb exposed.

Squid and eels. Squid, whole or as strips cut from the mantle (the skirtlike portion), is fine bait for a number of marine battlers. A whole squid, alone, can be used as shark bait, but more often it's employed as a kind of bonus, placed on the hook in addition to another bait. The hook's point and barb will have to be left exposed for this. The other bait in place, run the point and barb into the squid's body, leaving the arms to wave in the water. This doesn't have to be impaled as securely as the main bait. It's only an extra-added attraction.

Eels also come into play as bait for several salt-water game-sters, rigged whole, or in pieces, or just their skins (in combina-tion with an artificial). They can be rigged whole for sharks, but it has been my experience that they are not the best come-on for those prowlers, at least in daytime angling. I hastily add, though, that sharks and eels are active night feeders, so the latter are a logical after-dark bait. A live eel is preferred to a dead one. You'll need a fairly large specimen. Carefully hook the eel through the skin of the back in the body's forward portion—not too far forward, but enough to present the bait in a natural fashion, with plenty of free length to wiggle. Another stunt you can try is to rig a dead eel. Skin the critter first so that white flesh shows. Then run your hook through the body near the head.

PLACES WITH POTENTIAL   All the ocean is your shark hunting ter-ritory. To a much lesser extent, large bays, sounds, inlets, and channels also offer possibilities. But if you're a serious sharker, and want to be reasonably certain of catches, concentrate on the ocean. Out there is shark angling potential everywhere—offshore, inshore, and around the exits of big inlets.

The open sea is a limitless expanse, and its shark fishing po-tential is proportionately enormous. But there are no signs out there saying SHARKS HERE. The fact is that even with its huge potential, the ocean has areas as barren of sharks as the Sahara Desert. Conversely, you'll come across areas where they're con-centrated temporarily. Usually it's an abundance of food that has attracted them to that place.

Also because of the sea's vastness, and because many species do not school appreciably, sharks can be scattered widely. With-out a gimmick there are times when chances of contacting even one are overwhelmingly against you. Such a gimmick has been devised, and you'll learn about it shortly.

Tips: (1) Sharks tend to feed more actively at night, thereby increasing the odds in your favor. Night shark fishing has an eerie suspense all its own. It's great. Just be sure you and your boat are equipped for night navigation. (2) Abrupt dropoffs in the ocean floor often are productive areas. Navigation charts show them; depth sounders and other electronic gear help to locate them. The procedure is to drift and chum, back and forth, along the brink of the dropoff.

DRIFT CHUMMING   Although sharks are hooked by surfcasting, angling on jetties, and fishing at anchor with chum, far and away the most effective technique is to chum while drifting. Its obvious advantage is that it covers a lot of ground. In this coverage chumming aids immensely, extending the boat's reach, so to speak, by appealing to sharks' extraordinarily keen sense of smell.

Sharks' most highly developed sense is smell. *Sharks hunt primarily by scent.* They can detect sounds and vibrations. And they can see—up to a point; their eyesight isn't too good. It's their olfactory sense that counts.

Evidence suggests that their search-and-destroy operation works like this: First they pick up a scent—fish, chum, blood in the water, or whatever—on which they zero in. They follow that scent like a radar beam, gliding toward its sources. You'll see sharks moving their heads slowly from side to side as they swim up a chum line. They're equalizing the scent in their nostrils to keep on target. Somewhere en route they pick up vibrations from prey's movements. Maybe they're from a busy school, or from fish struggling on hooks. Now they can "lock in" on target. Finally, when they draw close enough, they see their intended victims. *Zap!*

So it's to that tremendously keen sense of smell that we appeal when we chum for sharks.

Various materials function as chum: ground-up fishes such as mossbunkers, whiting, trash species, etc.; small pieces of fish, practically all kinds; and even whole small fish when there's an abundant supply—like a whopping good catch of mackerel, for example. You also can chum with ground-up meat from a pilot whale or "pothead." Sharks find this "whaleburger" stuff enticing. White sharks are particularly fond of it. But it has a big drawback: You have to go out and harpoon your own pothead. Another drawback is that the International Game Fish Association prohibits the use of any kind of animal flesh as chum in record contention.

I doubt that you'll be using pilot whale meat as chum, unless you can latch onto some guy who harpoons them.

Your most practical chum for sharks—and it can be used for several other marine species as well—is ground mossbunkers. If ground 'bunkers are unobtainable, scout around to see if you can arrange for a commercial fisherman to save his trash fishes for you, and grind those.

Mix this pulp with a little sea water, just as you would for bluefish on mackerel. Don't forget to thaw it beforehand.

In reply to a question often asked, yes, blood from various creatures, chickens to cows, is chum material, mixed in with other stuff. But it isn't essential. There's some blood in ground-up fish pulp. Besides, there's the question of availability of the red liquid. Further, you'll run afoul of the IGFA if you use blood from any mammal.

ACTUALLY CHUMMING Having found a patch of ocean in which to try your luck, with tackle in readiness and your rigs baited, swing into action. Kill the boat's engine(s) and let the craft drift. Start your chum line.

I suggest this for any chumming from a drifting boat: Do it on the side of the cockpit *opposite* to the direction in which the craft is drifting. You may be doing it into the wind, but don't let that bother you. *Drop* the chum overboard, don't sling it. If you chum on the cockpit's other side—that is, the one in the direction you're drifting—the boat will run over the stuff and disperse it prematurely, lessening its efficiency.

Memo. A rule of thumb for chumming is to ladle some of the gop overboard, watch it, and when it starts to disappear, drop another ladleful. Adapt the same principle to pieces of fish, shrimp, and similar chum. Very important, *keep a chum line unbroken.* If you want to grab a sandwich or go to the head, get someone to take over chumming immediately. Breaks in a chum line can ruin it.

Varying lengths of time are required for a chum line to elicit response. You might be lucky enough to get a customer within ten or fifteen minutes of the first ladleful. On the other hand, you might have to wait an hour or more. There will be times when you chum for a couple of hours and get no results whatsoever. The main thing is to give the chum a fair chance to work. Two hours, I'd say, constitutes a fair chance. If you don't raise action

COMMON HAMMERHEAD SHARK (*Sphyrna zygaena*)

by then you can be reasonably sure there are no sharks in that vicinity. Shift to another location a couple of miles away. You'll be gambling, so you can go in any direction. At the new site drift, get a chum line going, and give it another whirl.

You may find action at the first spot you choose. Or you may have to move a couple of times. There will be days when you're hit with all the shark action you can handle. At the other extreme are trips when action is slow or you're blanked completely. Sometimes you'll have good action at a given place, then come back there the next day and find it devoid of fish. But there's one thing about sport fishing for sharks: In even just so-so seasons your chances for success are high.

Warning. Once a chum line is started, don't let anyone toss beer cans, sandwich wrappings, bottles, or other debris overboard. Not only is it littering, such objects might distract a shark moving in along the chum, particularly if they're shiny like a can or white like a piece of paper. He may ignore your baits to investigate, or even play with them. The risk is that he may shove off after he tires of his little game.

LINES READY! The best setup in drift chumming for sharks is to put three lines overboard: one for an upper level; a second rigged for an arbitrary intermediate depth; and a third for a lowermost plane, somewhere over the bottom. That strategy covers the three main depth corridors along which the sea wolves may be cruising.

You do *not* put any of the lines in outriggers. They go straight out from the boat.

To dangle two of those rigs, upper and middle, at the desired levels you'll need pieces of cork. These have to be only large enough to suspend the weight of your terminal outfit. To attach a hunk of cork to your rig, cut partway through the piece, just a simple knife cut. It only has to be deep enough to hold the cork in place. Simply pull your line into this slit.

"Why not fasten the cork more securely?" you ask. Because you want to be able to flip it off at a moment's notice. Occasionally even a darkish-colored cork will capture a shark's eye and he'll make a pass at it. If he seizes the cork, there goes your line. There goes your fish too, along with a rig. A cork float usually can be flipped free by vigorous movements of your rod tip.

Inflated balloons are employed as floats, but they're unsatisfactory because they can't be jettisoned at will if sharks go for them. You also can rig small blocks of buoyant styrofoam as floats, in the same manner as pieces of cork, but I don't recommend it. Styrofoam's bright whiteness is too much of an eye-grabber.

Distances between floats and hooks, and among the rigs themselves, are arbitrary and variable, and consequently open to experimentation. Water depths and current strength in areas fished are factors, governing not only where you'll place the floats, but also (as a result of their location) the distance between baited rigs. Keep leader lengths in mind too. The floats can always be adjusted as required.

I'll suggest a starting setup. You can vary it as needed. To keep things simple we'll say that you're using fifteen-foot leaders throughout. Okay?

Top rig. For openers, position the cork approximately twenty, twenty-five, or thirty feet above the snap swivel. Added to the leader length, fifteen feet, this means that your bait would dangle about thirty-five to forty-five feet down, *if it were straight up and down.* But it won't be perfectly vertical because of current thrust and the boat's drift, so it actually will be closer to the surface. You'll have to gauge those facts when making adjustments to cause the rig to ride higher or lower.

Middle rig. Use the same procedure to place a float on this line so that the rig will be suspended at some arbitrary level between the top and bottom rigs. This is almost pure experimentation. For a starter you can place the cork fifty to sixty feet on the line ahead of its snap swivel. Theoretically this gives you a total dangling length of sixty-five to seventy-five feet, if it were perfectly vertical. Its depth will be lessened by current and drifting.

Bottom rig. No float is used here. As in the cases of the other two rigs, the current's force and the boat's drifting will tend to thrust it upward anyway.

Note: Because of the two factors just mentioned, you may not need corks on *any* of the rigs when the drift is fast enough. Just be sure that the three rigs are on three different levels.

Baiting recommendations. If possible, try different baits at the outset of fishing. You have no way of knowing for sure beforehand what come-ons they'll favor. All you can do is equip yourself with an assortment of those that seem to be most effective in that area and gamble. Repeated strikes on one rig is a cue to change the other baits accordingly. I suggest a live bait—whiting, mackerel, or whatever—on the top rig. For the intermediate rig you can use a dead whole-fish bait—mackerel, whiting, etc.—but don't make it too big. The bottom rig also carries a dead whole-fish bait, and it can be somewhat larger than baits on the other two outfits: large whiting or mackerel; medium-size bonito; or small tuna or albacore. Or whatever fish you happen to have on hand. A large strip bait also can be rigged. Make it 12 or 14 inches long, 2 to 3 inches wide, 1 to 1½ inches thick. Split its free end to create 2 fluttering tails.

Setting the drag. This should be done before you put any rigs over.

You'll hear all kinds of procedures for adjusting a reel drag properly. Don't ignore them, but evolve your own procedure. Most methods are based on personal ideas anyway. The fact is that setting a reel drag is an individualized thing, best learned from experience. Several variables are involved: the reel and its type of brake; how the angler uses it; the rod and its degree of stiffness; the line's size; and the weights and combat characteristics of the fishes involved. It's something you have to learn by feel, through experience, like scratching an itch.

But this much always holds true: The tighter a drag is, the greater its resistance to a fish and the more it tires him. It also ups chances of a popped line. Conversely, the looser a drag is, the less its resistance to a fish, the more line he'll peel off, and the longer he'll fight. You're less apt to break a line with a softer-set drag, but chances of it being stripped of line are increased when you tie into a particularly long-running, hard-fighting scrapper.

Some anglers set a drag with the aid of small hand scales, the kind used for weighing catches. Tying their line to the scales' hook, they moor it or have someone hold it, then let some line peel off and rear back on the rod, tightening or loosening the drag until the scale registers five, ten, or fifteen pounds, or whatever reading they think is proper. There's no quarrel with this method, except that it isn't too practical with a star-type drag, the most common. After making such a setting with a star drag and hooking your fish, you'll probably adjust the drag as the battle progresses, after which it becomes difficult to come back to that original setting precisely because a star drag isn't calibrated. With a calibrated, quadrant-style brake, it's a different story.

Let it be hastily added, though, that when you become completely familiar with your star drag you will be able to return to desired original settings with reasonable accuracy. This comes through feel, which in turn stems from experience.

To help you get that feel, try a simple preliminary. Tie your line to a fixed object. Move away a short distance, letting line peel off. Take up any slack. Now lift up on your rod. You can tell by the way line peels off whether your drag is at either extreme, much too tight or too loose. Adjust accordingly and do it again. The idea is to repeat this business until you get the feel of your reel's drag. You'll know when settings are extreme. Somewhere in between is a satisfactory medium; and, if anything, a setting should favor a lighter side of medium than a heavier one. When they set a drag many fishermen forget that a tightening effect sets in after a certain amount of line has left the spool.

Actually, presetting the brake is mainly for the purpose of setting a striking drag, because there will be adjustments—tightening or loosening, as the case may be—during battle. This striking drag need only be strong enough to set the hook. Later it can be tightened to put more pressure on the fish, or slacked off somewhat if he runs hard. To set for striking drag, tie your line to a fixed object, get it taut, then lift up hard and fast with your rod. This simulates a fish taking off in a hurry when he feels the hook. A broken line will tell you that you've set your drag too tight. If line peels off its spool freely with a certain amount of hold-back feel, the drag should be all right for striking.

I'm talking about setting a drag for the bigger battlers, of course. With small fishes there won't be this fiddling around.

PUTTING YOUR RIGS OVERBOARD   *Top rig.* Pay out line until its cork is about 100 to 150 feet out in the chum slick. Try that distance for a starter.

Middle rig. Drop it over and let it drift out until its float is approximately halfway between the boat and the top rig's cork. That will be its starting position. There will be both vertical and horizontal distance between it and the top rig.

Bottom rig. Let this one go out until you figure it's somewhere near the sea floor (knowing the depth in that location will help). It won't be right on bottom—it doesn't have to be—but it should be lower than the other two rigs to cover a deep plane. Because it carries no float, this rig's line will be more nearly vertical than the others.

These are trial starting positions, purely arbitrary. Later, any or all of them can be adjusted as desired. Don't hesitate to experiment. The main thing is that they are separated vertically to cover three different levels. Give each position a fair chance to produce.

Important: Keep all three rigs right in the chum line as much as possible. This will be by-guess-and-by-golly to a certain extent, since you won't be able to see all the rigs. But you should be okay. Not only will the chum and rigs tend to drift in the same direction, but chum material fans out vertically as well as horizontally.

Tips: It frequently develops that larger sharks hit the lowermost rig, or maybe the middle one. So tackle for those two should be sufficiently sturdy. Small sharks may hit those deeper rigs too, in which case you won't realize maximum sport with fairly heavy tackle. But this too is a calculated risk, and it's better than having a real monster take hold on a light outfit.

Tackle for the three rigs can be in any combination of heavy, medium, and light you desire. I suggest a heavy outfit for the bottom rig, another heavy combo or perhaps a medium one (at the lightest) for the middle rig, and medium tackle for the top rig. If you insist on a light tackle outfit, use it on the top rig. There, at least, you may have a chance to quickly switch to heavier gear if you can see your fish. By the same token, you also can change from heavier to lighter gear under such circumstances.

Flat-calm days, without a whisper of a breeze and no current to speak of, pose a problem in getting any chum line started. You can do this (it's serviceable for any species, by the way): Start the boat's engine and *idle* ahead, in any direction. Have your ground-fish chum mixed with plenty of sea water, and ladle it out as you ease forward. You may have to chum rapidly to maintain an unbroken line, consuming a whole can in only ten or fifteen minutes, but you have no choice. Just before you get down to about the last couple of ladlefuls in that can, kill the boat's engine and chum as usual.

At the outset each reel will be in free spool with its clicker on. This gives leeway in case you have to pay out line to a slow-striking fish. With a fast hitter you can throw the reel into gear instantly. Leaving the clicker on provides enough resistance to prevent the current and the boat's drift from peeling line off the spool. If the boat's motion or current pulls line off the reels, despite the clickers' resistance, try this arrangement: Place each line in the jaws of a couple of spring-type clothespins, moored on short lengths of twine to bitts or cockpit rails or suitable weights in the cockpit. When a line is hit it pulls free.

Watch your chum line. Be alert for the appearance of a customer. He may first show 'way out yonder in the slick. Here's where it's an advantage to have a watcher on the flying bridge. Up higher, he can see farther. You also want to keep an eye on any of the cork floats you can see. Noticeable twitchings and bobbings could indicate nibblings of a shark down below.

TO STAND OR TO SIT   Some anglers battle as many opponents as possible standing up, even heavyweight gamesters going a couple of hundred pounds and more. But there's a limit. Bigger fish and heavier tackle call for a fighting chair. The rod's butt fits into a swiveling gimbal on the chair, and a harness goes across the angler's kidney region and snaps onto the reel, enabling him to bring his back muscles into action. The chair also has a foot rest so that its occupant can brace himself against his fish's power surges.

In case you've forgotten, we discussed stand-up fishing back in the albacore-bonito chapter (which see).

STAND BY! Sharks' approaches to baits vary considerably, governed to a great extent by species and their feeding mood at the moment. Active species—the mako is one—and hungry individuals tend to smack a bait hard. Slower and less-hungry sharks will be more leisurely, sometimes nosing your offering or toying with it before deciding on a taste. Occasionally they're really sneaky, fooling around so gently that they can scarcely be detected. This calls for patience on your part. You'll have to put up with their shenanigans until they either take the bait into their mouth or reject it and move off.

In any case, follow this rule: With a fast pickup of the bait, put your reel in gear and set the hook at once, if the force of the strike hasn't already planted it. With slower pickups you'll have to wait, play their game, maybe even feed them a little line, until you feel a pull that tells you they've taken the bait into their mouth. Now you can throw your reel into gear—don't worry about the clicker, you can turn that off later—and set the hook with a short, brisk, upward lift of your rod tip.

Tip: When sharks play hard-to-get we try a teaser. This is a whole dead fish—it can be any kind you have handy—on a length of cord. No hook. The cord is merely passed in through the fish's mouth, out under a gill cover, and tied.

A teaser is brought into play when you see your intended opponent swimming around the boat and ignoring your baits. Toss the teaser in his direction, preferably right in front of him. Don't let him get it. If he moves to take the fish, pull it away from him. Repeat this a few times and you may get him excited enough to wallop one of your baits.

THE BATTLE   When a hook is planted in a shark's mouth there won't be any doubts. He'll take off for distant points. (Immediately all other lines should be reeled in.) You'll have no choice but to let him go, taking maybe a hundred yards or more of line on that initial power drive. Don't try to stop him, or even slow his rush. That's folly rewarded by a popped line. Just pit the resistance of your rod and reel's drag against him, but always fight him with the rod, not the reel. That's what the rod is for.

Each kind of shark usually has its own blueprint for battle, subject to individual and unpredictable variations. Some keep the fight near the surface. Others go deep almost immediately. Still others battle through various levels, top to deep. Some are given to long first rushes, then gradually shortening ones. Others fight in a series of shorter, strong charges. Some sharks will roll up in the leader during the argument. There's nothing you can do about this, except hope they don't cause a weakening kink in the wire or use up enough leader to bring your line in contact with their rough hide.

Unfortunately, unlike billfishes such as sailfish and marlins, sharks are not inclined to leap when hooked. Only a very few species do. Makos are one. An acrobatic mako will jump three, six, or more times during a fight. Not all makos leap, however. On rare occasions you'll get a leap or two from a maverick of a species that isn't supposed to jump.

THRESHER SHARK (*Alopias vulpinus*)

Almost any shark is liable to change direction as a battle tactic. You must be ready for it, keeping your rod aimed in his direction so as not to inflict unnecessary strain on the stick's tip section. There are two maneuvers for which you must be especially alert.

One is the fish swinging in a wide arc as though to circle the boat. If he does go out and around you'll have to follow him. In stand-up fishing you can do this by changing your position in the boat. If you're in a fighting chair, have someone stand behind you to turn it so that your rod is pointed in the general direction of the fish. In wide-sweeping runs it may be necessary to start the boat's engine and swing her accordingly.

The other cute trick for which sharks are (in)famous is to abruptly change direction and move toward the boat. One danger here is that the fish will torpedo directly under the vessel, bringing your line in contact with cutting barnacles on her bottom or fouling it in her propeller or rudder, with equally disastrous results to the line. There's another hazard. If the fish swings toward the boat he may create a loop of slack in the line. This costs you control of your fish for the moment and also poses a possibility of his skin rubbing against the slack enough to chafe through your line.

In this situation take up any slack quickly and be prepared to follow him. If he dives under the boat you'll have to move fast, if you can get out of the fighting chair. Holding onto your tackle tightly, work your line around the transom, trying to keep it free of the craft's bottom, prop, and rudder. Walk it around to the other side, and carry on from there.

As with any fish, a battle with a shark is a matter of wearing down your opponent. It's a fair fight. He has a lot of things going for him, maybe more than you have for you. He's in his native element, and he can get around in it faster than you can in yours. If he has any size he's a lot stronger than you are, and I don't care if you're the world's champion weight lifter or a re-creation of John L. Sullivan. What's more, he has surprising reserves of strength. In a long, knock-down-drag-out fight, you might not be so sure of *your* reserves.

But you also have advantages. You too possess stamina (you *do*, don't you?). You put up resistance. And there's your tackle. The shark will be fighting against that constantly, with a certain amount of resistance from the boat's weight. It will be the combination of your tackle, arm and back muscles, and stubbornness that turns the tide of battle.

It will be a seesaw affair. At times he'll have the upper hand, peeling off line in long, uncontrollable rushes, or perhaps lying "doggo" and unmovable as he "locks his brakes and transmission" and pauses to summon strength. He'll try every trick at his command. In other phases you'll gain the upper hand, if only temporarily. Always you'll be an opportunist, feeling for signs of weakening or tiring in your opponent to regain some line. And so it will go give and take, back and forth, until finally you see line gradually coming back on your reel.

The near-naked spool. Even with a lot of line on a reel it sometimes happens that a shark or other large, very active gamefish will make long or deep runs that threaten to completely strip a reel of line. You'll see this, of course; and if there's a strong hint that he might run off with all your Dacron you'll have to take emergency steps immediately.

The boat's engine is started, and a buoy or other floating marker is tossed overboard to indicate the approximate end of the chum line (it will drift along with chum) so you can come back to it. Now the boat is maneuvered in the direction the fish is taking, literally chasing him down, while the angler cranks like a mad thing to regain line. When sufficient line has been retrieved, the boat's engine is shut down, and the battle is resumed.

If too much time hasn't elapsed, you can return to your chum line marker, go beyond it a way in the direction it's traveling to take care of a gap, and commence chumming again. The chances are that the chum line won't be lost entirely. You might even find a customer waiting when you return. A few sharks are obliging that way.

If it should occur that two anglers have fish on simultaneously (by rights it shouldn't, if others get their lines out of the water when a buddy has a fish on), and it becomes necessary to chase one's fish down to regain line, the other fisherman may have to be prepared to sacrifice his catch. If that unfortunate can pay out enough line to keep his fish until his companion can retrieve enough line, okay. Otherwise a decision will have to be made to cut either fish loose.

A *tip* for when fighting any strong fish of appreciable size: Don't ever try to "horse" or bully your fish toward the boat. If he should suddenly decide to take off, pop goes the weasel. You'll have to yield line when he demands it, but always you'll maintain resistance with your rod-and-reel drag. You may have to adjust and readjust your drag at intervals, slacking off a bit to compensate for less line on the spool, or tightening it a little when he starts to tire. When you feel decreasing resistance that tells you your fish is tiring, regain line by a series of pumping motions with your rod. Lean back, bringing your rod up near shoulder height. This will pull the fish toward you. Then lean quickly forward, cranking rapidly as you go to regain as much yardage as possible. As your fish is drawn closer to the boat your line will become gradually more vertical. Now you'll modify your pumping technique to lessen strain on the rod tip. When the line comes nearly vertical, modify your lifts to half pumps, bringing the rod up only to about a 45° angle instead of to shoulder height.

Combat goes into its closing stages when you have reeled your beast close enough to the boat that the wire leader breaks water. There should be someone standing by the gunnel to seize it. And whoever executes this step, called wiring-up, had better be wearing work gloves. Wire leader can mutilate bare hands.

As the battle approaches its wiring-up phase, three items should be in readiness.

One is a flying gaff. This is a gaff whose head or hook is designed to pull free from its handle when planted in a fish. To its hook should be secured about 10 feet of ³⁄₁₆-to-¼-inch nylon rope, the eye splice at its other end already on a bitt. To try to put this line on a bitt after a shark has been gaffed is not only difficult but downright dangerous. The holder could be yanked overboard or slammed against a gunnel with considerable force.

The other two items are a tail rope and a straight or fixed-head gaff. The former is a 10-foot length of ½-inch nylon rope with a freely running but dependable noose at one end and an eye splice at the other for placing on a bitt or cleat. This will hold the fish after gaffing. The straight gaff, with a needle-sharp hook, will be used to lift the fish's tail so the tail rope's noose can be slipped over it and pulled tight.

Tip. Every serious shark hunter carries an extra flying gaff. A satisfactory size for a flying gaff's head is a span of about 6 inches. Larger ones will do, but in the cases of small or very slender sharks they could encircle the body instead of penetrating it. It's also wise to carry 3 or 4 straight gaffs in sizes 3 to 4 inches across their hooks, and a couple of spare tail ropes.

WRAPPING IT UP   Whoever seizes the wire leader must be braced for last-minute power surges by the fish. If they occur—a distinct

possibility—he'll have to release his grasp or go for an im-
promptu swim. The angler also should be alert to such developments. He might have to battle his shark a while longer before
the leader again breaks water.

Once the wire is seized and it's apparent the shark isn't going
anywhere, someone sinks the flying gaff, using a hooking motion
to drive its point into the fish's back just behind the dorsal fin.
(*Don't* gaff a shark forward of the dorsal fin. With tension on
the gaff line and his tail still in the water, you might suddenly
find your toothy opponent in the boat with you.) The hook will
dig in, coming free of its handle, and the fish will be secured by
the gaff line on a bitt. If the shark rolls over and over in the leader
or threshes about violently during this and other landing procedures, let him simmer down before progressing to the next step.

Tip: Dusky and brown sharks have exceptionally tough hides.
For such species, therefore, a kind of reverse gaffing motion is
suggested. Instead of having the flying gaff's hook in the usual

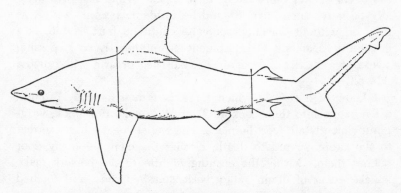

BROWN or SAND-BAR SHARK (*Carcharhinus milberti*)

position for planting in the fish's back, turn it upside down and
sink it in the sharks' underside in an area about opposite the
big dorsal fin.

Meanwhile, someone stands by with a straight gaff. This instrument is swung to hook into the base of the shark's tail, the
operator then lifting that fin out of water so a tail rope can be

slipped over it. When its noose is pulled tight and his powerful "propeller" is lifted out of the water, a fish is incapacitated considerably.

Now it becomes a matter of shifting the shark to the boat's ginpole and hoisting him out of the water with it. Ideally a ginpole should be equipped with two-sheave (wheel) blocks. Three sheaves in a pulley can cause the ropes to bind on each other if a shark threshes about. The shark is hoisted by means of a line around his tail, tail first, until his head is clear of the sea. A belly rope—a half inch or so, nylon—run around his middle and the ginpole will keep him from threshing and bouncing around. *Be careful when you put it on.* Sharks can turn and bite in a flash.

A WARNING AND SOME PROBLEMS *Never—repeat, never—bring a live shark into a boat.* Sharks are very tenacious of life. Some can remain alive for two hours or more out of water. A shark brought into a boat might die quietly after a minor commotion on hitting the deck. What's more likely, he'll appear to be dead but actually be very much alive. Should he suddenly become active, as they do without warning, someone could be hurt. A bite is a possibility. Damage to equipment is another. Even a passing swipe of a shark's hide against a bare leg or arm will rub the skin off.

I know of a case in which some fishermen foolishly brought a live mako into their cockpit. There the mako ran amok, wriggling violently all over the place. The anglers beat a hasty retreat to the cabin, scared to death, closing the companionway door behind them. During the ensuing nightmare the berserk mako knocked cans of chum galley west, smashed rods, and fetched up against the companionway with such force as to tear its knob out by the roots. The petrified anglers thought he was coming after them. Eventually the shark quieted down and they somehow managed to get him overboard. They were lucky. No one was injured. But that cockpit was a shambles.

By rights you shouldn't fish for sharks on open ocean in a little boat or in one not fully outfitted for big game fishing. And that outfitting should include a ginpole. If you can't haul your sharks

e water as a means of killing them you're going to have
...is.†

...cking a ginpole, there are a couple of alternatives.

One is to endeavor to get your shark out of water by lashing him to the outside of the hull—suspending him horizontally, with ropes around his head, middle, and tail. This is a tricky procedure at best. If you aren't skilled at it you could be wooing disaster. Furthermore, even if you do manage to get the beast securely lashed to the boat's side out of water it will be like having a giant rasp against the boat. His rough hide will do a job on the hull. Not only that, but he'll be in the way.

Another alternative is to get a tail rope on him and tow him backward to port. If the ride is long enough, towing that way may or may not kill him, but having to return to the dock will spell an end to that day's shark action.

Maybe you're asking, "What about killing the shark, then bringing him into the boat?" My reply is, if you can be *positive* the fish is dead and/or he's small enough to put in a fish box, it might be all right. But I still advise against bringing any shark into a boat. Sharks often are tough to kill, and not enough fishermen know how to be sure those rascals are dead.

Several ways to dispatch sharks have been tried: (1) repeated clubbing on the head; (2) towing backward so the fish literally drowns; (3) stabbing in the head, gill area, or body with a knife or icepick; (4) shooting with a pistol, rifle, or shotgun; and (5) simply letting him hang with his head out of water until he gives up the ghost.

You can forget methods (1) through (3). The chances are that clubbing will only give him a headache, slow him down temporarily. Not dependable. Towing backward works fairly quickly with a few, but takes an hour or more with others. Which is all right if you don't mind spending the time and fuel. Stabbing in the head generally isn't effective unless you hit the brain. And that isn't easy. The target area is comparatively small. Further, for safety's sake the weapon should be on a stick or pole of suit-

† Ginpoles have load limitations, and you should know the maximum weight capacity of yours. It's conceivable that you might one day conquer a shark either too heavy or too long to handle with that vertical boom, in which case you'll have to make do with an alternate procedure.

able length for you to stand clear. Stabbing in the gills w..
shark is still in the water will do a job, but it's slow and ca..
tract other sharks to tear your catch to shreds. Doing it aboard
boat is dangerous and messy. As for the body, I think you'd have
to stab your arms off before it took effect.

What about shooting? To begin with, it isn't sportsmanlike,
and it automatically disqualifies any fish in contention for IGFA
recognition. Second, it requires a fairly high-powered weapon,
and it doesn't do the job quickly unless you hit him in the brain.
I've seen a blue shark keep right on feeding in a chum slick after
being drilled completely through the body by a high-powered
rifle. Forget a .22-caliber weapon unless you can hit him smack
in the brain. The same goes for a shotgun, although a blast in the
gill area will give a shark pause for thought. Pistols are no good
except at close range and in the brain.

There are other problems. Most important is safety. Anyone
handling a weapon should have a cool head. Things can get
lively and exciting when a shark is brought alongside. Moreover,
a weapon's safety should be kept on until it is over the side and
aimed. With rifles there's a possibility of ricocheting bullets, a
distinct danger to any other boats that might be nearby (they
sometimes move closer to watch the landing). Let me tell you,
it isn't easy to hit a vital spot when the boat is bobbing and a
shark is threshing alongside. Still further, there's always a chance,
especially with a scattergun, of severing the leader. Don't snicker.
It happens. Last but not least, I don't think it's smart to have any
kind of loaded weapons aboard when there are kids.

In short, if shooting is to be used at all to dispatch sharks it
should be done only as a last resort. Preferably it shouldn't be
done at all.

How to kill a shark, then? Well, we've sure narrowed down
the methods. The only reasonably sure way left is to hang him
out of water until he dies. It takes time. Give him plenty. In the
event that you capture a specimen too large for that, your alternative is to tow him home backward. Just be sure the bitt taking
the tow line is strong enough.

There's only one way I know to determine with any certainty
that a shark is dead. Have everyone stand clear. Using a suitably
long stick or pole, nudge him directly in the eye. If there's any

movement at all, even if confined to the eye and only slight, that shark is still alive. Hang him up or leave him alone and try again later.

TARGETS AND SEASONS Drift chumming will account for many different kinds of sharks. The species and numbers of each naturally depend upon areas and seasons. The potential is great on both counts.

Although the critters are represented in cold waters by at least one species, the Greenland or gurry shark, kinds and quantities are greatest in temperate to tropical zones. It can be said, again speaking broadly, that variety increases with permanently warmer waters.

From the standpoint of sheer numbers of anglers, the biggest marine fishing theater in the United States, if not in the world, is that segment of the Atlantic Coast from New England to and including southernmost New Jersey. Let me cite that as a regional example of the kinds of sharks available to sport fishermen, together with their seasons.

Along that stretch of seaboard the over-all shark angling season extends from about late May or early June (given seasonably mild weather) on through September. Water temperatures, along with food supplies, play a big part; and with a reasonably mild autumn there can still be scatterings of sharks around offshore on into October. The peak period is from late June through August.

The region's list of potential opponents embraces the following:

1. *Makos.* Never too numerous (or, for that matter, plentiful enough), but present in worthwhile numbers during normal seasons. Any time from about mid- or late June into September. *Tip:* August and early September can be productive.

2. *Blues.* For numbers, the most common species in this region. Generally all over the place during the summer. Watch for them at or near the surface.

3. *Whites.* Most often just a few, and scattered at that. Any time after about the middle of June on through July and August. *Tip:* Keep your ears open for reports of pilot whales ("potheads") offshore. Sometimes the presence of white sharks seems linked

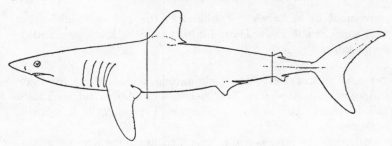

MAKO SHARK (*Isurus oxyrinchus*)

with them. Don't tangle with whites unless you have the heaviest tackle and know your business.

4. *Browns.* Fairly common, at least in Long Island's inshore-offshore ocean waters. Late spring on through the summer. *Tip:* I believe these sharks go in and out of Long Island's South Shore inlets to do their food shopping. You might try around the outside mouths of those gateways.

5. *Duskies.* Not overly plentiful, but certainly not rare either. A summer species. July and August probably best.

6. *Porbeagles.* Although there can be good numbers of them, they appear to be more restlessly migratory than the others. As a result, their showing within a given section of this region often is limited to about a month, even less, after which they probably move on. Offshore of Montauk they're usually the first of the warmer-water sharks to appear, along about the first or second week of May. They're caught in fair numbers for two or three weeks, then only occasionally thereafter for the remainder of the summer. If they follow a typical pattern, their appearances would be earlier to the south of Montauk and later in waters to the north. *Tip:* Porbeagles are members of a little group called mackerel sharks (along with the mako and white) because of their fondness for those fish. Conceivably, therefore, their appearances along progressively more northerly parts of the coast are timed with spring mackerel runs.

7. *Threshers.* Never really plentiful in this region, and catches are comparatively small. July, August, and early September are probably best.

8. *Tigers.* They're a tropical species. The scattered few that wander this far north are stragglers. You hear of one being boated occasionally—very occasionally. If there is a best bet as regards seasons hereabouts, it should be in August when offshore waters have had all summer to warm. Theoretically, southern New Jersey should be better than Long Island, with chances becoming even slimmer north of the island.

9. *Hammerheads.* There are five known species on the Atlantic Coast, including that monster, the great hammerhead, and the smaller common hammerhead. By and large, these sharks seem to favor tropical and semitropical waters over temperate regions. In comparison with other species, relatively few are caught by sport fishermen in that stretch from New Jersey to New England. Again, southern Jersey might have the best potential. July and August should be the months.

10. *Sand Tigers.* A common species hereabouts, and they can reach lengths of five and six feet. For some reason they seem reluctant to take hooks, and they're not a big item. Spring, summer, and fall are seasons with potential.

Many kinds of sharks are potential angling objectives. California has its Pacific mako plus several others. The Atlantic Coast from Delaware southward offers species mentioned above, and farther south, in that vast oceanic expanse that includes the Bahamas, Florida, and the Caribbean, there are still other species such as the silky, lemon, and blacktip sharks. The Gulf of Mexico has its variety too. And so it goes. If you follow procedures discussed in this book you'll be able to cope with any or all of them.

A king among sharks anywhere he's found is the mako. He's fast, powerful, aggressive, tough, and full of thunder and lightning in combat. Those qualities, coupled with his leaping ability, make him just about the most desirable shark. That's why bonus points usually are given for makos in shark tournaments.

Before we leave the subject of shark fishing I want to inject a note about double lines.

You'll hear about and see a double line used in fishing for many kinds of large battlers. All this consists of is a doubling of the line for about fifteen to thirty feet, according to IGFA regulations, above the swivel. Now, this adds strength to the terminal tackle system, but only when at least a couple of turns of double line are on the reel spool. Otherwise, the combination is only as strong as the single line. You can see why.

A double line offers an advantage when a large fish—tuna, marlin, shark, or whatever—is brought alongside for gaffing. With a few turns on the reel spool, a double line provides strength to hold against last-minute power surges and unruliness. Theoretically, in the case of sharks it offers another advantage, and that is a small extra measure of protection against chafing by the beasts' sandpaper hide. But this advantage is slight at best. If abrasion should cause one half of the double line to part, you're no better off than if you'd had a single line.

AT THE DOCK   Don't be careless when unloading sharks. Whenever possible, have them dead before taking them ashore for weighing, photographing, exhibiting, etc.

It's always wise to keep spectators clear. They're often bold in their ignorance. I've seen them, usually for the family's benefit, go over to a shark and open the brute's mouth to show the teeth, never questioning that the fish might still be alive. You have to be especially careful about youngsters. In their curiosity they have no fear at all. To really play it safe, it's for the good of all hands to give each shark that eye-prodding test before unloading. If there's any hint of life, warn spectators to keep clear until the fish finally does die or you can hasten the process with an icepick or knife in the brain.

Even dead sharks can cause injury if handled carelessly. I'm talking about their mouth and teeth. If you want to lift the mouth open to inspect the teeth, do it with the snout. Keep your fingers and hands out of the mouth. Quite often in dead sharks, particularly newly deceased ones, there's a nervous reflex action that can close the jaws like a trap. They might not amputate a finger, but those needle-sharp teeth can inflict painful punctures and cuts. Added to that is a danger of infection. I certainly wouldn't stick a hand inside a shark's mouth unless it was propped open with a block of wood, and even then I'd be wary of those teeth. If you must retrieve your hook (it really isn't worth it), go in the back door, through the gill region.

It should go without saying that the shark should be as dead as he ever will be before you start butchering the carcass or extracting souvenirs.

BONUSES Along with the sport of battling them, sharks offer sport fishermen other rewards.

Least troublesome of these are photographs. Pictures of the sharks you conquer not only are lasting mementos of trips, but also interesting conversation pieces. Most people are fascinated by them. Take along a couple to a party you suspect will be dull.

Shark teeth in themselves are eye-arresting souvenirs. They can be cut from the jaws, which are only cartilage. A superior method is to *carefully* boil the jaws to free them. You can exhibit your shark teeth by cementing them to a display board, with labels as to species, weights, dates, etc., or by imbedding them in clear plastic (there are home kits for this). They also can be fashioned into novel jewelry items such as tie clips and necklaces.

For an unusual, awesome trophy, the jaws can be dissected from the head—teeth left in place, of course—and prepared for mounting on a suitable plaque. Also on the plaque goes a small plate giving such data as kind of shark, size, where and by whom caught, etc.

Preparing head mounts and whole-fish mounts is a job for professional taxidermists. There are many such pros, some of whom specialize in fishes. To locate one of these specialists, inquire locally at a tackle shop or on the waterfront, or consult a classified telephone directory. Skippers usually know of one. A few of the larger taxidermy outfits have agents in key sport-fishing ports. The best and easiest procedure is to place the specimen in their hands. They'll take care of all details.

ON THE TABLE A big bonus from shark fishing is food. Regrettably, though, it's a benefit often overlooked or ignored.

Shark meat is eaten in many foreign countries, including England, Italy, Denmark, and Japan. Among species mentioned as edible are makos, threshers, porbeagles, duskies, hammerheads, dogfish (popularly, but erroneously, called "sand sharks"), blues, and whites.

The meat is not only nutritious, it can be every bit as flavorful as that from more widely used market fishes. In some cases, I believe, shark meat has a more delicate taste and is even superior. Makos, threshers, porbeagles, and dogfish have been cited as particularly good eating, along with meat from hammerheads and small duskies. My friend Jack Casey, a federal fisheries biologist specializing in shark research, comments in his booklet *Anglers' Guide to Sharks of the Northeastern United States, Maine to Chesapeake Bay* (U. S. Bureau of Sport Fisheries & Wildlife Circular No. 179, U. S. Government Printing Office, Washington, D.C. 20402): "All sharks found off the northeastern coast are edible. Elaborate preparations are not necessary, but culinary imagination is a helpful ingredient."

According to taste, some species are better eating than others. Personally, I don't think you'll ever go wrong with mako meat. Broiled as steaks, it's excellent. Smoked, it's a gourmet's item.

There's also this comment in the book *Guide to Commercial Shark Fishing in the Caribbean Area*, originally issued several years ago by the U. S. Department of the Interior: "Most shark flesh, if properly handled, can be made into tasty, wholesome food. It can be used fresh or salted. Well-prepared salted shark is equal in flavor to good-grade salted cod." An analysis of meat from a common species of dogfish, *Squalus acanthias*, mentioned in another report, said that it offers more protein and energy value than milk, eggs, oysters, and fishes such as mackerel and salmon.

Tip: Younger, smaller specimens are preferable to their older, larger brethren for eating purposes.

I won't take it upon myself to declare that *all* species of sharks are edible. They might very well be, but I don't know. Not enough have been consumed that extensively. I can tell you that several different kinds are edible; and the list undoubtedly will lengthen as fishermen become more adventuresome in dining. In any case, it seems a pity that this enormous source of food is largely ignored, especially in a world where thousands of people are protein-starved.

Shark meat can be prepared for the table in just about any of the culinary procedures employed for other kinds of fishes. It also can be kippered or, as already noted, salted or smoked.

Shark meat lends itself to steaking and broiling, like halibut and swordfish. It can be cloaked in an egg and cracker-crumb mixture and deep-fried, like flounder and sole fillets. It can be cooked in a chowder, like cod and haddock. It can be pan-fried like any other kind of fish. You can serve it plain or submerged in fancy sauces. It can be boiled, cooled, broken into little pieces, and served on a bed of lettuce as a seafood cocktail or salad, accompanied by mayonnaise, tartar sauce, or a lively concoction compounded from catsup and horseradish.

Another palate-tempting possibility is smoked shark. So far I've eaten only mako prepared in this manner, but I believe that any kind of shark with reasonably firm flesh—porbeagle, white, and other species in addition to the mako—should smoke satisfactorily. Try mako for openers. I think you'll agree that it's very tasty.

You might check around to learn if there's a commercial smokehouse in your area. It could come in handy, not only for shark meat, but also for such delicacies as smoked eels, whiting, tuna, white marlin, etc. Or you can construct a simple little smokehouse outside at home. It isn't difficult, but make sure beforehand that there are no local laws against it. Even easier and cheaper, buy one of those small, portable fish and game smoking units marketed nowadays.

And here's an idea: Foist some smoked mako, or, as hot hors d'oeuvres, small shark fish sticks, on friends at a cocktail party. Don't tell them what they're eating. Dream up a wild name such as South African salmon or Tibetan trout. Tell them it's imported, extremely hard to obtain, and awfully expensive. Unless I miss my guess, they'll devour every crumb. Later, if you want, you can break the truth to them. The expressions on their faces should be good for laughs. And if they're honest they'll admit they enjoyed it.

All I can say to you is, if you're a fish eater I'm sure you'll like shark.

Important last-minute bulletin—note: Investigation of the presence of harmful mercury in fishes was continuing as this book went to press. Findings, therefore, were not yet complete. However, evidence gathered at that time by Dr. James E. Alexander, senior research scientist at New York Ocean Science Laboratory, Montauk, pointed to *dangerous* mercury levels in mako meat.

Shark fishermen who eat their catches are urged to keep advised on findings as research continues. Meanwhile, when there's a shred of doubt about the safeness of consuming mako meat—or the flesh of *any* fish, *don't eat it.*

CHAPTER 20

Snappers:
Baygoing Firecrackers

You never hear about rod-'n'-reelers going out of their way to deliberately fish for pocket-size fluke, or midget marlin, or little *anything*, for that matter. Most anglers want their fish as large as possible, and the bigger the better for bragging purposes. If they latch onto any dwarfs of the species it's in the nature of poor luck.

I say you never hear of anglers purposely fishing for small ones. That isn't quite correct. Change that "never" to "hardly ever." An exception is bluefish. Little bluefish, familiarly known as snappers to the hook-and-line fraternity-sorority, are one young-of-the-species that lots of folks, especially youngsters, go out of their way to catch.

Few kinds of angling have such universal appeal for kids as snapper fishing. Comes that time in summer—say, around July or August—when word flashes along the Little People's own grapevine telegraph network that snappers are showing, you'll see them gravitating on foot or aboard bikes toward waterfronts. With a run under way, youngsters of many shapes and sizes, both sexes, stand, sit, squat, kneel, or assume any of the umpteen other positions kids can assume as they line creek and canal banks, perch on docks and piers, sit like gulls on a bay jetty, or bob in rowboats and small outboards to concentrate on the very serious business of jerking young bluefish from the water.

But don't get me wrong. Kids do not have a monopoly on this fun. Their elders like to dangle hooks for snappers too. The fact is that snapper fishing is fun for folks of all ages, eight to eighty . . . and if you happen to be six or ninety, that's all right too. Anyone who tries snappering is likely to return for more. It has a personality all its own.

SAMPLE SIZES Snappers represent the youngest age groups among bluefish—the youngest worth catching, that is.

Back in the chapter on that species I told you how bluefish are arbitrarily catalogued for sizes in an unofficial, flexible sorting. You'll hear occasional differences of opinion as to where one size group leaves off and another begins, with consequent overlapping; but this is of no consequence. The whole business is an informal arrangement anyway. The fish couldn't care less.

On one detail all fishermen agree: Snappers occupy the lowest rung of the bluefish size ladder. These are the juniors of the family—its grammar school kids, you might say. To qualify for the label "snappers" they range up to ¾ pound to 1 pound in lengths to 8 or 10 inches or thereabouts. After that they graduate into high school and become the family's teen-agers, with weights going to maybe 2 or 2½ pounds. Generally we speak of these more advanced individuals as "snapper-blues."

In size, snappers are a far cry from their seagoing big brothers. But don't let the disparity fool you. Snappers are endowed with the same killer instinct, relentless ferocity, and needle-sharp teeth. The only difference is that all these traits are incorporated in a smaller package.

Another habit shared by snappers and adult blues is their gregariousness, their traveling in large schools, like gigantic wolf packs. Again like their big brothers, snappers often move around swiftly in search of food. Victims of the adults' forays are menhaden, herring, and other schooling species. For snappers it's the same picture, miniaturized. The youngsters take on prey more their size, like spearing, killies, and so on.

Only in one major respect, perhaps, do the youngest and older blues differ in their hunting habits, and that is in wariness. Older bluefish tend to be more cautious and, I suspect, smarter. They develop a keener instinct, or maybe they're better attuned to danger, which is why they live to be adults. Snappers, on the other hand, exhibit the brashness of the young of all creatures, including man. Being green, "naïve" kids, they're less wary—more inquisitive and enthusiastic too, no doubt—and will venture boldly into much shallower water than their older kin. Consequently, it's often easier to locate and catch them.

SNAPPER SEASONS It's a paradoxical and unfortunate truth that, for all their importance to our sport and commercial fisheries, we know relatively little about the breeding pattern of blues. This is unfortunate because it directly affects the presence or absence and quantity of snappers.

Some authorities have been of an opinion that bluefish spawn in the ocean along about May or June. This fits in with more recent ideas, which broaden the period to extend from late spring on through July or August, with the usual variations according to regions. And there's a tendency to believe that at least some spawning also occurs in very large bays such as the Chesapeake.

That general timetable, late spring into summer, agrees with fact in one respect at least, because it's around July or August—again depending upon regions (and years)—that we first see baby blues starting to appear in bays. I'm entitled to a hunch, and mine is that bluefish spawn at sea, and perhaps in very big bays and open sounds; and that the babies infiltrate bays and other sheltered waters after a suitable nursery period in the ocean. While out there and still very small they probably can find food among plankton and other tiny organisms. Later, growing rapidly, perhaps they must shift to bays for prey that they're now better able to hunt and that are more suited to their nourishment. Maybe at that age they also favor the warmer waters of bays.

In any event, the babies grow rapidly. Under favorable conditions growth is so rapid as to be noticeable practically from week to week. It's as though they can't wait to grow up to join their elders in carnivals of mayhem. Given adequate food supplies, snappers attain lengths of four to six or seven inches by the end of their first summer, and ten to fifteen inches by that October.

The junior blues can, and sometimes do, start to show in bays and shallow arms of sounds before July is out, if weather is summery enough. At that time, though—and, in fact, during the first stages of their run, no matter when it starts—they're invariably much too small to catch, let alone keep. But growth is so fast that fishermen can afford to be patient for a couple of weeks until sizes improve. Traditionally August and September are snapper angling months. It's then that the midget battlers are at their season's peak for numbers and, especially in September, for sizes. Late July or early August usually launches the real parade of kids trudging or cycling toward waterfronts and into bait depots. This is a sure sign that snappers are in.

A LOT FOR A LITTLE   There's a lot to be said for snappering. It's healthful fun in salt air and sun. Catching fish is a certainty. Good numbers of them too. Snappers can be thicker than bugs under a damp rock. There's also sport, if you use the very lightest gear. On ultralight tackle, snappers are as lively as the dickens. To top it all off, these baby blues are fine eating—better than their bigger brothers, if you want my two cents' worth.

You can look until you're purple in the face and you won't find a kind of fishing that tolerates equipment simpler or cheaper than can be wielded in snappering. That's another of the sport's drawing cards. Still another is that it doesn't require a boat. Snappers can be caught from creek and channel banks, inlet shores, seawalls and bay jetties, piers, bridges, marina docks, and other shoreside structures. Let me hastily add, though, that a boat is a definite advantage; it covers more territory and heightens chances of contacting roving snapper schools.

For anyone who's budget conscious (and who isn't?), one of snapper fishing's stellar attractions is the utter simplicity and attendant inexpensiveness of the tackle needed. If you want you can use a little old handline, but it won't be as much fun as with a really skinny, bendy rod.

You must use the very lightest, most flexible rod you can lay your hands on. A fly rod is good. Ultralight fresh- and salt-water spinning rods and conventional "sticks" will give you some action too. Reels are correspondingly small and simple: a 1/0 for conventional rods, fly and spinning counterparts for the others. Lines are the very lightest. Fifty yards—even twenty-five—are more than enough. A point I'm trying to make here is that you don't have to strip off a lot of the line you may already have on a reel.

There's another outfit, simplest and cheapest of all, that I recommend highly for snappers.

For generations the badge of a snapper fisherman has been a long, very skinny bamboo pole, cut expressly for the purpose. Longer than many surf rods and tapering practically to a point, such a snapper pole practically bends with a breeze, has tremendous flexibility, and—very important—is sensitive to even the daintiest tugs on a bait. It's tough and durable too. Occasionally a bamboo pole will split, and where space is limited it's awkward to store because of its length (ideally it should lie flat when not in use so that it doesn't take a permanent bend), but with reasonable care it should last for many snappering seasons. And it will be the cheapest fishing rod you'll ever buy.

You don't *have* to get one of those bamboo poles, because any kind of light tackle will do. But there's something about a bamboo pole—this is sentiment and nostalgia, I suppose—that seems to make it belong in snapper fishing more than any other kind of tackle. I guess I figure that way because snappering is an old-fashioned sport, and a bamboo pole is an old-fashioned weapon. Someday I may just organize the SFPPOTBPISF—Society For Permanent Preservation Of The Bamboo Pole In Snapper Fishing.

If you choose a bamboo pole you won't need a reel. Your line is tied directly to its end. More about that when we get to rigging.

TERMINAL GEAR You'll require a couple of other items to complete your snapper-catching equipment. One is a float or bobber; the other, of course, is a hook.

Floats or bobbers rigged in snapper fishing used to be fashioned from cork. Nowadays they use plastic. Actually, they can be of any material that will float. A large, ordinary cork will do; or, in a pinch, a piece of styrofoam. The main thing is that it be buoyant enough to support the rig and remain visible at the surface. Store-bought floats, round and egg-shaped, can be obtained at any tackle shop.

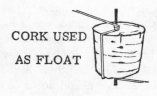

CORK USED
AS FLOAT

STANDARD
SNAPPER FLOAT

The float has two purposes. First and foremost, it suspends your rig at the desired depth below the surface. Second, it indicates when you have a bite. When a snapper fiddles with your bait he'll make the float dance. When he takes the bait, your float will vanish below.

Hooks for snappers *must be small*. The fish are little; so are their mouths. Hooks must match. Snapper hooks should have fairly long shanks; otherwise a short leader of fine wire is required. Like their big brothers, snappers come armed with sharp teeth that can sever line or regular leader material.

The Carlisle is one pattern rigged for snappers. It has a fairly long shank. Another design is the so-called Bridgeport snapper hook. Various other patterns also are used. If you don't have a memory for names, don't lose any sleep. Just ask a tackle emporium man or fishing station operator for snapper hooks.

More important than designs are hook sizes. Here you should gauge them to the sizes of the snappers currently running. In general, sizes go from about a No. 6 or so for the littlest fellows up to a No. 3 for the largest snappers. As in the case of flounders and other finned targets with small mouths, you'll be better off using a hook that's a bit undersized rather than one that's too big. Rig a hook that's too large and you might as well try to catch them with a tennis racket or a polo mallet. Obviously, they can't be caught on a hook that's too large to wrap a mouth around. Right?

Here again, don't be too concerned. If you're at all in doubt, specify snapper hooks when you buy them.

RIGGING AND BAITING Terminal tackle is the same whether you wield a bamboo pole or more elaborate equipment.

If you have a long-shank hook—I suggest sticking with this type for snappers—rig about three feet of light leader material between it and your line. It can be gut, monofilament, nylon, or whatever; and a mist color is good because of relatively lower visibility. If you persist in using a short-shank hook you'll have to interpose a foot or two of fine wire leader between it and your line. Connection of leader to line doesn't require a swivel.

Ready-made floats come with a centerpost or other arrangement for attachment to the line. Some have a couple of loops of wire to facilitate the process. If you're improvising with a piece of cork or styrofoam, shove a lollypop stick or wooden match through it to serve as a centerpost. A simpler technique here is to punch a hole through your improvised bobber and run the line through it, taking two or three turns around the float to secure it at the desired height. Or you can make a knife cut into the material, force your line into the cut, then take a turn or two around it. Either way, you rig your hook as before. Best is a float that allows for adjustment of its position on the line. You may have to change it from time to time.

Snappers do a lot of their feeding at or near the surface. Often

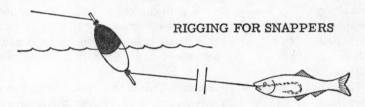

RIGGING FOR SNAPPERS

you'll be able to detect schools in the process by the rippling they cause. However you attach your float, do it so that your baited hook will be suspended about three feet below the surface. That's a good starting depth. Later, if necessary, the float can be adjusted so that the hook will hang closer to the surface or deeper. I wouldn't go too deep—say, no more than four feet— at the start.

If a bamboo pole is your weapon, tie your line to its skinny end, right near the tip. Just be sure to use enough line so that you can hold the pole at comfortable angle and reach the water, then add a couple of extra feet to let the float drift away a short distance. Your line length naturally will be determined by whether you're fishing from a rowboat or other small craft, close to the water, or from a low creek bank, or from a dock or bulkhead that's quite high above the water. Stages of the tide will have something to say too about how much line you'll need when fishing from shoreside structures. In any case, don't be excessive in the amount of line you use. That will make it more difficult to land your fish.

Snappers dine mainly on fishes smaller than themselves, vary-

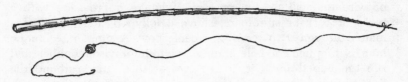

SNAPPER POLE

ing their menu with little shrimp and other critters of gulpable size. On hooks they'll accept small mummichogs or killies, alive or dead, and pieces of shrimp. I suppose bits of squid would get results too. I've always stayed with the old reliable for snappers, a spearing or silversides. You can't beat spearing as snapper bait. I believe spearing are superior to killies for snappers because their silvery bodies are better eye-catchers. Killies are somber green.

Spearing are sold in packages, which is the most common, convenient way to get them. Sometimes you can buy them alive at rowboat liveries and bait stations. Or, if you're ambitious, you can invest in a small hand seine, take along a friend, and net your own in shallow waters along bay shores. Packaged spearing are satisfactory. They'll do the job. Live spearing are preferable, however, because they're fresher. You'll never go wrong in any kind of fishing with the freshest possible bait. You won't be able to keep spearing alive on your hook—not for long, anyway—but you'll know that they're really fresh. The only trouble is that you won't always be able to buy live spearing.

Tip: Thaw your packaged spearing before use. A board-stiff bait fish doesn't look too interesting even to a hungry snapper. Thawing will bring back a certain amount of lifelike flexibility to give them a little body motion in the water. Another thing: Frozen baits may contain ice, which gives them buoyancy. In spearing it might be just enough to make them ride higher than desired.

You can impale a spearing on your hook in various ways. One is to thrust the hook in through the fish's mouth, feeding its point and barb far enough in to hide them inside the body. Another technique is to run the hook's point into the body under, and just ahead of, the tail and have it emerge at the body's center. Then you draw the spearing's tail up on the hook's shank, and feed the point in through the mouth to emerge again at the gills. Some anglers simply hook the little fish through the back, burying its point and barb inside. But I don't care for that method. It presents the bait in an awkward fashion. I prefer the first technique.

Snappers themselves can be used as bait if you run short of spearing or want to stretch your supply. Cut a small, narrow strip from the silvery belly and try that. Feed one end up on the hook's shank, then bury the point in the other end.

If you're baiting with live killies, use small ones and hook them just as you would for fluke (see the chapter on fluke).

Tip: Sometimes a shiny bit of foil, such as that from a pack of cigarettes, wrapped tightly around your hook's shank serves as an added attraction. It glitters, you see.

Did you ask about artificials for snappers? Even if you didn't, the answer is yes, they can be rigged. Small spinners and tiny spoons, such as those made for spinfishing and armed with hooks of appropriate size, will take snappers when cast into the right places. Slow trolling of small spinners and streamer flies also has been known to account for baby blues. In such techniques, though, you won't use a bamboo pole outfit, but will go to your other, regular tackle.

ULTRALIGHT TACKLE SPECIAL   Are you a light tackle *aficionado?* I have a lively stunt for you. You'll need a salt- or fresh-water fly rod and reel, with very light line to match. Rig as before, with a float. To complete your gear you'll need two killy cars, some spearing, and a chumpot filled with ground mossbunkers.

Before I give the details I must inject words of caution. *This stunt is not for children or nonswimmers. If you try it, always be careful of holes in the bottom. Feel your way slowly and cautiously as you go. Beware of ledges that drop off suddenly into deeper water, a distinct possibility along channels. Pay heed to strong currents.*

So much for the warning signs. Here we go.

Select a likely-looking place along a bay shore, creek, or channel, or on a sandy point where you can *safely* wade in water up to your waist. Put your 'bunker-filled chumpot in one killy car.

Tie this car to your waist with just enough line to let it float out away from you a few yards, yet not escape. In your second car, place the bait. (The water will help thaw it if it's frozen stiff.) This car is tied to your middle with a short piece of cord to keep it handy.

The procedure is to wade out from shore, letting your chumbearing killy car drift out away from you and allowing your baited rig to drift right along with it. Keep your rig close enough to the floating chumpot to take advantage of its contents as they seep out into the water. If there are snappers in that area you should see response in short order as your chum attracts them. With a fly rod you'll enjoy lively sport.

In this version of snapper fishing you can wield any kind of ultralight tackle. I suggest fly gear for maximum action, but spinning equipment is fine. You also can fish with one of those long bamboo poles, if it isn't too awkward for you to handle under the circumstances. For this fishing you might want to lop off a couple of feet—from the thicker end—for better wielding.

PLACES WITH PROMISE   During a run, snappers schools are scattered all over bays, coves, harbors, and other waterways. Often they're restless and moving fast as they seek or pursue food, turning up in one place one minute, then in another location some distance away the next minute. When they're really on the move they have to be hunted. This is when a boat offers a definite advantage over a shoreside location. But if you don't have access to a boat, don't stew. When snappers are plentiful, as they frequently are, good catches are made from shore.

Snappers often feed at the surface, creating a disturbance like full-fledged bluefish. And there may be seagulls around, freeloading on scraps. Keep an eye open for such signs.

Incidentally, there's no law against trying some chum for snappers at times other than in that stunt I mentioned earlier with the fly rod and killy cars. It could be helpful when the schools are scattered. You'll have to gauge the speed and strength of the existing current, though. It might be too fast and strong for practical chumming. Ground mossbunkers are one chum you might try. Although I've never used it for snappers, that canned jack mackerel (broken into tiny bits and mixed with sea water) and cats' fish food might work too. Small pieces of spearing, alone or as a supplement to some other chum, should help too.

When a tide is just past the halfway mark and climbing toward high water, snappers frequently will run up into creeks. These "cricks" are areas with potential. If you can find a spot where the crick makes a sharp bend, so much the better. Spearing and killies like to get in out of a tidal thrust, and they'll gather in the quieter water of the lee of such bends. Snappers are quite aware of this. You can stand on a bank or beach and let the current carry your rig toward the point of shore at the bend, or anchor your boat so that the rig drifts toward it.

When snappers are abundant you're likely to find them distributed over shoal areas and shellfish beds. But usually the more productive locations are around piers, ends of sand bars, points of land, and other sites where tidal currents are brisk enough to create little eddies and swirls as they rush by, and where water is roughly nine or ten feet to twenty-five or thirty feet deep at low tide. Areas around the inside mouths of inlets, bridge abutments, entrances to channels, junctions of channels or of channels and creeks, and the mouths of tidal rivers also offer promise under those conditions. What happens in such places is that currents not only convey little food fishes and tumble them about in confusion in eddies and swirls, but also churn up the bottom, dislodging tiny organisms that attract small fishes such as killies and spearing; and they, in turn, draw snappers.

Places with quieter water in the vicinity of piers and docks can produce too. If you've ever walked along a wharf or bulkhead flanking the relatively still waters of a canal or sheltered cove you've probably noticed schools of little fishes wandering about. They can attract snappers. The proof is the fishing for baby blues on municipal docks.

A canal dock where there's some tidal action can be good too. Examples are the docks and bulkheads strung out along Shinnecock Canal at Canoe Place (Hampton Bays), L.I. Shinnecock Canal links a chain of bays on Long Island's South Shore with the famed Peconics, and it's a first-class snapper fishing place. Anglers of all ages line its shores when a snapper run is in progress.

How to Catch Salt-water Fish

You'll also find that oceanfront piers can be productive locations at the height of a season—if you can find such a pier. The reasons are the same as for waters around sandbars, points of land, etc. Fast-moving tidal currents bear food. Snappers are alert to that, and wait for tidbits just beyond the eddies.

Every angling "rule" has its exception(s). But we can speak broadly and say that a generally productive time for snapper fishing is from about the midpoint of an incoming tide—say, about three hours before the flood stage—until approximately two hours after high water. Snappers tend to be more active during that period, you see.

GET THAT SKILLET READY! (Mama's little baby loves snappers.) Baby bluefish are delicious eating. I'd rather dine on them than on full-grown blues any day. Just thinking about them makes the salivary tide rise in my mouth.

All you need do to prepare snappers for cooking is gut 'em, scale 'em lightly, and cut off their heads and tails. When they're dressed, toss 'em into a frying pan with plenty of butter. I suppose they could be rolled in an egg and cracker crumb mixture before frying in a pan or hot deep fat, but I don't go for that "overcoat" on any kind of fish. Who needs it?

In my book, one of the most delightful ways to eat snappers is to cook them over a wood fire on a beach, then engulf them right there in the salt air.

CHAPTER 21

Striped Bass:
The "Addict" Makers

It borders on the impertinent to attempt to tell all about this extremely popular game fish in only a chapter. Forsooth, as they used to exclaim in ye olde days, 'tis difficult to compleatly cover this fine fishe in an entire booke.

What I'll do, therefore, is provide you with a distillate of salient details. First I'm going to tell you things about the species that will help you to understand Old Linesides. Then I'll add useful information about methods employed to catch the rascal. All this will swing the odds in your favor so you won't come home skunked, at least not every time.

Let me warn you, right at the outset, that striped bass fishing is invariably a gamble. It isn't one of the easier kinds of angling, because striped bass can be extremely unpredictable and maddeningly frustrating. But the rewards are great, not only in action and personal satisfaction, but also on a dinner plate. All of which adds up to the reasons striper hunting can get under your skin and make you an incurable fishing nut.

Now, if you still want to proceed, more power to you. But if you find that stripers have you biting your nails and talking to yourself, don't come chasing after me, sniveling and rubbing your runny nose on my sleeve.

PROFILE The striped bass is a ruggedly handsome fish. If you'll step into our aquarium here and glance at the profile sketch as we progress, I'll point up identification details.

Note that this species is rather stout-bodied. Look at the head. It's large, proportionately. This head comes equipped with a mouth of generous capacity and well-developed jaws, the lower of which projects slightly. Mouth size is a detail of importance

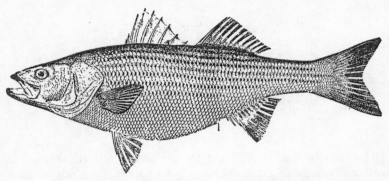

STRIPED BASS (*Roccus saxatilis*)

to fishermen, because it means that this bass can accept rather large baits and artificials. Our friend is nicely endowed with fins. On his back are two dorsals, approximately equal in length, but separate and distinct. His caudal fin or tail is well developed and characterized by a fairly deep, thick base and a markedly concave trailing edge.

As among so many fishes, the striper's color scheme is subject to certain variations among individuals, with age playing a part. In the main, though, it goes like this: Topside he's an olive greenish, greenish blue, or steel blue (sometimes so dark as to be almost black). Occasionally there are brown and grayish brown variations too. Farther down on the sides, the topside color changes to silvery or grayish silver, not infrequently with a brassy sheen. The belly is silvery, silver-white, or white. His fins have dusky tinges.

Cardinal among identification details are the longitudinal body markings that give the critter his name. On an average there are seven or eight of these narrow stripes running horizontally all along the back and sides. Sooty or smoky in color, they're formed by markings on the scales. The topmost stripe or two are most distinct. The others become progressively lighter and less defined.

A physical detail of magnetic interest to fishermen is the sizes striped bass attain. Drs. Henry Bigelow and William Schroeder mention definite record of specimens in the 125-pound class (!), of which "several" (!!) were commercially caught off Edenton, N.C., in April of 1891. Also noted by the same authorities are a 112-pounder, "which must have been at least 6 feet long," captured near Orleans, Mass., many years ago, and a 100½-pounder reported for Casco Bay, Me., quite a while back. They too must have been commercial fish.

If such huge stripers exist today, it isn't being proved by sport fishermen. Even the largest taken by rod-and-reelers are well under 100 pounds. But that's not to take anything away from the famous IGFA world-record 73-pounder extracted from Massachusetts waters by Charles B. Church 'way back in 1913. For decades Charley Church's king defied dethroning. The weight was matched a few years ago by another Massachusetts fish; but, alas, that bass had to be disqualified for official recognition, since IGFA rules had been violated.

Barring a new world record contender that could come down the pike, the largest stripers in sport-fishing catches are in the 60-pound class. Rhode Island has produced a few of these; so have Massachusetts, New Jersey, and New York. Sport-caught stripers in the 50-pound bracket, on the other hand, are far from uncommon. Anglers who have spent years in unsuccessful attempts to land such lunkers may challenge that declaration, but catches support it.

By and large, though, most of sport-caught stripers fall within a broad range extending from "shorts," up through small school fish of 4 or 5 pounds to 10 or 12, to individuals tipping scales at 30 to more than 40 pounds. Many fishermen are happy to nail stripers in the teens or 20s. For newcomers' benefit it should be mentioned that shorts are those bass under the legal minimum keeping size (16 inches from tip of snout to fork of tail in New York State, for example). You'll encounter a lot of those youngsters. Check on the minimum keeping length in your state.

The younger, smaller stripers commonly are nicknamed "schoolies" because of their habit of traveling in large groups. Size classification of stripers to qualify for this nickname is very flexible. Technically, any striped bass traveling in groups of appreciable numbers could be dubbed schoolies. Although schools can contain a mixture of sizes, including some hefties, the term "schoolies" in common use is intended to indicate smaller fish, those ranging from shorts up into, say, the teens and 20s.

BREEDING AND GROWTH   Of considerable importance to anglers is the fact that striped bass are anadromous, which is to say they spend most of their lives in salt water, but run up into fresh water to spawn. Catadromous fishes are the other way around. They spend much of their lives in fresh water, but run to sea to breed.

Female stripers are ready to reproduce when they mature at ages 4 to 6. Spawning takes place in the spring, with April to June being a peak period. As the time for breeding nears, males and females seek estuaries and tidal rivers, moving into brackish, then fresh, water. In spawning migrations they sometimes travel considerable distances upstream. In the Alabama River system, it's reported, they've been encountered as far as 300 miles from the nearest salt water. In California's Sacramento River they've been found 250 miles from the sea. Travels of 50 to 100 miles upstream in other rivers are known. In New York's Hudson River they've been known to journey all the way north to the capital city of Albany, roughly a 160-mile jaunt.

Each female may have anywhere from a few lovers to 30 or more in attendance at spawning, whereupon she shows her appreciation by being very prolific. Small females may discharge about 5,000 to 10,000 or 11,000 eggs. Their larger sisters can turn out 1,000,000 to 5,000,000 (for a 50-pounder). It's been said that a big, very conscientious lady might release up to 10,000,000. The eggs are fertilized in the water by the males.

Food supply is the prime factor determining their early growth. Bass fry of a particular year checked in Chesapeake Bay enlarged from 1 and a fraction inches in June to 3 and a fraction inches by the end of that summer. A batch of studied Hudson River fry showed about the same growth rate. Another study of Chesapeake Bay youngsters revealed lengths of 3¾ inches to as much as 8½ inches by their first birthday.

Here are some samples of subsequent growth rates, noted for Connecticut and Hudson River stripers: At age 2, 11 to 11½ inches that spring, adding another ½ inch or so by June, increasing to 14½ inches in October; at age 3, 13¾ inches in the spring, 18 inches by that October; and at age 4, 18¾ to 20¾ inches between springtime and autumn. Among Pacific Coast stripers, it has been calculated that 20-pounders are about 7 years old, while 30-pounders are 10 to 11; 40-pound individuals are 14, and 50-pounders are 17 or 18. A 1913 bulletin of the New York Zoological Society mentions a striper in the old New York Aquarium that lived to be 23 years old.

My friend Ed Migdalski at Yale has compiled an approximate length-weight ratio table that will give you an idea of the poundage of your catches if you have a tape measure (and you should have, because of legal minimum keeping sizes) but no scale:

Length in Inches	Weight in Pounds
12 to 13	¾
18 to 20	2¾ to 3
24	5
30 to 32	10 to 15
33 to 36	18 to 20
43	30
47, 48	40
50 to 51	50

(Above table from *Angler's Guide to the Salt Water Game Fishes, Atlantic and Pacific.*)

DISTRIBUTION Striped bass are a marine game fish known to U.S. Atlantic Coast residents since colonial days, even before we told England and George III we didn't want to belong to their old club anymore. There are New England writings about stripers' fighting and edibility qualities dating back to the 1600s. The chances are that the Narragansetts, Montauks, Shinnecocks, and other coastal Indians knew about striped bass long before that.

In bygone centuries the distribution of striped bass was easy to describe, since it was confined, so far as anyone knew, to the Atlantic seaboard. But subsequent studies over the years revealed that the species' over-all range extends from the St. Lawrence River and the Gulf of St. Lawrence down to northern Florida, as well as on the western shore of that state and in tidal and fresh-water rivers along the Gulf of Mexico's northern rim to Alabama, Mississippi, and Louisiana.

In recent years, thanks to the enormous, ever-increasing popularity of striped bass as a sport fish, the species' distribution has literally mushroomed all over the place, inland as well as in coastal areas. With the aid of modern fisheries procedures, striped bass are branching out. They no longer are considered primarily a marine species, but are already established as a sport fishery, or may one day be such, in such far-from-the-sea places as Kansas and Arizona. This is where the importance of their anadromous habits comes in. Striped bass can adapt themselves to lives in fresh water.

Experimental transplantings of stripers to set up branch populations in various parts of the United States began back in the 1800s.

Among the more notable were the transplants from New Jersey's Navesink River to San Francisco Bay in 1879–82. In San Francisco Bay adaptation was speedy. Not only did the newcomers settle down nicely, they thrived. Simultaneously, word of the species' excellence as a game fish spread rapidly in California. A new sport fishery was in the making.

How well stripers have prospered there is demonstrated dramatically by their spreading down into Southern California's waters and in the opposite direction up the seaboard to Oregon and Washington; they now constitute a major Pacific Coast rod-and-reel target.

Another dramatically successful adaptation of stripers to a new environment has occurred in South Carolina's huge Santee-Cooper river and reservoir system. It appears that waters within that system already harbored populations of bass, and those that were landlocked by dam construction continued on as though nothing had happened. Now linesiders are a much-sought sport fish in the Santee-Cooper network; and South Carolina has exported large quantities of young stripers for transplanting in other states.

On our Atlantic Coast the greatest numbers of striped bass dwell in that vast segment extending from southern Massachusetts (notably in the Cape Cod and Cuttyhunk sectors) southward to North Carolina. Included in that more or less continuous belt are: Rhode Island; both shores of Long Island Sound, Connecticut and Long Island sides, all the way down to its western reaches; Montauk and Block Island; Staten Island; Romer Shoals, a famous striper ground between New Jersey and Long Island's western South Shore; the entire New Jersey coast, with an accent on Sandy Hook and the surf, and including the Garden State's many bays; Delaware Bay; and the fertile Chesapeake Bay.

Generally conceded to be principal breeding-nursery regions within that stretch of coast are Chesapeake Bay and tidal tributaries, sections of Delaware Bay, lower Hudson River, and North Carolina's Pimlico Sound.

MIGRATIONS   Striped bass are migrators, and their movements on the Atlantic Coast are typical. Here the main migrations are coastwise. Schools swim up the seaboard on a northerly and somewhat easterly heading in the spring, then turn around and march on back in the fall.

Many bass undertake only relatively short trips. Others may travel the better part of the full route from, say, northern North Carolina to southern New England. Then there are local populations that move down out of estuaries or tidal rivers to the sea or some other convenient body of water such as a bay or sound in spring, then return in winter. This is a type of short-range journeying that goes on among stripers shifting between the lower Hudson River and Long Island Sound, and among bass "commuting" between New Jersey's rivers and the bays to which those rivers are tributary. Where rivers are long enough, stripers may satisfy their itch to travel by confining themselves to those stretches of water.

So all along the seaboard from North Carolina to Massachusetts you have the main coastwise migrations, plus a series of short-haul and more or less local movements.

SEASONS   It's important to you as a fisherman to know that striped bass migrate. It's also important to know *when* they move. These are details determining angling seasons.

Water temperatures are a big factor, along with spawning, in influencing their movements. Water temperatures, in turn, are affected by weather and warm or cold currents. Striped bass can tolerate a fairly wide range of temperatures, as evidenced by their wanderings as far north as the St. Lawrence River region and as far south as northern Florida. That range is roughly from a low of 43 to 46° F to highs going from about 77° F to as warm as 86° F. Extremes prompt them to move to warmer or cooler water, as the case may be. Warming water is prime mover in causing them to travel.

So it comes about that coastwise migrating schools arrive in progressively more northern regions at progressively later dates. Off North Carolina, schools start to move when temperatures reach somewhere around 44 to 46° F, according to Ed Migdalski. New Jersey can see a vanguard of these troops any time from late March on, with April a better bet. Before April is over, the first migrators usually have been reported for Long Island's South Shore. The same thing goes for Rhode Island. In Massachusetts the first schools generally start to show in May.

A similar situation takes shape among populations wintering locally; and in some instances it occurs before the first coastwise-traveling fish appear. In New Jersey, for instance, stripers may start trickling down out of their winter river areas into estuaries and bays as early as March's first or second week. Similarly, impatient striper buffs on Long Island's western South Shore have been known to contact a few bass by about mid-March. These probably are fish emerging from their hibernal headquarters in the Hudson River, although some could be individuals that wintered locally. So it goes all along the coast.

Remember: Striped bass timetables are unpredictable at best, and always subject to changes without notice.

Throughout that over-all range mentioned earlier, stripers are present from spring, through summer, into autumn. It's a period that spans at least six months and can stretch to as much as eight or nine between its extreme ends. During that time the fish build to a spring zenith, aided by migrating schools, then level off in a summer performance, finally building to an autumn peak as schools pass through on their return trip southward. Situations vary from region to region and season to season, but in general the best runs are in late spring and early fall. Summer fishing can be productive, but often it exhibits marked lulls as heat forces bass to abandon shallow local grounds for deeper, cooler places. Also during that spring-to-autumn period, sizes steadily increase. Usually the early phases of a spring showing are dominated by small stripers, fish under ten pounds. Often there's a large percentage of shorts. But as more and more bass depart their wintering areas and are joined by migrating schools, sizes begin to inch upward. You'll hear of specimens ten to fifteen pounds being caught, then some in the twenties. By and by, thirty-pounders appear in the catches, then forty-pounders, and so on, until weights reach the fifty-to-sixty-pound bracket.

Tapering-off of a year's run comes when autumn is well along. Their stay in a region can be prolonged by favorable weather and good food supplies, or shortened by severe storms or cold spells. So it comes about that stripers can still be around deep into November, or even early December, in some locales; or the fall run can be shot by early November. Too, the time of ringing down the curtain on an autumn run is generally somewhat earlier the farther north you go.

AN UNPREDICTABLE FEEDER   To anglers, the single most important striper habit is feeding. It governs what they'll accept as natural and artificial baits. But stripers' feeding patterns, unhappily, are vexing. They make sense to the fish, but sometimes they drive fishermen right up the walls.

It isn't that striped bass are fussy eaters. Quite the contrary. Not finicky in their dining, they gulp their way through a lengthy list of items that include marine worms, squid, shrimp, crabs, jellyfishes occasionally, and a wide assortment of lesser neighbors such as sand eels, American eels, menhaden, herring, whiting, spearing, and other kinds of young fishes that happen to be handy. At one time or another they'll respond to many of those as baits, with an accent on eels, sand launce, sandworms, bloodworms, and menhaden. They'll also snap at a number of artificials which, because of shape, color, and/or action, remind them of natural food.

But—here's the rub—there's no predicting with any assurance just what they'll like in a given place at a given time. This is one of the things that make striped bass so intriguing and such a test of skill, and so doggoned frustrating.

Although they're omnivorous, with a lusty appetite and roomy mouth, they'll often concentrate on a particular kind of food: a favorite, perhaps, or one particularly abundant at the moment. When stripers exhibit such favoritism it's up to anglers to determine (if they can) what that current fancy is, then select a natural bait or man-created lure most closely simulating it in appearance and/or action. Like the man said, it ain't easy.

Stripers are aggressive hunters. That's helpful for fishermen to know, because it influences techniques. Unfortunately, though (and that's what striped bass fishing is, a series of happy and unhappy circumstances, often contradictory), there's no handy rule that can be laid down as a guide to their feeding habits. If anything, stripers are more erratic (to us) and unpredictable in their dining customs than many other species. Each fisherman, therefore, formulates his own "rules," based on observations and experience. Always he does his utmost to select a come-on most closely matching whatever natural food appeals to bass at the time.

Here are some generalizations to illustrate:

Striped bass around Long Island, elsewhere too, often exhibit a feeding pattern associated with a particular part of a season. In spring along the island's southern coast, for instance, bass are caught by bottom fishing the surf with worm baits. At this time at least some of the fish are part of a customary northward migration. Why a preference for worms at this time? One theory is that the fish are tired from the swim north and just don't feel like exerting themselves in pursuit of fast-swimming prey. So they satisfy their hunger with marine worms, which are easier to seize. To do it they must forage along the sea floor where the worms reside, hence the bottom fishing technique.

Later in the season stripers are more willing to work for their supper. If the surf, we'll say, happens to offer an abundance of sand eels, they'll fill their bellies with those. Fishermen then rig a metal squid that looks something like a sand eel. This lure has a shallow body, which should be shiny to flash in the water, and a couple of gentle curves in simulation of the undulating form of a sand launce. Or the bass might be on a crab-eating kick, in which case a piece of shedder crab is good bait. When there's a run of mullet, stripers will feed on those, so the angler employs either a natural mullet bait or an artificial resembling that food fish. And so on.

Sometimes a clue to stripers' current feeding preference can be had when they're observed at the surface, chasing their victims clear of the water. Commonly this occurs when they're dining on mossbunkers or mullet. It's not infallible, though, because the bass might be glutting themselves on smaller fish that the mullet and 'bunkers also are raiding. In such instances the angler may have to experiment with a succession of lures until he finds one that approximates the little fish being attacked by the bass, or at least one that deludes the stripers into striking. These observations can be very frustrating. You'll see a school of linesiders right there on the surface, splashing and gallivanting around, yet you'll cast or troll everything but the kitchen sink without response. That too is one of many details making striped bass fishing fascinating. On the other hand, it adds to the satisfaction when you finally do make contact.

Like some other kinds of fishes, stripers' feeding patterns tend to vary according to their ages. They're always voracious and aggressive when hunger is upon them, but there are differences in the ways they hunt. Younger individuals, the so-called school stripers, travel in large schools, vigorously pursuing herring, mullet, spearing, and other small species. Their older and much larger brethren, in contrast, tend to seek food in smaller groups, or in twos to sixes, or even alone. They lurk in shadowy water around rocks, waiting for unsuspecting victims to swim their way or be carried past by currents. Or they prowl tide rips and around eddies looking for dinner, or cruise the bottom with a knowing eye to marine worms, crabs, and creatures they can capture with less effort. Like older humans, senior bass like to do things in an easier way whenever possible.

That difference in feeding procedures is a detail to remember. Another is that when stripers are gorging themselves on one particular kind of food they may ignore everything else. Still another feeding habit, especially when food is abundant, is to stuff their stomachs, then tear themselves away from the dinner table, so to speak, to give that food a chance to digest. They've had it for the time being, and nothing further in the way of chow is likely to appeal to them. Later they'll return to filling their

bellies again. That's why times arise during a great plentitude
of food, such as sand eels, when stripers will ignore any kind of
natural or artificial bait.

Often stripers' food of the hour can be learned by asking fishermen and skippers working the area. Or you can examine the
stomach contents of bass already caught. And you can always
inquire at a local tackle shop, fishing station, or bait depot. Tackle
shop operators are especially knowledgeable about currently
effective lures.

Important tip: Striped bass frequently are more active, notably
in feeding, during the period from sunset to sunrise, give or take
an hour either way, than during the day, when the sun is high.
There's a reason. It's at night that eels are more likely to be
around, and marine worms emerge from their burrows to see
what's going on in town. Other morsels are out wandering about
too. You'll frequently find that the better bass action is in the evening after sundown, then on through the predawn hours. Along
the same lines, you'll also discover that often during the day the
larger bass will go deeper, perhaps to avoid the heat and light
of the sun.

Tides also can be important. Certain phases of tides dislodge
food such as crabs and worms more readily than others. Consequently, bass feed more actively at such times. Whenever they're
actively feeding your lures have a better chance.

Don't get me wrong. Bass are caught by day too. Much depends
upon the availability of food.

OTHER HABITS   When quite young, up to about age two, stripers
congregate chiefly in small groups. After that, but while still
young, they show a fondness for togetherness and gather in large
schools, some of which contain thousands of individuals. These
are the "schoolies." Still later, when they reach the thirty-pound
mark and above, they're more likely to be encountered in small
schools again. The older they get, the more they seem to favor
progressively smaller groups. Finally, the heaviest fish, lunkers of
fifty pounds and more, find life more interesting when traveling
alone.

This doesn't mean that bass of various sizes do not intermingle.
You'll come across schools whose members represent a mixture of

sizes spanning a range from, let's say, five or six pounds up to more than thirty pounds. Such intermingling has led some ichthyologists to speculate that, except when migrating, striped bass schools do not hold together for any great length of time. During migrations their schools often are densely packed. When feeding in an area, however, schools tend to spread out, even scatter.

Fortunately for anglers, striped bass are primarily an inshore species. Although some schools may travel appreciable distances from land during various legs of their migrations, and certain numbers may wander offshore to elude winter cold, the vast majority of oceangoing bass stay comparatively close to the coast, except during spawning, when they run up into estuaries and rivers. There they can be found in an inshore belt that extends from the surf on out to no more than about four or five miles to seaward. These ocean travelers also are encountered in and around inlets; and they join local residents in bays and tributaries.

Inside mouths of inlets and their tributary channels, and bays and their connecting waterways, estuaries and other sheltered waters usually house small-to-medium linesiders, little schoolies, and shorts up to fish in the twenties. Tops among these is about thirty pounds or so. Heftier bass generally are caught in the surf, ocean, and large, open sounds, as well as in great bays such as the Chesapeake and Delaware.

PLACES WITH POTENTIAL—SOME BASICS   There are countless locations with striper fishing possibilities. I'll give you several starting points. They're generalities, but strong clues. They form a useful skeleton on which you can drape meat as you learn details of various areas you fish.

File these for openers:

1. Stretches of beach studded by boulders or masses of rock, totally or partially submerged. Rocks provide haven for food fishes that attract bass.

2. Sandy beaches along an oceanfront, as well as those flanking inlets. In such places there are small fishes such as sand eels; and waves and currents dislodge crabs, worms, etc. Stripers may

be feeding right in the breakers' white water or around sand bars just beyond the surf.

3. Inlets. Sections with striped bass potential include outside mouth, inlet proper, and inside portal. Often there's both surf-casting and boat action right in an inlet. Inlets draw stripers because a variety of lesser creatures either inhabit them or are carried through by tidal currents. For the same reasons, attention should be paid to points of land in inlets or flanking their mouths, and to sand bars just beyond them to seaward.

4. Points of land in general. These always should be considered. Sometimes small, bass-attracting fishes linger in the points' calmer waters, out of the current, or are swirled by in a tidal flow. Stripers aren't likely to miss a trick.

5. Rocky jetties and seawalls. These can be productive for the same reasons as rocky areas. Waters around bridge abutments, causeways, and trestles also harbor bass.

6. Bays and channels. Availability of food is a major factor here. Locations where there's a fairly brisk current—around points of land, etc.—are apt to be best.

7. Beds of mussels and other shellfishes. These have potential because they often contain marine worms and other critters that tickle striper palates.

8. Gardens of sedge grass and other marine vegetation in shallow bays. Stripers know that these locales provide refuge for little fishes, shrimp, crabs, etc. They'll hunt food there when a tide is high, then shift to deeper places as the tide drops. Similarly, bass will hang around floating patches of seaweed, looking for tidbits hiding therein.

9. Mouths of tidal rivers and estuaries. Stripers frequent such places, preying upon smaller fishes passing in or out. Usually the better fishing is on a side where the current is stronger. If there's a bar on that side, with breakers or agitated ("white") water, that has potential too.

10. Shoals and extensive sand bars or flats—in the ocean, sounds, large bays—covered by water even at low tide. Bass know that small food fishes fan out across those areas. Stripers also are aware that currents can bring chow their way in sloughs and cuts along the edges of such places. Maybe the water isn't deep enough

for bass on some shoals at low tide. Wait until high water or try the current-eroded gullies.

Important!: Study and thoroughly learn the characteristics of any area you plan to fish, whether by boat or from shore.

SURF FISHING

SEA "SIGNS" Personally, I think the most challenging, exciting, and self-satisfying way to catch striped bass is by surfcasting. It's also one of the toughest ways, a real test of know-how and skill. It puts an angler into a toe-to-toe slugfest with his opponent. The battle is tricky, right up until the fish is high and dry on the sand. But the rewards are great. Just being out there in the salt air, even under a gray sky, the song of the breakers throwing a white-water challenge, is glorious. The greatest bonus of all is the realization that you met a wild, elusive creature on *his* terms and whipped him.

Here's how you go about learning characteristics of a beach where you plan to surf fish:

Study the beach's general layout. Do it at various phases of the tide, low to high water. If there are sand dunes nearby, climb atop the highest one to study the water. Sometimes deep spots and shoals aren't readily visible from a flat beach, but can be detected from a dune. Get to know the exact locations of such variations in depths.

You'll be able to identify shallows, bars, sloughs, and deeper places by differences in water shades. Water over shoal areas is lighter. In addition to its darker shade, deeper water sometimes can be detected by a minimum of foam and breakers. Conversely, waves rearing up and curving shoreward out yonder beyond the beach indicate the obstructing influence of a sand bar.

In and around the seaward mouths of inlets and along ocean beaches some sand bars become more or less permanent features, while others shift. A storm can move sand bars around like checkers. In some locales sand bars are so shifty they can't be buoyed for navigation. It will pay you to keep tabs on such alterations, especially after severe storms.

Tip: Striped bass are fond of turbulent water, notably the so-called white water evidenced by foam and whitecaps. It spells food dislodged or tumbled their way. That's why a lively surf, generously decorated with bobbing whitecaps—but at the same time clear or at least comparatively free from churned-up sand, mud, and debris, which interfere with the visibility of lures and baits—holds more promise than a calm, slick-surface sea. Sometimes striper fishing is better after a storm for the same reason, so long as the water hasn't become too murky. Seaweed in a surf is an annoying nuisance to anglers because it gets fouled up in baits and lures, obscuring them. But the presence of seaweed *per se* isn't necessarily detrimental to striper fishing. The fact is that at times water well peppered with bits of weed produces better than clear water.

To your surf fishing lore you must add sea signs. Some of these will stand you in good stead when you're after bluefish and other gamesters too. Here they are, with their significance:

Sign 1. Birds "working." This means sea birds such as gulls flying low and swooping down toward the surface.

Interpretation: The presence of small fish chased to the top by larger predators, or maybe scraps of mossbunkers torn to shreds by marauding bluefish passing through. In either case, bass may be feeding on those tidbits. Watch for the silvery glint of little fish jumping clear of the water.

Your cue: Cast your lure as close to the scene of activity as possible, then retrieve it in lively fashion. Here a darting or surface-splashing artificial can be an advantage.

If birds are working beyond casting range, watch to see if they move in closer. Follow them down the beach if necessary.

Note: An absence of active birds doesn't necessarily rule out the presence of bass. Go on to Sign 2.

Sign 2. Surface disturbances. They may be distinct ripplings. If they spell fish they will be different from ripplings caused by wind in that they will be confined to a particular, comparatively small area. Too, they may be more violent than agitation caused by a breeze, and be punctuated by lightning-fast flashes of silver as small fish break water.

Interpretation: Bait fish pursued to the surface by predators (stripers, blues, others) attacking them from below.

Your cue: The same as for Sign 1.

Sign 3. A narrow corridor of water, long or fairly short, lighter color than the surrounding sea and running roughly parallel to the beach.

Interpretation: A sand bar and shoaler water. Between that bar and the beach may be one or more holes and/or a slough, a gullylike trough eroded by currents swirling around the bar. If holes or sloughs are present, their water will be darker and generally calmer than the rest. Stripers commonly seek food in these deeper places at low water or on an ebbing tide. At high tide, bass sometimes feed right on a sand bar, since the sweep of water over it dislodges food items.

If you can't detect deeper places along a bar's inshore edge, try to check its seaward side. Look for one that can be reached at low water or partway down on a tide. Fish bottom-feed in holes and sloughs along bars' outer rims.

Your cue: Holes and gullies along a bar's inshore and seaward edges are apt to be more productive if you use bait instead of artificials. However, a metal squid might draw response if it is allowed to drop into the bottom of a deep spot, then is retrieved slowly across it. At high tide, when there's a chance of bass feeding atop the sand bar, try casting for the bar, reeling your lure slowly across it.

Sign 4. Darker water indicating a hole or slough just off the beach, beyond which lies a sand bar (lighter shade) covered by a couple of feet of fast-moving water.

Interpretation: Large stripers have been known to prowl for food around such bars and in deeper holes.

Your cue: Both a metal squid and a baited hook can get results. If you're fishing a squid, cast out onto the bar and reel in line slowly, imparting a series of spasmodic jerks to the artificial. Continue to retrieve, letting the squid slide down off the bar into the trough's or hole's deeper water, then bring it in a little faster. When bait fishing in such places, cast out onto the bar and let the tide transport your rig into a deeper area, all the while keeping your line free of slack. When your rig gets down into the deeper water, let it rest a minute, then retrieve slowly.

Sign 5. A strip of darker water extending to seaward practically at right angles to the beach. It may be forty or fifty feet wide, or fifty yards, or more.

Interpretation: This is a channellike slough hollowed out by waves and currents, sometimes called a "sea puss" or "sloo." Stripers frequent these gullies because the currents creating the troughs also bring in food fishes.

Your cue: Probe different parts of the sea puss, casting out as far as you can each time and retrieving slowly. If slow retrieves bring no response, don't hesitate to vary your reeling tempo.

Sign 6. An expanse or strip of darker (deeper), somewhat calmer water on a long bar off the beach.

Interpretation: A groove or small channel cut into the bar by waves and currents. Bass prowl these hollows too.

Your cue: Try a metal squid, casting out as far as possible into the trough, then retrieve. If you're trying bait, use a round or ball-type sinker so that your rig can drift with the current.

Sign 7. Turbulent white water marking tide rips and areas where opposing currents collide. Locales where you'll see these signs include points of land, junctions of channels or of channels and inlets, around small islands, and places where the bottom shelves upward abruptly.

Interpretation: These are white water sites greatly favored by stripers. There's often an abundance of chow in such places, and you can be sure that bass, including some of the heftier individuals, are well aware of it. Here you also want to look for eddies and whirlpools indicating deeper places directly underneath. Stripers do their food shopping in those swirling waters too.

Your cue: Cast as close as you can to the rips, whirlpools, and eddies, or directly into them. Try varying your rate of retrieve.

Sign 8. Current-generated white water in other locations. Such sites include oceanfront jetties and groins (structures of wood or rock extending outward at right angles to a beach to check erosion), bridge abutments, and other structures in channels where there are brisk tides, and around the ends of seawalls and jetties in bays.

Interpretation: The same as for Sign 7.

Your cue: The same as for Sign 7.

Finally, there's this *tip:* When fishing is slow, cast out as far as you can, then retrieve ten to twenty feet or so of line at intervals. Experiment with your rates of retrieve. Mix 'em up—all slow, all fairly fast, alternately faster and slower, erratic, etc. Cover a fair section of beach in this fashion before shifting to another station.

Stripers can be prowling at the far end of your cast, or they might be in so close as to be practically flirting with the undertow. Often that backwash releases sandbugs and other morsels. Strikes can occur within fifty to a hundred feet of where you're standing. It depends upon location and circumstances, of course, but casting distance isn't necessarily a prerequisite of successful surf fishing (*beginners take note*) because fish may be feeding surprisingly close to the beach.

SURF FISHING ON THE BOTTOM

In the spring, as stripers arrive along some outer beaches during their vernal coastwise migrations, a considerable amount of fishing is done on the bottom, baiting with worms. Bloodworms often are preferred to sandworms in this surf bottom angling, and the bait should be alive so that it's absolutely fresh.

Two popular rigs will give you service in this method. One is the version detailed back in the chapter on bluefish, the Kronuch rig. The other is the time-honored fish-finder rig. A pyramid sinker is standard for either rig, especially on sandy bottom, where it holds well. However, when it's desirable for a rig to drift, or in rocky areas where a pyramid would be more likely to become snagged, a round sinker is substituted. In either case, three to five ounces of lead may be enough to hold bottom, or you may need more. You have to play it by ear, judging current and undertow strengths. Take along a variety of sinker weights.

The fish-finder outfit calls for a leader of monofilament or wire, according to preference. Mono is good. It can be about the same strength as the line, or somewhat heavier to be more abrasion-resistant if there are rocks in the area. Wire leaders in strengths to a No. 7 or No. 8 are used. Some anglers favor wire over mono in rocky places, and it's a must if bluefish are known to be around. Leaders range from approximately twelve to thirty or thirty-six

inches, again according to individual preference. A serviceable
size is twelve to twenty-four inches.

One end of the leader takes the hook. You can choose from
among several good patterns—O'Shaughnessy, *et al.* Size doesn't
have to be too precise, but it is gauged roughly to sizes of bass
currently running. The range is from a 2/0 up to maybe a 6/0 or
7/0. Your leader's other end is connected to the line through a
two-loop barrel swivel. Don't connect swivel and line yet. The
rig's fish-finder has to go on first.

All you need for the fish-finder subassembly is a two-loop barrel swivel or similar small ring connector serving the same purpose. If that connector comes with a snap arrangement to accept
the sinker, fine; otherwise you can attach a snap swivel to the
connector—or to the barrel swivel, if that's what you're using.
A snap swivel offers an advantage by letting you change sinkers
as needed.

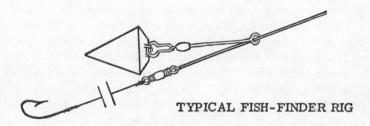

TYPICAL FISH-FINDER RIG

Now the fish-finder's barrel swivel or ring connector goes on
the line, and the line tied into the swivel on the leader. Got it?

The rig's fish-finder component must be free to slide on the
line, yet be stopped by the swivel between line and leader; otherwise its purpose won't be served. You'll see why in a minute.

A fish-finder rig casts readily. Momentum thrusts the sinker
right down to the swivel connecting line and leader, adding
weight at the rig to aid in casting. On bottom, the fish-finder
keeps your bait close to the floor where it should be, yet is free
to slide along the line when a fish strikes, letting him move with
the bait, unhampered by the sinker's weight. For this reason it's
particularly good with smaller fish. Also for the same reason, a
fish-finder is good when live bait is used.

Tip: There will be times in surf bottom fishing when crabs are a blinkin' nuisance. Reaching out with their claws, they'll snick off pieces of bait, even strip a hook nude, every chance they get. A way to minimize these forays is to put a small cork on the leader, just large enough to buoy the baited hook up out of the reach of crabs' eager claws.

BAITS AND BAITING Bloodworm is a surf bottom bait for stripers. Impale the worm on your hook in such a way as to give it some lifelike action. This is accomplished by letting a generous portion of the body trail out beyond the hook. Feed the hook's point in through the worm's mouth end, thence on through the body for about a third of its length, or enough to conceal the shank, then bring its point out through the worm's underside. *Tip:* To prevent the bait from "bunching up" on the hook's bend, thereby detracting from its natural appearance, rig a hook specially designed for this kind of baiting. It has tiny spikes on its shank that dig into the worm and keep it extended.

Sandworms also can be used via the method just outlined.

A juicy worm undulating in the water is an effective come-on, but it poses a problem. Bass can bite off that free end and escape the hook. Rig two hooks in tandem for these "short strikers." Open the eye of a ring-eyed hook just enough to get it on the bend of your original hook, then squeeze the eye closed. To bait, impale a worm on your first hook as before. Hook it only lightly on the trailing hook, or secure it with a few loops of thread or a small, thin rubber band.

Many surfcasters prefer using a single worm. Others employ two, both impaled on a single hook so that a sizable portion of their bodies dangle free in the water. The first worm is hooked as before, its body moved up on the shank as far as it will go. The second worm then is impaled in similar fashion. There's no law that says you can't add a trailing hook for one of those worms to take care of short strikers.

Even with lulls caused by the hot "dog days" of summer, there are always at least scatterings of stripers along an oceanfront, in bays and channels, and along beaches rimming sounds. But it's during warmer weeks that they display a feeding fickleness that makes them the despair of even the most ardent bass buffs.

At such times they're so unpredictable that scarcely anything can be offered as a dependable fishing guide. These are trying times, when it will pay you to look, listen, ask questions, and experiment on your own.

You may find, notably in the spring, that surf-run stripers are smacking bloodworms with gusto. Or their mood may have changed suddenly, with cut bait such as strips of squid, or maybe strips cut from the belly of a whiting, mackerel, or herring turning them on. Whether squid or fish belly, a strip about five or six inches long and three-quarters of an inch wide can be used. This strip is fed onto a hook much as you would a worm, leaving a generous portion to flutter in the water. Splitting its free end up the middle for an inch or two will create two waving tails. A strip bait can be kept extended by impaling it on one of those hooks with tiny spikes along its shank, or by securing it with thread. A two-hook tandem setup, like that rigged with a worm, can be used with a strip bait, the strip being only lightly impaled on the trailing hook.

One of the most versatile baits on the U.S. East Coast is squid. Whole, they're great for swordfish, marlin, and big stripers. As strips they catch weakfish, stripers, bluefish, and other battlers. It won't be easy, but get fresh squid whenever you can. Failing that, buy frozen squid in packages, allowing them to thaw before use. Strips cut from a squid's skirtlike mantle are good bait in surf bottom fishing for bass. You can rig the head, tentacles attached, as bait too. Cut it off just forward of the eyes, burying your hook inside the head so that the appendages flutter in the water.

During warmer months, especially when stripers are feeding in close to shore just beyond the tide line, clam bait gets results. A favorite is skimmers. They're shucked or shelled, of course, and the inner meat, the so-called body, is used. Small clams can be impaled on a hook whole. Larger skimmers are cut into generous pieces. Bury your hook in the clam until its point, barb, bend, and as much of the shank as possible are concealed. Because clams are soft-bodied, some anglers better secure them to a hook with a few loops of thread, particularly if some casting is involved. Skimmer clams also can be rigged in combination with a bloodworm, sandworm, squid strip, or other bait. Your true surfman fiddles with all kinds of combos. You should too.

One of the imponderables that can alter a surf fishing picture in warmer months is a bumper crop of sand eels. Striped bass gulp these little eellike fish with all the enthusiasm of a kid turned loose in a candy store. Apprised of one of those sand eel invasions, your cue is to bait with same, or at least to try a shiny metal squid shaped like a sand eel.

A natural sand eel is baited by thrusting your hook through the eyes and imbedding it in the body near the tail. It's a tough bait that stays on a hook quite well. Incidentally, a sand eel can be used in combination with a spinner as a trolling come-on for stripers. If you can get sand eels alive, so much the better. They're fairly hardy, and you can keep a supply alive for a while in a pail, or even on a bed of wet seaweed, in coolish weather, out of the sun.

Shedder crabs and soft crabs, alive and dead, also are effective striper baits. They're rigged whole or in generous pieces, roughly gauged to the sizes of the bass currently running. For smaller schoolies try a quarter- or half-size piece. For larger fish, bait the crab whole. If half a crab is to be used, bisect the critter straight down the middle, front to rear of shell. These halves can be cut into smaller pieces as desired. The only problem with chunks of crab is that they're hard to keep on the hook and tend to go to pieces after submersion for a while. Securing a piece to the hook with a few wrappings of thread will offset these drawbacks to a certain extent.

Few baits beat a whole shedder when big bass are on a crab-eating kick. There are various ways to put this bait on a hook. Each surf fisherman has his pet technique. One is to break off the swimmerettes, those flattened rear appendages, close to the body, then feed the hook in one resultant hole and out the other. Another procedure is to simply hook the crab through the rear part of his body between the swimmerettes. A third method is to pass the hook into the rear section of the body, through the carapace or upper shell, and bring the point out underneath. When whole soft crabs are used they can be secured further to the hook with a few loops of thread.

There are other baits for surf-run stripers. Shrimp, for example.

Two or three small sand shrimp are impaled on a hook head-first, and positioned until all or most of the hook is covered. The so-called sand bugs, also known variously as "sand crabs," "beach bugs," and "sand fleas," are another bass bait. These little critters, up to an inch or so long and identified by a tannish, rounded shell with "hairy" legs on the underside, are common along open, sandy beaches. There they usually reside in colonies, just below the sand's surface, at the tide line. They're a get-it-yourself bait, and can be dug as each wave recedes. Sometimes the waves' backwash does the digging for you, uncovering them to be scooped up. They'll stay alive in a container of damp sand for quite a while.

Sand bugs are used singly for small surf-run fishes such as kings, weaks, and little school stripers, and in twos, threes, or more for larger game. You can run your hook in through the underside and out the top. But do it carefully, or else you'll crack the shell or create too large a hole, making this bait that much more difficult to keep on a hook. Sand bugs won't stay put too well anyway, and should be secured with thread.

Heads of fishes such as mossbunkers or one of the herrings also are come-ons, the hook's bend and point buried inside from the back. Whole small fishes—mullet, menhaden, spearing, butterfish, and various members of the herring tribe—are rigged too. These are impaled in various ways, including simply thrusting the hook through both eyes. Larger specimens of bait fishes can be employed in chunks.

TECHNIQUE   Bait fishing the surf usually requires a more careful study of a beach than when using artificials. In other words, it's even more important to find places with potential beforehand. One reason is that some natural baits do not stand up under repeated casts and retrieves. Too, it's more a case of finding a place and dropping your offering into it, letting it lay, whereas much of artificials' effectiveness asserts itself when they're worked or retrieved. You'll have to exercise more care when casting natural baits. A smooth cast favors them. A cast with a snap or jerking motion can loosen them, even pull them free.

Once you feel your sinker hit bottom, and the rig comes to

rest, be alert to the slightest activity out there at the far end of your line. Like many of their contemporaries, stripers can be individualistic in their approaches to baits. Some—particularly bold, hungry schoolies—will wallop a bait with sufficient enthusiasm to hook themselves. Others (and this is common among older, more cautious linesiders) "tick" the bait or mouth it very warily; then, if they feel no resistance (here's where a fish-finder rig earns its keep), they swim away with it. You'll have to give him a chance to really get the bait in his mouth—you'll be able to feel it—then sock it to him.

Memo: A sand spike serves a good purpose. During lulls you can stick your rod in it and give your arms a rest, setting the reel's drag fairly lightly and leaving the reel's clicker on to provide an audible warning of a customer at your bait. Some anglers tie a small piece of cloth to their line just beyond the tiptop guide to further apprise them of any sneaky activity. All this is fine when fishing is slow or you want to take time out for chow, but don't overdo it. Keep your rod in hand most of the time so you can be Johnny-on-the-spot if there's the slightest response to your rig. Not only do you want to be aware of any nibblings, you also want to be apprised of the activities of bait thieves such as dogfish ("sand sharks") and crabs.

SURF FISHING—SQUIDDING

LURES AND RIGGING   If there's a time-hallowed artificial among Atlantic seaboard surfcasters, it's the metal squid. Its use, to no one's surprise, came to be known as squidding.

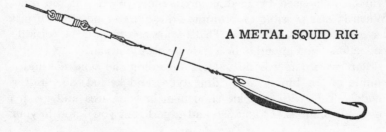

A METAL SQUID RIG

Metal squids comprise a family of lures all by themselves. Still referred to as block tin squids, or simply block tin or tin, these artificials are made from sufficiently heavy metal and come in an assortment of shapes, sizes, and weights, with or without chrome finish. Each is designed to simulate the general shape and/or action of some item of food on stripers' menu. There's that squid shaped like a sand eel I mentioned earlier, for instance, along with models intended to resemble butterfish, small herring, mullet, mossbunkers, etc. Some are broad, designed to ride fairly high when retrieved. Others, with keels, were developed to ride lower. Lots of times surf fishermen paint some of their squids a bright color—yellow, red, blue, or white—for added attraction. Yellow, by the way, is a good choice. It can be effective when the water is murky.

Every veteran surfcaster has his own ideas about the best kind of armament on a squid. Some favor a fixed hook, its shank imbedded rigidly in the lure's body. Others go for a swinging or dangling hook. Still others like a combination of both, and achieve it by bridling a ring-eye hook (the swinger) on the bend of the fixed hook. A metal squid can be used as is, with its hook nude. But it's apt to be more effective when the hook is decorated with a piece of pork rind (sold in jars for this purpose), a bucktail of natural or nylon hairs, or bits of feather in a bright color such as red. Here's another chance to experiment.

Squids are good surf lures because they're heavy for their size, and they cast nicely. They're particularly good when wind conditions make difficult the casting of larger, bulkier attractors such as big plugs and eel rigs. And they're often more effective than other artificials in rough-surf fishing.

Selection of a squid for the fish-catching assignment at hand will be influenced by feeding preferences of bass at the time. When it isn't possible to determine these preferences, you'll just have to try different types. That's your cue to build a versatile collection if you intend to be a serious surf fisherman.

Start with a few basic models, including the sand eel and a couple of the broad, high-riding types and keeled, deep-riding models. Talk with a tackle shop man in your area and get his recommendations. As you fish and experiment you'll add to your inventory, including some with fixed hooks, others with swinging hooks, painted and unpainted squids, and some whose tail hooks are garnished with feathers or bucktails. Keep a jar of pork rind in your tackle box. Get some natural squid strips too for hook decorating. Vary the weights of your squids. Those in the one- and two-ounce classes are for light tackle, and the latter weight also can be used with medium gear. Those going three ounces can be rigged for medium gear too. Heavier models naturally will require sturdier tackle. Hook sizes range from a 2/0 on the low side on up to 7/0 or 8/0, depending upon the weights of the bass currently running.

In rigging a squid you'll encounter variations—as usual. One arrangement calls for a couple of feet of monofilament or wire leader, with connection of line and leader made through a two-loop barrel swivel. If you're fishing in a rocky area you can rig wire for the leader, or monofilament in a heavier test than the line, say, up to about forty pounds. Otherwise a short length of mono, in about the same strength as the line or slightly heavier, will suffice. If bluefish are known to be in the same area as stripers, a wire leader is a precaution against their teeth.

THE METHOD   Effectiveness in squidding demands that the lure be placed right where there's striper feeding activity, or in a spot where it's suspected such activity may be occurring. Casting accuracy, therefore, is important; and so, to a certain extent, is timing.

When you see bass attacking bait fish, lob a metal squid in among them, or as close as possible to the action. When obvious signs are lacking, cast into the edges of tide rips, or work the white water where currents collide with each other or with boulders or large rocks. Don't overlook eddies and whirlpools, and white water swirling around a point of land. In a heavy surf that bounces your squid around too violently, watch the breakers' pattern and drop your lure between them.

Proper squidding requires practice. Casting accuracy and timing are only parts of the story. For maximum effectiveness, a squid's retrieve should be started the instant it hits the water. This is where timing comes in again. It isn't easy to halt the flow of line at the precise instant the squid hits the surface, throw the reel into gear, lift the rod tip to take up slack, then crank to begin the retrieve, all in a matter of seconds. If you're a greenhorn, your first attempts will be awkward, to say the least; and with conventional tackle you'll probably have backlashes to add to your woes. But don't be discouraged. We all went through that routine.

When stripers are bashing bait fishes at or near the surface, the indication is for one of the broader, shallower squids that will travel high when retrieved. That also holds true for shoal water and places with rocks or other bottom obstructions to snag the lure. Conversely, in turbulent water, in a violent surf, or where you want to probe deep in the rips, the call is for one of the narrower, deeper-keeled models that will go down to where it can do its job. Retrieve speed will regulate your squid's depth to a certain extent. Fast cranking while holding your rod tip up will bring a squid in along one of the upper levels. Slower reeling while holding your rod tip lower will cause the lure to ride at a deeper plane.

Ordinarily the retrieve speed in squidding is moderately rapid. Sometimes, though, a combination of fast and slower reeling, causing the lure to alternately ride higher and lower at variable speeds, will be more effective than a consistently fast retrieve. Tides and currents will be factors in your retrieve rates, and you'll learn to judge their effects. On some tides you may have to let your squid sink almost to the bottom before you start reeling in to get response. At other times, keeping the lure in rapid motion from the time it touches down on the surface will be the ticket. Adding an erratic, jerking motion to the lure is a variation you also should try. Always have control of that squid, keeping your line taut in case of a strike and to prevent the artificial from being thrust sideways by waves and currents.

"Traditionally" in some Atlantic Coast areas, striped bass feed on worms and/or cut baits in the spring, even on into summer. Also "traditionally," many surfcasters in those areas don't begin trotting out their squids much before July. But striped bass are apt to sneer at man-made traditions and ignore them by accepting metal squids much earlier.

PLUGS AND PLUGGING

SCHOOLS OF LURES The phoney baits we call plugs have been with us in one form or another for a long time. American Indians probably tossed pluglike artificials, shaped from wood and armed with bone hooks, to catch finned game in our seas, lakes, and rivers long before the first foreigner planted an exploratory foot on this continent.

After the Indians, from whom the idea undoubtedly was swiped, modern plugs had their genesis chiefly among inland anglers. Those fellows were unsung heroes. To them goes credit for years of inventing, field testing, and refining. From them, down through generations via circuitous routes and aided by still other unsung heroes among salt-water fishermen of long-gone decades, have come today's plugs. It's to all those anglers' credit that they did their job so well that some of the basic ideas remain unchanged.

ANATOMY AND FUNDAMENTALS Any plug consists of three indispensable components: a body fashioned from wood or other material (nowadays it's commonly plastic); hook armament; and a metal eye or swivel arrangement for attachment to leader or line. Everything else is window dressing, you might say. Many

VARIATION OF
PLUG RIGGING

refinements are incorporated in plugs to enhance their attractability. We considered them in the chapter on lures.

Whatever its design, construction, and trimmings, the prime purpose of any plug is to simulate, through action, shape, color scheme, and/or other physical attributes, an item of food appealing to the fish being sought . . . or at least delude them into thinking it's something to eat.

Start with a reasonably good selection of those models most frequently employed—and proven—in your area. You can shape this selection easily. Consult a local tackle emporium. Its operator knows what kinds of plugs that stripers are smacking. Too, tackle stores are fishermen's hangouts. Another way to shape your plug selection is by getting a consensus among your fellow anglers, preferably those with a lot of experience.

Physical dimensions and weights are details to consider when building your collection. The greater a plug's length and diameter (forgetting weight for a moment), the more difficult it is to cast when there's opposition from a breeze. Plug weights (forgetting length and diameter this time) enter into the picture because your tackle has to be capable of handling them. You have plenty of latitude, so don't worry. But you should match your plugs and other artificials as closely as possible to your equipment and the conditions under which you'll be fishing most of the time.

Lengths and diameters are inherent within various models; and those plugs are chosen according to the species hunted, fishing conditions, etc. In most instances those details will be taken care of "automatically," so to speak. Weights, therefore, may turn out to be the prime consideration. Here's a broad guide: the larger, heavier plugs, which can go up to about four ounces or so, for the stronger conventional tackle; medium weights, an ounce or two, for medium-caliber conventional gear and sturdier spinning equipment; and the lighter, smaller plugs, which grade on down to fractional-ounce models, for spinning tackle and light conventional outfits. As I said, you have leeway.

Commonly favored color patterns and finishes among salt-water models include silvery, the so-called blue mullet, mackerel, golden flash, and all-yellow. Wooden plugs are enameled; and in time fishes' teeth do a job on the finish, so it has to be retouched. Plastic plugs have colors and finishes built right into their bodies.

Hook arrangements on plugs are governed to a great extent by the models themselves. Hook sizes also vary according to models. To a certain extent they're gauged to the over-all size of a plug. They also are gauged properly for the kinds and sizes of finned game for which those artificials are intended. Hook sizes are therefore "automatic," you might say. Often fishermen change hooks and hook arrangements to suit themselves. All kinds of variations are possible. These modifications are done according to personal ideas. You'll find yourself fooling around with a few of your own.

If you buy sensibly you never need be concerned about investing money in a collection of plugs. These lures are versatile. Far from being limited to beach and jetty fishing for striped bass, they also give service in trolling and casting from boats. They'll catch battlers other than stripers too—bluefish, to cite but one. If you select wisely, guided by the experience and advice of others, you can assemble a versatile assortment of plugs without spending a lot of money. And with reasonable care they'll last for a long time. *Tip:* Carry spares of your most effective models. Lost plugs are a common casualty.

SOME BASIC TYPES   As inevitably as dawn follows the night and heartburn follows chili con carne, your kit of plugs eventually will include models of one or more of these basic types:

1. *Popping plugs* ("poppers"). These are near-surface lures. They're marketed in a good range of lengths and weights, which include jointed models. Their name-giving feature is a concavity at the front end whose resistance to water during retrieves creates a splashing, bubbling action and causes a popping or "plupping" sound to attract victims. Varying the concavity's shape and depth brings variations in the sounds they make. Some so-called poppers have a lip at their head end, instead of a concavity, to generate sonic effects. So here you have a combination of action and sound providing an attraction. Some models carry a skirt of natural hairs (bucktail) or nylon threads at the rear hook for still more attraction. Commonly their armament consists of two sets of treble hooks.

For effectiveness poppers rely on an ability to create an illusion of an injured sea inhabitant trying to escape enemies. Left alone, they float. Retrieved, they duck just below the surface and go into their act. Jerking, spasmodic retrieves add to the illusion of a crippled bait fish.

2. *Other surface plugs.* These are legion, coming in an enormous variety of shapes, sizes, colors, and weights. But they all

have one thing in common: They're designed to create a surface disturbance when reeled in. (Normally they float when not retrieved.) The type and intensity of their commotion are credited to their appendages. These include little propellers, fore and/or aft, dangling arm- and leglike gadgets, and metal tails that flap. Among the fishes they're intended to imitate are mullet, menhaden, herring, and other surface swimmers.

Surface plugs open the door to a lot of experimentation. They can be reeled in slowly and steadily, or rapidly, or at speeds in between, or in a series of retrieves and spasmodic jerks, etc.

3. *Subsurface models.* There's a big fleet of these too, with all kinds of designs, weights, actions, and so on. They usually float when not reeled in, and submerge when retrieved. They're designed to travel a foot or two or three down when in action, depending upon a bevel at their front end and retrieve speed. Wobbling, zig-zagging, or other erratic motions are their stock in trade. Also in this classification are darting plugs or darters. They float when at rest, and duck down to a shallow plane when reeled in. Their typical design calls for a tapered body with a notched or grooved head. It's this notching or grooving that imparts a tantalizing series of darts in different directions, like a small fish.

Subsurface plugs can be retrieved at varying speeds. You might arbitrarily start at a slow, steady rate, then speed it up if that doesn't elicit response. The slower they're reeled, the higher they ride. The faster they're cranked, the lower they travel. Another maneuver is to let them pop to the surface at intervals and make them twitch with your rod tip. That might get results when steady or variable-speed retrieves fail.

4. *Floating/diving, sinking models.* As their name implies, the former models float when at rest, and dive when retrieved. Most of these are designed to work at somewhat lower planes than subsurface plugs, riding at depths of, say, three to six feet or so. Their depth can be controlled by retrieve speed, and that is varied in experimentation. Plugs in this family have various movements when retrieved. Their advantage is that they can be put into play when stripers and other gamesters are not at the surface.

Sinking plugs submerge the instant they hit the water. They

too come in assorted shapes, sizes, types of action, etc. They're versatile in that they can be made to travel at different depths, bottom to higher planes, and their action can be varied, all by retrieve rate and working of the rod tip. They come in handy when bass are figured to be deep or at some intermediate level. The slower you reel them, the deeper they ride. By varying your reeling speed and working your rod tip you'll put these lures through many kinds of maneuvers, from bumping along the bottom, to swimming briskly at a higher plane, to moving spasmodically through the water.

5. *Deep riders.* Some of these float when at rest; others quickly sink when not retrieved. All of them dive deep when cranked in. They come with different built-in actions, and by making certain adjustments on the lure itself you will regulate its depth. Many underwater plugs have a metal lip at their forward end. This governs their riding depth, which you can alter by bending the lip. Broadly speaking, bending it downward will cause the plug to ride higher; conversely, bending it upward will cause it to ride deeper. Just remember that its traveling depth is the opposite of the direction you bend its lip.

Again the plug's depth and action are influenced by retrieve rate and rod movements. You'll usually have to experiment. Certain combinations are more effective with some models than with others.

Tip—for all plugs: Often manufacturers make recommendations as to how to best work the lures.

Speaking for all plugs, each type performs best under given sets of conditions. Here are examples:

In general, surface plugs are effective when there are small bait fish in the area, stripers are feeding in upper levels, and the water is relatively calm. They usually produce better during the day than after dark, although they will take some bass at night too. Subsurface and deeper-diving plugs usually are considered for night fishing and/or in water that isn't as clear as it is normally. Also in murky water, brightly colored (yellow, for example) or flashy models are more likely to draw attention than the darker-colored ones. Darker, less flashy lures are dependent to a great extent on clear water and daylight.

But always—I can't stress this enough—you want to try different models, day and night, under the widest possible range of conditions: clear water and murky, calm sea and rough surf, and so on. Fool around with variations too. Try adding weight on some section of the plug's body to alter its riding depth and action. Experiment with changes in color patterns too. With your own enamel you can dream up all kinds of color schemes: a single, solid color; combinations of two or more; even outrageous, multihued, "psychedelic" patterns. Test the value of certain refinements, such as adding a spinner blade to the tail end, or one or more spinners to the leader ahead of the lure, or a propeller to either end, or a dressing of the rear hook with bits of bright-colored feather, or a bucktail, or a gaudy-colored nylon skirt. The possibilities are practically unlimited, and among them you could come upon some real bass killers.

RIGGING PLUGS FOR SURF AND JETTY ACTION   The procedure is essentially the same as in rigging metal squids: line plus leader plus lure. You'll encounter variations along beaches and on jetties, of course, and you'll undoubtedly devise a few yourself.

Rigging centers around a leader of wire or monofilament (the former, or mono—in somewhat heavier gauge than the line, favored in rocky areas), twelve to thirty or thirty-six inches long, according to personal preference and sizes of fish involved. With wire, many anglers prefer the shorter lengths to facilitate handling and minimize chances of kinks. Attachment of leader to lure is made directly. Connecting of leader and line can be made in the same fashion or through a swivel. A swivel is desirable in the case of wire, optional with mono. A snap swivel at the free end of any leader (fitting into a small loop on the line) permits easy changing of lures.

It should go without saying that precious fishing time will be saved, especially at night, on a beach or jetty if lure-leader outfits are made up beforehand.

Tip: If you can't feel your plug or other artificial working properly, check it. It may have picked up some obscuring seaweed.

RIGGED EELS AND EELSKIN RIGS   In these lures we find a beautiful example of the logic underlying all baiting procedures. Striped bass are fond of eels—gastronomically, that is, not romantically. Therefore, eels are good bait for striped bass. Eels are most active at night, so it follows that they're best used for stripers during hours of near-darkness and darkness. Let me hastily add that eels and eelskin rigs will take linesiders by day too.

A rigged eel, as the term indicates, calls for a whole eel, used intact. For this purpose specimens measure from about eight to twelve or fourteen inches, and even up to sixteen, eighteen, or twenty inches for big bass. They're used both alive and dead.

RIGGED EEL

Live eels are favored by some striper buffs because of their movements in the water. An eel rigged in this live-bait fishing is hooked in the tail or—carefully—through the flesh of the back. They can be hooked through the "lips" too; but with their snakey wiggling they wrap themselves around the leader like ivy around a tree. That really fouls up things. The fact is that live eels are hard to handle, which is why most surf fishermen use them dead.

Rigging a whole eel has the anticipated variations, including these: (1) used as is, hooked through the head, maybe with a thin, narrow strip of lead wound around the head to weight it for greater depth; (2) more commonly than the foregoing, the eel is used plain, but with line, or sometimes small chain or wire, run lengthwise through the body to hold two or more hooks; (3) with a bullet-shaped weight—the metal head of an old feather lure will do—at the eel's head end, also for depth; (4) in combination with a keeled squid for depth and added action; (5) with a metal lip or wobble plate, similar to that on diving plugs, on the head end, also for depth and action.

You can buy eels alive or dead and place them in a large container of strong brine. Eels are tough baits anyway, because of their skin, and putting them in brine makes 'em even tougher. In that salt solution they'll keep for a long time. So you can rig a supply in advance during an off-season and have them ready to go when the festivities start.

Preparing rigged whole eels and eelskin rigs isn't listed under Fun and Games. You can save yourself trouble and mess by buying them already made up.

Rigged eels can be armed with two or three hooks, according to length. Two hooks are average. They range up to about an 8/o, in proportion to the sizes of the bass sought. These baits can account for lunkers going up to forty or fifty pounds and more.

One way to rig an eel is as follows:

You'll need an extra-long needle; an appropriate length of stringing material—stout twine, or chain made for this purpose, or, what will do, strong Dacron or monofilament line; a two-loop barrel swivel; and two hooks of suitable size.

The procedure: (1) Tie one hook to the free end of your stringing material. Attach your needle to its other end. (2) Thrust the needle into the eel's underside on its midline, a few inches from the tail end. Feed the needle lengthwise through the body, drawing the stringing material with it, and bring it out at the mouth. (3) Pull on the stringing material until the hook's shank is brought up inside the body. Part of its bend and the point will remain exposed. (4) Put that barrel swivel on the stringing material, then feed your needle back into the eel's mouth and make it emerge a couple of inches behind the gills on the bait's underside. (5) You're ready for the second hook. This step is a little tricky because you'll have to estimate how much of the remaining stringing material you'll need. Laying it alongside the eel will help. You need only enough to tie in the second hook and pull its shank up inside the body's underside, just as you did the first one, yet not leave too large a loop (the one carrying the swivel) at the eel's snout. (6) The stringing material's looped end is tied in a simple knot just far enough behind the swivel so the knot rests in the bait's mouth. (7) For the finishing touch, the eel's mouth is tied shut with a few loops of thread or light line.

In the foregoing technique both hooks emerge from the underside. Personally, I think it's as broad as it is long, but you also can rig an eel so that the rear hook is as before, but the leading hook comes out the bait's head. In this variation the trailing hook is positioned as before, and the stringing material brought lengthwise through the body and out the mouth. Just beyond the eel's snout, roughly the length of the hook's shank ahead of the snout, secure your second hook to the stringing material, and cut off any excess. Now thrust the hook upward through the eel's head, from underneath, just behind the eyes, and bring its point out through the top of the head. That hook's ring eye will serve as the place of attachment of your leader. A two-loop barrel swivel between leader and hook eye is optional.

Note: In both of the above techniques the hooks can be either a needle-eye or ring-eye type, with one exception. The only advantage of the former is that their shanks can be pulled into the bait's body easier. The exception is the leading hook in the second method, the one coming out the top of the head. Since it will serve as a place of attachment for the leader, it should be a ring-eye type.

Another eel-rigging procedure calls for a metal squid, specifically a kind created for this combination natural-artificial bait. This type of squid is a couple of inches long, a half inch or so wide, and carries a fixed hook of appropriate size. The hook's shank is imbedded in the squid, but is bent in such a way that it emerges from the lure's body at about the middle, leaving its ring eye exposed.

A matching hook is secured to the stringing material as before. The material is drawn lengthwise through the eel's body, pulling the rear hook's shank up inside, also as before. The string material then is tied to the ring eye of the squid's hook. With your rear hook in position, the squid's hook is thrust upward through the bait's head. That upper hook in place, the eel's head can be secured to the hook with a few loops of line, twine, or strong thread. This arrangement furnishes weight to carry the lure deep and also allows the eel a lifelike swimming motion.

When using a bullet-shaped head, such as salvaged from a discarded feather lure, for weight, the eel can be rigged with two hooks as outlined earlier, utilizing the hole running lengthwise through the metal head. But here the eel's head is cut off, and an inch or so of skin is peeled back to accommodate the metal substitute. Lashings of strong twine will keep the metal head in place. Metal lips and other gadgets designed to steer a bait deep and/or enhance its motion in the water can be added to the eel's head end in similar fashion.

Tip: This isn't orthodox, but I offer it as a contribution to your striped bass angling lore. Small flounders rigged like eels have been known to take stripers up to twenty pounds or so over a mud bottom.

Okay, so much for rigged whole eels. Now let's look at eelskin rigs.

If the name has led you to guess that these involve only the skin of eels, you've surmised correctly. Like rigged eels, these baits often are more effective at night than by day, for the same reason. Also like rigged eels, they can be bass killers.

There are two basic techniques. Just about all eelskin rigs are variations of one or the other. If you don't want to go to the messy fuss of procuring your own eels and skinning them, you can buy the skins already prepared.

Obviously there has to be some way to support and extend the skin, since there's no body flesh. That's what the two rigging methods have in common. Both allow water to flow through the skin when the bait is retrieved or trolled, distending it like a breeze fills an airport windsock, and cause it to imitate the appearance and behavior of the real McCoy.

One method calls for a metal squid with a ring or similar arrangement through which water can flow into the socklike skin.

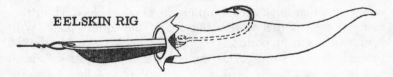

EELSKIN RIG

The larger open end of the skin is secured to the ring with line or stout thread. The squid's hook is brought out through the skin, top or bottom, according to how the hook is imbedded in the squid or as preference dictates (turn the squid upside down, if need be). If desired, a second hook can be added, bridled to the bend of the squid's hook with a short length of line or stout twine. It can emerge from the eelskin in the same or opposite direction of its predecessor.

The other basic procedure utilizes a weighted head, of which there are several kinds. They too have one thing in common: They have an aperture to let water flow into the skin and inflate it. With a weighted-head setup, one or two hooks may be secured to it by six to eight inches or so of leader wire or, as some anglers prefer, by a similar length of light chain made for this purpose. The eelskin is lashed to the weighted head, after which the hooks are thrust through the skin so that only their points, barbs, and a small section of their bends protrude. It's optional as to whether both hooks come out the skin's underside, or both through the top, or, as many of us like, the forward hook comes out the top and its mate comes out the bottom.

If you don't mind the fuss, you can prepare your own skins, thusly: Make a circular cut through the skin, completely around the eel, back of the head. Leaving the head on as a handle, peel the skin off, *intact*, like a sock. Eelskins can be stored in brine to preserve and toughen them. I'll tell you, though, it's less bother to buy 'em, pickled and ready.

Hook patterns and sizes for rigged eels and eelskin rigs are left to users' preferences, influenced by the sizes of the bass they're seeking. The O'Shaughnessy is a popular type, but there are several others. Whatever their pattern, sizes range up to a 7/o or 8/o. Match your hook sizes approximately to the weights of currently running stripers. Don't sweat out precision. Stripers have big mouths. Save the largest hooks for the biggest bass, and grade other sizes downward accordingly. A size one way or another isn't crucial, but it's important that your hooks be strong enough. It's better, I'd say, to go a bit on the larger side than the other way, especially if fairly heavy fish are known to be in the area.

Rigged eels, particularly those that are brine-preserved for a long time, become more limber with use, and so improve with age. Another thing: Rigged eels and eelskins actually seem to increase their potency as baits when they become smelly. The "riper" the better. This is one of relatively few exceptions to the rule in most angling that all baits should be as fresh as possible.

When rigged eels and eelskin rigs are attached to your line

you'll employ substantially the same setup as for plugs (see the section on plugs).

Rigged eels and their skin-only versions can be deadly for stripers; and, if worked properly, they often account for heavy-weights. That's why whole eels up to sixteen, eighteen, even twenty inches long, and skins in nearly the same lengths, come into play. They constitute big baits for big fish. But they have drawbacks. They demand suitably heavy tackle to cast, and even then are anything but easy to fling. With a fairly brisk breeze, moving parallel to the beach or against the caster, it can become practically impossible to get the lures out.

Since eels in their natural state are bottom feeders, it follows that imitative rigs should ride close to the bottom. To have your bait at an effective level and to be able to fish it properly, you'll base your choice between a rigged eel or a skin on local conditions such as the nature of the bottom, tides, current strengths, and type of surf. Thus, when current or tidal pull isn't too great, or when the surf is relatively quiet, a plain rigged eel, or one weighted slightly at the head, will do a job. At other times and in other places, when currents are powerful or a heavy surf is running, you may have to employ a heavier terminal setup, such as a rigged eel and metal squid combination, or an eelskin rig with a weighted head, to get your bait down where it belongs. Fishing under a variety of conditions will enable you to determine which outfit stands the better chance at a given time.

Whichever rig is selected, it should ride low over the bottom, even bouncing occasionally. (*Tip:* In rocky places you'll have problems, so carry spares.) Usually a retrieve is on the slow side, punctuated at intervals by short, smart movements of the rod tip. These maneuvers, together with current flow, impart a life-like action to the bait.

There's a detail that involves two schools of thought. One faction "polishes" eel baits before use, scraping them with a knife or rubbing them with steel wool to bring out a lighter, brighter color, which they consider more eye-catching to bass. The other school of thought says "Nuts to that!" (or words to that effect) and doesn't bother with the polishing. Both schools get their quota of fish. See which works better for you.

Rigged eels and eelskin rigs have a certain amount of versatility in that they can be trolled as well as cast. Moreover, they'll take marine gamesters other than striped bass. Bluefish, marlin, and swordfish have been caught on them; so have sharks, when the baits are fished in drift chumming.

SPECIAL Teasers of one kind or another have been used for years to excite fishes' attention and get them interested in baits. Teasers are effective in trolling for tuna, albacore, bonito, marlin, barracuda, and other finned game. As you now know, they work in shark fishing too. The type of teasing done in shark hunting is different than in trolling, but the idea is the same.

A teaser also has a place in surfing for striped bass. Results aren't guaranteed, but a teaser can stir up action when fishing is slow. As usual, the gimmick has a host of variations. I'll give you a few basics; then you can do some fooling around on your own.

A common bass teaser consists of a bit of bucktail or a couple of brightly colored feathers secured to a hook—a 2/0 to a 6/0 or 7/0 or 8/0, according to current bass sizes. That ensemble is tied to the swivel between line and leader via a few inches of strong leader material. Usually the connection to the swivel is made by means of a small snap fastener so that it can be removed easily. The plan is for this teaser to ride ahead of the main lure. It can be dressed up in various ways, if desired. Painting the windings that hold the bucktail or feathers to the hook a bright yellow is one refinement. Adding a piece of pork rind to the hook is another.

An alternate arrangement is to have the teaser *follow* the main lure. All this involves is tying sixteen to eighteen or twenty inches of leader material to the teaser's hook and securing the other end to the main lure's stern.

Since both operate on the same principle, I don't know if one arrangement is superior to the other. It's a matter of time, place, and the fish themselves, I suppose. Strangely enough, though, a striper sometimes will favor the teaser to the other offering. If you get in among a bunch of schoolies with that outfit, it's even possible to nail fish on both attractors.

A bad feature of the teaser is that it will add to your terminal rig's air resistance and reduce casting distance proportionately. But where you don't have to cast too far that's no great worry.

SURF AND JETTY TACKLE SUGGESTIONS

Both conventional tackle and spinning equipment are wielded in surf and jetty fishing for striped bass and other species. Conventional gear has served anglers well for generations, and has undergone steady improvement over the years. Spinning tackle has earned enormous popularity because of its greater ease in casting, the greater casting distance it achieves with less practice, and its freedom from annoying backlashes. The choice is yours. Maybe I can help you make up your mind.

We can lump conventional and spinning equipment together for purposes of simplification. The same general rules apply for both. Where there are differences I'll note them.

First of all, give consideration to the rod's over-all length. Surf rods come in lengths up to 12 feet. Some are even longer. It stands to reason that these rods can be wielded with varying degrees of ease and effectiveness according to the heights and builds of their wielders. Arm lengths and musculature play a part too. A little guy with short arms, for example, might have problems with really long sticks (unless, maybe, he's built like an orangutan). Conversely, a big, husky guy might feel as though he were fishing with a lollypop stick if he were to use one of the shorter rods.

If you're of average height and build, for a male or female, give thought to rods in the 8-to-9½- or 10-foot range. If you're on the slighter side of average, look to rods on the lower side of that general range I mentioned earlier. If you happen to be taller, and perhaps huskier, than average, you can investigate sticks going up to 12 feet.

If you happen to be 6½ feet tall with arms a foot long, or 5 feet tall with arms 4 feet long, you have problems.

Pay heed to butt lengths too. These are more or less standardized according to over-all rod lengths and are in proportion. They can go 24 or 26 inches or more. They're longer, proportionately, than those on boat rods to give leverage in casting.

The main thing about butt length to concern you is that it won't be too awkward for you to handle.

The point of my going into all this is to help you find a rod that feels comfortable in your hands, casts without prompting you to wonder if you're courting a hernia or contusions, does its job well, and doesn't tire you in prolonged use. You're going to live with that equipment through many hours on the beach.

How can you find a rod that's both comfortable *and* serviceable?

Part of that selection is going to be trial and error, naturally. For preliminaries, visit a tackle shop and heft surf rods on display. Ask the dealer's advice and recommendations. Another help is to hike along beaches. Look at the rods in service. Ask questions of their users. I wouldn't be surprised if you'd even get to try some of those rods. Look for a fisherman about your height and build. Ask about his experience with his particular tackle.

Opinion is divided as to which is superior, a one-piece stick or a two-piece model. Many seasoned beach fishermen favor the former because they feel its casting and fish-playing action are better. Their argument is that a certain amount of action is sacrificed in a two-piece rod because of the ferrule uniting its sections. Technically that's true, but for an average user the loss is minor. Besides, there are rods with glass ferrules that bend as the rods curve, eliminating any stiffness inherent in metal ferrules. A two-piece rod's advantage is that it can be stored and carried more easily. But that doesn't have to be a major factor. There are padded rod carriers that can be quickly installed on automobiles to transport long, single-piece models. In storage those sticks can be carefully laid flat.

The action of a rod's tip section, that length between butt handle and tiptop guide, is very important. Give thought to the kinds and weight ranges of the fishes you'll be seeking, places you intend to fish, casting distances required, and lures and lines you'll be using. You must consider whether most of your activity will involve light artificials or the heavier lures and natural baits. All that may sound complicated, but it isn't, really. Those details have a way of being satisfied "automatically."

You want a rod, conventional-type or spinning, that has "whip" to aid in casting, plus resiliency to absorb the shocks of battling a fish. You *don't* want extremes in either of those details. A rod that's too flexible will make it tougher to place your lures where you want them and control their movements afterward. At the other extreme is a rod with too much spine. Except, perhaps, with the heaviest terminal rigs, this type is that much more difficult to cast, and certainly isn't for a novice. It will kill a fish quicker too, because of its lower resiliency, thereby shortchanging you in the action department.

For maximum versatility a surf rod should have a tip section that combines sufficient resiliency for artificials in the 1- to 2½- or 3-ounce range with enough backbone to cast rigs carrying a 3- or 4-ounce sinker and a chunk of bait. At the same time it should possess the sturdiness to cope with opponents in a fairly wide range of sizes. There are such rods. Their versatility is achieved through the tapering of their tip sections. Here's how it works. The tip's outermost portion is sensitive enough to toss lighter artificials, yet strong enough to absorb the jolts of hard strikes and sudden power surges. Its middle part, becoming increasingly thicker, has sufficient whip to cast medium-weight lures and baits, plus muscle to handle hard-fighting battlers. And its lowermost portion, that closest to the butt, and still greater in diameter, combines backbone for good casting leverage and fish-fighting power with resiliency for handling heavier rigs.

Memo: Just as considerable casting distance won't always be a requirement, most of your surf-run opponents won't be lunkers. However, size potentials must be kept in mind. Surf stripers, for example, have been known to go up into the forty-pound, even fifty-pound, bracket. On the other hand, many of your surf-run gamefishes will be under ten pounds; some, such as kingfish, are as light as a pound and a half. You should be prepared for size extremes in areas you fish. If one outfit won't satisfy those demands, you'll have to invest in two, in appropriately different calibers. As I've said elsewhere, you can't always expect one rod-and-reel combo to satisfactorily handle all assignments, any more than you could expect the family sedan to serve equally well as a sports car and pickup truck.

The number of line guides on surf rods varies from three or four up to maybe eight or ten, depending upon whether they're the conventional or spinning type, and upon tip section lengths.

In this sport, the more guides the better. They keep the line away from the rod when it arches, thus preventing contact that could cut down on casting distance and increase line wear.

Once upon a time Calcutta cane and split bamboo were popular materials for surf rods. There may still be hard-nosed purists around who prefer them. But glass is the stuff today, and you can't beat it.

We explored details of what to look for in reels earlier. There's no need to repeat them here. But I do want to call your attention to one characteristic of surf models: They're usually built with wider-than-average spools. It's a decided advantage. Not only does it provide greater line capacity than that of reels of equivalent size, it also facilitates casts and retrieves. Too, with proper handling there's less chance of line "bunching up" in one part of the spool. Further, faster retrieves are made possible with conventional-type reels by greater gear ratios than on nonsurf models.

Interchangeability of spools is a desirable quality in a surf reel. It enables you to carry one, two, or more extra spools loaded with lines of different strengths, and readily switch from one to another as circumstances dictate. Another desirable quality is an easy take-apart feature. Surf reels take a beating from sand, spray, and water. By rights they should be disassembled and cleaned whenever they undergo such punishment. A quick-take-apart model makes the chore much simpler and easier.

Surf reels, conventional and spinning, come in a broad range of sizes, from small models designed for light spinning tackle on up to fairly large and sometimes heavy "mills" destined for the stoutest surf sticks. They're also available in a bewildering array of models. You won't go wrong with name brands. The choice of a particular model will take care of itself when you decide on a rod. Reel size, like maximum line strength, will be governed by the rod you select. Let desirable features—those you've learned from this book—help pinpoint a specific model. The main thing is that your reel and rod balance each other within reason.

SURF LINES There once was a rule of thumb that said: monofilament lines for spinning tackle, braided lines for conventional equipment. We've gotten away from that in all phases of salt-

water fishing. Improvements of lines and reels have made it possible to use those two types of lines interchangeably. The lighter
the tackle, the lighter the lines you must use. And the lighter the
lines, the smaller the lures you can fish. The stronger a line is,
the greater its diameter. And the greater a line's diameter, the
more its resistance to air, with commensurate reduction in casting
distance.

Understandably, line strengths are influenced by caliber of
tackle, weights of artificials and baits, and sizes of fishes involved.
In addition, there's that ever-present variable called angling skill.
Along beaches you'll see lines in several different strengths, from
10- or 12-pound test, even lighter sometimes, for lighter gear and
smaller fishes, up to 40- and 45-pound test when stouter tackle
and heavier game are the order of the day.

You'll have to make your selection according to the variables.
But I think you'll find that strengths within the following ranges
will take care of most of your surf assignments: for spinning
equipment, from 15- or 20-pound test to, say, 30 at the outside;
and between 20- and the 30s, perhaps 40-pound test at the outside, for conventional gear. As for quantity, the majority of surf
reels accommodate at least 150 to 200 yards or so of lines in the
popular strengths. That's enough for your needs.

Although leaders, as such, can be dispensed with when monofilament is used (except when monkeying around with scissor-
toothed bluefish), it's common practice among surf fishermen
to tie in 15 or 20 feet of somewhat heavier mono between terminal rig and line. The purpose of this is threefold: (1) With
lighter lines it lessens chances of breakage during a cast's initial
momentum, especially if the caster has a tendency to impart a
snap motion rather than make a continuously smooth, even sweep.
There's considerable strain on a line during the first swift propulsion of casting. Often surfers using conventional reels heighten
chances of breakage by keeping a thumb on the spool when casting. (2) Some of the more severe strain is imposed on a line when
the fish is being reeled in close, because this is when he's apt to
put up strong, desperate surges of resistance. That length of
stronger mono absorbs some of the strain. (3) That somewhat
heavier line provides extra protection against abrasion in rocky
areas.

JETTY FISHING   In our continuous struggle against the theft of shoreline by waves and currents, we have built numerous jetties, seawalls, and similar structures—one type is known as a groin (a smaller version of a jetty, usually extending to seaward at right angles to the beach)—along our coasts where erosion will gobble great chunks of shoreline.

Anglers quickly recognized the fishing potential of these structures. They provide a haven for many kinds of creatures such as little fishes, assorted crustaceans, and lesser forms of marine life. Moreover, below their waterline they accumulate a blanket of mussels and barnacles. All of these items, anchored and moving, comprise a magnetic attraction for sport fishes. Jetties and the like can be a happy hunting ground for striped bass, bluefish, northern whiting, blackfish, and other littoral species . . . and so for fishermen too. Jetty angling has established itself as a facet of surf fishing, and those who pursue it have acquired the friendly nickname, "jetty jockies."

Jetty fishing has its own advantages. There's the catch potential just mentioned. That, coupled with the positioning of such structures, means that casting distance usually isn't a factor in success. Jetties and seawalls extend fair distances out into the water. On oceanfronts they go well beyond the lines of breakers. In bays and similar locations they extend into channels, the thoroughfares traveled by fishes in searches for food. Often there are tide rips, current collisions, and other white-water agitation around these structures to attract striped bass. Sometimes there are also nearby sand bars with sluices and deep holes that yield fish. So there are occasions when a jetty jockey has a jump on his beachbound brother. When casting distance isn't a factor, jetty jockies have still another advantage in that they can get away with lighter, easier-to-handle tackle.

While I'm at it, I should point up the disadvantages of jetty fishing. Chiefly these involve certain dangers. I don't want to overdramatize them or give an impression that you take your life in your hands when fishing a jetty. 'Tain't so. By and large, you're safer on a jetty than when driving your car or even walking across a busy street. But you should be apprised of certain perils, if for no other reason than that they exist. Then, by exercising common sense and simple precautions, you can make those dangers almost as remote as being clouted by a meteorite.

Jetty fishing's principal danger lies in tricky footing. Most jetties are constructed from rocks. Dry rocks are bad enough to scramble over. Wet rocks, especially those with accumulations of vegetation, are as slippery as greased glass and extremely treacherous. While awaiting action you'll be wary. It's during the excitement of playing a fish that you have to watch out. Caution may go with the breeze. A penalty for carelessness is broken bones.

Another danger, nowhere nearly as common as the foregoing, is the possibility of being marooned on a jetty's seaward end by rising tides and/or a very rough surf. The outermost ends of jetties often are choice fishing sites. Watch your tides and a mounting surf caused by a stiffening wind. Don't find yourself isolated.

JETTY TACKLE   Because casting distance isn't a prerequisite, jetty rods are shorter than their beach fishing counterparts. Dimensions among typical jetty sticks range from 5 to 6 or 6½ feet for their tip sections and from 18 to 24 inches for their butts, giving over-all lengths of 6½ to 8½ feet. These shorter lengths are better suited to jetty operations, doubly so when climbing over rocks or perched like a mountain goat atop one with barely enough level surface to accommodate a brace of seagulls.

Jetty fishing's popularity has brought about rods designed primarily with that service in mind. These are sticks, I should add, that also can be used aboard boat and elsewhere. But the lack of need for casting distance also has brought considerable latitude to the conventional and spinning tackle wielded in jetty angling. Some fishermen make their all-purpose boat equipment serve them on those rock piles too. What's more, they catch fish.

If there's an "ideal" rod for a jetty jockey it has these attributes: It's within the length range mentioned a moment ago, with the lure- and bait-handling versatility noted for a good surf rod. It also possesses a nice balance between flexibility and backbone. The former is for maximum sport in playing a fish. The latter comes in handy when handling stubborn customers, such as blackfish, which have a habit of ducking into rocky crevices and defying you to dislodge them.

As in other kinds of fishing, the spinning and revolving spool

reels in jetty fishing balance their rods. The idea is to have an outfit that isn't cumbersome. An unwieldy outfit is not only awkward
under the circumstances, it can be an outright pain in the neck
when the angler has to climb among large rocks. A spinning reel
holding 150 to 200 yards of line up to 20-pound test or so is fine.
The same is true for a conventional model taking the same
lengths to 30-pound test or thereabouts.

Monofilament lines are popular among jetty jockies. It isn't
because braided lines can't be fished on the rock piles. They can.
But mono has a higher degree of abrasion resistance. That's important in places where lines are likely to come in frequent contact with rough surfaces. Protection against abrasion can be
increased by that gimmick of interposing 15 or 20 feet of somewhat heavier mono between terminal rig and line. If you'll be
doing appreciable jetty fishing with conventional tackle, get a
reel that can handle monofilament as well as braided line.

COME-ONS Many lures that get results in beach fishing for stripers also will nail bass from jetties. Among them are metal squids;
surface and subsurface plugs of various types, including poppers,
darters, propeller models, and the so-called mirror plugs; rigged
eels—6 to 8 inches long for smaller schoolies, and up to 12, 14,
or 16 inches for the big fellows; bucktails; and jigs in assorted
designs, including the hammered stainless steel models. Plugs
and jigs often have their tail hooks garnished with pork rind,
bucktails, or bits of bright-colored feather.

As always, selection of productive lures will be aided greatly
by inquiring locally and trying various models yourself. Note the
artificials used by other anglers. In time you'll assemble a good
basic selection. I say "basic selection" because there's only so
much gear you can tote on a jetty, and you're more or less isolated. It isn't always convenient to clomp back to your car
where you have other lures. That's why a standard accessory for
jetty work is a roomy shoulder bag. Jetty jockies favor this type
of carrier over a tackle box because it's less encumbering. In it
you can tote a reasonably wide assortment of artificials and other
necessities, including baits and bottom rigs if you intend to switch
off from striper pursuit, along with extra hooks, sinkers, leader
material, etc. A roomy bag also will have space for an extra reel

or two, or at least a couple of interchangeable spools of line, and maybe some chow.

Your inventory of lures for jetty striper fishing can include the following "standards": four to six plugs, varied surface and subsurface types; a few assorted bucktails; three or four jigs and an equal number of metal squids; three or four rigged eels in a separate, watertight bag, if your tackle can handle them; and a jar of pork rind.

HOW TO FISH A JETTY   Begin by looking on each jetty as a kind of self-contained fishing ground. Consider jetties as differing from each other in one or more aspects. You'll find that each has its own characteristics, good and bad. These traits may involve the way currents swirl around it at certain tides, for instance, or include a deep, swift channel along one edge, or a sand bar with a parallel cut nearby, or scattered deep pockets, etc.

It will pay to take time to study a jetty beforehand, looking for eddies, distinctive current patterns, and white water that spell potential bass spots. Remember too that stripers prowl in among large rocks forming the structure. Don't overlook places where waves churn up white water in their headlong rush toward the beach.

Since a jetty has several places with potential, there's a proper way to fish it if none are to be overlooked. And that is to cover it completely, both sides and outer end. To do this right you'll take up a series of casting stations along the jetty, making trial casts at each for maximum coverage.

There should be at least three satisfactory casts at each place you stop (casting station). Naturally, they should be in different directions. Here's a way to do it. Think of the jetty as a straight line. If you were to stand at any given point on either side of the jetty you could swing your rod horizontally through 180° of arc. Follow me? Okay, half that 180° arc is 90°. That would be when you're casting straight out in front of you. If you were to cast to either side, roughly halfway between the 90° and the side of the jetty, you'd be casting approximately in a 45° direction.

That's what you should do at each casting station as you progress out on a jetty. You can start on either side arbitrarily, but naturally you'll favor the side you think has the greater potential.

You can begin near the shoreside end. At each station where you give it a whirl you make your trial casts in three directions. It doesn't make any difference, but let's say your first flings are in a 45° direction toward the beach. No response. Okay, now try a couple at the 90° mark, directly out from you. If no action there, flip your lure in the 45° direction toward the jetty's seaward end. This is repeated at each place you elect to stop, on out to the end. The same thing goes for the jetty's other side, of course. Out on the end of the structure you'll probably have more than 180° through which to work, so you can try casts in four, five, six, or more different directions. Hopefully, you'll meet action before it becomes necessary to cover the entire jetty.

A jetty's roomiest, safest footing is usually along its top. Unfortunately, though, it isn't the best place from which to fish. To get the most from your casts you should be as close to the water *as you can operate safely*. This lower portion will better enable you to work your lures properly, play your fish, and bring them to gaff. Choose a dry, reasonably flat surface on which to stand. *Beware of wet rocks!*

Begin your coverage on one side near the beach end, where the waves begin to rear up before hurling themselves on the sand. Stripers can be feeding on sand eels and other bait fishes just beyond the breakers. Make your trial casts. You don't have to cast far. Any bass in the area are likely to be fairly close to the jetty, because that's where the food is. Cast your lure and work it in toward the jetty. There may be bass lurking right in among the rocks, practically at your feet. Plant your offering in a few places close alongside the jetty's base, and don't be too anxious to get your lure away from the rocks when you do. You might yank it away from a fish before he has a chance to grab it, or even see it. Lost lures are a calculated risk in this business. But it's worth the risk. It's also the reason you must have spares when fishing rocky areas.

If a station proves unproductive after a fair trial, move on to another, fifteen, twenty, or twenty-five feet farther along. Thoroughly cover places with potential. Work all the way out along one side, try the seaward end, then move shoreward along the jetty's other side, if necessary.

A jetty won't pay off in stripers every time, even for veteran jockies. There will be days mother didn't tell you about, when you're skunked, or when fishing is slow or only mediocre. There also will be days (and nights) when you have the good fortune to be on deck for a flurry. Those lively times make it all worthwhile.

In many instances tides will determine when you can fish a jetty. For example, one structure may have a lot of too-shallow water along one side at low tide. Often when oceanfront jetties are built, the beach literally follows them out to the end by building up along one side as coastwise currents deposit sand. If that piling-up is extensive, and there's a pretty good tide drop, much of one side may be too shallow at low tide. Your cue is to wait for high tide. Maybe you can fish the other side meanwhile. At the other extreme are jetties that are nearly submerged at high tide or by a combination of flood tide and rough surf. You'll have to save them for when the tide is lower.

Then there are jetties, notably those at inlets, where tidal currents have eroded a deep channel along one side of the structure. Often these channels are more productive when water is moving through them briskly. Other jetties have sand bars or shoals built up off their seaward ends. If these bars are within casting distance you can look for sluices and deeper spots to work at various tide stages.

To choose the right lures and work them properly in jetty fishing you'll have to pay attention to current directions and speeds. This is especially true when at an inlet. There's likely to be a strong flow along one side of the structure as the tide sweeps in or out. At other jetties—oceanfront and elsewhere—the main current action you'll have to reckon with is out at the end. There it may take the forms of swirls and eddies, rather than a continuous flow, as alongside an inlet jetty.

Current forces and directions become factors when you want to fish deep; and stripers frequently are taken near the bottom around jetties. If you cast in the direction of the current flow, the water's surge can thrust your lure upward, too high to be effective, when you retrieve. A better technique is to cast in the opposite direction. Here the tendency will be for the current to carry your lure toward you, and you'll have to continually take up slack; but at least you'll be able to get on bottom. Cast out

. . . let your lure hit bottom . . . take up slack . . . then retrieve, working the lure and letting it bounce along the sea floor. Rigged eels are worked the same way. So are the heavier artificials, such as metal squids, etc. Heavier lures are preferred in this technique because they find bottom and can be worked along it.

On jetties where there's no appreciable current, or on inlet structures when there's slack water between tides, you can work your favorite lures—plugs, bucktails, jigs, or whatever—in the customary manner. Pay attention to eddies and swirls at the jetty's outer end.

Inlets generally are productive of fish, in variety. Not only striped bass, but also bluefish, blackfish, weakfish, kingfish, and others. It's logical. These gateways are major highways for finned predators, with food as the magnet. They may be inbound or outbound in search of prey.

That leads into another jetty angling technique. This one can be productive for plugs, especially on an outgoing tide:

Select a casting station on the jetty's inlet side, or on its seaward end or close to it. Let your lure ride out toward the middle of the inlet, or cast it as far as you can in that direction. When it touches down and settles, allow the current to carry it a couple of hundred feet, and give it plenty of action. Once it's out there, let it rest a while. As long as it has some motion, you'll be able to feel it, it's working for you. If that doesn't get response, try retrieving it *across the current*. If you still haven't had a strike, repeat the entire procedure. Vary the distance you let the current transport your lure. Vary retrieve speeds too.

MISCELLANEOUS SURF AND JETTY GEAR   I've already mentioned a sand spike. Another beach fishing item is a pair of waders. There are different styles, but essentially surf waders are overgrown hip boots, coming up at least waist high, like a pair of pants, then continuing still higher in front like a pair of overalls, with a strap around the neck to hold them up. In warm water a swimsuit will do. But in spring and fall, when the water is downright frosty, you'll want waders. In case you've asked, yes, you can wear hip boots. But when you're out there clomping around in the breakers you're liable to forget that those boots don't go all the way up to your ears; and they're not very comfortable when they ship water, especially cold water.

Tip: Check your waders or boots periodically for leaks. Take them into a dark room and shine a flashlight inside them. Follow the manufacturer's instructions for mending.

The chances are that you won't wear boots or waders on a jetty unless there's a distinct chance of getting soaked below the waist. In any case, a pair of creepers or some form of nonskid safety footwear is a must, unless you get your kicks from risking a broken arm or worse. There are various kinds of footwear designed for this service. One type attaches to the bottoms of shoes or boots. They're inexpensive and are easily applied. Some jetty regulars cement golf shoe soles to their shoes or boots. And there's footwear made expressly for this use. All are designed for surer footing on slippery rocks; they're cheap insurance against possible injury or a dunking.

Sooner or later, on beach or jetty, you'll go night fishing. A flashlight in your tackle box or shoulder bag is a must. It has many uses: illuminating your way, for light when changing rigs or untangling backlashes, etc. A refinement is a fishing lamp you wear on your head. The idea was borrowed from coal miners. It leaves both hands free.

Essential in surf and jetty fishing is a gaff. The standard surf gaff is about two feet long and can be hung at the belt. For jetty action a couple of different lengths may be required. One, about the same size as a surf gaff, is for use when you can get close to the water. The other, which is anywhere from five to seven feet long, is for when you have to fish higher up on a jetty, because of its construction or because a rough surf is running. All these gaffs come in fixed-head models. Some telescope or jackknife into a more compact size for easier carrying. (I'm being optimistic, you see.)

Memo: Don't forget those other helpful items mentioned earlier: fisherman's pliers, stringer, sunglasses, a good knife, etc.

FISHING YOUR BASS FROM SHORE   Your battle starts with a strike. It also will end there if you don't keep your wits about you.

Hold your rod tip reasonably high, but don't try to poke out a star with it. This will let the rod absorb some of the shock of a smashing strike and the energetic fight that ensues, instead of throwing all the initial strain on the line alone. The rod's flexibility and resilience lessen chances of your line snapping under a stiff, sudden jerk, and also minimize possibilities of your hook ripping free of the mouth of a very hard-fighting opponent. To a certain extent the rod's resiliency also will take up some of the slack when your fish reverses direction suddenly or becomes gripped in the clutches of a breaker momentarily. But you still want to be prepared to crank rapidly if an appreciable amount of line slack develops. Bass can throw plugs easily enough; no sense in giving them a helping hand.

When you tie into a surf-running linesider you won't require the verification of witnesses. The strike is a solid *socko!* You'll find that you've invited yourself to a razzmatazz of a party, with no recess until the game battler has been reeled exhausted to the beach . . . or has escaped. You'll be matching muscle and tricks with two powerful opponents: the sea and one of its shrewd inhabitants.

When you get a strike, set your hook solidly. This is no time to be dainty. Plant the hook with a substantial upward lift of your rod tip. If you've nailed your fish, you'll know all about it. The bigger the bass, the more walloping that announcement will be.

In fishing dead baits you may encounter occasional stripers that "tick" or toy with your offering before mouthing it. Maybe they're not especially hungry. You'll have to give them time to really take the bait. If you don't get a strike after a reasonable chance, better check your rig. A bass or some other thief may have denuded your hook.

With live baits the strike usually is decisive, because here the stripers' intended targets are lively, trying to elude them. Responses to bullheads and other artificials generally are clear-cut and decisive too. With rigged eels or eelskins, especially when larger bass are involved, you may first feel a pronounced thump or bumping at the far end. Heavier linesiders sometimes "thump" (probably nosing around) a bait before taking it. You'll have to allow them time to grab it. A technique here is to throw your reel into free spool, letting a little line out to give some action to the bait. But stand by to re-engage the reel at an instant's notice when the fish actually takes hold. *Careful!* Don't let out too much line or you'll make it difficult to set the hook. Control the flow by keeping a thumb *lightly* on the spool.

You may be able to fight your bass successfully without moving outside a relatively small strip of beach. But if he's one of those wild hooligans that elects to carry out the naval engagement parallel to the beach, you'll have to go along with him. In any event, avoid retreating to higher sand. Slug it out with him where you are, moving only when required, and closer to the water if necessary. Keep your line as taut as you can to thwart any vigorous efforts to throw the hook.

Your reel's drag should be moderate at the most. Actually, the drag should be set beforehand, with care. Setting it too tight will cost you fish because of snapped lines. Not tightening it enough defeats the drag's purpose, which is to offer some resistance to the fish to aid in tiring him. A brake that is far too loose spells bad news in the form of slack when the fish runs.

Experience—some of the heartbreaking variety—will soon teach you just how much drag should be applied with the particular reel you're using. The proper amount is well under the line's breaking point, of course, and enough to aid in setting the hook. Later, if the fish is difficult to control, you can apply additional braking (easy does it, watch out for a painful line burn!) with your thumb. The drag adjustment can be tightened just a hair or two during the time you're playing a fish, but being precise under those circumstances is tricky, and doubly so when you're slugging it out with an obstreperous striper. And it can be fatal to your line if you misjudge. It's not advised until you're thoroughly familiar with your reel.

Often the smaller bass are the more active scrappers, whereas the larger fellows tend to be a slower, steadier, bulldog type of antagonist. There are exceptions, of course. And although your worthy opponent might peel off substantial line yardage in his first couple of dashes, his subsequent combat strategy is likely to involve a series of short or moderate runs, punctuated by power sprints to lower levels and seaward.

Always he'll reach into his bag of tricks. In addition to a continuous display of muscle, plus a few acrobatics if he happens to be one of the younger, friskier individuals, he'll shake his mighty head in attempts to throw the hook, and he'll streak for any rocks that are convenient. He might even swing himself broadside to the current to make things as tough as he can. And when he demands line he won't wait for the idea to be put to a vote.

But you'll have your innings too. By pitting the rod's spring action against him you'll be exerting your kind of pressure. Don't make the mistake of trying to "horse in" a striper of any size. He'll show you how wrong you can be. Play him. That's the sport. When he runs away with line he's only kidding himself, because the water drag on that line will help to tire him. Sooner or later the exertion of battle will gradually wear him down, and you'll be able to retrieve line.

Never write off your opponent. The closer you get him to the beach, the trickier he can become, especially if he's at all green or wild. More than once I've had green bass—schoolies of only ten pounds or so—leap clear of the water as I was trying to work them toward the beach.

This final stage can mean salvation for your striper if you don't handle him right. Beaching a fish in the surf has its tricky moments.

Let the surf give you a hand. Use incoming waves to your advantage, retrieving line as each one seizes the fish and moves him bodily toward the beach. *Take up any slack.* Keep your line taut, but let him drift back into the troughs between waves if need be, then reel in line as the next comber lifts him toward you. Never try to strong-arm a still-active bass through a surf to the beach. Such impatience is very likely to cost you your fish.

You shouldn't have any problem reeling in the smaller schoolies. Sometimes the breakers toss them right onto the sand for you in an apron of foam. This wave deal works with larger bass too, but it's risky. The waves that maroon your fish also recede; and as they do, they exert a sudden extra strain on the line, which may be all it needs, if it's fatigued, to cause it to part. You probably are aware that undertows can be strong. Their tumbling, suctionlike pull also has been known to get stripers all fouled up in leaders until *they* break. What can happen too is that a bass, hitting the sand, makes a desperate lunge oceanward as air sears his gills. When that occurs and he manages to take off, let him go; but keep your line taut and your rod tip high, and work him in again with the surf's aid.

Seasoned surfmen sometimes will work a bass in as close as they can (which in this case is right at their feet), then seize the fish by the gills to effect capture. It works, but it's not as easy as it sounds. It calls for good timing and fast movement; and if the angler isn't careful he can get a hook in his hand. This landing method isn't recommended unless you happen to be without a gaff.

And you shouldn't be. A small hand gaff is an important part of a surf fisherman's gear. Keep it handy. Lead the bass toward you. Have your gaff ready in one hand; work your fish within range, lifting your rod if necessary; then—*wham!*—let him have it. Make the shot count. If you miss, don't try to hold him in tight. Let a receding wave carry him, then work him into gaffing range again. Just be careful you don't knock the fish off the hook in your excitement. Don't let some well-intentioned helper seize the line while you attempt to gaff your fish. If the bass makes a last-minute power surge it could break the line.

FIGHTING YOUR BASS FROM JETTIES   This action has its own spicy moments. One presents itself when you go to plant your hook. If you're fishing fairly light tackle and you tie into a husky linesider, you'll have to give it everything you've got to set the hook. That accomplished, you're ready for the next problem. . . .

Rocks. I don't have to tell you what they do to line—and *tout de suite,* as the French say. If your striper goes deep around rocks, or ducks into a crevice, you have a headache. Be of good cheer, though. You won't have it long if your line saws against barnacles.

If your fish comes to the top, the only thing you have to worry about is whether or not he can send your hook flying when he shakes his head.

After a few preliminary maneuvers, which are likely to vary between going deep and showing at the surface where you'll see him, your bass probably will take off on a run. There's no choice but to let him go. The more line he takes, the more its water drag will tire him. Every striper has his own blueprint for battle; and the number, length, and intensity of his gallops are governed accordingly.

It's in these that you may be up against the next problems.

For instance, instead of running straight out from you, he might elect to dash toward the jetty's seaward end. You may have to follow him to keep your line clear of rocks and other obstructions, including fellow anglers and spectators. Doing this among irregularly shaped, often sloping masses of stone is tricky, so watch your step. No fish is worth a broken leg.

Or your opponent might decide to streak toward the beach. This is common. It will show how adept you are at controlling your fish. Your first impulse will be to follow him, with the idea of playing him from the beach. This can be done if you're close to the strand to begin with, but if you're any distance out on the jetty it can be a sucker trap. In the first place, that fish can swim a lot faster than you can scramble over jetties. What is equally factual, he might abruptly change direction and swing to seaward, leaving you 'way back yonder somewhere with your bare (red) face hanging out. Then you sure will have your work cut out for you, trying to keep your line away from the rocks. Instead of heading for the sand to play him through the waves, try to bring him under control from where you're standing. Try to lead him back toward you. It will be give and take, with a calculated risk of a ruptured line if the bass is of any size; but usually you'll be able to work him back toward the area where you hooked him.

It's tough sometimes with a rambunctious customer, even a comparatively small schoolie, especially if you're wielding the lighter-caliber gear so common on jetties. But with the right playing—letting him take line when he demands it, retrieving line when he slows—you'll do it. Keeping him near the top where waves can thrust him toward you will help to work him closer.

You want to bring him within gaffing range. And here's where a long-handled gaff is worth its weight in gold—or at least beer. Once you get your striper within that weapon's scope, let him have it. Give it to him *quickly* and accurately. Use a hooking motion toward you, rather than a downward swing. A split second's delay here, and the fish could be away on a run or be carried bodily out of range by a wave.

With your gaff planted, get the fish higher up on the jetty, where you can unhook him without concern about his flipping or slipping to freedom. Run your stringer, that length of clothesline or whatever, in through his big mouth and out under a gill cover. Once he's high and dry, secured on a stringer, you can remove the gaff and safely unhook him. Just be sure your catch is in a place where he can't flip himself back into the water or down into some deep crevice among the rocks where it would be difficult or hazardous, if not impossible, to retrieve him.

TROLLING

One way to precipitate an argument among striped bass regulars is by asking which is the superior way to catch the line-sided rascals, from shore or by trolling—"superior" meaning more sport, more productive, and (let's not forget this for ego's sake) more demanding of skill. You'll meet enthusiastic proponents of both techniques.

The fact is that each has its advantages and its own brand of superiority.

Personally, I think shoreside bassing is superior to trolling in that it provides a more primitive, gutsy, man-to-beast slugfest. Puts a guy more on his talents too. On the other hand, trolling has a superiority over shoreside angling in that it covers more ground and therefore is likely to account for greater numbers of fish. It's also a more comfortable, lazy way to fish.

Both methods account for heavy stripers, although boat fishing in general, which includes both trolling and casting, accounts for more of the heavyweights, in terms of man-hours of effort, than fishing from a beach or jetty. So, in a sense, comparing trolling with surfside and jetty operations boils down to a matter of quality (of combat) versus quantity (of catch). But don't let that sway you either way. As a striper buff you must try both methods. In the final analysis the better technique for you is the one giving you the most pleasure and satisfaction. You fish primarily for diversion. Quantity, in my opinion, isn't necessarily a criterion of good fishing.

TACKLE TALK You have latitude in your choice of rods for trolling, but certain things should be kept in mind when making a selection.

To begin with, any medium-caliber boat rod will serve. This is a stick with a tip section about 5 or 5½ feet long and a butt to suit individual taste. It will have at least 4 or 5 good ring guides, and its tiptop guide should be of the roller type for wire lines in deep trolling for stripers, bluefish, and other battlers. In fact, if you'll be fishing wire lines quite often, it won't do any harm to get a rod that has roller guides throughout.

Although any medium-caliber boat rod will serve in trolling, certain traits make some rods superior to others in this sport. One is real sturdiness without great cost to flexibility. It must have the capacity to absorb the stresses and strains of fighting muscular opponents. Trolling in itself, no fish on, imposes a strain on a rod. There's the weight of the line, plus water drag on it, plus the lure's weight and water resistance, plus the boat's forward motion.

Ideally, a trolling rod will have substantial spine where it counts, in the lower portion of its tip section, yet the outermost part of that section will have plenty of spring to give and take when setting a hook and playing a fish. Its butt and handle section should be long enough to provide good leverage, yet not be awkward to handle. Many trolling rods come equipped with a simple refinement that's handy when fishing from a fighting chair. It's a slotted metal cap on the butt's free end that fits securely into the chair's gimbal or rod socket.

A foregrip of cork or other good-grasping material is helpful. Even more important is a secure reel seat, one that reliably locks your reel in position. It's very exasperating to have a reel wobble in its seat when playing a fish.

I've been talking about conventional rods. "What about spinning rods in trolling?" you ask. I'm glad you brought that up.

Want my opinion? (Might as well take it, you've paid for it. You can accept it or try to disprove it, as you will.) Spinning rods, by and large, are unsatisfactory in trolling. They're too flexible. As I'll reiterate from time to time, spinning sticks are designed chiefly for casting, and in that they star. But the flexibility that suits them beautifully to casting, works against them in trolling. They may be too willowy to furnish the needed *zock!* when setting a hook. Many times you really have to slap it to a fish to plant your hook properly.

You'll see spinning rods used in trolling, and there are models with added spine to offset the flexibility drawback to a certain extent. There are even heavier-duty spinning rods employed in fishing for large game. But for the everyday type of trolling by an average angler I recommend conventional tackle. So we'll concentrate on that.

You have latitude in your selection of trolling reels too. Heddon, Garcia, Penn, and other leading manufacturers produce excellent models. I'll suggest some sizes and features.

For much of your fishing you might be able to get away with a 2/0, but more in balance with that rod I mentioned earlier, and huskier, is a 3/0 or 4/0. Your reel also must have the guts to withstand strains. They can be considerable. A smooth, dependable drag system is a must. Another important feature is a metal spool. Lines, notably monofilament, can exert extraordinary pressure on a reel spool when a fish is being fought. It's enough to break a plastic spool sometimes.

Optional refinements include an extra-large crank handle for better gripping. Another is a level wind mechanism that lays the line evenly on a spool as it's being retrieved; it's not essential, but handy, particularly in night fishing.

"What about lines?" you press.

Well, let me offer this profound thought, based on an invaluable lesson I learned through experience: Sport fishing is extremely difficult without lines. I make it a point never to be without them, except, maybe, when I go to the movies.

Okay, I'll be serious.

There's no point in rehashing all that business about different kinds of lines we've already covered. If you need a refresher course you can refer to the chapters on tackle and bluefish.

We'll simplify things here and avoid unnecessary repetition by saying that both braided and monofilament lines are used in striper trolling. Both will serve you as well in that technique as they will in others.

There will be times when you want to troll deep, really deep. Back in the chapter on bluefish you'll find devices to aid in this.

Also for deep trolling is wire line, discussed earlier. To that I'll add lead-core line. This has its own built-in weight. Through its center runs a metal core. Outside is a synthetic such as nylon. Lead-core line usually won't take your rig as deep as wire will, so the former is more for shallower depths. Lead-core line is more limber than wire, and therefore easier to handle; but if you want to go very deep with it you'll have to tie in a drail or trolling sinker.

If trolling eventually will be your main method, and you'll be doing quite a bit of it, it will pay you to have at least two complete outfits. On the reel of one you'd keep your regular trolling line. On the reel of its companion outfit you'd carry wire line for those occasions when you have to go deeper.

If you have to be satisfied with a single outfit meanwhile, my suggestion is that you keep its spool filled with Dacron or whatever you're using, and take along drails or a trolling planer for deep trolling. Even better, get yourself a reel with interchangeable spools so you're outfitted with lines of different strengths.

Thirty-pound line, fished properly, will handle most, if not all, the stripers with which you'll lock horns. But if you're a cautious soul who wants a margin of safety, especially when fish to fifty pounds or so are known to be about, there's nothing stopping you from going to line in the forty-to-fifty-pound bracket, *so long as your rod is rated to handle it.* One hundred fifty to two hundred yards should be ample.

TACKLE FOR SCHOOLIES The gear we've just discussed was suggested to equip you for larger bass, huskies up to forty and fifty pounds and even heftier. It also will give you action with what I'll call the larger mediums, those linesiders in the upper twenties and thirties, as well as with smaller medium-size fish and even the lighter schoolies. But the sport will be in proportion to the caliber of your tackle. Naturally you won't have as much fun with small stripers on an outfit more suited to their big brothers.

By rights, therefore, you should acquire a lighter outfit, a smaller-caliber version of the other, to accommodate stripers ranging from about five or six pounds up into the teens to twenty pounds or so. Its rod will be of about the same over-all length as the one I suggested earlier, but appreciably lighter and rated to handle lighter lines. Being lighter, it will have more flexibility. But it also must possess sufficient backbone to give you authority when you set the hook and play your fish.

The reel for your lighter outfit will be proportionately smaller to balance the rod. A 2/0 can do it. Or you can clamp on a 3/0 if it isn't unwieldy for that stick. In that way you can make one reel do for two rods.

It follows that the lighter outfit's lines will be lighter too. You probably won't go any heavier than about 20-pound test; and you won't go *that* heavy if your rod isn't rated for it. One hundred to 150 or 200 yards will be sufficient.

The chances are that most of your school striper hunting will be in comparatively shallow water, so there may be no call for wire or metal-core line. Trolling speed and the amount of line out will give you a certain amount of added depth if you need it. When you have to go deeper than usual, a trolling sinker of appropriate weight will put your rig where you want it.

TALKING ABOUT SIZES FOR A MOMENT   Much of your activity with striped bass, wherever caught and by whatever means, will involve schoolies. The accent, I suspect, will be on bass from barely over the legal minimum keeping length to about fifteen pounds.

But much depends upon where, when, and how often you fish, as well as on how much savvy you develop and how you apply it. The more you fish and the better you fish (the latter is usually the consequence of the former), the greater your chances of tying into larger bass. I don't know if you'll ever be fortunate enough to catch one of those sixty-pound bruisers. Maybe you will. You might even set a world record one day. I hope you do. But in the main, speaking frankly, you can consider yourself fortunate if you boat or beach thirty- and forty-pounders. That's nice striper fishing, make no mistake, and you can be proud of such catches. What's more, if you fish persistently and correctly, using every bit of lore at your disposal, your chances of nailing lunker-size bass are as good as the next guy's —a lot better than those of some fishermen I've seen.

TROLLING LURES AND RIGGING   There's a host of lures for trolling, so many that it's impossible to discuss them all. What we'll do, therefore, is look at some of the more popular and proven models. We'll start with those commonly brought into play for schoolies.

SPINNER BAITED WITH WORM

For years on both sides of Long Island Sound and elsewhere, a classic, old faithful rig has been one we call a spinner-and-worm combination. For schoolies it's a killer.

This rig is preceded by a leader. Its material and length are optional. You can't go wrong with monofilament. Its relatively low visibility is a help. It can be about the same strength as your line. A couple of pounds test either way doesn't make that much difference. Three or four feet are enough (some anglers use two). Attachment to the line can be made via a two-loop barrel swivel, or through a snap swivel to facilitate rig changes.

The rig itself consists of a 2/0 or 3/0 hook, just ahead of which are attached one or two, even three or four, spinner blades. These blades are available in chrome, stainless steel, pearl, and other finishes, and in varying shapes and sizes. Models known as the June Bug, Willow Leaf, and Cape Cod are popular, and there are others equally effective. Their function is to spin and flash in the water as they're trolled, catching a striper's eye and teasing him into making a pass at the baited hook. The bait in this case, the other half of the combo giving it its name, is sandworm, impaled on the hook in such a way as to stream out behind and flutter. A single worm will do. Two can be even better.

Usually the weight of spinner and worm will carry the rig deep enough. When a current is brisk enough to thrust the rig too high, a small pinch-on sinker or two affixed to the leader will compensate.

A spinner-and-worm combination is highly effective for school stripers ranging up into the teens in weight. It's also been known to take heavier bass. I had a twenty-four-pounder fall for the gimmick, and I've known it to capture linesiders up to about thirty pounds. What's more, these spinner-worm rigs sometimes are trolled for big bass when other come-ons fail.

Spinners are an effective added attraction; but some anglers either have an aversion to what they consider so much extra "hardware" or simply like to troll worms alone. Sandworms usually are favored, although bloodworms can be used. The rig is basically the same, including leader, as just outlined, minus the spinner blades. The worm is impaled on a 2/0 or 3/0 hook through its forward end, leaving most of it free to stream out astern and wiggle. Here again a single worm or a couple can be used.

Bucktails are school striper killers too. So are bullhead jigs. These two types of artificials come in various designs, finishes, colors, and weights. They're all effective at one time or another. Certain models may produce better than others at given times. Similarly, certain finishes and colors may be more effective than others on occasion. All I can say is, I've had no quarrel with a plain finish in yellow or white. But try as many as you can. As for weights, a half ounce to an ounce is fine.

A VARIATION OF BUCKTAIL RIGGING

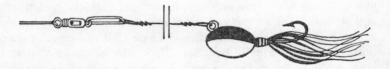

Rigging of bucktails and bullheads is a matter of personal preference. Variations are numerous. I'll give you one as a starter. You can vary it as you see fit:

A three- or four-foot length of leader material, such as monofilament, is attached to the line by a barrel swivel. The leader's other end is tied to the lure. Again you can substitute a small snap swivel for the barrel swivel for changing of rigs. That's all there is to it.

A finishing touch is to garnish the lure's hook with a strip of pork rind. Some bait and lure suppliers put out pork rind in colors. Yellow is good, especially when the water isn't as clear as it might be. But you won't go wrong with the natural whitish color. This pork rind is impaled on the hook like a worm and functions the same way, fluttering astern as it's trolled, hopefully waving an oncoming bass into grabbing himself a mouthful of hook. Sometimes it works. But sometimes stripers are crafty, biting off that pork rind just short of the hook. A second, smaller, trailing hook, bridled onto the bend of the first and imbedded in the free portion of the rind, usually takes care of short-strikers. You can try this stunt with a worm too.

Trolled plugs take their quota of striped bass. Here I'll have to leave the selection up to you. There are too many different kinds. You can make your choice from among poppers, underwater swimmers, models with propellers, etc., in lengths up to 4 and 5 inches long and weights to 1, 1¼ and 1½ ounces or so. And there are all kinds of finishes, in a rainbow of colors. Always ask around among trollers and tackle stores in the areas you fish, then assemble an assortment accordingly. Your plug kit should include representatives of both surface and subsurface types, with an accent on the former. Schoolies often feed or "gambol" at the top.

Still other kinds of artificials should be represented in your armament for school stripers. These include spoons. There's a small army of them in somewhat varying shapes. Lengths among the smaller models range from about 2 to 4 and 5 inches, and they're light. Typical among these are models with a single, fixed hook, 1/0 to 3/0. A popular finish is shiny chrome plate. Models that have known popularity over the years include the Pfleuger Record, Huntington Drone, and Acetta Pet.*

Spoons' effectiveness depends upon their action—spinning, wobbling, or whatever—and flash in the water. But many fishermen aren't content with these inherent qualities, so they dress up their spoons with bits of bright-colored feather, a piece of pork rind, or a small strip bait.

Other artificials rigged for school stripers include chromed jigs and block tin squids in two-to-five-inch lengths. These can be jigged as they're trolled to contribute to their action. Sometimes they too are decorated with pieces of bright feather and their hooks garnished with pork rind, worm, or a piece of strip bait.

In areas where eels offer a ready supply of food for bass—and

* Among salt- and fresh-water artificials of all kinds there is occasional discontinuing of certain models for one reason or another. However, you generally can locate a reasonable facsimile, or even a near-duplicate, under a different name.

these include bays, tidal creeks, and around the mouths of estuaries—rigged eels are effective for schoolies. Here the baits are smaller, about six inches long, but they're rigged just like their bigger brothers. They can be trolled by themselves or in combination with spoons or metal squids.

While I think of it—this goes for any kind of fishing and whatever the targets—if you buy an artificial that's "hot" for a while but then seems ineffective, hold onto it. The odds are that that lure, like styles in men's suits, will "come back" again.

NOTES ON RIGGING   Rigging of plugs, spoons, other artificials, and eels is subject to individual variations according to the users' ideas. But basically the setups follow the same blueprint: a leader of monofilament or other material, attached to the line through a barrel swivel or snap swivel, then the lure affixed to the leader. Many of the variations involve leader lengths, which can be two feet or more. Three to four feet is the length I've favored, but leaders can go to six, eight, or ten feet, and even more. I can't see any need for more than six to eight feet at the outside; but then, differences of opinion are what make horse racing, as they say.

Ordinarily the weights of most of these rigs will be enough to fish the lures at desired levels. When currents are strong enough to push them upward too high, small pinch-on sinkers on the leader will offset that thrust. When deep trolling is indicated, and the rig's weight alone isn't sufficient, a drail or trolling sinker of proper weight is incorporated between line and leader. It can be tied in directly, or, if you want to be able to remove it easily when conditions change, use a snap swivel arrangement.

FOR LARGER BASS   Just about all the artificials employed for schoolies also will take medium and heavier bass. The only major difference is that attractors rigged for the larger stripers are scaled upward in sizes and weights.

Plugs trolled for striped bass run a full gamut. They include surface swimmers, subsurface types, and deep runners. Among them are darters, poppers, "straight" swimmers, those with an intriguing side-to-side skitter, types with their own uniquely erratic action in imitation of frightened or injured bait fishes, etc.

From five and six inches long they go up through eight and ten inches to as big as twelve and fourteen inches among the whoppers, with a weight range from about two ounces to over four ounces. Many are single-piece plugs; others are jointed for more movement. Some have metal lips that bend upward or downward to regulate their traveling depths. Some have glass or painted eyes; others have propellers. Some produce distinctive sounds. And the variety of colors and finishes is awesome—mackerel, blue mullet, red and white, silvery, and so on, into the distance.

Their hook armament varies too. There may be a single swinging hook, or one or two sets of treble hooks. Some models carry three sets of treble hooks—one set forward near the lure's head end, another halfway to two-thirds of the way back, and the third set in a trailing position. Hook sizes graduate upward from 1/o or 2/o on smaller models to 5/o to 6/o or so on the big boys. Here again there are opportunities to add attraction by dressing the trailing hook(s) with pieces of bright feather or with a nylon or natural bucktail.

Remember what I said about asking questions and noting what other anglers use.

You should pay some heed to the sizes of the plugs and other artificials you select. In general you can be guided by that old rule of thumb: big lures for big fishes; smaller lures for smaller fishes. At the same time you should try to match for size, as closely as possible, food on which stripers dine in a given place at a given time. Since that menu changes, it follows that your plugs should be in graduated sizes accordingly.

Plugs trolled for stripers have to be rugged. The strain imposed on a lure by a strike and subsequent power surges of even a medium-size bass can be considerable, heightened by the boat's motion. Here's where through-wire construction in plugs shows its worth. It's also a good argument for triple-strength hooks on those plugs.

Earlier we talked about spoons, but I purposely saved one for special spotlighting. It's king of spoons for size, a come-on for lunkers up to fifty pounds and more. I'm talking about the bunker spoon, named for the mossbunker because of its shape and size. As schooling fish, mossbunkers frequently are targets of stripers'

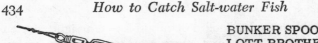

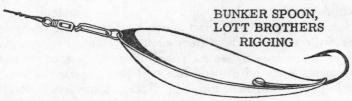

(No leader needed with mono line.)

food raids. Bunker spoons are either chrome-plated or of stainless steel for flash, in imitation of fishes' silvery sides. With their
shape, size, and action, they're intended to simulate the species
for which they're named.

Bunker spoons are quite heavy. Lengths range from six and
eight inches to nearly a foot, with widths of three or four inches
and more. Their body is roughly teardrop-shaped, and usually
somewhat concave for action in the water. Extending from the
tapered end is a hook that can go up to a husky 12/0, depending upon the spoon's size. Normally this hook is fixed; but, if preferred, this arrangement can be modified by substituting a
swinging hook. The bunker spoon is a trolling lure, and certain
models have a keellike refinement to give them greater stability
when towed.

We joke about bunker spoons. We say that if we can't hook
a striper with one we can club him to death with it. But their
effectiveness is no joke. Bunker spoons have a justified reputation
for being lethal to large stripers. They've accounted for many
linesiders in the forty- and fifty-pound classes. A couple of them
in graduated sizes should be among your trolling weapons.

Bunker spoons take some getting used to. Until then, their
sheer weight and surface area might delude you into thinking
you have a fish on. But that's minor.

A serious drawback is that their size and weight can cause
the hook to work itself loose as the fish is being fought, in which
case the striper might throw the lure and escape. Many a lunker
has been lost this way. Here's where the standard arrangement of
a fixed hook poses a problem. There's no give to it. That's why
some trollers modify the lure by substituting a swinging hook.
The alteration can be effected by minor surgery. After removal

of the fixed hook, by cutting off if necessary, a small hole is drilled through the spoon's tail end. Into this is placed a *strong* ring that will take a ring-eye hook of suitable caliber. And there's a further refinement. Some anglers feel that a swinging hook has a drawback in that it isn't always in the best position when a bass goes for the lure. Accordingly, they keep the swinging hook up in the position of the original fixed hook by means of a short piece of wire, stiff enough to do its job, yet give once a striper has taken the hook.

RIGGING NOTE Rigging plugs and spoons, including the monstrous bunker spoons, are substantially the same as for smaller artificials used on school stripers. I'll refer you back to that.

OTHER TROLLING LURES For stripers—and bluefish—there have come into service very popular lures known as surgical tubes. They're a fine addition to a bass troller's kit. They account for stripers ranging from small and medium schoolies on up to lunkers. Trolled deep on wire line, they nail hefty bluefish too.

As its name implies, a surgical tube lure is fashioned from a kind of tubing doctors might employ in blood transfusions and the like. Today it's a synthetic material, and it comes in several diameters and colors, including red, black, brown, amber, and an off-white. You can buy a few feet of it at a time, in diameters of ⅜-to-⅝ inch or so, then cut it into desired lure lengths. Red and black are common colors in use.

This tubing can be cut into lengths of anywhere from 2 or 3 inches in the smaller diameters, through 5 or 6 inches, to 12 or 14 inches in the larger diameters, scaled more or less to the sizes of the hooks involved and sizes of the bass sought. Shorter lengths and smaller diameters often are used in multiple-tube rigs, which we'll come to later.

The length of tubing is slipped over a long-shank hook of suitable size and secured. When trolled, water passing through the tube will distend it and give it action. The effect is not unlike that of a small eel. These surgical tubes also can be jigged in conjunction with weighted trolling heads or small metal squids.

Surgical tube lures are inexpensive to make. You can afford to carry several in your tackle box. Make them up in assorted lengths and different colors, with matching hooks. They're rigged like other artificials for striped bass.

It was inevitable that some fisherman would dream up a rig calling for more than one surgical tube. A result is a weird-looking assembly that has come to be nicknamed variously "Christmas tree," "umbrella rig," and "coat hanger." I don't know where it came from originally. I first used one at Montauk, where it has been a proven killer of striped bass and bluefish.

There are several versions, some so laden with tubes, hooks, and other hardware that they're fairly expensive to buy (and cheaper to fashion yourself). A common version goes like this:

Its starting point is a spreader, similar to that used in flounder fishing. It has a swivel at its top, middle, for tying to a line. Directly under that is a loop (to which a sinker would be connected in flounder angling). At each end of the spreader's two outstretched arms is another loop (for flounders these would take the hooks). The loops are for attachment of the tube lures.

The tubes' lengths, diameters, and colors are up to the builder. Arbitrarily, you might try, say, 4-to-5-inch lengths in a diameter of about ¼ inch. Red is a popular color. Black also is used. Some umbrella rigs carry a mixture of the two, not necessarily in any special ratio or arrangement. You can try these and other colors individually or in combinations to suit your experimental fancy. Each length of tubing is slipped over its hook's shank, like a sleeve, and secured. The hooks, of course, are of suitable size. Now each tube is a lure unto itself.

These lures are suspended in chainlike arrangements from each spreader loop. There can be three or more in each chain. To do the stringing you use short lengths of stainless steel or piano wire (remember, piano wire rusts). The lengths of wire between tube lures are according to each little old umbrella rig maker's preference, but they space the tubes a few inches apart—three, four, or five inches, maybe. Each "chain" begins with a short length of wire attached to a spreader loop, followed by a tube lure, then another piece of wire, another tube, and so on until the desired number of lures is suspended from each of the spreader's three loops.

This ensemble commonly is trolled on wire line to carry it deep for lunker-size stripers and blues. But it also can be trolled on other kinds of lines if greater depth isn't desired. The rig's weight will take it down a way. Also according to preference, a couple of feet of leader can be interposed between rig and line.

The umbrella rig may be wild-looking, even provoke mirth, but it's backed by a sound idea. It's made to simulate a small school of bait fish breezing through the water. It does a job on stripers and blues. I've seen it take double-headers of both species. And that, let me tell you, will keep you busy for a few minutes. I also should tell you that the umbrella rig has come in for a measure of scorn and criticism as being an unsportsmanlike rig because of its multiple lures, which could even foul-hook fish instead of catching them in approved fashion. Critics have a point, but I don't propose to get into that argument here. Personally, I could live without umbrella rigs, but everybody to his own opinion.

Rigged eels and eelskin rigs also come in for service in striper trolling, as they do in surfcasting. They're rigged in the same fashion as for beach fishing. There are the inevitable variations, one of which combines an eelskin with a small tin squid, three or four inches long. A whole eel or an eelskin can be rigged with leader, like one of the artificials. You might try these eel rigs at sundown, at night, or in predawn hours.

Natural squid is another trolling attractor for stripers. It's a durable bait because it's tough. Get fresh squid if you can; otherwise settle for the frozen stuff. Get squid of pretty good size. The strips you'll cut from it will be fairly long. Cut them from the squid's mantle. Make them eight or ten inches long, an inch or so wide, and shaped like a torpedo or an ellipse.

Use a ring-eye hook, up to an 8/o for larger bass. A small safety pin will secure the squid strip's front end to the hook's eye and help to keep it extended, after which the bait can be impaled on the hook's bend. A little belly in the strip between safety pin and hook will impart a flutter to the bait. Splitting the strip's trailing end for a couple of inches will create fluttering tails.

Still another come-on is the head of a mossbunker or a chunk of that fish, securely impaled on the hook. Rigging is the same as for any chunk bait.

COMBINATIONS   The sky's the limit here. I repeat for emphasis:
You can rig different artificials in varying combinations; the same
is true for natural baits, and for combinations of artificials and
natural baits. You're limited only by your imagination and
willingness to experiment.

Here, for example, is a strategy that has paid off:

This one is designed to troll for large and smaller stripers
simultaneously, using two outfits. One is a top-riding rig. This
might tow a popping plug to entice surface-feeding schoolies.
A second line, riding at a lower level (weighted, if necessary)
and somewhat behind the popper, trolls a bucktail. The theory
behind this dual setup is that the popper attracts and the bucktail catches. Larger bass have been known to smack the plug
too. The idea works. I've proved it myself.

A variation of the foregoing, trolled with sufficient success to
account for as many as 12 bass, the largest 14½ pounds, on a
single trip, and at least half a dozen per trip on occasions, including a 23-pounder, is essentially the same sort of deal. On the
higher of the two lines fished simultaneously, riding near the
top, is a plug—take your choice of type. A few feet below and
slightly astern of it, on its own line, is a bucktail baited with
pork rind. The latter is jigged constantly while trolling. Bass may
not hit the plug too often; usually they'll go for the bucktail. It
could be that the plug serves as an eye-catching teaser. When a
bass moves in to pursue, the bucktail is closer, so he hits that.

Another tandem outfit calls for a subsurface swimmer and a
jig, each with its own leader yoked in on a three-loop swivel.
This rig is trolled deep, the heavier jig often being allowed to
bounce along the bottom. Above and slightly behind it is the
lighter, more buoyant swimming plug. Again, a striper is more
apt to hit the jig, but response to either artificial is a possibility.
A theory is that this combo arouses bass because it gives an illusion of one fish (the plug) pursuing a smaller neighbor (the
jig).

Still another combination calls for an artificial and a natural
bait. In this arrangement a plug, usually a subsurface swimmer,
is tied into the line through a leader about two feet long. Tied
in at the point of attachment of that leader and line is a short
length of leader material, eight inches or so, with a single hook

on which is impaled a strip of squid or piece of pork rind. The squid or pork rind rides just ahead of the plug and at a slightly lower plane. Here stripers seem to favor the natural bait over the artificial, although they'll also hit the plug at times. Presumably this is another illusion of one critter pursuing a smaller victim.

TROLLING TECHNIQUES   Striper trolling can be enjoyed in a boat of any size, small outboards up to posh, twin-screw cruisers. It's been done from small, *oar-powered* craft by hard-nosed veterans convinced that underwater sounds from boat engines drive stripers into the next county. Along the same lines, there are striper regulars who favor electric outboard motors because of their quieter operation.

Striped bass are like Boston mackerel and certain other species in that you never know at what depth they may be encountered. The levels they prowl go from the very top all the way down to the floor. It isn't uncommon to see schoolies at the surface, their backs and tails breaking water as they feed on small fish or as they frolic. Often on such occasions they can be very frustrating, refusing to accept anything trolled or cast in their direction. Sometimes they travel along planes just below the surface, or at levels halfway between top and bottom. Or they may be down as far as they can get.

The result is that trolling frequently demands trial-and-error probing to find out where they are—from day to day. Altering the depth at which your lure travels will aid in this probing. It can be done in various ways. The simplest is to lengthen or shorten the amount of line you have out. Paying out more line will cause the lure to go deeper. Conversely, shortening it will bring the lure to a higher plane. Varying the boat's speed also will change a lure's depth. Go faster—*within reason!*—and the lure will ride higher. Go slower and your lure will drop to a lower level, unless it's a buoyant surface type.

The type of lure you fish also is a factor in its riding depth, as I brought out earlier. And there are those weighting devices—pinch-on sinkers, drails, etc.

Another simple way to vary the depths at which your lure rides is to make a wide, sweeping U-turn with the boat. This causes most lures to cut through different planes. Sometimes you'll get hits during the turn when trolling a straight course draws a blank.

Outriggers are a helpful accessory when trolling more than two lines, and they come in scaled-down models for outboard craft. With outriggers you can troll four lines—two directly from rods, two through the 'riggers to keep them away from the boat and the other rigs. Theoretically, the more lines out, the better, especially when you want to try different depths and assorted rigs. Depending upon the boat's size and the amount of room in her cockpit, two to six lines can be trolled simultaneously, but four are an ideal maximum.

Several factors will govern trolling distance astern: (1) type of lure fished; (2) water depths; (3) boat's speed; (4) desired traveling level of the lure; and (5) the angler's own theories. A recommendation for water up to twenty feet deep is about thirty yards from tip of rod to hook, and about twenty yards for water deeper than twenty feet. Try those suggestions for openers, making adjustments as you see fit and as circumstances dictate.

Trolling speeds also are variables. The same factors mentioned for trolling distances astern play a part here too, and you can add boat maneuvering requirements. Watching your lures is a helpful guide to proper trolling speeds. Incorrect trolling rate is often indicated by the depths at which they travel—too low or too high—and how they behave. If they're barely moving or not exhibiting the tactics for which they were designed (darting, diving, etc.), they're being trolled too slowly. Conversely, if they seem to have gone berserk—zigzagging wildly, spinning excessively, or otherwise performing in a fashion not characteristic of those lures—they're being trolled too fast.

Because of the variable influencing factors involved, it's impossible to lay down a universal speed for all boats for all occasions. *Experiment!* Suggested starting points are 4 or 5 knots (approximately 4.6 to 5.8 miles per hour, or 4 to 6 miles per hour in round figures) for school stripers, and 3 knots (about 3.5 miles per hour) to 4 knots for larger bass. Try your variations around those, favoring the slower speeds, if anything. You'll soon learn the proper trolling rate for your areas, especially after coming home fishless a few times.

There are areas with striped bass potential in inshore ocean zones, inlets, bays, estuaries, and rivers. They include tide rips, rocky places, edges of channels, river mouths, holes, dropoffs (where the bottom abruptly falls away to greater depth), coastwise belts just beyond the breakers, sloughs or gulleys along a beach or sand bar, and inlets proper, as well as around sand bars at their outside mouths.

As in all kinds of fishing, you'll realize the best trolling results when you become thoroughly familiar with the water involved. A depth sounder can be very helpful here, scanning the bottom for you to find holes, dropoffs, submerged rocks, etc. Once you become familiar with your instrument's performance, you'll be able to "read" the bottom to aid in determining an area's possibilities. You may even be able to detect schools for fish under the boat.

PRESENTATION OF LURES IN TROLLING *Tide rips* produce handsomely for trollers. They're detected readily by a surface disturbance marking the contrast between current and slower-moving or quiet water. Bass commonly lurk in the quieter water, waiting for food morsels to be swept their way.

Here the technique is to fish along the rips' edges, working your lure in that zone where the current meets calmer water. Ideally, your lure will be in the rips' edges while the boat travels off to one side. Change the boat's course every so often to cause your lure to cross back and forth across the rips' edges. The main thing is to maintain a speed that brings out the attractor's best action.

Inlets and mouths of estuaries. Your best bet in these locations is to troll across the flow, rather than in its long axis. Making a sweeping U-turn and altering the boat's course at intervals will give added coverage.

Trolling a dropoff. Follow the technique for edges of tide rips, working your lure so it covers that zone between the dropoff's edge and deeper water beyond.

Trolling a surf. There's often action at varying distances beyond the breakers, depending where and upon what stripers are feeding. Sometimes they're barely beyond the reach of casters, much to those anglers' vexation and frustration. The fish may be feeding at the surface or at different levels below. Experimenting with trolling depths is necessary when the bass can't be seen. *Caution!* This can be tricky, even dangerous, fishing. The boat must have an absolutely dependable engine. You may have to get away from the breakers in a hurry. Stay alert so you don't become so absorbed in fishing that you let wind or current sneak you into the breakers' clutches. In this activity it's smart to have a capable nonfishing member of the party at the controls. The same advice applies when fishing in rocky areas.

Working deep spots and gullies. Here there are assorted techniques. In the case of a hole, maneuver the boat so that your lure swings out over the edge into its deeper water. Slowing the boat slightly or lowering your rod tip will cause the lure to cut through a couple of different levels within the hole. Sloughs and gullies can be worked along their edges, letting the lure travel between the rim and deeper water. Stripers seek food in these places too. Use the same technique when fishing sand bars off an inlet or beach.

Tidal creeks, estuaries, and rivers. Look to the banks in these locations, trolling as close to them as it's safe to do. Bass often lurk in among vegetation near banks.

Trolling schools at the surface. Bold as they are in pursuit of prey, striped bass can be spooked by a boat barging into their midst at the surface. Your cue, therefore, is to approach a school cautiously. When within range, so to speak, but not so close as to scare the fish, skirt the school, maneuvering the boat so that your lure is swung in among the feeding linesiders. If the boat's course tows the lure out of the school, maneuver her to swing it in again. Work around the school's outer perimeter in this fashion. Above all, don't try to plow right through the group. When you get a fish on, it's a good idea to work him out of the school into open water so as not to alarm the others. Done properly, it's possible to fish a surfaced school for quite a while and extract several bass from it.

Popping plugs, high-riding spoons, and surface lures are recommended for trolling schools at the top.

OF TIME AND TIDES What I'm about to say applies to striped bass fishing in general.

Among striper regulars you'll hear all kinds of ideas about which are the best times and tides for action. In the surf angling fraternity, for example, you'll find buffs working beaches only during the dusk-to-dawn hours. But there are also eager beavers who fish during daylight hours too, or both day and night. And all those with at least a smidgin of talent get fish at one time or another. You'll find trollers, boat casters, and jetty jockies similarly divided according to what they consider the best times to fish. But I don't think that any striper regular—whatever his preferred method, but especially if he's a surfer—will argue against the predawn, dawn, sundown, early evening, and night hours being among the more productive times.

You'll find similar differences of opinion as regards tides. For these the fish are responsible in large measure. On one occasion they'll favor an incoming phase. At another time they'll bite halfway down on a tide. On another day they'll be active during the last half of the ebb phase. They've even been known to confound everybody by responding at low-water slack. Added to those is an old standby: two hours up on a tide—as it begins to rise, that is; then two hours down, as it starts to fall.

What it all boils down to is that the "best" tides are those that yield fish. Unfortunately, they constitute an unpredictable variable that can change from place to place, and even, depending upon the stripers' vacillating feeding moods, from day to day within the same locale. Therefore, since there's no way of *accurately* forecasting the best tide in a given area on a given day, the smart thing to do is try as many different phases as possible.

A *trolling tip:* Don't hesitate to give your lures added action by jigging them with your rod tip. Sometimes continuous jigging while trolling will spell the difference between fair and good results.

BOAT CASTING

In this procedure a boat becomes a mobile casting platform— like a small patch of beach, you might say, but not quite as steady.

Boat casting is a technique developed primarily for fishing surfaced schools of fishes—bass, blues, mackerel, or whatever, wherever they may be—in open sea or sound, inlet, bay, channel, or just beyond a curling surf. Its biggest advantage is mobility. If one spot doesn't produce, you move to another. It will give you a crack at fish that are inaccessible to shorebound anglers. It's also exciting and a good developer of casting skill. Moreover, it's effective, action-packed, and not infrequently superior to trolling for working a surfaced school.

TACKLE CHATTER You have plenty of leeway in your choice of weapons for boat casting. Both spinning and conventional types are employed. If you're a novice in casting, spinning gear offers an advantage, for reasons already detailed. But let me add that the advantage probably won't be great, since casting distance usually isn't a factor.

There's widespread preoccupation with light equipment in boat casting, chiefly because of the added action it affords. Self-appraisal of your fishing ability will be your guide to how light you can go. I'll say this: From the standpoint of gaining experience, there's more for, than against, your going to really light tackle, short of fly fishing equipment, if you're inexperienced . . . as long as you're prepared to lose fish and rigs.

As I said, casting distance isn't a prerequisite of success in this kind of fishing, a fact that erases a necessity for a long rod, whatever its type. The fact is that long rods are less desirable than shorter models here because aboard boat they can be awkward to wield, especially when you have companions intent upon the same objective.

In length, a rod well suited to boat casting for striped bass, bluefish, and other gamesters within the same broad size range is a conventional or spinning stick about six to seven feet long with a butt of eighteen to twenty inches. To be best fitted for its assignments this rod will combine lively resiliency in its tip section with good spine.

On this rod you'll mount a reel—conventional or spinning, as the case may be—to balance it. Balancing doesn't have to be precise, just within reason, unless you're a hard-nosed purist. It might be a 2/o or 3/o revolving spool type, or a spinning equivalent, a model in the medium or light-medium category. On it you'll wind enough line to fill its spool suitably. For actual use, 150 to 200 yards will be ample. Strengths can range up to about 30-pound test, depending upon rod and reel. Gauge your line strength roughly to sizes of the fish currently running. In many instances surfaced stripers are in the schoolie size range, often small; but you should allow for ever-present possibilities of fish in the 20- and 30-pound brackets being among them. By so doing you'll also allow for the largest bluefish. Stripers and blues often occupy the same areas.

A reliably smooth drag, one that won't become sticky or freeze, is important. There are refinements that are handy but not essential. On certain models there's an automatic gear shift that provides a higher speed for retrieves, then shifts to a lower rate by itself when playing a fish. There's that level-wind feature that feeds line evenly on the spool during retrieves. And there are reels that automatically shift from free spool to re-engaged gears in retrieves. All handy features, but they up the cost of reels.

Many anglers favor spinning tackle over conventional gear for boat casting, either because they feel they can cast better with it or because a more slender spinning rod gives them more action. In any case, the requirements for a spinning rod are the same as for its conventional counterpart. Here too you can find a rod that tapers from a very flexible tip, for a wide range of lures and baits, to a section with enough spine for the jobs at hand.

Mate that rod with a medium-size spinning reel, on which you can spool 150 to 200 yards of monofilament line in an appropriate strength. You shouldn't need line any heavier than about 30-pound test, if that heavy. For rocky places, however, keep these things in mind: A somewhat heavier than usual line provides some safeguard against abrasion; and monofilament generally resists damage by rubbing better than braided line.

LURES AND RIGGING You have a wide choice of artificials. Here's a sampling, with some notations:

Plugs. Many types and models are fished, but poppers and surface runners are often preferred when bass are at the top. Theoretically at least, any kind of surface or near-surface lure that creates a little ruckus or simulates a small bait fish has a chance of scoring. When stripers are feeding at some subsurface plane, a deeper-running plug is indicated. Those of the so-called mirror type will produce, among others. Weights range from fractional-ounce models, for lighter spinning outfits, up to 1½ or 2 ounces for conventional tackle.

Bucktails. Because they're compact and heavy for their size, they cast fast and straight. Also because of their weight, they can be effective when bass are bottom feeding, or cruising at levels not far off the bottom.

Chromed diamond jigs. These can be worked with a jigging motion when stripers are feeding deep. After casting, a jig can be worked on or near the bottom or jigged upward through various levels.

Other attractors. Spoons are one type. Metal squids are another. Small rigged eels also are used with effect. You also can fish natural bait in combination with an ordinary bottom rig, casting into a spot you think has possibilities.

Rigging of artificials for boat casting. This is essentially the same as for casting from shore (see that section). About the only difference—an individual matter—is that some anglers prefer shorter leaders, going to three feet or so, or even less.

When bluefish and striped bass occupy the same area, be prepared for the "choppers" by using a length of wire leader between line and lure (see the section on bluefish rigging).

LOCATIONS There are several. Rocky places, including waters around jetties, have potential. Cast in among the rocks or toward the jetty, but be prepared to move away. Often a zone paralleling an ocean front beach just beyond the breakers is fertile striped bass territory. Again you must be careful with the boat. Casting in toward a beach will nail bass, but it has dangers. You must be ready to move away from the breakers' clutch. Keep your craft's bow pointing to seaward. Don't let her aim her stern toward the waves or swing broadside to them. She could take on water.

Tide rips have possibilities too. So do sluices and current-eroded cuts around sand bars. Casting into the calmer water flanking a rip can bring results. In cuts around bars it often pays to try the bottom of a gulley, working a bucktail or other deep artificial along the floor.

Always you'll watch for seagulls, hovering over an area and swooping to pick up small bait fish driven to panic by marauding bass (or bluefish). This is usually a sign of a surfaced school. At other times you'll see a school of stripers raising a commotion or simply cruising around right at the surface. In either case your cue is to approach the school cautiously. Maintain a discreet distance so as not to spook them, then cast in among the fish. Here's where surface plugs can do a job. You may be able to drift with the school, staying outside its perimeter to work it for a nice take.

Artificial fishing reefs, more and more of which are being constructed on U.S. coasts, also have bass potential. A depth sounder is a valuable aid in pinpointing them. Once a reef is located, the boat can anchor or drift off to one side of it, with her anglers casting in toward it. Frequent checking of the depth sounder is necessary when drifting to maintain a position within casting reach of the reef. In similar fashion you also can work your way along the banks of channels, estuaries, and rivers, looking for rocks or gardens of vegetation that might harbor stripers.

CHUMMING

The once near-obsolete technique of chumming for striped bass has undergone an enthusiastic revival in several Atlantic Coast areas. It has been particularly effective in channels, notably in the vicinity of bridges. It also produces in inlets and around their bars.

I don't say it's typical for all areas, but for Long Island fishermen, by and large, chumming gets bass more consistently than surfcasting, and even more than trolling (except, possibly, on the island's North Shore and at Montauk) and boat casting at times. It usually doesn't account for big stripers. Invariably they're schoolies up into the teens, maybe early twenties, occasionally laced with fish to thirty pounds or so. But often it puts rewarding catches into the boats.

Striper chumming is a method with flexibility. It allows variations. This is good. It means opportunities to try different ideas and adapt the procedure to a given locale or set of conditions.

Although never widely popular, for some reason, it has been practiced in a number of Atlantic Coast regions, including New England's famed Cuttyhunk area and Martha's Vineyard, Maryland's Rock Hall, Bloody Point, Herring Bay, Holland Point, Sharps Island and Tilghman Island, and Virginia's York and Rappahannock rivers. Over the years New Jersey has had a quota of bass chummers too. And there's no reason why it shouldn't work anywhere.

BASICS   Several kinds of chum can be employed for stripers. On the list are clams, sandworms, mussels, bloodworms, shrimp (grass and sand varieties), assorted crabs, sand bugs, eels, and fishes of various species—menhaden, mullet, killies, spearing, etc. A chum that has been used with noteworthy success on Long Island is the skimmer or sea clam, which also is an effective bait in this technique. Some chumming items—marine worms and shrimp, to cite a couple—aren't practical because of their cost and/or availability. Clams other than skimmers will work, but it's expensive to feed stripers a buffet of little necks or cherrystones. Besides, skimmers are larger and yield more chum and bait.

Naturally you want to select something for chum that has been proved effective in the area, or at least is a food of stripers, whenever you can. Where chumming is very infrequent or nonexistent, you'll be on your own. Here you can try skimmers or shrimp, or, lacking those, one of the local fishes on which bass are known to dine. You may have to improvise with whatever is available locally. Results might be poor or a zero. On the other hand, you might just stumble on something superior to materials in use.

Given the right place, if you're willing to exert yourself, you can collect your own chum. Killies, spearing, and other small fishes can be caught along bay shorelines with a small hand seine. Crabs can be caught in traps or with crab nets. Small hand seines worked along bay shores and in tidal creeks and estuaries will collect shrimp. Hard-shell clams can be dug or treaded. (Skimmers are in the ocean. You can't get those without a dredge.) And sand bugs can be collected along a surf front. But such independence is time-consuming. It's a lot easier to buy chum whenever you can.

Some kinds of chum are distributed whole. Small shrimp are a case in point. Little fishes the size of killies, spearing, and butterfish can be cut into halves or pieces. The same is true with worms and crabs. Fishes the size of menhaden and mullet can be cut into chunks. Or you can try ground-up fish, such as the mossbunker pulp used for mackerel, bluefish, tuna, *et al.*

Your first step is to select a place you think might have potential. Study its current and wind conditions. If the current is too brisk, you might do better to try another area and come back to that place at a different stage of the tide. A current that's too fast not only will consume chum at an alarming tempo, it may also scatter it too rapidly to be effective. A strong breeze blowing in the same direction as the current can enhance this adverse effect. You also want to take stock of boat traffic. If it's too heavy, forget that spot, at least for the time being. Boats would be running back and forth across your chum line, cutting it.

Having chosen a satisfactory place, get your boat into position. Locate upcurrent from the spot you want to work, so that current flow will ferry your chum into it. Drift down toward the spot—engine off, if possible. When you're fifty yards or so from where you think response might lie, prepare to anchor. Ease your anchor into the water with a minimum of noise and commotion. If wind or current have any muscle, the boat is liable to swing on her anchor line, making your chum streak erratic at best, if not disrupting it to the extent that its effectiveness is erased. Strong breezes are especially apt to make a boat swing because they change directions at intervals. To prevent this pendulum effect, ease another anchor over at the stern to hold your craft in the desired position.

Current velocity will determine the frequency with which you'll distribute your chum. With striped bass you don't have to be as generous as with some other gamesters. In this instance heavy chumming actually can work against you by tempting bass to gather at the far end of the chum line. Once they get word of a hearty buffet coming their way, then discover they don't have to move to partake, they'll just stay out there and fill their stomachs, coming nowhere near your hook. Light chumming, in contrast, is a teaser, more persuasive in drawing stripers closer. But don't go to an extreme and skimp.

Whole small shrimp and pieces of fish, clams, mussels, crabs, etc., are dropped overboard a few at a time; three or four at a clip will do it. If you're using live chum, such as shrimp, sand bugs, or small crabs, pinch or crush them a bit (don't pulverize 'em!) before releasing; otherwise they'll scamper in all directions. Minced clams or mussels, ground fish, and other pulp chum can be ladled overboard at a pace commensurate with maintaining a light but continuous line. Remember, though, that unlike more solid forms of chum (fish pieces, etc.), this stuff starts to diffuse when it hits the water. Time the intervals between ladlings so that chumming isn't too heavy.

TACKLE, RIGGING, AND BAITS Light or medium spinning equipment is brought into play in this sport, and it provides action with a capital "A." In my opinion, however, a conventional outfit has marked advantages.

By way of a conventional combo I suggest a medium or light-medium boat rod. Here too it's the old story: The more flexibility it has in its tip section, the greater sport; but it must have some backbone too. On it would go a 2/o reel—3/o at the outside. Braided Dacron or monofilament line is fine; 150 to 200 yards are ample. Its strength, depending upon the caliber of the rod and what it's rated to handle, needn't exceed 30-pound test. Twenty-pound line is strong enough in most instances.

Rigging is elementary. All you need is three or four feet of leader of your choice—monofilament, let's say, if you're not fishing mono line already—in a strength approximating the line's. Attach a 2/o or 3/o hook at one end of the leader. Secure the leader's other end to your line through a two-loop barrel swivel.

Just as several kinds of chum have been used successfully for striped bass, so there is a selection of effective baits. You can choose from among any of the items I mentioned as chum earlier. To those you can add squid. Squid baits are cut in fluttery strips, three or four inches long and a half inch or so wide. Whenever you can, match your bait to your chum. You can be fairly generous in the sizes of your baits, since linesiders have big mouths.

For example, you can impale two or three shrimp, or a good-size piece of clam or fish, etc. You won't always be able to match bait and chum, of course. Here you can rig a squid strip, or impale two or three sandworms or bloodworms on your hook. Try combination baits too, especially when fishing is slow: shrimp and clam on the same hook, shrimp and a squid strip, and so on.

GOING TO IT   Okay. Your boat is anchored. A chum line has been started, and your goodies are being carried toward that place you think has bass. Maybe it's a rocky area, or a jetty, or a hole, or a deep cut alongside a sand bar. Get your baited rig overboard *in the chum line*. Have your reel in free spool, but keep your thumb lightly on the spool and stand ready to shift into gear to fight a fish. Let the current transport your rig away from the boat, amidst the chum line, toward the target area. Peel off a few feet of line if necessary to get it started. If the current is brisk, control the paying out of line by braking the spool lightly with your thumb; otherwise you're likely to launch the festivities with a bird's nest. If, on the other hand, the tidal flow is weak and doesn't carry your rig out satisfactorily by itself, hand-strip a few feet of line from the reel, let that pay out, and repeat until you judge that your baited hook is in the place you want to probe.

It's when currents are weak that a conventional or revolving-spool reel shows an advantage over its spinning counterpart. With the former you can hand-strip line more readily. Further, it's easier in this kind of angling to drive a hook home quickly at a strike with a conventional reel than with a spinning combo, with its rod flexibility and less accessible reel spool. With a conventional reel you can simply clamp your thumb down on its spool and lift with your rod tip, then throw the reel in gear for battle.

When your rig has traveled out as far as desired, retrieve line and repeat the entire cycle. *Tip:* Imparting extra action to the bait by jigging it with short, smart lifts of your rod tip during drifts and retrieves will give the enticer greater eye-catching movement. *Another tip:* Always keep your bait in motion as it drifts out and when it's being retrieved. You want it to simulate a live thing as much as possible. It won't look alive if you let it stand still. What's more, if you keep it in one spot the current's thrust is likely to push it upward out of the chum line, where it will lose effectiveness.

As in shark fishing, it will pay in striper chumming to begin the procedures with the hooks at somewhat different levels, within the chum line. Unlike the sharking arrangement, however, you don't leave the rigs at those depths, but wait to see which one elicits response, then change the others accordingly. This requires a bit of doing when you're fishing solo, but with a couple of companions it's the way to start.

None of the rigs should be very deep. The fact is that they'll probably all ride at near-surface levels, since the current will thrust them upward. They can be made to travel at desired depths by adding a small pinch-on sinker to take one rig deeper than its mates, outfitting another with a small float or piece of cork to carry it higher than the others, and leaving another rig as it is. Make your adjustments according to current strength and velocity, remembering that it's most important that all rigs be within the chum's sphere of influence.

A moment ago I said, "None of the rigs should be very deep." It should go without saying that if "scratching" the upper layers fails to produce, the rigs should be dropped lower in the chum. Keep in mind that there's a current thrust on the chum too.

OTHER PROCEDURES

FLY CASTING   Salt-water fly casting is a sport unto itself, one that provides maximum piscatorial combat thrills and excitement. Many kinds of marine gamesters are being caught on fly tackle—billfishes, tarpon, sharks, bonefish, and, well, you name it. But because of the ultralightness of the tackle involved, salt-water fly fishing imposes great demands on the skill of its followers. In that respect it's rather like a graduate course in college. It's a form of advanced learning.

Now, I don't mean to say that a less-experienced angler can't attempt it. But to me, a tyro going into salt-water fly fishing is being premature, to put it mildly. Therefore, since this book is written primarily for beginners and less-experienced fishermen,

I've studiously avoided dwelling on fly casting. Besides, it's a subject worthy of a book in itself.

I suggest that you leave salt-water fly fishing until such a time as you feel you've gained sufficient experience and ability with other equipment. Then you can graduate to the lightest-of-tackle action, with an intermediate step via light conventional and spinning equipment recommended.

FISHING WITH LIVE BAIT This is an action-packed technique. Among striped bass, as among marine game fishes in general, strikes on live bait often are more slam-bang than with other types of attractors. The reason is that the fish has to pursue the bait, which naturally is trying to escape. When he catches up with it he wants to cinch capture, no more nonsense. Furthermore, this "live-lining" for stripers and bluefish accounts for some of the larger rascals.

Many different kinds of small fishes have been employed in this method. A sampling of the lineup shows mossbunkers, eels, northern whiting, mackerel, killies, mullet, herring, and the young of several other species. The fact is that any small, satisfactorily agile fish probably would serve. The only problem with some species is keeping them alive on a hook.

Yes, there's a wide choice. But you can see a drawback—getting the live bait. Certain kinds, such as killies, can be purchased at rowboat stations and bait depots, or can be caught with small seines or dip nets. Others, such as eels, mackerel, herring, and whiting, can be hooked by do-it-yourselfers. The same is true for young bluefish (snappers) and porgies (sand porgies). But others, such as mullet and mossbunkers, are something else again.

Nor is procuring them the only hurdle. Having obtained them, you must keep them alive and kicking. That poses problems with certain types. Little fellas, like killies, stay alive very nicely in a bait car tied alongside the boat. Eels are rugged and will stay alive in a bucket if you give them some new water occasionally and protect them from the sun. But certain other species require a live-bait container of some sort. Ideally, this is either a built-in feature of the boat or a pump-powered portable well, with constantly circulating water. Portable bait wells (without pumps) and makeshift containers such as tubs, pails, and small watertight barrels also serve, but they're less satisfactory because their water must be replenished or renewed at intervals. Too, certain bait fishes are considerably less hardy than others in captivity.

A third drawback is keeping the bait alive on your hook. Care in handling has everything to do with success in this phase. Similarly, any bait fishes you catch must be unhooked with great care. In all instances do the job as quickly as possible to minimize exposure of the bait fish to air. Keep handling at a minimum.

There are assorted ways of hooking live baits. One is to pass the hook's point from under the chin upward through the two jaws, as close behind the mouth's firmer parts as possible.† This technique presents the bait in a reasonably lifelike manner. Another way is to pass the hook's point and bend through the flesh of the back—don't go too deep!—alongside the dorsal fin. It works, but it doesn't always present the bait in a lifelike fashion, since there can be a tendency for small fish to spin when so hooked.

There are still other methods of hooking live baits. So far as I'm concerned, they don't rate with the foregoing, but I'll mention them anyway.

One is to hook the bait on its side. Some anglers do it opposite the dorsal fin; others go farther forward. Another is to run the hook through the fish's eyes. This keeps a bait nosing into the current flow, as though battling it, but it understandably shortens its life (if it hasn't killed it outright). Still another method is to hook the bait through the fleshy part of the base of its tail. It's easy, fast, and least apt to harm the fish, but a bait moving backward through the water hardly looks natural, even to the most stupid predator. Besides, enough water rushing through the bait's gills in the wrong direction is apt to drown it.

Live crabs can be impaled on a hook in either of two ways. In one the hook is run through the body's rear part, between the swimmerettes. In the other method the hook is passed through a corner of the shell, in the rear where it's pointed. Soft-shell blueclaw crabs are good, if you can resist the temptation to fry them for your own consumption, but they can be difficult to get and expensive. The calico crab is another live bait for stripers.

† An aside to lady newcomers: Don't be squeamish. Fishes feel pain a lot less than you do.

Sandworms and bloodworms also can be employed as live bait. The hooking procedure is to pass the point through the forward end and bring it out about one-half to three-quarters inch beyond. This leaves most of the worm to dangle and wiggle in the water. In poor digging seasons, worms—especially bloodworms —often are small. When you get stuck with runts, impale two on your hook, side by side, as just described. Of the two kinds of worms, sandworms are better for this kind of fishing. Bloodworms tend to "bleach out" and lose their firmness after a while, becoming quite unappetizing-looking to a bass.

Live baits can be used in chumming, trolling (here they have to be exceptionally hardy types), boat casting, drifting, and fishing at anchor. They can be rigged to do their job at various levels. Tackle and rigging are the same as already described for those techniques.

Bottom fishing is a good live-bait technique because it can be put into service aboard boat or shoreside. A standard bottom rig and its variations are employed; these are discussed elsewhere in this book.

How you'll set up your terminal rig depends upon how far off bottom you want to fish. A leader generally is incorporated in a bottom rig for stripers, and its length can be two to four feet or even more. As I said, it depends upon how far off the floor you want to fish. The distance above bottom also can be regulated by how close to the rig's swivel, or how far away from it, you tie your sinker. These are variables you'll have to experiment with in various areas at different times.

Thirty-pound line should be strong enough; 100 to 150 yards will suffice. Your leader can be in about the same strength as the line. Match your hooks to the sizes of your baits, within reason. Don't go to either extreme. With larger bait fish you'll go up to at least a 5/0 or 6/0, maybe even to an 8/0. As usual, sinker weights will be governed by current strength and phase of the tide in that area. Bank-type sinkers will help on a muddy floor, while the pyramidal weights rigged in surf fishing will hold better on a sandy bottom. Also as when surf fishing on the bottom, a small piece of cork attached to your leader will buoy your baited hook up out of the reach of larcenous crabs.

Live mossbunkers have come in for a measure of attention as

striper bait, especially for the larger linesiders, if they can be had. These can be rigged for fishing at anchor, or even from shore, but they have proved to be particularly effective when drifted. Whole dead mossbunkers, or chunks of same, such as the head, also are used, and come in handy when live menhaden aren't available. These baits can be drifted or trolled slowly.

There are hooks with slender shanks especially designed for live bait fishing, good for when the baits are small. Unless they're extra-strong for their size, however, there's a risk of having them straightened out by a rambunctious striper of reasonable size.

MISCELLANEOUS BAITING NOTES—ALL TECHNIQUES

Some baits—squid strips are one—are tough and will remain in reasonably good condition on a hook for hours. Others, because of some inherent fragility, either fall off a hook or gradually disintegrate. Clams are a case in point. So are pieces of crab. Many fishermen secure such baits to their hooks either with a rubber band or a few lashings of strong thread. With soft baits this securing is an obvious necessity when casting them.

Whatever the bait used for striped bass, and whatever the method involved, it's a good idea to leave your hook's point and barb exposed after the bait has been impaled. The reason is that hook's point must be ready to penetrate instantly. Stripers can be real toughies to hook at the strike. Frequently it requires real *oomph* to drive the hook's point home. A layer of bait over the point and barb doesn't exactly help. It should go without saying that bass hooks must have needle-sharp points.

FINALLY, THE BONUS

Striped bass are superb eating. As with any other kinds of fishes, however, care must be exercised if they're to be at their peak for quality.

The first step is prevention of spoilage. In normally cooler climes during the early spring and in autumn this will be no great problem. It's during warmer weather that you have to worry.

Ideally, except in cold weather, fish should go on ice as soon as possible, preferably gutted beforehand. Aboard boat, one of those portable food and beverage carriers, or even an old box, with ice will serve. Steaking or filleting large bass will enable you to get more fish on ice. Lacking ice aboard boat, the next best bet is to put the fish in a shady place, such as a fish box, or cover them with a tarpaulin or wetted cloth. Throwing a bucket of water over the fish occasionally won't do any harm.

When you're fishing from shore the main thing is to get your fish out of the sun's heat, or at least out of its direct rays. Cover them if possible. A portable ice chest comes in handy for this protection. Lacking that, you'll have to improvise. On a surf beach without an ice chest, you can dig down until you hit damp, cool sand. Drop your fish in and cover them over. The sand above them will act as an insulator. Just make sure you mark the place.

If you have a long trip home by car in warm weather, ice your fish before you start. The two-bag procedure is good. Put the fish in one plastic bag, then place that inside another, packing crushed ice around it. This not only provides double insulation, it keeps ice water from the fish. I suggest gutting any fish before icing them down for an automobile trip home. It helps to minimize chances of spoilage. On arrival home, dress the fish and place them under refrigeration right away.

To repeat: It's always best to gut any fish as soon as possible after catching. I don't mean immediately after they've been hooked, but within a reasonable length of time. With striped bass I think you'll also find that it's easier to scale them soon after catching, while they're still wet. Their scales are tougher to remove after they've dried. If you intend to fillet and/or skin the fish, scaling isn't necessary.

COOKING   Striped bass recipes would fill a small book . . . well, a booklet anyway. Suffice it to say that linesiders can be cooked by any of several standard fish culinary procedures, with or without elaborate spicing, sauces, garnishes, or other trimmings. Methods include baking, frying, poaching, broiling, steaming, and stewing in a fish chowder. For my money, the best eating stripers are those from just over keeping size to five or six pounds or so, and I like 'em baked.

Keepers to five to seven or eight pounds can be baked whole, either plain or with a stuffing. Smaller schoolies are just right for broiling. Fish sticks and fillets can be fried, in a pan or in deep fat. Fillets also can be broiled or baked. Steaks can be broiled, baked, or fried.

No matter how you cook 'em—so long as they're cooked properly, of course—striped bass are a gastronomic delight. And if you want a treat among treats, cook your fresh-caught bass over a charcoal fire beside the sea. There's nothing, but nothing, quite like that banquet.

I'd like to wrap up this chapter with a little vignette:

My dad was a great fisherman all his life. He also was a pretty good cook. In his last years he lived on Shelter Island, a pretty isle nestled between Long Island's Orient and Montauk peninsulas. He enjoyed few things more than charcoal barbecuing steaks—fish and beef—outdoors at home beside the bay. One of his specialities was striped bass steaks. You never tasted anything like them. And here's a little twist. If there happened to be any of that fish left over, he and I liked it for breakfast, warmed in a frying pan with a little butter. Try it sometime.

CHAPTER 22

Broadbill Swordfish:
Majestic Loner

Although I doubt it, perhaps shrewd old Ma Nature was in a whimsical mood when she dreamed up the broadbill sword-fish, *Xiphias gladius*. At least it would seem that way, because a fish with a snout like a broadsword is stuff from which tall tales are spun. Be that as it may, the swordfish and his awesome weapon are very much a reality. What's more, he's one of the ocean's more interesting and, for anglers, most frustrating in-habitants.

This swordsman of the sea, a finned Scaramouche, belongs to a unique, regal family of fishes whose outstanding characteristic is a bony projection of the upper jaw that forms a hard, fairly sharp-pointed instrument known variously as a bill, spear, or, in this instance, a sword. It's from these terms for their weapons that members of the tribe get such collective group names as billed fishes or billfishes and speared fishes or spearfishes. In such blanket classifications the marlins (blue, white, black, striped), the Atlantic and Pacific sailfishes, and a species known as spear-fish all are "cousins" of the broadbill swordfish.

In scope, the distribution of broadbills is generous. The regal brutes are encountered in warm and temperate seas throughout our globe. On our side of the Atlantic Ocean their range stretches all the way from as far north as Newfoundland and Nova Scotia down to Argentina. On the U.S. side of the mighty Pacific Ocean they've been encountered from California's Santa Cruz Island on down to Chile.

Swordfish are oceanic in habit. You may run across one inshore, only a couple of miles off a beach, but usually contact is made well—even far—offshore. It's highly doubtful that you'll ever en-counter one in a sound or a bay in the sport-fishing theater. It would be a freak meet. For your purposes, consider swordfish as high seas wanderers.

Ichthyologist-oceanographer Edward C. Migdalski of Yale University has compiled some interesting notes about swordfish and their distribution in his excellent book *Angler's Guide to the Salt Water Game Fishes, Atlantic and Pacific,* a reference volume I recommend highly.

As Ed states, swordfish favor warm seas, and usually are found in their greater numbers in regions where water temperatures are above 60° F, but he adds that they can tolerate colder water than marlins will accept. Bearing that out is their presence in such chilly areas as Newfoundland and Norway. Ed also reports that broadbills have been caught on halibut setlines at depths as great as 1,200 feet. Further, he says that it isn't unusual for swordfish captured on the offshore banks of the Gulf of Maine to have deep-sea fishes in their bellies. Since those fishes are known to dwell below depths of 150 fathoms or 900 feet, it becomes obvious that broadbills do at least some of their food shopping at great depths beyond the continental shelves. Presumably they forage for food at many levels, from the sea floor on up.

In their very large eyes is evidence that they frequent great depths. Their eyes, it's theorized, are that big to gather whatever little light may be available in the eternal night far beneath the waves.

THE YOUNGSTERS AND THE MONSTERS To say that positive information about the spawning habits of *Xiphias gladius* is sparse is an understatement. But breeding must take place at sea, probably far offshore and perhaps at great depths. The usual procedure is followed. Mama Swordfish releases eggs in the water to be fertilized by Papa Swordfish. Incubation time probably is inversely proportional to water temperatures. Baby swordfish are quite unlike their elders in looks. In infancy the characteristic sword, as such, is yet to come. Both jaws are equally prolonged very early in life, and are outfitted with minute teeth.

Swordfish grow to great size, a fact that thus far has been proved more by commercial men than by recreational anglers. In the U.S. Atlantic sport fishery the broad average range is from about 175 pounds to 350 pounds. Once in a great while there are larger specimens hooked. I know of at least one 400-pounder. A few years ago a North American sport-fishing record, 608 pounds, was established by Long Island sportsman Walter Margulies.

Those two are magnificent fish, but even heavier brutes are recorded in commercial operations. Among the largest of those, mentioned by Bigelow and Schroeder, was a bruiser brought into Boston's wharves back in 1920. That monarch weighed 915 pounds *dressed*, and therefore, it's figured, must have gone better than 1,100 pounds in life. Unfortunately, the fish's over-all length wasn't measured, but the sword exceeded 5 feet, leading to an estimate of a total length of about 15 feet. Other heavyweights brought into Halifax and Boston during the 1920s and '30s by commercial fishermen included: One tipping the scale at 637 pounds, dressed, and estimated to have topped 750 when alive; a 644-pounder (dressed weight) that was 13 feet long; a specimen weighing 925 pounds before butchering; and another that went 650 pounds when dressed and was thought to have weighed in the vicinity of 800 pounds in the sea. There was also an 850-pounder recorded at Halifax, but it isn't known if this was the dressed weight or estimated live weight. And a 1,565-pound monster was harpooned off Chile.

On the basis of sport-fishing and commercial catches, Pacific broadbills—especially those caught off South America—grow larger than their Atlantic kin. My friend Albert van der Riet, a noted international big game angler with whom I spent a few days at his Cathedral Peak Hotel in South Africa's Drakensberg mountains, caught a broadbill in the 800-pound class off Iquique, Chile.

Potential sizes in our Atlantic Coast sport fishery go to at least 400 pounds, if not 500. Considering both Atlantic and Pacific seaboards of the United States and South America, there are undoubtedly broadbills that go well over 1,000 pounds. If you shoot for a world record you'll have to top 1,000. So you see, when you do combat with swordfish you're playing with some of the bigger boys.

A LONER   Their far-flung distribution belies the fact that broadbill swordfish seldom, if ever, could be described as abundant. But

I should hastily add that everything is relative. What I mean is, they're never as abundant as some of the schooling fishes with which we're familiar. Under favorable circumstances they can be numerous *for swordfish.*

When adults, swordfish aren't schoolers by nature. Although they may congregate in respectable numbers within a given region, they usually travel alone or, at the most, in pairs. Exceptions to that solitary habit may occur during their spawning season, but I don't know. One thing is for sure. Even with fairly good numbers (for them), the ocean's vastness makes it seem like they're few and far between.

You must think of them as loners, widely scattered; and you can count on having to hunt them every trip. You can consider yourself extremely fortunate if you ever stumble upon one without first having done appreciable scouting. More trips than not you'll wander all over the ocean without so much as seeing a broadbill. There will be even more trips when you won't catch one.

IDENTIFICATION AND HABITS   One would hardly have any difficulty identifying *Xiphias gladius* or separating him from other billfishes. The clincher, of course, is his sword, which is longer, wider, and thicker than the weapons worn by his billed relations. After that, and his size, other physical characteristics become redundant so far as identification is concerned.

In life he's a beauty. His back and upper sides are a rich blue, with variations ranging from a lighter shade to a dark cobalt, almost black. On the lower sides and belly the color gives way to a silvery or silvery white. Few fishes are more breathtaking than broadbills when seen breaching or greyhounding, or even swimming just below the surface. Unhappily, the colors fade soon after death, giving way to a nondescript, drab gray.

You'll note that the swordfish has a superbly streamlined body. If you gather from that that he's a fast swimmer, you surmise correctly. You'll note too that his most prominent fins are the first dorsal, roughly triangular with a concave trailing edge, and a very well-developed, crescent-shaped tail, a powerful propeller.

Pay particular attention to that big dorsal and the upper lobe

SWORDFISH (*Xiphias gladius*)

of his tail. Those are "indicators" you'll be looking for when scouting surfaced swordfish.

The broadbill's sword occupies about one-third its owner's total length. The lower jaw projects somewhat too and is pointed. His mouth is large, extending aft of the eyes.

Xiphias gladius is piscivorous, a fish eater. His menu lists such items as herring, mullet, menhaden, squid, butterfish, and blue-fish. He'll dine on many kinds of small fishes, including species residing at considerable depth. His appetite is lusty. He eats those menu items by the bucketful.

It's a common misconception that swordfish feed by spearing their prey, impaling a morsel on the sword like a guy stabbing an olive in a martini. Inspection of the weapon's broad, flat surface would show that this wouldn't be practical. Their manner of attack, as has been witnessed, is to barrel in among a school of intended victims and slash that sword from side to side in the manner of a cavalry saber to kill and stun their prey.

THE DUELIST Although a swordfish wields his "saber" mainly to obtain food, the big beast can bring it into play as a terrible weapon when needs arise.

Numerous are the accounts of broadbills charging small craft —even ships—when harpooned, hooked, or otherwise enraged. It's on record that the New Bedford, Mass., sailing vessel *Redhot* cooled off rapidly when she was sunk by the plank-breaking charge of a swordfish being brought alongside many years ago. Long Island's maritime history notes an incident in which a broadbill slammed his weapon clear through the bottom of a fishing schooner off Fire Island.

The annals of the sailing ship era are spiced with accounts of assaults on sizable vessels by wounded or enraged swordfish. Dr. William Hornaday, one of our most famous naturalists, wrote about a three-inch-thick, copper-sheathed ship's plank that had a sword thrust through it to the hilt. Such penetration, commented Dr. Hornaday, didn't testify so much to the weapon's hardness as it did to the great speed with which the beast charged. To completely penetrate three inches of seasoned, copper-sheathed oak, he estimated, would call for the swordfish to be hitting sixty miles per hour. Years ago when swordfish were harpooned commercially from dories there were several reported instances of infuriated broadbills attacking their tormentors.

It's generally conceded that they do not charge unless provoked. I've never heard of an instance of it in sport fishing. Nor have I ever heard of a case of an attack when a broadbill was hooked, or even harpooned.

FOES When small, swordfish probably are victimized by larger predators. But in adulthood, with their size, weapon, and speed, they have few natural enemies. Orcas or killer whales, for my money the most savage creatures in the sea, could spell bad news for swordfish in encounters. Some sharks definitely are foes. Makos probably are broadbills' worst enemies in nature.

Some years ago a team competing in the United States Atlantic Tuna Tournament out of Galilee, R.I., had a ringside seat at a one-sided encounter between a swordfish in the three hundred-pound class and a large mako off Block Island. This is how it went, swiftly:

The victim—the swordfish—unaware of impending disaster, was loafing along at the surface. Torpedoing in from dead astern, taking advantage of the blind spot in a swordfish's peripheral vision, came the raider. The first thing the shark did was amputate the broadbill's tail. Thus relieved of his means of propulsion, the victim was like a ship without a propeller, a helplessness of which you can be sure the mako was aware. His prey unable to escape, the shark set about demolishing him quickly. Great mouthfuls of flesh, estimated at thirty to fifty pounds apiece by the observers, disappeared into the attacker's maw. Within minutes it was all over. Only an angry red cloud of blood remained in the arena to mark the tragedy's site.

Outside of nature, broadbills' greatest foe is man—specifically, the commercial swordfisherman. All the recreational anglers in the world do not catch enough of these billfish to pose even a minor threat to the species. In bygone years, when broadbills were taken commercially by harpooning, the fish had a fighting chance. But then commercial operations adopted the Japanese method of long-lining. Carried out extensively, long-lining is a major menace to any species.

THE HUNT One of the world's greatest broadbill sport fisheries is in an east coast region that extends from the offing of eastern Long Island to the southern and western offshore waters of Massachusetts. (Another prime swordfishing region is on our Pacific seaboard, extending from Southern California on down along Mexico's great Baja California peninsula.) Among all the places in the world inhabited by swordfish, this is among the very few in which the royal billfish are seen on the surface or close to it. As a result, a fishing technique has been developed in which the broadbills are sighted first, and then the bait is presented.

In other words, swordfish are not trolled blind in this region. This is not to say that trolling blind hasn't been tried in some areas. In fact, a couple of winters ago in Key West, Fla., I saw a 300-pound broadbill that had been nailed by that method, but the catch was so unusual, either because of species or technique —or both—that it caused surprised comments on the docks. Although I've often wondered if deep trolling or drifting would produce a broadbill, I believe the odds in both are very high against the angler. Since the sighting-first method does pay off, I stick with that.

Yes, swordfish must be hunted. Since they're solitary and very widely scattered, an educated guess is that at least 99 percent of the time consumed in the sport fishery is invested in looking for them. The remaining 1 percent comes into the picture only if you're lucky enough to make contact. After many seasons of wandering around out there offshore, my eyes out on stalks staring at the dancing triangles of the waves, I'm convinced that in no other kind of angling does luck play so great a role as in swordfishing.

In the hunting method broadbills are cooperative in one way if in no other. They come to the surface to laze around in the warm water and feel the sun's rays, and maybe latch onto a few tidbits that do not require too much work to catch. When they do this they betray themselves to humans, because their dorsal fin and the upper lobe of their tail are exposed.

That's what you look for, those two fins; and if there's any sort of chop on the water it takes a bit of looking. Since the dorsal fin and upper lobe of the tail are more or less triangular, and small waves are triangular and darkish too, it's not uncommon to be fooled after hours of staring.

In those fins also lies a clue to differentiating between a swordfish and a surfaced white marlin. On the latter you'll see the tail, but you're not likely to glimpse his dorsal fin. A white marlin can hoist and lower his dorsal like a sail, and he generally doesn't erect it unless irked, alarmed, or excited about something, in which case you probably won't see him for long anyway, because he'll sound. A swordfish can't retract his dorsal fin as can other marlins and sailfishes.

What will fool you, at least until you gain experience, is to sight the dorsal fin and upper tail lobe of a shark 'way off yonder. Many an angler has had his blood pressure boosted by that, thinking he has spotted a broadbill. Blue sharks in particular are great for this deluding. Drawing closer or inspection through binoculars will reveal the differences. Look for the characteristically shaped dorsal fin and tail of a swordfish. They're quite different from those of sharks. You also want to look for a wobble in the tail's upper section that some sharks, notably blues, have. You won't see any wobble in a swordfish's tail. It's rigid.

SEASONS, HOURS, AND TIPS ON SIGHTING Swordfish are seasonal migrators. To date little is known of the routes and depths they travel during these coastwise treks northward. But since an occasional specimen is hooked in Florida's eastern offshore waters, and broadbills have been reported for Cuba, we can assume that they move through that oceanic region on their way from wherever they came.

In that prime swordfishing region from eastern Long Island and Block Island to southern Massachusetts they usually arrive in early June—if weather and water temperatures are seasonable, that is. For sport fishermen June is the month, first week on. From then into July they build to a peak, some lingering on into August, even a bit later, with warm weather, but in sharply decreased numbers. Their appearance in regions to the north of that is correspondingly later. In all regions they take off when there's a hint of cooler weather to come.

On our Pacific Coast the season is approximately the same, although there can be appreciable numbers of swordfish still around in September and even October. Then they disappear.

When they first show, they're so far offshore as to be beyond the practical reach of anglers, unless boats are equipped to remain at sea overnight. As the season progresses and coastal waters warm, swordfish move closer inshore. Once their run has established itself, they may be encountered anywhere from within just a few miles of the beach to thirty or more miles out.

An ideal swordfishing day is one when the sea is calm—the flatter, the better. A flat-calm sea better enables you to spot the fins of a surfaced swordfish. Even a slight chop increases sighting difficulties. You'll need all the good breaks you can get, believe me. In fact, if you're smart you'll confine your swordfishing efforts to such calm-ocean days whenever possible. It's less expensive and apt to be more rewarding. But don't be misled. That doesn't rule out days when there's a bit of a chop.

If there are "best" hours in which to hunt broadbills they occur between about 10:00 A.M. and 2:00 P.M., when the sun is at its zenith. Solar warmth helps draw them to the ocean's uppermost levels. I don't mean that you won't see broadbills earlier or later, but those are what I'd call optimum hours. I'd also better add that you can encounter swordfish at the top on cloudy days. Even so, you'll need all the spotting power you can muster. The more eyes looking, the better. Scan the sea constantly in all directions. If the boat has a tuna tower, so much the better. Its height will give appreciable advantage in spotting. There should be an observer up there, plus others on the flying bridge and in the cockpit.

TACKLE AND RIGS   Swordfishing tackle must be rugged. It's pitted against muscular fish of appreciable sizes, big boys that play marbles for keeps.

Conventional tackle is indicated, of course. You'll run across lighter-tackle buffs wielding 50-pound-caliber weapons for broadbills. Unless you have appreciable swordfishing experience under your belt, I suggest you don't go any lighter than 80-pound line. If you're new at the game, better use 130-pound line and matching tackle. Braided Dacron is good, but it's a matter of personal choice as to whether you fish that or monofilament in an equivalent strength.

The rod has to be rated to handle heavy lines, of course. One made to take 130-pound test lines naturally will accommodate 80-pound lines too. It will be a big-game stick with roller guides throughout and a husky butt section.

You'll need a lot of line. Four hundred or 500 yards aren't too much. Better yet, fill the reel spool. You can figure on at least a 9/0 reel. With a lot of 130-pound line you'd better look to a 10/0 or 12/0.

If you don't own such a big-game fishing outfit, give consideration to how much battling with heavyweights you'll do before you invest in one. These outfits come high. Until you make up your mind you might be better off chartering a boat that has big-game gear aboard.

You'll rig a leader between hook and line to protect against chafing-through, hits by the swordfish's weapon, etc. You have a choice of materials. Today many broadbill hunters have gone away from the cable leaders, in tests up to 450 pounds, once in vogue. The choice is more between stainless steel wire, about a No. 10 or No. 12, and 180-to-250-pound monofilament. Personally, I think it's six of one and half a dozen of the other, although monofilament is easier to handle than wire (which, you'll recall, can kink). Leader length is optional too. Fifteen to 20 feet should suffice. Some anglers go to 25. If you're world-record-minded, remember the IGFA limits on leader lengths.

For your hooks you can select from among several good patterns, including the Martu, Norwegian-made Mustad, Pfleuger-Sobey, Sobey, and others. You won't go wrong with any of the commonly used swordfish hooks. The range of sizes is 9/0 to

14/0, with a 12/0 about right. Hooks must be strong. You might be wise to consider triple-strength (3X or XXX) gauge.

The standard broadbill rig calls for one hook. There's also a tandem two-hook rig (always check IGFA specifications for two-hook ensembles if you're record-minded) that has proved lethal for broadbills. I'll tell you about that later.

Our illustration shows one way of attaching a cable leader. Note that ring-eye hooks are used. We'll talk about wire in the white marlin chapter.

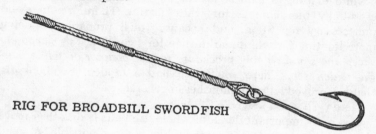

RIG FOR BROADBILL SWORDFISH

Rigging a cable leader calls for some work. Here a hook with a large enough ring eye is required. The cable's free end is fed through the eye—some fishermen loop it around the eye once as it passes through—then brought out alongside the leader for six or eight inches. The end is secured in three places with tight wrappings of copper wire or seized with strong twine. A finishing touch is to solder the end of the cable to the leader proper. A similar procedure is employed for making a loop on the cable's other end for attachment to the line. Usually this loop is made over a small thimble to keep it open.

Cable leaders come already prepared in various lengths and strengths. Some are sheathed in a plastic coating to protect the hands.

You'll probably go with a wire or mono leader, instead of cable. In any case, connection between leader and line is made through a suitably strong swivel. For large game fishes the end of the line often is doubled. Details are in the tuna chapter.

BAITS AND BAITING   For reasons best known to the fish, broadbills seldom respond to trolled artificial lures. Natural baits, on the other hand, are proven killers. At one time or another these baits have taken swordfish: squid, mullet, eels, mackerel, *balao* ("ballyhoo"), small bluefish, northern whiting, flying fish, and even small striped bass. Generally you won't go wrong with a fresh, plump squid, eight or twelve ounces to about a pound or so. Strictly fresh squid may be difficult to obtain, in which case you'll have to ride with the frozen stuff. Be sure to thaw it beforehand so it will be supple and lifelike.

Special note concerning whole-squid baits: These are not only killers for broadbill swordfish, but also for other kinds of billfishes —white marlin, to name one. Rigging of squid for swordfish is essentially the same as for white marlin. Therefore, to avoid unnecessary repetition, and because you'll probably be doing more hunting for white marlin than for swordfish, *I've purposely saved the squid rigging procedure for the chapter on white marlin—which see.* There you'll also find a tandem two-hook rig that has proved lethal to billfishes in general.

Here we'll go on to whole-fish baits.

The most important detail of whole-fish baits is that they move through the water in the most lifelike manner possible. A small fish going along sideways or backward hardly looks natural. Similarly, a very stiff bait also has to look rather odd to a predator. That leads to a couple of important recommendations. First, use fresh baits whenever you can. If you have to rig the frozen kind, thaw it thoroughly beforehand and remove the backbone to give the fish more action in the water.

Don't ever underestimate the sensibilities of any fish to the appearance of a bait. Don't think, as some anglers mistakenly do, that a fish will grab something simply because it's a bait. An offering that looks unnatural or weird can pass ignored, or even spook a fish. Look at it this way: Even if you were hungry, would you be attracted to a steak that was bright green, or a purple fried egg?

To debone a fish bait for broadbills you can follow a procedure long employed by my friend, the late Capt. Walter Drobecker, a Montauk charter skipper who was one of the best swordfishermen who ever lived.

Here's Walt's deboning and baiting technique:

1. Make a cut along the midline of bait fish's back, from just behind the head to the tail's base. Deepen this incision to lie alongside the backbone on both sides.

2. Remove the backbone in its entirety. Cut it loose and lift it out.

3. A shallow trench is left. Feed your hook in through the bait's mouth and bring it out in the vicinity of the start of the trench at the bait's head end. Make a little cut or two if necessary.

4. Lay that portion of your leader immediately adjacent to the hook in the groove formerly occupied by the backbone. Bury the hook in the bait's flesh approximately two-thirds of the way to the tail.

5. Complete your baiting by sewing shut the groove with the leader inside; also sew shut the fish's mouth. A stout needle and some twine or heavy thread will do it. The rig is now ready to go to work.

The common black eel is another effective billfish bait, for white marlin as well as for swordfish. A popular version of rigging this come-on is as follows:

1. A hook of appropriate size—gauged according to whether the target is a broadbill or white marlin, an 8/0 to 12/0 or 14/0 —is secured to about fifteen feet of hundred-pound test monofilament leader.

2. The hook's point is brought out through the eel's underside a couple of inches behind the head. This leaves most of the bait's body free to wiggle enticingly in the water. And that's all there is to it, except, possibly, the optional step of lashing the eel's mouth shut on the leader with a few coils of thread or twine.

The *balao* or ballyhoo is still another billfish-getter. As with all whole-fish baits, there are various ways of rigging a ballyhoo. Depending upon where you do your broadbill hunting or marlin fishing, this bait may or may not be available. In any case, the chances are high that you'll have to use the frozen stuff.

There's a two-hook ballyhoo rig that is as simple as it is effective. It goes like this:

1. Get yourself two ring-eye hooks of suitable size—say, 8/0 to 12/0, depending upon the fish sought.

2. Secure the first one to about fifteen feet of hundred-pound mono leader.

3. Open the eye of your second hook just enough to slip it around the first hook's bend. *Note:* The first hook will ride with its point upward. Bridle your second hook on the first so that its point rides *downward,* then squeeze its eye closed with pliers.

4. The second hook, its bend and point aimed downward, is fed in through the bait's mouth and made to emerge at the body's underside. How far back it comes out is determined by the length of the hook's shaft. To complete baiting, thrust your second hook upward through the fish's jaws so that its point emerges through the top of the head.

HUNTING STRATEGY   Swordfish are so few and far between that they must be hunted in a concentrated effort. The initial step in your strategy, therefore, is to find one.

This is when you begin to get an inkling that there are easier, more productive kinds of angling. It's also when it dawns on you that broadbilling can be frustrating. All this will put you to the test. Two of the greatest criteria of successful swordfishing are patience and persistence. Be prepared for many days when you won't so much as *see* one.

Patience and persistence are what separate the men from the boys in this game. They're the factors that make dyed-in-the-wool swordfishermen among the most indefatigable and optimistic anglers in the world. But the stakes, like the odds against, are high. To the winners go supreme angling rewards: magnificent sport and the prestige of catching one of the world's most highly desirable and seldom captured sport fishes.

Someone has calculated that out of fifty broadbills sighted an angler *might* get to present a bait to twenty, evoke a positive reaction from ten, hook four, and actually catch one. Following this arithmetical pattern, an average annual catch of fifty in all the nation's major sport swordfishing areas is a distillate of at least a thousand baiting attempts and a probable minimum of twenty-five hundred sightings.

Before you can so much as hope to do battle with a broadbill you must sight one at the surface. You now know what to look for. And when your eyes rivet themselves to that electrifying sight of the telltale dorsal fin and upper-tail lobe betraying a surfaced swordfish, the tricky part of your strategy begins. You're going to approach the fish and endeavor to get him interested in your bait.

THE APPROACH Having spotted a swordfish, you've hurdled the first set of odds against you. Now you're ready to tackle the second set.

Perhaps the single most important thing to keep in mind at this stage is that swordfish are unpredictable individuals. You have no way of knowing how they will react to your advances. What I'm saying is, your seeing one at the surface doesn't mean beans. It's an all-important start, true; but it also may be omega, *finis*. You have no way of knowing beforehand if a broadbill is even remotely interested in food or has filled his belly; or if he's ambitious or lethargic; or, even if he is hungry, whether or not your offering will appeal to him. You usually get the answers to these queries in short order.

The technique is to troll your bait as close as possible to the target, right across his line of vision. Naturally he has to see the come-on.

The approach calls for common sense and know-how on the part of the person at the helm. Some broadbills are quite bold— or stupid, if you prefer—and allow a boat to draw surprisingly close, as witness instances in which they're harpooned. Others may be boat-shy, or skittery, and spook easily. So the word is *caution*. Have the boat maneuvered so that your bait is towed right across in front of him, maybe twenty or twenty-five feet away, without the craft coming near enough to scare him into moving off or sounding. You may have to accomplish this by cutting across well in front of him on an angle. Or maybe you can do it with a wide-sweeping arc of the boat. In any case, don't draw any closer than you have to with the boat.

Above all, never try to tiptoe up behind a swordfish. Remember that blind spot in his vision, dead astern. If he should happen to turn his head and catch a glimpse of something big in his peripheral vision he won't stick around to say howdy.

Among these billfish there's appreciable variation in response to baits. One may come charging in, slashing at it with his sword.

This has been known to mangle a bait beyond use or even tear it off the hook. Another broadbill will move in almost leisurely. Still another will show complete indifference, even turning away as though in contempt. Sometimes a fiercely onrushing attack on a bait causes complications. If the fish's sword slides over the bait, he can grab it with his mouth. If his aim is careless, and the bait passes *over* the sword, there's nothing for his mouth to seize, and he might just be foul-hooked in the eye or upper body, which can spell trouble.

Years ago a common approach was to troll the offering across in front of a swordfish with the angler on the alert to throw his reel into free spool to give the bait a dropback when the critter showed interest. Needless to add, a lot depended upon the angler's reflexes and timing. That technique has been refined. Its basic principle is the same, but the procedure is different.

Instead of the squid, eel, or whatever being trolled past the broadbill, it's kept ready in the cockpit until the boat is about ready to make her pass. At that point the fisherman lets his bait drop about fifty or sixty to a hundred feet astern, where it is kept at that distance by someone in the party, or the mate on a charter boat, holding the line. The boat moves *slowly* across ahead of the broadbill. Whoever is holding the line strips off a sizable loop of it by hand from the reel and lets it trail in the water. As the boat passes the swordfish there comes one of the sport's moments of truth. It calls for judgment on the part of the fellow holding the line, because he may have to quickly shorten or lengthen the bait's distance astern to bring it within twenty to twenty-five or thirty feet of the fish.

Here comes another instant of judgment. Immediately before the broadbill has had an opportunity to actively respond to the bait, whoever is holding the line lets go. This is where that loop dragging in the water comes into service. Its slack becomes a dropback, causing the bait to pause to give the fish a chance to come after it, without throwing the reel into free spool. The person handling the line from the transom—it isn't the angler, remember—has to know what he's doing. As the boat moves away from the fish he hand-peels additional yardage from reel, letting it fall into the water and watching it constantly for any indications that the swordfish may be picking up the bait. That slack line straightens out promptly when he has seized the bait and is moving away with it.

It could happen, especially with a line handler who is inexperienced or has poor timing, that a swordfish will rush the bait swiftly and savagely before he can release the line. If it happens, and the swordfish hasn't hooked himself, the line will have to be given an instant dropback to delude the "customer" into thinking he has captured a tasty morsel. In a more leisurely approach his telltale fins may vanish momentarily as he goes below to investigate the bait. Watching the line will reveal the degree of his interest.

If the broadbill has viciously rushed the bait and missed, and a dropback brings no response, or if he reappears at the surface and obviously hasn't taken the bait, the entire baiting procedure has to be repeated . . . while everyone hopes he sticks around for another go. Before the next pass the bait should be checked to make sure it's intact on the hook. A mangled bait should be replaced.

One of the big dangers at this stage of the game is the angler's attempts to strike his fish prematurely. The eagerness is understandable, but it must be controlled. Trying to set the hook too soon only serves to yank the bait away. The fish could lose interest and disappear, thus abruptly ending the only opportunity that day—or maybe that season. An experienced line handler is in an excellent position to tell an angler when to set his hook. So is a seasoned swordfishing skipper, perched on the boat's bridge.

When there's no doubt that the swordfish has taken the bait and is moving away with it, the angler throws his reel into gear, and the boat moves ahead suddenly and fast to take up any slack. Then, when the angler feels the unmistakable line tension that tells him the fish is on, he rears back in the chair and strikes hard to set the hook. If he has indeed hooked a broadbill, the party gets under way in earnest.

Before we get to that combat here are a few useful notes:

Swordfish have tough bone in the area where the sword joins the head. But parts of their mouth are surprisingly soft. One of the reasons there are odds against a hooked broadbill being brought to gaff is that a hook planted in those parts can tear free.

A hook solidly set in that bony region of the upper jaw is something else again.

The reel's striking drag is a factor in setting the hook. In extremes it could be too light for effective penetration in hard bone or too heavy for the softer mouth parts. Since you have no way of knowing about where the hook is about to bite, you have to try what you hope will be a satisfactory medium. I'll pass along these suggestions: for 130-pound tackle, not over 20 pounds; for 80-pound line, about 16 pounds; for 50-pound tackle, 10 to 12 pounds. Tie your line to a hand scale, have someone hold it, then pull against it with your rod until the reel drag slips. Adjust drag to desired readings on scale.

One of the most suspenseful moments in all sport fishing is that interval during which a broadbill decides whether to pick up a bait or ignore it. It's also one of the most nerve-racking. All angling has no other moment quite like that when a swordfish is hooked. The second set of odds has been overcome.

COMBAT TIME The length and intensity of a swordfish's fight will depend upon his size, his disposition, the intensity of his resentment on finding his freedom curtailed, and how he has been hooked.

The "personality" of the fish and his physical condition at the time are important factors. As you'll learn, the stamina of big fishes varies considerably because of them. Thus one specimen might take twice—or half—as long to whip as another of the species and comparable weight. They're like boxers in this respect.

How your swordfish has been hooked can be a cardinal factor in the nature and duration of his resistance. For instance, if your hook has dug into his lower jaw in such a way as to interfere with his breathing by holding his mouth closed, the fight may be shortened appreciably. Similarly, if he has been gut-hooked (that is, if he has swallowed the bait down in his innards and the hook has found a tender spot), which I don't think is likely to happen if you've been alert, the battle probably won't last long. He'll go along with almost anything that eases the pressure on that hook. But if, on the other hand, you've hooked him firmly in his tough upper jaw, you're apt to be in for a long, rugged contest. Occasionally there are complications that prolong or shorten combat—such as foul-hooking in the eye or back, and the fish rolling up in the leader or getting it all tangled around his sword.

Usually a swordfish's first run or two are his longest and strongest, and he can peel off a couple of hundred yards of line at express train speed if he has a mind to. You'll have nothing to say about it, that's for sure. When he gets that first long spurt or two out of his system he'll probably settle down to a series of shorter but still powerful runs. He's likely to run and make a fuss at the surface periodically, which is a time when he can roll up in the leader.

During his great power surges you won't be able to stop him. For at least half the tug-o'-war he'll take more line than you can retrieve. The fight is give-and-take all the way, with him doing much of the taking. Should an especially tough, obstinate broadbill threaten to strip your reel of line (a dilemma that shouldn't arise if you start out with an adequate supply), you'll have to chase him down, a procedure described in the chapter on sharks —unless, of course, you can bring him under control before your yardage becomes critically low. The chances are that this situation won't pop up unless you start out with a ridiculously inadequate supply of line.

Every big fish plays the game his own way, often not according to rules man has set down. But sooner or later the fight settles into a routine seesaw pattern. Throughout this scrap you'll have to maintain respect for your opponent's softer mouth parts, in case your hook is imbedded there. Don't, whatever you do, try "horsing" tactics if he insists on running. Tend to your reel drag. Remember the increasing brake effect as more line leaves the spool. You may have to slack off a bit on your drag to compensate when you have a lot of line out, then tighten it later. Adjust and readjust when necessary, but only enough to keep steady pressure on your fish.

Note: Reels have been known to become very hot, because of drag friction, when a big fish repeatedly runs. A procedure here is to have someone standing alongside the fighting chair with a bucket of sea water, some of which can be poured over the reel at intervals to cool it. The big danger in a drag overheating is that it will "freeze" or bind tight. That ends a battle abruptly, usually by a popped line.

Combat with a swordfish is always exciting. Some broadbills resist less, or have less stamina, than others, but I've never known an argument with one that didn't have rugged phases. You may be lucky enough to get a bonus thrill in the form of a leap. Only a few broadbills jump, but when they do it's one of angling's greatest spectacles. The sight of that magnificent body skyrocketing out of the sea to glint in the sun, then fall back in a geyser of water and foam is an indelible fishing memory.

A swordfish will fight you every inch of the way. But in time there comes a point of no return for him, and the tide of battle gradually turns in your favor. The finned gladiator will tire. A decrease in his resistance will be noticeable, and eventually there will be more line coming in than going out. Always, though, you'll have to be alert for those surprising moments when he summons reserve strength for another run.

Finally, when the feel of it and that increasing amount of wet line on your reel inform you that you have him started toward the boat, the battle goes into its closing phase. Barring some calamity such as your leader or line snapping because of fatigue, or the hook letting go at the last minute before gaffing, the affair is just about over; and, tired as you might be, you find yourself sorry that it is.

THE INTRUDERS   In battles with many kinds of gamesters in a wide range of sizes your unseen foes will be sharks. Their threat becomes especially acute in the closing phases of combat, when your opponent tires. It increases sharply as the fish is being brought toward the boat for gaffing. Threshing movements and vibrations are shark attractors. Any bleeding is a long-distance telegraphed invitation to a free lunch.

I've seen marlin and yellowfin tuna, among others, severely mangled by sharks as they were being reeled toward the boat. More than half of one broadbill caught off Montauk disappeared down the gullets of sharks while being brought to gaff. Thanks to sharks, more than one fisherman has wound up with only the head of his catch.

Short of discouraging such piracy with a rifle or shotgun (*use extreme caution!*), which is generally ineffective unless the intruders are killed, there's little if anything that can be done in such attacks. Sometimes, when the hooked fish is brought close enough, skillful prodding with boathooks or long poles will help to fend off the raiders, but this has obvious limitations. About the only thing you can do is get your opponent on a ginpole or into the cockpit as quickly as possible. If that can't be done, for one reason or another . . . well, at least you had the sport of playing your fish.

I have to tell you a story about shark-discouraging methods. In retrospect it's humorous. At the time the parties involved weren't chuckling. The episode occurred in the Bahamas. Its heroes were two veteran anglers who shall remain nameless, since they probably took plenty of needling about it.

They were trying to bait a blue marlin when a large hammerhead shark glided into the scene. He was about as welcome as bubonic plague, and the fishermen conspired to get rid of him. Now, they happened to have some dynamite aboard—what for, I can't imagine, but there it was. They rammed a stick of it down inside a whole-fish bait, lighted the fuse, and tossed it to the hammerhead. Obligingly, the big shark gulped the bait. With diabolical timing he swam under the boat just as the dynamite let go. Its blast blew the craft's stern section right out of the water and sprang most of her seams. They had to race for shore, pumping like mad all the way, and barely made it to shallow water, where the boat sank.

A CLASSIC   Ernest Hemingway's famous "Old Man and the Sea" had a real-life counterpart, but with a much happier ending. In all swordfishing lore there are few other stories to match this one. I believe only two or three such incidents are on record. It's the saga of a sport fisherman who conquered a big broadbill singlehandedly, start to finish. Alone at the time, he baited the beast, fought him—all the while maneuvering the boat whenever necessary—gaffed him, and strung him up on a ginpole.

The fisherman was my late friend Capt. Walter Drobecker, charter skipper-guide and broadbill hunter *par excellence*. His amazing feat took place within a couple of miles of the beach near Shinnecock Inlet on Long Island's South Shore. It's a story that will be told and retold wherever broadbill hunters gather.

That particular day Walt was making a special trip with a brand-new forty-foot Pacemaker from Montauk to a marina on the Hudson River in Manhattan. Since it was the swordfish season and he'd be taking the outside ocean route to New York, Walt went prepared with some rigged squid baits. He was alone on board.

Walt was making knots west'ard, the Pacemaker's twin engines humming sweetly as Montauk Lighthouse dropped astern. He cut a course fairly close to shore, taking advantage of the lee of the beach. Then, as he came into the Hampton Bays sector, he saw a swordfish. The broadbill was well ahead of him at the time. Walt had vision that would make an eagle seem nearsighted. A surfaced swordfish galvanized him like a matador's *muleta* challenges a Moro bull.

Walt slowed the cruiser to a crawl and rushed down from the flying bridge. A squid bait was ready for presentation in seconds. Back up on the bridge he went, maneuvering his charge for a pass. Back down in the cockpit again, the boat running herself, he paid out line and trolled his squid temptingly across in front of the billfish. *Bingo!* Walt had him on.

During the hectic three hours or so that ensued Walt was busier than a juggler with body lice, all the while alternately playing his fish and rushing up and down between cockpit and flying bridge, where he could better watch his line, in attempts to divine the broadbill's next move and maneuver the boat accordingly. Picture arguing with an angry swordfish of considerable size and having to thrust the rod into a holder at intervals, dash up to the flying bridge to correct the boat's course, then hurry down to resume the fight.

So the incredible encounter went. Finally Walt got his opponent close enough to seize the leader with one hand and swing a flying gaff with the other. The fish thus secured, he could breathe a little easier, but now another problem presented itself. All that action had brought him to the brink of exhaustion. He was unable to hoist the big broadbill on the ginpole by himself. He solved the problem neatly. He fashioned a jury rig, using the boat's electric anchor winch, and the regal fish dangled from the Pacemaker's ginpole.

Walt guided the boat through Shinnecock Inlet and put in at Mickey Altenkirch's Canoe Place Dock on Shinnecock Canal in Hampton Bays. On Mickey's scales the broadbill weighed in at four hundred pounds even.

Walt was a few hours late getting to Manhattan, but no one seemed to resent it when he explained the delay. Even non-anglers in the crowd sensed that a bit of sport-fishing history had been made that day.

FROM SEA TO TABLE   For anglers the No. 1 detail of swordfishing is its challenge, with triumph, enormous satisfaction, and prestige as the rewards of success. There's another bonus, and you know it: Swordfish are excellent eating. I'm sure you've engaged one—or part of one, rather—with knife and fork, even though you may never have seen one in life. Personally, I'd rather have a broadbill as a headmount on a wall than as a steak on a plate, but for many folks it's the other way around.*

Photographs of your catch are another bonus, a permanent one, inexpensive and easy to obtain. Still another lasting memento is a trophy mount; but this is costly, even if only the head is involved (the average wallet and home are not likely to accommodate a whole-mounted broadbill).

If you want the head for a mount, remove it carefully and set it aside for a taxidermist's agent. Or, better yet, get him to do it for you. (Inquire locally about a taxidermist or his representative.) The sword alone makes a fine reminder of your victory, if you're not going to have the head mounted. Simply saw it off evenly, close to the head. Sometimes these "blades" are outfitted with a handle and hilt of wood to fashion a novel sword.

In any case, make provision for proper disposal of the carcass and discarded parts. Don't become a *persona non grata* by dump-

* I'm not going into a discussion of the subject of swordfish being rendered inedible by mercury contamination. Not because I brush it off as being minor. It isn't. I avoid it here because it's complex and has no place in these pages. I suggest you keep posted via current newspaper and magazine reports. Have up-to-the-minute information about contamination of swordfish meat by mercury and/or other possibly harmful chemical compounds before you consider eating any broadbill catch. Lacking such information or a positive okay from qualified authorities, or if you're at all in doubt, play it safe and don't eat the meat.

ing them indiscriminately or abandoning them on a dock. Any meat destined for the table should be iced down for the trip home and placed under satisfactory refrigeration until used.

Always have a camera along on a swordfishing trip. I don't care if it's the simplest kind of fixed-focus Kodak. Any action shots will add immeasurably to your record of the event. No matter what else you do with a swordfish you catch, you must have dockside pictures. On sport-fishing docks there's often available an aerosol can of white paint for spraying the weight and date on a fish for recording by a camera's lens. Be sure to get into the picture with your broadbill (it would take a tribe of Borneo head hunters to keep you out, eh?). How else are you going to be able to convince any skeptics when you brag about your triumph?

CHAPTER 23

Tuna, Bluefin Variety:
Schoolkids to Giants

I can't remember when I caught my first bluefin tuna. It was a long time ago. The occasion launched a one-sided romance of sorts that has endured ever since. I have no way of knowing how the fish feel about me (they've never said), but for yours truly it was delight at first catch.

For my money these fish, especially the youngsters nicknamed school tuna (a size classification I'll clarify in a moment), are among the finest kind of finned opponents. They're everyone's game fish.

FAMILY ALBUM Throughout our world's seas there are several different kinds of tunas. Recognized in addition to the bluefin are species with names such as big-eye, yellowfin or Allison, dogtooth, blackfin, tonggol, etc. As a family they're encountered in oceans all over the globe, including those lapping the shores of Africa, Australia, and Asia.

DISTRIBUTION We can sum this up in one word: worldwide. As Drs. Bigelow and Schroeder would say, bluefin tuna are cosmopolitan in warm, warm-temperate, and temperate regions of the Atlantic and Pacific oceans, the Mediterranean Sea, and the Indian Ocean. They're also found in the Caribbean, the North Sea, the Baltic Sea, the Black Sea, the Sea of Azov, and the Persian Gulf.

In the Atlantic their distribution is on both sides. We'll concentrate on those on our side of the big puddle. Here their range is from Newfoundland and southern Labrador on down to Bermuda, the Bahamas, the Caribbean Sea (including Cuba, Jamaica, and—at least in migrations—waters off Mexico's Yucatan

Peninsula), and the Gulf of Mexico. In many locales, particularly those in the northern extremes of their ranges, their appearance is according to seasons, and variations often are radical.

Bluefin tuna are long-range migrators. To give you a for-instance: Those that file past the Bahamas earlier in the year are thought to be the same fish that turn up in Nova Scotia in the fall. The same is thought to be true for the transient giant bluefins encountered for a couple of weeks in May off Mexico's Isla de Cozumel.

Their migrational patterns can be complex. Our knowledge of them still is riddled with gaps. However, thanks to the untiring efforts of researchers such as Frank Mather III of Woods Hole Oceanographic Institution, who has been studying bluefin wanderings along the Atlantic's North American side for years, those gaps are gradually being filled.

SIZES Bluefins come in a very wide range of sizes. These start somewhere around 5 or 6 pounds for the very young ones and go up to 1,000 pounds, if not more. Fully grown, they're the largest of all the tunas, by far.

This broad range of weights has spawned an unofficial size terminology among U.S. Atlantic Coast tuna hunters. It's arbitrary and flexible, and goes like this: Bluefins up to, say, 100, 125, or 150 pounds are referred to as "school tuna" because of their habit of traveling in sizable groups. The older individuals, 400 to 500 pounds and up, which tend to be loners or travel in smaller groups, are referred to as "giants." Oddly enough, there's never been a nickname for those bluefins in the size range between those extremes, say, above 150 pounds and under 400. But, as I said, the classification is purely informal anyway, quite flexible and arbitrary. The tendency today is to call any bluefin above 150 pounds a "giant."

They're all the same species. Differences are only a matter of sizes (and habits); and sizes, naturally, are a matter of ages. An approximate age-weight table goes as follows: 1 to 4 years old, 5 to 69 pounds; 4 to 9 years, 70 to 269 pounds; at least 9 years and older, 270 pounds and upward. School tuna are the young-sters. The intermediates are the bluefin family's teen-agers, you might say. The larger individuals are the grownups and senior citizens.

Among those senior citizens are some of angling's largest game. Only blue and black marlin, some of the sharks, and occasional swordfish encountered off South America's Pacific seaboard can top the largest bluefins. Their size potential goes to half a ton.

Interestingly, the ancient Romans seem to have been acquainted with giant bluefins. Pliny the Elder, a scholar and naturalist who wanted to study the cataclysmic eruption of Mount Vesuvius firsthand in A.D. 79 and got himself cooked in that big outdoor barbecue for his pains, wrote of Mediterranean "tunny" weighing 1,200 pounds. I doubt if old Pliny caught any himself, but he must have seen such specimens somewhere.

His observations on 1,000-pound tuna were substantiated more than 1,000 years later. In their excellent book *Fishes of the Gulf of Maine,* Drs. Bigelow and Schroeder mention "a length of 14 feet or more, and a weight of 1,400 pounds being rumored, with fish of 1,000 pounds not rare." They note a recorded Rhode Island giant, caught commercially along about 1913, that tipped the scale at 1,225 pounds, plus 4 or 5 brutes in the 1,200-pound class brought into Boston years ago, and a 1924 specimen said to have weighed 1,300 pounds. Then there's that king of them all—so far—originally mentioned by the Italian ichthyologist Sella in a 1931 marine science publication. It tells of a fairly well-authenticated instance of a bluefin caught off Narragansett Pier, R.I., more than 70 years ago that weighed "in the neighborhood of 1,500 pounds, was divided among the various hotels, and fed 1,000 people."

Many years were to pass before sport fishermen saw any tuna approaching 1,000 pounds. In 1950 an IGFA world record was set by a 977-pounder caught at St. Ann Bay, Nova Scotia. Not far behind that champ came a U.S. record established a year or two later by New Jersey angler Harry Brain aboard the late Capt. Buster Raynor's *Scamp* out of Montauk. That bruiser was recorded at 961½ pounds and was extracted from Rhode Island waters. There's no doubt in my mind that both of those giants weighed about 1,000 pounds in life, the lesser weights being due to loss of blood (tunas bleed a lot) and a certain amount of drying out.

For 20 years the St. Ann Bay giant reigned as IGFA best of species. Then, within a span of about 2 months, the mark was topped five times in rapid succession! Four of those fish were caught in Nova Scotia and Prince Edward Island waters. The fifth was caught offshore of Montauk. Most interesting, two of them topped the 1,000-pound mark for the first time in sport-fishing history. Both were captured in Nova Scotia's waters. One weighed 1,025 pounds; the other, 1,065 pounds.

A HANDY LENGTH-WEIGHT CHART   Ed Migdalski has come up with a table that aids in *estimating* the weights of bluefins at the time of boating. Ed based his chart on figures gathered during three seasons at Nova Scotia's famous tuna fishing center of Wedgeport, then modified it somewhat according to his own research. The table is from Ed's fine book, *Angler's Guide to the Salt Water Game Fishes, Atlantic and Pacific.*

Length in Inches	Weight in Pounds
55 to 60	110 to 140
61 to 65	150 to 185
66 to 70	190 to 205
71 to 75	208 to 250
76 to 80	260 to 290
81 to 85	320 to 400
86 to 90	440 to 500
91 to 95	510 to 560
96 to 100	570 to 650
101 to 105	670 to 700

IDENTIFICATION DATA   There are certain family characteristics that all tunas share. One of these is a superbly streamlined body. Among all sizes the body has a solid, muscular look, a feature that is accented by the giants' great bulk. Because of a certain resemblance to mackerel and their massiveness, really big blue-fins once were called "horse mackerel." Incidentally, the term "tunny" is still applied to tuna in British sport-fishing literature.

Fins also are an identification aid. This tuna has two dorsals. They're practically continuous, but different in shape and size. Contributing to its owner's magnificent streamlining, the first

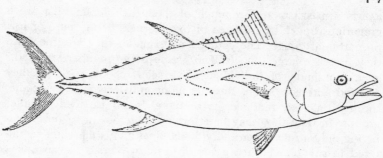

TUNA (*Thunnus thynnus*)

dorsal can be retracted into a slot on the back. The pectoral (side) and ventral (lower) fins are modest in size, the former being proportionately longer than wide. The anal fin approximates the second dorsal in shape and size, but is positioned farther aft. Prominent is the big caudal fin or tail, shaped like a quarter moon. Its base is very slender and carries a longitudinal keel on either side.

Anatomical features shared by many members of the tuna-albacore-bonito-mackerel tribe are two series of small processes called finlets. There's one row of these along the back's midline and another along the midline of the underside, both in the fish's stern section.

The bluefin's color scheme is conservatively handsome. His back is a dark, rich blue, midnight or almost black on some specimens, often with greenish or silver-gray reflections. On the sides this gives way abruptly to silver-gray, continuous on down to the belly. Sides and belly are brightened by an iridescent pink tinting, and may be marked by vague blotches and bands of silver. The gill covers are silvery. Noted for some specimens is a golden or yellowish band along the sides, extending from the snout partway along the body. Interestingly, this stripe disappears almost instantly when the fish is gaffed.

Although the bluefin's body carries small scales on its trunk section, its surface is amazingly smooth, almost like an enameled finish, to further minimize water resistance. Ma Nature was far ahead of man in streamlining when she designed this tuna.

HABITS AND SEASONS   For much of their life bluefin tuna are a gregarious bunch, the degree of togetherness being more or less proportional to age. The younger and smaller they are, the more they travel in large schools. These groups can number hundreds, even thousands, of individuals. I've seen schools so large they covered acres of ocean. But the older and larger they become, the greater their tendency is to travel in progressively smaller groups. In time they may hang around together in schools numbering only a few dozen individuals. Real giants may be encountered in small pods—just a few fish, or in pairs, or even alone. I should add, though, that I've seen large schools of giants in the five-hundred-to-eight-hundred-pound bracket as they migrated northward along the Yucatan Channel route past Mexico's Isla de Cozumel.

Most, if not all, the individuals within a given school of the younger fish are approximately the same size, give or take a few pounds. The younger the bluefins, the more this holds true.

The gregariousness of school tuna probably is for protection. There's safety in numbers, you know. Feeding habits may be a factor too. It might also explain why all the members of a school of the younger fish are so nearly the same in size.

An old tuna fisherman once theorized that bluefins' feeding habits change as they grow older. When very young and not too experienced as hunters, he figured, they dine on prey that they're better able to catch at that stage and while hunting in large schools. Later they acquire tastes for other food fishes and are better able to forage for themselves or at least in smaller packs. Accordingly, schools begin to dwindle. Still later, when the individuals grow really big, they require a diet of larger prey. At that time, perhaps, less speed is required because of the nature of their prey. Or maybe they no longer need the corraling tactics often employed by large schools of predators. Too, they probably have become still wiser in hunting procedures, so they start operating more independently. It sounds plausible.

Bluefins' diet embraces many kinds of smaller fishes, with an accent on those gathering in large schools. Availability is a factor. Tuna aren't fussy. Herring are one item on the menu. Bluefins devour them in huge quantities. The same is true for mackerel and mossbunkers. They also eat hake, sand eels, shrimp, dogfish, crabs on occasion, and assorted other small neighbors.

Strangely timid in some respects, even when attaining great size, they're voracious feeders and bold, swift hunters. It's reported that sometimes they're so persistent in pursuit of prey that they run into water too shallow and become stranded.

School tuna often betray their presence by finning at the surface or, more commonly, by creating a ruckus there as they feed. During a dining orgy they can be seen splashing and boiling, even leaping clear of the sea. Bluefins also will break the surface, even breach, when attacking a lure. It's been my experience, however, that such an approach is confined chiefly to youngsters. Giants may come near the top in a chum slick or when investigating a bait, creating a "boil" behind the boat, but they usually remain submerged. For some reason, school tuna do not leap once they're hooked; nor have I heard of any giants jumping once a hook bites in. But I witnessed leaping among those five-hundred-to-eight-hundred-pound brutes migrating past Cozumel. Fish that size hurling themselves out of the water is quite a spectacle. It's also recorded that bluefin tuna will leap when traveling on a definite course, at which time they all jump in the same direction. During a surface-feeding frenzy they breach in all different directions.

As eggs and infants and when very young, bluefins probably fall victim to all sorts of hungry neighbors, as well as to adverse environmental conditions, in considerable numbers. But their speed helps them to avoid many predators. That, coupled with increasing size, leaves them with relatively few finned foes as they grow older. Sharks and killer whales are their natural foes. Parasites and diseases extract a certain toll throughout life. Man is an enemy, of course, especially when he goes after them with large nets.

I won't go into the details of Atlantic bluefin spawning. Take my word for it, they're complex and contain gaps in knowledge. Suffice it to say that it seems fairly well established that the Mediterranean is a major breeding ground on the European side of the Atlantic. On our side the picture remains less distinct, although studies by the University of Miami's Marine Laboratory have pointed to various southern regions as spawning grounds.

These include the Straits of Florida, offshore of northwestern Cuba, and the Bahama Banks' western edge on the Gulf Stream. Bimini in the Bahamas and the Windward Passage in the Antilles are other areas mentioned.

Aided by lusty appetites, growth is quite rapid among bluefin tuna, especially when young. The following table, from the great *McClane's Standard Fishing Encyclopedia* (New York, Holt, Rinehart & Winston, Inc.), provides an approximate correlation of lengths and weights with ages:

Age in Years	Length in Inches	Weight in Pounds
To 3 months	13	1½
1	23	8½
2	31	22
3	39	40
4	47	69
5	55	100
6	61	140
7	67	185
8	73	240
9	79	300
10	85	360
11	91	430
12	96	510
13	101	600
14	105	690

Bluefin tuna are extensive wanderers. Their migration patterns are complicated and not yet fully understood. We know enough about them, however, to have some idea of how they move up and down the Atlantic Coast of North America.

In addition to an inborn urge to wander, their migrations are influenced by such environmental factors as availability of food, water temperatures, and salinity. Their appearing in progressively more northern waters is timed accordingly. They are ocean-going fish, although they're known to move into deeper bays and sounds when so inclined. Probably because of the salinity or saltiness factor, they haven't been reported for brackish water. Throughout their U.S. East Coast range they may be encountered anywhere from fairly close inshore to many miles offshore, depending upon region, local conditions, and time of year. According to Drs. Bigelow and Schroeder, the smaller bluefins "seem rather closely restricted to regions where the surface layer is warmer than 60 to 62° F," while large individuals can and do tolerate lower temperatures. As an example of the latter, Bigelow and Schroeder cite the eastern side of the Gulf of Maine, where summer-visiting bluefins encounter water temperatures no higher than about 50–54° F, even in August.

A simplified version of their northward migration has them starting somewhere down in the vast Caribbean region, tracing a course through Yucatan Channel past Cuba. As their movement progresses, some may move into the Gulf Stream, while others choose a route closer to the Bahamas and Bermuda, traveling roughly northwestward. Up the Atlantic Coast they come, apparently at various distances from shore, past North Carolina's Cape Hatteras, then along the New Jersey coast to Long Island and New England, finally getting to Nova Scotia and beyond.

Bluefin tuna have been reported around Jamaica for much of the year, but seem to be most plentiful there in March and April. Commercial fishermen on Cozumel, Mexico, say that schools of giants pass through there in May, which is when I saw them. According to Bigelow and Schroeder again, "they appear earliest on the Bahamian side of the Straits of Florida in the first or second week in May; next off New Jersey, off Long Island, off southern New England, and in Cape Cod Bay in June. But they have been reported well within the Gulf of Maine by the last week of May, or nearly as early as in Bahamian waters. This, with the added fact that they are not known to approach the American coast anywhere between the Bahama Channel and North Carolina or Virginia, suggests that we may have two separate populations, a southern and a northern." In any case, bluefin tuna move right along.

Reports of school tuna well offshore of New Jersey and Long Island can come any time in June, even early in the month. The time varies from year to year and may not be until July. Although there probably are some giants around by midsummer, they usually aren't anticipated in eastern Long Island, Block Island, and Rhode Island waters until about August. August and September are prime months for the biggies offshore of Montauk, around Block Island, and on such famed Rhode Island tuna grounds as

Watch Hill, Rosie's Ledge, and Nebraska Shoals. It's significant that two major East Coast contests, the U. S. Atlantic Tuna Tournament and the Rhode Island Tuna Tournament, are scheduled during September's first half.

Late August and September bring giant bluefins to Soldiers Rip and other tuna grounds off Wedgeport, Nova Scotia. In recent years September and October have been productive months in Nova Scotia and off Prince Edward Island, and that 1,065-pound world record I mentioned earlier was set during the first week of November.

School tuna remain in the northerly segments of their range well into September, and even later, if waters remain warm enough. There have been seasons, two of them in a row not long before this book was written, when there were "freak" runs of school tuna off Long Island's western South Shore as late as the first week in November. That brought about a strange situation. Some Sheepshead Bay boats were still racking up school bluefins while others had started sailing for cod! Showings as late as that aren't to be counted on, however.

Bluefin tuna of varying sizes, small schoolies to giants, can be encountered along northern segments of their North American range on into autumn. After that they "vanish," presumably turning around and heading offshore and southward to warmer climes. It's thought that on those return jaunts they travel very far offshore and/or very deep. My speculation is that some may linger even into winter in the deeper and therefore warmer waters of such submarine gorges as Hudson Canyon and Block Canyon. If they do, though, it's academic so far as most sport fishermen are concerned. It's a long offshore run to those ravines, and the North Atlantic is notoriously surly in winter.

Now let's get down to bluefin fishing facts. For these I'll divide the tuna into schoolies and giants, since the angling techniques vary.

SCHOOL TUNA

The kids of the bluefin tuna family are fast, powerful, and extremely lively. I've never encountered a sluggish school tuna.

They offer an excellent fight. A scrap with an individual of 25 to 50 pounds, especially on lighter tackle, will give you a good workout and plenty of action. And it's just long enough. It doesn't go into one of those arm-straining, drawn-out tests of endurance often experienced with heavyweight game fishes.

Pound for pound, school tuna can take their place among the best battlers. Some favor albacore as being a mite tougher. Well, maybe, but so far as I'm concerned that's open to debate. I never cease to marvel at the power in young bluefin tuna, even smaller specimens going 10 to 15 pounds.

THE TACKLE Conventional gear is indicated. You can match its caliber to the sizes of the fish currently running. Here the uniform weight among individuals in a given school is helpful, and with some experience you'll be able to make educated guesses as to weights when you see them at the surface.

Be advised, though, that during one day's trip it's possible to contact schools between which there are wide differences in weights. You might troll one group whose tuna are in the 20-to-25-pound bracket, then come across a school of 75- or 100-pounders. Under those circumstances, if you're fishing an outfit gauged to, say, schoolies up to 50 pounds or so, you'll be able to handle even somewhat heavier fish, but you'll sacrifice some action when you tie into smaller scrappers such as common bonito, albacore, and younger bluefins. Conversely, if you're geared to smaller tuna, let's say under 30 pounds, you could risk a broken line if you encounter larger battlers. Follow me?

Similarly, for reasons just noted, trolling blind for school tuna is a calculated risk.

By rights, therefore, it's not a bad idea to have a couple of outfits of different calibers to cope with a wider range of sizes. (On a charter boat the skipper will have them.) Braided Dacron is excellent line for tuna trolling. Three hundred yards should be ample. Two hundred or 250 yards will take care of most assignments, since school tuna aren't tremendously long-running fish; but 300 yards will give a margin of safety in the case of some of the larger ones.

Match your line strengths approximately to the weights of schoolies currently in the area. Unless you're a seasoned tuna hunter or light-tackle buff, 40- or 50-pound test line will handle most of the schooling bluefins you meet. I mean, those are reasonably safe strengths. Later, when you've undergone sufficient baptism by fire, you can graduate to lighter stuff. If really heavy school tuna, those in the 75-pound-and-up range, are known to be in the neighborhood, your cue might be to go to lines heavier than 40- or 50-pound test. In such situations, which occur as a season progresses, you could have two outfits ready, one with 40-pound line and another with, say, 80-pound Dacron for the heftier rascals.

As always, your rod should be graded according to the line strength involved. Your reel, of course, should reasonably balance the rod. Its size will be governed by the strength and amount of line used. Suggestions are a 3/0 or 4/0 for tuna of 30 pounds or less, a 4/0 to 6/0 for those over 30 and to 60 pounds, and a 6/0 to 9/0 for fish upward of 60. Those are what I'd call conservative, "safe" specifications. There's nothing to prevent you from going lighter, your ability permitting. Needless to add, the reel, like your rod, must be rugged enough to absorb the punishment meted out by hard fighters, and a dependable drag is a must.

LURES AND RIGGING   Artificials are the come-ons.

Years ago a popular school tuna lure was a cedar jig (detailed in our chapter on lures). You'll be wise to carry at least a couple of cedar jigs in different sizes in your bag of tricks.

Much used today are feather lures. They too are versatile, accounting for various kinds of tunas, along with bluefish, albacore, bonito, and other species. Lures with skirts of nylon fibers, instead of natural feathers, also can be used; but I prefer those with natural feathers.

These come in several colors. Here's a sampling: all white; red and white; yellow; white and blue; green and yellow; black and white; and a kind of pinkish orange called tangarine. Whatever the nature of the skirt, natural feathers or a man-made substitute, it's affixed to a bullet-shaped metal head, chromed for brightness and carrying a pair of painted or glass eyes for added realism. This assembly is slid down a leader until the hook, attached to the leader, is inside the skirt.

A wire leader is employed. For school tuna you can rig about 8 to 10 or 12 feet. I wouldn't go less than about 8, nor more than 12. A 10-foot length is a good medium. You can use either stainless steel or piano wire, according to preference. Size No. 7 should do. Attachment of your hook to this wire has been detailed elsewhere.

One of the advantages of feather lures and their variations is that they allow for latitude in choice of hook pattern and size. There are several good patterns: Mustad, Sobey, Pfleuger-Sobey, Eagle Claw, Martu, etc. Sizes I generally suggest are: 7/o or 8/o for school tuna up to about 40 pounds; 9/o for fish over 40 to 100 pounds; 10/o for any over 100 to 150 pounds. Double- and triple-strength hooks offer an added margin of protection against straightening out. A triple-strength 8/o or 9/o should take care of just about all the larger school bluefins you run up against. *Tip:* These tuna have a mouth of good size. Using the largest hook possible for fish of a given weight will lessen the tendency of the hook to pull (or straighten) out.

A snap swivel is recommended over a barrel swivel for attachment of leader to line. You guessed it. A snap swivel facilitates changing of lures, something you may have occasion to do before finding a winner on a given day.

If you try a cedar jig or other artificial whose attachment to the leader is made via a small eye or loop in the lure's head end, connection is made by means of a small loop in the wire, after which another loop is made in the leader's free end for connection with a snap swivel on your line.

LURE LORE When hungry, school tuna will respond to a variety of artificials. This gives you *carte blanche* to experiment.

School tuna will go for bright, shiny attractors. I've known them to be taken on those flat, shiny, metal beer can openers to which a hook of suitable caliber had been soldered. I don't recommend such novelties, but you get the idea. Sometime, when more conventional attractors fail to get response, you might try one of the larger spoons, one with a lot of glitter. I wouldn't be surprised if a couple of shiny spinner blades attached just ahead of a feather or cedar jig might serve as an added eye-catcher.

Speaking of whimsical tuna lures, I've heard tell that school bluefins have been caught on a shaving brush (a "feather" or "bucktail" of sorts) and even a toothbrush. Although such weird lures do not come recommended, they serve to point up the fact that school tuna will bite on almost anything when in a real feeding frenzy. Conversely, I should add hastily, there are times when they're not in the mood and consequently refuse to bite on *anything*.

SCRATCHING FOR TUNA　Trolling is the most popular school tuna fishing technique. In this, feathers are the most widely employed lures. This combination, trolling and feathers, is highly effective. It's also versatile, accounting for tuna of other species, bluefish, assorted bonitos and albacores, and other gamesters.

In trolling for school bluefins there are preparations that will heighten your chances of success:

1. Get four lines out, if possible. Actually, you can troll as many as six—two from outriggers and four from rods, but four is a good maximum. Two more than that have only the advantage of letting you experiment with some other lures. In any case, what you're doing here is testing to determine what artificial the tuna fancy that day. Try feather lures in different color combos—at least one of which should be red and white—on all the lines. Or rig three with feathers and the fourth with a cedar jig.

If your boat has outriggers, use them for two of the lines, trolling the remaining lines from rods, which can be placed in holders until there are hits. Or all the lines can be trolled from rods. Set the reels at a striking drag. Leaving their clickers on will give you an audible signal of a strike.

Whatever type of lure or color combination gets the first hit is a clue to change the others accordingly.

2. Experiment with trolling distances astern at the start of fishing. School tuna aren't especially shy when it comes to grabbing a lure fairly close to a boat. Put one artificial out about twenty to twenty-five feet, another at forty feet or so, a third at fifty to sixty feet, and one at seventy or seventy-five feet as starters. Vary these distances occasionally if action isn't forthcoming.

3. These fish like to hunt prey on the move, which is why troll-

ing is productive. They're bold, aggressive hunters. Frequently when pursuing lures they'll come right up into the boat's wash. You may even see them hit. For some reason, the bubbly, foamy water churned up by a boat's propeller is an attraction for school tuna. We capitalize on it by towing a bucket, fish basket, or old automobile tire close to the boat's transom to create even more wake. The lures are trolled so that they move as much as possible within that white trail.

No one knows why a boat's wake entrances young bluefins. Maybe it piques their curiosity. Or perhaps the invasion of their domain annoys or arouses them to a degree that they must rush in to find out what the heck is going on here. Charter skipper Carm Marinaccio, who has caught and helped catch more school tuna than anyone else I know, once suggested that a boat's propeller and/or water pressure changes it causes, kills or stuns small fishes, which attract tuna. Or, he added, it might be a combination of several things. Anyway, it works.

AT THE READY Uncountable thousands of school bluefins journey northward off the U.S. East Coast. It may be that many ride right along with the Gulf Stream or travel along its offshore and inshore edges, enjoying the transportation and food advantages of that great "ocean river," as the University of Miami's famed oceanographer Dr. F. G. Walton Smith so aptly calls it. En route northward, they swing closer to the coast, seeking food in enormous eddies that curl shoreward from the Gulf Stream and in waters nearer the seaboard. Those eddies, composed of warmer water and carrying food fishes, probably are instrumental in luring the tuna inshore.

During the early phase of a bluefin run in some regions boats may have to venture fifty miles or more offshore before finding fish. I remember one early June dawn with Capt. Carm Marinaccio on his *Duchess II* out of Freeport, L.I., when we didn't encounter schools until we had sailed all night and were about eighty miles off Jones Inlet. Later, food supplies and water temperatures being favorable, the schools move progressively closer to shore until some may be encountered only a few miles off the beach. But always their location changes as they move swiftly hither and yon. This is your cue to be on constant watch for signs of surface activity.

You never know where you might contact them. An ideal— and common—situation is to find them at the top, preferably in an eating mood. But there will be times when you cover acres of sea without sighting such activity, and then, out of desperation if nothing else, you'll try "scratching"—trolling blind—for them with hopes that your artificials will raise them from lower levels. This can be either rewarding or very frustrating. Sometimes contact will be established in fairly short order, with the angry buzzing of reels' clickers announcing strikes. At other times you'll patrol for miles and get nothing more than a boat ride, or maybe pick up a few stray bonito or albacore as consolation prizes. Or maybe, if you're lucky, blind trolling will raise fair numbers of albacore or bonito. Always when trolling blind you should maintain a sharp lookout for surface signs betraying school tuna. In season in the right places you should also watch for the telltale fins of swordfish and white marlin (and I hope you'll be prepared for such possibilities by having the proper baits aboard).

Along stretches of our Atlantic Coast the Gulf Stream is beyond the practical reach of all but the fastest sport-fishing boats, unless they're large enough and expertly handled, and weather is favorable, to make overnight trips. I suspect that the Gulf Stream proper carries several species of warmer-water fishes—maybe even sailfish—to northerly latitudes, but reaching them is often a problem. The next best things are the huge eddies that curl shoreward. These are worthy of exploration.

What frequently happens is that the eddies branch off, so to speak, from the Gulf Stream's main flow and curl toward land. Eventually they sever connection with the Stream entirely to become large, individual masses of water, transported at the whims of currents and winds. They usually can be detected by a brighter blue color than that of the surrounding ocean. That difference can be startling. Often an eddy's water is clearer too; and if you can check it with a thermometer you'll probably find that it's warmer than the sea surrounding it. Frequently an eddy will be flecked with sprigs and masses of golden yellow sargassum weed, carried northward by the ocean river from southern climes. For a while the eddies retain their identity. Eventually they're absorbed by the surrounding ocean. While they retain their identity they can harbor food fishes that attract larger game, and not uncommonly they contain sport species that are normally found much farther south.

Often school tuna aren't inclined to feed at the top during the earliest phase of their seasonal debut, thereby depriving fishermen of such helpful signs as a surface commotion. Under these circumstances a hope is to raise them by blind trolling. As you do, you can look for birds such as the so-called tuna hags (shearwaters, related to the petrels and albatrosses) busy at the sea's surface.

Later, as ocean waters warm, the young bluefins frequently feed at the top. Then you look for a surface ruckus and birds working. You may see tuna breach, along with the fish they're pursuing. Binoculars will save you from being fooled by wind-generated riffles 'way off yonder.

THE APPROACH Having spotted promising signs, head for the area and stand by for action, your lures out. Response can come suddenly and in large chunks. Don't be surprised if all your lures are hit almost simultaneously.

You'll hear varying opinions as to the proper trolling speeds for school tuna. Suggested speeds, when a school is sighted and when trolling blind, is about six or seven knots (just under seven to eight miles per hour). Here again you can experiment, but don't go to extremes. School tuna are fast swimmers, but I wouldn't go much over those suggested speeds. Don't drop down to crawling slowness either. You want to impart lively action to your lures.

When you approach a surfaced school don't barge pell-mell into its midst. These tuna aren't overly boat-shy, but the bulk and sound of a boat barreling right in among them is apt to scare them into diving. Instead, maneuver to skirt the school's edges, swinging your lures in among the fish. It takes practice, but if it's done properly you may be able to work a school for a good catch.

Some schools are approached without driving them down. Others are easily spooked and promptly submerge before you can get to them. In the latter situation you have two courses of action. One is to watch for the fish to reappear some distance away and have another go at them. The other course of action goes into effect immediately. It's a procedure I learned from the late Capt. Walter Drobecker of Montauk. There's no guarantee, but you have everything to gain. Head your boat in the same direction the school appeared to be moving when last seen. Run right over the spot where you saw them. With a little luck the fish will come right up behind the boat and smack your lures. This maneuver involves guesswork, since you have no way of knowing if the group changed direction right after it sounded. But believe me when I say it's well worth a try. I've nailed tuna that way when I'd all but written off a school that had spooked.

Tip: Always carry duplicates of the more effective artificials.

CHUMMING Trolling is such a popular school tuna technique that it has overshadowed chumming, a method that has produced some lively action on our Atlantic Coast in bygone years. Even some tuna-fishing veterans may not be aware of the fact that chumming is productive when young bluefins are around in numbers. Basically it works the same as the now passé commercial-tuna-fishing procedure used by the clippers before the era of big nets. In that technique the tuna clipper approached a school and ladled large quantities of live anchovies or other bait overboard to create a feeding frenzy among the tuna, whereupon they wildly hit the unbaited jigs tossed at them by fishermen wielding reelless cane poles.

In chumming the boat can be at anchor or allowed to drift. The latter has an advantage in that it covers more territory. Ground mossbunkers are a good chum, and the standard method of ladling it overboard is used. Once a chum line is established, the lures are cast out into it or simply allowed to drift into it as line is paid out. Then the rigs are retrieved and cranked toward the boat but not out of water, after which that whole process is repeated. The idea is to keep the attractors in motion, as in trolling.

Natural baits usually are employed in this tuna chumming, although artificials should work on occasion. The baits can be chunks of mossbunker, whole butterfish, or small ling, whiting, or mackerel, used whole.

Chumming for school tuna also can raise albacore, bonito, and bluefish—and sharks.

Tuna chumming tackle must be as strong as that wielded in trolling. After all, the battlers are the same; only the method has changed. If anything, I think tuna chumming tackle should be a bit more rugged than trolling equipment, because there's likely to be a greater variation in sizes among bluefins drawn by chum than those in schools whose individuals are more or less uniform in size. Too, chumming has been known to attract the larger fish that travel alone or in small groups. The fact is that chumming is a technique for catching giant tuna.

You'll have to gauge your gear as closely as you can to the tuna known to be in the area. If you have two or more outfits, including one for real heavyweights, fine. But if you're working with only one outfit you might be wise to strike a kind of arbitrary in-between, selecting weapons able to handle fish upward of fifty pounds. Fifty-to-eighty-pound Dacron, at least three hundred yards of it, on a 6/o reel mounted on a properly rated rod, would comprise a satisfactory compromise.

Based on sizes of tuna reported for the area, you'll have to decide how heavy (or light) you want to go with your tackle. Stouter gear is going to cost you some action with smaller tuna and any bonito or albacore that wander into your chum line, but at least you'll be ready for some of the heavier bluefins. If there's any chance of giants being around, you should have a heavy-duty outfit standing by. It's very frustrating to see a giant tuna in your chum and realize that you don't have weapons heavy enough to argue with him.

Rigging and method are essentially the same as for bluefish chumming, with understandable differences, such as stronger line and terminal tackle. A wire leader is rigged. Its length is optional. Six to eight or ten feet is about right. Its strength ranges from that of a No. 7 to No. 13, influenced by the sizes of the tuna you figure you might contact. The same thing goes for hook sizes. A 7/o to 9/o should take care of most of your opponents, except, possibly, the giants. For those you'll find details later on in this chapter.

SMACKO! When a school tuna hits, he does so with enthusiasm. It can be a wallop that will jiggle your teeth, and he usually hooks himself with the force of his impact. A short, brisk, upward lift of your rod tip, although generally not necessary, will assure planting the hook.

Your reel has been preset at about striking drag. You may have to adjust your drag somewhere along the line, easing off or tightening it a little as the situation demands. If you haven't yet acquired the feel of adjusting your drag as required, ask the aid of an experienced angler beforehand. Let him set it for you, then leave it alone unless he advises otherwise. With the smaller school tuna, if your drag has been set reasonably well, you probably won't have to go through adjustments and readjustments. But when you tie into the larger schoolies, you may have to make some changes.

At a strike—or strikes—the boat's engine is thrown into neutral, and the argument is on. It's really something when two, three, or four lines are hit simultaneously.

A school tuna will fight in a series of moderately long and short rushes in any and all directions. I wouldn't say that he tears off for what seems like half a mile, like a tarpon, nor does he jump, but he makes some good, brisk runs. One minute you'll be battling him not too far below the surface; seconds later he'll drill his way downstairs. Although not a long-distance runner like some sportsters, his resistance will be marked by surprisingly strong power surges.

Periodically he'll slow down, giving you an opportunity to retrieve some line. You may regain a couple of feet or several yards before he gets ornery again. When he slows or pauses, you can pick up line by leaning back with your rod to pull the fish toward you, then quickly bending forward, cranking to take up any slack you've created. Don't try that during one of his rushes, however. Bad news. Don't forget that your rod is there to do a good share of the fighting, aided by the reel's drag. As one old-timer remarked, "Try to play a tuna with the reel alone and he'll make you look like a monkey."

Tip: Action with school tuna is heightened considerably by fighting the fish standing up. But it isn't recommended to inexperienced anglers, especially when the larger school bluefins are involved. And under no circumstances should it be tried without a gimbal belt.

Your "debate" with a school tuna will be a back-and-forth affair. It can consume ten or fifteen minutes or more. It all depends upon the size and stamina of your opponent, the caliber of tackle you're wielding, and how you play him. Easing off on your reel brake naturally gives him more freedom to run and consequently extends the action. Conversely, setting up on the drag a little tighter than ordinarily (*careful!*) tires the fish faster and shortens the fight. No matter how long it takes, you'll agree that a tussle with a school tuna is well worth the price of admission.

As the battle nears its closing phase, someone should be standing by with an appropriately sturdy, sharp-pointed straight gaff. Whoever is handling the gaff also will grab the wire leader when it breaks water. And he'd better be wearing some kind of work gloves, because wire is murder on bare hands—laceration line, we call it. Even when you've reeled your tuna close enough to the boat to be seen, he'll still have plenty of vinegar and can take off on another run.

When the swivel breaks water the gaffer will seize the leader with one hand, pulling the fish upward if necessary, then swing his weapon with the other hand.

I like to swing a gaffed tuna right into a fish box or other container. These fish bleed like stuck pigs, and for a few minutes after release from a gaff they beat a lively tattoo with their tails and bodies. If they're not in a container they'll spatter blood all over the place, including you. That's messy and makes for slippery footing.

Tip: If you get tuna blood, or any fish blood, on your clothes, remove it immediately while it's still wet. Cold water will take it out. I use sea water. If that blood is allowed to dry, no amount of cleaning will ever get it out.

ONE OF THE BEST Matching muscles with school tuna is lively sport. Pound for pound, they rate with the fightingest fishes of all. And they're just right for the angler who wants plenty of action but not the long, drawn-out tug-o'-war that often comes with big tuna and other heavyweight game fishes.

Not only are school tuna great sport, they also can be prepared in several ways for the table. They can be filleted and stored in a deep freeze, or cooked and packed in jars for the freezer.

Or they can be cooked in a number of ways just as they come from the water.

Tuna are very bloody fish. Many anglers who eat their catches (or someone else's tuna) maintain that the blood imparts an objectionably strong flavor to the meat. I'm with them. What some of us in that school of thought do is gut the fish and encourage bleeding as soon as possible after catching—action permitting, of course. Later much of the remaining blood can be removed by bleaching the fillets in cold, salted water (milk has been used for this too), after which they can be cooked as desired.

There, I've tried to cover every detail. The rest is up to you. Go out the first chance you get and hook yourself some school tuna. Hey, wait a second . . . I'll get my gear and go with you!

GIANT TUNA

Behold, a lord among fishes, a member of the undersea kingdom's royalty, the giant bluefin tuna! Thousands of tunafish sandwiches on the hoof!

This bulky bluefin, the mightiest of all tunas, along with the bigger sharks, billfishes, and some other finned leviathans, are to sport fishermen what elephants, grizzly bears, and rhinos are to hunters. They're among the sea's monarchs, salt water's big game.

Giant bluefins are the same species, *Thunnus thynnus*, as the so-called school tuna. The only differences, along with those of habits, are size and age. The giants, of course, are the family's grownups and senior citizens.

Dockside spectators ogling a giant bluefin hanging from a scale sometimes ask, "How old would a fish that big be?" An Italian researcher named Sella had that question too, and set out to find answers. In subsequent studies of Mediterranean bluefins he capitalized on an "age indicator" built into the fish. Their vertebrae have concentric circles, like those of a tree trunk. Similarly, each one represents a year of life. By counting the annual rings of bluefin vertebrae, ichthyologist Sella was able to come up with approximate size-age relationships.

On an average, he discovered, young bluefins weighing 10 pounds are a year old. By the time they're 2 this weight more than doubles, to 21 pounds. (These are all averages.) An 88-pounder is about 5 years old, and reaches approximately 128 pounds at age 6. By their 10th birthday Mediterranean bluefins are above 300 pounds (320 was Sella's average). Those individuals going 400 to 450 pounds have been around 12 years, he said. He figured 500-pounders to be in their 13th year, while those from 616 to 660 pounds are about 14. At that rate, Mediterranean specimens in the 700-, 800-, and 900-pound classes would be roughly 15, 16, and 17 years old, while 1,000-pounders would be at least 18, old enough to vote in some places.

These brutes are all muscle. No flab there. Unlike some of the huge groupers, whose resistance can be like that of a parked truck, giant tuna possess power commensurate with their bulk. And they use it.

WEAPONS It won't surprise anyone to learn that tackle for giant tuna has to be rugged. Except, maybe, for the smaller giants, 80-pound line equipment could be considered as being on the light side. Real biggies can be taken on such gear, even lighter, but it's for seasoned combat veterans. Unless you fit into that category, stay with the heavy-duty gear. You can go as light as you dare later.

Until such time as you feel ready to go with 80-pound line or lighter, I suggest you use 130-pound line, and tackle matched to it. Rods of this caliber have roller guides throughout. They also have a suitably thick, strong butt section, obviously needed. Some of these rods have the usual straight butt. Others, according to anglers' preference, come with an aluminum butt section that is bent at an angle. Considering the pull of a large tuna and the butt's use for leverage, the strain on that section of a rod can be tremendous. I've seen butts break under it.

These big-game sticks also are equipped with double-locking reel seats to keep the "winch" securely in place. The reel has to be large enough, with suitably strong guts, to handle lines of 80-pound test and upward to 130. Reel sizes range from 10/0 to 12/0. You may even see an occasional 14/0. Not only does the reel's spool have to be able to handle line in the higher strengths, it must also accommodate sufficient yardage of it, which is to say upward of 400 or 500 yards among the larger sizes.

Suggestion: Because such heavy-duty tackle runs into money, you might better do your big-game fishing from charter boats that provide those weapons. Later, if you decide that big-game angling is your cup of tea, you can invest in your own gear. By then you probably will have garnered enough savvy to guide you in its selection.

Heavy-caliber tackle necessitates a fighting chair with a gimbal in which the rod's butt can rest. That helps support the equipment's weight. To complete the outfit there should be fighting harness. A typical harness consists of a wide band of leather or canvas that goes across the lower portion of its wearer's back, and has straps that lock onto the reel by means of snaps. A harness takes much of the strain off the angler's arms and distributes it across his back and shoulders. It also enables him to bring more of his muscles into play.

A basic giant tuna rig calls for these components: wire leader, about a No. 12; a heavy-duty barrel swivel of suitable strength (you won't need a snap swivel in this instance); a piece of cork or equally buoyant float big enough to support most of the terminal rig's weight; and a ring-eyed hook, 12/0 to 14/0. The length of the wire leader varies according to the rigger. Twelve to fifteen feet should do. Watch your IGFA regulations if you're trying for a record.

GIANT TUNA RIG

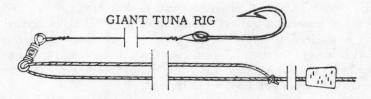

Here's a "standard" method of assembling the terminal outfit:

1. Double the end of your line, the end carrying the swivel, for about fifteen feet. Run that end through one of your swivel's loops, bring it up to double it for fifteen feet or so, and secure it

to the main line with a nonslip knot. Doubling a line in this fashion is for extra strength and to provide a measure of protection against chafing-through. That added strength doesn't go into effect until some of the double line is back on the reel, and it's an advantage when you have your fish close alongside the boat, a time when extra line strength can come in handy. Otherwise, so far as extra strength is concerned, a double line doesn't mean beans, since the maximum strength of any line-leader combination is that of its weakest component. As for added protection against chafing, a doubled line does afford it to a certain extent. Still, if one part of that double line is chafed through, the result is the same as with a single line.

2. Attach your wire leader to the barrel swivel's other eye, fashioning a small loop.

3. Affix your ring-eyed hook to the leader's free end. Use a small loop here too.

That completes your terminal tackle, except for the cork or float, which we'll come to in due time.

BAITING AND CHUM Various kinds of fishes have been used, whole or in large pieces, for giant bluefin tuna. They include mossbunkers, herring, mackerel, butterfish, northern whiting, and so on. A small whole mossbunker, or half a large one, is a good come-on, particularly when the same fish is used as chum. Herring are baits employed on Nova Scotia's world-famed tuna grounds. Other small fishes have been used successfully in various locales. If you're tuna fishing in a strange region, without benefit of a guide or experienced skipper, inquire locally as to what kinds of baits the giants in that area favor.

Whatever bait is impaled on the hook, it can be in generous portions. That doesn't necessarily mean that better results will follow with a bigger bait. Don't try to foist some monstrosity on your intended prey, but use a good-size bait. The big bluefins have a mouth to match their appetite. If you're baiting with half a fish or a generous piece, impale it securely on your hook, leaving point and barb buried. Whole fish, dead or alive, can be impaled by methods already described.

Theoretically at least, almost any kind of fish, ground into a mushy pulp, will serve as chum. The list includes whiting, ling, and . . . well, you name it. Anglers have obtained trash fishes from commercial netters and used those successfully. But you're not likely to go wrong with ground mossbunkers or herring. 'Bunkers are used a lot. Don't stint on the quantity of chum you take along on a tuna trip. I wouldn't take less than three or four large cans. If you want to play it safe, take more. Often you can arrange for dockside cold storage for any that may be left over.

Provided the current isn't too swift, or the wind doesn't move you along too fast, there's nothing to prevent you from trying drift-chumming for giant tuna. A popular preference, however, is to chum with the craft at anchor. In this procedure a buoy is secured to the upper end of the anchor line so the mooring can be found later. It may be necessary to detach the anchor line so that the boat is able to "chase down" a particularly powerful, long-running giant.

Mix your ground-fish chum with sea water to the consistency of thick stew and ladle it overboard according to the procedures detailed elsewhere in this book. Give your chum line a reasonable chance to produce before you shift to another area.

I once learned a bitter lesson in chumming patience. What made it worse was that the affair wasn't my fault. Let me tell you the sad story (try not to sob louder than the background music).

Four of us were fishing a then-celebrated giant tuna ground known as the Mud Hole, a deep-water area between Long Island and New Jersey. We had plenty of chum, at least six big cans of it. After dropping anchor on a rim of the Mud Hole, we got a good chum line going right into area. We tried a couple of different places around the Hole without so much as seeing a tuna.

We knew there were big ones in there. Early afternoon found us chumming at a new location at the Mud Hole. We kept ladling the ground mossbunker pulp overboard, occasionally beefing it up with small chunks of butterfish. Time passed . . . nothing. Finally our host, the boat's owner, said, "Let's call it quits, boys. This place is deader than a [censored] today." The rest of us would have liked to stay another hour or two, maybe at least get a strike. But he wanted to return to port. Reluctantly we started to crank in our lines.

We had two full cans of 'bunker chum and considerable bait left. I had to bite my tongue when our host dumped all that stuff overboard. "What a waste!" I griped to myself. But that wasn't the half of it. Just as the last rig was coming in—it wasn't more than twenty-five or thirty feet beyond the transom—a giant boiled up right behind it. The surprised angler continued reeling; and that, coupled with the force of the tuna's hit, tore the bait off the hook. To add insult to injury, our newcomer paused long enough to give us a good look at him, goggle-eyed.

Talk about being up a creek without a paddle! There we had a giant right astern—500 pounds if he weighed an ounce—practically begging for a bait, and we had nothing to give him. Seconds later he vanished into the dark green.

Let that be a lesson to you.

ACTION By now you can see the difference between two techniques commonly employed in fishing for school tuna and for their beefier brothers. Although chumming also can be employed for school-size bluefins, trolling artificials is a more popular method. Chumming at anchor or drifting has proved very effective in nailing giants in many major giant tuna areas from Nova Scotia to waters off Long Island's South Shore and the Bahamas.

For our close look at giant tuna fishing let's conjure up a situation in which you're the angler. Got your imagination percolating? Okay. Presto, you're out after big bluefins.

You're aboard a forty-footer. It's a beautiful morning (we might as well ask for good weather while we're imagining). There's no wind chop yet. That may come later with an afternoon breeze. Right now the sea is calm . . . an occasional low, lazy ground swell, maybe, but otherwise the ocean is almost like a limitless bowl of grayish-green Jell-O.

The boat's hook, a buoy attached to the upper end of its line, has found bottom and dug in. Once she swings the way she's going to ride, someone starts a chum line. Over the side go gobs of fish pulp, hitting the water with a soft "plop" and drifting away in a widening fan as the stuff scatters.

You bait your hook with half a big mossbunker. On your line, maybe ten to fifteen or twenty feet above the leader, is that cork or float I mentioned earlier in connection with rigging. Now you'll see its purpose. Adjustable along your line, it will help to keep your rig in among the chum where it belongs. (*Note:* This use of a cork is optional and subject to conditions at the time. The current's thrust may be such that it will keep your rig where you want it without a float.) Over goes your baited rig, line trailing behind it.

Your throne, the fighting chair, awaits. Into it you go, placing the notched end of your rod butt in the chair's gimbal. You get into a harness and snap its straps into place on the reel fittings made to receive them. You get yourself comfortable, seeing that the chair's back and footrest are adjusted to suit you.

Now you wait. Your rig is out there in the chum, well astern. The chummer continues to dish out his strong-smelling stew. You stare into the depths and wonder how long it will be before one of those big blue beasts becomes interested in your offering. This waiting interval is in the lap of the piscatorial gods. If you're very fortunate, it might be under an hour. Or it might be much longer. Or response might not come at all in that place.

The boat gently lifts on small swells rolling in from far off yonder. Funny, you never noticed how quiet it is out here. All you hear is the soft lap of water as it caresses the hull, and a gurgling, almost sensuous sound as wavelets splash around the boat's exhaust exit. Minutes tick by in normal fashion at first. Enjoy those standard sixty-second minutes while you can. If response is slow in coming, they're likely to lengthen.

All eyes are aimed in the direction of the chum line. This is where action will come. You tighten your arm muscles in anticipation. For a while the waiting is made more tolerable by excited suspense. But then, as the minutes tick by—slower, now— you begin to wonder if there are any tuna in this place. The wonder might even give way to skepticism. It's at this stage that I've seen an angler unharness himself, leave his rod in the fighting chair holder, and go wandering around the boat. This is a calculated risk. Should a big bluefin hit without being spotted beforehand, scrambling into the chair, struggling to get the rod into the gimbal, and trying to don the harness can be rough.

For something to do, you check your drag. It's okay, preset for striking. The sun is getting warmer. You sit back, take a couple of deep lungfuls of sea air, and relax. Then, maybe, just as you're comfortably loggy in the sunshine and have decided that this is really living, even without tuna, the pleasant lolling is shattered rudely by a shout from the bridge. There's a tuna in the chum! In an instant the cockpit's atmosphere becomes electric.

From the chair you can't see the giant, but other eyes have zeroed in on him from the bridge. There's a great, dark form out there, moving in. You brace yourself. Someone whistles softly and mutters, "He's a good one." Your breath catches in your throat.

Any instant now. You thrust your legs firmly against the fighting chair's footrest. Then, a silent swirl of water shows at the surface, and . . . *crash!* the brute hits. Behind you, you hear someone yell, "Sock it to him!" You rear back with your rod, arm muscles bulging. The hook has been driven home solidly. Your rod arcs downward, and already you feel the fish's power. In split seconds, thoughts flash across your mind that the whole outfit will be yanked out of your hands, or maybe you'll go with it, harness and all, right out of the chair and over the transom like a hurdler. I suspect that such thoughts have crossed many an angler's mind in the first encounter with a giant tuna.

What happens next is anyone's guess. Each giant is an unpredictable individual. Some of the big fellows have been known to move away with surprising slowness—but very deliberate. Others can tear away like mad things, peeling off two hundred or more yards of line. Still others go deep, taking line until you think they'll never halt.

Your fish decides to take off. You've adjusted your reel's drag for good resistance in playing the fish, but he isn't at all impressed. Away he goes. Your rod takes a greater bend as you hang on for dear life. It's now that you especially appreciate the harness and chair's footrest. Line disappears from your reel in a blur. It looks as though he's boring deep. Further tightening of the drag now could be fatal. There's no stopping this rush. Is this big lummox ever going to stop? Already you're beginning to feel the strain in your arms and shoulders, and the thought flashes in your skull that this is only the start of the party. Well, at least you have him on . . . or is it the other way around? One thing is for certain, this could be a long, drawn-out affair. You resign yourself to it as even more line zips down into the sea.

You haven't noticed, but the boat is free of her anchor now. The distance between the boat and her bobbing anchor line buoy widens as the big fish tows the cruiser. Someone is behind you, keeping the chair and your rod aimed toward the opponent.

The long, downward power rush slows, then stops. Your muscular adversary is 'way down there, gathering wits and muscle while deciding what to do next. During this pause you try to retrieve a little line. Nothing doing. He won't budge.

Abruptly the brief recess is over. Your rod jerks spasmodically as more yardage leaves the reel. Another brief pause, then more line melts from the spool. Inwardly you groan at the prospect of having to get it all back. Maybe you think about the guys who have been on rods five and six hours with giant bluefins, or about the unfortunates who fought their fish for who knows how long, only to lose them when a line or leader finally parted because of fatigue.

Working a stubborn giant up from the depths is rugged business, but you stay with it, arms protesting. Every time your opponent pauses for a breather or a decision, you endeavor to put some line back on your reel. It's uphill all the way. You retrieve a yard; he takes it back, and more.

This seesawing in favor of the tuna goes on for a while. By and by (you've lost track of time) you seem to be gaining an advantage. You note with some satisfaction that cranking is retrieving more yardage now, but you're still earning every inch of it.

Don't get your hopes up. It's at this stage that he can suddenly throw his engine into gear and swing off on an arcing tangent, or maybe bore deep again. The boat maneuvers to keep you aimed at your fish. He streaks away with twenty, twenty-five yards, or fifty or more, then slows. You lean back, bend forward, and crank, lean back, come forward, and crank. Every time he slows and stops you bear down on that reel. From the feel of things you sense that maybe, just maybe, he's tiring. Along about this time you could run right smack into a Mexican standoff. He's not moving, but you're not regaining line. This is a chance for you to take a little breather. You grin weakly when a companion asks you if you have a match, or makes a crack about your fixing a sandwich while you're "resting."

Whoops! Recess is over. Away goes your bluefin again. Back

and forth the argument continues. He demands line. Then you sneak some of it back, dripping, on your reel. You're having a tough time "balancing the books"—his amount of line against yours—to break even. Thirty minutes have long since widened into an hour, and that first hour is behind you.

You've heard that these bruisers have no fixed blueprint for battle. This beast underscores the point by changing direction again. He swings around to the boat's starboard side, curving in toward you and giving you a chance to pick up some line as the craft maneuvers. Just as you get lined up with him, he slows and stops. But you can't budge him. Your back and shoulders are beginning to feel as though someone drove over them with a square-wheeled wagon. Your arms are two appendages running from your shoulders to the tackle, but you're not sure they're still attached to you.

Without advance notice there's more action. At one stage he abruptly turns toward the boat, probably to ease your hook-and-line pressure. It's a chance to retrieve line, and you do it fast to take up that slack he created. A hundred feet or so astern he goes deep, giving you a worry about the possibility of his torpedoing under the boat before she can get out of his way. This would be bad news indeed. Your line could foul in the prop or rudder or, equally disastrous, be drawn tight across barnacles on her bottom and keel. Here's where the fellow at the controls has to be on the ball, easing the boat ahead on a short spurt if a run beneath her seems imminent.

Fortunately, your fish changes his mind for the umpteenth time and swerves away in a new direction. You lose line to another run. But now there's a glimmer of encouragement, because this dash is noticeably shorter and less forceful than others. He's finally beginning to tire. Now you can tighten your drag a bit.

The advantage is shifting in your favor. You rear back with your rod, lean forward, and crank as fast as you can. Slowly, foot by foot, line creeps back on the spool. Off in the background a voice comments, "You've got him comin'." Just about then the giant shows how wrong everyone can be by summoning reserve strength to tear away on another spurt. With him goes the line you just regained, plus extra yardage as a penalty for your overconfidence.

Back you go to the tug-and-crank routine, setting up on your drag a little more. One hour has become two, and you're working on the third.

But you're heartened. There's no doubt about it, he *is* tiring (and not a minute too soon, you figure). With the three-hour mark approaching, you've gained the upper hand. Slowly at first, then a trifle more steadily, line builds on the spool, dribbling brine in your lap. The veins in your hands and forearms stand out like crooked blue spaghetti as you doggedly grind the reel crank. Your fish is bushed all right, but still game. Even now you're not getting him for nothing.

All hands are watching this closing phase. Now they're giving you vocal encouragement. The beginning of your leader isn't very far away when they see him, a dark, broad-shouldered form down there in the green. "He's a beaut!" someone yips. "Keep him comin'." Someone else ventures an estimate as to his weight. You wish you could see him, but you still have your hands full. Suddenly your line changes course in the water, swinging you in the chair. The big boy is summoning all his remaining strength for a final bid. Abruptly your line stops cutting the water, twitches the rod, and goes in the opposite direction. No chance to crank. You hold on. When he slows, you work your reel some more. At the transom, leaning over for a better look, is someone with a flying gaff, its line secured to a cleat.

Hallelujah! Your leader breaks water! The gaffer reaches out and seizes the double line, then the wire, with a gloved hand, pulling upward. Seconds later the needle-sharp head of his weapon flashes downward and sinks into the tuna's back. There's a commotion as he surfaces briefly. Spray flies in all directions, his tail thumps against the boat's hull, and blood runs into the sea.

Now your prize is alongside. You unsnap the harness, put your rod in the fighting chair's holder, and go to the gunnel. You peer down at your defeated opponent. He looks enormous.

His powerful caudal fin throwing water every time it breaks the surface, your giant is maneuvered to the craft's ginpole. A stout rope running to a block atop this vertical boom is secured to his tail. Backs and arms go to work. The boat lists as the magnificent, gleaming, blue-and-silver form emerges from the sea. A red tinge marks his point of departure. Minutes later the huge fish is eased down into the cockpit, his tail hammering out a final tattoo. He's a beauty, all right. This is sport-fishing's moment of truth. You're frankly proud of your accomplishment; but maybe, as you look down at that tremendous example of nature's work, you're also just a mite sorry you won.

"How much do you figure he weighs?" you ask. "Should go about 500" is the educated appraisal of one of the more experienced tuna hunters aboard. (Later, on the dock, a scale reads 523.) Headed for port, you park in the fighting chair and admire your prize. Tomorrow your arms and shoulders probably will feel as though they'd been worked over with a ball bat, but you couldn't care less. Tomorrow you also can start to talk about this encounter. There's also a fleeting thought that you might never catch another bluefin as large, but you don't give a hoot about that either. You've had this one battle, and it's something to remember for a long, long time.

Then you get to thinking. There will be tomorrows. Maybe your next bluefin will be even larger.

NOTES ON OTHER METHODS   Trolling also is a technique employed for giant tuna in some areas—Bimini, Bahamas, to name one. Whole-fish baits are rigged. These, in addition to some of those already mentioned, include ballyhoo and bonefish in southerly waters. Trolling rigs, in one variation or another, are put into service. Tackle is gauged to the fish as in chumming, and/or in whatever caliber the angler sees fit to wield.

Another technique that has been used, notably in Nova Scotia, is a variation of chumming. It's basically the same as that employed while drifting or at anchor, with one difference. In this procedure the boat drifts into a spot where tuna have been sighted or contacted, and a fairly heavy chum line is established. Often pieces of fish are dropped overboard in generous quantity, along with occasional whole fish as teasers. When this chumming has attracted a big tuna to the boat's vicinity, a baited rig is tossed to the fish. The angler, of course, is in a fighting chair, ready to go. This method has accounted for giants to at least 400 or 500 pounds.

FIGHTING TIME   Since every giant tuna is an individual, there's no
way of predicting how long a scrap with one will last. So much
depends upon the fish's physical condition at the time—and therefore his fighting spirit and stamina, and the tackle involved and
the angler wielding it.

I can cite some extremes. A Long Island friend of mine was
on a rod for six hours with an estimated 600-pounder (then lost
the fish when his fatigued line broke). Still more awesome, from
a time standpoint, was an encounter between famed woman
caster Joan Salvato Wulff and a bluefin in the 500-pound class in
eastern Canadian waters. Joan was on the rod for about 13 hours
(she got her fish), but she was using 50-pound line. At the other
extreme was a brief tussle involving another Long Island friend
of mine, fishing columnist Hugo Uhland, at the U. S. Atlantic
Tuna Tournament off Point Judith, R.I., several years ago. Hugo
brought a 500-pound-class bluefin to gaff in 15 minutes, a tourney
record at the time. He was fishing with 130-pound line. I should
add that Hugo is built like a bull.

As you can see, fighting times vary greatly. Here are a few
more: 2 hours, 48 minutes for a 500-pounder; 1 hour, 3 minutes
for a 350-pounder; 20 minutes for a fish going 390 pounds; 1 hour,
23 minutes for a 400-pounder (mine); and 46 minutes for one
weighing 450 pounds. Note those differences in times for the
500- and 450-pounders. So it goes. For that reason I suggest you
make no shoreside appointments for days you go giant tuna
fishing.

WRAPUP   You'll have all the knock-down, drag-out action you
could want with bluefin tuna, whatever their sizes. And you can
write your own postscript to the action.

You'll want to photograph your catches, of course. Some of your
school-size fish you may want to take home for the table. Along
the line you'll probably want to have one of them mounted.
Should you latch onto a giant, you'll wonder what to do with the
carcass after pictures have been snapped. Unless the brute is to
be mounted (which isn't likely unless you're prepared to spend
a good piece of change for the job and have a place to hang such
a trophy), there are two alternatives. One is to have the carcass taken to sea the next day for disposal. The other, much bet-

ter, is to follow a procedure adopted by some tournaments. What they do is arrange for hospitals and charitable institutions to take the fish. This eliminates waste and provides a lot of people with fresh seafood.

Before we leave the subject of tuna I also should mention that in some ports, where such facilities are available, it may be possible to arrange for your catches to be canned, each tin carrying a label bearing your name. I knew a guy who did that for years. Such facilities aren't readily available, I must tell you, but if you can find a cannery, it's an excellent way to have your tuna preserved for future consumption while also providing a novel, practical gift for relatives and friends.

CHAPTER 24

Weakfish:
They're Anything but Weak

Many rod-'n'-reelers have been fooled by misleading implications in this species' name. I should quickly add, though, that the name can be either an unfair misnomer or aptly descriptive, depending upon which of the fish's characteristics you happen to be discussing.

If you're talking about his fighting talents, the name suits him about like "puny" fits a professional football tackle. Anyone who has had even a 1½- or 2-pound weak on his line has known this species' reluctance to be caught. And anyone who has been fortunate enough to tie into one of those robust 8-to-12- or 13-pound "tide runners" that used to draw anglers from far and wide to Long Island's famed Peconics in autumn has met a game fish *par excellence,* one matched by few other marine rod-benders of comparable size. The weakfish is a champ in his own right. Angling history is peppered with instances of lost or fractured tackle to prove it.

So the "weak" in "weakfish" has nothing whatsoever to do with his combat ability.

The truth of the matter is that the name was bestowed upon this gray-blue-silver beauty because of his delicate mouth tissues. They're almost paperlike in their fragility, leading to the old nickname "papermouth." A hook can rip free of these parts with ease, especially under the force of his strike, often a humdinger. The delicateness of his lips and other mouth parts also makes the weakfish a very tricky customer to play. He can be a real challenge.

IDENTIFICATION AND FAMILY ALBUM   Scientifically this species is listed as *Cynoscion regalis.* His most popular angling name is weakfish, often shortened to "weak." That handle, weakfish, is so common that I doubt if you'll ever hear of such nicknames as *squeteague* (Indian), yellowfin, and gray trout. "Sea trout" is another nickname, but it seldom is applied to the northern weakfish.

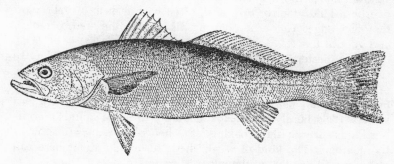

WEAKFISH (*Cynoscion regalis*)

There are standards of beauty for all wild creatures, even orangutans. Among fishes the weak is handsome. He's nicely formed. His body is on the slender side—not too deep, that is (compare his with the porgy's, for example), being about one quarter as deep as it is long. Flattened only slightly from side to side, it's gracefully tapered.

His mouth is quite large, a detail of interest to anglers, with a protruding lower jaw that contributes to the longish appearance of his head. Small, thin scales extend forward onto the head.

He possesses a full complement of fins: Two dorsals, the first sail-shaped and with spines, the second being lower, more uniform in height, softer, and with rays; two pectorals; two ventrals; one anal fin; and, but of course, one caudal fin or tail, characterized by a well-developed base and slightly concave trailing edge. Differences in profile, along with his first dorsal fin and other physical features, separate him from the kingfish, in whose company he's often found (or vice versa).

The weak's color pattern is neat, if not gaudy, and subject to the usual variations. Along his back the color is apt to greenish, dark olive, or a mixture of blue and green. The sides carry blue,

purple, green, and lavender tones, with a copper or golden tinge.
Speckling the uppersides and back are small, vaguely defined
dots of black and/or dark green, sometimes interspersed with
tiny bronze spots. His underside may be silvery, white, or grayish-
white. His dorsal fins are smoky or dusky, sometimes tinged with
yellow (hence the nickname yellowfin). The well-developed tail
can be a kind of olive or dusky, often with a dash of yellow on
its lower edge. Yellowish coloring also marks the anal, pectoral,
and ventral fins.

This gamester is catalogued with a family called Scianidae. In
the family with him are several species of croakers, drumfishes,
and other kinds of weaks. A close relative is the spotted weakfish, *Cynoscion nebulosus*, or spotted sea trout of our southern
waters. It's a family known for its ability to make sounds of various kinds—drumming, croaking, etc.—hence the names of some of
its members. The kind of weakfish we're talking about here can
produce sounds too, but the talent is limited to males.

DISTRIBUTION AND SEASONS   This species' over-all general range is
on the U.S. Atlantic Coast from Massachusetts southward to the
Carolinas and even down to Florida's eastern shores. Stragglers
may wander into northern New England waters and even beyond. Their greatest population concentrations are usually within
that expanse between Chesapeake Bay on the south and New
Jersey and New York to the north. Chesapeake Bay is a great
weakfish region. Other concentrations are noted for Delaware
Bay, New Jersey's littoral zones and bays, and Long Island's Great
Peconic, Little Peconic, and Gardiners Bays.

In more southerly parts of their range, say, from the Carolinas southward, some weakfish may be encountered in coastal
waters through the better part of the year. But weaks dislike
cold water, and their appearances are governed accordingly in
progressively more northern areas. In other words, in those regions, the sooner that inshore ocean zones and bays absorb spring
warmth, the sooner the weaks are likely to make their debut that
year.

In the Chesapeake Bay sector, a weakfishing season can start
in April and continue deep into fall, through November in some
years. In New Jersey and Long Island waters they usually begin

to appear in May or thereabouts (somewhat earlier in New Jersey than in New York). Throughout that segment they can stay on into October. The first frost or two generally wraps it up. In southern New England, June is apt to bring the start of a run, with the fish sticking around into September.

Water temperatures are a cardinal factor in the weakfish timetable. As you can see, they determine how soon the fish will appear and when they will leave, thereby dictating the lengths of their visits in various regions.

Comes autumn, they begin to run away from a falling thermometer, departing bays, channels, sounds, and shallow close-inshore (surf) zones. Evidence indicates that they move well offshore—some of them southward as well—into greater depths, where a substantial layer of sea above them acts as an insulator against winter cold. Another sport fishing season is over.

FEEDING HABITS AND OTHER MANNERISMS   Natural foods of *Cynoscion regalis* include killies, spearing, butterfish, small porgies, herring, and other available little fishes. They gobble shrimp and marine worms too, along with squid, crabs, and assorted lesser critters.

Weakfish are a schooling species, especially when young. Their schools vary widely in size, from small to large. Of interest is an enormous weakfish school cited by Drs. Bigelow and Schroeder. This school was observed 'way back in July of 1881 off Rockaway Beach, L.I., and was so large that three menhaden steamers netted some 200,000 pounds of weakfish, 1½ to 3 feet long.

Weakfish also are a coastal breed, tending to stay close inshore during warmer months. They exhibit a fondness for clean, sandy bottom, but food searches take them into bays, harbors, and salt-water estuaries. Channels are part of their habitat too. They're also found in small salt-water creeks, such as those zigzagging through salt marshes and into tiny bay islands. Weaks will venture into river mouths, but apparently have no inclination to run up into fresh water like striped bass.

Essentially they're shoal water fish—seldom, according to Bigelow and Schroeder, going deeper than 5 or 6 fathoms in summer. They probably favor shallow water because of its warmth. Weakfish are quite sensitive to cooling waters. Sudden, radical drops in temperatures undoubtedly would kill them if there were no escape. Rising and falling water temperatures are factors in their movements.

Food too, of course. Weakfish, as you'll discover, go food shopping at various levels, from the surface, where they can be seen, down through intermediate levels, to near-bottom depths. They're active feeders. When current food supplies offer crabs, mollusks, and other bottom residents, they forage along the bay floor or right in a surf. When hunting some of the smaller fishes they're likely to be feeding in the upper levels to the top. When neither of those depth extremes is particularly productive, they'll scout planes in between. These are details of importance to anglers. Levels at which weaks are feeding not only determine the most timely fishing techniques, but also provide opportunities to match baits to whatever comprises their diet at the time.

LOVEMAKING, GROWTH, AND SIZES AMONG WEAKFISH   There are at least two, probably three, major weakfish spawning areas on our Atlantic Coast. One is Long Island's Peconic Bay system. Another, believed greater than that for volume production, is the Chesapeake. It's also believed that Delaware Bay may be an important breeding region because quantities of weakfish eggs have been found there. Peconic spawning can occur in May. Possibly it takes place in June too, and may even extend into July. For Chesapeake weaks the vital process occurs at about the same time, give or take a couple of weeks. Presumably that schedule would hold for Delaware Bay too. Water temperature is a factor in spawning.

Female weakfish release eggs in great numbers during breeding. A good thing it is, too, because the odds against many of the ova reaching the hatching stage are high. Water temperature is a potential foe. If it goes too low, the eggs die. The water's salinity or saltiness also enters the picture. Radical changes can be lethal. Cold rainstorms are bad news too. And always there are the hungry predators who have a gustatory fondness for neighbors' eggs and kids. Mortality among weakfish ova and infants often is high.

Weakfish eggs are fertilized in the water by the males in standard fish fashion. Not very romantic, but it's the best procedure they've found so far. At fertilization, a weakfish egg is about 1/125 inch in diameter. Usually 3 or 4 days are required for hatching, under average bay conditions. Water temperatures are either a catalyst or a retarder. During its stay inside the egg the embryonic weakfish subsists on tiny droplets of oil, a box lunch thoughtfully provided by mother. When hatched, weakfish are less than 1/12 inch long, which is pretty small to go poking around in the world.

A weakfish that gets past infancy can consider himself (or herself) lucky—for the moment. The same old perils—predatory enemies, hostile environmental conditions—are still around the next corner. The death rate among infant weakfish is great.

All things being favorable, goodly numbers survive, despite the odds, and advance from a precarious infancy to an equally chancey childhood. If conditions are in their favor, the larval fish grow rapidly, attaining a length of about 8 inches at the end of their first year. By spring of their second year they're approximately 10 inches long. From then on they develop at the rate of roughly 2 inches annually, with greatest growth in summer.

Drs. Bigelow and Schroeder have mentioned unconfirmed reports of weakfish as large as 30 pounds. But such specimens, as those two good scientists would be the first to point out, are veritable monsters for this species. Personally, I've never even heard of a 20-pound weak, sport or commercially caught. But then, I didn't live in the 1800s, when great sizes were recorded for several species. Weakfish in the 17-to-19-pound bracket are of world-record caliber. The fact is that during recent decades any weaks approaching 8 or 10 pounds have been something to write home about.

Here's a table of average, approximate length-weight ratios:

Length in Inches	Weight in Pounds
12 to 14	⅔ to 1
14 to 16	1 to 1½
16 to 18	1¼ to 1¾
18 to 20	1⅔ to 2½
22 to 23½	3½ to 4⅓
25½ to 27½	5 to 6
30 to 32	9½ to 11

LONG AGO AND FAR AWAY   No talk about weakfishing could be complete without mention of the sport's golden era in the Peconics. That's in the musty past now, but it never will be forgotten by those who knew it.

Peconic weakfishing's golden age began back in the 1920s when a handful of professional charter and party boat skippers began trickling into the region. From Princess Bay, S.I., came the late Capt. Emil Kreuder, later to sail his *Sea Lark* from Babylon on Long Island's South Shore. Also from down to the west'ard came the late Capt. John Boshler. John and his boat *Doris,* sailing from Bay Shore, L.I., became legendary in weakfishing. I believe that John was the greatest weakfishing skipper-guide of them all. For years he maintained a meticulous record of every one of his weakfishing trips, neatly jotted by dates in a big ledger, complete with notations about numbers and weights of weaks caught, tides, weather, even hook sizes.

Also to the Peconics gravitated my friend Capt. Carm Marinaccio, later to pilot his charter boat *Duchess II* out of the Freeport (L.I.) Boatmen's Association dock for many years. Carm was a young lad then, full of vinegar. He'd been mating on public fishing boats out of Long Beach, down to the west'ard, and now was embarked on what was to become a three-decade career as a charter captain. For him, and for John and Emil, as well as for the Tuthills and Warners and other natives of that region and a long parade of anglers, the Peconics were to provide truly historic weakfishing in years to come. It was fabulous. Unhappily, it also was long ago and far away, possibly gone forever.

A fisherman could boat all the big weaks he wanted in those days. And when I say "big" I mean rod-benders going 12 or 13 pounds and better. Runs lasted all summer and on into September, until frost made the fish think about other places. It was during the latter part of the run that the big slammers, called tide runners, often were hooked.

One time I was writing an article on weakfishing for a magazine, so I set up an interview with John Boshler and Emil Kreuder at the latter's home. We sat at a round, old-fashioned dining room table, illuminated by an orange glow from one of those elaborate fixtures with colored glass panels and suspended from the ceiling by a chain. John had a kind of burly build, with a roundish, jovial face. Emil was on the slight side, with white hair and sharp features. Both their faces had been tanned by sun, wind, and weather to the color and toughness of top-grain cowhide. Between them they had better than a century of sport-fishing experience. They were in their seventies, I guess.

All I had to do was prime the pump. I fed the old-timers a couple of lead-in questions, then sat back. Well sir, Emil and John got to reminiscing about long-gone weakfishing days in the Peconics, and I believe they forgot I was there. Their talk about fifteen-to-seventeen-pounders being caught regularly and in numbers was enough to make a modern weakfisherman want to ram his head into a wall. I remember Emil chuckling, "Why, a fisherman would've been laughed off the dock if he came in with a little five-pounder."

Yes indeed, "fabulous" is a word for that golden era in the Peconics. So is "tragic." There was so much waste among sport fishermen that it was pitiful. A grim fact is that many a weakfish —up to and beyond ten pounds, mind you—was left to smell up a dock or be planted as fertilizer in a home garden, or maybe make a garbageman wish he'd gone into another business. We'll never know how many of those superb game fish were so wasted. There was pressure from commercial fisheries in the Peconics too, but at least bona fide netters had a logical reason for taking weaks in wholesale lots.

All sorts of theories have been propounded to explain the demise of that great Peconic weakfishery of long ago. I offer mine. In my humble opinion it was killed by a combination of things: wasteful overfishing by thoughtless anglers; increasing commercial fishing pressures; and, possibly, some less-than-average spawning years in between. I think increasing commercial fishing of Chesapeake Bay was a factor too. The Chesapeake has always been thought to contribute substantially to Peconic weakfish populations through migration. Maybe when those commercial operations to the south were stepped up they provided a *coup de grâce*. It must be remembered too that both sport fishermen and netters took female weakfish, the breeders, many laden with roe.

But that's all academic now. A great sport fishery died.

Sure, there are weakfish in the Peconics, New Jersey bays, in the surf, channels, and elsewhere. In fact, Long Island weakfish seemed to be staging a comeback as this book was being written, but it was nothing to match that action of long ago. Hopefuls have wondered out loud if the Peconic weakfishery might just come somewhere near its golden era. I'd like to be optimistic, and say I hope so.

METHODS, RIGGING, AND BAITS We'll scan these first, then go to tackle. I can start by saying that there's an assortment of weak-fishing techniques.

Top fishing with a shrimp chum line. Capt. Emil Kreuder said this one had its origin on Princess Bay, S.I., along about the turn of the century. I sure couldn't argue with him. I know, though, that over the years it has been a popular method.

As Emil set it up, the rig consisted of a nylon or gut leader (he favored nylon), 2 to 3½ feet long. On that is tied a single hook; the leader and line then are connected with or without a two-loop barrel swivel. Today you could use monofilament in

BOSHLER TOP FISHING RIG

place of the nylon or gut. John Boshler employed substantially the same outfit, except that he dispensed with a swivel, tying the leader directly to a small loop in the line. "The less hardware the better" was John's philosophy.

Various patterns of hooks can be rigged for weakfishing. Captains Kreuder and Boshler favored O'Shaughnessys. In days when hefty weaks were around, fishermen varied hook sizes according to the weights of fish in the current run, going to a 3/0 or so. But John and Emil rigged a 1/0 for just about all weakfish. Today you shouldn't have to worry about going stronger than that—a 2/0 at the outside for the largest weaks.

This top fishing rig is used with or without small weights or with or without a cork float, all depending upon current strengths. The idea is to keep the rig in the chum line as much as possible.

If a current is strong, it will tend to thrust your baited rig toward the surface, even to the very top. This is undesirable because it lifts your hook up and away from the chum line. Chum, you must remember, tends to sink as it goes out. When a current forces your rig too high, weight it a little. There are small, fractional-ounce sinkers just for this. One type, called split shot, is round and has a slot, into which the leader or line fits. A split shot is placed where desired, then squeezed shut to keep it there. Another kind of weight, called a pinch-on sinker, is installed in the same fashion. You may require only one such weight, or current strength may necessitate a couple of them. They can be added to the rig a foot or so above the leader. Capt. John Boshler used to add his to the loop in the line.

If the current is light, and your rig sinks too deep or won't drift away properly, it may be necessary to add a small cork float to your rig. This will help to buoy the rig at the proper depth in the chum line and also aid in carrying the rig away from the boat. *Note:* Use of a heavy float with light tackle should be avoided. It will interfere with setting the hook.

Baits employed in weakfishing the top with chum include shrimp, sandworm, and bloodworm, according to the feeding fancy of the fish on a given day. Although it's ideal to have those three kinds of attractors aboard to cover possibilities, you usually won't go wrong with shrimp.

These shrimp aren't the luscious kind starred in seafood cocktails, but small local species known variously as grass shrimp, sand shrimp, etc. They're particularly good bait when also used as chum, a case of matching bait to chum, you see. I suppose you could use the eatin' kind of shrimp, cut into pieces, as a substitute bait and chum for weakfish, but would that be expensive!

The local shrimp are an excellent weakfish attractor, but there are times when they're difficult to obtain or are available only in limited quantities. I suggest pieces of sandworm, or, as second and third choices, pieces of bloodworm or squid.

Baited artificials also are rigged in top fishing for weaks. One is a pearl squid, its hook garnished with a piece of shrimp or worm. Another artificial, one whose weight is helpful in counteracting a strong current's upward thrust, is a mackerel jig. This too can be baited with shrimp or worm. The lure is tied directly to the end of your leader. An alternate means of connection is through a small barrel swivel or a small snap swivel (for changing of lures). But if you're of Capt. John Boshler's the-less-hardware-the-better school of thought, you'll dispense with swivels and make the connection directly. Having known John, I'd say that's better.

Chumming is practically a must in this weakfishing technique. The first step is to anchor your boat properly. With an eye to wind and current directions and strengths, put one anchor out at her bow. Let her swing until she's settled, then put out another anchor in the stern to hold her approximately in line with the intended chum procession. *Tips:* Ease your anchors into the water, don't drop them with a splash. Weakfish tend to be noise-shy. And when you anchor, do it in such a way that boats won't cut across your chum line and spoil its effect.

Boat anchored, commence chumming. For a good chum line you need a freely flowing current, but preferably one that isn't too swift. Drop your shrimp overboard, whole, in clusters of four or five at a time, spacing each cluster a foot or so apart. The frequency, naturally, will be dictated by current velocity. If the current is fairly fast, drop your shrimp from the bow. That will buy you a little time before they scatter too much. If, on the other hand, the current is slow or the tide is at near slack water stage, jettison your shrimp clusters as close as you can to your rig.

Tips: Take along plenty of shrimp if you can get them. You're more likely to wind up with too few than too many. If you're working with live shrimp you should pinch them to kill them before dropping them overboard; otherwise they'll scatter immediately, and there goes your chum line.

Shrimp are about the best weakfish chum. But if you can't obtain them, you'll have to improvise. Here are some substitutes: mossbunkers; sardines; killies; porgies; snappers; spearing; clams; and mussels. Even the shells of shedder crabs have been used, but they can be more difficult to obtain than shrimp. Whichever of the foregoing items is used, it should be chopped very fine. It should be doled out sparingly, because it sinks readily and is apt to attract sea robins and other pests.

If you have only a small amount of shrimp you can stretch it by mixing with any of the foregoing substitutes. Sometimes the same effect is achieved by adding uncooked oatmeal to the chum. Oatmeal by itself has been used too; so have bread crumbs and boiled rice; even egg shells, although they have an obvious limitation, unless you're wild about hard-boiled eggs. The oddest weakfish chum I ever came across was oatmeal mixed with whale oil. This too has an obvious limitation . . . unless you have a friend who's a whale hunter. What you could do, though, is try raw oatmeal mixed with some kind of fish oil.

In top fishing the rig is allowed to drift out in the chum line for a distance of 100, 150, or 200 feet—more, if the current will carry it. There are two reasons for this distance. One is that it gets the rig away from the boat, lessening chances of the weaks being spooked. The other is that weakfish are more apt to bite on a retrieve than when a rig is drifting out. Letting your rig be carried away gives just that much more opportunity of a hit during retrieves.

Captain Boshler always followed this procedure at the start of fishing: The *Doris* anchored and a chum line going, he'd have his rigs at varying depths near the surface, but still within the chum line. Varying their depths is accomplished by adding small weights—or corks, as the case may be—as outlined earlier. When the first weak came into the *Doris,* John noted the depth and had his anglers adjust their rigs accordingly. I recommend trying it.

If your rig tends to sink while riding out, tighten your line a bit every so often. Retrieve your rig slowly, jigging it or making it twitch to impart some movement to your offering. Keep your rig within the chum line's scope as much as possible at all times.

What about drifting with chum, instead of fishing at anchor? Well, it has the usual advantage of covering more ground and giving motion to the bait or lure. However, current and wind conditions have to be such that drifting is slow. Even then, you'll use more chum. Today there's still another drawback in many bay and channel areas: too much boat traffic.

Bottom fishing at anchor. This is another popular weakfishing technique. Weakfish cruise at various levels. Bottom fishing accounts for them when they're deep. *Tip:* There's nothing to stop you from trying it in combination with top fishing at anchor.

A favored gimmick in this bottom fishing is a high-low rig. One of the best is the Peconic version.

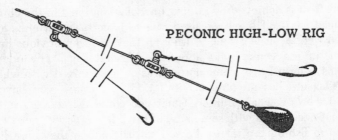

PECONIC HIGH-LOW RIG

The Peconic high-low rig has minor variations, but they're all basically the same setup. As its name implies, this arrangement calls for two hooks. A high hook is tied into the line via a two-loop barrel swivel, anywhere from three or four to six feet above the sinker (which is on the end of your line, of course). The low hook is attached, also through a swivel, one to three feet above the sinker, depending upon the upper hook's location. Since they'll be on leaders, you want to minimize the chances of their tangling with each other.

You can see this outfit's advantages. It can be rigged and baited to entice weakfish swimming at either or both of two levels above the bottom. Or the high hook can be rigged and baited for weakfish, while its lower companion is set up for a bottom species, such as porgies.

Fished exclusively for weaks, the rig's low hook is given a leader (mono or gut) two to three feet long, and the high hook has one of four to five feet in length. Connections to the line are made through swivels. Hooks can be baited with any of these: shrimp; sandworm; bloodworm; strip of squid; live killy; hard or soft clam; a piece of shedder or soft crab; or a strip of fish such as mossbunker, porgy, snapper, herring, or even sea robin (one use for these pests). If shedder or soft crab is used, select a small or medium-size one. Peel off the shell and cut the crab in half. Break off the legs and cover the hook's point and barb with one of them.

Combination baits also are used. Put a shrimp, killy, or worm on the hook, then hide its point and barb with a piece of clam. Or run the hook lengthwise through a strip of squid, four inches or so long and about a half inch wide, so that about an inch to an inch and a half dangles freely; cover the hook's point with a shrimp. Or put a hard or soft clam on the hook, then impale a live killy through the lips, as for fluke. Try combinations of your own too.

Tip: Squid strips, shrimp, sandworms, and shedder crab are among good weakfish baits, but you'll have no way of knowing what the battlers will favor on a given day. A variety of baits, therefore, is an advantage. Regardless of what is used, though, *it should be as fresh as possible.*

If the high-low outfit is rigged for two species, weakfish and another, the top hook can remain as described, but appropriate changes must be made in the low hook and its rigging, according to the kind of fish sought. If porgies are that hook's target, for example, a hook of suitable size (see the chapter on porgies) is incorporated. It will have a snell of gut or other material about ten inches long, replacing the two-to-three-foot leader for weaks. Then, instead of being tied into the line one to three feet above the sinker, as it would be for weakfish, it's attached, via a swivel, not more than six inches above the sinker.

The sinker for a high-low rig preferably should be one that holds bottom, yet doesn't remain anchored in one spot. A bank type can be rigged, but a round or oval sinker with a built-in swivel is superior because it permits the rig to move with the current each time it's lifted. As usual, current strength will determine proper sinker weight. The main thing is that it be heavy enough to hold bottom.

Bottom fishing for weaks consists of letting the sinker touch the bay or channel floor, then lifting the rig a little so that the current will carry it a few feet. This settling-lifting-settling process is repeated until 150 to 200 or more feet of line have paid out. Sometimes a strike won't occur until the rig is out quite a distance. When a suitable amount of line has been let out, the rig is retrieved slowly by again repeatedly lifting the rig slightly with your rod and allowing it to hit bottom. A retrieve is a good test of whether or not your sinker is heavy enough. You should be able to feel it thump. If no hit occurs during a retrieve, go through the whole business again.

Bottom fishing, drifting. This is merely a variation of the foregoing method. Here the best sinker is one of those round types I described a moment ago, just heavy enough to hold bottom against the boat's movement and current thrust. One rig calls for a single hook, a 1/0 on an eighteen-to-twenty-four-inch leader, tied in about six inches above the sinker. If you're a two-hook addict, tie the second about twenty-four inches above the first, using a three-loop swivel and a short leader (12 inches or so). This second hook can be productive of kingfish, often encountered in the same areas as weaks.

The procedure consists of running your boat up into the wind, killing her engine(s), and letting her drift. Some weakfishing buffs favor drifting over fishing at anchor because of the former's advantages, but there are limits to its practicality in places with a lot of boats.

OTHER METHODS In weakfishing there's pretty good leeway in techniques. Added to those already detailed are the following:

Surfcasting. This method is most productive after a run has established itself. As when surf angling for any gamester, it's good sport. However, it generally isn't as productive of as many weaks as boat fishing.

The terminal tackle is a fish-finder rig (described in the chapter on striped bass), or some version thereof. Worthwhile baits include sandworm, bloodworm, and a piece of shedder crab (which, for casting purposes, can be secured to the hook with a few windings of thread). I think you'll find that appreciable casting distance isn't a major requirement.

Jigging. A combination of drifting and jigging will lure weakfish. The procedure calls for a small, shiny, metal jig, armed with a hook of suitable size (1/0 or so), on a short leader (mono will do), twelve to twenty-four inches long. Attachment to the line is made through a barrel swivel.

The jig is left unbaited, the angler relying on its flash, glitter, and a jigging motion to do the attracting. A chrome-plated jig is preferred, but a lead model is okay if its surface has been scraped or sandpapered to bring out a shine. The technique is to drift across shallower areas where weakfish may be feeding on small bait fishes, the angler alternately raising and lowering his rod tip through a range of a few inches in a constant jigging motion. The depth at which jigging is done will depend upon how far below the surface the fish are traveling at the time, so a little experimentation may be required. You may have to rig a slightly heavier lure or add a little weight ahead of it to carry the hook at a lower plane.

Trolling. Small weaks, about ¾ pound to 1½ or 2 pounds, laced with 3-pounders on occasion, often knock around in sizable groups. Trolling is a way to contact these roving bands. A simple, basic trolling rig is fished, the come-on usually being a spinner, like a June Bug, Willow Leaf, or Cape Cod, its hook baited with sandworm. That outfit also will account for school-size striped bass. Other artificials rigged for weakfish trolling include small spoons, bucktails, metal squids, and small plugs of the surface, near-surface, or diving types.

TACKLE STORE   In selection of equipment you have latitude, so give way to preferences. As usual, the lighter the gear, the greater the action. Just keep in mind that most of the weaks you're likely to encounter will be under 5 pounds, so gauge your weapons accordingly.

Here are suggestions, by methods (in each case I'm speaking of conventional gear; spinning tackle will be considered separately):

Fishing the top with chum. A light rod with plenty of whip, 5½ to 6 feet long. A 1/o reel will do, on which you can spool braided Dacron or monofilament line up to about 10-pound test. You shouldn't need more than 150 yards.

Bottom fishing, at anchor or drifting. You can wield a light boat rod here too. It should have lively resiliency for good action. It also should have some spine, because a fairly heavy rig is involved. Reel and line are the same as for top angling.

Trolling. Tackle here is of the same caliber as that wielded in the foregoing methods.

Jigging. Again, the tackle is of the same caliber as that used in the foregoing methods.

Surfcasting. A light surf combo will do fine: a rod with a tip section to about 6½ feet long and a butt length to suit your ease in handling, with a reel to match. Although good whip in the tip section is helpful in casting, distance probably won't be a major factor. The fact is that in many areas—notably on jetties, piers, breakwaters, and beaches shelving off abruptly into deeper water—you may be able to get by with an all-purpose boat rod or a bait-casting stick.

Spinning tackle. This gear fills light-tackle, great-flexibility specifications neatly. A 7-foot rod with matching reel and 150 yards of monofilament line in strengths up to 10- or 12-pound test should handle assignments in all techniques. Personally, I prefer conventional tackle for bottom fishing and trolling. But if you have only one outfit—say, a light-to-medium spinning combo—by all means use it.

Hooks. Whatever the tackle or method, hook sizes for weakfish will be about the same—except, possibly, those on spinfishing artificials, which may run smaller than hooks rigged for natural baits.

Weakfish possess fairly roomy mouths, so hook sizes aren't as much of a worry as for small-mouthed species such as flounders and little bay porgies. Furthermore, in the absence of really large weaks, you don't have to concern yourself with the practice of gauging hook sizes to weights of fish currently running.

As noted earlier, a 1/0 hook should handle all the weaks with which you'll exchange arguments. When small school weaks, less than a pound to 1½ pounds (sometimes referred to as "spikes"), predominate, you can go to a No. 1, which is a trifle smaller than a 1/0. In the other direction, if the fish appear to be going to 5 pounds and heavier, you can go to a 2/0, although a strong 1/0 will do.

THE GAME   A weak's approach to a bait is generally with enthusiasm. But the degree of that enthusiasm varies among individual fish and according to the depths at which they're hooked.

A strike is usually strongest near the surface, probably because prey sought in those upper levels are active and fast. It can be a smashing wallop. A good-size weak can hit with a jarring strike like a bluefish's. I'm sure weaks often take baits on the run, because of their food hunting habits, and keep right on going.

These jolting hits are great sport, but they pose certain dangers. One is that the impact may rip the hook right out of the fish's delicate mouth parts. Another, less likely but possible, especially with larger weaks, is that a strike can come with such suddenness and force as to yank a rod right out of the angler's hands. Don't snicker. It has happened. I know of an instance. This luckless fellow had a brand-new outfit, an expensive Christmas gift, which he was using for the first time. Obviously he wasn't alert, because the very first strike jerked it out of his hands and into the bay's depths. There's another message in there: I don't recommend leaving a rod leaning against a gunnel, unattended, when weakfishing. I've seen anglers very nearly lose outfits that way too.

If weakfish fought to the bitter end with the intensity that often characterizes their strikes, they'd be among the scrappiest sportsters of all. But that's asking a bit much, even for characters as energetic as these. Usually their first run is their best, and it's a dandy. After that they tire gradually. But don't ever underestimate them. They never really surrender completely. In time their strength ebbs, but you'll earn weakfish every foot of the way. They display their determination in fast, sudden, unpredictable dashes of varying lengths. They might fight wide of the boat, or tear off on wild tangents, or even turn toward you. These eccentric rushes, coupled with an ever-present threat of the hook ripping free, make weakfish tricky customers to bring to boat.

Often weaks strike with sufficient energy to hook themselves. There are also occasions when they take a bait in what, for them, is fairly genteel fashion. Then they move away, usually slowly but sometimes quickly, without any great show of muscle. In such instances it will be up to you to set the hook. Tighten your line carefully, feeling for the fish's weight. Once you detect that —a steady pull indicates he has taken your bait—a lift of your rod tip will plant the hook.

If, on the other hand, when tightening your line cautiously you feel a series of spasmodic jerks or irregular pulls, he's probably toying with your offering and hasn't taken the hook yet. Now comes a test of your patience and self-control. Feed him line slowly, gingerly. Avoid any movements of rod or line that could yank the bait away from him. You might think he's never going to stop teasing, and his antics may necessitate paying out twenty yards or more of line, a little at a time. Stay with him. Give him a chance to mouth the bait and take the hook. If you play it right, he'll eventually accept the bait, get the hook, and streak off.

There will also be times when weaks play their part very cagily, approaching a bait in almost dainty fashion, "ticking" or nibbling it. This is his contribution to a little war of nerves. You'll have no choice but to go along with him. Attempting to set your hook at once is usually futile. Moreover, it could yank the bait away, causing him to lose interest if he isn't especially hungry. Instead, pay out six to eight feet of line quickly. The current will move your bait along, enticing him to seize it (you hope). You may have the fidgets before your wily opponent figures enough is enough, already, and finally grabs the bait. Now it's important that you don't be overeager. Give him an opportunity to make his weight felt on the line before you try to set the hook. If the nibbling ceases and there's no further evidence of his presence, better check your bait. You probably have a nude hook.

As with other battlers, you fight a weakfish primarily with your rod, not rod and reel. Take advantage of your rod's flexibility. During the vigorous phases of playing, forget that your reel has a crank. Control the fish with your rod. For maximum sport keep your drag or brake at a minimum. If you can, regulate the flow of line from your reel with *light* thumb pressure, rather than with the drag, giving him line slowly or rapidly as he demands it. Using your thumb as a brake calls for some experience—with any fish. Pressure that's too heavy can mean a skin burn, or, in the case of a sufficiently strong fish, a skin burn or popped line. Pressure that's 'way too light can lead to backlashes when the fish run.

It's in weakfishing that light, springy rods really come into their own. Not only do they afford maximum action, they give with the fish to absorb shocks and at the same time favor the weak's delicate mouth parts. Sensitivity is another advantage of a light, very resilient rod. It keeps the angler apprised of his opponent's maneuvers, telegraphing sudden movements and changes of direction much better than a heavier, stiffer rod. Therein, incidentally, lies the reason that split-bamboo rods were so popular in weakfishing.

You always must be alert for the favorite weakfish tactic of changing direction suddenly, causing slack in the line. This, as many an angler has learned to his sorrow, can mean goodbye fish. A weak's mouth parts are bound to be torn a bit, no matter how carefully he's played; and even a little slack could let the hook fall out or give the fish a chance to shake it free. When slack occurs, reel it in quickly, stepping backward or raising your rod tip to temporarily absorb some of the slack while you work the reel's crank.

Don't be too anxious to work on him with your reel crank. You'll be able to tell when he's tiring. Then, and only then, should you attempt to retrieve appreciable amounts of line. Don't make the error of trying to crank in a weakfish when he wants to go. You'll be asking for a ripped-out hook. Similarly, you'll have to be ready for sudden, unexpected sprints.

Tip: Always have a landing net with you on weakfishing trips. Remember the fragile mouth parts. They don't become any tougher for the battle. Many weaks have been played successfully, only to be lost during attempts to swing them out of the water without a landing net. When you bring your fish within range, keep normal tension on the line and slip the net under him *while he's still in the water.* If you try to net him in midair, you could knock him free. That's been done too.

MISCELLANEOUS NOTES ABOUT PLACES AND THINGS   1. Among locations frequented by weakfish are tide rips, channels, inlets, sloughs, holes, and shelving beaches. Keep in mind that they come right into a surf for food too. At dusk and at night they can be hooked around bridges and sometimes from piers and docks.

Quiet creeks ambling through salt marshes also will yield weaks. In such areas a likely spot is the junction of two marsh-lined creeks. Here you should look for a pool above the streams' convergence and quietly anchor above it; or fish from a bank if the pool is accessible. Try a surface rig, baited with shrimp, a squid strip, or a piece of shedder crab. Let the rig be carried along by the current, a foot or so below the surface, on down to the pool.

2. Weakfish adapt readily to local feeding conditions. They like to feed at or near the surface, hunting active prey. They may even be seen at the very top, nonchalantly swimming around with their dorsal fins partly exposed ("finning").

When food is more bountifully stocked on or near the bottom, they prowl there, seeking worms, crabs, and other tidbits. Thus you may find bottom-cruising weaks close to the surface in very shallow places. Similarly, they may be on the bottom, yet not deep, in little creeks where they go to search for shrimp, killies, and other small fishes.

When food supplies are inadequate at the top and bottom, weakfish scout levels in between. Here the problem is to find the depth at which they're prowling, so experimentation is indicated. Current strength may be a factor in dangling a bait at the proper level, once you find it, in which case weight your rig or suspend it from a small float, as circumstances demand.

3. Tides and winds play important roles in successful weakfishing. It's helpful to know that the fish tend to feed on tidal ebbs and flows, such as that period extending from an hour before high water until two hours after the turn of the tide, and that winds out of a southerly quarter can be beneficial. However, a fact is that tides and winds are variables whose effects can change from place to place and time to time. The physical layout of an area—shoals, bars, deep spots, etc.—is another factor that has to be considered. Combining all these variables in a generalization is impossible. Personal experience, asking questions locally, keeping your eyes open, and experimentation all go to make the best teacher. It will pay you to inquire about specific weakfishing grounds in the locale to be fished. Queries will bring valuable information about baits and methods too.

4. Your success in different techniques will vary. Sometimes one will produce while all others fail or account for poor results. That's another good argument for asking questions and experimenting. I'll add this: By and large, boat fishing, whatever the technique involved, produces more consistently, with better results, than any shoreside weakfishing.

5. When drifting or trolling, note the place where you contact fish by lining it up with landmarks on the nearest shore. You want to be able to pass over that spot again.

6. I've told you that weakfish are inclined to be noise-shy, and I've cautioned you about dropping your anchor with a splash. Along the same lines, avoid thumping and bumping sounds aboard boat. They can be transmitted to the water through her

hull. And don't row or cruise under power over an area to be fished.

7. Just as you want other boats to respect your chum line, avoid crossing theirs. If you come up on a place where other craft are getting weakfish, do it very quietly and maintain a respectable distance.

EDIBILITY Weakfish are good eating, but their flesh loses firmness and flavor rather rapidly after catching. To minimize these losses, place them on ice immediately after catching; then clean them as soon as possible and keep them iced until you get home.

Another prefreezing suggestion, one offered by Ed Migdalski for weakfish, goes like this: Skin your weaks and dip them in a solution composed of four fluid ounces of concentrated lemon juice in a gallon of tap water. Immerse them for fifteen to twenty seconds, then allow any excess to drain off before wrapping. He adds that it isn't absolutely necessary to skin the weaks; they can be scaled instead. When weakfish aren't destined for freezing they can be dunked in a solution of three fluid ounces of concentrated lemon juice in a gallon of water to help preserve firmness and flavor.

You can cook weakfish whole or as fillets by any of the popular methods. Preparations beforehand naturally include gutting and removal of head and fins. The skin can be left on whole fish or removed, as desired. If left on, you'll have to scale your catch. Once cooked, all that's left is the nicest kind of action with knife and fork.

CHAPTER 25

White Marlin: Another Member of Game Fish Royalty

"Marlin" is a magic word in sport fishing. It electrifies anglers everywhere. And well it should, because these billfishes, kin of sailfishes and swordfish, are regal gamesters indeed.

Unhappily, the word "marlin" also engenders confusion at times, for ichthyologists still aren't in solid agreement as to how many distinct species there are. I'm not going to involve you in that running hassle. It's been going on for years. The fact is that I don't like to touch it myself, even with a ten-foot pole—or a twenty-foot Hungarian either, for that matter. It's too confusing when it comes to the species' Latin scientific names (the black marlin, for example, has at least four). Besides, I doubt if you'd rattle off those chunks of Latin anyway.

Suffice it here to provide a generally accepted list of common names, letting ichthyologists and taxonomists (scientists who worry about classifications of creatures) fall where they may. It will serve your purposes.

Here are the marlins, with names that will identify them: Atlantic blue marlin; black marlin; Pacific blue marlin; striped marlin; and white marlin. In recent years the name Bermudian marlin has been introduced as representing still another species, but that one is being argued, and probably will be for decades. It also has been reported that two kinds of striped marlin have been distinguished, but that also is in the realm of debate.

What we're interested in chiefly in this chapter is white marlin (scientifically labeled *Makaira albida* by some, *Tetrapturus albidus* by others—see what I mean?). This is the most abundant species of marlin on the U.S. East Coast.

CLOSE-UP He's the smallest member of the marlin family. Most specimens racked up by rod-'n'-reelers are within the weight range of 45 or 50 pounds to 70 or 75. But larger fish to 80 and 100 pounds are boated occasionally, and once in a while there are even heavier whites in the 110-to-130-pound bracket reported. Those are king-size representatives of the breed, as was the 161-pounder claiming an IGFA world record.

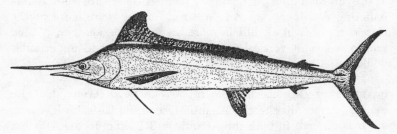

WHITE MARLIN (*Makaira albida*)

The white marlin's weight range might seem like minor-league stuff when compared with the size potentials of his blue and black cousins, both of which go above 1,000 pounds. But don't let that fool you. He may be the smallest member of his family, but he's no Little Lord Fauntleroy on a line. No sir!

Typical of marlins, whites have a superbly streamlined body and a hard, bony extension of the upper jaw to form a pointed bill. Although this is nowhere near as long and broad as the swordfish's weapon, or even as big, proportionately, as that of some of the other marlins, the white can use his "dirk" with equal efficiency to obtain food. So far as I know, he wields it in similar fashion.

Details of his fins—their number, shapes, and positioning—are like those of other marlins. Also like those cousins, he has a comparatively large tail, crescentic in profile. Typical of marlins are two dorsal fins, the first being much longer and higher than the second, and shaped rather like an elongated sail. In fact, the white's first dorsal can be raised and lowered like a sail. There's a noticeable difference in this first dorsal of the white and its counterparts on other marlins. Its apex is rounded, whereas on the others it's pointed.

In color the white marlin is a rich blue along the back and

upper sides, sometimes with a greenish cast. The lower sides
and belly are white and silvery.

Tip: White and blue marlins of comparable size can be confused with each other. One point of difference is that rounded
tip of the white's first dorsal. His first anal fin is similarly rounded.
Those fins on a blue are distinctly pointed. There are other differentiating details too, apart from sizes, but these are more subtle.
For one, the white's bill is more slender. For another, a blue
marlin has faint vertical markings on his back and upper sides
while still alive.

DISTRIBUTION AND SEASONS   So far as can be determined, white
marlin are peculiar to the Atlantic Ocean, unlike sailfish, which
are encountered in both the Atlantic and Pacific. In the Atlantic,
whites are found with respectable frequency on our side of the
big puddle and in its eastern reaches.

On our side of the Atlantic their general range is from southern
New England to southern Florida and the Caribbean, including
the waters around Bermuda and the Bahamas, and in the Gulf
of Mexico. They've been recorded as far up the North American
seaboard as Nova Scotia, but appearances beyond southern New
England are in the nature of straggling. At the other end of their
range they've been reported as far south as southern Brazil; and
there has developed a lively sport fishery for them off Venezuela
(in September), with boats sailing from La Guiara. It has been
suggested, and I agree, that as more angling is done off South
America's eastern shores we probably will hear of white marlin
catches in other areas.

In the North Atlantic, white marlin have been noted for waters around the Azores and the island of Madeira, off France
and Portugal, and in the Mediterranean. In the eastern South
Atlantic Ocean whites reportedly have been caught in South
Africa's Walvis Bay and offshore of Cape Town.

White marlin fancy warm and warm-temperate waters. On
the United States' East Coast their centers of greatest abundance
lie within that expanse between Florida and the offing of Delaware Bay. Maryland's waters can be particularly productive of
white marlin during the warmer months. In fact, that state's

Ocean City bills itself as the White Marlin Capital of the World, and so far I've heard no challengers.

The fact is that during a normal season offshore of Ocean City, in an area known as Jack Spot, you might very well have all the white marlin action you can handle. The Jack Spot grounds comprise an area roughly 5 by 2 miles, lying some 22½ miles southeast by east of Ocean City Inlet, with water depths of approximately 45 to 60 feet. I believe Jack Spot and environs have to be among the greatest white marlin territories of all.

In more northerly sections of their range, to Block Island and Massachusetts, they're strictly summer visitors. Thereabouts they do not usually appear much before late June. If food supplies and water temperatures remain satisfactory, they linger throughout the summer, even well into September if weather doesn't turn too chilly.

In this region, which must be broadened to include New Jersey and eastern Long Island, they show in considerable numbers. That stretch of New Jersey coast from Cape May to Atlantic City has fairly consistent action with white marlin from season to season. And there's an offshore zone extending from just west of Shinnecock Inlet on Long Island's South Shore to the east of Block Island which, because of seasonal yields of white marlin and swordfish, has been dubbed Billfish Alley.

I must quickly add, however, that the quality of white marlin runs throughout the region from New Jersey to Massachusetts can vacillate and reach extremes of both want and plenty. Offshore of eastern Long Island, for example, summers have brought showings that were little short of phenomenal for that area, with boats sighting several during a single day and docking with as many as three or four each. During one such bonanza the ocean was alive with baby mackerel, unquestionably a feast that attracted and held the billfish. At the other pole are seasons in that sector when white marlin are widely scattered and almost as scarce as the proverbial hen's teeth.

I've even seen radical variations in numbers of whites within a season in that region. I recall one July week in particular. On Saturday and Sunday white marlin were all over the place off Shinnecock Inlet and eastward to Montauk, "so thick," as Hampton Bays skipper Ted Squires put it, "you could walk on 'em."

Ted purposely was exaggerating, but you get the idea. On Saturday we sighted several. I nailed a 55-pounder, and the boat had another tipping the scale at 60½. The next day, in the same sector, we again saw a flock of whites. I baited one, but failed to score. Later I hooked and released a white estimated at about 50 pounds. A companion hooked and lost a fish, and we all had a go at baiting of others. The following Tuesday we trolled an inshore-offshore belt from Shinnecock Inlet to Montauk Light and didn't see one.

White marlin are migratory. And that, coupled with their estimated times of arrival in various locales, is about the extent of our knowledge of their travels.

During winters they provide sport off Florida and in the Bahamas. In those regions the broad timetable is from January until June, with peak action often occurring between mid-April and mid-June. As the calendar marches deeper into spring, then into summer, the billfish show in progressively more northern regions, moving coastwise past the Carolinas, Virginia, and Maryland to New Jersey and New York, then on to southern New England. With the passage of late summer and consistent hints of impending cooler weather, these marlin gradually retreat offshore and southward.

HUNTING TECHNIQUE   I use the word "hunting" advisedly, because the procedure is substantially the same as for broadbills—that is, you look for them at the surface. Although I suppose you could troll blind for white marlin, and I've known them to take a bait suspended from a kite (yes, a kite) while drifting for sharks, a popular method is to sight the fish first, then present a bait.

Like swordfish, white marlin hunt food near the surface, and often loaf there, taking life easy. At a distance the give-away you'll look for is the dark upper section of his crescent-shaped tail. You may or may not see his first dorsal. The chances are you won't, unless he's aroused. At a distance you can differentiate between a white marlin and a shark by the latter's exposure of both his dorsal fin and the upper lobe of his tail, as well as by the differences in shapes of those fins on white marlin and sharks. Remember that a surfaced swordfish shows portions of both his dorsal fin and tail.

Discerning between surface-cruising white marlin and blue marlin (you should be so fortunate!) from a distance can be difficult unless you can get a look at the first dorsal—remember the difference in tips—or unless you can get some idea of the fish's size (fully grown blues are much larger) through binoculars.

Once a white has been pinpointed at the sea's surface, the procedure follows the same blueprint as for swordfish. The craft moves discreetly within a respectful distance of the fish, alert so as not to spook him, then trolls a bait or artificial lure as close as possible across in front of him.

WEAPONS AND RIGGING Understandably, tackle for white marlin is lighter than swordfishing gear, there being considerable differences in bulk and power between the two species.

The choice of tackle is up to you. Overall, white marlin weapons range from ultralight salt-water fly fishing outfits to medium-caliber and heavier conventional and spinning gear. The lighter you go, the more critical of your skill you'll have to be. Ultralight, or even light, tackle isn't recommended unless—or until—you've had appreciable experience and are prepared to lose fish, and maybe fracture a rod or two. Spinning tackle is used by some anglers, but, because of the method involved—trolling—I don't recommend spinning tackle for these fish.

Unless you're already in the category of fishermen well seasoned in the use of light gear, I suggest you stay with conventional tackle and go no lighter than 30-to-50-pound line. Lean toward the latter if you want an extra margin of safety. Braided Dacron and mono lines are fished, but some anglers object to mono because of its stretch. Give yourself plenty of line, at least 300 yards.

Rods must be rated to handle the strength of line used. Reels must be large enough to accommodate sufficient yardage of that line, and they range from 4/0 to 6/0 with lines in 30-, 40-, and 50-pound classes. Don't go to an extreme in heavy gear. Really heavy tackle will wear the fish down more quickly and subtract a lot of the sport. It also can deter white marlin from jumping, thereby erasing one of this game's biggest thrills. Tackle in the 30-to-50-pound, or at least in the 40-to-50-pound, category will handle all the whites you'll encounter.

You'll need a wire leader. You can rig either stainless steel or piano wire, but remember their respective shortcomings. Every white marlin fisherman has his own ideas regarding leader strength. As I've pointed out, though, the maximum strength of any line-leader combination is that of its weakest component. Thus, if you link 50-pound line with, say, 100-pound test wire, the maximum strength of that combo is 50 pounds. So why bother with unnecessarily heavy wire that only complicates matters by being harder to handle? For white marlin you should be able to go as low as No. 7 wire, or even No. 6, and you shouldn't have to use wire any stronger than No. 8 or No. 9. The strengths of these diameters (stainless steel first, then piano or music wire) are: No. 6, 58 and 60 pounds; No. 7, 69 and 76; No. 8, 86 and 93; No. 9, 104 and 114 pounds. Fashion a 15-foot leader from your wire, allowing enough extra for loops for attachment.

Instead of wire, if you want, you can fashion a leader from monofilament. Some anglers do it. Mono won't give as much protection as wire against the roughness of a marlin's bill, but it's easier to handle. A 15-foot leader is enough. For some added protection against chafing, use mono in somewhat greater strength than your line.

For marlin you can rig 6/0 to 9/0 hooks, gauging them roughly to weights of the fish currently running. Go to an 8/0 or 9/0 if you want to cover the possibilities of heavier fish. Any of the time-proven patterns are fine. It should be a strong hook, of course, and should have good penetrating power in case it's planted in the marlin's bony jaws. Its point must be kept needle-sharp. And for the rigging procedure described here you'll require a hook of the ring-eye (not needle-eye) type.

A common method of securing hook to wire leader calls for passing the wire through the hook's eye, then completing a twist as detailed in the section on shark rigging. The result is a swinging hook. A small loop, with a similar twist arrangement, will be made later for attachment to a snap swivel on your line. If you're using monofilament instead of wire as a leader, knots will be substituted for the twists.

When we get into the mechanics of baiting I'll show you a tandem rig.

BAITS AND BAITING White marlin are swift, active feeders, aggressive in pursuit of food. They dine on squid, eels, mackerel, small dolphin, anchovies, jacks, and a variety of little fishes. So there's fair latitude in the choice of natural baits. The list of potential attractors is lengthened further by the fact that their fast aggressiveness makes them respond to artificials. It also points up trolling as a desired technique.

White marlin have been taken with several kinds of natural baits. They include whole squid, whole small fishes, eels, and strips cut from various species.

Many kinds of marine battlers consider squid a choice morsel. They're high on the white marlin's bill of fare. I don't think you can beat them as bait for these billfish. Fresh squid are the best, but, alas, not readily obtainable. Unless you run offshore and catch them yourself or make an arrangement to obtain them, you'll have to buy them frozen in packages.

There are assorted ways of rigging a whole squid for billfishes such as white marlin and swordfish. I've always used that employed with outstanding success by Hampton Bays, L.I., tackle man Mickey Altenkirch, a veteran marlin and broadbill hunter. It has worked for me. It'll do the same for you. Here's how it goes:

Assemble its components: your terminal tackle—a hook attached to its wire (or monofilament) leader; a whole squid of 6 to 8 ounces; a small cork, about ¾ inch long and ½ inch in diameter at its wider end; and a small pinch-on sinker.

Put the rig together as follows:

1. With a needle make a small tunnel (it only has to be large enough to accommodate the leader) lengthwise through the cork's center. With the cork's larger end pointing toward the hook, feed your leader through the tunnel. Move it down to within a few inches of the hook for the time being.

2. Put your pinch-on sinker on the leader between hook and cork. For the moment squeeze it shut only enough to hold it on

the leader, but not enough to prevent it from being freely adjustable. The rig is now ready for baiting.

3. Stretch out your squid (doing this on the dining room table or a sofa isn't recommended). Lay your rig right alongside it, with the squid's pointed end (that end of the body opposite the tentacles) aimed away from the hook. Lay the rig alongside the bait in such a way that the squid's eyes are at about the level of the hook's bend. Got it?

4. Shift the cork on the leader so that its smaller end is about ½ inch farther down on the leader than the squid's pointed end. (The cork is going to be *inside* the squid, so you must allow for that.) The next step is to adjust the pinch-on sinker so that it lies right against the cork's wider end. There it's pinched tight to prevent the cork from moving down the leader.

5. Feed your leader's free end up underneath the squid's skirt-like mantle, all the way up into the critter's pointed end. (Now you can see why we didn't put a loop on that end of the leader earlier.) You want the leader to emerge at that end of the bait. With wire you usually can locate and guide it with one hand as you thrust it through and out with the other. With monofilament you'll have to make a hole with a needle or a tiny slit with a knife point. The leader should be made to emerge somewhere near the center of the squid's pointed end.

6. Your leader now is lying inside the squid in the long axis of its body. Pull it on out until the cork is drawn as far up inside the pointed end as it will go. With the cork up snug against the inside, thrust your hook through the squid's head, between the eyes, and bring its point out the other side so that the bait's head rests at approximately the middle of the hook's bend. The hook's point and barb will be exposed, but the squid isn't squawking and the marlin won't find out until it digs into him, so why should you worry?

7. To complete the baiting, secure the squid's head to the hook with a couple of turns of light twine or heavy thread, tied just above the eyes. You don't have to draw the loops too tight.

See the purpose of the moored cork inside? With that thrust against the squid's pointed end, and the lashing around the head, your bait is kept extended and lifelike. Were it not for the cork, trolling would cause the squid to "bunch up" on the hook.

8. Last, to finish your rig, make a small loop in the leader's free end. With wire you can use a haywire or bailing wire twist for this. With monofilament you'll have to resort to a knot. Either way, the loop needs to be only large enough to take the snap swivel that will be tied to your line. Here again a snap swivel is preferable to the barrel type because it permits rapid changing of rigs. When a billfish mutilates your bait beyond further use you want to be able to get another out in a hurry.

Tip: Because baits can be mangled, or even torn off a hook entirely, it's wise to have at least three rigs baited beforehand and ready to go.

BAITING WITH SQUID FOR SWORDFISH   As mentioned back in the chapter on broadbills, I purposely saved these details for this chapter. It's basically the same arrangement as for white marlin.

There are only a few variations:

1. For broadbills you'll use a larger squid, one weighing eight to twelve ounces, or even a pound.

2. No cork or pinch-on sinker is used. You'll learn why in a moment.

3. The bait is stretched out alongside the rig as before, and the leader is fed up inside the mantle as far as it will go. If the leader is wire, you may be able to thrust it on through the squid's pointed end. But if it's heavy monofilament or cable, it will be difficult or impossible to shove through, and out of the question if the leader is cable with a loop already incorporated in its free end. So you'll have to give it an assist by making a small incision where you want the leader to emerge. Make the cut only large enough to accommodate the leader's end. Pull it on through.

4. The squid is stretched out on the leader, its pointed end aimed away from the hook, so its tentacles dangle, until its eyes are even with the hook's bend. The incision you made is sewed shut with light twine, after which the twine's free end is secured to the leader with a series of half hitches. These half hitches are a substitute for that cork and pinch-on sinker you used in the white marlin rig, and serve the same purpose, keeping the bait extended and lifelike. Here's how to place those half hitches: Make the first three about three inches ahead of the squid, the

second three about an inch beyond those, and three more an inch beyond that. Pull them all tight as you go. You can secure the end of the twine with a simple knot or cement it to the leader with clear nail polish.

5. In the last step you thrust the hook through the squid's head between the eyes, then lash it with a few turns of twine or heavy thread.

Tips on squid baits: (1) I've seen anglers—and skippers—keep rigged squids in a bucket of sea water while awaiting use. A better procedure is to keep them in plastic wrappers on ice, taking them as needed. (2) In addition to their appeal to several game fishes, squid are excellent bait because their tough flesh makes them durable on a hook. But this durability has a drawback in trolling. After a couple of hours of being towed around they tend to harden, which detracts from their natural appearance. For best results they should be replaced before this occurs. And don't bother to refreeze baits that have been trolled.

A TANDEM SQUID RIG My friend and fellow fishing writer Mark Sosin of New Jersey, an angler of enormous experience, wrote a feature article about this for *Sportfishing* magazine, and it's an excellent addition to offshore lore. It's particularly effective on swordfish. Larger marlins and tuna go for it too. Reports are that it also will take sharks. It should nail white marlin too. The specifications I'm about to give you are for a rig for the larger game fishes. Just scale down the sizes of the squid and its hooks and the strength of its leader for white marlin, according to those details I gave you earlier.

For a leader here you can rig wire, heavy-duty monofilament line, or a combination of the two. I'm going to suggest that you stay with wire all the way.

Leader strength is dictated by the angler's convictions. On big-game rigs it ranges up to a No. 12 wire (174-pound test in stainless steel, 198 pounds in piano wire), even to No. 15 (240 pounds in stainless steel, 288-pound test in music wire) for heavyweights. Much depends upon the species and sizes of battlers hunted. The IGFA enters the scene when it comes to lengths. For catches to be eligible for world-record recognition by that body, leaders must be no longer than 15 feet for lines up to and including 50-pound test, and no longer than 30 feet for lines over that.

Further, the IGFA bans the use of more than one hook unless certain requirements are met—e.g., two hooks are maximum and *they must be at least one hook length apart.* Properly fashioned, this tandem rig conforms with IGFA regulations.

Now for Mark Sosin's method of rigging a tandem squid.

To begin, hook sizes are gauged to squid sizes. The latter, in turn, are matched roughly to the sizes of the finned game involved. This outfit will take squid anywhere from about 8 inches long to 15 or 18 (approximate measurements, from the pointed or forward end to where the arms join the head, *not* including the ten appendages). For the smaller of these squids, rig 6/o to 8/o hooks. For the larger baits you can go to 10/o or 12/o. The steps in this method are as follows:

1. This outfit calls for two ring-eye hooks, one to be imbedded in the squid's body, the other to transfix its head. Secure the body hook to the end of your leader. Fasten the second hook on a piece of wire of the same strength as the leader, and about 12 inches long. Don't attach it yet. Stretch out the squid, tentacles pointing in the direction of the leader's hook end, "belly" side up. (You can tell the underside from the back by those two triangular fins. They're more or less flush with the back.) Place your hooks alongside it for spacing. Both hooks will emerge on the underside in the finished rig.

2. Eventually the body hook will be inside the squid, but with its bend and point exposed. Bend and point will emerge about 2½ to 4 inches or so (depending upon bait length) from the squid's pointed end. Place that hook alongside the bait accordingly.

3. The second, or head, hook will be attached to the body hook's eye, and be thrust through the squid's head between the eyes. Lay your second hook beside the bait at that level. Secure its piece of wire to the body hook's eye, cutting off any excess. Now the hooks are in tandem.

4. Slide a small egg-shaped sinker (it has a hole running lengthwise) down the leader, bringing it up against the attachment of

the body hook. Lay the rig alongside the bait again. You'll see the sinker's purpose in a minute.

5. With a knife's point make a small incision through the squid's mantle where the body hook will emerge. Feed your wire leader up inside the mantle and force it out the bait's pointed end, as nearly dead center as possible. Draw the wire all the way through, until the egg sinker comes up snug against the inside. This sinker serves the same purpose as that cork and pinch-on sinker in the white marlin rig—it helps to keep the bait extended.

As you draw the wire through to bring the sinker snugly in position, the body hook naturally will come with it. A deboner or similar tube will facilitate feeding this hook up inside the body. Insert the tube through that incision you made for the body hook, bring it down to cover the hook's point, and pull the hook into position.

6. If you've done everything right so far, the sinker will be snugly in place up inside the squid's forward-riding end, the body hook's bend and point will emerge through the incision, and the head hook will be about at the level of the squid's eyes. Thrust that lower hook through the center of the bait's head so that its point emerges on the same side as the body hook. To help support the squid's head (and its hook), sew it to the body with a single loop of stout twine, preferably white or off-white for inconspicuousness.

7. There's a little more sewing to secure the bait for trolling and against onslaughts of attacking billfishes. (I'll bet you never thought you'd be a tailor.) Use stout twine. Here too a white or off-white will make the stitches less conspicuous. So will neatness. Sew through the squid's mantle on both sides of hook and sinker, using X-shaped stitches. Just a few will do. Tie the ends and snip off any excess. A small loop on the leader's free end will connect it, via a barrel swivel or snap swivel, to the line.

The completed tandem rig will have both hooks emerging on the bait's underside, and it should troll with its hooks downward. When the rig is properly made, its hooks will lie more or less flat against the body, making the bait easier to swallow.

The first couple of times you fashion this rig your eyes will be darting back and forth between bait and directions, and it may seem complicated. Actually it isn't. After you've done it a few times you'll be able to put a tandem rig together in nothing flat—well, almost.

OTHER WHITE MARLIN ATTRACTORS Whole fish are effective. These include mackerel, eels, mullet, small jacks, etc. Mosey about local waterfronts and inquire about what that area's whites are feeding on. Often fishermen and skippers open their catches' stomachs to determine this. What fishes feed upon, naturally, influences bait selections.

Again, baits should always be as fresh as possible (that goes for those used for most species of game fishes). Except for eels, you can rig whole-fish baits in any one of several different methods in use in sport-fishing theaters throughout the world. One is detailed in our chapter on swordfish. Others are shown here in illustrations. As usual, frozen baits should be thawed first, and deboning (also detailed elsewhere) will aid their flexibility in the water.

There are several ways to rig eels too. This is about the simplest:

Run the free end of your wire leader—without its loop for attachment to the line—in through the bait's mouth, making it emerge on the belly's midline about a third of the way back from the head. Attach your hook with a haywire twist, then pull its shank up into the bait's body, leaving part of its bend and the point exposed. The point will be aimed forward. Since you're using a ring-eyed hook, you may have to make a tiny incision to facilitate this step. With the hook drawn up inside the eel's body, close the bait's mouth with light twine or strong thread, using any excess to secure the head to your leader with a series of half hitches.

Strip baits, as their name implies, are strips cut from fishes, squid, and the like. In this instance we're talking about strips cut from fishes. Many different species can be used: mackerel, bluefish, dolphin, etc. Strips should be cut from the lighter undersides to give them maximum visibility. Rig generous strips for white marlin. Cut them a good six or eight inches long and an inch or so wide. Split their trailing end up the middle for two or three inches to create fluttering tails.

ARTIFICIALS   I've seen best luck with white marlin via natural baits, notably whole squid. But that's *my* experience. The billfish will respond to artificials. They'll react to feather lures, the same types rigged for tuna, in various color combinations. They've also been known to go for shiny spoons of various kinds. And I hear tell that a fake plastic squid will work, but I figure, Why use a phoney when the real McCoy is available? Try a fake squid if you want, but give preference to the genuine article.

By all means carry an assortment of artificials with you on white marlin trips. You should have them along for other game-sters such as tuna and dolphin anyway. So far as white marlin are concerned, let any selection of artificials be guided by advice from local skippers, fishermen, and tackle shop people.

GET READY, GET SET . . .   White marlin aren't especially boat-shy, so you don't have to troll your offering too far astern. Fifty to seventy-five feet or so will do it. I've seen squid work as close as twenty-five to thirty feet off a transom. It seems to help to have the come-on skittering, zigzagging, etc., in the white, bubbly water of a boat's wake. As with school tuna, this water agitation apparently piques the whites' curiosity. The extra action it imparts to a bait helps too.

Speaking of white marlin not being especially boat-shy, I have to tell you a funny little story. Half a dozen of us were offshore one day hunting whites. We had trolled for two or three hours without so much as a sign of a fish, but all hands—some on the bridge, one guy in the tuna tower, and others in the cockpit—were looking hard. Not a fin to be seen. Then some guy in the cockpit let out a yell and pointed. Believe it or not, right along-side us, not fifteen feet off our port gunnel and cruising in the same direction as the boat, was a white marlin! All hands had been so busy staring into the distance that they had missed this fish right alongside. P.s.: Before we could get a bait to him, he vanished. Presumably he exited laughing.

Tip: Outriggers provide an opportunity to experiment with various attractors and trolling distances simultaneously. With two outriggers and two more lines trailing from rods, you have four lure-and-trolling-distance combinations.

In case you're asking, it's possible to raise white marlin by trolling blind. However, it's common procedure to sight the fish at the surface first. Actually you'll be doing both, since you're trolling blind between sightings.

It's like swordfishing. Spotting a white marlin at the surface, the boat maneuvers to tow the lures across in front of the fish so he sees them. There's no telling which one he'll favor (if any). Hopefully, he'll think one of them is an interesting luncheon item and take off after it, throttle open. Here the bait is close enough astern that the entire drama of the fish's pursuit and attack can be watched. Few angling sights are as exciting as that of a billfish zeroing in on a bait, and sometimes the suspense is heightened by the fish abruptly switching his attention from one lure to another. I've seen billfish shift back and forth among three or four lures, as though undecided which one to grab. Anglers have to be alert when this occurs. The fisherman whose lure he takes is the one who will play him.

Watching a billfish zero in on a lure can aid in judging when to set the hook. Be advised, though, that if you're the one in the fighting chair you won't witness the approach like someone topside on the flying bridge. So if they offer suggestions, pay heed. For this, and to aid in maneuvering, it's good to have someone up on the bridge.

A white marlin's approach to a bait is quite like that of other billfishes. Generally they come up directly behind it. But they also can come in from an angle, depending on the boat's course. He might seize the offering quickly, as soon as he gets within grabbing range. Or he may slash at it with his bill, using that weapon in his method of killing or stunning prey trying to elude him. Watching the approach is a thrill in itself. As many times as I've seen it, I still get a charge.

If the billfish seizes the bait right off the bat, without preliminaries, and you figure he has it in his mouth, set your hook by raising your rod tip and rearing back in the chair. You'll know if you've sunk the hook home. You'll also know if you've miscalculated. Often, setting the hook in a billfish is aided by the boat zooming ahead in a short spurt.

If, on the other hand, he proceeds to fiddle around with the bait, tapping or hitting it with his bill, and dropping behind it, it's a cue to throw your reel into free spool. This allows the bait to drop back, deluding the marlin into thinking he's captured a tidbit. Let the bait or artificial drop back to the fish. Keep your thumb *lightly* on the reel spool so the dropback doesn't cause a backlash. The last thing in the world you want now is a line tangle. Don't exert excessive pressure on the spool. Let the line drop back freely. Be ready to remove your thumb when he takes the bait. If you're pressing on that spool when he takes off, with your reel in free spool, you'll have a peachy line burn—*and* a bird's nest.

While this book was being written I went to Australia to get material and photographs for a magazine article about the fishing for giant black marlin done along the Great Barrier Reef off northern Queensland. I interrupt to mention it here because those boats use an automatic dropback that's interesting. Very simple too. All they do is leave several yards of slack between the rod tip and the clip that holds the line on the outrigger. In fact, the slack drags in the water. When a fish strikes, the line pulls free of the outrigger clip, and that slack becomes an automatic dropback. It works fine. But I have to add that those monstrous black marlin (they go to at least fifteen hundred pounds, and two thousand-pounders are sought) don't mess with a bait. They come up behind it and—CRASH!—that's it. With a white marlin tapping a lure he'd have to hit it hard enough to pull the line out of the outrigger clip for the automatic dropback to function.

All right, back to your fish . . .

As in swordfishing, from the baiting on, there should be close coordination between angler and whoever is handling the boat. Someone standing behind the fighting chair to keep it turned toward the fish at all times is helpful too.

The dropback business and what happens thereafter often add up to touch and go. Conceivably the fish could lose interest and shove off. Or, what's more likely at that stage, he'll mouth the bait. It will be up to you to judge when he has really taken it. Within a split second you'll throw your reel into gear and set your hook—in that order. The battle is on the instant your hook digs in.

. . . GO! On his initial run a white marlin might strip off a hundred yards or more of line. You'll have no choice but to let him go. Any attempt to slow him will end the encounter right then and there. Bide your time, ride with him. Wait for signs of his slowing and tiring. It's the old story: You yield line when the fish demands it, take it back when you figure you can safely do so. Originally you will have set your reel drag for striking strength —enough, that is, for force to sink the hook. Don't go to an extreme in tightness in this, thinking you'll be that much more certain to plant the hook. This could cost you a broken line or, with heavy enough line, a fractured rod, when the fish runs.

As the scrap goes on, you may have to adjust your drag, easing off and/or tightening it a little, as situations warrant. Don't go to extremes in either direction. Generally speaking, the lighter the tackle, the greater the need for just the right setting in each phase of a battle. This concern lessens with the heavier gear because of its sheer muscle and the greater strength of the lines involved. Here the rod's strength and the weight of, and water drag on, appreciable line yardage combine in a drag effect. They help to kill a fish more quickly than lighter tackle. Proper setting of a drag isn't an exact science. Rather, it requires a certain "feel," a kind of seventh (or is it eighth?) sense that comes with experience.

Stand-up fishing for white marlin is good for the ego. It makes an angler feel more rugged than when sitting in a fighting chair. It's also a more exciting way to battle an opponent, and naturally provides more mobility when a fish tears away on erratic runs. The angler can better stay on top of his fish, so to speak. And if he becomes fatigued he can always sit in a fighting chair. But it can be tough, with either light tackle or heavier equipment: with the former because the fight lasts longer, with the latter because it isn't the easiest to handle and it seems to become heavier as time goes on. *Repeat:* No stand-up fishing should be attempted without a gimbal belt.

White marlin are splendid game fish, noted for putting on a dazzling show. It can be quite an extravaganza, consisting of long, swift runs and shorter, rod-bending power surges, breathtaking leaps clear of the sea, and mad "tail walking" along the surface. They have their own brand of maneuvers and acrobatics, and they're magnificent.

A duel with a white marlin calls for skill, make no mistake. Its duration varies with each fish and can last fifteen minutes, thirty minutes, or more. The length of the argument is influenced by many things—how he's hooked, for example. If the hook is planted in his hard upper jaw in such a way that he can breathe with reasonable normalcy, the fight's duration will be in proportion to his stamina. If he's hooked in the lower jaw in such fashion that it interferes with his breathing, the fight will be shortened. Similarly, gut-hooking shortens fighting time. Caliber of tackle is another factor. So is the angler's skill. And always there are the fish themselves, with their individual degrees of toughness, trickiness, and determination.

A MOMENT OF TRUTH   When your superior strength swings the tide of combat to your favor, wet line will gradually pile up on the reel as you crank your fish toward the boat. But don't write him off yet. He could still have tricks and enough reserve energy to play them. "Green" or wild fish can become suddenly rambunctious in the closing phase. You may have some more line-retrieving to do before you're through. When he's finally had it—is really exhausted—you'll reel the valiant warrior alongside the boat.

Now you'll have to make a decision. Do you want that fish? I'm not talking about a possible record-size marlin. No decision there. What I mean is, do you want that fish for a mount? If not, wouldn't you prefer to be a sportsman and, having had your sport, release him? I hope you make the latter decision in most instances, even at the sacrifice of photographs of your catch back at the dock. (Sometimes it's possible, handling the fish with care, to lift him clear of the water by his bill—with gloves!—for a quick picture with you alongside, then release him unharmed.) I hate to see any fish killed simply for dockside photographs. If your marlin is gut-hooked or otherwise badly injured, or even nearly dead from exhaustion, it's more merciful to bring him in, rather than turn him loose to become the prey of sharks.

The marlin can be released just by snipping the leader. If you can tag him before release, so much the better. Don't worry about a hook in his jaws. It will rust out in time.

If you decide to keep your white marlin for mounting, the fish is reeled alongside, close enough for someone to grasp the leader —with gloves here too—and pull him to the surface. If he becomes wild, let him simmer down before attempting to bring him inboard. Then he can be landed with or without a straight gaff. Small whites can be brought aboard boat by grasping the bill with gloved hands. Larger whites may require two aides to do the lifting, or one guy on the bill and another with a gaff. Once in the boat, the white can be quieted or dispatched mercifully by sharp blows on the head just above the eyes with a heavy, blunt instrument. There's a billy for this purpose. Some fishermen use a ball bat.

When it's all over, there he'll be, conquered but no less majestic in defeat.

You can feel fortunate to whip a single white marlin on a given trip. There may be occasions when you bring a second, even a third or fourth, to boat. On those red-letter occasions the sporting thing to do is release the fish, especially if you already have one in the boat. More and more, tournaments are accenting releases of billfishes—with tagging. Some even pay more points for releasing than for boating.

NOTE FOR EPICURES Generally speaking, white marlin aren't considered edible. There may be seafood eaters somewhere (like Japan) who drool over marlin steaks, but I've never known an angler to take home fresh marlin for the table. I can tell you, though, that the meat is delicious when smoked. If you have one of those home smoking devices, or contact with a local smokehouse, try smoked white marlin. If your fish is to be mounted, you can slay two birds with the same rock by making arrangements with the taxidermist's agent to salvage some of the meat before what's left is shipped.

CHAPTER 26

Epilogue: So Long for Now

I hope you've enjoyed this book. More important, I hope it helps you to get an ever-increasing amount of pleasure from fishing. Incidentally, all the basic techniques in marine angling are covered in your book here. Suited to each species, they can be used for *all* salt-water fishes.

Before we part company I'd like to leave you with a digest of what I hold to be ten cardinal guides to good fishing.

1. *Fish!* No one has invented a satisfactory substitute for experience. Get out there and fish at every opportunity. That's the best course to becoming a good fisherman.

2. *Look, listen, and learn.* Watch other anglers. Study their methods, gimmicks, and catches. Listen when veterans talk. Keep your mind receptive to ideas, especially new ones. You can always learn something about fishing.

3. *Ask questions.* Speak with experienced anglers, boat captains, and mates, fishing station operators, bait depot men, and tackle shop personnel. Don't be afraid to fire questions at them. You'll not only learn things, it will be a tonic for their ego.

4. *Experiment!* Every detail of sport fishing is the result of experimentation along the way. Never hesitate to try ideas of your own, even if they seem outlandish. If you see something you think can be improved, try to improve it.

5. *Study your places.* Learn everything you can about areas you fish. And remember that it can be just as important to find out why one location *doesn't* produce as it is to learn why another does. These are among the details that add to your knowledge of fishes and fishing and will save wasted time and effort.

6. *Be thorough.* The old saying that anything worth doing is worth doing well is as valid today as when coined. Anything learned well is more enjoyable, more profitable, and more satis-

fying. It's to be expected that a lack of thoroughness is what makes perpetual duffers, in any endeavor. You don't want to be just a fisherman, you want to be a *good* fisherman.

7. *Use common sense.* This applies to fishing itself, to your conduct as a true sportsman, and to matters of safety.

8. *Observe common courtesy.* We go fishing to enjoy ourselves. Simple courtesy enhances that enjoyment for everyone. The avoidance of littering of waters, docks, and beaches is part of it.

9. *Give the other fellow a hand.* Got a good idea? Share it with fellow anglers. Help beginners whenever you can. Remember, you were a novice yourself once upon a time.

10. *Above all, be a sportsman.* Consider others' angling future as well as your own by not overfishing and by carefully returning undersized fish to the water unharmed. Become familiar with marine ecological problems in your area and their solution. Help whenever you can. And always be an active part of fisheries conservation. That's where the responsibility for successful preservation of our fisheries resources lies, with each one of us.

That's it for now. Perhaps we'll meet on a dock someday, or off there on the deep sea, or on an oceanfront beach, or in a tackle shop or at an outdoorsmen's show. I sure hope so.

It has been fun being with you, if only in print.

Good fishing! Best of luck!

Index

R